ANALYTICAL SOURCEBOOK OF CONCEPTS IN DRAMATIC THEORY

ANALYTICAL SOURCEBOOK OF CONCEPTS IN DRAMATIC THEORY

Oscar Lee Brownstein
and Darlene M. Daubert

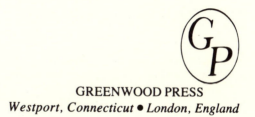

GREENWOOD PRESS
Westport, Connecticut ● *London, England*

Library of Congress Cataloging in Publication Data

Main entry under title:

Analytical sourcebook of concepts in dramatic
theory

  Bibliography: p.
  Includes indexes.
   1. Drama—History and criticism—Indexes.
I. Brownstein, Oscar Lee. II. Daubert, Darlene M.
Z5781.A55   [PN631]   801′.952   80-1200
ISBN 0-313-21309-7 (lib. bdg.)

Library of Congress Catalog Card Number: 80-1200
ISBN: 0-313-21309-7

First published in 1981

Greenwood Press
A division of Congressional Information Service, Inc.
88 Post Road West, Westport, Connecticut 06881

Printed in the United States of America

10 9 8 7 6 5 4 3 2 1

CONTENTS

vi   Contents

ACKNOWLEDGMENTS

The authors are indebted to the following for permission to quote from:

Building a Character. Copyright 1949 by Elizabeth Reynolds Hapgood. ©️ Copyright renewed 1977 by David Ten Eych Hapgood. Copyright under the International Copyright Union. All rights reserved under Pan-American Copyright Union. Used by permission of the publishers, Theatre Arts Books, 153 Waverly Place, New York, N.Y. 10014.

Creating a Role. ©️ 1961 by Elizabeth Reynolds Hapgood. All rights reserved. Copyright under the International Copyright Union. All rights reserved under Pan-American Copyright Union. Used by permission of the publishers, Theatre Arts Books, 153 Waverly Place, New York, N.Y. 10014.

The Theatre and its Double, by Antonin Artaud, translated by M. C. Richards. Copyright 1958 by M. C. Richards. Extracts reprinted by permission of Grove Press and John Calder, publishers.

Major Critical Essays [of G. B. Shaw]. Extracts reprinted by permission of The Society of Authors on behalf of the Bernard Shaw Estate.

Brecht on Theatre, edited and translated by John Willett. Copyright ©️ 1957, 1963, and 1964 by Suhrkamp Verlag Frankfurt am Main. This translation and notes ©️ 1964 by John Willett. Reprinted by permission of Hill and Wang (a division of Farrar, Straus and Giroux, Inc.) and Eyre Methuen, publishers.

"A Short Description of a New Technique of the Art of Acting Which Produces the Effect of Estrangement," by Bertolt Brecht. Extracts reprinted by permission of *World Theatre* and the International Theatre Institute, publisher.

Encyclopédie, translated by Daniel C. Gerould. Copyright 1964 by Daniel C. Gerould. Extracts reprinted by permission of the translator.

"Theatre for Learning," "On Chinese Acting," and "On Unrhymed Lyrics in Irregular Rhythms," by Bertolt Brecht, *Tulane Drama Review*, Nov. 1957 and Sept. 1961. Extracts reprinted by permission of *Tulane Drama Review*.

The Use of Poetry and the Use of Criticism, by T. S. Eliot. Extracts reprinted by permission of Faber and Faber Ltd. and Harvard University Press, publishers.

Dramatic Essays of the Neo-Classic Age, edited by H. H. Adams and Baxter Hathaway. Extracts reprinted by permission of Columbia University Press, publisher.

Luigi Pirandello: On Humor, translated and annotated by Antonio Illiano and Daniel P. Testa. Studies in Comparative Literature, The University of North Carolina Press, publishers.

The authors wish to thank the Council on the Humanities, Yale University, for an A. Whitney Griswold Humanities Research Award to Oscar Brownstein toward prepublication expenses for this book.

INTRODUCTION

Concern with theories of the drama is primarily a European phenomenon and that is owed largely to the man to whom this volume might be dedicated: Aristotle. Much of the dramatic theory written in the past twenty-five hundred years looks very like comments written in the margins of Aristotle's *Poetics*. Aristotle was first in the field, and he was unusually thoughtful and sensible. Yet the continued domination of his ideas, his categories, and his vocabulary is a rather remarkable, even curious, phenomenon in its own right. (See Notes on the Format, note 5.)

Perhaps it was inevitable. We learn to talk with the words we have been taught, and it was Aristotle who taught us to talk about drama. The beginnings of modern drama in the Renaissance were accompanied by a stream of translations, commentaries, and extrapolations of the *Poetics*; perhaps only architecture among the arts—and for much the same reason—became so self-conscious, theoretical, and prescriptive so quickly. Plays were examined in the light of the classical theories of Aristotle, that is, as those theories were perceived by contemporary observers. Aristotle gave us a vocabulary, but his words mean what we think they mean.

Because medieval culture imbued these perceptions of Aristotle's theories, the earliest translations and explications of the *Poetics* imported much that was alien in fact or in spirit. In the retrospect of five hundred years we can see the scholastic moralism, rationalism, and mechanistic psychology that Scaliger and Castelvetro brought to their understandings of Aristotle; it is not so easy to see the effects of our own presuppositions, of course.

Although Aristotle first raised many of the substantive issues that have since engaged dramatic theorists, the commentaries themselves created a new issue that has sometimes seemed more important: namely, what did Aristotle really mean? For instance, the question ''what is dramatic action?'' became ''what was Aristotle's concept of dramatic action?'' Therefore more fundamental issues were difficult to raise, such as whether ''action'' is the most useful metaphor, or, even more fundamental, what *is* the nature of the dynamic unity of drama? While there may be many ways to achieve a unity of concrete elements, feelings, and ideas, is there a single way that is uniquely dramatic or that is especially congenial to drama? The thrust toward definition as an end in itself hardened assumptions and deflected thought from exploration.

The intellectual clout of the classical revival and the sophistication of Aristotle's insights gave enormous authority to those theorists who spoke in Aristotle's name and who protected their authority with demonstrations of arcane scholarship (linguistic and historical knowledge, on the whole, rather than critical and philosophical thinking). The most rationalistic and mechanistic features of Aristotle's thought were emphasized, and it was given a cast more consistent with the prescientific rationalism of medieval theology than with Greek philosophy. The result of the classifications and extrapolations of Renaissance and Enlightenment theorists, carried further by each successive expositor, was the creation of a system as rigid as the table of atomic weights. But the progressive distillation of neoclassic theory had a good result. When a logic is followed to its end, any false premises will carry the seeds of their ultimate destruction: as they become increasingly clear and lose their protective vagueness and flexibility, they also lose their insulation from the realities of experience.

Eventually even an innately conservative thinker, if he was a man of such determined common sense as Samuel Johnson, found his reason rebelling. To justify that rebellion Johnson resorted to a principle of knowledge even more fundamental and revolutionary in its implications for dramatic theory than his rejection of the Unities of Time and of Place: his argument was grounded neither on authority nor, in the first instance, on reason but on consultation with his own sensibility. He (like Aristotle) observed what actually happened to his own perception in the presence of a play.

Johnson was not a revolutionary nor did he seek to be; it was A. W. Schlegel who accepted that role. In his campaign to further the cause of romantic drama, which he identified with Shakespeare, Schlegel attacked Aristotle as the symbol as well as the source of neoclassical drama. Though he sought completely non-Aristotelean principles on which to found a new aesthetic for the theater, to a very great extent his thinking was confined within Aristotelean categories and to Aristotelean issues. But ironies abound if one cares to look for them: hardly more than a century after Schlegel another German revolutionary, Bertolt Brecht wished to further the cause of "epic theater" (which he associated with Shakespeare) by attacking Aristotle as the symbol and source of romantic drama. It might seem that efforts to reject him merely affirm Aristotle's domination over the theory of the drama.

However, beyond the superficial appearances of change, where old concepts are simply called by new names, beyond actual change induced by new solutions to old problems, there may be more fundamental transformations in progress in the body of dramatic theory. These changes may provide quite different ways of conceiving the art object, its nature, its purposes, and its elements. For instance, Aristotle treats drama as a species of literature—as the superior form of poetry; later theorists seem increasingly, and with ever-widening implications, to perceive drama as a performing art. In consequence, Spectacle, which for Aristotle was the last and least artistic of the elements of drama, has become a central concern of aesthetic investigation. Where previously the art object could be located simply and with certainty in the play script, most later theorists seem to locate the art object in the produced play. Indeed, a further step seems to be in process: just as the center of interest for understanding the art object has moved from the words on paper to enactment, now that center seems to be moving toward what J. L. Styan has called "shifting impressions"—the dynamic interactions that take place between the stage and the auditorium. It is clear that the role of the spectator has been quietly (often unconsciously) reconceived: once seen as an onlooker who was to be pleased, and then (by Romantic and Realistic theorists) as an intruder to be ignored, the spectator is generally considered by contemporary theorists as a participant in a creative dialogue.

Whatever the trends, and however the user of this volume assesses them, the format chosen is intended to make easily available both the specific detail of ideas and arguments and their place in the larger contexts of the development of thought about drama. This analytical source book—using common categories for the purpose of comparison—provides access to the works of thirty-three important theorists. The seventy-three categories (supplemented by an index which creates additional categories) have been established as devices for access to the material and should not be considered as absolute classifications: the categories are storage bins, not Platonic Forms. The headnote with each category stipulates boundaries.

The storage bin idea best applies to the first, and largest in number, of the three kinds of category employed here:

The first kind of category provides a topical or issue-directed location for a number of concepts: for example, PLOT, or ACTION. In these categories there is not one theoretical concept but many. It should be noted that categories of this kind are not coextensive; some are more inclusive than others, both in their area of concern and in their logical subordination. For instance, concepts of the dramatic protagonist (*see* HERO) are specific applications, usually with additional qualifications, of the broader concepts of dramatic characterization (*see* CHARACTER). In addition, the FLAW category is subordinate to HERO.

Another kind of category focuses on a particular concept that is associated with a specific theorist or group of theorists: for example, ALIENATION, DECORUM or OBJECTIVE CORRELATIVE. In general, the statements quoted under these headings attempt to explain or exemplify one concept rather than to argue alternative concepts.

The third kind of category is perhaps the most problematic; it identifies some of the philosophical premises which are explicit, or seem clearly implicit, in the language of the theorists: for example, IDEALISM or REALISM. These ideas seem sufficiently significant to the development of dramatic theory to warrant the inclusion of materials not classifiable under categories of dramatic concepts. (In some regards AESTHETIC is such a philosophical category.)

The choice of the format of this book has necessarily involved trade-offs. No writer wishes to be quoted out of context, but the context created by the writer is not the only one that is relevant or useful to the reader's full comprehension of an idea. By excluding the original contexts, which are available elsewhere, this volume compensates by enabling the user to quickly associate an idea with others: with the history of similar ideas; with the writer's own related ideas from different works; with the ideas of other writers of that period; and with more fundamental philosophical or theoretical assumptions. This does not mean that the original contexts can be safely ignored, however. While an extract may make some tendencies of a theorist's thought clearer, and while historical comparison may make even slight shifts in language significant, the problem of framing and communicating difficult ideas pushes the theorist to the limits of his language. We assume that the user wants to understand the intended meaning of the passages quoted, not merely to learn what words were used. So the reader, too, must beat against the limits of language. Therefore, the editors urge that this book be employed as a reference to the texts surveyed and as a specilized kind of index and supplement to them—but not as a substitute for them. In this way nothing of the original will be lost and much may be gained. For this reason we have attempted to restrict our sources to those most widely available (but, obviously, without total success).

It should be noted that extracts were taken only from those works cited in the bibliographies (see the Guide to Authors), which does not preclude the relevance of passages from other works by these authors; nor should the reader presume that every passage of conceivable relevance has been extracted from the cited works. Again, this volume is intended to aid and not to substitute for the reader's own examination and analysis of works of dramatic theory.

As a further aid we suggest this work may be useful as:
1. A quotation finder.
2. A topical index to the works surveyed.
3. A historical dictionary.
4. A thesaurus of a sort, in which the use of a single term for different concepts can be identified as well as the use of different terms for a single concept.

5. A supplement to the study of theoretical works:

   a) by which some part of a theorist's work may be related to the whole;

   b) by which selected theoretical works, including those not surveyed for this volume, may be related to an historical context.

6. An analytical tool for the identification of the premises, lines of reasoning, and attitudes of dramatic theorists:

   a) Some of the most basic of a theorist's assumptions may be found under nondramatic headings such as AESTHETIC, AUTHORITY, EVOLUTIONISM, FUNCTIONALISM, IDEALISM, RATIONALISM, and REALISM.

   b) In addition, some categories which primarily concern dramatic theories may be especially suggestive of a theorist's basic premises, such as AFFECT, CON-FLICT, DRAMA, GENRE, INSTRUCTION, PLEASURE, RULES, SPECTA-CLE, and so on.

   c) Moreover, many of the references in the Index of Terms and Topics may be useful for identifying theoretical assumptions; such as Organic Form, Philosophy, History, and so on.

   d) Similarly, the Index of Names and Titles may be an aid to the discovery of what a theorist points out for special praise or dispraise, suggesting his affinities or antipathies.

   e) Finally, the chronology of the citations within a category may suggest historical precedents and influences.

NOTES ON THE FORMAT

The headings of the entries convey a great deal of information in succinct form, which may produce some initial confusion. The following brief description of the general principles of organization should aid in the clarification of the format.

Below the title of a category the entries are listed chronologically. The heading of each entry contains the date of the entry, its author, and the bibliographical code (and page numbers) for its source. When an extract is quoted, this is followed by a reference to the volume, number, and pages of the source. If the material the reader seeks is quoted under a different category title elsewhere in this book, it can be found through the cross-references provided.

1. The following example shows three typical entries, two of which involve cross-references; the superscript letters refer to the explanations given after the example.

ACTION[a]

1888[b]   **Nietzsche.**[c]   *See* under WILL[d]   (NW 138-40).[e]
1913[b]   **Shaw**[c]   SMCE[f]

We now have plays . . . which begin with discussion and end with action, and others in which the discussion interpenetrates the action from beginning to end. . . . [Some] plays were passionate arguments from beginning to end. The action of such plays consists of a case to be argued.[g]   (138-39)[h]

See also Shaw under THOUGHT[d]   (SMCE 137-39).[e]

   (a) The category title under which the entries appear.
   (b) The date of the entry: all entries are arranged chronologically (*see* note #3, below).
   (c) The author of the extract.
   (d) A cross-reference to the category where the extract is quoted.
   (e) The bibliographical code and page numbers of the original source. To find the quotation for the first entry, look first for category WILL, then for the year 1888, then for Nietzsche, etc.

(f) When the entry contains the quotation, the bibliographical code appears as the last element of the heading. The bibliographical code refers to the bibliographies in the Guide to Authors (*see* below, note #4).

(g) All quotations are presented as they appear in the sources; internal omissions are indicated by ellipses (*see* below, note #2).

(h) Internal or final parenthetical numbers refer to the page (or volume, number, and page) of the source. When a cross-reference for the same author follows a quoted extract (as here in the Shaw entry) the date of the citation is that of the whole entry (1913 in this example).

2. Occasionally the quoted material has been rearranged to clarify the author's reasoning when that reasoning is clear in the context of the source but would be distorted by the extraction of the most succinct and precise statements. In these few instances the page references to the sources indicate the original order.

3. Because some of the material quoted was not published until long after the statements were written (or, sometimes, spoken) the extracts are dated according to their origin when that can be reasonably well determined.

4. The Guide to Authors provides biographies of the theorists, bibliographies of their work, and indexes to the quoted extracts from their work. The biographies are brief, intended only to establish a basic historical context, especially as that pertains to intellectual history. The bibliographies include only the works surveyed for this volume and only those from which extracts are quoted; the titles of the works are alphabetized according to the bibliographical codes used in the entries. The Authors' Indexes provide simplified references to the quotations from their work, permitting rapid identification of each author's ideas under the major categories.

5. Aristotle's *Poetics* has been treated as a special case among the works surveyed, both because of the relative completeness of its presentation in this volume and because alternative translations are provided. As noted in the Introduction, the *Poetics* has been extraordinarily significant in the development of dramatic theory; even Aristotle's casual comments, and misunderstandings of them, have had a seminal importance. The primary translation of the *Poetics* is that of S. M. Butcher which is the most commonly used and widely available, but it has been supplemented here by extracts from a more recent translation by Gerald Else. These supplements provide either alternative or additional language. The Else translations appear in brackets, followed by the bibliographical code EP and a page reference. When the bracketted language follows a word or phrase in Butcher's translation which has been set in *italics*, Else's translation is an alternative: thus, "of a certain *length* [bulk: EP 203] . . ." presents an alternate translation of Aristotle's language.

BIBLIOGRAPHIC ABBREVIATIONS

The following is an alphabetical list of bibliographic codes, shortened titles, and the authors' names under which the full citation may be found. Complete bibliographic information is provided in the Guide to Authors (pp. 471-519), under the name of each author.

AA	Aristotle, *De Anima*
AAS	d'Aubignac, *The Whole Art of the Stage*
AM	Aristotle, *Metaphysics*
ANE	Aristotle, *Nicomachean Ethics*
AP	Aristotle, *Poetics* (trans, Butcher)
APA	Aristotle, *Parts of Animals*
APO	Aristotle, *Politics*
AR	Aristotle, *Rhetoric*
AT	Artaud, *Theatre and Its Double*
AW	Addison, *Works*
BBA	Brecht, "Theatre for Learning"
BBAn	Brecht, "A Short Description of a New Technique..."
BBB	Brecht "On Chinese Acting"
BBBG	Brecht, "A Little Organum for the Theater"
BBEB	Brecht, "A Model for an Epic Theatre"
BBG	Brecht, "On Unrhymed Lyrics in Irregular Rhythms"
BBT	Brecht, *Brecht on Theatre*
BLD	Brunetière, *The Law of the Drama*
CBL	Coleridge, *Biographia Literaria*
CCSL	Coleridge, *Seven Lectures on Shakespeare*
CDENA	Corneille, "Discourse on Tragedy..."
CDT	Corneille, "A Discourse on Tragedy"
CDTU	Corneille, "Third Discourse on the Three Unities"
CFD	Corneille, "First Discourse..."
CL	Chekhov, *Letters*
CLF	Chekhov, *Letters on the Short Story...*
CLSW	Coleridge, *Lectures upon Shakespeare...*
CMC	Coleridge, *Miscellaneous Criticism*
CP	Castelvetro, *Theory of Poetry*
CSC	Coleridge, *Shakespearean Criticism*
CSD	Corneille, "Second Discourse on Tragedy..."
CSNL	Coleridge, *Shakespeare...Notes and Lectures*

CSP	Corneille, *Seven Plays*
CTU	Corneille, "A Discourse on the Three Unities"
DDE	Diderot, *Encyclopedia*
DDP	Diderot, *On Dramatic Poetry*
DPA	Diderot, *The Paradox of Acting*
DW	Dryden, *Works*
EEE	Eliot, *Elizabethan Essays*
EJD	Eliot, *John Dryden*
EOPP	Eliot, *On Poetry and Poets*
EP	Aristotle, *Poetics* (trans. Else)
EPD	Eliot, *Poetry and Drama*
ESE	Eliot, *Selected Essays*
ESW	Eliot, *The Sacred Wood*
ETVP	Eliot, *The Three Voices of Poetry*
EUP	Eliot, *The Use of Poetry* . . .
GCE	Goethe, *Conversations with Eckermann*
GED	Goethe, "Epic and Dramatic Poetry"
GLE	Goethe, *Literary Essays*
HAP	Horace, *Ars Poetica*
HFA	Hegel, *Philosophy of Fine Art*
HW	Hazlitt, *Works*
JBW	Jonson, *Works*
JD	Jonson, *Discoveries*
JL	Johnson, *Lives of the English Poets*
JS	Johnson, *Shakespeare*
JW	Johnson, *Works*
LSPW	Lessing, *Selected Prose Works*
MP	Molière, *Plays*
NBT	Nietzsche, *The Birth of Tragedy*
NDD	Nietzsche, *The Dawn of Day*
NEG	Nietzsche, *Early Greek Philosophy*
NEH	Nietzsche, *Ecce Homo*
NGM	Nietzsche, *The Genealogy of Morals*
NHH	Nietzsche, *Human-All-Too-Human*
NHH2	Nietzsche, *All-Too-Human, Part II*
NJW	Nietzsche, *The Joyful Wisdom*
NTI	Nietzsche, *Twilight of the Idols*
NTS	Nietzsche, *Thoughts Out of Season*
NTS2	Nietzsche, *Thoughts Out of Season, Part II*
NW	Nietzsche, *Will to Power* (trans. Ludovici)
NWP	Nietzsche, *Will to Power* (trans. Kauffmann)
NZ	Nietzsche, *Thus Spake Zarathustra*
POH	Pirandello, *On Humor*

PPSC	Pirandello, ''Preface to *Six Characters*''
RP	Racine, ''Prefaces''
SAA	Shaw, *The Author's Apology*
SALOP	Shaw, *Androcles*...
SAP	Stanislavski, *An Actor Prepares*
SAS	Stanislavski, *The Art of the Stage*
SBC	Stanislavski, *Building a Character*
SCL	Schlegel, *Lectures*
SCP	Shaw, *Complete Prefaces*
SCR	Stanislavski, *Creating a Role*
SDC	Shaw, *Dramatic Criticism*
SDDGM	Shaw, *The Doctor's Dilemma*
SDP	Sidney, *The Defense of Poesy*
SEP	Strindberg, ''An Effective Play''
SGCR	Shaw, *Geneva*...
SKDC	Stanislavski, et al, *Discipline or Corruption*
SL	Stanislavski, *Legacy*
SMD	Strindberg, ''On Modern Drama...''
SMCE	Shaw, *Major Critical Essays*
SMDLS	Shaw, *Misalliance*...
SMS	Shaw, *Man and Superman*
SOL	Strindberg, *Open Letters*...
SP	Scaliger, *Poetics*
SPC	Shaw and Campbell, *Correspondence*
SPPU	Shaw, *Plays: Pleasant and Unpleasant*
SS	Shaw, *On Shakespeare*
SSPP	Strindberg, *Plays*
STPB	Shaw, ''Preface,'' *Plays of Brieux*
STPP	Shaw, *Plays for Puritans*
STT	Sarcey, *Theory of the Theater*
THEL	Taine, *History of the English Literature*
TLA	Taine, *Lectures on Art*
VAWP	deVega, *The New Art of Writing Plays*
VE	Voltaire, *Essays*
VW	Voltaire, *Works*

ANALYTICAL SOURCEBOOK OF CONCEPTS IN DRAMATIC THEORY

ACTION

The statements contained here concern the element of dynamic unity in drama when that is conceived generally as "action," following Aristotle's terminology (see also CONFLICT, FORM, FORWARD MOVEMENT, and UNITY). Traditionally considered an objective characteristic of drama, most recently this element has come to be treated as a phenomenon of the perception of drama: that it is the mental activity induced in the spectator, rather than the physical activity represented on the stage, which is the essential quality. Renaissance concepts of Unity of Action are included here. For the Unities of Time and Place see THE THREE UNITIES. For discussions of physical activity as such, see SPECTACLE.

4th cent. B.C.   Aristotle   AP

Tragedy is an imitation, not of men, but of an action and of life, and life consists in action, and its end is a mode of action, not a quality. *Now character determines men's qualities* [The dramatic persons have certain qualities by nature of their "characters": EP 251], but it is by their actions that they are happy or the reverse. Dramatic action, therefore, is not with a view to the representation of character: character comes in subsidiary to the actions. Hence the incidents and the plot are the end of tragedy; and the end is the chief thing of all. Again, without action there cannot be a tragedy; there may be without [expressions of: EP 252] character.... Thus Tragedy is the imitation of an action, and of the agents with a view to the action. (25-29)...Unity of plot does not...consist in the unity of the hero. For infinitely various are the incidents in one man's life which cannot be reduced to unity; and so, too, there are many actions of man out of which we cannot make one action.... Homer ...seems to have happily discerned the truth. In composing the Odyssey he did not include all the adventures of Odysseus...incidents between which there was no necessary or probable connexion: but he made the Odyssey, and likewise the Iliad, to centre round an action that in our sense of the word is one. As therefore, in the other imitative arts, the imitation is one when the object imitated is one, so the plot, being the imitation of an action, must imitate one action and that a whole.... (33-35)...Of all the [simple: EP 323] plots and actions the episodic are the worse.... Tragedy is an imitation not only of a complete action, but of events *inspiring* [replete with: EP 323] fear or pity.... Plots are either Simple or Complex, for the actions in real life, of which plots are an imitation, obviously show a similar distinction. An action which is one and continuous . . . I call Simple when the change of fortune takes place without Reversal of the Situation and without Recognition. (37-39) . . . A perfect tragedy should . . . be arranged not on the simple but the complex plan. It should, moreover, *imitate actions which excite pity and fear* [be an imitation of fearful and pitiable happenings: EP 364], this being the distinctive mark of tragic imitation. (45) . . . [The double action] is accounted best because of the weakness of the spectators; for the poet is guided in what he writes by the wishes of his audience. The pleasure, however, thence derived is not the true tragic pleasure. (47-49)

See also Aristotle under CHARACTER (AP 27-29, 69), DRAMA (AP 13, 107-11), MAGNITUDE (AP 91-93), MOTIVATION (ANE 329-31), PLOT (AP 25-29, 37-39, 39-41, 45-49, 65-67), PROBABILITY (AP 95-97), THOUGHT (AP 69-71), TRAGEDY (AP 23-25), UNITY (AP 33-35).

1561   Scaliger   SP

Aeschylus [had a] pompous style, but with little variety of plot, and little, if any, novelty; he showed simply one manner, tenor and treatment. But the tragedy that can fill the spectator, and send him away satisfied, allows of more than one issue. . . . The outcome [of a tragedy] is either calamitous or associated with misfortune: joy of bad men turned to sorrow, grief of good men to joy, but with peril or injury from exile, judgment, carnage, or revenge. (62)

See also Scaliger under CHARACTER (SP 82), INSTRUCTION (SP 82-83).

1570   Castelvetro   CP

It was Aristotle's opinion that the plot of tragedy and comedy ought to comprise one action only, or two whose interdependence make them one. . . . But he ought to have justified this, not by the fact that the plot is incapable of comprising more actions, but by the fact that the extreme temporal limit of twelve hours and the restriction of place for the performance, do not permit a multitude of actions . . . nor indeed do they permit the whole of one complete action, if it is of any length: and this is the principal reason and the necessary one for the unity of action. (89) . . . No drama can be praiseworthy, which has not two actions, that is two plots, though one is principal and the other accessory. (90) . . . The plot of epic and tragic poetry ought to comprise not only human action, but indeed human action magnificent and of a king. . . . As tragedy must tell of the action of a king, it follows that such action must really have happened, for we cannot create a king, who never existed, by our imagination, nor can we attribute actions of such a king; indeed we cannot even attribute to a really historic king actions which he never performed: for history would give us the lie. (113)

See also Castelvetro under CHARACTER (CP 102-103, 104), UNITY (CP 90-91).

1609   de Vega   **VAWP**

Bear in mind that [the] subject should contain one action only, seeing to it that
the story in no manner be episodic; I mean the introduction of other things
which are beside the main purpose; nor that any member be omitted which
might ruin the whole of the context. There is no use in advising that it should
take place in the period of one sun, though this is the view of Aristotle; but we
lose our respect for him when we mingle tragic style with the humbleness of
mean comedy. Let it take place in as little time as possible, except when the
poet is writing history in which some years have to pass; these he can relegate
to the space between the acts, wherein, if necessary, he can have a character go
on some journey; a thing that greatly offends whoever perceives it. But let not
him who is offended go to see them. (30-31)

1641   Jonson   **JD**

As a house, consisting of diverse materialls, become one structure, and one
dwelling; so an Action, compos'd of diverse parts, may become one *Fable*.
. . . For *example*, in . . . *Sophocles* his *Ajax*: *Ajax* depriv'd of *Achilles's*
Armour . . . rageth and turnes mad. In that humour he doth many sensless
things. . . . Returning to his Sense, he growes asham'd of the scorne, and kills
himself; and is by the *Chiefes* of Greekes forbidden buriall. These things agree,
and hang together, not as they were done; but as seeming to be done, which
made the Action whole, intire, and absolute. (105)

1657   d'Aubignac   **AAS**

I call Truth of the Theatral Action, the whole story of the Play, so far as it is
considered a true one, and that all the Adventures in it are look'd upon as being
come to pass. . . . All that in the Play either is consider'd as a part, or has a
necessary dependence upon the Story, ought to be of the truth of the Action;
and 'tis by this Rule that one ought to Examine the probability of all that's done
in the Play. . . . And one naturally approves of all that ought to have been don[e]
according to the truth, though it be a suppos'd story, and one condemns all that
one thinks contrary to truth, or not becoming the actions of life. (1: 43-
44) . . . 'Tis one of *Aristotle's* Rules, and without doub[t] a very Rational one,
that a Dramatick Poem ought to comprehend but one Action; and he does very
pertinently condemn those, who make a Play of the whole Story, or life of a
Hero. For though we speak but of one principal Part, on which all the other
Events, bad and good, do depend; yet there are divers subordinate Actions.
. . . 'Tis certain, that the Stage is but a Picture or Image of Humane Life; and as
a Picture cannot shew us at the same time two Originals, and be an accomplished Picture: it is likewise impossible that two Actions, I mean principal
ones, should be represented reasonbly by one Play. (2: 81) . . . [Tragedy:] 'Tis
called a *Drama*, which signifies an action. . . . And indeed all the Discourses of

Tragedy ought to be as the Actions of those that appear upon the Stage; for there to speak, is to act, there being not there any speeches invented by the Poet to shew his Eloquence. (3: 11-12)

See also d'Aubignac under PROBABILITY (AAS 2: 76), THREE UNITIES (AAS 2: 111-13, 116-17).

1600   Corneille   CDTU

There must be one complete action . . . but it can evolve only through several other incomplete actions, which serve as progressions and keep the spectator in a pleasant state of suspense. The playwright must contrive this suspense at the end of each act in order to render the action continuous. . . . Each act must leave an expectation of something that will be shown in the one that follows it. (235)

See also Corneille under COMEDY (CFD 141), COMPLICATION (CTU 816).

1664   Racine. See under UNITY (RP 154).

1668   Dryden. See under UNITY (DW 1, 2: 86-87).

1679   Dryden   DW

The following properties of the action [of tragedy] are so easy, that they need not my explaining. It ought to be great, and to consist of great persons, to distinguish it from comedy; where the action is trivial, and the persons of inferior rank. The last quality of the action is, that it ought to be probable, as well as admirable and great. It is not necessary that there should be historical truth in it; but always necessary that there should be a likeness of truth, something that is more than barely possible, *probable* being that which succeeds or happens oftener than it misses. . . . This action thus described, must be represented, not told, to distinguish dramatick poetry from epick. (1, 2: 268-69).

See also Dryden under TRAGEDY (DW 1, 2: 266-67).

1711   Addison. See under PLOT (AW 1: 72).

1712   Addison   AW

Action should have three Qualifications in it. First, it should be One Action. Secondly, it should be an entire Action; and Thirdly, it should be a great Action. (1: 385) . . . The fable of every poem is, according to Aristotle's division, either simple or implex. It is called simple when there is no change of fortune in it; implex, when the fortune of the chief actor changes from bad to good, or from good to bad. The implex fable is thought the most perfect: I suppose, because it is more proper to stir up the passions of the reader, and to surprise him with a greater variety of accidents. The implex fable is therefore of two kinds: in the first, the chief actor makes his way through a long series of dangers and difficulties, until he arrives at honour and prosperity, as we see in the stories of Ulysses and Aeneas; in the second, the chief actor in the poem falls from some eminent pitch of honour and prosperity, into misery and disgrace. Thus we see Adam and Eve sinking from a state of innocence and happiness, into the most abject condition of sin and sorrow. The most taking tragedies among the ancients, were built on this last sort of implex fable, particularly the tragedy of Oedipus, which proceeds upon a story, if we may believe Aristotle, the most proper for tragedy that could be invented by the wit of man. . . . This kind of implex fable, wherein the event is unhappy, is more apt to affect an audience than that of the first kind. (1: 427)

1730 Voltaire. *See* under LANGUAGE (VE 283), RULES (VE 282), THREE UNITIES (VE 280-81).

c. 1745-1752 Voltaire. *See* under TRAGEDY (VW 19: 141).

1758 Diderot   **DDP**

You cannot put too much action and movement into a farce. . . . Less in gay comedy, still less in serious comedy, and almost none at all in tragedy. The less true to life a type is, the easier the task of making it rapid in action, and "warm." You have heat at the expense of truth and what is beautiful in human nature. . . . Although the movement of a play varies according to the different types [of drama], the action progresses in the same manner with all; it never stops, even during the entr'actes. It is like a mass of rock set loose from a mountain-top, whose speed increases as it descends, bounding headlong past every obstacle. If this comparison be just, if discourses decrease in inverse proportion to the action, the characters ought to speak a great deal at first and act a great deal toward the end. (291-92)

   See also Diderot under CLOSURE (DDP 291), COMPLICATION (DDP 291); compare with CHARACTER (DDP 290).

1765 Johnson. *See* under THREE UNITIES (JS 25, 27, 29).

1797 Goethe. *See* under DRAMA (GED 337-338), PLOT (GED 338).

1808 Schlegel   **SCL**

Aristotle requires the same unity of action from the epic as from the dramatic poet . . . and says that the poet must not resemble the historian, who relates contemporary events, although they have no bearing on one another. Here we have [an] . . . express demand [for a] connexion of cause and effect between the represented events. . . . This is nearly all that is to be found in the *Poetics* . . . on

Unity of Action. A short investigation will serve to show how very much these anatomical ideas [see MAGNITUDE SCL 1808 . . . ''founded on the quality of our organs.'' . . .], which have been stamped as rules, are below the essential requisites of poetry. . . . What is action? . . . In the higher, proper signification, action is an activity dependent on the will of man. Its unity will consist in the direction toward a single end; and to its completeness belongs all that lies between the first determination and the execution of the deed. This idea of action is applicable to many tragedies of the ancients . . . but by no means to all; still less does it apply to the greater part of modern tragedies, at least if the action be sought in the principle characters. . . . But further . . . we must include the resolution to bear the consequences of the deed with heroic magnanimity, and the execution of this determination will belong to its completion. . . . Farther, there could be no complication of the plot without opposition, and this arises mostly out of the contradictory motives and views of the acting personages. If, therefore, we limit the notion of an action to the determination and the deed, then we shall, in most cases, have two or three actions in a single tragedy. Which now is the principle action? Every person thinks his own the most important, for every man is his own central point. . . . We see . . . a new condition in the notion of action, namely, . . . the idea of moral liberty, by which alone man is considered the original author of his own resolutions. For, . . . the resolution, as the beginning of action, is not a cause merely, but is also an effect of antecedent motives. . . . [This is] the *unity* and *wholeness* of Tragedy . . . of the ancients; namely, its absolute beginning is the assertion of Freewill, and the acknowledgement of Necessity is its absolute end. But we consider ourselves justified in affirming that Aristotle was altogether a stranger to this view; he nowhere speaks of the idea of Destiny as essential to Tragedy. In fact, we must not expect from him a strict idea of action as a resolution and deed. . . . It is evident . . . that he, like all the moderns, understood by *action* something merely that takes place. (239-42)

 See also Schlegel under COMPLICATION (SCL 253-54), DRAMA (SCL 30-32), THREE UNITIES (SCL 236-51, 305).

c. 1820   Hegel   HFA

Action is . . . the executed will, which is at the same time *recognized*, recognized, that is, not merely in its origin and point of departure from the soul-life, but also in respect to its ultimate purpose. In other words, all that issues from the action, issues, so far as the personality in question is concerned, from [the character] himself, and reacts thereby on his personal character and its circumstances. . . . It is only when thus regarded that Human action asserts itself as *action* in the supreme sense, that is, as actual execution of ideal intentions and aims with the realization of which the individual agent associates himself as with   himself,   discovers   himself   and   his   satisfaction   therein.   (4:

52) . . . The end and content of an action is only dramatic by reason of the fact that on account of its defined character, in the distinctive qualities of which the personality itself can alone lay hold of it under definite conditions, it calls into being in other individuals other objects and passions opposed to it. . . . If . . . this essential content of human feeling and activity is to assert itself as dramatic it must in its specialization *confront* us as distinct ends, so that in every case the action will inevitably meet with obstruction in its relation to other active individuals, and fall into subjection to changing conditions and contradictions, which alternately prejudice the success of their particular fulfillment. The genuine content, the essential operative energy throughout may therefore very well be the eternal forces, . . . the divine and the true. . . . What we have here is the divine in its community . . . as concrete existence in its realization, invited to act and charged with movement. (4: 253-54) . . . Unity . . . of *action* is the one truly inviolable rule. . . . Every action must without exception have a *distinct* object which it seeks to achieve. It is through his action that man enters actively into the concrete actual world, in which also the most universal subject-matter is in its turn accepted in the poetic work and defined under more specific manifestations. . . . Unity will have to be sought for in the realization of an end. . . . The circumstances adapted to dramatic action are . . . of a kind that the individual end meets with obstruction at the hands of other [characters], and this for the reason that a contradictory end stands in its path, which in its turn equally strives after fulfillment, so that it is invariably attached to the reciprocal relation of conflicts and their devolution. Dramatic action in consequence rests essentially upon an action that is involved with *resistance,* and the genuine unity can only find its *rationale* in the entire movement . . . in such a way as to resolve the opposition implied. Such a resolution has, precisely as the action itself has, an external and an inside point of view. . . . A true end is . . . only then consummated where the object and the interest of the action, around which all revolves, are identified with the individuals concerned, and absolutely united in them. . . . No doubt in the particular end, which resolves the colliding factors, the possibility of fresh interests and conflicts may be presented; it is, however, the *one* collision with which the action is concerned. (4: 259-61) . . . If we go back to the most primitive of those so-called mysteries, morality plays and farces . . . from which the romantic drama issued, we find that these present no action in that original Greek sense of the term, no outbreak, that is, of opposing forces from the undivided consciousness of life and the god-like. (4: 317)

See also Hegel under CHARACTER (HFA 4: 173-74, 252), DRAMA (HFA 4: 249-50, 251, 261-62, 278-80, 321-23), FORM (HFA 4: 262-63), TRAGEDY (HFA 4: 295-99, 312-15), UNIVERSALITY (HFA 4: 252-53).

1827 Goethe. *See* under TRAGEDY (GCE March 28).

1864   Taine   TLA

What we call intrigue or action . . . is simply a series of events and an order of situations arranged with a view to manifest characters, to probe natures to their depths, to bring up to the surface profound instincts and unknown faculties which the monotonous current of habit prevents from emerging into day, in order to measure, as in Corneille, the force of their will and the grandeur of their heroism, in order to expose, as in Shakespeare, the lusts, madness, and fury, the strange devouring monsters which blindly rage and roar in the depths of our hearts. (318-19)

1888   Nietzsche *See* under WILL (NW 138-40).

1894   Brunetière   BLD

The proper aim of the novel, as of the epic . . . is to give us a picture of the influence which is exercised upon us by all that is outside of ourselves. The novel is therefore the contrary of drama. . . . It is thus that one can distinguish action from motion or agitation . . . ; and that is certainly worthwhile. Is it action to move about? Certainly not, and there is no true action except that of a will conscious of itself, conscious, as I was saying, of the means which it employs for its fulfillment, one which adapts them to its goal, and all other forms of action are only imitations, counterfeits, or parodies. The material or the subject of a novel or of a play may therefore be the same at bottom; but they become drama or novel only by the manner in which they are treated; and the manner is not merely different, it is opposite. One will never be able, therefore, to transfer to the stage any novels except those which are already dramatic; and note well that they are dramatic only to the extent to which their heroes are truly the architects of their destiny. (75-76)

1913   Shaw   SMCE

We now have plays . . . which begin with discussion and end with action, and others in which the discussion interpenetrates the action from beginning to end. . . . [Some] plays were passionate arguments from beginning to end. The action of such plays consists of a case to be argued. (138-39)
   See also Shaw under THOUGHT (SMCE 137-39).

c.1930   Stanislavski   SCR

"Action" is not the same as "miming," it is not anything the actor is pretending to present, not something external, but rather internal, nonphysical, a *spiritual activity*. It derives from an unbroken succession of independent processes; and each of these in turn is compounded of desires or impulses aimed at the accomplishment of some objective. (48)
   See also Stanislavski under CONFLICT (SCR 80), MOTIVATION (SCR 51), SUBTEXT (SCR 77-79).

1931-1936   Artaud   AT

After sound and light there is action, and the dynamism of action: here the theatre, far from copying life, puts itself whenever possible in communication with pure forces. And whether you accept or deny them there is nevertheless a way of speaking which gives the name of 'forces' to whatever brings to birth images of energy in the unconscious, and gratuitous crime on the surface. (82)

1936   Stanislavski   SAP

All action in the theatre must have an inner justification, be logical, coherent, and real. (43)

See also Stanislavski under FORWARD MOVEMENT (SAP 258), SUB-TEXT (SAP 256).

1938   Stanislavski   SBC

Action—real, productive action with a purpose is the all-important factor in creativeness, and consequently in speech as well! To speak is to act. . . . Your job is to desire to instill your inner visions in others, and that desire breeds action. (118)

See also Stanislavski under SUBTEXT (SBC 108-109), THOUGHT (SBC 176).

1938   Brecht   BBEB

Our demonstrator [that is, the actor in Epic Theatre] derives his characters entirely from their actions. He imitates their actions and thereby permits us to judge them. A theatre that follows him in this respect is making a complete break with the practice of conventional theatre, which derives actions from character. Thus the conventional theatre shields actions from criticism. (430)

AESTHETIC

The statements quoted here suggest their author's concepts of the nature of beauty or of art or of artistic value. See also DISINTERESTEDNESS, DRAMA, IMAGINATION, IMITATION, ORDER, PLEASURE, and TASTE. See RULES head note.

4th cent. B.C.   Aristotle   APA

Having already treated of the celestial world . . . we proceed to treat of animals. . . . If some have no graces to charm the sense, yet even these, by disclosing to intellectual perception the artistic spirit that designed them, give immense pleasure to all who can trace links of causation and are inclined to philosophy. Indeed, it would be strange if mimic representations of them were [not] attractive, because they disclose the mimetic skill of the painter or sculptor, and the original realities themselves [are] more interesting, to all at any rate who have eyes to discern the reason that presided over their formation. (16-17) . . . Absence of hap-hazard and conduciveness of everything to an end are to be found in Nature's works in the highest degree, and the resultant end of her generation and combinations is a form of the beautiful. (17)

    See also Aristotle under DISINTERESTEDNESS (ANE 85), FORM (AP 31-33, 89), IMITATION (AP 15), MAGNITUDE (AP 91-93), PLEASURE (ANE 597-99). PROBABILITY (AP 105-107), SPECTACLE (AP 29-31).

c.20 B.C.   Horace   HAP

He has won every vote who has blended profit and pleasure, at once delighting and instructing the reader. (479)

1561   Scaliger   SP

Horace most aptly said, ''he carries every vote who mingles the useful with the pleasing,'' for poetry blends all its energies to these two ends, to teach and to please. Now to realize these ends one's work must conform to certain principles. In the first place his poem must be deeply conceived, and be unvaryingly self-consistent. Then he must take pains to temper all with variety, for there is no worse mistake than to glut your hearer before you are done with him. . . . The third poetic quality . . . is what I term vividness. . . . By vividness I mean a certain potency and force in thought and language which compels one to be a willing listener. The fourth is winsomeness, which tempers the ardency of this last quality, of itself inclined to be harsh. Insight and foresight, variety, vividness and winsomeness these, then, are the supreme poetic qualities. (53)

1570   Castelvetro   CP

The artistic is that in the invention of which the artist suffers labour and exercises his genius greatly; and the inartistic, that in the invention of which he does not employ much subtlety of genius, as the inartistic of itself is capable of being seen by any ordinary wit. (28)

See also Castelvetro under IMITATION (CP 37-38, 43-44).

1641   Jonson   JD

There is no doctrine will doe good, where nature is wanting. (29) . . . *Poetry*, and *Picture*, are Arts of a like nature; and both are busie about imitation. It was excellently said of *Plutarch*, *Poetry* was a speaking Picture, and *Picture* a mute Poesie. For they both invent, faine, and devise manie things, and accommodate all they invent to the use, and the service of nature. Yet of the two; the Pen is more noble, than the Pencill. For that can speake to the Understanding; the other, but to the Sense. They both behold pleasure, and profit, as their common Object; but should abstaine from all base pleasures, lest they should erre from their end: and while they seeke to better mens minds, destroy their manners. They are both borne *Artificers*, not made. Nature is more powerful in them than study. *Whosoever* loves not *Picture*, is injurious to Truth: and all the wisdom of *Poetry*. Picture is the invention of Heaven: the most ancient, and most a kinne to Nature. It is it selfe a silent worke: and alwayes of one and the same habit: Yet it doth so enter, and penetrate the inmost affection (being done by an excellent Artificer) as sometimes it o'ercomes the power of speech, and oratory . . . *In Picture*, light is requir'd no lesse than shadow: so in stile, height, as well as humbleness. (59-60)

1695   Dryden. *See* under RULES (DW 3: 322).

1697   Dryden. *See* under THREE UNITIES (DW 3: 430-31.).

1712   Addison   AW

There is nothing that makes its way more directly to the soul than beauty, which immediately diffuses a secret satisfaction and complacency through the imagination, and gives a finishing to any thing that is great or uncommon. The very first discovery of it strikes the mind with an inward joy, and spreads a cheerfulness and delight through all its faculties. There is not perhaps any real beauty or deformity more in one piece of matter than in another, because we might have been so made, that whatsoever now appears loathsome to us might have shown itself agreeable; but we find by experience that there are several modifications of matter, which the mind, without any previous consideration, pronounces at first sight beautiful or deformed. Thus we see that every different species of sensible creatures has its different notions of beauty, and that each of them is most affected with the beauties of its own kind. . . . There is a second kind of beauty that we find in the several products of art and nature, which does not work in the imagination with that warmth and violence as the beauty appears in our proper species, but is apt however to raise in us a secret delight, and a kind of fondness for the places or objects in which we discover it. This consists either in the gaiety or variety of colours, in the symmetry and proportion of parts, in the arrangement and disposition of bodies, or in a just mixture and concurrence of all together. Among these several kinds of beauty the eye takes most delight in colours. (2: 139-40) . . . If we consider the works of nature and art as they are qualified to entertain the imagination, we shall find the last very defective in comparison of the former; for though they may sometimes appear as beautiful or strange, they can have nothing in them of that vastness and immensity, which afford so great an entertainment in the mind of the beholder. The one may be as polite and delicate as the other, but can never show herself so august and magnificent in the design. There is something more bold and masterly in the rough careless strokes of nature, than in the nice touches and embellishments of art. The beauties of the most stately garden or palace lie in a narrow compass, the imagination immediately runs them over, and requires something else to gratify her; but in the wild fields of nature, the sight wanders up and down without confinement, and is fed with an infinite variety of images, without any certain stint or number. For this reason we always find the poet in love with the country life, where nature appears in the greatest perfection, and furnishes out all those scenes that are most apt to delight the imagination. (2: 142)

See also Addison under IMAGINATION (AW 2: 138-39), IMITATION (AW 2: 142).

1730   Voltaire   VE

The principles of all the arts, which depend on imagination, are simple and easy; they are based upon nature and reason. (279)

See also Voltaire under THREE UNITIES (VE 280-81).

1751   Johnson   JW

We pronounce things beautiful because they have something which we agree, for whatever reason, to call beauty, in a greater degree than we have been accustomed to find it in other things of the same kind; and that we transfer the epithet as our knowledge increases, and appropriate it to higher excellence, when higher excellence comes within our view. (2: 431)

1755-1780   Diderot. *See* under ILLUSION (DDE 289).

1767-1769   Lessing. *See* under TASTE (LSPW 279).

c.1781   Johnson. *See* under IMITATION (JL 3: 255).

1798   Goethe. *See* under ILLUSION (GLE 52-57).

1804   Coleridge. *See* under ILLUSION (CSC 1: 178-81).

1808   Schlegel   SCL

Whoever is acquainted with the procedure of true genius, how it is impelled by an almost unconscious and immediate contemplation of great and important truths, and in no wise by convictions obtained mediately, and by circuitious deductions, will be on that ground alone extremely suspicious of all activity in art which originates in an abstract theory. (233) . . . The text [of the *Poetics* of Aristotle] is very much corrupted. . . . Very different is it with the *Rhetoric* . . . [which] is undoubtedly genuine, perfect and easily understood. But how does he consider the oratorical art? As a sister of Logic. . . . When we see how Aristotle, without allowing for imagination or feeling, has viewed oratory only on that side which is accessible to the understanding, and is subservient to an external aim, can it surprise us if that he has still less fathomed the mystery of poetry, that art which is absolved from every other aim but its own uncondi-tional one of creating the beautiful by free invention and clothing it in suitable language? . . . Lessing thought otherwise. But what if Lessing, with his acute analytical criticism, split . . . on the same rock [as Aristotle]? This species of criticism is [effective] when it exposes the contradictions for the understanding . . . but it could hardly rise to the idea of a work of art created by the true genius. . . . Were I to select a guide from among the ancient philosophers, it would undoubtedly be Plato, who acquired the idea of the beautiful not by dissection, which can never give it, but by intuitive inspiration, and in whose works the germs of a genuine Philosophy of Art, are everywhere scattered. (237-38) . . . The ancient art and poetry rigorously separate things which are dissimilar; the romantic delights in indissoluble mixtures; all contrarities: nature and art, poetry and prose, seriousness and mirth, recollection and anticipation, spirituality and sensuality, terrestial and celestial, life and death, are by it blended together in the most intimate combination. . . . The whole of the ancient poetry and art is . . . a *rhythmical nomos* (law), an harmonious promulgation of the permanently established legislation of a world submitted to a beautiful order and reflecting in itself the eternal images of things. Romantic poetry, on the other hand, is the expression of the secret attraction to a chaos which lies concealed in the very bosom of the ordered universe, and it is perpetually striving after new and marvelous births; the life-giving spirit of primal love broods here anew on the face of the waters. The former is more simple, clear, and like to nature in the self-existent perfection of her separate works; the latter, notwithstanding its fragmentary appearance, approaches more to the secret of the universe. For Conception can only comprise each object separately, but nothing in truth can ever exist separately and by itself; Feeling perceives all in all at one and the same time. (342-43)

    See also Schlegel under FORM (SCL 340), POETRY OF THE THEATRE (SCL 36-37), STYLE (SCL 370-71), UNITY (SCL 242-45).

1810   Coleridge. *See* under TASTE (CLSW 369-70).

1813   Hazlitt. *See* under IMAGINATION (HW 1: 134).

1814   Hazlitt. *See* under EVOLUTIONISM (HW 1: 160-61).

1815   Hazlitt   **HW**

If we were asked . . . what it is that constitutes historic expression or ideal beauty, we should answer, not . . . abstract expression or middle forms, but consistency of expression in the one, and symmetry of form in the other. (2: 228)

1815   Coleridge   **CBL**

The BEAUTIFUL, contemplated in its essentials, that is, in *kind* and not in *degree*, is that in which the *many*, still seen as many, becomes one. Take a familiar instance, one of a thousand. The first on the window-pane has by accident crystallized into a striking resemblance of a tree or a seaweed. With what pleasure we trace the parts, and their relations to each other, and to the whole! . . . Nor will our pleasure be less, should the caprice of the crystallization represent some object disagreeable to us, provided only we can see or fancy the component parts each in relation to each, and all forming a whole. . . . The most general definition of beauty, therefore, is . . . Multëity in Unity. (2: 232) . . . It seems evident then, first, that beauty is harmony, and subsists only in composition, and secondly, that the first species of the agreeable can alone be a component part of the beautiful, that namely which is naturally consonant with our senses by the pre-established harmony between nature and the human mind; and thirdly, that even of this species, those objects only can be admitted (according to rule the first) which belong to the eye and ear, because they alone are susceptible of distinction of parts. Should an Englishman gazing on a mass of cloud rich with the rays of the rising sun exclaim, even without distinction of, or reference to its form, or its relation to other objects, how beautiful! I should have no quarrel with him. First, because by the law of association there is in all visual beholdings at least an indistinct subsumption of form and relation: and, secondly, because even in the coincidence between the sight and the object there is an approximation to the reduction of the many into one. But who, that heard a Frenchman call the flavor of a leg of mutton a beautiful taste, would not immediately recognize him for a Frenchman, even though there should be neither grimace or characteristic nasal twang? The result, then, of the whole is that the shapely (i.e., *formosus*) joined with the naturally agreeable, constitutes what, speaking accurately, we mean by the word beautiful (i.e., *pulcher*). (2: 233-34) . . . The safest definition, then, of Beauty, as well as the oldest, is that of Pythagoras: THE REDUCTION OF MANY TO ONE—or, as finely expressed by the sublime disciple of Ammonius. . . . *The sense of beauty subsists in simultaneous intuition of the relation of parts, each to each, and of all to a whole: exciting an immediate and absolute complacency, without intervenence, therefore, of any interest, sensual or intellectual.* The BEAUTIFUL is thus at once distinguished both from the Agreeable, which is beneath it, and from the GOOD, which is above it: for both these have an interest necessarily attached to them: both act on the WILL, and excite a desire for the actual existence of the image or idea contemplated: while the sense of beauty rests gratified in the mere contemplation of intuition, regardless whether it be a fictitious Apollo, or a real Antinous. (2: 238-39) . . . Now Art, used collectively for painting, sculpture, architecture and music, is the mediatress between, and reconciler of, nature and man. It is, therefore, the power of humanizing nature, of infusing the thoughts and passions of man into every thing which is the object of his contemplation; color, form, motion, and sound, are the elements which it combines, and it stamps them into unity in the mould of a moral idea. (2: 253) . . . What is beauty? It is, in the abstract, the unity of the manifold, the coalescence of the diverse; in the concrete it is the union of the shapely (*formosum*) with the vital. In the dead organic it depends on regularity of form, the first and lowest species of which is the triangle with all its modification, as in crystals, architecture, etc.; in the living organic it is not mere regularity of form, which would produce a sense of formality; neither is it subservient to any thing beside itself. It may be present in a disagreeable object, in which the proportion of the parts constitutes a whole; it does not arise from association, as the agreeable does, but sometimes lies in the rupture of association; it is not different to different individuals and nations, as has been said, nor is it connected with the ideas of the good, or the fit, or the useful. The sense of beauty is intuitive, and beauty itself is all that inspires pleasure without, and aloof from, and even contrary to, interest. (2: 256-57)

    See also Coleridge under IMITATION (CBL 2: 256), ORDER (CBL 2: 262).

1816 Hazlitt   HW

It is about sixty years ago that Sir Joshua Reynolds . . . advanced the notion, which has prevailed very much ever since, that Beauty was entirely dependent on custom, or on the conformity of objects to a given standard. Now, we could never persuade ourselves that custom, or the association of ideas, though very powerful, was the only principle of the preference which the mind gives to certain objects over others. Novelty is surely one source of pleasure. ... Nor can we help thinking, that, besides custom, of the conformity of certain objects to others of the same general class, there is also a certain conformity of objects to themselves, a symmetry of parts, a principle of proportion, graduation, harmony ... which makes certain things naturally pleasing or beautiful, and the want of it the contrary. ... [Beauty] is in some way inherent in the object. ... The idea that all pleasure and pain depend on the association of ideas is manifestly absurd: there must be something in itself pleasurable or painful, before it could become possible for the feelings of pleasure or pain to be transferred by association from one object to another. (68) ... Motion is beautiful as it implies either continuity or gradual change. The motion of a hawk is beautiful, either returning in endless circles with suspended wings, or darting right forward in one level line upon its prey. ... All motion is beautiful that is not contradictory to itself, that is free from sudden jerks and shocks,—that is either sustained by the same impulse, or gradually reconciles different impulses together. (71) ... Mr. Burke, in his Essay on the Sublime and Beautiful, has very admirably described the bosom of a beautiful woman, almost entirely with reference to the ideas of motion. Those outlines are beautiful which describe pleasant motions. (1: 72)

See also Hazlitt under SUBJECT (HW 1: 75-76).

c. 1817 Coleridge. See under UNITY (CBL 2: 258).

1818   Hazlitt   HW

The best general notion which I can give of poetry is, that it is the natural impression of any object or event, by its vividness exciting an involuntary movement of imagination and passion, and producing, by sympathy, a certain modulation of the voice, or sounds, expressing it. ... Poetry is the language of the imagination and the passions. It relates to whatever gives immediate pleasure or pain to the human mind. It comes home to the bosoms and businesses of men; for nothing but what so comes home to them in the most general and intelligible shape, can be a subject for poetry. Poetry is the universal language which the heart holds with nature and itself. He who has a contempt for poetry, cannot have much respect for himself, or for any thing else. ... [Poetry] has been the study and delight of mankind in all ages. Many people suppose that poetry is something to be found only in the books, contained in lines of ten syllables, with like endings: but wherever there is a sense of beauty, or power, or harmony, as in the motion of a wave of the sea, in the growth of a flower. ... there is poetry, in its birth. ... There is no thought or feeling that can have entered into the mind of man, which he would be eager to communicate to others, or which they would listen to with delight, that is not a fit subject for poetry. ... Poetry is that fine article within us, that expands, rarefies, refines, raises our whole being. . . . Man is a poetical animal: and those of us who do not study the principles of poetry, act upon them all our lives. (5: 1-2) . . . If poetry is a dream, the business of life is much the same. If it is a fiction, made up of what we wish things to be, and fancy that they are, because we wish them so, there is no other nor better reality . . . Poetry . . . is an imitation of nature, but the imagination and the passions are a part of man's nature. We shape things according to our wishes and fancies, without poetry; but poetry is the most emphatical language that can be found for those creations of the mind 'which ecstacy is very cunning in.' Neither a mere description of natural objects, nor a mere delineation of natural feelings, however distinct or forcible, constitutes the ultimate end and aim of poetry, without the heightenings of the imagination. The light of poetry is not only a direct but also a reflected light, that while it shews us the object, throws a sparkling radiance on all around it: the flame of the passions, communicated to the imagination, reveals to us, as with a flash of lightning, the inmost recesses of thought, and penetrates our whole being. Poetry represents forms chiefly as they suggest other forms; feelings, as they suggest forms or other feelings. Poetry puts a spirit of life and motion into the universe. It describes the flowing, not the fixed. It does not define the limits of sense, or analyze the distinctions of the understanding, but signifies the excess of the imagination beyond the actual or ordinary impression of any object or feeling. The poetical impression of any object is that uneasy, exquisite sense of beauty or power that cannot be contained within itself; that is impatient of all limit. (5: 3) . . . Poetry is only the highest eloquence of passion, the most vivid form of expression that can be given to our conception of any thing, whether pleasurable or painful, mean or dignified, delightful or distressing. It is the perfect coincidence of the image and the words with the feeling we have, and of which we cannot get rid in any other way, that gives an instant 'satisfaction to the thought.' This is equally the origin of wit and fancy, of comedy and tragedy, of the sublime and pathetic. (5: 7-8)

See also Hazlitt under FORWARD MOVEMENT (HW 5: 10).

c.1820   Hazlitt   HW

Beauty does not consist in a medium, but in gradation or harmony. It has been the fashion of late to pretend to refer everything to association of ideas . . . [but] association implies something to be associated, and if there is a pleasing association, there must be first something naturally pleasing from which the secondary satisfaction is reflected, or to which it is cojoined. The chirping of a sparrow is as much a rural and domestic sound as the notes of the robin or the thrush, but it does not serve as a point to link other interests to because it wants beauty in itself. . . . Those who deny that there is a natural and pleasing softness arising from harmony or gradation, might as well affirm that sudden and abrupt transitions do not make our impressions more distinct as that they do not make them more harsh and violent. Beauty consists in gradation of colours or symmetry of form (conformity): strength or sublimity arises from the sense of power, and is aided by contrast. The ludicrous is the incoherent, arising, not from a conflicting power, but from weakness or the inability of any habitual impulse to sustain itself. (2: 463)

c.1820   Hegel   HFA

Fine art is not art in the true sense of the term until it is . . . free, and its *highest* function is only . . . satisfied when it has established itself in a sphere which it shares with religion and philosophy, becoming thereby merely one mode and form through which the Divine, the profoundest interests of mankind, and spiritual truths of widest range, are brought to consciousness and expressed. . . . The world, into which the profundity of thought penetrates, is a supersensuous one, a world which to start with is posited as a Beyond in contrast to the immediacy of ordinary conscious life and present sensation. It is the freedom of reflecting consciousness which disengages itself from the immersion in the *"this side,"* or immediacy, in other words sensuous reality and finitude. But the mind is able, too, to heal the *fracture* which is thus created in its progression. From the wealth of its own primary resources it brings into being the works of fine art as the bond of mediation between that which is exclusively external, sensuous, and transitory, and the medium of pure thought, between Nature and its finite reality, and the infinite freedom of a reason which comprehends. (1: 8-9) . . . It is . . . [the] entire sphere of the empirical world, whether on its personal side or its objective side, which we ought . . . to call in a stricter sense than when we apply the term to the world of art, merely a show or appearance, and an even more unyielding form of deception. It is only beyond the immediacy of emotional life and that world of external objects that we shall discover reality in any true sense of the term. (1: 10)

See also Hegel under IDEALISM (HFA 1: 2-3, 4: 265-67).

1824   Hazlitt. *See* under IDEALISM (HW 9: 405), UNIVERSALITY (HW 9: 402).

1830   Hazlitt. *See* under IDEALISM (HW 9: 429-30, 431-32, 432), IMITATION (HW 9: 425).

1863-1867   Taine   THEL

A work of literature is not a mere play of imagination, a solitary caprice of a heated brain, but a transcript of contemporary manners, a [specimen] of a certain kind of mind. [One can] retrace, from the monuments of literature, the style of man's feelings and thoughts for centuries back. [Three different sources contribute to our understanding of the literary monument—race, milieu, and period.] (1) . . . Art is a kind of philosophy made sensible, religion a poem taken for true, philosophy an art and a religion dried up, and reduced to simple ideas. There is therefore, at the core of each of these three groups, a common element, the conception of the world and its principles; and if they differ among themselves, it is because each combines with the common, a distinct element: now the power of abstraction, again the power to personify and to believe, and finally the power to personify and not believe. (15) . . . Every kind of human production . . . literature, music, the fine arts, philosophy, science, statecraft, industries . . . has for its direct cause a moral disposition, or a combination of moral dispositions: the cause given, [these works] appear; the cause withdrawn, they vanish: the weakness or intensity of the cause measures their weakness or intensity. They are bound up with their causes, as a physical phenomenon with its condition, as the dew with the fall of the variable temperature, as dilatation with heat. (18)

See also Taine under EVOLUTIONISM (THEL 18-19), DRAMA (THEL 20).

1864   Taine   TLA

Suppose . . . we should be able to mark clearly and precisely the various intellectual conditions which have led to the birth of Italian painting—its development, its bloom, its varieties and decline. Suppose the same undertaking successful with other countries, and other ages, and with the different branches of art, architecture, sculpture, painting, poetry and music. Suppose that through the effect of all these discoveries, we succeed in defining the nature, and in marking the conditions of existence of each art, we shall then have a complete explanation of the Fine Arts, and of art in general; that is to say, a philosophy of the Fine Arts—what is called an *aesthetic* system. This is what we aim at, . . . and nothing else. (36) . . . My sole duty is to offer you facts, and show you how these facts are produced. The modern method, which I strive to pursue, and which is beginning to be introduced in all the moral sciences, consists in considering human productions, and particularly works of art, as facts and productions of which it is essential to mark the characteristics and seek the causes, and nothing more. Thus understood, science neither pardons nor proscribes; it verifies and explains. (37) . . . The end of a work of art is to manifest some essential or salient character, consequently some important idea, clearer and more completely than is attainable from real objects. Art accomplishes this end by employing a group of connected parts, the relationships of which it systematically modifies. In the three imitative arts of sculpture, painting, and poetry, these groups correspond to real objects. (76) . . . That established, . . . we see, on examining the different parts of this definition, that the first is essential and the second accessory. An aggregate of connected parts is necessary in all art which the artist may modify so as to portray character; but in every art it is not necessary that this aggregate should correspond with real objects, it is sufficient that it exists. If we therefore meet with aggregates of connected parts which are not imitations of real objects, there will be arts which will not have imitation for their point of view. This is the case, and it is thus that architecture and music are born. (76-77) . . . Man, in many respects, is an animal endeavoring to protect himself against nature and against other men. He is obliged to provide himself with food, clothing, and shelter, and to defend against climate, want, and disease. To do this he tills the ground, navigates the sea, and devotes himself to different industrial and commercial pursuits. . . . After so many inventions and such labor, he is not yet emancipated for his original condition; he is still an animal, better fed and better protected than other animals; he still thinks only of himself, and of his kindred. At this moment a superior life dawns on him—that of contemplation, by which he is led to interest himself in the creative and permanent causes on which his own being and that of his fellows depend, in the leading and essential characters which rule each aggregate, and impress their marks on the minutest details. Two ways are open to him for this purpose. The first is Science, by which, analyzing these causes and these fundamental laws, he expresses them in abstract terms and precise formula; the second is Art, by which he manifests these causes and these fundamental laws no longer through arid definitions, inaccessible to the multitude, and only intelligible to a favored few, but in a sensible way, appealing not alone to reason, but also to the heart and senses of the humblest individual. Art has this peculiarity that it is at once *noble* and *popular*, manifesting whatever is most exalted, and manifesting it to all. (82-84) . . . *A work of art is determined by an aggregate which is the general state of the mind and surrounding circumstances.* (87) . . . All things equal in other respects, the work which expresses a beneficent character, is superior to the work which expresses a malevolent character. If, in two given works, both exhibit, with the same talent in execution, natural forces of like grandeur, that which represents to us a hero is better than that which represents to us a dolt; and in this gallery of living works of art, which form the definitive museum of the human mind, you will see established, according to our new principle, a new order of ranks. At the lowest step of all are the types preferred by the literature of realism and by the comic drama; that is to say, simpletons and egotists—limited, weak and inferior natures. They are those, in fact, encountered in ordinary life, or those that can be turned into ridicule. (273-74).

   See also Taine under CHARACTER (TLA 307), HERO (TLA 180, 351-53), UNITY (TLA 332-33).

1871 Nietzsche   NBT

The continuous development of art is bound up with the duplexity of the *Apollonian* and the *Dionysian*: in like manner as procreation is dependent on the duality of the sexes, involving perpetual conflicts with only periodical intervening reconciliations. . . . It is in connection with Apollo and Dionysus, the two art deities of the Greeks, that we learn that there existed in the Grecian world a wide antithesis, in origin and aims, between the art of the shaper, the Apollonian, and the nonplastic art of music, that of Dionysus: both these so heterogeneous tendencies run parallel to each other, for the most part openly at variance, and continually inciting each other to new and more powerful births, to perpetuate in them the strife of this antithesis . . . till at last, by a metaphysical miracle of the Hellenic will, they appear paired with each other, and through this pairing eventually generate the equally Dionysian and Apollonian art-work of Attic tragedy. . . . Let us conceive them first of all as the separate art-worlds of *dreamland* and *drunkenness*. . . . (21-22)

See also Nietzsche under AFFECT (NBT 57-58), DRAMA (NBT 67), ILLUSION (NBT 57-58), TRAGEDY (NBT 127), UNITY (NBT 27), WONDER (NBT 25-26).

1873   Nietzsche. *See* under METAPHOR (NEG 178-88).

1875   Shaw. *See* under DRAMA (SMCE 315-16).

1875   Nietzsche. *See* under CONFLICT (NTS 128-30), POETRY OF THE THEATRE (NTS 149-50).

1882   Nietzsche   **NJW**

In regard to all aesthetic values I now avail myself of this radical distinction: I ask in every single case, "Has hunger or superfluity become creative here?" At the outset another distinction might seem to recommend itself more. . . . whether the desire for rigidity, for perpetuation, for *being* is the cause of the creating, or the desire for destruction, for change, for the new, for the future— for *becoming*. . . . The desire for *destruction*, change and becoming, may be the expression of overflowing power, pregnant with futurity (my *terminus* for this is of course the word "Dionysian"); but is may also be the hatred of the ill-constituted, destitute and unfortunate, which destroys, and *must* destroy, because the enduring, yea, all that endures, in fact all being, excites and provokes it. . . . The will to *perpetuation* requires equally a double interpretation. It may on the one hand proceed from gratitude and love:—art of this origin will always be an art of apotheosis, perhaps . . . clear and kindhearted as with Goethe, and spreading a Homeric brightness and glory over everything (in this case I speak of *Apollonian* art). It may also, however, be the tyrannical will of a sorely-suffering, struggling or tortured being, who would like to stamp his most personal, individual and narrow characteristics, the very idiosyncrasy of his suffering, as an obligatory law and constraint on others; who, as it were, takes revenge on all things, in that he imprints, enforces and brands *his* image, the image of his torture, upon them. (334-35)

1887   Nietzsche. *See* under AFFECT (NGM 130-31), DISINTERESTED-NESS (NGM 131).

1887   Chekhov. *See* under REALISM (CL 57).

1888   Nietzsche   **NTI**

Nothing is beautiful; man alone is beautiful: all aesthetic rests on this piece of ingenuousness, it is the first axiom of this science. And now let us straightway add the second to it: nothing is ugly save the degenerate man—within these two first principles the realm of aesthetic judgments is confined. . . . Ugliness is understood to signify a hint and a symptom of degeneration: that which reminds us however remotely of degeneracy, impels us to the judgment "ugly." (75-76)

1888   Neitzsche   **NW**

Metaphysics, religion, morality, science—all these things are but the offshoot of [man's] will to art, to falsehood, to a flight from "truth," to a denial of "truth." This ability, this artistic capacity *par excellence* of man—thanks of which he overcomes reality with lies—is a quality which he has in common with all other forms of existence. He himself is indeed a piece of reality, of truth, of nature: how could he help being also a piece of genius in prevarication. . . . [This] is the profoundest and highest secret motive behind everything relating to virtue, science, piety and art. . . .Love, enthusiasm, "God"—are but subtle forms of ultimate self-deception; they are but seductions to life and to the belief in life! In those moments when man was deceived, when he befooled himself and when he believed in life: Oh, how this spirit swelled within him! Oh, what ecstasies he had! What power he felt! And what artistic triumphs in the feeling of power! (289-90)

1890   Chekhov   **CL**

Of the word "art" I am terrified, as merchants' wives are terrified of "brim-stone." When people talk to me of what is artistic and inartistic, of what is dramatic and non-dramatic, of tendency, realism, and so on, I am bewildered, hesitatingly assent, and answer with banal half-truths not worth a brass farthing. I divide all works into two classes: those I like and those I don't. I have no other criterion, and if you ask me why I like Shakespeare and don't like Zlatovratsky, I don't venture to answer. (137)

1894   Brunetière. *See* under WILL (BLD 81).

1897   Shaw   **SDC**

Vital art work comes always from a cross between art and life: art being of one sex only, and quite sterile by itself. (259)

1903   Shaw   **SMS**

All this academic art is far worse than the trade in sham antique furniture; for the man who sells me an oaken chest which he swears was made in the XIII century, though as a matter of fact he made it himself only yesterday, at least does not pretend that there are any modern ideas in it; whereas your academic copier of fossils offers them to you as the latest outpouring of the human spirit, and, worst of all, kidnaps young people as pupils and persuades them that his limitations are rules, his observances dexterities, his timidities good taste, and his emptiness purities. And when he declares that art should not be didactic, all the people who have nothing to teach and all the people who don't want to learn agree with him emphatically. (xxxvi)

1908   Pirandello. *See* under GENRE (POH 22-32). HUMOR (POH 31 ff.), ILLUSION (POH 63-64, 66-67).

1909   Shaw. *See* under GENRE DEFINITION (STPB xx).

1919   Eliot. *See* under OBJECTIVE CORRELATIVE (EEE 61).

1921   Eliot   **ESW**

It is said that the stage can be used for a variety of purposes, that in only one of them perhaps is it united with literary art. . . . But where you have "imitations of life" on the stage, with speech, the only standard that we can allow is the standard of the work of art, aiming at the same intensity at which poetry and the other forms of art aim. (61)
    See also Eliot under THOUGHT (ESW 61).

1924   Eliot. *See* under IMITATION (EEE 11).

1930   Brecht   **BBT**

Why this obstinate clinging to the pleasure element? This addiction to drugs? Why so little concern with one's own interests as soon as one steps outside one's own home? . . . We have seen that opera is sold as evening entertainment, and that this puts definite bounds to all attempts to transform it. We see this entertainment has to be devoted to illusion, and must be of a ceremonial kind. (40-41)

1931-1936   Artaud   **AT**

    We abolish the stage and the auditorium and replace them by a single site, without partition or barrier of any kind, which will become the theater of the action. A direct communication will be re-established between the spectator and the spectacle, between the actor and the spectator, from the fact that the spectator, placed in the middle of the action, is engulfed and physically affected by it. This envelopment results, in part, from the very configuration of the room itself. (96) . . . To speak of the spectacle's character as true illusion or of the direct and immediate influence of the action on the spectator will not be hollow words. For this diffusion of action over an immense space will oblige the lighting of a scene and the varied lighting of a performance to fall upon the public as much as upon the actors—and to the several simultaneous actions or several phases of an identical action in which the characters, swarming over each other like bees, will endure all the onslaughts of the situations and the external assaults of the tempestuous elements, will correspond to the physical means of lighting, of producing thunder or wind, whose repercussions the spectator will undergo. However, a central position will be reserved which, without serving, properly speaking, as a stage, will permit the bulk of the action to be concentrated and brought to a climax whenever necessary. (97)

See also Artaud under POETRY OF THE THEATRE (AT 12).

1938   Stanislavski. *See* under UNITY (SBC 61).

1940   Brecht   **BBT**

The rejection of empathy is not the result of a rejection of the emotions, nor does it lead to such. The crude aesthetic thesis that emotions can only be stimulated by means of empathy is wrong. None the less a nonaristotelian dramaturgy has to apply a cautious criticism to the emotions which it aims at and incorporates. Certain artistic tendencies like the provocative behavior of Futurists and Dadaists and the icing-up of music point to a crisis of the emotions. . . . Fascism's grotesque emphasizing of the emotions, together perhaps with the no less important threat to the rational element in Marxist aesthetics, led us to lay particular stress on the rational. Nevertheless, there are many contemporary works of art where one can speak of a decline in emotional effectiveness due to their isolation from reason, or its revival thanks to a stronger rationalist message. (145)

1948   Brecht   **BBBG**

The goal [of Epic theatre] was a theater of the scientific age, and when its planners found it hard to borrow or steal enough from the arsenal of existing aesthetic concepts to keep the aesthetes of the press at arm's length any longer, they simply threatened "to develop an intellectual discipline out of the means of pleasure and to convert certain institutions from place of entertainment into organs of information." (Notes on *The Rise and Fall of the City of Mahagonny*) —in other words, to depart from the realm of the merely pleasurable. Aesthetics [was] the heritage of a class grown depraved and parasitic. . . . Nevertheless, what was practiced as the theater of a scientific age was not science but theater. With the innovations accumulated during the time of the Nazis and the war, when opportunities for practical demonstration ceased, it is now feasible to examine the place of this species of theater in aesthetics, or at any rate to indicate the outlines of a possible aesthetics for it. . . . Let us . . .—though many people will regret it—retract our intention of departing from the realm of the pleasurable. Let us announce our intention of settling down in this realm—though even more will regret it. Let us consider the theater as a place of entertainment, as it should be considered in an aesthetics, and let us inquire what kind of entertainment we can accept. (13-14)

See also Brecht under DRAMA (BBBG 13, 14, 19-20, 24), PLEASURE (BBBG 15), STYLE (BBBG 23, 39-40).

1956   Brecht. *See* under THOUGHT (BBT 277, 279).

AFFECT

Contained here are statements concerning the perception of drama, describing the mental impressions that it induces or the mechanisms by which the impressions are created. In general the treatment of aesthetic perception evolves from something like a "stimulus-response" model to one which is more nearly phenomenological. At first the significant condition is the object itself, which, if of a certain kind, will produce certain responses automatically —or at least should do so for the "right reader." By the mid-twentieth century, however, theorists seem to assume that response is multidimensional, relativistic, indeterminate, and intersubjective, the significant condition being the specific perceptual process which determines the object that is perceived, the nature of the stimulation "it" produces, and the responses that result. See also ALIENATION, CATHARSIS, DISTANCE, FEAR, FORWARD MOVEMENT, HUMOR, IDENTIFICATION, ILLUSION, INSTRUCTION, IRONY, OBJECTIVE CORELLATIVE, OBJECTIVITY, PITY, PLEASURE, SURPRISE, SUSPENSE, TASTE, and WONDER.

4th cent. B.C.   Aristotle   AR

The Affections are those things, being attended by pleasure or pain, by which men are altered in regard to their judgments;—as anger, pity, fear, and the like, with their opposites. (69)

4th cent. B.C.   Aristotle   APO

In addition to this common pleasure [of music for recreation], felt and shared by all (for the pleasure given by music is natural, and therefore adapted to all ages and characters), may it not have also some influence over the character and the soul? It must have such an influence if characters are affected by it. And that they are so affected is proved in many ways, and not least by the power which the songs of Olympus exercise; for beyond question they inspire enthusiasm, and enthusiasm is an emotion of the ethical part of the soul. Besides, when men hear imitations, even apart from the rhythms and tunes themselves, their feelings move in sympathy. Since then music is a pleasure, and virtue consists in rejoicing and loving and hating aright, there is clearly nothing which we are so much concerned to acquire and to cultivate as the power of forming right judgments, and of taking delight in good dispositions and noble actions. Rhythm and melody supply imitations of anger and gentleness, and also courage and temperance, and of all the qualities contrary to these, and of the other qualities of character, which hardly fall short of all the actual affections, as we know from our own experience, for in listening to such strains our souls undergo a change. The habit of feeling pleasure or pain at mere representations is not far removed from the same feeling about realities. (1340a: 1-25)

See also Aristotle under ACTION (AP 37-39, 45, 47-49), AESTHETIC (APA 16-17), DRAMA (AP 107-11), EXPOSITION (AR 182), FORM (AP 31-33), IMITATION (AP 97-101, and APO 1340a: 11-25), MAGNITUDE (AP 91-93), METAPHOR (AR 167-68), PLOT (AP 25-29, 39, 45-49, 49), PROBABILITY (AP 35-37), RECOGNITION (AP 41-43), REVERSAL (AP 41-43, 67-69), SPECTACLE (AP 29-31, 61), SUBJECT (AP 53), THOUGHT (AP 69-71), TRAGEDY (AP 23-25), VARIETY (AP 93).

c.20 B.C.   Horace   HAP

Not enough is it for poems to have beauty: they must have charm, and lead the hearer's soul where they will. As men's faces smile on those who smile, so they respond to those who weep. If you would have me weep, you must first feel grief yourself: then . . . will your misfortunes hurt me: if the words you utter are ill suited, I shall laugh or fall asleep. Sad tones befit the face of sorrow; blustering accents that of anger; jests become the merry, solemn words the grave. (459)

See also Horace under DECORUM (HAP 459-61), DRAMA (HAP 479), DRAMATIZATION (HAP 465-67), IMITATION (HAP 477), STYLE (HAP 459, 479).

1561   Scaliger. See under ACTION (SP 62), AESTHETIC (SP 53), INSTRUCTION (SP 82-83), THREE UNITIES (SP 60).

1570   Castelvetro   CP

Poesy was founded for the delight of the ignorant mob and the common people, and not for the delight of the learned. (73) . . . There is no possibility of making the spectators believe that many days and nights have passed, when they themselves obviously know that only a few hours have actually elapsed: they refuse to be so deceived. (86)

See also Castelvetro under DRAMA (CP 60-61), FUNCTIONALISM (CP 68), GENRE (CP 105), HERO (CP 110-11), IMAGINATION (CP 114-15), TRAGEDY (CP 95-96, 98).

c.1583   Sidney   SDP

[The poet] excelleth history, not only in furnishing the mind with knowledge, but in setting it forward to that which deserveth to be called and accounted good; which setting forward, and moving it well-doing, indeed setteth the laurel crown upon the poet as victorious, not only of the historian, but over the philosopher, howsoever in teaching it may be questionable. For suppose it be granted—that which I suppose with great reason may be denied—that the philosopher, in respect to his methodical proceeding, teach more perfectly than the poet, yet do I think that no man . . . [can] compare the philosopher in moving with the poet. And the moving is of a higher degree than teaching, it may by this appear, that it is well nigh both the cause and effect of teaching; for who will be taught, if he be not moved with desire to be taught? And what so much good doth that teaching bring forth—I speak still of moral doctrine—as that it moveth one to do that which it doth teach? (22) . . . I have known men, that even with reading Amadis de Gaule, which, God knoweth, wanteth much of a perfect poesy, have found their hearts moved to the exercise of courtesy, liberality, and especially courage. Who readeth Aeneas carrying old Anchises on his back, that wisheth not it were his fortune to perform so excellent an act? Whom do not those words of Turnus move, the tale of Turnus having planted his image in the imagination? (24) . . . Infinite proofs of the strange effects of [poetry] might be alleged. . . . The one of Menenius Agrippa, who, when the whole people of Rome had resolutely divided themselves from the senate with apparent show of utter ruin, though he were, for that time, an excellent orator, came among them upon trust either of figurative speeches or cunning insinuations, and much less with far-fet maxims of philosophy. . . . He telleth them a tale, that there was a time when all the parts of the body made a mutinous conspiracy against the belly, which they thought devoured the fruits of each other's labor; they concluded they would let so unprofitable a spender starve. In the end, to be short . . . with punishing the belly they plagued themselves. This, applied by him, wrought such effect in the people, as I never read that ever words brought forth but then so sudden and so good an alteration; for upon reasonable conditions a perfect reconcilement ensued. (25) . . . How much [tragedy] can move, Plutarch yieldeth a notable testimony of the abominable tyrant Alexander Pheraeus; from whose eyes a tragedy, well made and represented, drew abundance of tears, who without all pity had murdered infinite numbers, and some of his own blood; so as he that was not ashamed to make matters for tragedies, yet could not resist the sweet violence of a tragedy. And if it wrought no further good in him, it was that he, in despite of himself, withdrew himself from hearkening to that which might mollify his hardened heart. (29)

See also Sidney under COMEDY (SDP 28), GENRE (SDP 50), INSTRUCTION (SDP 15-16, 17-18, 20, 26), TRAGEDY (SDP 28-29).

1601   Jonson See under SYMBOL (JBW).

1605   Jonson See under POETIC JUSTICE (JBW).

1609   de Vega   **VAWP**

Equivoke and the uncertainty arising from ambiguity have always held a large
place among the crowd, for it thinks that it alone understands what the other
one is saying. Better still are the subjects in which honor has a part, since they
deeply stir everybody; along with them go virtous deeds, for virtue is everywhere loved; hence we see, if an actor chance to represent a traitor, he is so
hateful to everyone that what he wishes to buy is not sold him; but if he is loyal,
they lend to him and invite him, and even the chief men honor him, love him,
seek him out, entertain him, and acclaim him. (35-36)

    See also de Vega under MAGNITUDE (VAWP 32), VARIETY (VAWP
30).

1611   Jonson. Compare with RATIONALISM (JBW).

1641   Jonson   **JD**

[Among the virtues of "the true Artificer":] How he doth raigne in mens
affections; how invade, and breake in upon them; and makes their minds like
the thing he writes. (33)

    See also Jonson under AESTHETIC (JD 59-60), MAGNITUDE (JD 102),
SURPRISE (JD 35).

1648   Corneille. *See* under AUTHORITY (CSP 8-9).

1657   d'Aubignac   **AAS**

[Spectators] never go from the Theatre without carrying along with them the
Idea of the Persons represented; the knowledge of those Virtues and Vices, of
which they have seen the Examples; their memory repeating continually to them
those Lessons which have been derived to them, from sensible and present
objects. (1: 6)...The Poet considering in his Play the Representation or
Spectacle of it, does all that he can to make it agreeable to the Spectators; for
his business is to please them. And therefore he shall preserve all the noblest
Incidents of his Story, he shall make all his Actors appear with the best
Characters he can, he shall employ the finest Figures of Rhetorick, and the
Moving'st Passions, observing to hide nothing that ought to be known and
please, and to shew nothing that ought to be hid, and may offend; and in fine,
he shall try all means to gain the esteem and admiration of the Audience. (1:
37-38) . . . We are not to forget . . . that if the Subject is not conformable to the
Customs and Manners, as well as Opinions of the Spectators, it will never take,
what pains soever the Poet himself take, and whatsoever Ornaments he employs to set his Play off. For all Dramatick Poems must be different, according
to the People before whom they are represented; and from thence often
proceeds that the success is different, though the Play be still the same. (2:

69-70) . . . All passions that are not founded upon Opinions and Customs conformable to those of the Spectators, are sure to be cold, and of no effect, because they being possessed with an Opinion contrary to the Action of the Player, cannot approve of any thing he says or does in another sense. (3: 44)

See also d'Aubignac under DRAMA (AAS 1: 4, 7), EXPOSITION (AAS 3: 15-16), INSTRUCTION (AAS 1: 5, 3: 32-33), PATHOS (AAS 3: 40-44), POETIC JUSTICE (AAS 1: 5-6), SPECTACLE (AAS 3: 95-98), SUBJECT (AAS 2: 64, 68-69), THREE UNITIES (AAS 2: 111-13).

1660   Corneille   CFD

According to Aristotle, the sole end of dramatic poetry is to please the audience. . . . [He says] that in order to find that pleasure which is fitting to the audience, the poet must follow the precepts of the art and give that pleasure according to them. (159)

See also Corneille under ACTION (CDTU 235), CHARACTER (CFD 144-46), CLOSURE (CFD 143, 148), PLOT (CSP 197-98), POETIC JUSTICE (CFD 141), RULES (143-44), THREE UNITIES (CDENA 32, CTU 817).

1663   Molière   MP

Judgment and good sense have no exclusive place in theatres. Standing or seated, men may have poor opinions, but, as a general thing, I'd rather trust the approbation of the pit; for the reason, that among those who fill it are many who are capable of judging a play by rules of art, and others who judge by the best method of judging, which is by its effect on them—not by blind prejudice, or silly complaisance, or foolish prudery. (6: 324)

1665   Dryden. See under STYLE (DW 1, 2: 19-20).

1668   Dryden   DW

Short speeches and replies are more apt to move the passions and beget concernment in us, than [long speeches]; for it is unnatural for any one in a gust of passion to speak long together, or for another in the same condition, to suffer him, without interruption. Grief and passion are like floods raised in little brooks by a sudden rain; they are quickly up; and if the concernment be poured unexpectedly in upon us, it overflows us: but a long sober shower gives them leisure to run out as they came in, without troubling the ordinary current. (1, 2: 88)

See also Dryden under DRAMA (DW 1, 2: 160), DRAMATIZATION (DW 1, 2: 90-93), STYLE (DW 1, 2: 85-86).

1668   Racine. See under FLAW (RP 154-55).

1669   Molière   **MP**

I do not see that there is any crime in being moved by the sight of honest passion. The absolute insensibility to which [my critics] seek to raise our souls is a lofty stage of virtue; but I doubt if human nature has the strength to attain to such perfection, and I submit that it may be better to rectify and calm men's passions than seek to crush them altogether. (2: 37-38)

    See also Molière under COMEDY (MP 2: 31-32).

1670   Racine. *See* under UNITY (RP 155).

1671   Dryden. *See* under COMEDY (DW 1, 2: 191-92), POETIC JUSTICE (DW 1, 2: 198-201).

1674   Racine   **RP**

Certain people have . . . censured me for that very simplicity [of plot] I strove so diligently to attain: they believed that a tragedy so denuded of intrigue could not be according to the rules of dramatic art. I wished to know whether the tragedy had bored them, and learned that they all admitted that it had not, but had moved them, and that they would willingly witness it again. What more could they demand? I beg them to think well enough of themselves not to believe that a play which stirs them and gives them pleasure, *can* be absolutely at variance with the rules. The principal rule is to please and to stir; all others are simply means to arrive at that end. . . . Let them leave to us the trouble of interpreting Aristotle's theory of poetry, and reserve for themselves the pleasure of weeping and being moved. . . . (156)

1679   Dryden. *See* under HERO (DW 1, 2: 270-271, 277), INSTRUCTION (DW 1, 2: 274), PLOT (DW 1, 2: 288), TRAGEDY (DW 1, 2: 266-67).

1695   Dryden. *See* under IMITATION (DW 3: 322-25).

1697   Dryden. *See* under TRAGEDY (DW 3: 430-31).

1711   Addison. *See* under DRAMATIZATION (AW 1: 75), PLOT (AW 1: 72), POETIC JUSTICE (AW 1: 71-72) SPECTACLE (AW 1: 74-75, 77-78); compare with THOUGHT (AW 1: 70).

1711   Dryden. *See* under MORALITY (DW 1, 2: 309-10).

1712   Addison   **AW**

Those who have laid down rules for rhetoric or poetry, advise the writer to work himself up, if possible, to the pitch of sorrow which he endeavors to produce in others. There are none therefore who stir up pity so much as those who indite their own sufferings. Grief has a natural eloquence belonging to it, and breaks out in more moving sentiments than can be supplied by the finest imagination. Nature on this occasion dictates a thousand passionate things which cannot be supplied by art. It is for this reason that the short speeches or sentences which we often meet with in history make a deeper impression on the mind of the reader than the most laboured strokes in a well-written tragedy. Truth and matter of fact sets the person actually before us in the one, whom fiction places at a greater distance from us in the other. (120)

See also Addison under ACTION (AW 1: 427) AESTHETIC (AW 2: 139-40), DRAMA (AW 2: 184), FORM (AW 2:227), IMAGINATION (AW 2: 138-39); compare with THOUGHT (AW 2: 41).

1725   Voltaire   VE

A plot regularly conducted will contribute but little [to satisfy the cool deliberate reader]; and though it should be affecting, yet even that will not be sufficient: all poetical performances, though ever so perfect in other points, must necessarily displease if the lines are not strong and harmonious, and if there does not run through the whole a continued elegance and inexpressible charm of verse, that genius only can inspire, that wit alone can never attain, and about which people have agreed so ill. (277)

c.1749   Voltaire. See under COMEDY (VW 10, 1: 280).

1751   Johnson. See under AESTHETIC (JW 2: 431), HERO (JW 3: 242).

1755-1780   Diderot. See under CHARACTER (DDE 288, 291), COMEDY (DDE 287, 288-89), SUBJECT (DDE 287), TRAGEDY (DDE 291).

1758   Diderot   DDP

The theatre is the only place where the tears of the virtuous man and the rogue are mingled. There the mean man regrets the injustices he has committed, feels sorry for the evil he has done, and is indignant toward a man of his own sort. But the impression is made, and it remains in the hearts of each of us, in spite of ourselves. The evil man leaves his seat less disposed to do evil than if he had listened to a severe and pitiless orator. . . . I don't want clever maxims on our stage, but impressions. . . . The greatest poet is he whose work remains long in our minds. Oh, dramatists, the true applause which you seek is not the hand-clapping which follows a brilliant verse, it is rather that profound sigh that brings relief. But there is another impression to make, a more violent one, . . . and that is to make your audience feel ill at ease. Their minds will be troubled, uncertain, distracted, and your spectators be like those who in the presence of an earthquake see the walls of their homes rock, and feel the earth yawn before them. (289-90)

See also Diderot under DRAMA (DDP 287-89), RULES (DDP 298); compare with IDEALISM (DDP 298, 299).

1759 Johnson. See under UNIVERSALITY (JW 1: 222).

1765 Johnson   **JS**

Through all the denominations [that is, genres] of drama, *Shakespeare's* mode of composition is the same; an interchange of seriousness and merriment, by which the mind is softened at one time, and exhilarated at another. But whatever be his purpose, whether to gladden or depress, . . . he never fails to attain his purpose; as he commands us, we laugh or mourn, or sit silent with quiet expectation, [or] in tranquility without indifference. (18)

See also Johnson under GENRE (JS 16).

1766 Lessing. See under IMITATION (LSPW 23),TRAGEDY (LSPW 31).

1767-1769 Lessing   **LSPW**

The only unpardonable fault of a tragic poet is this, that he leaves us cold; if he interests us he may do as he likes with the little mechanical rules. (273) . . . Pity and fear are those passions which we, not the acting personages, feel in tragedy; they are those passions through which the acting personages touch us, not those which draw upon them their own misfortunes. There might be a play in which they both exist. But as yet I know no play, in which the commiserated person has been plunged into misfortune by the means of misconceived pity and misconceived fear. (419)

See also Lessing under CLOSURE (LSPW 377), DRAMA (LSPW 233, 426), GENRE (LSPW 248,425), LANGUAGE (LSPW 393-94), THOUGHT (LSPW 329), TRAGEDY (LSPW 415).

1778 Diderot   **DPA**

Have you ever thought on the difference between the tears raised by a tragedy of real life and those raised by a touching narrative? You hear a fine piece of recitation; by little and little your thoughts are involved, your heart is touched, and your tears flow. With the tragedy of real life the thing, the feeling and the effect, are all one; your heart is reached at once, you utter a cry, your head swims, and the tears flow. These tears come of a sudden, the others by degrees. And here is the superiority of a true effect of nature over a well-planned scene. It does at one stroke what the scene leads up to by degrees, but it is far more difficult to reproduce its effect; one incident ill given would shatter it. Accents are more easily mimicked than actions, but actions go straighter to the mark.

This is the basis of a canon to which I believe there is no exception. If you would avoid coldness you must complete your effect by action and not by talk. (17-18)

   See also Diderot under CONVENTION (DPA102).

1797   Goethe   GED

The contemplative listener [play spectator] is in reason found to remain in a state of constant sensuous exertion; he must not pause to meditate, but must follow in a state of passionate eagerness; his fancy is entirely put to silence; no claims may be made upon it, and even that which is narrated must be so placed before the eyes of the spectator as though it were actually taking place. (339)

1808   Schlegel   SCL

The object proposed [by a dramatic work] is to produce an impression on an assembled multitude, to rivet their attention, and to excite their interest and sympathy. In this respect the poet's occupation coincides with that of the orator. . . . (37) The dramatic poet . . . must from the very commencement, by strong impressions, transport his hearers out of themselves, and, as it were, take bodily possession of their attention. . . . The grand requisite in a drama is to make [its] rhythm perceptible in the onward progress of the action. When this has been effected, the poet may all the sooner halt in his rapid career, and indulge the bent of his own genius. . . . The poet's great art lies in availing himself of the effect of contrasts, which enable him at one time to produce calm repose, profound contemplation, and even the self abandoned indifference of exhaustion, or at another, the most tumultous emotions, the most violent storm of the passions. . . . The dramatic poet is, more than any other, obliged to court external favour and loud applause. But of course it is only in appearance that he thus lowers himself to his hearers; while in reality, he is elevating them to himself. . . . (38) In ordinary intercourse men exhibit only the outward man to each other. . . . The orator and the dramatist find means to break through [the] barriers of conventional reserve. While they transport their hearers into such lively emotions that the outward signs thereof break forth involuntarily, every man perceives those around him to be affected in the same manner and degree, and those who before were strangers to one another, become in a moment intimately acquainted. . . . Almost inconceivable is the power of a visible communion of numbers to give intensity to those feelings of the heart which usually retire into privacy. The faith in the validity of such emotions becomes irrefragible from its diffusion; . . . all hearts and minds flow together in one great and irresistible stream.(39) . . . Why does [Greek] Tragedy select subjects so awfully repugnant to the wishes and the wants of our sensuous nature? . . . Some have said that the pleasure of such representations arises from the comparison we make between the calmness and tranquillity of our own situation, and the storms and perplexities to which the victims of passion are exposed. But when we take a warm interest in the persons of a tragedy, we cease to think of ourselves; and when this is not the case, it is the best of all proofs that we take but a feeble interest in the exhibited story, and that the tragedy has failed in its effect. Others again have had recourse to a supposed feeling for moral improvement, which is gratified by the view of poetical justice in the reward of the good and the punishment of the wicked. But he for whom . . . dreadful examples could really be wholesome, must be conscious of a base feeling of depression [not] genuine morality, and would experience humiliation rather than elevation of mind. Besides, poetical justice is by no means indispensible to a good tragedy . . . if only the balance be preserved in the spectator's own consciousness by the prospect of futurity. Little does it mend the matter to say with Aristotle, that the object of tragedy is to purify the passions by pity and terror. . . . Commentators have never been able to agree as to the meaning of this proposition. . . . Lessing gives a new explanation of his own and fancies he has found in Aristotle a poetical Euclid. . . . Supposing, however, that tragedy does operate this moral cure in us, still she does so by the painful feelings of terror and compassion: and it remains to be proved how it is that we take a pleasure in subjecting ourselves to such an operation. Others . . . say that we are attracted to theatrical representations from the want of [excitement in] our everyday life. Such a craving does exist . . . but to it we must equally attribute the fights of wild beasts among the Romans. No, it is not the sight of suffering which constitutes the charm of tragedy. . . . The satisfaction . . . must be ascribed either to the feeling of the dignity of human nature, excited in us by such grand instances of it as are therein displayed, or to the trace of a higher order of things, impressed on the apparently irregular course of events, and mysteriously revealed in them; or perhaps to both these causes conjointly. The true reason, therefore, why tragedy need not shun even the harshest subject is, that a spiritual and invisible power can only be measured by the opposition which it encounters from some external force capable of being appreciated by the senses. The moral freedom of man, therefore, can only be displayed in a conflict with his sensuous impulses: so long as no higher call summons it to action, it is either actually dormant within him, or appears to slumber, since otherwise it does but mechanically fulfil its part as a mere power of nature. It is only amidst difficulties and struggles that the moral part of man's nature avouches itself. If, therefore, we must explain the distinctive aim of tragedy by way of a theory, we would give it thus: that, to establish the claims of the mind to a divine origin, its earthly existence must be disregarded as vain and insignificant, all sorrows endured and all difficulties overcome. (67-69)

   See also Schlegel under CHARACTER (SCL 268-69), CLOSURE (SCL 136,254), DRAMA (SCL 30-32,44), EXPOSITION (SCL 272-73), FOR-

WARD MOVEMENT (SCL 119), GENRE (SCL 44-46), MORALITY(SCL 39), POETIC JUSTICE (SCL 254), THOUGHT (SCL 69-70), UNITY (SCL 242-45); compare with MAGNITUDE (SCL 239).

1808   Coleridge. *See* under DRAMA (CSC 1: 177).

c.1810   Coleridge. *See* under GENRE (CLSW 74), PROBABILITY (CLSW 73).

1811   Coleridge. *See* under THREE UNITIES (CCSL 99).

1811-1812   Coleridge. *See* under UNITY (CLSW 20).

1814   Hazlitt. *See* under IMITATION (HW 1: 162).

1815   Coleridge   **CBL**

During the first year that Mr. Wordsworth and I were neighbors, our conversations turned frequently on the two cardinal points of poetry, the power of exciting the sympathy of the reader by a faithful adherence to the truth of nature, and the power of giving the interest of novelty by the modifying colours of imagination.... It was agreed that my [poetic] endeavours should be directed to persons and characters supernatural, or at least romantic; yet so as to transfer from our inward nature a human interest and a semblance of truth sufficient to procure for these shadows of imagination that willing suspension of disbelief for the moment, which constitutes poetic faith. (2: 5-6)

 See also Coleridge under AESTHETIC (CBL 2: 233-34, 256-57), DRAMA (CBL 2: 220-21; FORWARD MOVEMENT (CBL 2: 10-11), PROBABILITY (CBL 2: 189), STYLE (CBL 2: 51) UNITY (CBL 2: 10-11, 11).

1815   Hazlitt. *See* under TRAGEDY (HW 1: 13).

1816   Goethe. *See* under DRAMATIZATION (GLE 185-86).

1816   Hazlitt. *See* under IMITATION (HW 1: 72-74, 75), UNITY (HW 1: 76).

1817   Hazlitt   **HW**

[Actors] teach us when to laugh and when to weep, when to love and when to hate, upon principles and with a good grace! Wherever there is a playhouse, the world will go not amiss. The stage not only refines the manners, but it is the best teacher of morals, for it is the truest and most intelligible picture of life. It stamps the image of virtue on the mind by first softening the rude materials of which it is composed, by a sense of pleasure. It regulates the passions by giving a loose to the imagination. It points out the selfish and depraved to our detestation, the amiable and generous to our admiration; and if it clothes the more seductive vices with the borrowed graces of wit and fancy, even those graces operate as a diversion to the coarser poison of the experience and bad example, and often prevent or carry off the infection by inoculating the mind with a certain taste and elegance. To shew how little we agree with the common declamations against the immoral tendency of the stage on this score, we will hazard a conjecture, that the acting of the Beggar's Opera a certain number of nights every year since it was first brought out, has done more towards putting down the practice of highway robbery, than all the gibbets that ever were erected. A person, after seeing this piece is too deeply imbued with a sense of humanity, is in too good humor with himself and the rest of the world, to set about cutting throats or rifling pockets. Whatever makes a jest of vice, leaves it too much a matter of indifference for any one in his sense to rush desperately on his ruin for its sake. (1: 153-54)

See also Hazlitt under IMITATION (HW 1: 153).

1818   Hazlitt. *See* under AESTHETIC (HW 5: 1-2, 3), FORWARD MOVEMENT (HW 5: 10), IMAGINATION (HW 5: 4, 8-9), LANGUAGE (HW 5: 8, 12-13), NOVELTY (HW 5: 362).

1818   Coleridge. *See under* THOUGHT (CLSW 329-30).

1819   Hazlitt   HW

Tears may be considered as the natural and involuntary resource of the mind overcome by some sudden and violent emotion, before it has had time to reconcile its feelings to the change of circumstances: while laughter may be defined to be the same sort of convulsive and involuntary movement, occasioned by mere surprise or contrast (in the absence of any more serious emotion), before it has time to reconcile its belief to contradictory appearances. If we hold a mask before our face, and approach a child with this disguise on, it will at first, from the oddity and incongruity of the appearance, be inclined to laugh; if we go nearer to it, steadily, and without saying a word, it will begin to be alarmed, and be half inclined to cry: if we suddenly take off the mask, it will recover from its fears, and burst out a-laughing. . . . The alternation of tears and laughter, in this little episode in common life, depends almost entirely on the greater or less degree of interest attached to the different changes of appearance. The mere suddenness of the transition, the mere baulking our expectations and turning them abruptly into another channel, seems to give additional liveliness and gaiety to the animal spirits; but the instant the change is not only sudden, but threatens serious consequences, or calls up the shape of danger, terror supersedes our disposition to mirth, and laughter gives place to tears. (8: 6)

See also Hazlitt under HUMOR (HW 8: 5, 7-8, 15).

c.1820   Hegel   HFA

It is an essential part of the definition of the dramatic composition that it should possess the vitality able to command a favourable popular reception. . . . (4: 271) Now, in the *first* place, the ends, which in a dramatic work come into conflict and are resolved out of such conflict, either possess a general human interest, or at least have at bottom a pathos which is of a valid and substantive character for the people for whom the poet creates his work. . . . (4: 272) In proportion as a dramatic work accepts for its content wholly specific rather than typical characters and passions, conditioned, that is, exclusively by definite tendencies of a particular epoch of history, instead of mainly concerning itself with human interests substantive in all times, to that extent, despite of all its other advantages, it will be more transitory. And, *further*, it is necessary that universal human ends and actions of this kind should emphasize their poetic individualization to the point of animated life itself. Dramatic composition does not merely address itself to our sense of vitality, a sense which even the public certainly ought to possess, but it must itself, in all essentials, offer a living actual presence of situations, conditions, characters and actions. [In respect to local environment, customs, usages and other matters which affect the visual representation of action] dramatic individualization ought to be either so thoroughly poetical, vital, and rich with interest that we can discount what is alien to our sense, and feel ourselves attracted to the performance by this vital claim on our attention, or it should not pretend to do more than present such characteristics as external form, which is entirely outshone by the spiritual and ideal characteristics which underlie it. . . . More important than this external aspect is the vitality of the *dramatis personae*. Such ought not to be merely specific interests personified. . . . Abstract impersonations of particular passions and aims are wholly destitute of dramatic effect. A purely superficial (4: 273) individualization is equally insufficient. Content and form in such cases, as in the analogous type of allegorical figures, fail to coalesce. . . . (4: 274) As a matter for our *final* consideration in this place there is the relation in which the *poet* is placed to the general public. . . . We might imagine that the poet must perforce withdraw himself in the drama by reason of the very fact that he brings action before us in its sensuous presence, and makes the characters speak and active in their own names. . . . Such an impression is only, however, very partially valid. . . . The drama is exclusively referable in its origin to those epochs, in which the personal self-consciousnss (4: 275) . . . has already reached a high degree of development. . . . What we seek to recognize in the complete work is quite as much the product of the self-aware and original creative force, and by reason of this art and virtuosity of a genuine poetic personality. It is only thereby that dramatic productions attain to the genuine excellence of their artistic vitality and definition, as contrasted with the actions and events of natural life. From the opposite point of view the general public, too, if it has itself preserved a true sense of meaning of art, will not submit to have placed before it in a drama the more accidental moods and opinions, the peculiar tendencies and the one-sided outlook of this or that individual. ... It has a right to demand that in the course and final issue of the dramatic action, whether of tragedy or comedy, what is fundamentally reasonable and true should be vindicated. ... The dramatic poet must in the profoundest sense make himself master of the essential significance of human action and the divine order of the world, and along with this of a power to unfold this eternal and essential foundation of all human characters, passions and destinies in its clarity as also in its vital truth. It is no doubt quite possible that a poet ... may under particular circumstances find himself in conflict with the restricted and uncultured ideas of his age and nation. In such a case the responsibility for such a disunion does not rest with himself, but is a burden the public ought to carry. He has the single obligation to follow the lead of truth and his own compelling genius, the ultimate victory of which, provided it is of the right quality, is no less assured than that of ultimate truth itself universally. (4: 276-77)

    See also Hegel under COMEDY (HFA 4: 301-304), FORM (HFA 4: 262-63), GENRE DEFINITION (HFA 4: 305-308), PATHOS (HFA 4: 268-69), POETRY OF THE THEATRE (HFA 4: 289-91),TRAGEDY (HFA 4: 300-301); compare with CATHARSIS (HFA 4: 298-300), HERO (HFA 4: 320-21).

c.1820 Hazlitt. *See* under AESTHETIC (HW 2: 463).

1824 Hazlitt. *See* under UNIVERSALITY (HW 9: 402).

1826 Goethe. *See* under UNITY (GCE July 26).

1827 Goethe   **GCE**

Wednesday, Jan. 31. "[Manzoni] has too much respect for history. ... The poet must know what effects he wishes to produce, and regulate the nature of his characters accordingly. ... " Wed. March 21. "Such acts of violence [as Philoctetes deprived of his bow, and Oedipus of his daughter,]" said Goethe, "give an opportunity for excellent altercations, and such situations of help-lessness excited the emotions of the audience, on which account [Sophocles], whose object it was to produce an effect upon the public, liked to introduce them."

    See also Goethe under INSTRUCTION (GLE 130), VARIETY (GCE Jan. 31); compare with CATHARSIS (GLE 105).

1830   Hazlitt. *See* under METAPHOR (HW 9: 431).

1863-1867   Taine. *See* under DRAMA (THEL 20).

1864   Taine. *See* under AESTHETIC (TLA 82-84), CHARACTER (TLA 274-76), STYLE (TLA 321).

1871   Nietzsche   **NBT**

A. W. Schlegel . . . advises us to regard the chorus [of classical Greek drama] . . . as the essence and extract of the crowd of spectators,—as the "ideal spectator." . . . We . . . are astonished the moment we compare our well-known theatrical public with this chorus, and ask ourselves if it could ever be possible to idealise something analogous to the Greek chorus out of such a public. We tacitly deny this, and now wonder as much at the boldness of Schlegel's assertion as to the totally different nature of the Greek public. For hitherto we always believed that the true spectator, be he who he may, had always to remain conscious of having before him a work of art, and not an empiric reality: whereas the tragic chorus of the Greeks is compelled to recognise real beings in the figures of the stage. . . . Are we to own that he is the highest and purest type of spectator, who, like the Oceanides, regards Prometheus as real and present in body? And is it characteristic of the ideal spectator that he should run on the stage and free the god from his torments? We had believed in an aesthetic public, and considered the individual spectator the better qualified the more he was capable of viewing a work of art as art, that is, aesthetically. . . . (57-58) . . . The Dionysian Greek desires truth and nature in their most potent form;—he sees himself metamorphosed into the satyr. The revelling crowd . . . rejoices, swayed by such moods and perceptions, the power of which transforms them before their own eyes, so that they imagine they behold themselves . . . as satyrs. The later constitution of the tragic chorus is the artistic imitation of this natural phenomenon, which of course required a separation of the Dionysian spectators from the enchanted Dionysians. However, we must never lose sight of the fact that the public of the Attic tragedy rediscovered itself in the chorus of the orchestra, that there was in reality no antithesis of public and chorus. The Schlegelian observation must here reveal itself to us in a deeper sense. The chorus is the "ideal spectator" in so far as it is the only *beholder*, the beholder of the visionary world of the scene. A public of spectators, as known to us, was unknown to the Greeks. In their theatres the terraced structure of the spectators' space rising in concentric arcs enabled every one . . . to *overlook* the entire world of culture around him, and in surfeited contemplation to imagine himself a chorist. (64-65) . . . To the dithyrambic chorus [when characters were added to tragedy] is now assigned the task of exciting the minds of the hearers to such a pitch of Dionysian frenzy that, when the tragic hero appears on the stage, they do not behold in him, say, the unshapely masked man, but a visionary figure, born as it were of their own ecstasy. . . . (70) Let us picture [the spectator's] trembling anxiety, his agitated comparisons, his instinctive conviction . . . with which the spectator, excited to Dionysian frenzy, saw the god approaching on the stage, a god with whose sufferings he had already become identified. He involuntarily transferred the entire picture of the god . . . to this masked figure and resolved its reality as it were into a phantasmal unreality. (71) . . . Why should the artist be under obligation to accommodate himself to a power [the audience] whose strength is merely in numbers? And if by virtue of his endowments and aspirations he feels himself superior to every one of these spectators, how could he feel greater respect for the collective expression of all these subordinate capacities than for the relatively highest-endowed individual spectator? (90)

   See also Nietzsche under DRAMA (NBT 60-61), EXPOSITION (NBT 98-100), TRAGEDY(NBT 127,159-60).

1873   Nietzsche. *See* under METAPHOR (NEG 178-88).

1875   Shaw. *See* under DRAMA (SMCE 315-16).

1875   Nietzsche. *See* under POETRY OF THE THEATRE (NTS 149-50), 177, 177-78).

1876   Sarcey   STT

In themselves, events are not cheerful and they are not sad. They are neither. It is we who impregnate them with our sentiment or color them to our liking. (32) . . . It is not then with events, matter inert and indifferent, that we should concern ourselves, but with the public which laughs or weeps according as certain cords are toucht in preference to others. (33) . . . Most of those who rebel·against the sustained seriousness of tragedy, who advocate the mixing of the tragic and the comic in the same play, have set out with the idea that is thus things happen in reality and that the art of the dramatist consists in transporting reality to the stage. (34) . . . We are not at all concerned to know whether in real life the ludicrous is mingled with the terrible. . . . That is the one truth which no one questions and which has never been questioned. But the point at issue is altogether different. Twelve hundred persons are gathered together in the same room and form an audience. Are these twelve hundred persons likely to pass easily from tears to laughter and from laughter to tears? Is the playwright capable of transporting the audience from the one impression to the other? And does he not run the risk of enfeebling both impressions by this contrast? (36-37) . . . The human soul is not flexible enough to pass readily from one extreme of sensation to the contrary one. These sudden jolts overwhelm it with painful confusion. (38) . . . He [the dramatist] does not seek to reproduce the truth, but to give the illusion of truth to the . . . spectators. . . . When these . . .

spectators are entirely overwhelmed with grief they cannot believe that joy exists; they do not think about it; it displeases them when they are torn suddenly from their illusion in order to be shown another aspect of the same subject. (40-41)

See also Sarcey under GENRE (STT 48-49), STYLE (STT 49-50), UNITY (STT 41-42, 45, 53).

1878   Nietzsche. See under HUMOR (NHH 173), IMITATION (NHH 193-94).

1880   Nietzsche. See under STYLE (NHH 2: 62-63).

1881   Nietzsche. See under MORALITY (NDD 237-38).

1882   Nietzsche   **NJW**

What do I care for the drama! What do I care for the spasms of its moral ecstasies, in which the "people" have their satisfaction! What do I care for the whole pantomimic hocus-pocus of the actor! . . . It will now be divined that I am essentially antitheatrical at heart. . . . In the theatre we are only honest in the mass; as individuals we lie, we belie even ourselves. We leave ourselves at home when we go to the theatre; we there renounce the right to our own tongue and choice, to our taste, and even to our courage as we possess it and practise it within our own four walls in relation to God and man. No one takes his finest taste in art into the theatre with him, not even the artist who works for the theatre: there one is people, public, herd, woman, Pharisee, voting animal, democrat, neighbour and fellow-creature; there even the most personal conscience succumbs to the leveling charm of the 'great multitude'; there stupidity operates as wantonness and contagion. . . . (329-30)

1883   Chekhov   **CLF**

April. You have a story in which a young wedded couple kiss all through dinner, grieve without cause, weep oceans of tears. Not a single sensible word; nothing but *sentimentality*. And you did not write for the readers. You wrote because *you* like that sort of chatter. (69)

1886   Chekhov. See under LANGUAGE (CLF 70-71).

1887   Nietzsche   **NGM**

Kant, just like other philosophers, instead of envisaging the aesthetic problem from the standpoint of the experiences of the artist (the creator), has only considered art and beauty from the standpoint of the spectator, and has thereby imperceptibly imported the spectator himself into the idea of the "beautiful"!

But if only the philosophers of the beautiful had sufficient knowledge of this ''spectator''!—Knowledge of him as a great fact of personality, as a great experience, as a wealth of strong and most individual events, desires, surprises, and raptures in the sphere of beauty!... The contrary was always the case. And so we get from our philosophers, from the very beginning, definitions on which the lack of a subtler personal experience squats like a fat worm of crass error, as it does in Kant's famous definition of the beautiful. (130-31)

1888   Stringberg   **SSPP**

Turning to the technical side of the composition, I have tried to abolish the division into acts. And I have done so because I have come to fear that our decreasing capacity for illusion might be unfavourably affected by intermissions during which the spectator would have time to reflect and to get away from the suggestive influence of the author-hypnotist. My play will probably last an hour and a half, and as it is possible to listen that length of time, or longer, to a lecture, a sermon, or a debate, I have imagined that a theatrical performance could not become fatiguing in the same time. ... The form of the present play [*Miss Julie*] is not new, but it seems to be my own, and changing aesthetical conventions may possibly make it timely.... In the meantime I have resorted to three art forms that are to provide resting-places for the public and the actors, without letting the public escape from the illusion induced. All these forms are subsidiary to the drama. They are the monologue, the pantomime, and the dance (20-21)

   See also Strindberg under SPECTACLE (SSPP 23).

1888   Nietzsche. *See* under IMITATION (NW 255-56), TRAGEDY (NEH 70-73, NTI 119-20).

1888   Chekhov. *See* under THOUGHT (CL May 30).

1889   Strindberg. *See* under THREE UNITIES (SMD 16).

1898   Shaw. *See* under SPECTACLE (SMCE 220).

c.1900   Strindberg. *See* under PLOT (SEP 574-75)

1902   Shaw. *See* under MORALITY (SAA 33).

1908   Pirandello. *See* under IRONY (POH 79-80).

1909   Shaw. *See* under DRAMA (STPB xxiv).

1913   Shaw. *See* under CLOSURE (SMCE 139-40, 142-43, 145), THOUGHT (SMCE 137-39).

1918-1922   Stanislavski   **SAS**

An audience eagerly looks forward to getting something new and beautiful, something that exercises a great power of attraction over them. . . . (226) Every art in which the time element plays an important part must possess the power of attracting the unflagging attention of the spectators. (228)

1919   Eliot. *See* under CONVENTION (ESE 28), OBJECTIVE CORRELATIVE (EEE 61).

1926   Brecht. *See* under EPIC THEATRE (BBT 14-15).

1928   Eliot. *See* under THREE UNITIES (ESE 45).

1931   Brecht. *See* under CHARACTER (BBT 56).

1931-1936   Artaud. *See* under AESTHETIC (AT 96, 97), METAPHOR (AT 71), POETRY OF THE THEATRE (AT 120-21).

1932   Eliot. *See* under THREE UNITIES (EUP 45-46), UNITY (EJD 60), VARIETY (EJD 61, EUP 41).

c.1932   Brecht. *See* under GEST (BBT 104-105).

1933   Eliot   **EUP**

The ideal medium for poetry, to my mind, and the most direct means of social 'usefulness' for poetry, is the theatre. In a play of Shakespeare you get several levels of significance. For the simplest auditors there is the plot, for the more thoughtful the character and conflict of character, for the more literary the words and phrasing, for the more musically sensitive the rhythm, and for auditors of greater sensitiveness and understanding a meaning which reveals itself gradually. And I do not believe that the classification of audience is so clear-cut as this; but rather that the sensitiveness of every auditor is acted upon by all these elements at once, though in different degrees of consciousness. At none of these levels is the auditor bothered by the presence of that in which he does not understand, or by the presence of that in which he is not interested. (153)

1933   Stanislavski. Compare with IDEALISM (SL 134).

1935   Brecht. *See* under GEST (BBT 86).

c.1936 **Brecht.** *See* under EPIC THEATRE (BBA 20-21), WONDER (BBB 131).

1938 **Stanislavski** SBC

The spectators will be more affected than the actor, [who] will conserve all his forces in order to direct them where he needs them most of all: in reproducing the inner life of the character he is portraying. (70).

See also Stanislavski under ACTION (SBC 118).

1940 **Brecht.** *See* under AESTHETIC (BBT 145).

1943 **Eliot.** *See* under STYLE (EOPP 17).

1948 **Brecht** BBBG

Observe the effect that [today's] theatre has on its spectators. . . . One sees rather immobile faces in a peculiar condition. Their muscles seem to tighten in severe strain whenever they are not relaxed in severe exhaustion. These theater-goers have little truck with each other. They sit together like men who are asleep but having unquiet dreams. . . . True, they have their eyes open. But they don't watch, they stare. They don't hear, they are transfixed. . . . Watching and hearing are *activities* . . . but these people seem released from all activity. They seem to be *people to whom something is being done.* . . . As for the world therein depicted, the world from which segments have been cut to feed these moods and movements of feeling, it [is] . . . put together out of a few wretched ingredients—a piece of cardboard, a morsel of mimery, a scrap of text. . . . With this feeble copy of the world they can move the feelings of their well-attuned spectators much more than the world itself can. . . . All that matters to the spectators in these theaters is that they can exchange a contradictory world for a harmonious one, a world not exactly known for one that can be "dreamt up." (21-23)

See also Brecht under STYLE (BBBG 23, 39-40).

1951 **Eliot** EPD

In the theatre, the problem of communication presents itself immediately. You are deliberately writing verse for other voices, not for your own, and you do not know whose voices they will be. You are aiming to write lines which will have an immediate effect upon an unknown and unprepared audience, to be interpreted to that audience by unknown actors. . . . And the unknown audience cannot be expected to show any indulgence towards the poet. Every line must be judged by a new law, that of dramatic relevance. (24-25)

See also Eliot under STYLE (EPD 10-11, 13, 20-21).

1952   Brecht   **BBT**

[Mother] Courage has learnt nothing from the disasters that befall her. . . . But even if Courage learns nothing else at least the audience can, in my view, learn something by observing her. . . . The question of choice of artistic means can only be that of how we playwrights give a social stimulus to our audience (get them moving). To this end we should try out every conceivable artistic method which assists that end, whether it is old or new. (229)

1956   Brecht. *See* under THOUGHT (BT 277, 279).

ALIENATION

Brecht's notion of "alienation" seems to have evolved from an antiempathic stylistic device into a kind of theatrical metaphor which, by making the familiar strange, achieves the enlightened perception Nietzsche calls "estrangement."

See also *EPIC THEATRE, GEST;* compare with *IDENTIFICATION, ILLUSION.*

1878   Nietzsche   NHH

ESTRANGED FROM THE PRESENT.—There are great advantages in estranging oneself for once to a large extent from one's age, and being as it were driven back from its shores into the ocean of past views of things. Looking thence toward the coast one commands a view, perhaps for the first time, of its aggregate formation, and when one again approaches the land one has the advantage of understanding it better, on the whole, than those who have never left it. (389)

1922   Brecht   BBT

I hope in *Baal* and *Dickicht* I've avoided one common artistic bloomer, that of trying to carry people away. Instinctively, I've kept my distance and ensured that the realization of my (poetical and philosophical) effects remains within bounds. The spectator's 'splendid isolation' is left intact . . . he is not fobbed off with an invitation to feel sympathetically, to fuse with the hero and seem significant and indestructible as he watches himself in two simultaneous versions. A higher type of interest can be got from making comparisons, from whatever is different, amazing, impossible to take in as a whole. (9)

1929   Brecht   BBT

If I choose to see Richard III I don't want to feel myself to be Richard III, but to glimpse this phenomenon in all its strangeness and incomprehensibility. (27)

1935   Brecht. *See* under DISTANCE (BBT 86).

c.1936   Brecht   BBA

[In the Epic Theatre] nothing permitted the audience any more to lose itself through simple empathy, uncritically (and practically without any consequences) in the experiences of the characters on the stage. The presentation exposed the subject matter and the happenings to a process of de-familiarization. Defamiliarization was required to make things understood. When things are ''self-evident'', understanding is simply dispensed with. The ''natural'' had to be given an element of the *conspicuous*. Only in this way could the laws of cause and effect become plain. Characters had to behave as they *did* behave, and at the same time be capable of behaving otherwise. (19-20)

1936   Brecht   BBT

[In Piscator's production of *The Good Soldier Schweik*] the performer's self-observation, an artful and artistic act of self-alienation, stopped the spectator from losing himself in his character completely, i.e., to the point of giving up his own identity, and lent a splendid remoteness to the events. Yet the spectator's empathy was not entirely rejected. The audience identifies itself with the actor as being an observer, and accordingly develops his attitude of observing or looking on. (92-93)

1936   Brecht   BBB

To look at himself is for the [Chinese] performer an artful and artistic act of self-estrangement. Any empathy on the spectator's part is thereby prevented from becoming total, that is, from being a complete surrender. An admirable distance from the events portrayed is achieved. This is not to say that the spectator experiences no empathy whatsoever. He feels his way into the actor as into an observer. In this manner an observing, watching attitude is cultivated. ... [The Chinese performer] eschews complete transformation. He confines himself ... to merely *quoting* the character. ... It gets harder all the time for our actors to consummate the mystery of complete transformation. Their subconscious minds' memory is getting weaker all the time. ... It is difficult for the actor to generate certain emotions and moods in himself every evening and comparatively easy to render the outward signs that accompany and denote these emotions. Certainly the transference of these emotions to the spectator, the emotional contagion, does not take place automatically. The ''alienation effect'' enters in at this point, not in the form of emotionlessness, but in the form of emotions which do not have to be identical with those of the presented character. The spectator can feel joy at the sight of sorrow, disgust at the sight of anger. We speak of rendering the outward signs of emotions as a way of effecting alienation. This procedure may, however, fail to do so. The actor can so render these signs and select these signs that, on the contrary, emotional contagion follows, because the actor *has*, while rendering the signs, generated in himself the emotions to be presented. ... To act [in a manner that disassociates the emotions of the actor from those of the character] is more healthy and, it seems to us, more worthy of a thinking being. It calls for a considerable knowledge of men, a considerable general intelligence, and a keen grasp of what is socially important. Obviously, a creative process is going on here too. And one of a higher sort, since it belongs to the sphere of consciousness. Obviously the alienation effect in no way presupposes an unnatural style of acting. One must at all costs not think of what is called Stylization. On the contrary the success of the alienating effect is dependent on the lightness and naturalness of the whole procedure. And when the actor comes to examine the truth of this performance—a necessary operation, which gives Stanislavski a lot of trouble—he is not merely thrown back on his natural sensibility. He can always be corrected by reference to reality. Does an angry man really speak like that? Does a guilty man sit like that. He can be corrected, that is, from without, by other people. His style is such that nearly every sentence could be *judged* by the audience. Nearly every gesture is submitted to the approval of the audience. . . . It is difficult, when watching the Chinese act, to rid ourselves of the strangeness that they arouse in us because we are Europeans. One must be able to imagine they achieve the alienation effect also in their Chinese spectators. But . . . we must not allow ourselves to be disturbed at the fact that the Chinese performer creates an impression of mystery for a quite different purpose. . . . A technique which is taken from the realm of magic can be used to combat magic with. The Chinese performer may intend to use the alienation effect to make the events on stage mysterious, incomprehensible, and uncontrollable to the audience. And yet this effect can be used to make the events mundane, comprehensible, and controllable. . . . Whoever finds the formula $2 \times 2 = 4$ obvious is no mathematician, neither is the man who doesn't know what the formula means. The man who viewed a lamp swinging on a rope with astonishment at first and found it not obvious but very remarkable . . . such a man approached the understanding of the phenomenon. . . . A technical feature like the alienation effect in Chinese acting can be studied with profit only by those who *need* such a feature for particular social purposes. As charm, novelty, finesse, and formalistic frivolity it could never become significant. . . . In the German epic theatre the alienation effect was employed not only through the actors but also through the music (choruses and solos) and the decor (placards, film, etc.). The aim was the *historification* of the events presented. . . . The bourgeois theatre . . . sifts out from its materials the time element. The presentation of the human beings stops with the so-called Eternally Human. . . . Events on the stage are all one long cue, the cue for the Eternal Answer, the inevitable, usual, natural, human answer. . . . Such a philosophy may acknowledge the existence of history but it is an unhistorical philosophy. . . . To regard man as a variable which, moreover, controls the milieu, to conceive of the liquidation of the milieu in relationships between men—these notions spring from a new mode of thought, historical thought. . . . Our history-making theatre . . . siezes on the special, the particular, on what needs investigation. . . . It can only be done if the alienation effect is brought off. . . . A new theatre will find the alienation effect necessary for the criticism of society and for historical reporting on changes already accomplished. (131-36)

1936   Brecht   BBT

Certain incidents in the play should be treated as self-contained scenes and raised—by means of inscriptions, musical or sound effects and the actors' way of playing—above the level of the everyday, the obvious, the expected (i.e., alienated).(101)

    See also Brecht under ILLUSION (BBB 130), WONDER (BBB 131).

1938   Brecht   BBEB

Briefly, [the A-effect (Alienation-effect)] has to do with a technique which confers on the human events to be presented the stamp of the conspicuous, of something requiring an explanation, something not obvious, not simply natural. The aim of the A-effect is to make of the spectator an active critic of society. (432)

c. 1940   Brecht   BBAn

The following is an attempt to describe a technique of the art of acting which was used in some theatres in order to estrange from the spectators the events to be presented. The purpose of this technique, to be called hereafter "E-Effect" (abbreviation for the Effect of Estrangement) was to induce an enquiring, critical attitude on the part of the spectators towards the events shown. The means employed were artistic. A prerequisite for the use of the "E-Effect" is that the stage and auditorium shall be cleared of all "magic" elements and that no "hypnotic field" may be set up. No attempt was therefore made to reproduce the atmosphere of any particular place on the stage, such as a room at dark or a street in autumn. . . . [When in the epic theatre a definite atmosphere needs to be represented . . . the atmosphere itself must be "estranged": n.1, p. 20.] . . . It was not the purpose to entrance the public and to give it the illusion of witnessing a natural, unrehearsed event. . . . The tendency of the public to throw itself into such an illusion must be neutralized through specific artistic means. [. . . Showing the (sources of stage lighting) openly is important, for it can be one of the means of preventing unwanted illusion. It will hardly prevent the necessary concentration: n. 2, p.21.] A prerequisite for the achievement of the "E-Effect" is that the actor shall openly play to the audience. The conception of a fourth wall which invisibly separates stage and audience, thus creating the illusion that what happens on the stage is really happening, without any audience, must of course be dropped. [. . . (The actor) has . . . to tell (his spectators) something and to show them something, and this attitude of one merely informing and demonstrating should be the basis of all he does. . . . He will imitate another person, but not to such a degree as if he were that person,

not with the object of being himself forgotten in the process: n.3, pp. 21-22.]
The contact between public and stage customarily arises, as is well known, on
a basis of intuitive sympathy. . . . This is the chief aim of [the conventional
actor's art]. . . . A technique which seeks to bring about the "E-Effect" must
be diametrically opposed to the technique which seeks for intuitive sympathy.
. . . The actor on the stage will not identify himself completely with the
character he is to represent. He is not Lear, Harpagon, Schweik—he shows
them. . . . Once complete transformation has been abandoned, the actor no
longer speaks his text like an improvisation, but like a quotation. . . . There are
three aids which . . . may serve to bring about an "estrangement" of the actions
and sayings in the person to be represented.

1. A transposition into the third person.
2. A transposition into the past tense.
3. The speaking aloud of stage directions and commentaries. . . .

. . . Since he does not identify himself with the person he represents, he can
choose a particular point of view regarding him, and even invite the spectator
(who also was not asked to identify himself with the character) to criticize the
person represented [the artist's task . . . in portraying intense agitation, is to do
it in such a way that the "witness" (in this case the spectator) remains capable
of observation: n.10, p.24.)] Thus the actor's point of view is that of a social
criticism. . . . His playing . . . becomes a colloquy (about social conditions)
with the audience he is addressing. He invites the listener, according to the
class to which he belongs, to justify or condemn these conditions. It is the
purpose of the "E-Effect" to estrange *the* social gesture underlying all events.
By social gesture is meant all expression by mime and gesture of social
relationships among people of a certain epoch. . . . The actor must play the
events as historical events. Historical events happen once only, are transitory
and linked to definite epochs. . . . Constant change [of each succeeding epoch]
"estranges" us from the behaviour of those born before us. This distant and
objective attitude . . . the actor must take up in relation to the events and
patterns of behaviour of the present time. It is his task to "estrange" these
events and persons from us. Everyday [things] . . . carry implications of naturalness for us because of their familiarity. Their "estrangement" serves to
make them remarkable to us. Science has built up a careful technique of
imitation in the face of events customarily taken for granted and never doubted;
and there is no reason why art should not take over this immeasurably useful
attitude. . . . As regards emotion, attempts with the "E-Effect" . . . have shown
that this manner of acting, too, arouses emotions, though of a different kind to
those aroused in the conventional theatre. [The rejection of intuition does not
come from a rejection of emotions, nor does it lead to this. The thesis of
common aesthetics, that emotions can only be liberated by way of intuition, is

wrong. Yet a non-Aristotelian drama must weigh with careful criticism the emotions which it seeks to bring about and embody. We may sense a crisis of emotions in certain tendencies of the arts. . . . Postwar German drama had already taken the decisive turn to rationalism in the last years of the Weimar Republic. Nazism with its grotesque emphasis on emotions, no less perhaps than a threatened decline of rationalism in Marxist aesthetics, led us to underline all national elements heavily. Yet . . . a great part of contemporary art has declined in emotional power because it eschewed reason, and . . . the renaissance of emotional power arose directly from increased rational tendencies. . . . Emotions have always had a definite class basis. . . . The linking of certain emotions with certain interests is not too difficult if one looks for the relevant interests in the emotional impact of works of art. . . . It seems that emotions which accompany the progress of society can continue to live on for a long time as emotions linked with interests, and in works of art to have a more enduring life than might be expected . . . : n. 16, pp. 28-29.] A critical attitude on the part of the spectator is a thoroughly artistic attitude. [For many . . . to contradict and to remain distant seems incompatible with artistic pleasure. Of course there is also in artistic pleasure a higher level at which savouring is critical, yet the criticism here is relevant only to artistic matters. It is a very different matter to regard critically, argumentatively, distant[ly], not only the world's artistic representation but the world itself: n. 17, p. 29.] . . . The "E-Effect" . . . has nothing to do with the usual kinds of "styliza-tion." The principal advantages of an epic theatre utilizing the "E-Effect" with its sole purpose of showing the world in an interpretable way, are . . . its naturalness, its earthiness, its humour and its renunciation of all mystical elements that still cling to the conventional theatre as a remnant from former times. (15-20)

See also Brecht under GEST (BBAn 18).

1948 Brecht   BBBG

An alienating image is one which makes a circumstance recognizable and at the same time makes it seem strange. The ancient and medieval theatres alienated their characters by using masks . . . and the Asiatic theater still uses musical and pantomimic alienation effects. The effects undoubtedly prevented em-pathy: yet the technique rested on hypnotically suggestive foundations. . . . The social aims of the ancient effects were entirely different from ours. . . . The old alienation effects remove the thing which is imaged entirely from the influence of the spectator, make it appear unalterable. . . . New alienations should only remove [the seal of familiarity] from occurrences . . . which . . . prevent them from being tampered with. . . . What has not changed for a long time seems to be unchangeable. We are aways coming across something which is so obvious that we do not bother to understand it. . . . In order that [a person] may be able to call [the familiar] into question with as much zeal as he now accepts it, he would have to develop that alien vision with which the great Galileo looked at a chandelier swinging like a pendulum: he was amazed at its oscillations, as though he had not expected them to be like that, as though they were not self-evident; hencè he came to the formulation of physical laws. This vision, as difficult as it is productive, must be stimulated by the theater's images of men's life together. The theater must astonish its audience, and it does so by means of a technique which alienates what is accepted. . . . This technique permits the theater to use the method of the new science of society, dialectical materialism. (26-27)

   See also Brecht under DISTANCE (BBBG 28),GEST (BBBG 33, 35, 35-36, 39), IDENTIFICATION (BBBG 25, 28), ILLUSION (BBBG 28-29), MOTIVATION (BBBG 26), PLOT (BBBG 17, 35, 36), STYLE (BBBG 23, 39-40).

1949   Brecht   **BBT**

[The] possibility of objectively presenting a major state operation was due precisely to the fact (fatal in another respect) that the old play [*Antigone*] was historically so remote as to tempt nobody to identify himself with its principal figure. . . . Its elements of epic form were a help, and provided something of interest to our theatre on their own account. Greek dramaturgy uses certain forms of alienation, notably interventions by the chorus, to try and rescue some of that freedom of calculation which Schiller is uncertain how to insure. (210)

1951   Eliot. Compare with STYLE (EPD 13).

c.1952   Brecht. *See* under HERO (BBT 247).

AUTHORITY

As a support for theoretical positions—or, indeed, as their source—the authority of the ancients is employed most commonly by Renaissance theorists and most unskeptically by the Italian and French, whose weak native theatres were virtually swept away by the classical revival. See also RULES.

1561   Scaliger. *See* under IDEALISM (SP 52), TRAGEDY (SP 40).

1570   Castelvetro. *See* under DRAMA (CP 67), IMITATION (CP 37-38, 43-44, 78); compare with CATHARSIS (CP 123), IMAGINATION (CP 114-15), SPECTACLE (CP 83).

1609   de Vega. *See* under ACTION (VAWP 30-31).

1641   Jonson   **JD**

I know *Nothing* can conduce more to letters, than to examine the writings of the *Antients*, and not to rest in their sole Authority, or take all upon trust from them; provided the plagues of *Judging*, and *Pronouncing* against them, be away; such as *envy, bitternesse, precipitation, impudence,* and *scurrile scoffing*. For to all the observations of the *Ancients*, wee have our owne experience: which, if wee will use, and apply, wee have better means to pronounce. It is true that they opened the gates, and made the way that went before us; but as Guides, not Commanders. (7-10) . . . Nothing is more ridiculous, then to make an Author a *Dictator*, as the schooles have done *Aristotle*. The dammage is infinite, [that] knowledge receives by it. For to many things a man should owe but a temporary beliefe, and a suspension of his owne Judgement, not an absolute resignation of himselfe, or a perpetuall captivity. (80)

1648   Corneille   **CSP**

[Aristotle] has treated the art of poetry with such skill and judgment that the precepts he has left us on this subject are for all times and all peoples; and . . . he goes straight to the heart's reactions whose nature does not change. He has shown what emotions tragedy should stir in the hearts of its spectators; he has sought the necessary conditions both in the characters portrayed and the events introduced to effect these emotions; for this purpose he has left us the means which would have produced their effect everywhere since the creation of the world . . . and for the rest, that places and times may alter, he . . . has not even prescribed the number of acts, which has been laid down by Horace a long time after him. (8-9)

1657 d'Aubignac   AAS

[To write a good play the Poet] must begin with applying himself to the reading of *Aristotle's* Poeticks, and those of *Horace*, and he must read them attentively, and meditate upon them; then he must turn over those that have made Commentaries upon them, as *Castelvetro* in *Italian*, who in his Jargon says very fine things, *Hieronymus Vida, Heinsius, Vossius, la Menardiere*, and a great many more; and let him remember, that *Scaliger* alone says more than all the rest. . . . I add to these Authors *Plutarch, Athenaeus, and Lilius Giraldus*, who all in many places have touch'd the Chief Maxims of the Stage; in a word, [the Poet] must not let slip any thing of the Ancients, without examining every period of them. (1: 30)

    See also d'Augignac under ACTION (AAS 2: 81), RULES (AAS 1: 22-26)

1660 Corneille. *See* under PROBABILITY (CFD 139), RULES (CFD 139-40 and CDENA 32).

1663 Molière. Compare with RULES (MP 6: 344).

1669 Molière   MP

If we are willing to listen to the testimony of antiquity it will tell us that the most celebrated philosophers praised comedy, even those who made profession of austere virtue and rebuked incessantly the vices of their age. It will show us that Aristotle devoted his evenings to the theatre, and took pains to reduce to precepts the art of writing comedy. (2: 35)

1670 Racine   RP

I think of [the great men of antiquity whom I have taken for my models] actually as spectators. When we take our inspiration from them we should always ask ourselves, "What would Homer or Vergil say, if they were to read these lines? What would Sophocles say if he saw this scene?" (155)

1671 Dryden. *See* under POETIC JUSTICE (DW 1, 2: 198-201).

1674 Racine. *See* under AFFECT (RP 156).

1695 Dryden. *See* under RULES (DW 3: 318-19).

1713 Addison   AW

There is no rule in Longinus which I more admire, than that wherein he advises an author, who would attain to the sublime . . . to consider, when he is engaged in his composition, what Homer or Plato, or any other of those heroes in the learned world, would have said or thought upon the same occasion. . . . I may, at least, venture to say, with Dr. Dryden, where he professes to have imitated Shakespeare's style, that, in imitating such great authors, I have always excelled myself. (3: 148-49)

1730   Voltaire. *See* under THREE UNITIES (VE 280-81).

1751   Johnson. Compare with RULES (JW 3: 240).

1758   Diderot. Compare with IDEALISM (DDP 298), RULES (DDP 298).

1765   Johnson. *See* under THREE UNITIES (JS 24).

1767-1769   Lessing   LSPW

If I may think that I have rightly explained Aristotle's teaching, then I may also believe that my explanation has proved that the matter itself cannot possibly be otherwise than Aristotle teaches. (467)

1808   Schlegel   SCL

[Renaissance scholars], who were chiefly in the possession of . . . knowledge [of the classics], and who were incapable of distinguishing themselves by works of their own, claimed for the ancients an unlimited authority, and with great appearance of reason, since they are models in their kind. Maintaining that nothing could be hoped for the human mind but from an imitation of antiquity, in the works of the moderns they only valued what resembled, or seemed to bear a resemblance to, those of the ancients. . . . But in the fine arts, mere imitation is always fruitless; even what we borrow from others, to assume a purely poetical shape, must, as it were, be born again within us. . . . Art cannot exist without nature, and man can give nothing to his fellow-men but himself. . . . Authority is avowed with . . . little disguise as the first principle of the French critics. (235)

Compare with Schlegel under AFFECT (SCL 67-69), NOVELTY (SCL 50), RULES (SCL 235, 236).

1876   Sarcey. *See* under STYLE (STT 49-50).

1903   Shaw. Compare with AESTHETIC (SMS xxxvi).

1940   Brecht. *See* under AESTHETIC (BBT 145).

CATHARSIS

What Aristotle intended as initial approximations of a definition of CATHAR-SIS have remained his fullest definitions. The term has generated some later attempts at definition but has been most productive of confusion and controversy. See also CLOSURE, PLEASURE, and WONDER.

4th cent. B.C.   Aristotle   **APO**

Music should be studied, not for the sake of one, but of many benefits, that is to say, with a view to (1) education, (2) purgation (the word 'purgation' we use at present without explanation, but when hereafter we speak of poetry [that is, in *The Poetics*], we will treat the subject with more precision); music may also serve (3) for intellectual enjoyment, for relaxation and for recreation after exertion. . . . Feelings such as pity and fear, or, again, enthusiasm, exist very strongly in some souls, and have more or less influence over all. Some persons fall into religious frenzy, whom we see as a result of the sacred melodies— when they have used the melodies that excite the soul to mystic frenzy— restored as though they had found healing and purgation. Those who are influenced by pity or fear, and every emotional nature, must have a like experience, and others in so far as each is susceptible to such emotions, and all are in a manner purged and their souls lightened and delighted. The purgative melodies likewise give an innocent pleasure to mankind. Such as the modes and the melodies in which those who perform music at the theatre should be invited to compete. But since the spectators are of two kinds—the one free and educated, the other a vulgar crowd composed of mechanics, labourers, and the like—there ought to be contests and exhibitions instituted for the relaxation of the second class also. And the music will correspond to their minds; for as their minds are perverted from the natural state, so there are perverted modes and highly strung and unnaturally coloured melodies. A man receives pleasure from what is natural to him, and therefore professional musicians may be allowed to practice this lower sort of music before an audience of a lower type. (1341 b: 36 - 1342 a: 29)

 See also Aristotle under TRAGEDY (AP 23-25).

1561   Scaliger. Compare with TRAGEDY (SP 40).

1570   Castelvetro   **CP**

[Aristotle adopted the notion of catharsis] only incidentally and for a special purpose, namely, to defend tragedy from Plato's imputations. (120) . . . If poetry has been fashioned primarily for delight and not for utility, why in one species of poetry, i.e, in tragedy, is utility sought? Why is not delight sought here principally without meddling with utility, which ought to be of no account whatever? (123)

See also Castelvetro under TRAGEDY (CP 95), WONDER (CP 80).

1660   Corneille   CDENA

Pity concerns the interest of the person whom we see suffering, the fear which follows it concerns our own person. . . . The pity for a misfortune, where we see the fall of people similar to ourselves, brings to us a fear of a similar [misfortune]. This fear brings us to a desire of avoiding it, and this desire to purging, moderating, rectifying, and even eradicating in ourselves the passion which, before our eyes, plunges into this misfortune the persons we pity. (3)

1660   Corneille   CDT

I doubt whether [the purgation of the passions ever takes place] even in those plays which have the conditions which Aristotle demands. They occur in *le Cid*, and are the cause of its great success: Rodrigue and Chimène . . . fall into distress by the human frailty of which we too are capable, like them; their misery arouses pity, and costs the spectators so many tears that this is in-contestable. Our pity ought to give us fear of falling into like misfortune, and purge us of the over-plus of love which is the cause of their disaster, and makes us deplore them; but I do not know that it gives us that, or purges us, and I am afraid that the reasoning of Aristotle on this point is but a pretty idea. . . . It is not requisite that [pity and fear] always serve together, . . . it suffices . . . that one of the two bring about the purgation; with it understood, never-theless, that pity does not arrive without fear, [but] that fear may be effective without pity. (816)

See also Corneille under INSTRUCTION (CDF 140-41).

1679   Dryden. *See* under DRAMA (DW 1, 2: 269).

1697   Dryden. *See* under TRAGEDY (DW 3: 430-31).

1711   Addison   AW

As a perfect tragedy is the noblest production of human nature, so it is capable of giving the mind one of the most delightful and most improving entertain-ments. A virtuous man (says Seneca) struggling with misfortunes, is such a spectacle as gods might look upon with pleasure; and such a pleasure it is which one meets with in the representation of a well-written tragedy. Diversions of this kind wear out of our thoughts every thing that is mean and little. They cherish and cultivate that humanity which is the ornament of our nature. They soften insolence, sooth affliction, and subdue the mind to the dispensations of

Providence. It is no wonder therefore that in all the polite nations of the world, this part of the drama has met with public encouragement. (1: 69-70).

1712   Addison. *See* under IMAGINATION (AW 2: 138).

1767-1769   Lessing   **LSPW**

[Since] Aristotle's doctrine of the purification . . . rests in nothing else than in the transformation of passions into virtuous habits, and since according to our philosopher each virtue has two extremes between which it rests, it follows that if tragedy is to change our pity into virtue it must also be able to purify us from the two extremes of pity, and the same is to be understood of fear. Tragic pity must not only purify the soul of him who has too much pity, but also of him who has too little; tragic fear must not alone purify the soul of him who does not fear any manner of misfortune but also of him who is terrified by every misfortune, even the most distant and most improbable. Likewise tragic pity in regard to fear must steer between this too much and too little, and conversely tragic fear in regard to pity. (421)

1808   Schlegel. *See* under AFFECT (SCL 67-69).

1815   Hazlitt. *See* under TRAGEDY (HW 1: 13).

1817   Hazlitt   **HW**

The circumstances which balances the pleasure against the pain in tragedy is, that in proportion to the greatness of the evil, is our sense and desire of the opposite good excited; and that our sympathy with actual suffering is lost in the strong impulse given to our natural affections, and carried away with the swelling tide of passion, that gushes from and relieves the heart. (1: 271-2)

c.1820   Hegel   **HFA**

[It is] the famous dictum of Aristotle that the true effect of tragedy is to excite and purify *fear* and *pity*. By this statement Aristotle did not mean merely the concordant or discordant feeling with anybody's private experience, a feeling simply of pleasure or the reverse, an attraction or a repulsion, that most superficial of all psychological states. . . . For in a work of art the matter of exclusive importance should be the display of that which is conformable with the reason and truth of Spirit. . . . And consequently we are not justified in restricting the application of this dictum of Aristotle merely to the emotion of fear and pity, but should relate it to the principle of the *content*, the appropriately artistic display of which ought to purify our feelings. Man may, on the other hand, entertain fear when confronted with that which is outside him and finite; but he may likewise shrink before the power of that which is the essential and absolute subsistency of social phenomena. That which mankind has therefore in truth to fear is not the eternal power and its oppression, but the ethical might which is self-defined and its own free rationality, and partakes further of the eternal and inviolable, the power a man summons against his own being when he turns his back upon it. And just as fear may have two objectives, so also too compassion. The first is just the ordinary sensibility—in other words, a sympathy with the misfortunes and sufferings of another, and one which is experienced as something finite and negative. Your countrified cousin is ready enough with compassion of this order. The man of nobility and greatness, however, has no wish to be smothered with this sort of pity. For just to the extent that it is merely the nugatory aspect, the negative of misfortune which is asserted, a real depreciation of misfortune is implied. True sympathy, on the contrary, is an accordant feeling with the ethical claim at the same time associated with the sufferer—that is, with what is necessarily implied in his condition as affirmative and substantive. Such pity as this is not, of course, excited by ragamuffins and vagabonds. If the tragic character, therefore, just as he aroused our fear when contemplating the might of violated morality, is to awake a tragic sympathy in his misfortune, he must himself essentially possess real capacity and downright character. It is only that which has a genuine content which strikes the heart of a man of noble feeling, and rings through its depths. Consequently we ought by no means to identify our interest in the tragic *dénoument* with the simple satisfaction that a sad story, a misfortune merely as misfortune, should have a claim upon our sympathy. . . . Such pictures of lamentation and misery merely rack the feelings. A veritable tragic suffering, on the contrary, is suspended over active characters entirely as a consequence of their own act, which as such not only asserts its claim upon us, but becomes subject to blame through the collision it involves, and in which such individuals identify themselves body and soul. (4: 298-300)

1827   Goethe   GLE

"After a course of events arousing pity and fear, the action closes with the equilibration of these passions." In the foregoing translation [from Aristotle's definition of tragedy], I believe I have made this hitherto dubious passage clear. . . . Could Aristotle . . . be really thinking of the effect, indeed the distant effect, upon the *spectator*? By no means! He speaks clearly and definitely: . . . the tragedy must close *on the stage* with an equilibration, a reconciliation, of these emotions. By "catharsis" he understands this reconciling culmination, which is demanded of all drama. (105)

1871   Nietzsche   NBT

At the most essential point [in the drama the] Apollonian illusion [that the Dionysian is in its service] is dissolved and annihilated. The drama, which, by the aid of [Dionysian] music, spreads out before us with such inwardly illumined distinctness in all its movements and figures, that we imagine we see the texture unfolding on the loom as the shuttle flies to and fro—attains as a whole an effect which *transcends all Apollonian artistic effects*. In the collective effect of tragedy, the Dionysian gets the upper hand once more; tragedy ends with a sound which could never emanate from the realm of Apollonian art. (166)

See also Nietzsche under TRAGEDY (NBT 127, 159-60).

1878   Nietzsche   **NHH**

OLD DOUBTS ABOUT THE EFFECT OF ART.—Should pity and fear really be unburdened through tragedy, as Aristotle would have it, so that the hearers return home colder and quieter? Should ghost-stories really make us less fearful and superstitious? In the case of certain physical processes, in the satisfaction of love, for instance, it is true that with the fulfilment of a need there follows an alleviation and temporary decrease in the impulse. But fear and pity are not in this sense the needs of particular organs which require to be relieved. And in time every instinct is even *strengthened* by practice in its satisfaction, in spite of that periodical mitigation. It might be possible that in each single case pity and fear would be soothed and relieved by tragedy; nevertheless, they might, on the whole, be increased by tragic influences, and Plato would be right in saying that tragedy makes us altogether more timid and susceptible. (190-91)

1888   Nietzsche   **NW**

What is tragic?—Again and again I have pointed to the great misunderstanding of Aristotle in maintaining that the tragic emotions were the two depressing emotions—fear and pity. Had he been right, tragedy would be an art unfriendly to life . . . something generally harmful and suspicious. Art, otherwise the great stimulus of life, the great intoxicant of life, the great will to life, here becomes a tool of decadence, the handmaiden of pessimism and ill-health (for to suppose, as Aristotle supposed, that by exciting these emotions we thereby purged people of them, is simply an error). Something which habitually excites fear or pity, disorganises, weakens, and discourages: and suppose Schopenhauer were right in thinking that tragedy taught resignation (i.e., a meek renunciation of happiness, hope, and the will to live), this would presuppose an art in which art itself was denied. . . . This theory may be refuted in the most coldblooded way, namely, by measuring the effect of a tragic emotion by means of a dynamometer. The result would be a fact [that could not be misunderstood]: that tragedy is a tonic. (285-286)

See also Nietzsche under TRAGEDY (NTI 119-20).

1931-1936   Artaud   **AT**

The theatre is a disease because it is the supreme equilibrium which cannot be achieved without destruction. It invites the mind to share a delirium which exalts its energies; and we can see, to conclude, that from the human point of view, the action of theatre, like that of plague, is beneficial, for, impelling men to see themselves as they are, it causes the mask to fall, reveals the lie, the slackness, baseness, and hypocrisy of our world; it shakes off the asphyxiating inertia of matter which invades even the clearest testimony of the senses; and in revealing to collectivities of men their dark power, their hidden force, it invites them to take, in the face of destiny, a superior and heroic attitude they would never have assumed without it. (31-32)

1935   Brecht   BBT

The drama of our time still follows Aristotle's recipe for achieving what he calls catharsis (the spiritual cleansing of the spectator). In Aristotelian drama the plot leads the hero into situations where he reveals his innermost being. All the incidents shown have the object of driving the hero into spiritual conflicts.
. . . Non-Aristotelian drama would at all costs avoid bundling together the events portrayed and presenting them as an inexorable fate, to which the human being is handed over helpless despite the beauty and significance of his reactions; on the contrary, it is precisely this fate that it would study closely, showing it up as of human contriving. (87)

See also Brecht under IDENTIFICATION (BBT 87).

CHARACTER

If the action is the most basic image of drama, the agents of the action, the dramatis personnae, *are the images that compose that image. But the eternal problem of art, to balance the claim of the individual element against that of the larger form in which the element functions, is especially acute in drama; character is insubordinate, making appeals to external reality (resemblance) and to our egos (identification) that threaten the aesthetic integrity of the form. Aristotle asserts the primacy of form over character, and theorists have generally followed him even when—as in the flood tide of romantic drama— any real effect of that primacy was cancelled. See DECORUM, EMOTION, FLAW, HERO, IDENTIFICATION, MOTIVATION, PATHOS, SUBTEXT, and WILL.*

4th. cent. B.C.   Aristotle   AP

By Character [*ethos*] I mean that in virtue of which we ascribe certain [moral: EP 238] qualities to the agents. (25) . . . Dramatic action . . . is not with a view to the representation of character: character comes in as subsidiary to the actions. . . . Again, without action there cannot be a tragedy; there may be [tragedy] without [expressions of: EP 252] character. The tragedies of most of our modern poets *fail in the rendering of character* [are "character"-less: EP 252]; and of poets in general this is often true. It is the same in painting; and here lies the difference between Zeuxis and Polygnotus. Polygnotus delineates character well: the style of Zeuxis is devoid of *ethical quality* [expression of character: EP 252]. Again, if you string together a set of speeches expressive of character, and well finished in point of diction and thought, you will not produce the *essential tragic effect* [function of tragedy: EP 252] nearly so well as with a play which, however deficient in these respects, yet has a plot and artistically constructed incidents. . . . Novices attain to finish of diction and precision of portraiture before they can construct a plot. . . . Plot, then, is the first principle, and, as it were, the soul of tragedy: Character [portrayal: EP 252] holds second place. A similar fact is seen in painting. The most beautiful colours, laid on confusedly, will not give as much pleasure as the chalk outline of a portrait. Thus Tragedy is the imitation of an action, and of the agents mainly with a view to the action. . . . Character is that which reveals moral purpose, showing what kinds of things a man chooses or avoids. Speeches, therefore, which do not make this manifest, or in which the speaker does not choose or avoid anything whatever, are not expressive of character. (27-

29) . . . In respect of character there are four things to be aimed at. First, and most important, it must be good. Now any speech or action that manifests moral purpose of any kind will be expressive of character: the character will be good if the purpose is good. This rule is relative to each class. *Even a woman may be good* [There is in fact such a thing as a good woman: EP 455] and also a slave; though the woman may be said to be an inferior being, and the slave [as a class: EP 455] quite worthless. The second thing to aim at is *propriety* [appropriateness: EP 455]. There is a type of manly valour; but valour in a woman, or unscrupulous cleverness, is inappropriate. Thirdly, *character must be true to life* [is naturalness (''likeness''): EP 455]: for this is a distinct thing from goodness and propriety, as here described. The fourth point is con-sistency: for though the subject of the imitation, who suggested the type, be inconsistent, still he must be consistently inconsistent. (53-54) . . . As in the structure of the plot so too in the portraiture of character, the poet should aim at either the necessary or the probable. Thus a person of a given character should speak or act in a given way, by the rule either of necessity or probability; just as this event should follow that by necessary or probable sequence. (56) . . . Again, since Tragedy is an imitation of persons who are above the common level, the example of good portrait painters should be followed. They, while reproducing the distinctive *form* [appearance: EP 475] of the original, make a likeness which is true to life and yet more beautiful. So too the poet, in representing men who are irascible or indolent, or who have defects of character, should *preserve the type and yet ennoble it* [make them like that but morally good: EP 475]. (57) . . . The chorus too should be regarded as one of the actors: it should be an integral part of the whole and *share in the action* [an aid to him in winning the competition: EP 551], in the manner not of Euripides but of Sophocles. As for the later poets, their choral songs pertain as little to the subject of the piece as to that of any other tragedy. They are, therefore, sung as mere interludes. . . . (69)

See also Aristotle under ACTION (AP 25-29), IMITATION (AP 11-13), PITY (AP 49-53), PLOT (AP 25-29, 45-49), PROBABILITY (AP 35-37), RECOGNITION (AP 41-43) THOUGHT (AP 29, 69-71), TRAGEDY (AP 21-23, 23-25).

4th cent. B.C.   Aristotle   AR

Ethical proof is wrought when the speech is so spoken as to make the speaker credible; for we trust good men more and sooner, as a rule, about everything; while, about things which do not admit of precision, but only of guesswork, we trust them absolutely. Now this trust, too, ought to be produced by means of the speech,—not by a previous conviction that the speaker is this or that sort of man. . . . It might be said that almost the most authoritative of proofs is that supplied by character. (6) Since praise is founded upon actions, and it is distinctive of the good man to act according to moral choice, we must try to show that our man acts by moral choice. (40) The speakers themselves are made trustworthy by three things; for there are three things, besides demonstrations, which make us believe. These are, intelligence, virtue and goodwill. (69) The condition of effecting this is to know what gives "êthos." One way, then, is to make the "êthos" being determined by the quality of this purpose, and the quality of the purpose by the end. Hence mathematical discourses have no moral character, since they have no moral purpose, for they have no moral end. But the Sokratic discourses have such a character, since they deal with moral subjects. Different moral traits go with each character. (188-89)

4th cent. B.C.   Aristotle   ANE

Acts done in conformity with the virtues are not done justly or temperately if they themselves are of a certain sort, but only if the agent also is in a certain state of mind when he does them: first he must act with knowledge; secondly, he must deliberately choose the act, and choose it for its own sake; and thirdly the act must spring from a fixed and permanent disposition of character. . . . Thus although actions are entitled just and temperate when they are such acts as just and temperate men would do, the agent is just and temperate not when he does these acts merely, but when he does them in the way that just and temperate men do them. (85-87) . . . Choice is manifestly a voluntary act. But the terms are not synonymous, the latter being the wider. Children and the lower animals as well as men are capable of voluntary action, but not of choice. Also sudden acts may be termed voluntary, but they cannot be said to be done by choice. . . . A man of defective self-restraint acts from desire but not from choice; on the contrary, a self-restrained man acts from choice and not from desire. . . . (129) We may wish for what cannot be secured by our own agency . . . ; but no one chooses what does not rest with himself, but only what he thinks can be attained by his own act. Again, we wish rather for ends than for means, but choose the means to our end. . . . Nor yet can [choice] be a matter of opinion . . . [which] we distinguish . . . by its truth or falsehood . . . but choice is distinguished rather as being good or bad. . . . (131) For it is our choice of good or evil that determines our character, not our opinion about good or evil. (133)

1561   Scaliger   SP

[Aristotle] says that there cannot be a tragedy without action, though there may be one without disposition. Under the circumstances, I would here translate [ethos] by 'character,' for he says that the tragic poets of his day usually constructed plots that lacked delineation of character. . . . But if . . . [ethos] means 'an inclination to a certain course of action,' and this is excluded from tragedy, the action will be altogether fortuitous, and wholly dependent on chance. (82)

See also Scaliger under COMEDY (SP 38), TRAGEDY (SP 39).

1570   Castelvetro   **CP**

Poets who make tragedies without character and thought, do not really imitate human action; for in the operation of human action, character and thought are always revealed, though sometimes more, sometimes less. (102) . . . If the plot is the end of tragedy and of all poetry, if it is not a thing accessory to character, but on the contrary, character is accessory to plot, then many authors of great fame, ancient and modern, including Julius Ceasar Scaliger, have gravely erred in their opinion that it was the intention of good poets like Homer and Vergil to depict and demonstrate to the world, let us say, an indignant captain as excellently as possible, a valiant soldier, a wise man, and their moral natures; with much more of the same twaddle: for if this were true, then character would not be, as Aristotle says, secondary to action, but action would be secondary to character. Moreover, such subject could not be really poetic: it is much rather philosophic. (102-103) . . . Though character is not part of the action, yet it accompanies it inseparably, being revealed together with the action: hence character ought not to be considered as a part separate from the action, for without it the action would not be performed. (104)

c. 1583 Sidney. *See* under COMEDY (SDP 28).

1604   Jonson   **JBW**

In Picture, they which truly understand,
Require (besides the likeness of the thing)
Light, Posture, Height'ning, Shadow, Coloring,
All which are parts commend the cunning hand;
And all your Book (when it is thoroughly scann'd)
Will well confess; presenting, limiting,
Each subt'lest Passion, with her source, and spring,
So bold, as shows, your Art you can command.
But now, your Work is done, if they that view
The several figures, languish in suspense,
To judge which Passion's false, and which is true,
Between the doubtful sway of Reason,' and sense;
'Tis not your fault, if they shall sense prefer,
Being told there, Reason cannot, Sense may err.

Prefatory poem, Wright's *The Passions of the Mind in General*

1609   deVega. *See* under IMITATION (VAWP 34).

1657   d'Aubignac. *See* under TRAGEDY (AAS 4: 146-47).

1660   Corneille   **CFD**

The second part of the poem, [according to Aristotle] is *Manners*. Aristotle
prescribes four conditions: that they be good, suitable, similar and equal. . . . I
cannot imagine how one can conceive "good" to mean "virtuous." Most
poems . . . would remain in a pitiful state if one cut out all . . . bad or vicious
characters, or characters stained by some weakness which does not comport
with virtue. . . . If I may . . . conjecture on what Aristotle requires . . . I believe
it is the brilliant and elevated character of a criminal or virtuous habit. Just as
much as is proper and suitable to the person that one presents. . . . All
[Cleopatra's] crimes are accompanied by a loftiness of soul which has something so high in it that, while one despises her actions, one admires the source
from which they spring. . . . Another idea comes to me concerning what
Aristotle means by this goodness . . . that [the characters] must be as virtuous as
possible, so that they do not exhibit the vicious and criminal . . . if the subject
. . . does not require it. . . . In the second place, morals must be suitable. . . .
The poet must consider the age, dignity, birth, occupation and country of those
whom he paints . . . also that he may verify and then show what he wants his
public to love, and eliminate those [things] he wants him to hate, because it is
an infallible maxim that to achieve success one must get the audience on the
side of the important characters. . . . The quality of [likeness] . . . refers particularly to the people which history or fable teaches us to know and which we
must always depict such as we find them. . . . He who should depict . . . Medea
as a mild and humble woman would commit himself to public ridicule. . . .
There remains to speak of equality, which forces us to keep in our character the
manners which we gave them in the beginning. . . . Inequality can enter into it
all the same, not only when we bring persons of a light and uncertain spirit, but
also when in keeping the equality inside, we show inequality on the exterior,
according to the occasion. . . . That is what Aristotle calls "manners," un-
equally equal.(144-46)
       See also Corneille under COMEDY (CFD 141), SUBJECT (CFD 142-
43).

1664   Racine. *See* under SUBJECT (RP 154).

1668   Dryden. *See* under IMITATION (DW 1, 2: 82-83), VARIETY (DW 1,
2: 89).

1669   Molière. *See* under COMEDY (MP 2: 31-32).

1670   Racine. *See* under MAGNITUDE (RP 155).

1671   Dryden. *See* under POETIC JUSTICE (DW 1, 2: 198-201).

1679   Dryden.   DW

[Manners] may be all comprised under these general heads: First, they must be apparent; that is, in every character of the play some inclinations of the person must appear; and these are shown in the actions and discourse. Secondly, the manners must be suitable or agreeing to the persons; that is, to the age, sex, dignity, and the other general heads of manners: thus, when a poet has given the dignity of a king to one of his persons, in all his actions and speeches that person must discover majesty, magnanimity, and jealousy of power; because these are suitable to the general manners of a king. The third property of manners is resemblance; and this is founded upon the particular characters of men, as we have them delivered to us by relation or history: that is, when a poet has the known character of this or that man before him, he is bound to represent him such, at least not contrary to that which fame has reported him to have been. . . . The last property of manners is, that they be constant and equal, that is, maintained the same through the whole design. . . . The characters are no other than the inclinations as they appear in the several persons of the poem: a character being thus defined,—*that which distinguishes one man from another* . . . A character cannot be supposed to consist of one particular virtue, or vice, or passion only; but it is a composition of qualities which are not contrary to one another in the same person: thus the same man may be liberal and valiant, but not liberal and covetous. . . . Yet it is still to be observed, that one virtue, vice, and passion, ought to be shewn in every man, as predominant over all the rest; as covetousness in Crassus, love of his country in Brutus; and the same in characters which are feigned. (1, 2: 275-77)

See also Dryden under HERO (DW 1, 2: 277), PITY (DW 1,2: 270).

1711   Addison. *See* under GENRE DEFINITION (AW 1: 361).

1758   Diderot   DDP

I consider a passion, a well developed character, culminating in the exhibition of all his strength, much more important than that combination of incidents which goes to make up the tissue of a play in which the characters and audience are equally jostled and bandied about. That sort of thing is . . . foreign to good taste and grand effects. (290)

See also Diderot under IDEALISM (DDP 298, 299), PLOT (DDP 292, 296).

1755-1780   Diderot   DDE

The comic poet will . . . undertake a very special study of the divers temperaments of men. He will observe how these temperaments are nonetheless modified by the kind of life, the external relationships, the social obligations, the duties, and the other circumstances. In order to arouse our attention, he will create contrasts among the temperaments, duties, passions, and situations; he will often present to us the conflict between reason and inclination; he will unmask before our eyes the rogue and the hypocrite, and he will show them to us in their true colors; he will put the decent, honest man in the various crucial situations of life, and he will take care to place him in a light which will give us high regard and affection for him. (288) . . . It is to wrong the human heart and to misjudge nature to believe that nature needs titles to move us. The sacred names of friend, father, lover, spouse, son, mother, brother, sister, in a word man, with interesting manners and morals—these are the touching qualities. What matters the station, name, birth of the unfortunate person who has been drawn into the snares of gambling by his compliance toward unworthy friends and by the enticement of their example, and who now groans in prison devoured by remorse and by shame? If you ask what he is, I answer you: he was a virtuous man, and to make his sufferings worse, he is a husband and father: his wife whom he loves and by whom he is loved pines away, reduced to extreme indigence, and she can offer only tears when her children ask for bread. In the accounts of heroes, one could hardly find a situation more touching, more moral, in brief more tragic. (291)

See also Diderot under COMEDY (DDE 288-89).

1765 Johnson. *See* under UNIVERSALITY (JS 11-12).

1767-1769 Lessing   LSPW

We wished to investigate [Diderot's claim] . . . that tragedy had individuals, and comedy species, that is to say whether it is true that the persons in a comedy must seize and represent a great number of men while at the same time the hero of tragedy is only this or that man, only Regulus or Brutus or Cato. . . . (456-57) Aristotle has refuted this error two thousand years ago and pointed to the truth of the essential difference between history and poetry. . . . (457) It is unquestionable that Aristotle makes no distinction between the personages in tragedy and in comedy in regard to their generality. . . . All persons of poetic imitation without distinction, are to speak and act not only as would become them individually and alone, but as each of them would and must speak or act according to the nature of the circumstances. . . . In this generality is the sole reason why poetry is more philosophical and instructive than history. . . . (458) The characters in tragedy must be as general as the characters in comedy. (467)

1797 Goethe   GED

The characters [of epic poetry and tragedy] will appear to greatest advantage if they are represented as having attained a certain stage of development, when self-activity or spontaneity makes them still appear dependent upon themselves alone, and when their influence makes itself felt, not morally, politically, or mechanically, but in a purely personal way. (338)

1808   Schlegel   SCL

In conception [the essence of Greek tragedy] was ideal . . . ; this, however, must not be understood as implying that all its characters were depicted as morally perfect. In such a case what room could there be for that contrast and collision which the very plot of a drama requires?—They have their weaknesses, errors, and even crimes, but the manners are always elevated above reality, and every person is invested with as high a portion of dignity as was compatible with his part in the action. But this was not all. The ideality of the representation chiefly consisted in the elevation of everything in it to a higher sphere. Tragic poetry wished to separate the image of humanity which it presented to us, from the level of nature to which man is in reality chained down, like a slave of the soil. . . . The Greeks . . . in their artistic creations, succeeded almost perfectly, in combining the ideal with the real, . . . an elevation more than human with all the truth of life, and in investing the manifestation of an idea with energetic corporeity. (66) . . . Whatever is dignified, noble, and grand in human nature, admits only of a serious and earnest representation; for whoever attempts to represent it, feels himself, as it were, in the presence of a superior being, and is consequently awed and constrained by it. The comic poet, therefore, must divest his characters of all such qualities; he must place himself without the sphere of them; nay, even deny altogether their existence, and form an ideal of human nature the direct opposite of that of the tragedians, namely, as the odious and base. But as the tragic ideal is not a collective model of all possible virtues, so neither does this converse ideality consist in an aggregation, nowhere to be found in real life, of all moral enormities and marks of degeneracy, but rather in a dependence on the animal part of human nature, in that want of freedom and independence, that want of coherence, those inconsistencies of the inward man, in which all folly and infatuation originate. The earnest ideal consists of the unity and harmonious blending of the sensual man with the mental, such as may be more clearly recognised in Sculpture, where the perfection of form is merely a symbol of mental perfection and the loftiest moral ideas, and where the body is wholly pervaded by the soul, and spiritualized even to a glorious transfiguration. The merry or ludicrous ideal, on the other hand, consists in the perfect harmony and unison of the higher part of our nature, with the animal as the ruling principle. Reason and understanding are represented as the voluntary slaves of the senses. . . . (148-149) . . . Old Comedy introduced living characters on the stage, by name and with all circumstantiality . . . [but] such historical characters . . . have always an allegorical signification, and represent a class; and as their features were caricatures in the masks, so, in like manner, were their characters in the representation. But still this constant allusion to a proximate reality, which not only allowed the poet, in the character of the chorus, to converse with the public in a general way, but also to point the finger at certain individual spectators, was essential to this species of poetry. . . . As the New Comedy had to give to its representation a resemblance to a definite reality, it could not indulge in such studied and arbitrary exaggeration as the old did. It was, therefore, forced to seek for other sources of comic amusement, which lie nearer the province of [tragedy], and these it found in a more accurate and thorough delineation of character. In the characters of the New Comedy, either the *Comic of Observation* or the *Self-Conscious and Confessed Comic* will be found to prevail. The former constitutes the more refined, or what is called High Comedy, and the latter Low Comedy or Farce. . . . There are laughable peculiarities, follies, and obliquities, of which the possessor himself is unconscious, or which, if he does perceive them, he studiously endeavors to conceal, as being calculated to injure him in the opinion of others. Such persons consequently do not give themselves out for what they actually are; their secret escapes from them unwittingly, or against their will. Rightly, therefore, to portray such characters, the poet must lend his own peculiar talent for observation, that we may fully understand them. His art consists in making the character appear through slight hints and stolen glimpses, and in so placing the spectator, that whatever delicacy of observation it may require, he can hardly fail to see through them. (183-84) . . . If the effeminacy of the present day is to serve as a general standard of what tragical composition may properly exhibit to human nature, we shall be forced to set very narrow limits indeed to art, and the hope of anything like powerful effect must at once and forever be renounced. If we wish to have a grand purpose, we must also wish to have the grand means, and our nerves ought in some measure to accommodate themselves to painful impressions, if . . . our mind is thereby elevated and strengthened. The constant reference to a petty and puny race must cripple the boldness of the poet. . . . Shakespeare lived in an age extremely susceptible of noble and tender impressions, but which had yet inherited enough of the firmness of a vigorous olden time, not to shrink with dismay from every strong and forcible [character] painting. . . . If the delineation of all his characters, separately considered, is inimitably bold and correct, he surpasses even himself in so combining and contrasting them, that they serve to bring out each other's peculiarities. This is the very perfection of dramatic characterization: for we can never estimate a man's true worth if we consider him altogether abstractedly by himself; we must see him in his relations with others; and it is here that most dramatic poets are deficient. Shakespeare makes each of his principal characters the glass in which the others are reflected, and by like means enables us to discover what could not be immediately revealed to us. (268-69) . . . Characterization is merely one ingredient of the dramatic art, and not dramatic poetry itself. It would be improper in the extreme, if the poet were to draw our attention to superfluous traits of character, at a time when it ought to be his endeavour to produce other impressions. . . . Shakespeare's messengers, for instance, are for the most part mere messengers, and yet not common, but poetical messengers: the messages which they have to bring is the soul which suggests to them their language. (364)

    See also Schlegel under ACTION (SCL 239-42), COMEDY (SCL 309-10), PLOT (SCL 181-82).

1811-1812   Coleridge. *See* under UNIVERSALITY (CSNL 91).

1813   Goethe   **GLE**

It is said that [Shakespeare] delineated the Romans with wonderful skill. I cannot see it. They are Englishmen to the bone: but they are human, thoroughly human, and thus the Roman toga presumably fits them. . . . It is just his neglect of the outer form that makes his works so vital. (177) . . . No one has shown . . . better than [Shakespeare] the connection between Necessity and Will in the individual character. The person . . . is under a certain necessity; he is constrained, appointed to a particular line of action; but . . . he has a will, which is unconfined and universal in its demands. Thus arises an inner conflict, and Shakespeare is superior to all other writers in the significance with which he endows this. But now an outer conflict may arise, and the individual through it may become so aroused that an insufficient will is raised through circumstances to the level of irremissible necessity. . . . Hamlet through the agency of the ghost, Macbeth through the witches. . . . (182)

1815   Coleridge   **CBL**

I adopt with full faith the principle of Aristotle, that poetry as poetry is essentially *ideal*, that it avoids and excludes all *accident*; and its apparent individualities of rank, character, or occupation must be *representative* of a class; and that the *persons* of poetry must be clothed with *generic* attributes, with the *common* attributes of the class: not with such as one gifted individual might *possibly* possess, but such as from his situation it is most probable beforehand that he *would* possess. (2: 33-34) . . . Say not, that I am recommending abstractions: for these class-characteristics, which constitute the instructiveness of a character, are so modified and particularized in each person of the Shakespearean Drama, that life itself does not excite more distinctly that sense of individuality which belongs to real existence. Paradoxical as it may sound, one of the essential properties of geometry is not less essential to dramatic excellence, and . . . Aristotle has accordingly required of the poet an involution of the universal in the individual. The chief differences are, that in geometry it is the universal truth itself, which is uppermost in the consciousness, in poetry the individual form in which the Truth is clothed. (2: 159) . . . The ideal consists in the happy balance of the generic with the individual. The former makes the character representative and symbolical, therefore instructive; because *mutatis mutandis*, it is applicable to whole classes of men. The latter gives it *living* interest; for nothing *lives* or is *real*, but as definite and individual. (2: 187)

1817   Hazlitt. *See* under COMEDY (HW 1: 313), EMOTION (HW 1: 259).

c.1820   Hegel   **HFA**

The drama...has to exhibit situations, and the spiritual atmosphere that belongs to them, as definitely motivated by the individual character, which is charged with specific aims, and which makes these an effective part of the practical content of its volitional self-identity. The definition of soul-life, therefore, in the drama passes into the sphere of impulse, the realization of personality by means of active volition, in a word, effective action; it passes out of the sphere of pure ideality, it makes itself an object of the outer world, and inclines itself to the concrete facts of the epic world. . . . A character which is dramatic plucks for himself the fruit of his own deeds. (4: 252)...The *dramatis personae*...ought not to be merely specific interests personified, which is only too frequently the case of the hands of modern dramatists. Such abstract impersonations of particular passions and aims are wholly destitute of dramatic effect. A purely superficial individualization is equally insufficient. Content and form in such cases, as in the analagous type of allegorical figures, fail to coalesce. Profound emotions and reflections, imposing ideas and language offer no real compensation. Dramatic personality ought to be, on the contrary, vital and self-identical throughout, a complete whole, in short, the opinions and characterization of which are consonant with the aims and action. It is not the breadth of particular traits which is here of first importance, but the permeating individuality, which synthetically binds all in the central unity, which it in truth is, and displays a given personality in speech and action as issuing from one and the same living source, from which every characteristic, whether it be of idea, deed or manner of behaviour, comes into being. That which is merely an aggregate of different qualities and activities, even though such be strung together in one string, will not give us the vital character we require. . . . Among later writers Shakespeare and Goethe are preeminently famous for the vitality of their characterizations. . . . But...the task of dramatic creation is not completed with the presentment of vital characterization. Goethe's *Iphigeneia* and *Tasso* throughout are good enough examples of this poetic excellence—and yet they are not, if we look at them more strictly, by any means perfect examples of dramatic vitality and movement. . . . Unquestionably the display and expression of the personal experience of different characters in definite situations is not by itself sufficient; we must have real emphasis laid on the collision of the *ultimate ends* involved, and the forward and conflicting movement which such imply. . . . Dramatic effect is action simply as action; it is not the exposition of personality alone, or practically independent of the express purpose and its final achievement. . . . In the drama . . . the self-concentration of its principle is most asserted relatively to the particular collision and its conflict. (4: 273-75) . . . Critics have . . . recognized the nature of the chorus [of Greek tragedy] to the extent of maintaining that in it we find an attitude of tranquil meditation over the whole, whereas the characters of the action remain within the limits of their particular object[ives] and situations, and, in short, receive in the chorus and its observations a standard of valuation . . . in much the same way as the public . . . and within the drama itself, an objective representative of its own judgment upon all that is represented. . . . The chorus is, in truth, there as a substantive and more enlightened intelligence, which warns us from irrelevant oppositions, and reflects upon the genuine issue. But . . . it is by no means a wholly disinterested person, at leisure to entertain such thoughts and ethical judgments as it likes as are the spectators. . . . The chorus is the actual substance of the heroic life and action itself: it is, as contrasted with the particular heroes, the common folk regarded as the fruitful heritage, out of which individuals . . . grow and whereby they are conditioned in this life. Consequently, the chorus is peculiarly fitted to a view of life in which the obligations of State legislation and settled religious dogmas do not, as yet, act as restrictive force in ethical and social development, but where morality only exists in its primitive form of directly animated human life, and it is merely the equilibrium of unmoved life which remains assured in its stability against the fearful collisions which the antagonistic energies of individual action produces. . . . It does not, therefore, practically co-operate in the action; it executes by its action no right against the contending heroes; it merely expresses its judgment as a matter of opinion. . . . Just as the theatre itself possesses its external ground, its scene and environment, so, too, the chorus, that is the general community, is the spiritual scene. . . . In contrast to the chorus, the *second* fundamental feature of dramatic composition is that of *individuals* who act in *conflict* with each other. In Greek tragedy it is not at all the bad will, crime, worthlessness, or mere misfortune, stupidity, and the like, which act as incentive to such collisions, but rather . . . the ethical right to a definite course of action. Abstract evil neither possesses truth itself, nor does it arouse interest. At the same time, when we attribute ethical traits of characterization to the individuals of the action, these ought not to appear merely as a matter of opinion. It is rather implied in their right or claim that they are actually there . . . on their own account. (4: 315-18)

   See also Hegel under ACTION (HFA 4: 252), AFFECT (HFA 4: 273), CLOSURE (HFA 4: 323-25), COMEDY (HFA 4: 327-30), DRAMA (HFA 4: 248, 249-50, 261-62), GENRE (HFA 4: 256, 293, 294), GENRE DEFINITION (HFA 4: 305-308), IDEALISM (HFA 4: 265-67), LANGUAGE (HFA 4: 264-65), TRAGEDY (HFA 4: 295-99, 300-301, 312-15), UNIVERSALITY (HFA 4: 252-53).

1821-1822   Hazlitt   HW

There are various ways of getting at a knowledge of character—by looks, words, actions. The first of these, which seems the most superficial, is perhaps the safest, and least liable to deceive: nay, it is that which mankind, in spite of their pretending to the contrary, most generally go by. Professions pass for nothing, and actions may be counterfeited: but a man cannot help his looks. "Speech," said a celebrated wit, "was given to man to conceal his thoughts." The mouth of Cromwell is pursed up in the portraits of him, as if he was afraid to trust himself with words. . . . A man's whole life may be a lie to himself and others: and yet a picture painted of him by a great artist would probably stamp his true character on the canvas, and betray the secret to posterity. (4: 303)

1827   Goethe   GCE

Wed. March 21. Goethe . . . spoke about the characters of Creon and Ismene [in *Antigone*] and on the necessity for these two persons for the development of the beautiful soul of the heroine. "All that is noble," said he, "is in itself of a quiet nature, and appears to sleep until it is aroused and summoned forth by contrast. Such a contrast is Creon, who is brought in, partly on account of Antigone, in order that her noble nature and the right which is on her side may be brought out by him, partly on his own account, in order that his unhappy error may appear odious to us. But, as Sophocles meant to display the elevated soul of his heroine even before the deed, another contrast was requisite by which her character might be developed; and this is her sister Ismene."

See also Goethe under AFFECT (GCE Jan. 31).

1864   Taine   TLA

[The "literature of realism" and "comic drama" involve characters of "limited, weak and inferior natures." "Almost all good romances" use characters "that can be turned into ridicule."] Great artists, however, on whom the exigences of their class of subjects, or a love of strict truth, imposed studies of. this sad kind, have made use of two artifices to conceal the mediocrity and repulsiveness of the characters they have figured. They have either made of them accessories or contrasts, which serve to bring out some principal figure in stronger relief . . . ; or they have turned our sympathies against the personage, causing him to descend from one mishap to another, exciting against him the disapprobatory and vengeful laugh, purposely showing off the unlucky consequences of his inaptitude, and hunting out and expelling from life the defect which dominates in him. The spectator, become hostile, is satisfied; he experiences the same pleasure in seeing folly and egotism crushed, as he does in seeing an expansion of goodness and strength; the banishment of an evil is worth a triumph of the good. This is the great resource of the comedians, but novelists likewise make use of it; and you may see its success . . . in the *Précieuses*, the "Ecole des Femmes," the "Femmes Savantes," and numerous other pieces by Molière. . . . The spectacle, nevertheless, of these belittled or crippled spirits ends by leaving in the reader's mind a vague sentiment of weariness and disgust, and even irritation and bitterness. When they are very numerous in a work, and occupy the prominent place, one is disheartened. (274-76) . . . According as characters are more important or beneficient they hold a higher place and raise to a higher rank the works of art by which they are expressed. Note that importance and beneficence are two phases of a single quality, namely, *force*, considered in turn in relation to others and to itself. In the first case it is more or less important according as it resists greater or lesser forces. In the second case it is baneful or beneficent according as it borders on its own weakness or on its own extension. (307)

See also Taine under ACTION (TLA 318-19), AESTHETIC (TLA 76, 76-77, 82-84, 273-74), CLOSURE (TLA 319), HERO (TLA 180, 351-53), IMITATION (TLA 56-58), MAGNITUDE (TLA 323-24).

1871   Nietzsche   NBT

The character is not for [the true poet] an aggregate composed of a studied collection of particular traits, but an irrepressibly live person appearing before his eyes, and differing only from the corresponding vision of the painter by its ever continued life and action. (66)

See also Nietzsche under IMAGINATION (NBT 66), TRAGEDY (NBT 127).

1878   Nietzsche   NHH

CREATED INDIVIDUALS—When it is said that the dramatist . . . *creates* real characters, it is a fine deception and exaggeration. . . . As a matter of fact, we do not understand much about real, living man, and we generalize very superficially when we ascribe to him this and that character; this *very imperfect* attitude of ours towards man is represented by the poet, inasmuch as he makes into men (in this sense ''creates'') outlines as *superficial* as our knowledge of man is superficial. There is a great deal of delusion about these created characters of artists; they are by no means living productions of nature, but are like painted men, somewhat too thin, they will not bear a close inspection. And when it is said that the character of the ordinary living being contradicts itself frequently, and that one created by the dramatist is the original model conceived by nature, this is quite wrong. A genuine man is something absolutely *necessary* (even in those so called contradictions), but we do not recognise this necessity. The imaginary man, the phantasm, signifies something necessary, but only to those who understand a real man only in a crude, unnatural simplification, so that a few strong, oft-repeated traits, with a great deal of light and shade and half-light about them, amply satisfy their notions. They are, therefore, ready to treat the phantasm as a genuine, necessary man, because with real men they are accustomed to regard a phantasm, an outline, an intentional abbreviation as the whole. . . . Plastic art wishes to make character visible on the surface; histrionic art employs speech for the same purpose, it reflects character in sounds. Art starts from the natural *ignorance* of man about his interior condition. . . . (163-64)

1888   Strindberg   **SSPP**

In the course of the ages the word character has assumed many meanings. Originally it signified probably the dominant groundnote in the complex mass of the self, and as such it was confused with temperament. Afterward it became the middle-class term for an automaton, so that an individual whose nature had come to a stand-still, or who had adapted himself to a certain part in life—who had ceased to grow, in a word—was named a character; while one remaining in a state of development—a skillful navigator on life's river, who did not sail with close-tied sheets, but knew when to fall off before the wind and when to luff again—was called lacking in character. And he was called so in a depreciatory sense, of course, because he was so hard to catch, to classify, and to keep track of. This middle-class notion about the immobility of the soul was transplanted to the stage, where the middle-class element has always held sway. There a character became synonymous with a gentleman fixed and finished once for all—one who invariably appeared drunk, jolly, sad. And for the purpose of characterisation nothing more was needed than some physical deformity like a club-foot, a wooden leg, a red nose. (14) . . . I do not believe, therefore, in simple characters on the stage. And the summary judgments of the author upon men—this one stupid, and that one brutal, this one jealous, and that one stingy—should be challenged by the naturalists, who know the fertility of the soul-complex, and who realise that "vice" has a reverse very much resembling virtue. (15) . . . If [my minor] characters have seemed mere abstractions to some people, it depends on the fact that ordinary men are to a certain extent impersonal in the exercise of their callings. This means that they are without individuality, showing only one side of themselves while at work. And as long as the spectator does not feel the need of seeing them from other sides, my abstract presentation of them remains on the whole correct. (19)

1888   Chekhov   **CL**

Oct. 27. You say that the hero of my "Party" is a character worth developing. Good Lord! I am not a senseless brute, you know, I understand that. I understand that I cut the throats of my characters and spoil them, and that I waste good material. . . . [But one cannot take the time to write each story as one would like.] And so in planning a story one is bound to think first about its framework: from a crowd of leading or subordinate characters one selects one person only—wife or husband; one puts him on the canvas and paints him alone, making him prominent, while the others one scatters over the canvas like small coin, and the result is something like the vault of heaven: one big moon and a number of very small stars around it. But the moon is not a success because it can only be understood if the stars too are intelligible, and the stars are not worked out. And so what I produce is not literature. (100-102)

1888   Chekhov   CL

Dec. 30. In my description of Ivanov there often occurs the word "Russian."
. . . When I was writing the play I had in mind only the things that really
matter—that is, only the typical Russian characteristics. Thus the extreme
excitability, the feeling of guilt, the liability to become exhausted are purely
Russian. . . . Ivanov and Lvov appear to my imagination to be living people. I
tell you honestly, in all conscience, these men were born in my head, not by
accident, not out of sea foam, or preconceived "intellectual" ideas. They are
the result of observing and studying life. The stand in my brain, and I feel that I
have not falsified the truth nor exaggerated it a jot. If on paper they have not
come out dear and living, the fault is not in them but in me, for not being able to
express my thoughts. (118-19)

　　See also Chekhov under THOUGHT (CL May 30).

1889   Chekhov   CL

Jan. 7. I have been cherishing the bold dream of summing up all that has
hitherto been written about whining, miserable people, and with my Ivanov
saying the last word. (119)

1890   Chekhov. *See* under OBJECTIVITY (CL 141).

1894   Brunetière. *See* under ACTION (BLD 75-76).

1895   Shaw. *See* under GENRE DEFINITION (SDC 48-49).

1896   Shaw   SDC

The tradition of the stage is a tradition of villains and heroes. . . . The true
villain [is] the man whose terrible secret is that his fundamental moral impulses
are by some freak of nature inverted, so that . . . cruelty, destruction, and
perfidy are his most luxurious passions. . . . The average normal man is covetous, lazy, selfish; but he is not malevolent. . . . He only does wrong as a
means to an end, which he always represents to himself as a right end. (135)

1908   Pirandello   POH

It is clear that the parodic intention inevitably infuses caricature into the form,
since he who wants to imitate someone else must necessarily capture his most
conspicuous traits and insist on them; and such insistence inevitably produces
caricature. (49) . . . Parody and caricature are unquestionably motivated by the
writer's satiric or simply burlesque intention. Satire and mockery consist in a
ridiculous alteration of the model; consequently they are measurable only if
related to the qualities of the model and particularly to those qualities which are
most markedly conspicuous and which represent an exaggeration already in the

model itself. The writer of a parody or caricature will insist on these markedly noticeable features; he will highlight them, and exaggerate what is already exaggerated. In order to achieve this, the artist is inevitably bound to strain his expressive means and alter his sketch, his voice or, at any rate, his expression, in a strange, clumsy and even grotesque fashion. In short, parody requires that violence be done to art and to its serious norms. When working with a blemish or defect of art or nature, exaggeration is the only means to achieve laughter. The end result of this exaggeration must necessarily be something monstrous, something that, considered in and by itself, is devoid of truth and consequently of beauty; to understand its truth and therefore its beauty, it is necessary to examine the end result of a parody by relating it to the original model. Thus, we leave the sphere of pure fantasy. In order to laugh at or ridicule the blemish or defect, we must also jest with the tools of art; we must be conscious of our game, which may be cruel, or may not have any malicious intentions, or may even have serious intentions as in the case of Aristophanes and his caricatures. (59-60) . . . It is true that when a poet is genuinely successful in giving life to one of his characters, this character lives independently of its author, so much so that we can imagine it in other situations in which the author never intended to place it, and see it behave according to its own inner laws—laws which not even the author would have been able to violate; it is true that this character, in which the author was instinctively successful in gathering, unifying, and vivifying so many individual characteristics and so many random elements, can later become what is usually called a 'type', something that was not a part of the author's intention at the moment of creation. (86)

See also Pirandello under HUMOR (POH 142-43).

1908   Strindberg   SOL

The character is, of course, the essence of a human being's *inner* life: his inclinations, his passions, his weaknesses. If the character actor emphasizes the nonessential externals or tries to express the uniquely individual inner qualities of the role by means of strong external means the interpretation easily becomes a caricature, and instead of creating a character he creates a travesty. People often equate character with the type or the original model and demand consistency in the characterization. But there are inconsistent characters, disjointed, broken, erratic characters. (29)

1909   Shaw. *See* under GENRE DEFINITION (STPB xx, xxii-xxiii).

1919   Eliot   EEE

Jonson's characters conform to the logic of the emotions of their world. They are not fancy, because they have a logic of their own; and this logic illuminates the actual world, because it gives us a new point of view from which to inspect it. (79)

1921   Shaw   **SPC**

When you play Shakespeare, dont worry about the character, but go for the music. It was by word music that he expressed what he wanted to express; and if you get the music right, the whole thing will come right. . . . If you want to know the truth about Lady Macbeth's character, she hasnt one. There never was no such person. She says things that will set people's imagination to work if she says them in the right way: that is all. I know: I do it myself. (248-49)

1930   Eliot   **EEE**

Dramatic characters may live in more than one way. . . . Characters should be real in relation to our own life, certainly as even a very minor character of Shakespeare may be real; but they must also be real in relation to each other; and the closeness of emotional pattern in the latter way is an important part of dramatic merit. (121-22)

c.1930   Stanislavski. *See* under ACTION (SCR 48), SUBTEXT (SCR 51).

1931   Brecht   **BBT**

The epic actor's efforts to make particular incidents between human beings seem striking (to use human beings as a setting), may also cause him to be misrepresented as a short-range episodist by anybody who fails to allow for his way of knotting all the separate incidents together and absorbing them in the broad flow of his performance. As against the dramatic actor, who has his character established from the first and simply exposes it to the inclemencies of the world and the tragedy, the epic actor lets his character grow before the spectator's eyes out of the way he behaves. [The elements of behavior] do not altogether add up to a single unchangeable character but to one which changes all the time and becomes more and more clearly defined in course of "this way of changing." This hardly strikes the spectator who is used to something else. How many spectators can so far discard the need for tension as to see how, with this new sort of actor, the same gesture is used to summon him to the wall to change his clothes as is subsequently used to summon him there in order to be shot, and to realize that the situation is similar but the behaviour different? An attitude is here required of the spectator which roughly corresponds to the reader's habit of turning back in order to check a point. Completely different economies are needed by the epic actor and the dramatic. (The actor Chaplin, incidentally, would in many ways come closer to the epic than to the dramatic theatre's requirements.) (56)

1931-1936   Artaud. *See* under DRAMA (AT 116), THOUGHT (AT 41).

1935   Brecht. *See* under IDENTIFICATION (BBT 87); compare with CATHARSIS (BBT 87).

c.1936   Brecht. *See* under EPIC THEATRE (BBA 20-21).

1938   Brecht. *See* under ACTION (BBEB 430).

1938   Stanislavski. *See* under THOUGHT (SBC 169-71).

c.1940   Brecht. *See* under ALIENATION (BBAn 15-20).

1942   Eliot. *See* under STYLE (EOPP 33).

1948   Brecht   **BBBG**

Everyone responds differently according to his times or class; if he lived at another time, or were still young, or lived on the dark side of life, he would unfailingly respond otherwise. But he would respond just as emphatically, and just as everyone in the situation would. The question arises whether there are further differences in responses. Where is the man who is alive and unique, that is, the man who is exactly like the other people in his situation? It is clear that the theatrical image must bring him to light, and it will do so when the element of contradiction is incorporated into the image. The "historicizing" image will have something in common with sketches which show traces of other movements and traits around the finished figure. (25) . . . The unity of the character is to be depicted in a manner that makes individual characteristics contradict each other. (30)

   See also Brecht under ALIENATION (BBBG 26-27), GEST (BBBG 33, 35, 35-36, 39), ILLUSION (BBBG 28-29), UNIVERSALITY (BBBG 30).

1953   Eliot. *See* under STYLE (ETVP 4, 8, 9-10).

1956   Brecht. *See* under IDENTIFICATION (BBT 277-78).

CLOSURE

The need for the satisfaction of aesthetic closure in dramatic art is more often assumed than argued and its nature is more often asserted than demonstrated. For some theorists it seems to be the creation of a sense of finality, a clear punctuation mark at the end of the dramatic sentence. Others seem to require a perceived wholeness to the work for which the addition of the missing element —like the keystone in the arch—provides closure. Still others find closure satisfactorily realized only with a comprehensive epiphany, an insight that encompasses the work in a new vision. Whether as punctuation, wholeness, or epiphany, the means for achieving closure seem to be either content centered (resolutions of story, conflict, or character biography), or theme centered (the resolution of moral or philosophical issues), or form centered (the completion of a design that is externally or internally determined in an effort to realize an ideal model or an affective strategy). Such categories as ACTION, AES-THETIC, AFFECT, CONFLICT, FORM, ORDER, THOUGHT, and UNITY suggest what it is that the theorists believe requires resolution. See also CATHARSIS and POETIC JUSTICE as specific concepts of closure.

4th cent. B.C.   Aristotle   AP

The Unravelling [or *Dénouement*] is that which extends from the beginning of the change to the end. (65)
    See also Aristotle under COMPLICATION (AP 65), PLOT (AP 65-67).

1561   Scaliger. *See* under ACTION (SP 63), TRAGEDY (SP 39, 40).

1570   Castelvetro   CP

The solution of the plot ought to be brought about by the plot itself, i.e., the striking of the danger and the ceasing of the difficulty should themselves be constituents of the plot following the nature of the danger and of the difficulty by necessity or by verisimilitude. (99)
    See also Castelvetro under TRAGEDY (CP 96-97, 98).

1609   deVega   VAWP

See the connection from the beginning until the action runs down; but do not permit the untying of the plot until reaching the last scene; for the crowd, knowing what the end is, will turn its face to the door and its shoulder to what it has awaited three hours face to face; for in what appears nothing more is to be known. (32) . . . Let the scenes end with epigram, with wit, and with elegant verse, in such wise that, at his exit, he who spouts leaves not the audience disgusted. (34)

1657 d'Aubignac   AAS

I Do not think it necessary here to trouble my self about the explication of [the] word *Catastrophe*. 'Tis taken ordinarily, I know, for some sad calamitous disaster, which terminates some great design, for my part I understand by this word a sudden change of the first Dispositions of the Stage, and the return of Events, which change all the Appearances of the former Intrigues, quite contrary to the expectation of the Audience. Comedies have generally happy *Catastrophes*, or at least they end in some buffoonery or fooling . . . ; but as for serious Tragedies, they always end either by the Misfortune of the Principal Actors, or by a Prosperity such as they could wish for. (2: 131)

    See also d'Aubignac under EXPOSITION (AAS 3: 15-16), TRAGEDY (AAS 4:140).

1660 Corneille   CFD

[Tragedy and Comedy] have this in common, that the action must be complete and finished; that is, in the event which finishes it the spectator must be so clearly informed of the feelings of all who have had a part in it that he leaves with his mind quiet and doubting of nothing. . . . For comedy, Aristotle demands as the only precept that it may have as ending, the enemies becoming friends. Which must be understood in a . . . general sense [as] a reconciliation. . . . We must be careful, however, that this agreement does not come by a simple change of will but by an event which furnishes the occasion for it. Otherwise there would be no great art to the "dénouement" of a play. . . . It needs a considerable motive. . . . (143) . . . One must if one can reserve all the climax and even defer it until the end. The more one defers it the more the mind will remain in expectancy and the desire to know to which side it will turn, creates the impatience which causes it to be received with more pleasure. . . . The listeners who know too much have no more curiosity, and their attention wanes during all the rest, which tells nothing new. (148)

    See also Corneille under SURPRISE (CSP 109).

1710 Addison   AW

An *anti-climax* [is] an instance of which we have in the tenth page; where [the author] tells us, that Britain may expect to have this only glory left her, "that she has proved a farm to the Bank, a province to Holland, and a jest to the whole world." I never met with so sudden a downfall in so promising a sentence; a jest to the whole world, gives such an unexpected turn to this happy period, that I was heartily troubled and surprised to meet with it. (3:263)

1711 **Addison.** *See* under STYLE (AW 1:70).

1758   Diderot   DDP

He who undertakes to develop two intrigues at once labors under the necessity of unravelling them at the same moment. If the principal intrigue ends before the other, that other cannot stand alone; or if the subsidiary plot ends first, either the characters disappear, or else they are brought in again without sufficient motive, and the play is mutilated and leaves a frigid impression. (291)

1765   Johnson. *See* under FORM (JS 24-25).

1767-1769   Lessing   LSPW

I am far removed from believing with the majority of those who have written on the dramatic art that the *dénouement* should be hid from the spectator. I rather think it would not exceed my powers to rouse the very strongest interest in the spectators even if I resolved to make a work where the *dénouement* was revealed in the first scene. Everything must be clear for the spectator, he is the confidant of each person, he knows everything that occurs, everything that has occurred. (377)

1808   Schlegel   SCL

It is impossible . . . for a piece to have less action, in the energetical sense of the word [than Euripides's *Troades*]: it is a series of situations and events, which have no other connection than that of a common origin in the capture of Troy, but in no respect have they a common aim. The accumulation of helpless suffering, against which the will and sentiment even are not allowed to revolt, at last wearies us, and exhausts our compassion. The greater the struggle to avert a calamity, the deeper the impression it makes when it bursts forth after all. . . . In the ceaseless demands which this play makes on our compassion the pathos is not duly economized and brought to a climax. . . . (136) . . . In many French tragedies I find . . . a Unity for the Understanding, but the Feeling is left unsatisfied. Out of a complication of painful and violent situations we do, it is true, arrive at last, happily or unhappily, at a state of repose; but in the represented course of affairs there is no secret and mysterious revelation of a higher order of things; there is no allusion to any consolatory thoughts of heaven, whether in the dignity of human nature successfully maintained in its conflicts with fate, or in the guidance of an over-ruling providence. To such a tranquilizing feeling the so-called poetical justice is partly unnecessary, and partly also . . . very insufficient. (254)
       See also Schlegel under UNITY (SCL 242-245).

c.1820   Hegel   HFA

The higher conception of reconciliation in tragedy is . . . related to the resolution of specific ethical and substantive facts from their contradiction into their true harmony. The . . . accord is established . . . under very different modes [:] [1.] If it is the onesidedness of the pathos . . . of a particular individual . . . [which must] be abrogated then it is this individual which, to the extent that his action is exclusively identified with this isolated pathos, must perforce be stripped and sacrificed. For . . . if this unity is not secured . . . on its own account, the individual is shattered. [a] The most complete form of this development is possible when the individuals engaged in conflict . . . stand fundamentally under the power of that against which they battle and consequently infringe that which [for their safety] they ought to respect. Antigone, for example, lives under the political authority of Creon . . . so that her obedience to the royal prerogative is an obligation. But Creon also . . . is under obligation to respect the sacred ties of relationship, and only by breach of this can give an order that is in conflict with such a sense. In consequence of this we find immanent in the life of both that which each respectively combats, and they are seized and broken by that very bond which is rooted in the compass of their own social existence. . . . Among all the fine creations of the ancient and the modern world . . . the ''Antigone'' of Sophocles is from this point of view in my judgment the most excellent and satisfying work of art. [b] The tragic issue does not, however, require in every case as the means of removing both over-emphasized aspects, and the equal honour which they respectively claim, the downfall of the contestant parties. The ''Eumenides'' does not end . . . with the death of Orestes, or the destruction of the Eumenides[;] . . . Apollo . . . will have Orestes released from . . . punishment and honour bestowed on both himself and the Furies. [2.] As a contrast to this type of objective reconciliation [in which both sides are destroyed or both vindicated] . . . the individual concerned in the action may . . . surrender his one-sided point of view. [a] In this betrayal by personality of its essential pathos, however, it cannot fail to appear destitute of character; and this contradicts the masculine integrity of such plastic figures. The individual, therefore, can only submit to a higher Power . . . to the effect that while on his own account he adheres to such a pathos, the will is nevertheless broken in its base obstinacy by a god's authority. In such a case the knot is not loosened, but, as in the case of Philoctetes, it is severed by a *deus ex machina*. [b] More beautiful than the above rather external mode of resolution we have the reconciliation more properly of the soul itself. . . . The most perfect example of this in ancient drama is to be found in the . . . ''Oedipus Coloneas'' of Sophocles. (4: 323-25)

See also Hegel under ACTION (HFA 4: 259-61), DRAMA (HFA 4: 254-55, 261-62, 321-23), FORM (HFA 4: 262-63), FORWARD MOVEMENT (HFA 4: 262), PLOT (HFA 4: 264), TRAGEDY (HFA 4: 295-99, 300-301).

1827 Goethe. *See* under REVERSAL (GCE March 21).

1864   Taine   **TLA**

Portions of a scene are grouped together in view of a certain effect; all effects are combined in view of a dénouement; the entire story is constructed in view of the natures which we wish to bring upon the stage. The noteworthy class and the visible character are due to the qualities which converge or persist in them; this convergence of the entire character and of its successive situations manifests the essence of the character, and even its elements in drawing it out to a definite success or to a final overthrow. (319) . . . In a picture, in a statue, in a poem, in an edifice, and in a symphony all the effects should converge to one point. The degree of this convergence marks the place of the work. (311) All things equal in other respects, they will be more or less beautiful according to the greater or less completeness of the convergence of effects in them. (324)

1871   Nietzsche. *See* under DRAMA (NBT 60-61).

1887   Chekhov   **CLF**

Oct. The plot [of *Ivanov*] is complicated and not silly. I finish up each act as if it were a story: the action goes on quietly and peacefully, and at the end I give the audience a sockdologer. All my energy was spent on a few really brisk, forceful climaxes; but the bridges joining these are insignificant, loose, and not startling. (129)

1889   Chekhov   **CLF**

May 8. The first act may last as long as a whole hour, but the rest should not be more than twenty minutes each. The crux of a play is the third act, but it must not be so strong a climax as to kill the last act. (171)

1898   Shaw. Compare with CONFLICT (SCP 729)

c.1900   Strindberg. *See* under PLOT (SEP 574-75).

1909   Shaw   **STPB**

The tradition of the catastrophe [is] unsuitable to modern studies of life: the tradition of an ending, happy or the reverse, is equally unworkable. The moment the dramatist gives up accidents and catastrophes, and takes 'slices of life' as his material, he finds himself committed to plays that have no endings. The curtain no longer comes down on a hero slain or married: it comes down when the audience has seen enough of the life presented to it to draw the moral. . . . (xv-xvi)
   See also Shaw under GENRE DEFINITION (STPB xx).

1913   Shaw   **SMCE**

Since [*A Doll's House* conquered Europe] the discussion has expanded far
beyond the limits of the last ten minutes of an otherwise "well made" play.
The disadvantage of putting the discussion at the end was not only that it came
when the audience was fatigued, but that it was necessary to see the play over
again, so as to follow the earlier acts in the light of the final discussion, before
it became fully intelligible. [See ACTION 1913 Shaw (SMCE 138-
39)] . . . The natural is mainly the everyday; and its climaxes must be, if not
everyday, at least everylife, if they are to have any importance for the spectator. (139-40) . . . Shakespeare survives by what he has in common with
Ibsen, and not what he has in common with Webster and the rest. . . . We have
progressed so rapidly on this point under the impulse given to drama by Ibsen
that it seems strange now to contrast him favorably with Shakespeare on the
ground that he avoided the old catastrophes which left the stage strewn with the
dead. . . . The post-Ibsen playwrights apparently think . . . homicides and suicides . . . forced. In Tchekov's *Cherry Orchard*, for example, where the sentimental ideals of our amiable, cultured Schumann playing propertied class are
reduced to dust and ashes by a hand not less deadly than Ibsen's because it is so
much more caressing, nothing more violent happens than that the family
cannot afford to keep up its old house. (142-43) . . . The writer who practices
the art of Ibsen . . . discards all the old tricks of preparation, catastrophe,
dénouement, and so forth without thinking about it. . . . Ibsen substituted a
terrible art of sharpshooting at the audience, trapping them, fencing with them,
aiming always at the sorest spot in their consciences. Never mislead an
audience, was an old rule. But the new school will trick the spectator into
forming a meanly false judgment, and then convict him of it in the next act,
often to his grievous mortification. When you despise something you ought to
take off your hat to, or admire and imitate something you ought to loathe, you
cannot resist the dramatist who knows how to touch these morbid spots in you
and make you see that they are morbid. . . . And though he may use all the
magic of art to make you forget the pain he causes you or to enhance the joy of
the hope and courage he awakens, he is never occupied in the old work of
manufacturing interest and expectation with materials that have neither novelty,
significance, nor relevance to the experience or prospects of spectators. (145)

1948   Brecht. *See* under PLEASURE (BBBG 15).

COMEDY

The following passages express or clearly imply a theory of the comedic form of drama and its characteristics as an exercise in GENRE DEFINITION. Compare with TRAGEDY. For theories of the comic, see HUMOR.

4th cent. B.C.   Aristotle   **AP**

Comedy is . . . an imitation of *characters of a lower type* [relatively worthless characters: EP 183]—not, however, in the full sense of the word bad, the Ludicrous being merely a subdivision of the ugly. It consists in some *defect* [mistake: EP 183] or ugliness which is not painful or destructive. To take an obvious example, the comic mask is ugly and distorted but does not *imply* [cause: EP 183] pain. (21)

   See also Aristotle under IMITATION (AP 11-13), PROBABILITY (AP 35-37).

1561   Scaliger   **SP**

Why does Horace question whether or not comedy is poetry? Forsooth, because it is humble, must it be denied the title of poetry? Surely an unfortunate ruling! So far from comedy not being poetry, I would almost consider it the first and truest of all poetry, for comedy employs every kind of invention, and seeks for all kinds of material. (17) . . . Comedy is a dramatic poem, which is filled with intrigue, full of action, happy in its outcome, and written in a popular style. An inaccurate definition of the Latin comedy described it as "a plot free from the suggestion of danger, dealing with the life and affairs of the private citizen." [1] This definition covers other, non-dramatic stories. . . . [2] There is always the suggestion of danger in comedy, although the outcome is invariably tame. . . . Further, there is not only danger in comedy, but violence at the hands of panderers, rivals, lovers, servants, or masters. . . . [3] This definition would not admit the official class, wearers of the toga, for they are not private citizens. [4] Finally, the definition would embrace mimes and dramatic satires. (38)

   See also Scaliger under SUBJECT (SP 57, 69), TRAGEDY (SP 39).

1570   Castelvetro   **CP**

[The ludicrous, which is the source of comedy, entails no sense of injury or destruction; comedy is an unmixed pleasure,] being moved by pleasing things appealing to the sentiments or the imagination. [Its subject is] human turpitude, either of mind or of body; [but if the former] arising from folly, not from vice, [and if the latter] neither painful nor harmful. (134)...[Comic] plot comprises only actions possible to happen, those which have actually happened having no place at all. (136)

See also Castelvetro under SUBJECT (CP 134-35), TRAGEDY (CP 96-97).

c.1583 Sidney   SDP

The comedy is an imitation of the common errors of our life, which [the poet] representeth in the most ridiculous and scornful sort that may be, so as it is impossible that any beholder can be content to be such one. Now, as in geometry the oblique must be known as well as the right, and in arithmetic the odd as well as the even; so in the actions of our life who seeth not the filthiness of evil, wanteth a great foil to perceive the beauty of virtue. This doth the comedy handle so, in our private and domestic matters, as with hearing it we get, as it were, an experience what is to be looked for of a niggardly Demen, of a crafty Davus, of a flattering Gnatho, of a vain-glorius Thraso; and not only to know what effects are to be expected, but to know who be such, by the signifying badge given them by the comedian. And little reason hath any man to say that men learn evil by seeing it so set out; since . . . there is no man living, but by the force truth hath in nature, no sooner seeth these men play their parts, but wisheth them *in pistrinum*, although perchance the sack of his own faults lie so behind his back, that he seeth not himself to dance the same measure,— whereto yet nothing can more open his eyes than to find his own actions contemptibly set forth. (28)

1605 Jonson. See under POETIC JUSTICE (JBW).

1609 de Vega   VAWP

True comedy has its end established like every kind of poem or poetic art, and that has always been to imitate the actions of men and to paint the customs of their age. (25)

See also de Vega under ACTION (VAWP 30-31), IMITATION (VAWP 25), STYLE (VAWP 27, 32-33).

1641 Jonson   JD

The parts of a Comedie are the same with a *Tragedie*, and the end is partly the same. For the both delight, and teach. Nor, is the moving of laughter alwaies the end of *Comedy*, that is rather a fowling for the peoples delight, or their fooling. For, as *Aristotle* saies rightly, the moving of laughter is a fault in Comedie, a kind of turpitude, that depraves some part of a mans nature without a disease. As a wry face without paine moves laughter, or a deformed vizard, or a rude Clowne, drest in a Ladies habit, and using her actions, wee dislike, and scorne such representations; which made the ancient Philosophers ever thinke laughter unfitting in a wise man. . . . As, also it is divinely said of *Aristotle*, that to seeme ridiculous is a part of dishonesty, and foolish. So that, what either in the words, or Sense of an Author, or in the language, or Actions of men, is awry, or depraved, doth strangely stirre meane affections, and provoke for the most part to laughter. And therefore it was cleare that all insolent, and obscene speaches, jest upon the best men; injuries to particular persons; perverse, and sinister Sayings (and the rather unexpected) in the Old Comedy did move laughter; especially when it did imitate any dishonesty; and scurrility came forth in the place of wit: which who understands the nature and *Genius* of laughter, cannot but perfectly know. . . . Jests that are true and naturall, seldome raise laughter, with the beast, the multitude. They love nothing, that is right and proper. The farther it runs from reason, a possibility with them, the better it is. What could have made them laugh, like to see *Socrates* presented, that Example of all good life, honesty and vertue, to have him hoisted up with a Pullie, and there play the Philosopher, in a basquet. . . . This was *Theatricall* wit, right Stage-jesting, and relishing a Play-house, invented for scorne, and laughter; whereas, if it had favour'd of equity, truth, perspicuity, and Candor, to have tasten a wise, or a learned Palate, spit it out presantly; this is bitter and profitable, this instructs, and would informe us: what needs wee know any thing, that are nobly borne, more then a Horse-race, or a hunting-match, our day to break with Citizens, and such innate mysteries. This is truly leaping from the Stage, to the Tumbrell againe, reducing all witt to the Originall Dungcart. (99-101)

1657   d'Aubignac   AAS

[Ancient] Comedy was the picture of the Actions of the people, in which were generally represented the Debaucheries of young people, with the tricks and acts of Slaves and Courtezans, full of Railleries and Jests, and ending in Marriages, or some other pleasant Adventure of common life; and this Poem was so much confin'd to represent a popular life, that the style of it was to be low and mean, the expressions taken out of the mouths of ordinary people; the passions were to be short, and without violence. In a word, all the Intrigues were to be upheld by flight and cunning, and not by the sublime and marvellous part of humane life. (4: 141) . . . [Ancient] *Tragedy* and *Comedy* were two Poems so distinct, that not only the Adventures [and] Persons . . . of the one, had nothing common with the other; but even the *Tragedians* never acted Comedys, nor the *Comedians Tragedy*: They were as it were two different Trades or Professions. (4: 146) . . . The chief distinctive mark of these two Poems was the matter of their Incidents, and the condition of the persons in each Poem; for where Gods and Kings acted according to their gravity and dignity, that was call'd *Tragedy*; but when the *Intrigues* of the Stage were founded upon the tricks and behavior of young *Debauchees*, Women and Slaves, that was Comedy. (4: 147)

    See also d'Aubignac under TRAGEDY (AAS 4: 146-47).

1660   Corneille   CFD

[Aristotle] speaks only of tragedy, since all that he says of it is applicable to comedy also, and that the difference in these two kinds of poetry consists only in the dignity of the characters and in the actions which they imitate and not in the manner of the imitation nor in the things which serve the imitation. (141)

    See also Corneille under SUBJECT (CFD 142-43).

1668   Dryden   DW

For comedy, repartee is one of its chiefest graces; the greatest pleasure of the audience is a chace of wit, kept up on both sides, and swiftly managed. (1, 2: 88-89)

    See also Dryden under IMITATION (DW 1, 2: 126-27).

1669   Molière   MP

If any one will take pains to examine my comedy [*Tartuffe*] candidly, he will see that my intentions are wholly innocent; that the play does not, in any sense, laugh at those things which we ought to revere; . . . and that I have used all the art and all the care I possibly could in distinguishing the character of the hypocrite from that of truly pious men. For this very purpose, I employed two whole acts in preparing the way for my scoundrel. The audience is not kept for one moment in doubt; he is known for what he is from the start; and, from end to end, he does not say one word, he does not do one act, which will not show to the spectators the nature of a bad man, and bring into relief that of the goodman to which I oppose him. (2: 31-32) . . . The purpose of comedy is to correct the vices of men. . . . We have evidence that the stage has great virtue as a public corrective. But the finest shafts of serious morality are often less effective than those of satire; nothing corrects the majority of men so well as a picture of their faults. The strongest means of attacking vice is by exposing it to the laughter of the world. We can endure reproof, but we cannot endure ridicule. We are willing to be wicked, but not to be absurd. (2: 32-33) . . . We have only to strip off the veil of ambiguity and look at what comedy really is, to see whether or not it is condemnable. We shall discover, I think, that being neither more nor less than a witty poem, reproving the faults of men by agreeable lessons, it cannot be censured without great injustice. (2: 34-35)

1671   Dryden   DW

Farce . . . consists principally of grimaces. . . . I detest those farces, which are now the most frequent entertainment of the stage. . . . Comedy consists, though of low persons, yet of natural actions and characters; I mean such humours, adventures, and designs, as are to be found and met with in the world. Farce, on the other side, consists of forced humours, and unnatural events. Comedy presents us with the imperfections of human nature; farce entertains us with what is monstrous and chimerical: the one causes laughter in those who can judge of men and manners, by the lively representation of their folly or corruption; the other produces the same effect in those who can judge of neither, and that only by its extravagancies. The first works on the judgment and fancy; the latter on the fancy only: there is more of satisfaction in the former kind of laughter, and in the latter more of scorn. . . . In short, there is the same difference betwixt farce and comedy, as betwixt an empirick and a true physician: both of them may attain their ends, but what the one performs by hazard, the other does by skill. And as the artist is often unsuccessful, while the mountebank succeeds,—so farces more commonly take the people than comedies. For to write unnatural things, is the most probable way of pleasing them, who understand not nature; and a true poet often misses of applause, because he cannot debase himself to write so ill as to please his audience. (1, 2: 191-92)

See also Dryden under POETIC JUSTICE (DW 1, 2: 198-201).

1679   Dryden. See under ACTION (DW 1, 2: 268-69).

1715   Addison   **AW**

Productions of wit and humour, as have a tendency to expose vice and folly, furnish useful diversions to all kinds of readers. The good or prudent man may, by these means, be diverted, without prejudice to his discretion, or morality. Raillery, under such regulations, unbends the mind from serious studies, and severer contemplations, without throwing it off from its proper bias. It carries on the same design that is promoted by authors of a graver turn, and only does it in another manner. It also awakens reflection in those who are the most indifferent in the cause of virtue or knowledge, by setting before them the absurdity of such practices as are generally unobserved, by reason of their being common or fashionable. . . . By entertainments of this kind, a man may be cheerful in solitude, and not be forced to seek for company every time he has a mind to be merry. . . . Compositions of this nature, when thus restrained . . . show wisdom and virtue are far from being inconsistent with a politeness and good humour. They make morality appear amiable to people of gay dispositions, and refute the common objection against religion, which represents it as only fit for gloomy and melancholy tempers. (3: 244)

1725   Voltaire. See under SUBJECT (VE 278-79).

1738   Voltaire   **VW**

Comedy should be an exact representation of manners. (10, 1: 270)

c.1749   Voltaire   **VW**

Comedy . . . may be impassioned, may be in transport, or in tears, provided at the same time that it makes the good and virtuous smile; but if it was entirely destitute of the *vis comica*, if, from beginning to end, it had nothing in it but the serious and melancholy, it would then be a species of writing very faulty and very disagreeable. (10, 1: 280)

1755-1780   Diderot   **DDE**

Comedy is the imitation of manners and morals in terms of action. . . . The starting point of comedy is the malice natural to all men. When the short-comings of our fellow men are not pathetic enough to arouse passion, revolting enough to create hatred, or dangerous enough to inspire fear, we regard these shortcomings with a self-satisfaction mixed with contempt. These images make us smile if they are depicted with delicacy. If the srokes of this malicious joy, as striking as they are unexpected, are sharpened by surprise, these images make us laugh. From this propensity to seize hold of the ridiculous, comedy derives its power and its resources. It would undoubtedly be more beneficial if we could transform this vicious self-satisfaction into a philosophical pity; but it has proved easier and more certain to make human malice serve to correct the other vices of mankind—much as the sharp edges of the diamond are used to polish the diamond itself. This is the goal which comedy sets for itself; and the theatre is for vice and the ridiculous what the courts of justice and the scaffolds are for crime—the place where it is judged and where it is punished. (287)
. . . The misuse of comedy is to make the most serious professions appear ridiculous and to strip important people of that mask of solemnity which protects them from the insolence and malignity of envy. . . . Fops, pretentious bluestockings, and similar useless beings who are nuisances to society are comic subjects. But doctors, lawyers, and all those who perform a useful service must be respected. There is nothing objectionable about presenting *Turcaret* on the stage, but there perhaps is about performing *Tartuffe*. . . . True piety loses a great deal because of the ridicule that is cast on hypocritical bigots. (288-89)

    See also Diderot under INSTRUCTION (DDE 288), SUBJECT (DDE 287).

1758   Diderot. *See* under ACTION (DDP 291-92), GENRE DEFINITION (DDP 287), TRAGEDY (DDP 296, 297).

1767-1769   Lessing   **LSPW**

Comedy is to do us good through laughter; but not through derision; not just to counteract those faults at which it laughs, nor simply and solely in those persons who possess these laughable faults. Its true general use consists in laughter itself, in the practice of our powers to discern the ridiculous, to discern it easily and quickly under all cloaks of passion and fashion; in all admixture of good and bad qualities, even in the wrinkles of solemn earnestness. (307)

1778   Diderot. *See* under GENRE DEFINITION (DPA 49-50).

1808   Schlegel   SCL

Tragedy is the highest earnestness of poetry; Comedy altogether sportive. Now earnestness . . . consists in the direction of the mental powers to an aim or purpose, and the limitation of their activity to that object. Its opposite, therefore, consists in the apparent want of aim, and freedom from all restraint in the exercise of the mental powers; and it is therefore more perfect, the more unreservedly it goes to work, and the more lively the appearance there is of purposeless fun and unrestrained caprice. Wit and raillery may be employed in a sportive manner, but they are also both of them compatible with the severest earnestness. . . . The New Comedy . . . represents what is amusing in character, and in the contrast of situations and combinations; and it is the more comic the more it is distinguished by a want of aim: cross-purposes, mistakes, the vain efforts of ridiculous passion, and especially if all this ends at last in nothing; but still, with all this mirth, the form of the representation itself is serious, and regularly tied down to a certain aim. In the Old Comedy the form was sportive, and a seeming aimlessness reigned throughout; the whole poem was one big jest, which again contained within itself a world of separate jests, of which each occupied its own place, without appearing to trouble itself about the rest. In tragedy . . . the monarchical constitution prevails. . . . Comedy, on the other hand, is the democracy of poetry, and is more inclined even to the confusion of anarchy than to any circumscription if the general liberty of its mental powers and purposes, and even of its separate thoughts, sallies, and allusions. (147-48) . . . The very principle of Comedy necessarily occasioned that which in Aristophanes has given so much offence; namely, his frequent allusions to the base necessities of the body, the wanton pictures of animal desire, which, in spite of all restraints imposed on it by morality and decency, is always breaking loose before one can be aware of it. . . . The infallible and inexhaustible source of the ludicrous is the . . . ungovernable impulses of sensuality in collision with higher duties; or cowardice, childish vanity, loquacity, gulosity, laziness, etc. Hence, in the weakness of old age, amorousness is the more laughable, as it is plain that it is not mere animal instinct, but that reason has only served to extend the dominion of the senses beyond their proper limits. In drunkness, too, the real man places himself, in some degree, in the condition of the comic ideal. . . . As Tragedy delights in harmonious unity, Comedy flourishes in a chaotic exuberance; it seeks out the most motley contrasts, and the unceasing play of cross-purposes. It works up, therefore, the most singular, unheard-of, and even impossible incidents, with allusions to the well-known and special circumstances of the immediate locality and time. The comic poet, as well as the tragic, transports his characters into an ideal element: not, however, into a world subjected to necessity, but one where the caprice of inventive wit rules without check or restraint, and where all laws of reality are suspended. He is at liberty, therefore, to invent an action as arbitrary and fantastic as possible; it may even be unconnected and unreal, if only it be calculated to place a circle of comic incidents and characters in the most glaring light. In this last respect, the work should, nay, must, have a leading aim, or it will otherwise be in want of *keeping* [unity]; and in this view also the comedies of Aristophanes may be considered as perfectly systematical. But then, to preserve the comic inspiration, this aim must be made a matter of diversion, and be concealed beneath a medley of all sorts of out-of-the-way matters . . . The Parabasis [of Old Comedy] must, strictly speaking, be considered as incongruous with the essence of dramatic representation; for in the drama the poet should always be behind his dramatic personages. . . . But it is . . . consistent with the essence of the Old Comedy, where not merely the subject, but the whole manner of treating it was sportive and jocular. The unlimited dominion of mirth and fun manifests itself even in this, that the dramatic form itself is not seriously adhered to, and that its laws are often suspended. . . . (149-51) . . . The kind of moral which we may in general expect from Comedy . . . is an applied doctrine of ethics, the art of life. . . . The higher comedies of Molière contain many admirable observations happily expressed, which are still to the present day applicable. . . . In this sense Menander was also a philosophical comic writer; and we may . . . place the moral maxims which remain of his by the side . . . of those of Molière. But no comedy is constructed of mere apothegms. The poet must be a moralist, but his personages cannot always be moralizing. And here Molière appears to me to have exceeded the bounds of propriety: he gives us in lengthened disquisitions the *pro* and *con* of the character exhibited by him; nay, he allows these to consist, in part, of principles which the persons themselves defend against the attacks of others. Now this leaves nothing to conjecture; and yet the highest refinement and delicacy of the comic of observation consists in this, that the characters disclose themselves unconsciously by traits which involuntarily escape from them. . . . The endless disquisitions of Alceste and Philante . . . are serious, and yet they cannot satisfy us as exhausting the subject; and as dialogues which at the end leave the characters precisely at the same point as at the beginning, they are devoid in the necessary dramatic movement. . . . In a word, [the most admired pieces of Molière] are too didactic, too expressly instructive; whereas in Comedy the spectator should only be instructed incidentally, and, as it were, without its appearing to have been intended. (309-10)

See also Schlegel under CHARACTER (SCL 183-84), DISTANCE (SCL 184-86), GENRE DEFINITION (SCL 176-79), PLOT (SCL 181-82), THREE UNITIES (SCL 305).

1815   Hazlitt   HW

The question which has often been asked, *Why there are so few good modern Comedies*? appears in a great measure to answer itself. It is because so many excellent Comedies have been written, that there are none written at present. Comedy naturally wears itself out—destroys the very food on which it lives; and by constantly and successfully exposing the follies and weaknesses of mankind to ridicule, in the end leaves itself nothing worth laughing at. It holds the mirror up to nature; and men, seeing their most striking peculiarities and defects pass in gay review before them, learn either to avoid or conceal them. It is not the criticism which the public taste exercises upon the stage, but the criticism which the stage exercises upon public manners, that is fatal to comedy, by rendering the subject matter of it tame, correct, and spiritless. We are drilled into a sort of stupid decorum, and forced to wear the same dull uniform of outward appearance; and yet it is asked, why the Comic Muse does not point, as she was wont, at the peculiarities of our gait and gesture, and exhibit the picturesque contrast of our dress and costume, in all that graceful variety in which she delights. (1: 10)

1817   Hazlitt   HW

[Shakespeare] gives the most amusing exaggeration of the prevailing foibles of his characters, but in a way that they themselves, instead of being offended at, would almost join in to humour; he rather contrives opportunities for them to shew themselves off in the happiest lights, then renders them contemptible in the perverse construction of the wit or malice of others. There is a certain stage of society in which people become conscious of their peculiarities and absurdities, affect to disguise what they are, and set up pretensions to what they are not. This gives rise to a corresponding style of comedy, the object of which is to detect the disguises of self-love, and to make reprisals on these preposterous assumptions of vanity, by marking the contrast between the real and the affected character as severely as possible, and denying to those, who would impose on us for what they are not, even the merit which they have. This is the comedy of artificial life, of wit and satire, such as we see it in Congreve, Wycherly, Vanbrugh, etc. To this succeeds a state of society from which the same sort of affectation and pretense are banished by a greater knowledge of the world or by their successful exposure on the stage; and which by neutralising the materials of comic character, both natural and artificial, leaves no comedy at all—but the *sentimental*. Such is our modern comedy. There is a period in the progress of manners anterior to both these, in which the foibles and follies of individuals are of nature's planting, not the growth of art or study; in which they are therefore unconscious of them themselves, or care not who knows them, if they can but have their whim out; and in which, as there is no attempt at imposition, the spectators rather receive pleasure from humouring the inclinations of the persons they laugh at, than wish to give them pain by exposing their absurdity. They may be called the comedy of nature, and it is the comedy which we generally find in Shakespear. (1: 313)

1818   Coleridge. *See* under GENRE DEFINITION (CLSW 87).

c.1820   Hegel   HFA

The general basis of comedy is . . . a world in which man has made himself, in his conscious activity, complete master of all that otherwise passes as the essential content of his knowledge and achievement; a world whose ends are consequently thrown awry on account of their own lack of substance. A democratic folk, with egoistic citizens, litigous, frivolous, conceited, without faith or knowledge, always intent on gossip, boasting and vanity—such a folk is past praying for; it can only dissolve in its own folly. But it would be a mistake to think that any action that is without genuine content is therefore comic because it is void of substance. People only too often in this respect confound the merely *ridiculous* with the true comic. Every contrast between what is essential and its appearance, the object and its instrument, may be ridiculous, a contradiction in virtue of which the appearance is absolutely cancelled, and the end is stultified in its realization. A profounder significance is, however, implied in the comic. There is, for instance, nothing common in human crime. The satire affords a proof of this, to the point of extreme aridity, no matter how emphatic may be the colours in which it depicts the condition of the actual world in its contrast to all that the man of virtue ought to be. There is nothing in mere folly, stupidity, or nonsense, which in itself necessarily partakes of the comic, though we all of us are ready enough to laugh at it. And as a rule it is extraordinary what a variety of wholly different things excite human laughter. Matters of the dullest description and in the worst possible taste will move men this way; and their laughter may be excited quite as much by things of the profoundest importance, if only they happen to notice some entirely unimportant feature, which may conflict with habit and ordinary experience. Laughter is therefore little more than an expression of self-satisfied shrewdness; a sign that they have sufficient wit to recognize such a contrast and are aware of the fact. . . . What on the other hand is inseparable from the comic is an infinite geniality and confidence capable of rising superior to its own contradiction, and experiencing therein no taint of bitterness. . . . It is the happy frame of mind, a hale condition of soul, which, fully aware of itself, can suffer the dissolution of its aim and realization. . . . The kind of content which characterizes and educes the object of comic action . . . [:] On the *one* hand there are human ends and characters essentially devoid of substantive content and contradictory. They are therefore unable to achieve the former or give effect to the latter. Avarice, for example, not only in reference to its aim, but also in respect to the petty means which it employs, is clearly from the first and fundamentally a vain shadow....If anyone identifies *seriously* his personal life with a content so essentially false, . . . [and] if the same is swept away as his foot-hold, the more the life collapses in unhappiness —in such a picture as this what is most vital to the comic situation fails, as it does in every case where the predominant factors are simply on the one side the painfulness of the actual conditions, and on the other scorn and pleasure in such misfortune. There is therefore more of the true comic in the case where . . . the individual himself, when he falls short [of his intrinsically mean and empty aims], does not experience any real loss because he is conscious that what he strove after was really of no great importance, and is therefore able to rise superior with spontaneous amusement above the failure. A situation which is the reverse of this occurs where people vaguely grasp at aims and a personal impression of real substance, but in their own individuality, as instruments to achieve this, are in absolute conflict with such a result. In such a case what substance there is only exists in the individual's imagination . . . [and] for this very reason involves . . . action and character in a contradiction, by reason of which the attainment of the imaged end . . . is rendered impossible. An example of this is the "Ecclesiazusae" of Aristophanes, where the women who seek to advise and found a new political constitution, retain all the temperment and passions of women as before. We may add to the above two divisions of classifications, as a distinct basis for yet *another*, the use made of external accident, by means . . . of which situations are placed before us in which the objects desired and their achievement . . . are thrown into a comic contrast, and lead to an equally comic resolution. But inasmuch as the comic element wholly . . . depends upon contradictory contrasts . . . the action of comedy requires a *resolution* with even more stringency than the tragic drama. In other words, . . . the contradiction between that which is essentially true and its specific realization is more fundamentally asserted. Comedy . . . viewed as genuine art, has not the task set before it to display through its presentation what is essentially rational as that which is intrinsically perverse and comes to nought, but on the contrary as that which neither bestows the victory, nor ultimately allows any standing ground to folly and absurdity, that is to say the false contradictions and oppositions which also form part of reality. The masculine art of Aristophanes, for instance, does not turn into ridicule what is truly of ethical significance . . . namely genuine philosophy, true religious faith, but rather the spurious growth of the democracy, in which the ancient faith and the former morality have disappeared, such as the sophistry, the whining and querulousness of tragedy . . . ; in other words, it is those elements directly opposed to a genuine condition of political life, religion, art, which he places before us in their suicidal folly. (4: 301-304) . . . That which is comic is . . . in general terms the subjective or personal state, which forces and then dissolves the action which issues from it by its own effect into and in contradiction, remaining throughout and in virtue of this process tranquil in its own self-assurance. Comedy possesses . . . a soul [that is] to the fullest extent and eventually reconciled, a joyous state, which, however much it is instrumental in the marring of its volitional power, and, indeed, in itself comes to grief, by reason of its asserting voluntarily what is in conflict with its aim, does not therefore lose its general equanimity. A personal self-assurance of this character, however is . . . only possible in so far as the ends proposed . . . include nothing that is on its own account essentially substantive; or, if they do possess such an intrinsic worth, it is adopted and carried out intentionally under a mode which is totally opposed to the genuine truth contained . . . so that in this respect . . . it is merely that which is itself essentially of no intrinsic importance, but a matter of indifference which is marred, and the individual remains just as he was an unaffected. We should . . . be careful to notice the distinction whether the individuals in the play are aware that they are comic, or are so merely from the spectator's point of view. It is only the first class that we can reckon as part of the genuine comedy in which Aristophanes was a master. . . . A character is only placed in a ridiculous situation, when we perceive that he himself is not serious in what is actually of such a quality in his purpose and voluntary effort. . . . The comic comes . . . into play among classes of a lower social order in actual conditions of life, among men who remain much as they are, and neither are able or desire to be anything else; who while incapable of any genuine pathos, have no doubt whatever as to what they are and do. At the same time the higher nature that is in them is asserted in this that they are not with any seriousness attached to the finite conditions which hem them in, but remain superior to the same and in themselves essentially steadfast and self-reliant against mishap and loss. . . . The keynote that we find in [Aristophane's] various creations is the imperturbable self-assurance of [the] characters one and all, which becomes all the more emphatic in proportion as they prove themselves incapable of carrying into effect that which they project. Our fools here are so entirely unembarrassed in their folly, and also the more sensible among them possess such a tincture of that which runs contrary to the very course upon which they are set, that they all, the more sensible with the rest, remain fixed to this personal attitude of prodigious imperturbility, no matter what comes next or where it carries them. . . . What . . . is in the fullest sense resolved in [Aristophanes's] comedies is . . . not the divine and what is of ethical import, but the thoroughgoing upside-down-ness which inflates itself into the semblance of these substantive forces. (4: 327-30)

See also Hegel under GENRE (HFA 4: 256, 260, 293) TRAGEDY (HFA 4: 300-301).

1864   Taine   TLA

[Comic] writers, undertaking to depict men as they are, were obliged to portray them incomplete, mixed up and inferior, most of the time abortive in their character, or distorted by their condition. . . . It is the quality of comic drama to lay bare human deficiencies. (274)

    See also Taine under AESTHETIC (TLA 273-74).

c.1900   Shaw   SS

[When] the comic poet [became] less and less a fellow of infinite jest and more and more a satirical rogue and a discloser of essentially tragic ironies, the road was open to a sort of comedy . . . more tragic than a catastrophic tragedy. . . . Comedy has become the higher form. The element of accident in Tragedy has always been its weak spot; for though an accident may be sensational, nothing can make it interesting or save it from being irritating. In its tragedy and comedy alike, the modern tragi-comedy begins where the old tragedies and comedies left off. (254)

    See also Shaw under TRAGEDY (SS 253).

1909   **Shaw.** *See* under GENRE DEFINITION (STPB xx, xxii-xxiii).

1912   **Shaw.** *See* under SUBJECT (SALOP 67-68).

COMPLICATION

Anything that impedes the immediate resolution of a problem, a story, or a form creates structural complexity. While it might be precisely that impedence which ultimately distinguishes prose from poetry, dramatic theorists have generally perceived "complications" to be merely a practical problem of the intrigue or the plot.

4th cent. B.C.   Aristotle   AP

By Complication I mean all that extends from the beginning of the action to the *part which marks the turning point* [scene which is the last before the shift: EP 517] to good or bad fortune. (65)

> *See also* Aristotle under PLOT (AP 55-57, 65-67).

1660   Corneille   CTU

[In comedy] the unity of action consists . . . in a unity of intrigue, or of obstacle to the designs of the principal actors; as to tragedy, in a unity of peril, whether the hero succumb to it or escape. I do not mean that several perils may not be combined, in the latter, or several intrigues or obstacles, in the former, provided that one lead inevitably into another; the passing of the prime danger then does not complete the action, because it produces a secondary danger. . . . (816)

> *See also* Corneille under ACTION (CDTU 235).

1668   Dryden. *See* under UNITY (DW 1, 2: 86-87).

1711   Addison. *See* under PLOT (AW 1: 72).

1758   Diderot   DDP

A simple plot, an action taken up toward its end in order that everything should be heightened in its effect, a catastrophe invariably imminent, which is only kept back by a simple and true circumstance; strong passions; tableaux; one or two characters firmly drawn. . . . Sophocles required no more. (290-91) . . . Once the situations are known, the complicated play loses its effect. If a play were meant to be produced only once . . . I should say to the poet: "Complicate as much as you like. . . . " And even were I to allow as many complications as possible, the play would contain only the [single] action. (291)

1797   Goethe. *See* under PLOT (GED 338).

1808   Schlegel   SCL

[The French critics] prescribed the same simplicity of action as the Grecian Tragedy observed, and yet rejected the lyrical part, which is a protracted development of the present moment, and consequently a stand-still of the action. . . . If we deduct from the Greek Tragedies the choral odes and the lyrical pieces which are occasionally put into the mouths of individuals, they will be nearly one-half shorter than an ordinary French tragedy. Voltaire . . . complains of the great difficulty in procuring materials for five long acts. How now have the gaps arising from the omission of the lyrical parts been filled up? By intrigue. While with the Greeks the action . . . rolls on uninterruptedly to its issue, the French have introduced many secondary characters almost exclusively with the view that their opposite purposes may give rise to a multitude of impeding incidents, to keep our attention, or rather our curiosity, to the close. There was now an end . . . of everything like simplicity; still they flattered themselves that they had, by means of an artificial coherence, preserved at least a unity of the understanding. (253-54)

See also Schlegel under ACTION (SCL 239-42).

c. 1820   Hegel. Compare with DRAMA (HFA 4: 261-62).

c. 1930   Stanislavski. *See* under CONFLICT (SCR 80).

CONFLICT

With the rise of the romantic movement, the industrial revolution, and the development of ideas of natural selection a new view of drama (and of human existence) emerged: that drama imitates life that is seen as an unremitting competitive struggle for physical or spiritual survival. Since the early nineteenth century the "conflict theory" of drama has dominated dramatic criticism and, to a considerable degree, the practice of playwrights. It is a central assumption of most twentieth-century dramatic theory. See HERO and WILL.

1808 Schlegel. *See* under ACTION (SCL 239-42), AFFECT (SCL 67-69), CHARACTER (SCL 66), COMPLICATION (SCL 253-54), UNITY (SCL 242-45).

c.1810 Coleridge. *See* under DRAMA (CLSW 116).

1813 Goethe. *See* under CHARACTER (GLE 182).

1819 Hazlitt. *See* under HUMOR (HW 8: 7-8).

c.1820 Hegel   **HFA**

[Whereas Classical drama presents] simple conflicts, we now meet with the variety and exuberance of the characters . . . the unforeseen surprises of the new and complicated developments of plot, the maze of intrigue, the contingency of events . . . which . . . accentuates the type of romantic art in its distinction from the classic type. But . . . the whole ought to continue to be both dramatic and poetical. In other words, on the one hand, the harshness of the collision, which has to be fought through, ought to be visibly obliterated, and on the other, pre-eminently in tragedy, the predominant presence of a more exalted order of the world, whether we adopt the conception of Providence or Fatality, ought to plainly discover itself in and through the course and issue of the action. (4: 311-312) . . . [The scope of the content of the dramatic action in Greek drama], although capable of great variety of detail, is not in its essential features very extensive. The principle source of opposition, which Sophocles in particular, in this respect following the lead of Aeschylus, has accepted and worked out in the finest way, is that of the *body politic*, the opposition, that is, between ethical life in its social universality and the family as the natural ground of moral relations. These are the purest forces of tragic representation.

It is, in short, the harmony of these spheres and the concordant action within the bounds of their realized content, which constitutes the perfected reality of the moral life. In this respect I need only recall to recollection the ''Seven Before Thebes'' of Aeschylus and, as a yet stronger illustration, the ''Antigone'' of Sophocles. Antigone reverences the ties of blood-relationship, the gods of the nether world. Creon alone recognizes Zeus, the paramount Power of public life and commonwealth. . . . A content of this type retains its force through all times, and its presentation, despite all difference of nationality, vitally arrests our human and artistic sympathies. Of a more formal type is that second kind of essential collision, an illustration of which in the tragic story of Oedipus the Greek tragedians especially favoured. Of this Sophocles has left us the most complete example in his ''Oedipus Rex,'' and ''Oedipus in Colonos.'' The problem here is concerned with the claim of alertness in our intelligence, with the nature of the obligation implied in that which a man carries out with a volition fully aware of his acts as contrasted with that which he has done in fact, but unconscious of and with no intention of doing what he has done under the directing providence of the gods. . . . Crimes of this description, inasmuch as they were neither referable to a personal knowledge or volition, were not deeds for which the true personality of the perpetrator was responsible. . . . Other collisions . . . are comparatively speaking less important. (4: 318-20)

　　See also Hegel under ACTION (HFA 4: 253-54, 259-61, 317), AFFECT (HFA 4: 272ff.), CHARACTER (HFA 4: 273-15, 315-18), CLOSURE (HFA 4: 323-25), DRAMA (HFA 4: 249-50, 251, 254-55, 278-80, 321-23), FORM (HFA 4: 262-63), GENRE (HFA 4: 256, 293, 294), GENRE DEFINITION (HFA 4: 305-308), LANGUAGE (HFA 4: 264-65), TRAGEDY (HFA 4: 295-99, 300-301, 312-15).

1827　Goethe. *See* under AFFECT (GCE MARCH 21), TRAGEDY (GCE March 28).

1871　Nietzsche. *See* under AESTHETIC (NBT 21-22), MORALITY (NBT 78-79).

1875　Nietzsche　　　　　　　　　　　　　　　　　　　**NTS**

For us, Bayreuth [that is, Wagnerian opera] is the consecration of the dawn of the combat [against the philistinism of State and Society]. No greater injustice could be done to us than to suppose that we are concerned with art alone, as though it were merely a means of healing or stupefying us, which we make use of in order to rid our consciousness of all misery that still remains in our midst. In the image of this tragic art work at Bayreuth, we see, rather, the struggle of individuals against everything which seems to oppose them with invincible necessity, with power, law, tradition, conduct, and the whole order of things established. Individuals cannot choose a better life than that of holding themselves ready to sacrifice themselves and die in their fight for love and justice. The gaze which the mysterious power of tragedy vouchsafes us neither lulls nor paralyses. . . . How . . . would it be possible to endure this feeling of . . . insufficiency if one were not able to recognise something sublime and valuable in one's struggles, strivings and defeats, if one did not learn from tragedy how to delight in the rhythm of the great passions, and in their victim? Art is certainly no teacher or educator of practical conduct: the artist is never in this sense an instructor or adviser. . . . The strife it reveals to us is a simplification of life's struggle; its problems are abbreviations of the infinitely complicated phenomena of man's actions and volitions. (128-30)

1882 Nietzsche. *See* under AESTHETIC (NJW 334-35).

1886 Nietzsche. *See* under WILL (NZ 134-36).

1888 Nietzsche   **NW**

The will to power [which underlies all life] can manifest itself only against *obstacles*; it therefore goes in search of what resists it—this is the primitive tendency of the protoplasm when it extends its *pseudopodia* and feels about it. The act of appropriation and assimilation is, above all, the result of a desire to overpower . . . until at last the subjected creature has become a part of the superior creature's sphere of power. . . . (130)

1894 Brunetière   **BLD**

The . . . law [of the theatre] provides . . . the possibility of defining with precision the dramatic species . . . and for that it is only necessary to consider the particular obstacle against which the will struggles. If these obstacles are recognized to be insurmountable, or reputed to be so, as were, for example, in the eyes of the ancient Greeks, the decrees of Fate; . . . as are, for us, the laws of nature, or the passions aroused to frenzy . . . ;—it is tragedy. The incidents are generally terrifying, and the conclusions sanguinary, because in the struggle which man undertakes to make against fate, he is vanquished in advance, and must perish. Suppose now that he has a chance of victory, just one, that he still has in himself the power to conquer his passion; or suppose that, the obstacles which he is striving to overcome being the work of his fellow men, as prejudice, for example, or social conventions, a man is for that very reason capable of surmounting them,—that is the drama properly speaking, romantic drama or social drama. . . . Change once more the nature of the obstacle, equalize, at least in appearance, the conditions of the struggle, bring together two opposing wills, Arnolphe and Agnès, Figaro and Almaviva, Suzanne d'Ange and Olivier de Jalin—that is comedy. . . . But instead of locating the obstacle in an opposing will, conscious and mistress of its acts, in a social convention or in the fatality of destiny, let us locate it in the irony of fortune, or in the ridiculous aspect of prejudice, or again in the disproportion between the means and the end,—that is farce. . . . The general law of the theatre is defined by the action of a will conscious of itself; and the dramatic species are distinguished by the nature of the obstacles encountered by this will. (77-80)

See also Brunetière under GENRE (BLD 77-80).

1898   Shaw   SCP

Unity, however desirable in political agitations, is fatal to drama; for every drama must present a conflict. The end may be reconciliation or destruction; or, as in life itself, there may be no end; but the conflict is indispensable: no conflict, no drama. . . . The obvious conflicts of unmistakable good with unmistakeable evil can only supply the crude drama of villain and hero, in which some absolute point of view is taken, and the dissentients are treated by the dramatist as enemies to be piously glorified or indignantly vilified. (729)

1898   Shaw   SMCE

You cannot dramatize a reaction by personifying the reacting force only. . . . You must also personify the established power against which the new force is reacting; and in the conflict between them you get your drama, conflict being the essential ingredient in all drama. (217)

1902   Shaw. *See* under THOUGHT (SAA 43).

1908   Pirandello. *See* under HUMOR (POH 142-43).

1913   Shaw   SMCE

In the new plays, the drama arises through a conflict of unsettled ideals. . . . ambitions. The conflict is not between clear right and wrong: the villain is as conscientious as the hero, if not more so: in fact, the question that makes the play interesting (when it is interesting) is which is the villain and which the hero. (139)

c.1930   Stanislavski   SCR

No movement, striving, action is carried out on the stage, any more than in real life, without obstacles. One runs inevitably into the countermovements and strivings of other people, or into conflicting events. . . . Life is an unremitting *struggle*, one overcomes or one is defeated. The collision and conflict of . . . two opposing through actions constitute the dramatic situation. (80)

1931-1936   Artaud   AT

Like the plague, the theatre is a formidable call to the forces that impel the mind by example to the source of its conflicts. (30)

See also Artaud under THOUGHT (AT 41); compare with DRAMA (AT 70), IDEALISM (AT 50-51).

CONVENTION

The term "convention" is used in the theatre to refer to two distinct concepts, both of which—because they often address the same object—are included here. The first usage, akin to that in law and diplomacy, is that of a stated or tacit agreement (between theatre artists and spectators) providing for limits and permissions: that while accepted rules operate, certain things will stand for certain realities. The second usage is an expression of a negative judgment connoting obsolescence or triteness, often asserted polemically in order to replace conventions of which the attacker is painfully conscious with conventions of which he is not conscious at all.

1609   de Vega. *See* under STYLE (VAWP 27).

1616   Jonson. Compare with REALISM (JBW).

1660   Corneille. *See* under EXPOSITION (CFD 147).

1672   Dryden. *See* under ILLUSION (DW 1, 2: 218).

1711   Addison   **AW**

Another mechanical method of making great men, and adding dignity to kings and queens, is to accompany them with halberds and battle-axes. Two or three shifters of scenes, with the two candle-snuffers, make up a complete body of guards upon the English stage; and by the addition of a few porters dressed in red coats, can represent above a dozen legions. I have sometimes seen a couple of armies drawn up together upon the stage, when the poet has been disposed to do honour to her generals. It is impossible for the reader's imagination to multiply twenty men into such prodigious multitudes, or to fancy that two or three hundred thousand soldiers are fighting in a room of forty or fifty yards in compass. Incidents of such a nature should be told, not represented.
. . . I should, therefore, in this particular, recommend to my countrymen the example of the French stage, where the kings and queens always appear unattended, and leave their guards behind the scenes. I should likewise be glad if we imitated the French in banishing from our stage the noise of drums, trumpets, and huzzas. (1: 75)

    See also Addison under SPECTACLE (AW 1: 74, 77-78), STYLE (AW 1: 70).

1767-1769   Lessing   LSPW

We moderns, who have abolished the chorus, who generally leave our personages between four walls, what reason have we to let [our characters] employ . . . stilted rhetorical speech notwithstanding? Nobody hears it except those whom they permit to hear it, nobody speaks to them but people who are involved in the action, who are therefore themselves affected and have neither desire nor leisure to control expressions. (393)

    See also Lessing under LANGUAGE (LSPW 393-94).

1778   Diderot   DPA

People come not to see tears, but to hear speeches that draw tears; because this truth of nature. is out of tune with the truth of convention. Let me explain myself: I mean that neither the dramatic system, nor the action, nor the poet's speeches, would fit themselves to my stifled, broken, sobbing declamation. You see that it is not allowable to imitate Nature, even at her best, or Truth too closely; there are limits within which we must restrict ourselves. (102)

1808   Schlegel   SCL

In . . . English and Spanish plays . . . certain signs . . . were agreed on which served to denote the change of place, and the docile imagination of the spectators followed the poet whithersoever he chose. (256)

    See also Schlegel under RULES (SCL 236, 259), SPECTACLE (SCL 256-57).

1816   Hazlitt. *See* under AESTHETIC (HW 1: 68).

c.1820   Hegel. *See* under LANGUAGE (HFA 4: 264-65).

1876   Sarcey   STT

[The theater's] business is to represent life to a crowd. This crowd performs in some sort for dramatic art the function of the flat surface in painting. It requires the intervention of similar tricks, . . . of conventions. . . . [For example,] the representation of life that we can exhibit before a crowd cannot then exceed an average of six hours in length. That is a fact of absolute necessity. . . . The action represented evidently lasts more than six hours. . . . It will be necessary to resort to conventions in order to give the impression that a long time has elapst when we have only six hours at our disposal. (26-27) . . . Facts and sentiments drawn from reality and transported just as they are to the stage [would appear grotesque]. It is absolutely necessary to accommodate them to the particular disposition of mind which results among people when they assemble in the form of a crowd, when they compose an audience. Therefore deceptions—conventions—are essential. Among these conventions some are permanent, others temporary and changeable. The reason is easy to understand. The audience is composed of individuals; and among individuals there are sentiments—in very small number, it is true,—which are general and universal, which we find in varying degrees among all the civilized peoples who alone have developed a dramatic art. Likewise there are prejudices (in still smaller number) which we encounter in all times and in all countries. These sentiments, these prejudices, or in a word, these ways of looking at things, always remaining the same, it is natural that certain conventions, certain tricks, should be inherent in all drama, and that they should be establisht as laws. On the contrary there are other sentiments, other prejudices, which are changeable, which vanish every time one civilization is succeeded by another, and which are replaced by different ways of seeing. (28-29) . . . Dramatic art is the sum total of the conventions, universal or local, permanent or temporary, by the aid of which in representing life in the theater the audience is given the illusion of truth. (30)

1894   Brunetière. *See* under RULES (BLD 69).

1908   Strindberg. *See* under FORM (SOL 19).

1919   Eliot   **ESE**

A speech in a play should never appear to be intended to move us as it might conceivably move other characters in the play, for it is essential that we should preserve our position of spectators, and observe always from the outside though with complete understanding. (28)

1931-1936   Artaud   **AT**

The Balinese, who have a vocabulary of gesture and mime for every circumstance of life, reinstate the superior worth of theatrical conventions, demonstrate the forcefulness and greater emotional value of a certain number of perfectly learned and above all masterfully applied conventions. . . . These mechanically rolling eyes, pouting lips, and muscular spasms, all producing methodically calculated effects which forbid any recourse to spontaneous improvisation, these horizontally moving heads that seem to glide from one shoulder to the other as if on rollers, everything that might correspond to immediate psychological necessities, corresponds as well to a sort of spiritual architecture, created out of gesture and mime but also of the evocative power of a system, the musical quality of a physical movement, the parallel and admirably fused harmony of a tone. (55)

1948   Brecht. *See* under IMITATION (BBBG 16); compare with AFFECT (BBBG 21-23).

1951   Eliot. *See* under STYLE (EPD 20-21).

DECORUM

The notion of decorum of character that developed in Renaissance theory attempted to identify a rule for consistency in character just as the THREE UNITIES attempted the same for plot and GENRE attempted it for style. See STYLE headnote.

4th cent. B.C.   Aristotle   AP

The second thing to aim at is *propriety* [appropriateness: EP 455]. There is a type of manly valour; but valour in a woman, or unscrupulous cleverness, is inappropriate. (53)

   See also Aristotle under PROBABILITY (AP 35-37), STYLE (AP 101), UNIVERSALITY (AP 35).

4th cent. B.C.   Aristotle   AR

Each class of men, and each disposition, has a style suited to it. 'Class' may represent a difference of age, as between boy, man, and old man; or the difference of sex; or the difference between Laconian and Thessalian. By dispositions I mean those things which give a definite character to a man's life; not every disposition gives such a character. Now, if the speaker's words are appropriate to the disposition, he will represent the character; for the educated man would not use the same words, nor use them in the same way, as the boor. (160)

c.20 B.C.   Horace   HAP

Be the work what you will, let it at least be simple and uniform. (453) . . . If the speaker's words sound discordant with his fortunes, the Romans, in boxes and pit alike, will raise a loud guffaw. Vast difference will it make, whether a god be speaking or a hero, a ripe old man or one still in the flower and fervour of youth, a dame of rank or a bustling nurse. . . . Either follow tradition or invent what is self-consistent. If haply, when you write, you bring back to the stage the honouring of Achilles, let him be impatient, passionate, ruthless, fierce. . . . Let Medea be fierce and unyielding, Ino tearful, . . . Orestes sorrowful. If it is an untried theme you entrust to the stage, and if you boldly fashion a fresh character, have it kept to the end even as it came forth at the first, and have it self-consistent. (459-61) . . . If you want an approving hearer, one who waits for the curtain, and will stay in his seat . . . you must note the manners of each age, and give a befitting tone to shifting natures and their years. The child, who by now can utter words and set firm step upon the ground, delights to play with his mates, flies into a passion and as lightly puts it aside, and changes every hour. The beardless youth . . . finds joy in horses and hounds . . . slow to make needful provision, lavish of money, spirited. . . . With altered aims, the age and spirit of the man seeks wealth and friends, becomes a slave to ambition, and is fearful of having done what soon it will be eager to change. Many ills encompass an old man, whether because he seeks gain, and then miserably holds aloof from his store and fears to use it, or because, in all that he does, he lacks fire and courage, is dilatory and slow to form hopes, is sluggish and greedy for a longer life. . . . Many blessings do the advancing years bring with them; many, as they retire, they take away. So, lest haply we assign a youth the part of age, or a boy that of manhood, we shall ever linger over traits that are joined and fitted to the age. (463, 465)

1605   Jonson. *See* under THREE UNITIES (JBW).

1609   de Vega   **VAWP**

If the king should speak, imitate as much as possible the gravity of a king; if the sage speaks, observe a sententious modesty; describe lovers with those passions which greatly move whoever listens to them; manage soliloquies in such a manner that the recitant is quite transformed, and in changing himself, changes the listener. Let him ask questions and reply to himself, and if he shall make plaints, let him observe the respect due to women. Let not ladies disregard their character, and if they change costumes, let it be in such wise that it may be excused; for male disguise is usually very pleasing. (33-4)
  See also de Vega under IMITATION (VAWP 34).

1619   Jonson   **JCD**

[Jonson's] Censure of the English Poets was this, that Sidney did not keep a Decorum in making everyone speak as well as himself. (3)

1641   Jonson. *See* under METAPHOR (JD 73).

1731   Voltaire. *See* under RULES (VE 282).

1758   Diderot. *See* under LANGUAGE (DDP 292).

1767-1769   Lessing   **LSPW**

We are justified in demanding purpose and harmony in all the characters a poet creates. . . . Harmony; for nothing in the characters must be contradictory; they must ever remain uniform and inherently themselves; they must express themselves now with emphasis, now more slightly as events work upon them, but none of the events must be mighty enough to change black to white. (326)
  See also Lessing under MOTIVATION (LSPW 239).

1819   Hazlitt. *See* under HUMOR (HW 8: 11).

1824   Hazlitt. *See* under IDEALISM (HW 9: 405).

1830   Hazlitt. *See* under IDEALISM (HW 9: 429-30).

1864   Taine. *See* under IMITATION (TLA 56-58), STYLE (TLA 322-23).

1948   Brecht. Compare with CHARACTER (BBBG 30), IDENTIFICATION (BBBG 17, 25, 28, 30).

DISINTERESTEDNESS

A negative concept, but a crucial one in the aesthetics of those who accept it, is that art must have neither general utility nor personal interest. Emmanuel Kant, in his Critique of Judgment, *is the best known and fullest expositor of this position of disinterestedness. However, the concept was not without precedent nor, once expressed, has it been without critics. DISTANCE is a more limited but often related concept.*

4th cent. B.C.   Aristotle   AM

[As arts multiplied], some were directed to the necessities of life, others to recreation, [and] the inventors of the latter were naturally always regarded as wiser than the inventors of the former, because their branches of knowledge did not aim at utility. (981b 17)

4th cent. B.C.   Aristotle   ANE

Every art and every investigation, and likewise every practical pursuit or undertaking, seems to aim at some good: hence it has been well said that the Good is That at which all things aim. (It is true that a certain variety is to be observed among the ends at which the arts and sciences aim; in some cases the activity of practising the art is itself the end [such as flute-playing], whereas in others the end is some product over and above the mere exercise of the art [such as house-building]; and in the arts whose ends are certain things beside the practice of the arts themselves, these products are essentially superior in value to the activities. (3) . . . Works of art have their merit in themselves, so that it is enough if they are produced having a certain quality of their own. (85)

1641   Jonson   JD

There be some men are borne only to sucke out the poyson of bookes. . . . And such as they that only rellish the obscene, and foule things in *Poets*: Which makes the profession taxed. But by whom? men, that watch for it, (and had they not had this hint) are so unjust valuers of Letters; as they thinke no Learning good, but what brings in gaine. It shewes they themselves would never have beene of the professions they are; but for the profits and fees. But, if an other Learning, well used, can instruct to good life, informe manners; no less perswade, and leade men, then they threaten, and compell, and have no reward, is it therefore the worse study? (41-42)

1778   Diderot   DPA

[The great actor] must have a deal of judgment. He must have in himself an unmoved and disinterested onlooker. He must have, consequently, penetration and no sensibility. . . . If the actor were full, really full, of feeling how could he play the same part twice running with the same spirit and success? (7-8)

1808   Schlegel. *See* under AFFECT (SCL 67-69)

1815   Coleridge. *See* under AESTHETIC (CBL 2: 238-39, 256-57).

1816   Hazlitt   HW

The best things, in their abuse, often become the worst; as so it is with poetry when it is diverted from its proper end. Poets live in an ideal world, where they make everything out according to their wishes and fancies. They either find things delightful or make them so. They feign the beautiful and grand out of their own minds, and imagine all things to be, not what they are, but what they ought to be. They are naturally inventors, creators of truth, of love, and beauty: and while they speak to us from the sacred shrine of their own hearts . . . they cannot be too much admired and applauded: but when, forgetting their high calling, and becoming tools and puppets in the hands of power, they would pass off the gewgaws of corruption and love-tokens of self-interests as the gifts of the Muse, they cannot be too much despised and shunned. We do not like novels founded on facts, nor do we like poets turned courtiers. Poets, it has been said, succeed best in fiction: and they should for the most part stick to it. Invention, not upon an imaginary subject, is a lie: the varnishing over the vices or deformities of actual objects is hypocrisy. Players leave their finery at the stage-door, or they would be hooted; poets come out into the world with all their bravery on, and yet they would pass for *bona fide* persons. (1: 151-52)

1817   Hazlitt   HW

Tragedy . . . substitutes imaginary sympathy for mere selfishness. It gives us a high and permanent interest, beyond ourselves, in humanity as such. It raises the great, the remote, and the possible to an equality with the real, the little and the near. It makes man a partaker with his kind. It subdues and softens the stubbornness of his will. It teaches him that there are and have been others like himself, by showing him as in a glass what they have felt, thought, and done. It opens the chambers of the human heart. It leaves nothing indifferent to us that can affect our common nature. It excites our sensibility by exhibiting the passions wound up to the utmost pitch by the power of imagination or the temptation of circumstances; and corrects their fatal excesses in ourselves by pointing to the greater extent of sufferings and of crimes to which they have led others. Tragedy creates a balance of the affections. It makes us thoughtful spectators in the lists of life. It is a refiner of the species; a discipline of humanity. The habitual study of poetry and works of imagination is one chief part of a well-grounded education. (1: 200)

c. 1820 Hegel. *See* under AESTHETIC (HFA 1: 8-9).

1830 Hazlitt   **HW**

The *ideal* . . . is nothing but the continued approximation of the mind to the *great* and the *good*, [and] in the attainment of this object it rejects as much as possible not only the petty, the mean, and disagreeable, but also the agony and violence of passion, the force of contrast, and the extravagance of imagination. It is a law to itself. It relies on its own aspirations after pure enjoyment and lofty contemplation alone, self-moved and self-sustained, without the grosser stimulus of the irritation of the will, privation, or suffering. (9: 431)

1887 Nietzsche   **NGM**

"That is beautiful," says Kant, "which pleases without interesting." Without interesting! Compare this definition with this other one, made by a real "spectator" and "artist"—by Stendhal, who once called the beautiful *une promesse de bonheur*. Here, at any rate, the one point which Kant makes prominent in the aesthetic position is repudiated and eliminated—*le desinteressement*. Who is right, Kant or Stendhal? When, forsooth, our aesthetes never get tired of throwing into the scales in Kant's favour the fact that under the magic of beauty men can look at even naked female statues "without interest," we can certainly laugh a little at their expense: . . . Pygmalion was not necessarily an "unaesthetic man." (131)

1888 Nietzsche   **NW**

Error reached its zenith when Schopenhauer taught: *in the release from passion and in will alone* lay the road to "truth," to knowledge; the intellect freed from will *could not help* seeing the true and actual essence of things. The same error in art: as if everything became *beautiful* the moment it was regarded without will. (105-106)

1900 Shaw. *See* under ILLUSION (STPP xiv).

1908 Pirandello   **POH**

The difference between [the creation of our own lives] and artistic creation consists only in the fact that the former is *interested* and the latter *disinterested*, which explains why one is very common while the other is not.

Interested implies an objective of practical utility, while disinterested means that its goal is within itself; the former aims at obtaining something, while the latter wills itself for itself. (64)

See also Pirandello under ILLUSION (POH 63-64).

1913   Shaw. Compare with THOUGHT (SMCE 137-39).

1918-1922   Stanislavski. *See* under IDEALISM (SAS 105-106).

1930   Brecht. Compare with AESTHETIC (BBT 40-41).

DISTANCE

"Distance" has long been used in English to indicate interpersonal remoteness (Shakespeare, The Lover's Complaint: *"She kept . . . cold distance").* *Early in this century Edward Bullough adopted that usage in his proposal that a "Psychical Distance" (a degree of emotional disinterestedness) is essential to the perception of an object as art. Included in this category of Distance are observations that an awareness of fiction either enhances or permits artistic pleasure.*

4th cent. B.C.   Aristotle   AP

Objects which in themselves we view with pain, we delight to contemplate when reproduced with minute fidelity: such as the forms of the most ignoble animals and of dead bodies. The cause of this . . . is that to learn gives the liveliest pleasure, not only to philosophers but to men in general. . . . (15)

   See also Aristotle under IMITATION (AP 15), PITY (AR 91).

1712   Addison   AW

The pleasure of [the] secondary views of the imagination are of a wider and more universal nature than those it has when joined with sight; for not only what is great, strange, or beautiful, but any thing that is disagreeable when looked upon, pleases us in an apt description. Here, therefore, we must inquire after a new principle of pleasure, which is nothing else but the action of the mind, which compares the ideas that arise from words with the ideas that arise from objects themselves. . . . For this reason, therefore, the description of a dunghill is pleasing to the imagination, if the image be represented to our minds by suitable expressions; though, perhaps this may be more properly called the pleasure of the understanding than of the fancy, because we are not so much delighted with the image that is contained in the description, as with the aptness of the description to excite the image. But if the description of what is little, common, or deformed, be acceptable to the imagination, the description of what is great, surprising, or beautiful is much more so; because here we are not only delighted with comparing the representation with the original, but are highly pleased with the original itself. (2: 148) . . . If we consider . . . the nature of [the secondary] pleasure [of the imagination], we shall find that it does not arise so properly from the description of what is terrible, as from the reflection we make on ourselves at the time of reading it. When we look at such hideous objects, we are not a little pleased to think we are in no danger of them. We consider them at the same time, as dreadful and harmless; so that the more frightful appearance they make, the greater is the pleasure we receive from the sense of our own safety. In short, we look upon the terrors of a description with the same curiosity and satisfaction that we survey a dead monster. . . . It is for the same reason that we are delighted with the reflecting upon dangers that are past, or in looking on a precipice at a distance, which would fill us with a different kind of horror, if we saw it hanging over our heads. . . . This is, however, such a kind of pleasure that we are not capable of receiving, when we see a person actually lying under the tortures that we meet with in a description; because, in this case, the object presses too close upon our senses, and bears so hard upon us, that it does not give us time or leisure to reflect on ourselves. Our thoughts are so intent upon the miseries of the sufferer, that we cannot turn them upon our own happiness. Whereas, on the contrary, we consider the misfortunes we read in history or poetry, either as past or as fictitious; so that the reflection upon ourselves rises in us insensibly, and overbears the sorrow we conceive for the sufferings of the afflicted. (2: 149)

See also Addison under AFFECT (AW 2: 120), IDENTIFICATION (AW 2: 149).

1765   Johnson. See under ILLUSION (JS 28).

1766   Lessing. See under IMITATION (LSPW 23).

1778   Diderot   **DPA**

For imaginary beings we have not the consideration we are bound to have for real beings. (49)

See also Diderot under AFFECT (DPA 17-18).

1808   Schlegel   **SCL**

Oppressed by the consciousness of the proximity and reality of the represented story, the mind cannot retain that repose and self-possession which are necessary for the reception of pure tragical impressions. [Myths] . . . came to view at a certain remoteness; and surrounded with a certain halo of the marvellous. The marvellous possesses the advantage that it can, in some measure, be at once believed and disbelieved: believed insofar as it is supported by its connexion with other opinions; disbelieved while we never take such an immediate interest in it as we do in what wears the hue of the every-day life of our own experience. (72) . . . To keep the spectators in mirthful tone of mind Comedy must hold them as much as possible aloof from all moral appreciation of its personages, and from all deep interest in their fortunes, for in both cases an entrance will infallibly be given to seriousness. . . . The poet avoid[s this] by always keeping within the province of the understanding, [contrasting] men with men as mere physical beings, just to measure on each other their powers, [especially] their mental powers. . . . In this respect Comedy bears a very near affinity to Fable: in the Fable we have animals endowed with reason, and in Comedy we have men serving their animal propensities with their understanding. . . . Aristotle describes the laughable as an imperfection, an impropriety which is not productive of an essential harm. Excellently said! for from the moment that we entertain a real compassion for the characters, all mirthful feeling is at an end. Comic misfortune must not go beyond an embarrassment. . . . The comic effect [of physical abuse] arises from our having herein a pretty obvious demonstration of the mind's dependence on external things. . . . [In Tragedy] the resolution remains unshaken amid all the terrors of annihilation; the man perishes but his principles survive; [in Comedy] the corporeal existence remains, but the sentiments suffer an instantaneous change. (184-86) . . . In France the young men of quality who sat on the stage lay in wait to discover something to laugh at; . . . all theatrical effect requires a certain distance, and when viewed too closely appears ludicrous. . . . (256)

See also Schlegel under GENRE (SCL 44-46), IRONY (SCL 369-70), THOUGHT (SCL 69-70); compare with DRAMA (SCL 44).

1811-1812   Coleridge   CCSL

If we want to witness mere pain, we can visit the hospitals: if we seek the exhibition of mere pleasure, we can find it in ballrooms. It is the representation of it, not the reality, that we require, the imitation, and not the thing itself; and we pronounce it good or bad in proportion as the representation is an incorrect, or a correct imitation. The true pleasure we derive from theatrical performances arises from the fact that they are unreal and fictitious. If dying agonies were unfeigned, who, in these days of civilisation, could derive gratification from beholding them? (25)

1813   Hazlitt. See under IMAGINATION (HW 1: 134).

1815   Hazlitt. See under TRAGEDY (HW 1: 13).

1815   Coleridge. See under IMITATION (CBL 2: 256, 258).

1818   Coleridge. See under IMITATION (CSC 1: 115).

1871   Nietzsche   NBT

[A] . . . valuable insight into the significance of the [Greek] chorus [has] been displayed by Schiller in the celebrated Preface to his Bride of Messina, where he regarded the chorus as a living wall which tragedy draws round herself to guard her from contact with the world of reality, and to preserve her ideal domain and poetical freedom. It is with this . . . that Schiller combats the ordinary conception of the natural, the illusion ordinarily required in dramatic poetry. He contends that while indeed the day on the stage is merely artificial, the architecture only symbolical, and the metrical dialogue purely ideal in character, nevertheless an erroneous view still prevails in the main: that it is not enough to tolerate merely as a poetical license *that* which is in reality the essence of all poetry. The introduction of the chorus is, he says, the decisive step by which war is declared openly and honestly against all naturalism in art. . . . It is indeed an "ideal" domain . . . upon which the Greek satyric chorus, the chorus of primitive tragedy, was wont to walk, a domain raised far above the actual path of mortals. The Greek framed for this chorus the suspended scaffolding of a fictitious *natural state* and placed thereon fictitious *natural beings*. It is on this foundation that tragedy grew up, and so it could of course dispense from the very first with a painful portrayal of reality. (58-60) . . . [In the] extremest danger of the will, *art* approaches, as a saving and healing enchantress; she alone is able to transform [the] nauseating reflections on the awfulness or absurdity of existence into representations wherewith it is possible to live: these are the representations of the *sublime* as the artistic subjugation of the awful, and the *comic* as the artistic delivery from the nausea of the absurd. The satyric chorus of the dithyramb is the saving deed of Greek art. . . . (62)

    See also Nietzsche under AFFECT (NBT 57-58, 64-65), ILLUSION (NBT 57-58), TRAGEDY (NBT 159-60).

1887   Nietzsche   **NGM**

Oh, this ghostly beauty! With what enchantment it seizes me! . . . The enchantment and the most powerful effect of women is, to use the language of philosophers, an effect at a distance, an *actio in distans*; there belongs thereto, however, primarily and above all,—distance! (99)

1908   Pirandello. *See* under HUMOR (POH 113).

1935   Brecht   **BBT**

[In the epic theatre] the spectator is given a chance to criticize human behaviour from a social point of view, and the scene is played as a piece of history. The idea is that the spectator should be put in a position where he can make comparisons about everything that influences the way in which human beings behave. This means, from the aesthetic point of view, that the actors' social gest becomes particularly important. The arts have to begin paying attention to the gest. (Naturally this means socially significant gest, not illustrative or expressive gest.) The gestic principle takes over, as it were, from the principle of imitation. (86)

c.1936   Brecht. *See* under EPIC THEATRE (BBA 18-19).

1948   Brecht   **BBBG**

We say that man . . . need not remain as he is. He is to be regarded not only as he is but also as he might be. . . . This means that it is not enough for me simply to put myself in his place; . . . I must put myself at some distance from him. This is why the theater must *alienate* what it shows. (28)

1951   Eliot. *See* under STYLE (EPD 13).

c.1956   Brecht   **BBT**

Our enjoyment of old plays becomes greater, the more we can give ourselves up to the new kind of pleasures better suited to our time. To that end we need to develop the historical sense (needed also for the appreciation of new plays) into a real sensual delight. When our theatres perform plays of other periods they like to annihilate distance, fill in the gap, gloss over the differences. But what comes then of our delight in comparisons, in distance, in dissimilarity—which is at the same time a delight in what is close and proper to ourselves? (276)

DRAMA

For most theorists the nature of drama is identical with its function. The broadest distinction among theorists continues to lie between those for whom pleasure is the end (the characteristics of drama being functional to it, even including social value) and those for whom social value is the end (which even pleasure serves).

See also AESTHETIC, INSTRUCTION, and PLEASURE.

4th cent. BC.   Aristotle   AP

The name of "drama" is given to such poems [as those by Sophocles and Aristophanes], *as representing action* [because they are imitating men acting: EP 102]. (13) . . . The question may be raised whether the Epic or Tragic mode of imitation is the higher. If the more refined art is the higher, and the more refined in every case is that which appeals to the better sort of audiences, the art which imitates anything and everything is manifestly most unrefined. The audience is supposed to be too dull to comprehend unless something of their own is thrown in by the performers, who therefore indulge in restless movements. Bad flute-players twist and twirl, if they have to represent "the quoit-throw" or hustle the [chorus leader] when they perform the "Scylla." Tragedy, it is said, has this same defect. . . . We are told that Epic poetry is addressed to a cultivated audience, who do not need *gesture* [dance figures: EP 634]; Tragedy, to an inferior public. Being then unrefined, it is evidently the lower of the two. . . . This censure attaches not to the poetic but to the histrionic art; for gesticulation may be equally overdone in epic recitations . . . or in lyrical competition. . . . Next, all action is not to be condemned—any more than all dancing—but only that of *bad performers* [low characters: EP 639]. Such was the fault found . . . for representing degraded women. Again, Tragedy like Epic poetry produces its effect without *action* [movement (performance): EP 639]; it reveals its power by mere reading. If, then, in all other respects it is superior, this fault is not inherent in it. And superior it is, because it has all the epic elements—it may even use the epic metre—with the music and spectacular effects as important accessories; and these produce the most vivid pleasures. Further, it has the vividness of impression in reading as well as in representation. Moreover, the art attains its end within narrower limits; for the concentrated effect is more pleasurable than one which is spread over a long time and so diluted. What, for example, would be the effect of the Oedipus of Sophocles, if it were cast into a form as long as the Iliad? Once more, the Epic imitation has less unity; . . . any Epic poem will furnish subjects for several tragedies. Thus if the story adopted by the poet has a strict unity, it must either be concisely told and appear truncated; or, if it conform to the Epic canon of length, it must seem weak and watery. <Such length implies some loss of unity,> if, I mean, the poem is constructed out of several actions, like the Iliad and the Odyssey, which have many such parts, each with a certain magnitude of its own. Yet these poems are as perfect as possible in structure; each is, in the highest degree attainable, an imitation of a single action. If, then, Tragedy is superior to Epic poetry in all these respects, and moreover, fulfills its specific function better as an art—for each art ought to produce, not any chance pleasure, but the pleasure proper to it . . . —it plainly follows that Tragedy is the higher art, as attaining its end more perfectly. (107-11)

c.20 B.C.   Horace   HAP

Poets aim to either benefit, or to amuse, or to utter words at once both pleasing and helpful to life. . . . He has won every vote who has blended profit and pleasure, at once delighting and instructing the reader. (479)

1561   Scaliger   SP

The end [of poetry] is the giving of instruction in pleasurable form, for poetry teaches, and does not simply amuse, as some used to think. Whenever language is used, the purpose, of course, is to acquaint the hearer with a fact or with the thought of the speaker, but because primitive poetry was sung, its design seemed merely to please; yet underlying the music was that for which the music were merely the sauce. In time this rude and pristine invention was enriched by philosophy, which made poetry the medium of its teaching. (2) . . . [Philosophical exposition, oratory and drama] all have one and the same end—persuasion. . . . Its end is to convince, or to secure the doing of something. (3)

    See also Scaliger under INSTRUCTION (SP 82-83), THREE UNITIES (SP 60).

1570   Castelvetro   CP

The function of the good poet is, through observation and insight, to imitate the truth of the accidents of humanity's lot, leaving the discovery of the hidden truth of natural and accidental things to the philosopher and scientist. (41) Beyond this, there is another reason more easily apparent, why the matter of sciences and the arts cannot be the subject of poetry: for poetry was invented solely for delight and recreation, to delight and to recreate the minds of the uncultured mob and the common people, and they do not understand subtle reasons and arguments removed from vulgar use, such as philosophers adopt in investigating truth and scientists in formulating sciences. Hence, not understanding, they would have no pleasure and delight, but on the contrary displeasure. (60-61) . . . Poetry was fashioned principally for delight, and not for utility, as Aristotle has shown. (66) Let those who think that poetry aims at teaching, or at teaching and delighting together, let those see that they do not set themselves up against Aristotle, who assigns to the aim of poetry nothing but delight. (67)

See also Castelvetro under CATHARSIS (CP 123), FUNCTIONALISM (CP 68), WONDER (CP 80).

c.1583   Sidney   SDP

To all them that, professing learning, inveigh against poetry, may justly be objected that they go very near to ungratefulness, to seek to deface that which, in the noblest nations and languages that are known, have been the first light-giver to ignorance, and first nurse, whose milk by little and little enabled them to feed afterwards of tougher knowledges. . . . Let learned Greece in any of her manifold sciences be able to show me one book before Musaeus, Homer, and Hesiod, all three nothing else put poets. Nay, let any history be brought that can say any writers were there before them, if they were not men of the same skill, as Orpheus, Linus, and some other are named, who, having been the first of that country that made pens deliverers of their knowledge to their posterity, may justly challenge to be called their fathers in learning. (2-3)

See also Sidney under THREE UNITIES (SDP 47-48).

1605   Jonson. See under POETIC JUSTICE (JBW).

1609   Jonson. See under IMITATION (JBW).

1641   Jonson   JD

The study of [Poesy] (if wee will trust Aristotle) offers to mankinde a certaine rule, and Patterne of living well, and happily; disposing us to all Civill offices of Society. If wee will believe Tully, it nourisheth, and instructeth our Youth; delights our Age; adornes our prosperity; comforts our Adversity. . . . And, wheras they entitle Philosophy to bee a rigid, and austere Poesie: they have (on the contrary) stiled Poesy, a dulcet, and a gentle Philosophy, which leades on, and guides us by the hand to Action, with a ravishing delight and incredible Sweetness. (90-91)

1657   d'Aubignac   AAS

We are not . . . to imagine that . . . publick Spectacles [theatrical performances] afford nothing but a vain Splendour, without any real Utility; for they are a secret Instruction to the People of many things, which it would be very hard to insinuate into them any other way. (1: 4) . . . Whether out of consideration of procuring that Joy and Content to Mankind, which makes their greatest Felicity, and without which they can relish no other Happiness; or whether to shew the greatness of a state, either in Peace or War; to inspire the People with

Courage, or to instruct them in the Knowledge and practice of Virtue; or lastly, to prevent Idleness (one of the greatest mischiefs of a State) Princes can never do any thing more advantage[ou]s for their own Glory, nor for their Peoples Happiness, than to found, settle, and maintain at their own Charges, publick spectacles. (1: 7)

See also d'Aubignac under INSTRUCTION (AAS 1: 5).

1660   Corneille   CFD

It is impossible to please according to the rules without at the same time supplying [utility]. It is a fact that from one end to the other of Aristotle's Poetics not once does he make use of this word; on the contrary, he says that the end of drama is the pleasure we experience in observing the actions of men imitated. He prefers that part of the drama which has to do with the [plot] rather than with the "manners" portrayed, because the former contained what was most pleasing, like the [Recognitions] and the [Reversals]. . . . But let us remember that we learned from Horace that we cannot please the greatest number unless we include in our work [some element of utility]. . . . [It is therefore] a useless dispute regarding the value of plays. . . . (140)

See also Corneille under AFFECT (CFD 159).

1663   Molière. See under RULES (MP 6: 344).

1668   Dryden   DW

[Lisideius] conceived a play ought to be, *A just and lively image of human nature representing its passions and humours, and the changes of fortune to which it is subject; for the delight and instruction of mankind.* This definition . . . was . . . well received. . . . (1, 2: 43) Delight is the chief, if not the only, end of poesy: instruction can be admitted but in the second place; for poesy only instructs as its delights. It is true, that to imitate well is a poet's work; but to affect the soul, and excite the passions, and above all to move admiration, which is the delight of serious plays, a bare imitation will not serve. (1, 2: 160)

1669   Molière. See under COMEDY (MP 2: 31-32).

1671   Dryden. See under POETIC JUSTICE (DW 1, 2: 198-201).

1674   Racine. See under AFFECT (RP 156).

1679   Dryden   DW

To instruct delightfully is the general end of all poetry. Philosophy instructs, but it performs its work by precept; which is not delightful, or not so delightful as example. To purge the passions by example, is therefore the particular instruction which belongs to tragedy. (1, 2: 269)

See also Dryden under INSTRUCTION (DW 1, 2: 274).

1695   Dryden   **DW**

The principal end of painting is to please, and the chief design of poetry is to instruct. In this the latter seems to have the advantage of the former; but if we consider the artists themselves on both sides, certainly their aims are the very same: they would both make sure of pleasing, and that in preference to instruction. (3: 311)

See also Dryden under INSTRUCTION (DW 3: 310-11).

1711   Dryden   **DW**

The parts of a poem, tragick or heroick, are, 1. The fable itself. 2. The order or manner of its contrivance, in relation to the parts to the whole. 3. The manners, or decency of the characters, in speaking or acting what is proper for them, and proper to be shewn by the poet. 4. The thoughts, which express the manners. 5. The words, which express those thoughts. (1, 2: 302-303) . . . The Chief end of the poet is to please; for his immediate reputation depends on it. The great end of the poem is to instruct, which is performed by making pleasure the vehicle of that instruction; for poesy is an art, and all arts are made to profit. (1, 2: 307)

See also Dryden under MORALITY (DW 1, 2: 309-10).

1711   Addison. *See* under CATHARSIS (AW 1: 69-70).

1712   Addison   **AW**

Were our English stage but half so virtuous as that of the Greeks and Romans, we should quickly see the influence of it in the behaviour of all the politer part of mankind. It would not be fashionable to ridicule religion; or its professors; the man of pleasure would not be the complete gentleman; vanity would be out of countenance; and every quality which is ornamental to human nature would meet with the esteem which is due to it. If the English stage were under the same regulations the Athenian was formerly, it would have the same effect that it had, in recommending the religion, the government, and public worship of its country. Were our plays subject to proper inspections and imitations, we might not only pass away several of our vacant hours in the highest entertainment, but should always rise from them wiser and better than we sat down to them. . . . It is to be hoped, that some time or other we may be at leisure to restrain the licentiousness of the theatre, and make it contribute its assistance to the advancement of morality, and to the reformation of the age. As matters stand at present, multitudes are shut out from this noble diversion, by reason of those abuses and corruptions that accompany it. . . . The Athenian and Roman plays were written with such regard to morality, that Socrates used to frequent the one, and Cicero the other. (2: 184)

1730   Voltaire. *See* under THREE UNITIES (VE 280-81).

1731   Voltaire   **VE**

The stage, whether occupied by tragedy or comedy, exhibits a living picture of the human passions. (283)

1755-1780   Diderot. *See* under COMEDY (DDE 287), INSTRUCTION (DDE 288), TRAGEDY (DDE 291).

1758   Diderot   **DDP**

The duties of man, as well as his follies and vices, offer a rich field to the dramatist, and serious dramas will succeed everywhere, but more especially with a people whose manners and customs are corrupt. They will go to the theatre in order to escape the evil-doers by whom they are surrounded in life; there will they find people with whom they would care to live; there they will see mankind as it really is, and they will become reconciled with it. . . . "Is human nature good, then?"

Yes, my friend, very good. . . . Everything is good in nature. . . . It is our miserable conventions that pervert and cramp mankind, not human nature. . . . What art could be more harmful that that which should make me an accomplice of evil man? But on the other hand, what art more precious than that which leads me, imperceptibly, to take an interest in the lot of the good man, taking me out of the quiet and soothing position I now enjoy, and forces me into the refuge where he has gone, to take part in the trials which it has pleased the poet to throw across his path in order to try his mettle? How mankind would be benefited were all the arts of imitation to seek a common end, and come together with laws forcing us to love virtue and despise vice! (287-89)

See also Diderot under GENRE DEFINITION (DDP 287).

1765   Johnson. *See* under MORALITY (JS 21).

1766   Lessing. *See* under TRAGEDY (LSPW 31).

1767-1769   Lessing   **LSPW**

It is not easy to convert a touching little story into a touching drama. True, it costs little trouble to invent new complications and to enlarge separate emotions into scenes. But to prevent these new complications from weakening the interest or interfering with probability; to transfer oneself from the point of view of a narrator into the real standpoint of each personage; to let passions arise before the eyes of the spectator in lieu of describing them, and to let them grow up without effort in such illusory continuity that he must sympathise, whether he will or no; this it is which is needful. . . . (233) . . . All species of poetry are intended to improve us; it is sad that it should be necessary to have to prove this, still sadder that there are poets who even doubt it. But all species of poetry cannot improve all things, at least not everyone as perfectly as another, but what each can improve most perfectly, and better than any other species—that alone is its peculiar aim. (418) . . . The dramatic form is the only one by which pity and fear can be excited, at least in no other form can these passions be excited to such a degree. (426)

See also Lessing under COMEDY (LSPW 307), PROBABILITY (LSPW 236), THOUGHT (LSPW 329).

1797   Goethe   GED

The epic poet and the dramatic poet are both subject to the general laws of poetry, and especially to the laws of unity and progression. Furthermore, they deal with subjects that are similar, and they can avail themselves of motives of either kind. The great and essential difference between them, however, lies in the fact that, whereas the epic poet describes an action as being altogether past and completed, the dramatic poet represents it as actually occurring. . . . Neither [epic nor dramatic poetry] can lay exclusive claim to [forms, subjects or themes]. (337-38)

1804   Coleridge   CSC

The most important and dignified species of [the poetic] genus is, doubtless, the STAGE [which] . . . may be characterized (in its *Idea*, or according to what it does, or ought to, *aim* at) as a combination of several, or of all the fine arts to an harmonious whole having a distinct end of its own, to which the peculiar end of each of the component arts, taken separately, is made subordinate and subservient; that, namely, of imitating reality (objects, actions, or passions) under a *semblance* of reality. Thus, Claude imitates a landscape at sunset, but only as a *picture*; while a forest-scene is not presented to the audience as a *picture*, but as a forest: and tho' in the *full* sense of the word we are no more *deceived* by the one than by the other, yet are our feelings very differently affected, and the pleasure derived from the one is not composed of the same elements as that afforded by the other, even on the supposition that the *quantum* of both were equal. In the former, it is a *condition* of all genuine delight, that we should *not* be deluded; in the latter, stage-machinery [has for] its very purpose . . . to produce as much illusion as nature permits. (1: 177).

See also Coleridge under ILLUSION (CSC 1: 178-181).

1808   Schlegel   SCL

Poetry, taken in its widest acceptation, as the power of creating what is beautiful, and representing it to the eye or the ear, is a universal gift of Heaven, being shared to a certain extent even by those whom we call barbarians and savages. Internal excellence is alone decisive, and where this exists, we must not allow ourselves to be repelled by the external appearance. Everything must be traced up to the root of human nature: if it has sprung from thence, it has an undoubted worth of its own; but if, without possessing a living germ, it is merely externally attached thereto, it will never thrive nor acquire a proper growth. (18-19) . . . What is dramatic? To many the answer will seem easy: where various persons are introduced conversing together, and the poet does not speak in his own person. This is, however, merely the external foundation of the form; and that is dialogue. But the characters may express thoughts . . . without operating any change on the other . . . ; in such a case, however interesting the conversation may be, it cannot be said to possess a dramatic interest. . . . Action is the true enjoyment of life, nay, life itself. Mere passive enjoyments may lull us into a state of listless complacency. . . . Of all diversions the theatre is undoubtedly the most entertaining. Here we may see others act even when we cannot act to any great purpose ourselves. The highest object of human activity is man, and in the drama we see men measuring their powers with each other . . . influencing each other by their opinions, sentiments and passions and decisively determining their reciprocal relations and circumstances. The art of the poet accordingly consists in separating from the fable whatever essentially does not belong to it, whatever . . . interrupts the progress of important actions, and concentrating within a narrow space a number of events calculated to attract the minds of the hearers and to fill them with attention and expectation. In this manner he gives us a renovated picture of life. . . . The dramatic poet must renounce [narrative] expedients; but for this he is richly recompensed in the . . . [impersonation of] each of his characters in his story . . . by a living individual; that this individual should, in sex, age, and figure, meet as near as may be the prevalent conceptions of his fictitious original, nay, assume his entire personality; that every speech should be delivered in a suitable tone of voice, and accompanied by appropriate action and gesture; and that those external circumstances should be added which are necessary to give the hearers a clear idea of what is going forward. . . . All this brings us to the idea of *theatre*. It is evident that the very form of dramatic poetry, that is, the exhibition of an action by dialogue without the aid of narrative, implies the theatre as its necessary complement. (30-32) . . . The dramatic poet, as well as the epic, represents external events, but he represents them as real and present. In common with the lyric poet he also claims our mental participation [in emotion], but not in the same calm composedness; the feeling of joy and sorrow which the dramatist excites is more immediate and vehement. He calls forth all the emotions which the sight of similar deeds and fortunes of living men would elicit, and it is only by the total sum of impressions which he produces that he ultimately resolves these conflicting emotions into a harmonious tone of feeling. . . . He must decidedly take part with one or other of the leading views of human life, and constrain his audience also to participate in the same feeling. (44) . . . The French has endeavored to form their tragedy according to a strict idea; but instead of this they have set up merely an abstract notion. They require tragical dignity and grandeur, tragical situations, passions, and pathos, altogether simple and pure, and without foreign appendages. Stript thus of their proper investiture, they lose much in truth, profundity, and character; and the whole composition is deprived of the living charm of variety, and of the magic of picturesque situations, and of all ravishing effects which a light but preparatory matter, when left to itself, often produces on the mind by its marvelous and spontaneous growth. With respect to the theory of the tragic art, they are at the very same point that they were in the art of gardening before . . . Lenotre. All merit consisted . . . in extorting a triumph from nature by means of art. They had no other idea of regularity than the measured symmetry of straight alleys, clipped edges, etc. Vain would have been the attempt to make those who laid out such gardens to comprehend that there could be any plan, any hidden order, in an English park, and demonstrate to them that a succession of landscapes, which from their gradation, their alternation, and their opposition, give effect to each other, did all aim at exciting in us a certain mental impression. (273)

c.1810   Coleridge   CLSW

The first form of poetry is the epic, the essence of which may be stated as the successive in events and characters. This must be distinguished from narration, in which there must always be a narrator, from whom the objects represented receive a coloring and a manner;—whereas in the epic, as in the so-called poems of Homer, the whole is completely objective, and the representation is a pure reflection. The next form into which poetry passed was the dramatic;—both forms have a common basis with a certain difference, and that difference not consisting in the dialogue alone. Both are founded on the relation of providence to the human will; and this relation is the universal element, expressed under different points of view according to the difference of religions, and the moral and intellectual cultivation of different nations. In the epic poem fate is represented as overruling the will, and making it instrumental to the accomplishment of its designs. . . . In the drama, the will is exhibited as struggling with fate, a great and beautiful instance and illustration of which is the *Prometheus* of Aeschylus; and the deepest effect is produced, when the fate is represented as a higher and intelligent will, and the opposition of the individual as springing from a defect. (116)

    See also Coleridge under ILLUSION (CLSW 73), RULES (CLSW 72-73).

1815   Coleridge   CBL

The common essence of all [art] consists in the excitement of emotion for the immediate purpose of pleasure through the medium of beauty; herein contradistinguishing poetry from science, the immediate object and purpose of which is truth and possible utility. (The sciences indeed may and will give a high and pure pleasure; and the Fine Arts may lead to important truth, and be in various ways useful in the ordinary meaning of the word; but these are not the direct and characteristic ends, and we define things by their peculiar, not their common properties. (2: 220-21)

1816 Goethe   GLE

We must distinguish closely related poetic *genres*, however often they may be confused and merged together in actual treatment. . . . *Epic* requires the verbal delivery to the crowd through the mouth of an individual; *dialogue*, conversation in a narrow circle, where the crowd may eventually listen; *drama*, conversation bound up with action, even if enacted only before the imagination; *play*, all three together, in so far as they appeal to the sense of vision, and can be embodied under certain conditions of personal presence and stage-setting. (185)

1816 Hazlitt   HW

The object of poetry is to please: this art naturally gives pleasure, and excites admiration. (1: 152)

1817 Hazlitt   HW

If the stage is useful as a school of instruction, it is no less so as a source of amusement. It is the source of the greatest enjoyment at the time, and a never-failing fund of agreeable reflection afterwards. The merits of a new play, or of a new actor, are always among the first topics of polite conversation. One way in which public exhibitions contribute to refine and humanise mankind, is by supplying them with ideas and subjects of conversation and interest in common. (1: 154)

   See also Hazlitt under AFFECT (HW 1: 153-54).

1818 Hazlitt   HW

The end and use of poetry, ''both at the first and now, was and is to hold the mirror up to nature,'' seen through the medium of passion and imagination, not divested of that medium by means of literal truth or abstract reason. (5: 8)

1820 Hazlitt   HW

Dramatic poetry . . . is essentially individual and concrete, both in form and in power. It is the closest imitation of nature; it has a body of truth; it is ''a counterfeit presentment'' of reality; for it brings forward certain characters to act and speak for themselves, in the most trying and singular circumstances. It is not enough for them to declaim on certain general topics, however forcibly or learnedly—this is merely oratory, and this any other characters might do as well, in any other circumstances: nor is it sufficient for the poet to furnish the colours and forms of style and fancy out of his own store, however inexhaustible. (8: 417)

c.1820   Hegel   HFA

The reason that dramatic poetry must be regarded as the highest phase of the art of poetry, and, indeed, of every kind of art, is due to the fact that it is elaborated, both in form and substance, in a whole that is most complete. For in contrast to every other sort of sensuous *materia*, whether it be stone, wood, colour, or tone, that of human speech is the only medium fully adequate to the presentation of spiritual life; and further, among the particular types of the art of articulate speech, dramatic poetry is the one in which we find the objective character of the Epos essentially united to the subjective principle of the lyric. In other words, it presents directly before our vision an essentially independent action as a definite fact, which does not merely originate from the personal life of character under the process of self-realization, but receives its determinate form as the result of the substantive interaction in concrete life of ideal intention, many individuals and collisions. . . . In order that the entire art-product may receive the full animation of life, we require its complete scenic representation. (4: 248) . . . The demand of the drama, in its widest sense, is the presentation of human action and relations in their actually visible form to the imaginative consciousness, that is to say, in the uttered speech of living persons, who in this way give expression to their action. Dramatic action, however, is not confined to the simple and undisturbed execution of a definite purpose, but depends throughout on conditions of collision, human passion and characters, and leads therefore to actions and reactions, which in turn call for some further resolution of conflict and disruption. What we have consequently before us are definite ends individualized in living personalities and situations pregnant with conflict. (4: 249-50) . . . [As an historically evolved synthesis of the epic and lyric] points of view, drama has in the *first* place, following in this respect the Epos, to bring before our vision an event, action or practical affair. But . . . the factor of bare externality must be obliterated, and in its place the self-conscious and active personality is posited as the paramount ground and vital force. The drama, in short, does not take exclusive refuge in the lyric presence of soul-life, as such stands in contrast to an external world, but propounds such a life in and through *its* external realization. And in virtue of this the event does not appear to proceed from external conditions, but rather from personal volition and character; it receives in fact its dramatic significance exclusively in its relation to subjective aims and passions. . . . Consequently the dramatic action in question must submit to a process of development and collision with other forces. (4:251) . . . The drama, it matters not in what form it may be shaped, will have to propound to us the vital energy of a principle of Necessity which is essentially self-supporting, and capable of resolving every conflict and contradiction. Consequently, we have before every thing else the demand . . . that to the fullest extent [the poet must be] awake to that ideal and universal substance which is at the root of human ends, conflicts and destinies. . . . The spiritual powers . . . assert themselves in dramatic poetry in consonance with their simple substantive content as pathos altogether, and as apart from individual characters. The drama is, in fact, the resolution of the one-sided aspect of these powers, which discover their self-stability in the dramatic character. (4: 254-55) . . . Dramatic poetry is . . . not satisfied with merely *one* situation [as lyric poetry is]; it presents the ideal world of emotional life or intelligence in active self-assertion as a totality of circumstances and ends of very various characters, which expresses . . . all that . . . passes in such an inward world. In comparison with the lyrical poem, the drama reaches out to and is completed in a far more extensive embrace of subject matter. . . . Yet more important . . . is the nature of the *dramatic progression* as opposed to the mode of the epic's devolution. . . . The true dramatic progression is a *continuous* movement *onwards* to the final catastrophe. . . . Episodical scenes, . . . which only impede the action, are contrary to the nature of the drama. (4: 261-62) . . . Poetry, alone among the arts, completely dispenses with the sensuous medium of the objective world of phenomena. Inasmuch moreover as the drama does not interpret to the imaginative vision the exploits of the past, or express an ideal personal experience to mind and soul, but rather is concerned to depict an action in all the reality of its actual presence, it would fall into contradiction with itself if it were forced to remain limited to the means, which poetry, simply as such, is in a position to offer. The present action no doubt belongs entirely to the personal self, and from this point of view complete expression is possible through the medium of language. From an opposite one, however, the movement of action is toward objective reality, and it requires the complete man to express its movement in his corporeal existence, deed and demeanour, as well as the physiognomical expression of emotions and passions, and not only these on their own account, but in their effect on other men, and the reactions which are thereby brought into being. Moreover, in the display of individuality in its actual presence, we require further an external environment, a specific *locale*, in which such movement and action is achieved. Consequently dramatic poetry, by virtue of the fact that no one of these aspects can be permitted to remain in their immediate condition of contingency, but have all to be reclothed in an artistic form as phases of fine art itself, is compelled to avail itself of the assistance of pretty well all the other arts. The surrounding scene is to some extent, just as the temple is, an architectonic environment, and in part also external Nature, both aspects being conceived and executed in pictorial fashion. In this *locale* the sculpturesque figures . . . are presented with the animation of life, and their volition and emotional states are artistically elaborated, not merely by means of expressive recitation, but also through a picturesque display of gesture and of posture and movement, which, in its objective form, is inspired by the inward soul-life. . . . Poetry in its simplicity, [may be contrasted] with the external dramatic execution . . . : *First*, there is the dramatic poetry, whose object is to restrict itself to the ordinary ground of poetry, and consequently does not contemplate the theatrical representation of its productions. *Secondly*, we have the genuine art of the theatre, to the extent, that is, in which it is limited to recitation, play of pose and action, under the modes in which the language of the poet is able throughout to remain the definitive and decisive factor. *Lastly*, there is the type of reproduction, which admits the employment of every means of scenery, music and dance, and suffers the same to assert an independent position as against the dramatic language. (4: 278-80) . . . The true course of dramatic development consists in the annulment of *contradiction* viewed as such, in the reconciliation of the forces of human action, which alternately strive to negate each other in their conflict. . . . Misfortune and suffering [are] not the final issue, but rather the satisfaction of spirit . . . in complete accord with reason, . . . shaken by the calamitous result to the heroes, but reconciled in the substantial facts. . . . Ancient tragedy [is] . . . concerned with the appearance of the affirmative reconciliation and with the equal validity of both powers engaged in actual conflict, when the collision actually took place. [Demonstrated is not] a blind destiny, . . . a purely irrational, unintelligible fate . . . [but] rather . . . the rationality of destiny. . . . Fate drives personality back upon its limits, and shatters it when it has grown overweening. An irrational compulsion, however, an innocence of suffering would rather excite indignation in the soul of the spectator than ethical tranquility. . . . The . . . conception of reconciliation in tragedy is . . . related to the resolution of specific ethical and substantive facts from their contradiction into their true harmony. (4: 321-23).

　　See also Hegel under DRAMATIZATION (HFA 4: 280-82), FORWARD MOVEMENT (HFA 4: 262), LANGUAGE (HFA 4: 264-65).

1863-1867　Taine　　　　　　　　　　　　　　　　　　　**THEL**

Literary works . . . are instructive because they are beautiful; their utility grows with their perfection; and if they furnish documents, it is because they are monuments. The more a book represents visible sentiments, the more it is a work of literature; for the proper office of literature is to take note of sentiments. The more a book represents important sentiments, the higher is its place in literature; for it is by representing the mode of being of a whole nation and a whole age, that a writer rallies round him the sympathies of an entire age and an entire nation. (20)

1864　Taine. *See* under ACTION (TLA 318-19), HERO (TLA 180).

1871   Nietzsche   **NBT**

The most immediate effect of the Dionysian tragedy, [is] that the state and society, and, in general, the gaps between man and man give way to an overwhelming feeling of oneness, which leads back to the heart of nature. The metaphysical comfort,—with which, as I have here intimated, every time tragedy dismisses us—that, in spite of the perpetual change of phenomena, life at bottom is indestructibly powerful and pleasurable, this comfort appears with corporeal lucidity as the satyric chorus, as the chorus of [fictitious] natural beings, who live ineradicable as it were behind all civilization, and who, in spite of the ceaseless change of generations and the history of nations, remain forever the same. (60-61) . . . We talk so abstractly about poetry, because we are all wont to be bad poets. At bottom the aesthetic phenomenon is simple: let a man but have the faculty of perpetually seeing a lively play and of constantly living surrounded by hosts of spirits, then he is a poet: let him but feel the impulse to transform himself and to talk from out of the bodies and souls of others, then he is a dramatist. (67) . . . This enchantment [of a community of unconscious actors, who mutually regard themselves as transformed among one another] is the prerequisite of all dramatic art. In this enchantment the Dionysian reveller sees himself as a satyr, *and as satyr he in turn beholds the god*, that is, in his transformation he sees a new vision outside him as the Apollonian consummation of his state. With this new vision the drama is complete. According to this view, we must understand Greek tragedy as the Dionysian chorus, which always disburdens itself anew in an Apollonian world of pictures. The choric parts, therefore, with which tragedy is inter-laced, are in a manner the mother-womb of the entire so-called dialogue, that is, the whole stage-world, of the drama power. . . . The drama . . . is a dream-phenomenon throughout, and, as such, epic in character: on the other hand, however, as objectivation of a Dionysian state, it does not represent the Apollonian redemption in appearance, but, conversely, the dissolution of the individual and his unification with primordial existence. Accordingly, the drama is the Apollonian embodiment of the Dionysian perceptions and in-fluences, and is thereby separated from the epic as by an immense gap. (68-69)
    See also Nietzsche under IDENTIFICATION (NBT 67).

1875   Shaw   **SMCE**

The worthy artist or craftsman is he who serves the physical or moral senses by feeding them with [works] . . . which call the heightened senses and ennobled faculties into pleasurable activity. The great artist is he who goes a step beyond the demand, and, by supplying works of a higher beauty and a higher interest than have yet been perceived, succeeds after a brief struggle with its strange-ness, in adding this fresh extension of sense to the heritage of the race. This is why we value art. (315-16)

1876   Sarcey   **STT**

In regard to the theater there is one fact which cannot fail to strike the least attentive; it is the presence of an audience. The word play carries with it the idea of an audience. We cannot conceive of a play without an audience. Take one after the other the accessories which serve in the performance of a dramatic work—they can all be replaced or suppressed except that one. (22) . . . It is an indisputable fact that a dramatic work, whatever it may be, is designed to be listened to by a number of persons united and forming an audience, that this is its very essence, that this is a necessary condition of its existence. . . . The audience is the necessary and inevitable condition to which dramatic art must accomodate its means. (24-25)

See also Sarcey under CONVENTION (STT 26-27), IMITATION (STT 20-21).

1882   Nietzsche. See under AFFECT (NJW 329-30).

1888   Strindberg. See under IDENTIFICATION (SSPP 11-12).

1889   Chekhov   **CLF**

Jan. 4. You write that the stage lures you because it resembles life. . . . Is this so? But I think that the theatre lures you and me and shrivels Shcheglov up, because it is a form of sport. Where there is success or failure there is sport and hazard. (141)

1894   Brunetière. See under ACTION (BLD 75-76).

1902   Shaw. See under MORALITY (SAA 33), THOUGHT (SAA 43).

c.1908   Strindberg. See under ILLUSION (SOL 128, 263).

1909   Shaw   **STPB**

Life as it appears to us in our daily experience is an unintelligible chaos of happenings. . . . It is the business of [the great dramatist] to pick out the significant incidents from the chaos of daily happenings, and arrange them so that their relation to one another becomes significant, thus changing us from bewildered spectators of a monstrous confusion to men intelligently conscious of the world and its destinies. (xxiv)

1913   Shaw   **SMCE**

When Ibsen began to make plays, the art of the dramatist had shrunk into the art of contriving a situation. And it was held that the stranger the situation, the better the play. Ibsen saw that, to the contrary, the more familiar the situation, the more interesting the play. . . . He gives us not only ourselves, but ourselves in our own situations. The things that happen to his stage figures are things that happen to us. . . . Changes in technique follow inevitably from these changes in the subject matter in the play. (144)

See also Shaw under CLOSURE (SMCE 139-40, 142-43, 145), THOUGHT (SMCE 137-39).

1918-1922 Stanislavski. See under IDEALISM (SAS 104, 105-106).

1921 Eliot   **ESW**

From the point of view of literature, the drama is only one among several poetic forms. . . . Nevertheless, the drama is perhaps the most permanent, is capable of greater variation and of expressing more varied types of society, than any other. (55) . . . The essential is not, of course, that drama should be written in verse. . . . The essential is to get upon the stage this precise statement of life which is at the same time a point of view, a world—a world which the author's mind has subjected to a complete simplification. I do not find that any drama which "embodies a philosophy" of the author's (like *Faust*) or which illustrates any social theory (like Shaw's) can possibly fulfil the requirements. (61-62)

See also Eliot under AESTHETIC (ESW 61).

1931-1936 Artaud   **AT**

The theater, like the plague, is in the image of . . . carnage and . . . separation. It releases conflicts, disengages powers, liberates possibilities, and if these possiblities and these powers are dark, it is the fault not of the plague nor of the theater, but of life. (31) . . . One therefore understands that the theater, to the very degree that it remains confined within its own language and in correlation with it, must break with actuality. Its object is not to resolve social or psychological conflicts, to serve as a battlefield for moral passions, but to express objectively certain secret truths, to bring into the light of day by means of active gestures certain aspects of truth that have been buried under forms in their encounters with Becoming. To do that, to link the theater to the expressive possibilities of forms, to everything in the domain of gestures, noises, colors, movements, etc., is to restore it to its original direction, to reinstate it in its religious and metaphysical aspect, is to reconcile it with the universe. (70) . . . The theater as we practice it can therefore be reproached with a terrible lack of imagination. The theater must make itself the equal of life—not an individual life, that individual aspect of life in which CHARACTERS triumph, but the sort of liberated life which sweeps away human individuality and in which man is only a reflection. The true purpose of the theater is to create Myths, to express life in its immense, universal aspect, and from that life to extract images in which we find pleasure in discovering ourselves. . . . May it free *us*, in a Myth in which we have sacrificed out little human individuality, like Personages out of the Past, with powers rediscovered in the Past. (116)

    See also Artaud under CATHARSIS (AT 31-32), IDEALISM (AT 50-51), METAPHOR (AT 27-28).

1932   Eliot   **EJD**

I shall not venture here to investigate the nature of the *dramatic* in poetic drama, as distinguishable from the *poetic* in poetic drama; only to point out that the problem is much more of a tangle than it looks. For instance, there is *that which expressed in word and action is effective on the stage without our having read the text before*: that might be called the *theatrically dramatic*; and there is also the "poetically dramatic," that which, when we read it, we recognize to have dramatic value, but which would not have dramatic value for us upon the stage unless we had already the perception of it from reading. *Theatrically* dramatic value in verse exists when the speech has its equivalent in, or can be projected by, the action and gesture and expression of the actor; *poetic* dramatic value is something dramatic in essence which can only be expressed by the word and by the reception of the word. (29)

1935   Brecht. *See* under CATHARSIS (BBT 87).

c.1936   Brecht. *See* under EPIC THEATRE (BBA 20-21).

1938   Stanislavski   **SKDC**

Entertainment must be one of the main weapons of struggle against war and an international means of safeguarding peace throughout the world. True entertainment is the best means of communication between people. It reveals and makes their innermost feelings understood. (10)

1943   Eliot. *See* under STYLE (EOPP 17).

1948   Brecht   **BBBG**

[Epic theatre] defended its prediliction for social attitudes by pointing to social attitudes in generally accepted works of art, inconspicuous there only because they were accepted attitudes. . . . It accused the markets of evening entertainment of having become a mere branch of the drug traffic. False images of the social scene on the stage (including those of naturalism so-called) drew from it a demand for scientifically accurate images. . . . It scornfully rejected the cult of the Beautiful (which went along with a dislike for learning and a contempt for utility) particularly since nothing beautiful was being produced. (13) Let us consider the theater as a place of entertainment, . . . and let us inquire what kind of entertainment we can accept.

Theater consists in this: living images of historical or fictitious events taking place among men placed before us, for the purpose of entertainment. ...[Pleasure] is the noblest function we have found for theater. (14)... Science and art have a common ground... since both exist to make the life of men easier: the one *sus*tains and *main*tains, the other *enter*tains. In the coming age, art will find entertainment in the new productivity which can so much improve our sustenance and maintenance and which, once it is not interfered with, may itself be the greatest of all enjoyments. (19-20)... We need a theater that makes possible the feelings, insights, and impulses permitted by the historical context in which the actions at times take place. But we also need a theater that employs and generates ideas and feelings capable of playing a part in the transformation of the context itself. (24)

See also Brecht under PLEASURE (BBT 15).

c.1956   Brecht. *See* under EPIC THEATRE (BBT 276, 281).

1956   Brecht. *See* under THOUGHT (BBT 277).

DRAMATIZATION

Under this heading is collected judgments and arguments concerning what should be presented in action, what should be presented in language, and what principles are involved.

See also *ACTION, EXPOSITION, and SPECTACLE.*

c.20 B.C.   Horace   HAP

Either an event is acted on the stage, or the action is narrated. Less vividly is the mind stirred by what finds entrance through the ears than by what is brought before the trusty eyes, and what the spectator can see for himself. Yet you will not bring upon the Stage what should be performed behind the scenes, and you will keep much from our eyes, which an actor's ready tongue will narrate anon in our presence; so that Medea is not to butcher her boys before the people, nor impious Atreus cook human flesh upon the stage. . . . Whatever you thus show me, I discredit and abhor. (465-67)

1657   d'Aubignac. *See* under ACTION (AAS 3: 11-12), AFFECT (AAS 1: 37-38), EXPOSITION (AAS 3: 15-16), MOTIVATION (AAS 1: 39).

1665   Dryden   DW

[Horace] directly declares his judgment, that every thing makes more impression presented than related. Nor, indeed, can any one rationally assert the contrary; for if they affirm otherwise, they do by consequence maintain, that a whole play might be as well related as acted: therefore, whoever chooses a subject that enforces him to relations, is to blame; and he that does it without the necessity of the subject, is much more. (1, 2: 18-19)

1668   Dryden   DW

I must acknowledge . . . that the French have reason to hide that part of the action which would occasion too much tumult on the stage, and to choose rather to have it made known by narration to the audience. Farther, I think it very convenient . . . that all incredible actions were removed; but, whether custom has so insinuated itself into our countrymen, or nature has so formed them to fierceness, I know not; but they will scarcely suffer combats and other objects of horrour to be taken from them. And indeed, the indecency of tumults is all which can be objected against fighting: for why may not our imagination as well suffer itself to be deluded with the probability of it, as with any other thing in the play? For my part, I can with as great ease persuade myself that the blows are given in good earnest, as I can, that they who strike them are kings or princes, or those persons which they represent. . . . If we are to be blamed for shewing too much of the action, the French are as faulty for discovering too little of it: a mean betwixt both should be observed by every judicious writer, so as the audience may neither be left unsatisfied by not seeing what is beautiful, or shocked by beholding what is either incredible or undecent. (1, 2: 90-93)

1679   Dryden. *See* under ACTION (DW 1, 2: 268-69).

1711   Addison   AW

A good poet will give the reader a more lively idea of an army or a battle in a description, than if he actually saw them drawn up in squadrons and battalions, or engaged in the confusion of a fight. Our minds should be opened to great conceptions, and inflamed with glorious sentiments by what the actor speaks more than by what he appears. Can all the trappings of equipage of a king or hero, give Brutus half that pomp and majesty which he receives from a few lines in Shakespeare? (1: 75)

1778   Diderot. *See* under AFFECT (DPA 17-18).

1797   Goethe. *See* under AFFECT (GED 339).

1808   Schlegel. *See* under EXPOSITION (SCL 272-73).

1816   Goethe   GLE

Shakespeare's works are . . . highly dramatic; by his treatment, his revelation of the inner life, he wins the reader; the theatrical demands appear to him unimportant, and so he takes it easy, and we, spiritually speaking, take it easy with him. We pass with him from place to place; our power of imagination provides all the episodes which he omits. We even feel grateful to him for arousing our imagination in so profitable a way. Since he exhibits everything in dramatic form, he renders easy the working of our imaginations; for with the "stage that signifies the world" we are more familiar than with the world itself, and we can read and hear the most phantastic things, and still imagine that they might pass before our eyes on the stage. This accounts for the frequently bungling dramatizations of favorite novels. (185-86)

c.1820   Hegel   HFA

The true sensuous medium . . . of dramatic poetry is . . . not only the human voice and the spoken word, but the entire man. . . . It is a feature of modern notions . . . to regard the organization of drama with a view to its theatrical reproduction as unessential and subsidiary. . . . The result is that the greater number of more recent dramas are unable ever to find a stage, and the simple reason for this is that they are undramatical. . . . We affirm that it is only to an action, the dramatic course of which is admirably adapted to theatrical representation, that we are to attribute such intrinsic dramatic worth. . . . [Modern] poets to some extent deliberately fashion their work exclusively for the reader's perusal. [It is true that indifference to mere] features of external form, which are implied in the so-called knowledge of the stage, . . . does not lessen the poetical worth of a dramatical production. . . . A knowledge and aptitude of this nature is neither indicative of any poetical superiority or the reverse. . . . There are, however, other features relative to which the poet, in order to be truly dramatical, must have the animated reproduction visibly present in its substance, must make his *dramatis personae* speak and act conformably thereto, that is, in complete congruity with an actually present realization. Viewed in this light theatrical reproduction is a real test. For in the presence . . . of a sound and artistic public the mere speeches . . . , if dramatic truth is not asserted, will not hold water. . . . Let [the public] retain its own essentially sterling common sense, and it will only be satisfied in those cases where characters express themselves and act precisely as the reality of life no less than art demands and necessitates. (4: 280-82)

1829   Goethe   GCE

Wed., Feb. 4. ''Writing for the stage . . . is something peculiar, and he who does not understand it thoroughly, had better leave it alone. Every one thinks that an interesting fact will appear interesting on the boards,—nothing of the kind! Things may be very pretty to read, and very pretty to think about; but as soon as they are put upon the stage the effect is quite different, and that which has charmed us in the closet will probably fall flat on the boards.

1896   Chekhov   CLF

Dec. 14. You classify plays into those which can be performed, and those which can be read. Into which class would you put ''Bankrupt,'' particularly the act during the whole of which Dalmatov and Mikhailov carry on a conversation about book-keeping, and nothing else, and do this successfully? I think that when a good actor plays a closet-drama, the play becomes one that can be performed. (153)

EMOTION

The following statements are concerned with the representation of emotion, either by description or by enactment (for the arousal *of emotion,* see *AFFECT).*

4th cent. B.C. Aristotle. *See* under IDENTIFICATION (AP 61-63), IMITATION (APO 1340a: 11-25), RECOGNITION (AP 41-43, 57-61), TRAGEDY (AP 23-25).

c.20 B.C. Horace. *See* under DECORUM (HAP 459-61).

1682 Dryden. *See* under STYLE (DW 2: 329).

1711 Dryden. *See* under MORALITY (DW 1, 2: 309-10).

1725 Voltaire. *See* under LANGUAGE (VE 277-78), SUBJECT (VE 278-79).

1731 Volatire. *See* under DRAMA (VE 283), SUBJECT (VE 284).

c.1749 Voltaire. *See* under COMEDY (VW 10,1: 280).

1755-1780 Diderot   **DDE**
To keep passion in check within us, it is not a matter of making us see that it is fatal to others, but of making us see that it is fatal to ourselves. . . . Of all the active passions love is the most theatrical, the most interesting, the most fruitful in producing touching scenes, the most useful in showing its dreadful excesses. (291)
    See also Diderot under CHARACTER (DDE 291), TRAGEDY (DDE 291).

1758 Diderot. *See* under STYLE (DDP 288).

1765 Johnson. *See* under UNIVERSALITY (JS 11-12).

1766 Lessing. *See* under TRAGEDY (LSPW 31).

1767-1769 Lessing. *See* under IMITATION (LSPW 399), LANGUAGE (LSPW 393-94).

1778   Diderot. *See* under ILLUSION (DPA 14-15,16-17,22, 74).

1816   Hazlitt. *See* under SUBJECT (HW 1: 75-76).

1817   Hazlitt   **HW**

The greatest strength of genius is shewn in describing the strongest passions: for the power of the imagination, in works of invention, must be in proportion to the force of the natural impressions, which are the subject of them. (1: 271) It has been said, and we think justly, that the third act of *Othello* and the first three first acts of *Lear*, are Shakespear's great masterpieces in the logic of passion: that they contain the highest examples not only of the force of individual passion, but of its dramatic vicissitudes and striking effects arising from the different circumstances and characters of the persons speaking. We see the ebb and flow of the feeling, its pauses and feverish starts, its impatience of opposition, its accumulating force when it has time to recollect itself, the manner in which it avails itself of every passing word or gesture, its haste to repel insinuation, the alternate contraction and dilatation of the soul, and all ''the dazzling fence of controversy'' in this mortal combat with poisoned weapons, aimed at the heart, where each wound is fatal. (1: 259)

c.1820   Hegel. *See* under ACTION (HFA 4: 253-54), DRAMA (HFA 4: 249-50, 254-55, 261-62, 278-80), PATHOS (HFA 4: 268-69).

1827   Goethe. *See* under CATHARSIS (GLE 105).

1864   Taine. *See* under ACTION (TLA 318-19), IDENTIFICATION (TLA 101).

1875   Nietzsche. *See* under POETRY OF THE THEATRE (NTS 177-78).

1881   Nietzsche. *See* under MORALITY (NDD 237-38).

c.1900   Strindberg. *See* under PLOT (SEP 574-75).

1919   Eliot. *See* under CHARACTER (EEE 79), OBJECTIVE CORRELA-TIVE (EEE 61), STYLE (ESE 29).

1926   Brecht   **BBT**

I aim at an extremely classical, cold, highly intellectual style of performance. I'm not writing for the scum who want to have the cockles of their hearts warmed. (14)

1926 Eliot. *See* under STYLE (EEE 167).

c.1930 Stanislavski. *See* under ACTION (SCR 48), MOTIVATION (SCR 51,55), SUBTEXT (SCR 51, 52,77-79).

1933 Stanislavski. *See* under IDEALISM (SL 134).

1936 Stanislavski **SAP**

What is more important than the actions themselves is their truth and our belief in them. The reason is: Wherever you have truth and belief, you have feeling and experience. You can test this by executing even the smallest act in which you really believe and you will find that instantly, intuitively and naturally, an emotion will arise. (139)

    See also Stanislavski under IMITATION (SAP 163).

1936 Brecht. *See* under ALIENATION (BBB 131-36).

1938 Stanislavski. *See* under AFFECT (SAP 70), THOUGHT (SBC 169-71).

1940 Brecht. *See* under GEST (BBAn 18).

c.1944 Brecht **BBT**

The epic theatre isn't against the emotions; it tries to examine them, and is not satisfied just to stimulate them. It is the orthodox theatre which sins by dividing reason and emotion, in that it virtually rules out the former. As soon as one makes the slightest move to introduce a modicum of reason into theatrical practice its protagonists scream that one is trying to abolish the emotions. (162-63)

c.1952 Brecht **BBT**

Emotions[:] Aiming to avoid artificial heat, we [of the Berliner Ensemble] fall short in natural warmth. We make no attempt to share the emotions of the characters we portray, but these emotions must none the less be fully and movingly represented, nor must they be treated with coldness but likewise with an emotion of some force. . . . If actors in other theatres overplay the moods and outbursts of their characters that does not allow us to underplay them; nor may we overplay the story, which they are apt to underplay. (248-49)

EPIC THEATRE

Brecht's idea for a new drama was not entirely without precedent, nor did it remain a static or unexamined concept in his mind. The notion evolved throughout his career, and his writings just before his death suggest that he saw Epic Theater as a step toward the development of something further, which he calls "dialectical theater."
    See also *ALIENATION, GEST*.

1797   Goethe. Compare with IMITATION (GED 338), SUBJECT (GED 338).

c.1810   Coleridge. *See* under UNITY (CLSW 17).

1926   Brecht   **BBT**

[B.B.] I don't let my feelings intrude in my dramatic work. It'd give a false view of the world. I aim at an extremely classical, cold, highly intellectual style of performance. I'm not writing for the scum who want to have the cockles of their hearts warmed.

Q. Who do you write for?

[B.B.] For the sort of people who just come for fun and don't hesitate to keep their hats on in the theatre.

Q. But most spectators want their hearts to flow over. . . .

[B.B.] The one tribute we can pay the audience is to treat it as thoroughly intelligent. It is utterly wrong to treat people as simpletons when they are grown up at seventeen. I appeal to the reason.

Q. But the intellectual mastery of the material is just what I sometimes feel to be lacking with you. You don't make the incidents clear.

[B.B.] I give the incidents boldly so that the audience can think for itself. That's why I need a quick-witted audience that knows how to observe, and gets its enjoyment from setting its reason to work. . . .

Q. But sometimes it can confuse the audience. They lose the thread of the material.

[B.B.] If so then it's the fault of the modern theatre, which takes anything that would repay analysis and plays it for its mystic meaning. . . . Proper plays can only be understood when performed. But we've got to get away from the prevailing muzziness. . . . I'm for epic theatre! The production has got to bring out the material incidents in a perfectly sober and matter-of-fact way. Nowadays the play's meaning is usually

blurred by the fact that the actor plays to the audience's hearts. The figures portrayed are foisted on the audience and are falsified in the process. Contrary to present custom they ought to be presented quite coldly, classically and objectively. For they are not a matter for empathy; they are there to be understood. Feelings are private and limited. Against that reason is fairly comprehensive and to be relied on. (14-15)
See also Brecht under EMOTION (BBT 14).

1930   Brecht. *See* under AESTHETIC (BBT 40-41).

1931   Brecht. *See* under CHARACTER (BBT 56).

1935   Brecht. *See* under CATHARSIS (BBT 87), DISTANCE (BBT 86), IDENTIFICATION (BBT 87).

c. 1936   Brecht   **BBA**

The expression "epic theatre" seemed self-contradictory to many people, since according to the teachings of Aristotle the epic and the dramatic forms of presenting a story were considered basically different from one another. The difference between the two forms was by no means merely in the fact that one was performed by living people while others made use of a book—epic works, like those of Homer and *minnesingers* of the Middle Ages, were likewise theatrical performances, and dramas like Goethe's *Faust* or Byron's *Manfred* admittedly achieved their greatest effect as books. Aristotle's teachings themselves distinguished the dramatic from the epic form as a difference in construction, whose laws were dealt with under two different branches of aesthetics. The construction depended [on the] way in which the works were presented to the public, either on the stage or through a book, but nevertheless, apart from that, "the dramatic" could also be found in epic works and "the epic" in dramatic works. The bourgeois novel in the last century considerably developed "the dramatic," which meant the strong centralization of plot and an organic interdependence of the separate parts. The dramatic is characterized by a certain passion in the tone of the exposition and a working out of the collision of forces. . . . The epic, in contrast to the dramatic, could practically be cut up with a scissors into single pieces, each of which could stand alone. . . . Technical achievements enabled the stage to include narrative elements in dramatic presentations. The potentialities of projection, the film, the greater facility in changing sets through machinery, completed the equipment of the stage and did so at a moment when the most important human events could no longer be so simply portrayed as through personification of the driving forces or through subordinating the characters to invisible, metaphysical powers. . . . The stage began to narrate. The narrator no longer vanished with the fourth wall. Not only did the [environment] make its own comment on stage happenings through large screens . . . ; the actors no longer threw themselves completely into their roles but maintained a certain distance from the character performed by them, even distinctly inviting criticism. (18-19)

Dramatic Form	*Epic Form*
The stage "incarnates" an event.	It relates it.
Involves the audience in an action, uses up its activity.	Makes the audience an observer, but assures its activity.
Helps it to feel.	Compels it to make decisions.
Communicates experiences.	Communicates insights.
The audience is projected into an event.	Is confronted with it.
Suggestion is used.	Arguments are used.
Sensations are preserved.	Impelled to level of perceptions.
The character is a known quantity.	The character is subjected to investigation.
Man unchangeable.	Man who can change and make changes.
His drives.	His motives.
Events move in a straight line.	In "irregular" curves.
Natura non facit saltus.	Facit saltus.
The world as it is.	The world as it is becoming.

The audience in the dramatic theatre says:

Yes, I have felt that too.—That's how I am.—That is only natural.—That will always be so.—This person's suffering shocks me because he has no way out.—This is great art: everything in it is self-evident.—I weep with the weeping, I laugh with the laughing.

The audience in the epic theatre says:

I wouldn't have thought that.—People shouldn't do things like that.—That's extremely odd, almost unbelievable.—This has to stop.—This person's suffering shocks me, because there might be a way out for him.—This is great art: nothing in it is self-evident.—I laugh over the weeping, I weep over the laughing. (20-21)

See also Brecht under STYLE (BBB 132).

c.1944   Brecht. See under EMOTION (BBT 162-63).

1948   Brecht. See under AESTHETIC (BBBG 13-14), CHARACTER (BBBG 25, 30), DRAMA (BBBG 13, 14, 19-20, 24), IDENTIFICATION (BBBG 17, 25, 28, 30), ILLUSION (BBBG 28-29), PLOT (BBBG 17, 35,36), STYLE (BBBG 23,39-40), SUBJECT (BBBG 21), UNIVERSALITY (BBBG 30).

c.1956   Brecht   **BBT**

(a) If we now discard the concept of EPIC THEATRE we are not discarding that progress towards conscious experience which it still makes possible. It is just that the concept is too slight and too vague for the kind of theatre intended; it needs exacter definition and must achieve more. Besides, it was too inflexibly opposed to the concept of the dramatic, often just taking it naively for granted, roughly in the sense that ''of course'' it always embraces incidents that take place directly with all or most of the hallmarks of immediacy. In the same slightly hazardous way we always take it for granted that whatever its novelty it is still theatre, and does not turn into a scientific demonstration. (b) Nor is the concept THEATRE OF THE SCIENTIFIC AGE quite broad enough. The Short Organum may give an adequate explanation of what is meant by a scientific age, but the bare expression, in the form in which it is normally used, is too discredited. (276) . . . An effort is now being made to move from the epic theatre to the dialectical theatre. In our view and according to our intention the epic theatre's practice—and the whole idea—were by no means undialectical. Nor would a dialectical theatre succeed without the epic element. All the same we envisage a sizeable transformation. (281)

See also Brecht under PLOT (BBT 240-41).

EVOLUTIONISM

Acknowledged or unacknowledged, whether modeled on the life of an individual organism or on the history of a living species, the evolutionary premise has had considerable influence on the theories of many thinkers. Essentially, it is a metahistorical view that suggests some form of determinism linking otherwise independent events to produce a pattern analogous to a natural life cycle.

4th cent. B.C.   Aristotle   AP

Whether Tragedy *has as yet perfected its proper types* or not; and whether it is to be judged [both: EP 149] in itself, *or* [and: EP 149] in relation also to the audience,—this raises another question. Be that as it may, Tragedy—as also Comedy—was at first mere improvisation. The one originated with *the authors of* the Dithyramb, the other with those of the phallic songs. . . . Tragedy advanced by slow degrees; each new element that showed itself was in turn developed. Having passed through many changes, it found its *natural form* [inherent nature: EP 149] and there it stopped. . . . Once dialogue had come, *Nature herself* [the very nature of the genre: EP 164] discovered the appropriate [meter]. (17-19)
      See also Aristotle under AESTHETIC (APA 17).

1808   Schlegel. *See* under GENRE (SCL 46-47), LANGUAGE (SCL 366).

c.1810   Coleridge. *See* under DRAMA (CLSW 116), UNITY (CLSW 117).

1814   Hazlitt   HW

It is often made a subject of complaint and surprise, that the arts in this country, and in modern times, have not kept pace with the general progress of society and civilisation in other respects, and it has been proposed to remedy the deficiency by more carefully availing ourselves of the advantages which time and circumstances have placed within our reach, but which we have hitherto neglected, the study of the antique, the formation of academies, and the distribution of prizes. First, the complaint itself, that the arts do not attain the progressive degree of perfection which might reasonably be expected from them, proceeds on a false notion, for the analogy appealed to in support of the regular advances of art to higher degrees of excellence totally fails; it applies to science, not to art. Secondly, the expedients proposed to remedy the evil by adventitious means are only calculated to confirm it. The arts hold immediate communication with nature, and are only derived from that source. When that original impulse no longer exists, when the inspiration of genius is fled, all the attempts to recall it are no better than the tricks of galvanism to restore the dead to life. . . . Nothing is more contrary to the fact than the supposition that in what we understand by the *fine arts*, as painting and poetry, relative perfection is only the result of repeated efforts, and that what has been once well done constantly leads to something better. What is mechanical, reducible to rule, or capable of demonstration, is progressive, and admits of gradual improvement: what is not mechanical or definite, but depends on genius, taste, and feeling, very soon becomes stationary or retrogade, and loses more than it gains by transfusion. . . . The greatest poets, the ablest orators, the best painters, and the finest sculptors that the world ever saw, appeared soon after the birth of these arts, and lived in a state of society which was, in other respects, comparatively barbarous. Those arts, which depend on individual genius and incommunicable power, have always leaped at once from infancy to manhood, from the first rude dawn of invention to their meridian height and dazzling lustre, and have in general declined ever after. This is the peculiar distinction and privilege of each, of science and of art; of the one, never to attain its utmost summit of perfection, and of the other, to arrive at it almost at once. (1: 160-61)

1815   Hazlitt. *See* under TRAGEDY (HW 1: 13).

c.1820   Hegel. *See* under DRAMA (HFA 4: 251).

1863-1867   Taine   **THEL**

Given a literature, philosophy, society, art, group of arts, what is the moral condition which produced it? What [are] the conditions of race, epoch, circumstance, the most fitted to produce this moral condition? There is a distinct moral condition for each of these formations, and for each of their branches; one for art in general, one for each kind of art—for architecture, painting, sculpture, music, poetry; each has its special germs in the wide field of human psychology; each had its law, and it is by virtue of this law that we see it raised, by chance, as it seems wholly alone, amid the miscarriage of its neighbours, like painting in Flanders and Holland in the seventeenth century, poetry in England in the sixteenth, music in Germany in the eighteenth. At this moment, and in these countries, the conditions have been fulfilled for one art, not for others, and a single branch has budded in the general barrenness. (18-19)
    See also Taine under AESTHETIC (THEL 1, 18).

1864   Taine   **TLA**

At highly cultivated and very refined epochs, in nations somewhat decrepit, . . . in Greece, in the saloons of Louis XIV, and in our own, appear the lowest and the truest types, a comic and realistic literature. At mature epochs, when society is at its full development, when man stands midway in some grand career, in Greece in the fifth century (B.C.), in Spain and in England at the end of the sixteenth, in France in the seventeenth century and to-day, appear the robust and enduring types, a dramatic and philosophic literature. In the intermediary epochs, which are on the one side a maturity and on the other a decline . . . [,] the two ages commingle through a reciprocal encroachment, and each of them engenders the creations of the other, together with its own. But creations truly ideal are fertile only in primitive and simple epochs; and it is always at remote ages, at the origin of peoples, amidst the dreams of human infancy, that we must ascend in order to find heroes and gods. (283-84)

See also Taine under AESTHETIC (TLA 36), GENRE (TLA 104).

1888   Nietzsche. Compare with WILL (NW 138-40).

c.1900   Shaw. *See* under TRAGEDY (SS 253).

EXPOSITION

*Traditionally a special challenge to the general principle of DRAMATIZA-
TION has been the need to provide story information, especially the "givens"
of a situation from which a drama may proceed. The discussions included here
are concerned with what is to be provided, by what means, and to what
purpose.*

4th cent. B.C.   Aristotle   AR

In drama and in epos, the introduction is an indication of the subject, in order
that the hearers may know it beforehand, and that their thoughts may not be in
suspense;—for the indefinite bewilders;—so that he who puts the opening (as
it were) into the hand of the listener, makes it immediately easy for him to
follow the story. . . . In the same way the tragic poets explain the action; if not
directly, as Euripides does, at all events somewhere in a prologue: as
Sophokles—
    "My father was Polybos. . . ."
And so in Comedy. This, then, is the essential and proper task of the proem,—
to explain the object of the work. (182)
    See also Aristotle under THOUGHT (AP 69-71).

c.1583   Sidney. *See* under THREE UNITIES (SDP 49).

1657   d'Aubignac   AAS

Narrations which happen in a Drammatick Poem, do generally regard two sorts
of things; either those which have happened before the opening of the Stage,
wheresoever they came to pass; nay, though it be long before; or else they
regard those things which happen off of the Scene in the Contexture of the
Theatrical action, after once the Stage is open, and within the Extent of time
that it requires. As to the first sort which are brought into the body of the Poem,
for the better understanding of things which happened before the opening of
the Stage, they may regularly be us'd in the beginning of the Play, that they
may give a Foundation to the whole Action, and prepare the Incidents, and by
that means facilitate to the spectator the understanding of all the rest; or else
they may be made use of toward the end of the Poem, and serve to the
Catastophe, or the untying and opening of all the Plot. . . . As for those things
which happen in the course of the Action, the recital of them is to be made as
they happen; or if it be thought necessary, or more pleasing to delay them,

there must be us'd some Art to feed the Spectators desire of knowing them without impatience. . . . We must remember besides, that these Recitals or Narrations are introduced only to instruct the Spectator about what passes off the Scene; for to relate either those things that have been seen, or might have been seen, as being suppos'd to have been done upon the Stage, would certainly be very ridiculous; and besides, those things that give ground to these Incident Narrations, ought to be very considerable, or else they are to be avoided, and the thing to be insinuated into the Audience by some words scattered here and there either before or after. (3: 15-16)

   See also d'Aubignac under MOTIVATION (AAS 1: 39).

1660   Corneille   CFD

[The] first act was called the prologue in Aristotle's time and ordinarily one made it the opening of the subject, to instruct the listener in all that happened before the beginning of the action, and in all that he would have to know in order to understand what he was going to see. [Euripides boldly exposes information at the beginning with a god or a principal character in soliloquy.] I do not mean to say that when an actor speaks he cannot inform the listener about many things but he must do so through the passion which moves him, and not through a simple narration. . . . The *poet* especially must remember that when an actor is alone in the theater it is taken for granted that he is thinking to himself, and speaks but to let the listener know what he thinks. Therefore it would be an unforgivable error if another actor should by this means learn his secret. (147)

   See also Corneille under UNITY (CFD 147).

1765   Johnson   JS

Narration in dramatick poetry is naturally tedious, as it is unanimated and inactive, and obstructs the progress of the action; it should therefore always be rapid, and enlivened by frequent interruption. (22)

1767-1769   Lessing   LSPW

The advantage possessed by native customs in comedy rests on the intimate acquaintance we have with them. The poet does not first need to acquaint us with them; he is therefore relieved from all requisite descriptions and hints, he can at once let his personages act in accordance with their customs without first having tediously to describe these customs. Native customs therefore facilitate his labour and enhance the illusion of the spectator. . . . The tragic poet . . . too has reason to facilitate his labour as much as may be, and not to squander his strength on side issues but to husband it for the main object. For him too all depends on the illusion of the spectator. It may be replied that tragedy does not greatly need customs, that it can completely dispense with them. But in that case it does not need foreign customs, and of the little it desires to have and to show of customs, it will still be better if these are taken from native customs rather than from foreign ones. (484-85)

See also Lessing under SURPRISE (LSPW 380-82).

1797   Goethe. See under PLOT (GED 338).

1808   Schlegel   SCL

The expositions or statements of the preliminary situation of things . . . [in French drama] generally consist of choicely turned disclosures to the confidants, delivered in a happy moment of leisure. That very [French] public whose [alleged] impatience keeps the poets and players under such strict discipline, has, however, patience enough to listen to the prolix unfolding of what ought to be sensibly developed before their eyes. . . . To me it seems that their whole system of expositions, both in Tragedy and in High Comedy, is exceedingly erroneous. Nothing could be more ill-judged than to begin at once to instruct us without any dramatic movement. At the first drawing up of the curtain the spectator's . . . interest has not yet been excited; and this is precisely the time chosen by the poet to exact from him an earnest of undivided attention to a dry explanation,—a demand which he can hardly be supposed ready to meet. . . . How admirable . . . are the expositions of Shakespeare and Calderon! At the very outset they lay hold of the imagination; and when they have once gained the spectator's interest and sympathy they then bring forward the information necessary for the full understanding of the implied transactions. (272-73)

See also Schlegel under DRAMA (SCL 30-32).

1825   Goethe. See under THREE UNITIES (GCE Feb. 24).

1871   Nietzsche   NBT

The Euripidean *prologue* [is an example of his] rationalistic method. Nothing could be more opposed to the technique of our stage than the prologue in the drama of Euripides. For a single person to appear at the outset of the play telling us who is, what precedes the action, what has happened thus far, yea, what will happen in the course of the play, would be designated by a modern playwright as a wanton and unpardonable abandonment of the effect of suspense. Everything that is about to happen is known beforehand; who then cares to wait for it actually to happen? . . . The effect of tragedy never depended on epic suspense . . . but rather on the great rhetero-lyric scenes in which the passion and dialectics of the chief hero swelled to a broad and mighty stream. Everything was arranged for pathos, not for action. . . . But . . . so long as the spectator has to divine the meaning of this or that . . . his complete absorption in the doings and sufferings of the chief persons is impossible, as is likewise breathless fellow-feeling and fellow-fearing. The Aeschyleo-Sophoclean tragedy employed the most ingenious devices in the first scene to place in the hands of the spectator as if by chance all the threads requisite for understanding the whole: a trait in which that noble artistry is approved, which as it were masks the *inevitably* formal, and causes it to appear as something accidental. But nevertheless Euripides . . . placed the prologue even before the exposition, [so that the poetic beauties and pathos of the exposition would not be lost to the spectator,] and put it in the mouth of a person who could be trusted; some deity . . . to guarantee the particulars of the tragedy to the public. . . . (98-100)

1909   Shaw. *See* under GENRE DEFINITION (STPB xx, xxii-xxiii).

FEAR

Of the special affective theories, those concerned with the evocation of a response of fear or dread from the spectator are among the earliest. In general, these theories suggest an interconnection of effect and structure in drama; because fear is anticipatory it invests the spectator's emotional force in a play's futurity. See also AFFECT, FORWARD MOVEMENT; compare with PITY.

4th cent. B.C.   Aristotle   AP·

Fear [is aroused] by the misfortune of a man like ourselves. (45)

4th cent. B.C.   Aristotle   AR

Fear may be defined as a pain or trouble arising from an image of coming evil, destructive or painful; for men do not fear *all* evils,—as, for instance, the prospect of being unjust or slow; but only such evils as mean great pains or losses, and these, when they seem, not distant, but close and imminent. We do not fear very distant things; thus, all men know that they will die, but because it is not near, they do not care. If, then, fear is this, such things must be fearful as appear to have a great power of destroying, or of doing harms which tend to great pain. Hence the signs, too, of such things are fearful, since the dreaded thing seems near; for this is danger, the approach of something dreaded. (81) . . . Now, if fear is attended by an expectation of some destructive suffering, it is plain that no one fears unless he thinks that something will happen to him; nor does he fear things, which he does not think will happen, or persons, at whose hand he does not expect them, or at times when he does not expect them. It follows, then, that those who fear are those who expect to suffer something—and this from certain persons and in a certain form and at a certain time. (82).

   See also Aristotle under ACTION (AP 37-39, 45) CATHARSIS (APO 1341b: 36-1342a: 29), ILLUSION (AA 123), PITY (AR 91), POETIC JUSTICE (AP 48-49), TRAGEDY (AP 23-25)

1570   Castelvetro. *See* under HERO (CP 110-11), TRAGEDY (CP 98).

1660   Corneille. *See* under CATHARSIS (CDT 816, CDENA 3).

1711   Dryden. *See* under PITY (DW 1, 2: 307).

1712   Addison. *See* under DISTANCE (AW 2: 149).

1758   Diderot. *See* under TRAGEDY (DDP 296, 297).

1767-1769   Lessing   **LSPW**

[Commenting on translations of Aristotle's *Poetics* that use the word ''terror'' instead of ''fear'':] The word which Aristotle uses meant fear; fear and pity, he says, should be evoked by tragedy, not pity and terror. It is true that terror is a species of fear, it is a sudden overwhelming fear. But this very suddenness, this surprise which is included in the idea of terror, plainly proves that those who here substituted the word terror for fear, did not comprehend at all what kind of fear Aristotle meant. (404) . . . [Aristotle's] fear is by no means the fear excited in us by misfortune threatening another person. It is the fear which arises for ourselves from the similarity of position with that of the sufferer; it is the fear that the calamities pending over the sufferers might also befall ourselves; it the fear that we ourselves might thus become objects of pity. In a word this fear is compassion referred back to ourselves. (407)

   See also Lessing under AFFECT (LSPW 419), DRAMA (LSPW 426), PITY (LSPW 409, 412), SURPRISE (LSPW 380-82).

1827   Goethe   **GCE**

Sat., July 21. ''Fear may be of two sorts; it may exist in the shape of alarm [*Angst*], or in that of uneasiness [*Bangigkeit*]. The latter feeling is awakened when we see a moral evil threatening, and gradually overshadowing, the personages . . . ; but alarm is awakened, in reader or in spectator, when the personages are threatened with physical danger. . . . The feeling of alarm is necessarily of a material character, and will be excited in every reader; but that of admiration is excited by a recognition of the writer's skill, and only the connoisseur will be blessed with this feeling.

1888   Nietzsche. *See* under CATHARSIS (NW 185-86).

FLAW

The notion of the "tragic flaw" is still sometimes debated. This category contains statements most directly relevant to that issue.

4th cent. B.C. Aristotle   AP

[The tragic protagonist must be] a man who is not eminently good and just, yet whose misfortune is brought about not by vice or depravity, but by some error or frailty. (45)

4th cent. B.C. Aristotle   ANE

If a man does an injury of set purpose, he is guilty of injustice, and injustice of the sort that renders the doer an unjust man. . . . Similarly one who acts justly on purpose is a just man; but he acts justly only if he acts voluntarily. Of involuntary actions some are pardonable and some are not. Errors not merely committed in ignorance, but caused by ignorance are pardonable; those committed in ignorance, but caused not by that ignorance but by unnatural or inhuman passion, are unpardonable. (303-305, 1136a: 1-11)

4th Cent. B.C. Aristotle   AR

Those acts are equitable, which are to be excused. It is equitable not to take the same account of mistakes, of wrongs, and of misfortunes: misfortunes being things which could not be reckoned upon, and which do not result from vice; mistakes, things which might have been reckoned upon, but which do not result from vice; wrongs, things which were reckoned upon, and which resulted from vice. It is equitable to excuse human failings. (58-59)

    See also Aristotle under HERO (AP 45-47).

1660 Corneille. *See* under CATHARSIS (CDT 816).

1668 Racine   RP

[Some] would have us recast all the heroes of antiquity and make them paragons of perfection. I think their intention . . . admirable, but I beg them to remember that it is not for me to change the laws of the drama. Horace tells us to describe Achilles as ferocious, inexorable, violent—as he actually was. And Aristotle, far from asking us to portray perfect heroes, demands on the contrary that tragic characters—whose misfortunes bring the tragic catastrophe —should be neither wholly good nor wholly bad. He does not want them to be extremely good, because the punishment of a good man would excite indignation rather than pity in the audience. . . . They must therefore . . . fall into misfortune through some fault which allows us to pity without detesting them. (154-55)

1695   Dryden   DW

As [the] idea of perfection is of little use in portraits, or the resemblances of particular persons, so neither is it in the characters of comedy and tragedy, which are never to be made perfect, but always to be drawn with some specks of frailty and deficience; such as they have been described to us in history, if they were real characters, or such as the poet began to shew them at their first appearance, if they were only fictitious or imaginary. The perfection of such stage-characters consists chiefly in their likeness to the deficient faulty nature, which is their original: only . . . in such cases there will always be found a better likeness and a worse, and the better is constantly to be chosen; I mean in tragedy, which represents the figures of the highest form amongst mankind. (3: 307)

See also Dryden under IDENTIFICATION (DW 3: 308)

1731   Voltaire. *See* under SUBJECT (VE 284).

1755-1780   Diderot. *See* under MOTIVATION (DDE 290).

1871   Nietzsche. Compare with HERO (NBT 73-74).

FORM

The discussions presented under this heading concern the general structure or shape of drama, whether this is produced by external requirements or internal forces. Generally, these concepts are premised either on a natural order which the structure reflects—natural to human experience, or to the intuitive genius of the artist, or to a genre, or to an internal logic—or on an expressive function of form that is the deliberate creation of the structure of the work. See also PLOT as the means for producing that structure.

4th cent. B.C.   Aristotle   **AP**

According to our definition, Tragedy is an imitation of an action that is complete, and whole and of a certain magnitude; for there may be a whole that is wanting in magnitude. A whole is that which has a beginning, a middle, and an end. A beginning is that which does not itself follow anything by causal necessity, but after which something naturally is or comes to be. An end, on the contrary, is that which itself naturally follows some other thing, either by necessity, or as a rule, but has nothing following it. A middle is that which follows something as some other thing follows it. A well constructed plot, therefore, must neither begin nor end as *haphazard* [an accidental point: EP 282], but conform to these principles. Again, a beautiful object, whether it be a living organism or any whole composed of parts, must not only have an orderly arrangement of parts, but must also be of a *certain magnitude* [size which is not accidental: EP 283]; for beauty depends on *magnitude and order* [size and arrangement: EP 283]. Hence a very small . . . organism cannot be beautiful. . . . Nor . . . can one of vast size . . . ; for as the eye cannot take it all in at once, the unity and sense of the whole is lost for the spectator. . . . So in the plot, a certain length is necessary, and a length which can be easily embraced by the memory. The *limit* [norm: EP 286] of length in relation to dramatic competition and sensuous presentment is not part of artistic theory. . . . But the *limit* [norm: EP 286] as fixed by the nature of the drama itself is this:—the greater the *length* [magnitude: EP 286], the more beautiful will the piece be by reason of its size, provided that the whole be perspicuous. And to define the matter roughly, we may say that the proper magnitude is comprised within such limits, that the sequence of events according to the law of probability or necessity, will admit of a change from bad fortune to good, or from good fortune to bad. (31-33) . . . [Like tragedy, epic ought] to be constructed on dramatic principles. It should have for its subject a single action, whole and complete, with a beginning, middle and an end. It will thus resemble a living organism in all its unity, and produce the pleasure proper to it. (89)

4th cent. B.C.   Aristotle   AM

"A whole" means (1) that from which is absent none of the parts of which it is said to be naturally a whole, and (2) that which so contains the things it contains that they form a unity; and this in two senses—either as being each severally one single thing, or as making up the unity between them. (1023b: 26-31) . . . Of quanta that have a beginning and a middle and an end, those to which the position does not make a difference are called totals, and those to which it does, wholes. (1024a: 1-4)

4th cent. B.C.   Aristotle   APA

Everything that Nature makes is means to an end. For just as human creations are the products of art, so living objects are manifestly the products of an analogous cause or principle, not external but internal. . . . Order and arrangement and constancy are much more plainly manifest in the celestial bodies than in our own frame; while change and chance are characteristic of the perishable things of earth. Yet there are those who . . . hold that the heaven was constructed to be what it is by chance and spontaneity; the heaven, in which not the faintest sign of haphazard or of disorder is discernible! (8)

    See also Aristotle under ORDER (AM 1076a:1, 1090b: 20), UNITY (AP 33-35).

1570   Castelvetro. *See* under FUNCTIONALISM (CP 68).

1660   Corneille. *See* under ACTION (CDTU 235).

1711   Dryden   DW

The meaning [or order] is, that a fable ought to have a beginning, middle, and an end, all just and natural; so that that part, e.g., which is the middle, could not naturally be the beginning or end, and so of the rest; all depend on one another, like the links of a curious chain. (1, 2: 303)

1712   Addison   AW

When I read an author of genius who writes without method, I fancy myself in a wood that abounds with a great many noble objects, rising one among another in the greatest confusion and disorder. When I read a methodological discourse, I am in a regular plantation, and can place myself in its several centres, so as to take a view of all the lines and walks that are struck from them. You may ramble in the one a whole day together, and every moment discover something or other that is new to you; but when you have done, you will have but a confused, imperfect notion of the place: in the other your eye commands the whole prospect, and gives you an idea of it as is not easily worn out of the memory. Irregularity and want of method are only supportable in men of great learning or genius, who are often too full to be exact, and therefore choose to throw down their pearls in heaps before the reader, rather than be at the pains of stringing them. Method is of advantage to a work, both in respect to the writer and the reader. In regard to the first, it is a great help to his invention. . . . His thoughts are . . . more intelligible, and better discover their drift and meaning, when they are placed in their proper lights, and follow one another in a regular series, than when they are thrown together without order and connexion. There is always an obscurity in confusion; and the same sentence that would have enlightened the reader in one part of the discourse, perplexes him in another. For the same reason, likewise, every thought in a methodological discourse shows itself in its greatest beauty, as the several figures in a piece of painting receive new grace from their disposition in the picture. The advantages of a reader from a methodological discourse are correspondent with those of the writer. He comprehends everything easily, takes it in with pleasure, and retains it long. (2: 227)

See also Addison under AESTHETIC (AW 2: 139-40, 142); compare with IMAGINATION (AW 2: 138-39, 140).

1765　Johnson　　　　　　　　　　　　　　　　　　　　　**JS**

[Shakespeare] has well enough preserved the unity of action. . . . His plan has commonly what *Aristotle* requires, a beginning, a middle, and an end; one event is concatenated with another, and the conclusion follows by easy consequence. . . . The general system makes gradual advances, and the end of the play is the end of expectation. (24-25)

1789　Goethe. *See* under IMITATION (GLE 59-61).

1808　Schlegel　　　　　　　　　　　　　　　　　　　　　**SCL**

In Grecian art and poetry we find an original and unconscious unity of form and matter; in the modern, so far as it has remained true to its own spirit, we observe a keen struggle to unite the two, as being naturally in opposition to each other. (27) . . . We must understand the exact meaning of the term form, since most critics, and more especially those who insist on a stiff regularity, interpret it merely in a mechanical, and not in an organical sense. Form is mechanical when, through external force, it is imported to any material merely as an accidental addition without reference to its quality; as for example, when we give a particular shape to a soft mass that it may retain the same after its induration. Organical form, again, is innate; it unfolds itself from within, and acquires its determination contemporaneously with the perfect development of the germ. . . . In the fine arts, as well as in the domain of nature—the supreme artist—, all genuine forms are organical, that is determined by the quality of the work. In a word, the form is nothing but a significant exterior, the speaking physiognomy of each thing, which, as long as it is not disfigured by a destructive accident, gives a true evidence of its hidden essence. (340) . . . It was . . . the prevailing tendency of the time which preceded our own, . . . to consider everything having life as a mere accumulation of dead parts, to separate what exists only in connexion and cannot otherwise be conceived, instead of penetrating to the central point and viewing all the parts as so many irradiations from it. Hence nothing is so rare as a critic who can elevate himself to the comprehensive contemplation of a work of art. (360)

    See also Schlegel under CHARACTER (SCL 148-49), COMEDY (SCL 149-51), GENRE (SCL 46-47), GENRE DEFINITION (SCL 176-79), POETRY OF THE THEATRE (SCL 36-37), UNITY (SCL 242-45).

1811-1812   Coleridge. *See* under PLEASURE (CCSL 17).

1815   Coleridge   **CBL**

Poetry, even that of the loftiest and, seemingly, that of the wildest odes, had a logic of its own, as severe as that of science; and more difficult, because more subtle, more complex and dependent on more and more fugitive causes. In the truly great poets . . . there is a reason assignable, not only for every work, but for the position of every word. (1: 4)

    See also Coleridge under AESTHETIC (CBL 2: 233-34, 238-39, 256-57), ORDER (CBL 2: 262), UNITY (CBL 2: 11).

1815   Hazlitt. *See* under AESTHETIC (HW 2: 228).

1816   Hazlitt. *See* under AESTHETIC (HW 1: 68).

1818   Hazlitt. *See* under AESTHETIC (HW 5: 3).

c.1820   Hegel   **HFA**

We may divide the course of the dramatic work most naturally by simply following the stages implied in the notion of dramatic movement. . . . In this connection Aristotle long ago remarks that a whole is that which possesses a beginning, a middle, and a conclusion. . . . Now no doubt in the reality of our experience every action includes many presuppositions which makes it a difficult matter to decide the exact point where we may find the true commencement. Insofar, however, as dramatic action rests esssentially on a definitive state of collision, the right point of departure will lie in the situation, out of which the future devolution of that conflict, despite the fact that it has not yet broken out, will none the less in its further course issue. The end . . . will then be attained when the resolution of the discord and its development is secured in every possible respect. In the midway condition between origination and end we have the conflict of ends, and the struggle of individual persons in collision. These different sections are . . . the *acts* of the piece. . . . With regard to their number, three such acts for every kind of drama is the number that will adapt itself most readily to intelligible theory. (4: 262-63)

See also Hegel under PLOT (HFA 4: 264).

c.1820   Hazlitt. *See* under AESTHETIC (HW 2: 463).

1824   Hazlitt. *See* under IDEALISM (HW 9: 405).

1864   Taine   TLA

The artist, in modifying the relationships of parts, modifies them understandingly, purposely, in such a way as to make apparent the *essential character* of the object, and consequently its leading idea according to his conception of it (64) . . . [This essential character is what philosophers call the *essence* of things] which must be made as perceptible as possible. In order to accomplish this the artist must suppress whatever conceals it, select whatever manifests it, correct every detail by which it is enfeebled, and recast those in which it is neutralized. (73)

See also Taine under AESTHETIC (TLA 76, 76-77, 87), HERO (TLA 180), IMITATION (TLA 56-58).

1908   Strindberg   SOL

In drama we [of the intimate theatre] seek the strong, highly significant motif, but with limitations. We try to avoid in the treatment all frivolity, all calculated effects, places for applause, star roles, solo numbers. No predetermined form is to limit the author, because the motif determines the form. Consequently: [there is] freedom in treatment, which is limited only by the unity of the concept and the feeling for style. (19)

1908   Pirandello. *See* under HUMOR (POH 35), RULES (POH 29-30), STYLE (POH 36), THOUGHT (POH 30-31).

1919   Eliot. *See* under STYLE (ESE 29).

1921   Eliot   ESW

To create a form is not merely to invent a shape, a rhyme or rhythm. It is also the realization of the whole appropriate content of this rhyme or rhythm. (57)

1925   Pirandello   PPSC

The Mother [in *Six Characters*] declares . . . the particular value of artistic form—a form which does not delimit or destroy its own life and which life does not consume—in her cry to the Manager. If the Father and Step-Daughter began their scene a hundred thousand times in succession, always, at the appointed moment, at the instant when the life of the work of art must be expressed with that cry, it would always be heard, unaltered and unalterable in its form, not as a mechanical repetition, not as a return determined by external necessities, but on the contrary, alive every time and as new, suddenly born *thus forever*! embalmed alive in its incorruptible form. . . . All that lives, by the fact of living, has form, and by the same token must die except the work of art which lives forever in so far as it *is* form. (372)

1938   Stanislavski. *See* under THOUGHT (SBC 169-71), UNITY (SBC 61).

FORWARD MOVEMENT

This category is concerned with the "futurity" or progressiveness of drama: the use of tempo, foreshadowing, patterns, styles, or subject matters to create curiosity, hypothesis-formation, answer-seeking, purposiveness, expectation, suspense, and so on. For dread, see FEAR; for anticipation of formal qualities, see CLOSURE, FORM, GENRE, and ORDER. Compare with SURPRISE.

1609   **de Vega.** *See* under SURPRISE (VAWP 34).

1657   **d'Aubignac.** *See* under SUBJECT (AAS 2: 68-69), UNITY (AAS 2: 89).

1660   **Corneille.** *See* under ACTION (CDTU 235), SURPRISE (CSP 109).

1668   **Dryden.** *See* under UNITY (DW 2, 2: 86-87), VARIETY (DW 1, 2: 89).

1712   **Addison.** *See* under SURPRISE (AW 2: 312).

1758   **Diderot.** *See* under ACTION (DDP 291-2), COMPLICATION (DDP 291).

1765   **Johnson.** *See* under WONDER (JS 32-33).

1767-1769   **Lessing.** *See* under SURPRISE (LSPW 377-78, 380-82).

1797   **Goethe.** *See* under PLOT (GED 338).

1808   **Schlegel**   SCL

As he frequently rejected all the incidents which were generally known [in the myths, Euripides] was reduced to the necessity of explaining in a prologue the situation of things in his drama, and the course which they were to take. Lessing, in his *Dramaturgie*, has hazarded the singular opinion that it is a proof of an advance in the dramatic art, that Euripides should have trusted wholly to the effect of situations, without calculating on the excitement of curiosity. For my part I cannot see why, amidst the impressions which a dramatic poem produces, the uncertainty of expectation should not be allowed a legitimate place. The objection that a piece will only please in this respect for the first time, because on an acquaintance with it we know the result beforehand, must be easily answered: if the representation be truly energetic, it will always rivet the attention of the spectator in such a manner that he will forget what he already knew, and be again excited to the same stretch of expectation. (119)

See also Schlegel under ACTION (SCL 239-42), AFFECT (SCL 39), COMEDY (SCL 309-10), DRAMA (SCL 30-32), EXPOSITION (SCL 272-73), PLOT (SCL 181-82), UNITY (SCL 242-45).

1815   Coleridge   CBL

Philosophic critics of all ages coincide . . . in equally denying the praises of a just poem, on the one hand, to a series of striking lives or distichs, each of which, absorbing the whole attention of the reader to itself, becomes disjoined from its context, and forms a separate whole, instead of a harmonizing part; and, on the other hand, to an unsustained composition, from which the reader collects rapidly the general result unattracted by the component parts. The reader should be carried forward, not merely or chiefly by the mechanical impulse of curiosity, or by a restless desire to arrive at a final solution; but by a pleasurable activity of mind excited by the attractions of the journey itself. Like the motion of a serpent . . . at every step he pauses and half recedes, and from the retrogressive movement collects the force which again carries him onward. (2: 10-11)

See also Coleridge under NOVELTY (CBL 2: 262), UNITY (CBL 2: 10-11).

1818   Hazlitt   HW

It should seem that the argument which has been sometimes set up, that painting must affect the imagination more strongly, because it represents the image more distinctly, is not well founded. We may assume without much temerity, that poetry is more poetical than painting. . . . Painting gives the object itself; poetry what it implies. Painting embodies what a thing contains in itself: poetry suggests what exists out of it, in a manner connected with it. But this last is the proper province of the imagination. Again, as it relates to passion, painting gives the event, poetry the progress of events: but it is during the progress, in the interval of expectation and suspense, while our hopes and fears are strained to the highest pitch of breathless agony, that the pinch of the interest lies. (5: 10)

1819   Hazlitt. See under HUMOR (HW 8: 7-8).

c.1820   Hegel   HFA

The true dramatic progression is a *continuous* movement *onwards* to the final catastrophe. This is clear from the simple fact that it is in the *collision* that we find the emphatic turning point. In consequence of this we have the twofold view of, in the first place, a general strain towards the outbreak of this conflict, and, secondly, the necessity implied in this discord and contradiction of views, ends, and activities, that they should find some resolution to which they are driven forwards. By this we do not mean that mere celerity of forward movement is simply in itself beautiful in the dramatic sense. On the contrary, the dramatic poet should leave himself room to supply every situation on its own account with all the motives which it truly implies. Episodical scenes, however, which only impede the action, are contrary to the nature of the drama. (4: 262)

See also Hegel under ACTION (HFA 4: 253-54, 259-61), CHARACTER (HFA 4: 252, 273-75), DRAMA (HFA 4: 261-62), FORM (HFA 4: 262-63), PLOT (HFA 4: 264).

1826   Goethe. *See* under SYMBOL (GCE July 26).

1882   Nietzsche. *See* under AESTHETIC (NJW 334-35).

1894   Brunetière. *See* under WILL (BLD 73, 75).

c.1900   Strindberg. *See* under PLOT (SEP 574-75).

1918-1922   Stanislavski. *See* under AFFECT (SAS 226, 228).

c.1930   Stanislavski. *See* under CONFLICT (SCR 80), MOTIVATION (SCR 51, 55, 79), SUBTEXT (SCR 51, 77-79).

1936   Stanislavski   **SAP**

That inner line of effort that guides the actors from the beginning to the end of the play we call the *continuity* or the *through-going action*. This through line galvanizes all the small units and objectives of the play and directs them toward the super-objective. From then on they all serve the common purpose. (258)

See also Stanislavski under SUBTEXT (SAP 256).

1938   Stanislavski   **SBC**

The tempo-rhythm of a whole play is the tempo-rhythm of the through line of action and the subtextual content of the play.... The actor seeks the rightly balanced distribution of tempo-rhythm along the whole through line of action in a play. (211-12)

See also Stanislavski under THOUGHT (SBC 169-71, 176).

1953   Eliot. *See* under STYLE (ETVP 9-10).

FUNCTIONALISM

By this term we wish to identify expressions (or rejections) of attitudes and arguments that consider particular artistic elements in terms of their fulfillment of a purpose beyond their independent values. Functionalism stands in contrast, for instance, with an imitative standard (for which the resemblance of the artistic element to an external object is the criterion of judgment), an ideal standard, or a "local" aesthetic standard for consideration of particular elements.

4th cent. B.C.   Aristotle   **APO**

The nature of a thing is its end. For what each thing is when fully developed, we call its nature, whether we are speaking of a man, a horse, or a family. Besides, the final cause and end of a thing is the best, and to be self-sufficing is the end and the best. (1252b: 32-36)

   See also Aristotle under ACTION (AP 25-29), AESTHETIC (APA 16-17, 17), CHARACTER (AP 27-29), FORM (APA 8), IMITATION (AP 97-101), PROBABILITY (AP 105-107), STYLE (AP 101, 105).

1570   Castelvetro   **CP**

An error in the very essence of poetic art is justifiable, if the end is reached thereby. (67) . . . In constructing the plot we should have no regard for the beginning, the middle, or the end of the action forming the plot, but the action or a part of it being taken, we should diligently consider if it is capable of doing what we seek to do, that is, if it is capable of delighting the spectators.(68)

   See also Castelvetro under ACTION (CP 89).

1657   d'Aubignac. *See* under THREE UNITIES (AAS 2: 97-99).

1674   Racine. *See* under AFFECT (RP 156).

1679   Dryden. *See* under INSTRUCTION (DW 1, 2: 274).

1695   Dryden. *See* under INSTRUCTION (DW 3: 310-11).

1711   Dryden. *See* under MORALITY (DW 1, 2: 309-10).

1751   Johnson. *See* under RULES (JW 3: 240-41).

1758   Diderot. *See* under PLOT (DDP 292, 296).

1765   Johnson. *See* under GENRE (JS 16), THREE UNITIES (JS 30).

1767-1769   Lessing. *See* under GENRE (LSPW 380).

1808   Schlegel. *See* under CHARACTER (SCL 364); compare with AESTHETIC (SCL 237-38).

c.1820   Hegel. *See* under CHARACTER (HFA 4: 252), TRAGEDY (HFA 4: 312-15).

1826   Goethe. *See* under UNITY (GCE July 26).

1827   Goethe. *See* under AFFECT (GCE Jan. 31); compare with THOUGHT (GCE March 28).

1864   Taine. *See* under FORM (TLA 73), HERO (TLA 180), UNITY (TLA 332-33).

1888   Nietzsche   **NW**

If all unity were only unity as organization. But the "thing" in which we believe was *invented* only as a substream to the various attributes. If the thing "acts," it means: we regard *all the other* qualities which are to hand, and which are momentarily latent, as the cause accounting for the fact that one individual quality steps forward—that is to say, *we take the sum of its qualities* —*x*—as the cause of the quality *x*; which is obviously *quite* absurd and imbecile! (67)

Compare with Nietzsche under WILL (NW 138-40).

1913   Shaw. *See* under DRAMA (SMCE 144).

1936   Stanislavski. *See* under SUBTEXT (SAP 256).

1951   Eliot. *See* under STYLE (EPD 10-11).

GENRE

These discussions deal with the significance of distinguishing drama by species and with the principles for making such distinctions. For applications, see COMEDY, GENRE DEFINITION, and TRAGEDY.

4th cent. B.C.   Aristotle   AP

I propose to treat of Poetry in itself and of its various kinds, noting the essential quality of each. . . . Epic poetry and Tragedy, Comedy also and Dithyrambic poetry, and the music of the flute and lyre in most of their forms, are all in their general conception modes of imitation. They differ, however, from one another in three respects,—the medium, the objects, the manner or mode of imitation, being in each case distinct. There are persons who, by conscious art or mere habit, imitate and represent various objects through the medium of colour and *form* [shapes: EP 17], or again by the voice; so in [epic, tragedy, comedy, dithyrambic poetry, and music], taken as a whole, the imitation is produced by rhythm, *language, or "harmony"* [speech and melody: EP 17], either singly or combined. (7) . . . The objects of imitation are men in action, and . . . it follows that we must represent men either better than in real life, or as worse, or as they are. . . . Now it is evident that each of the modes of imitation above mentioned will exhibit these differences, and become a distinct kind in imitating objects that are thus distinct. (11) . . . The same distinction marks off Tragedy and Comedy; for Comedy aims at representing men as worse, Tragedy as better than in actual life. There is still a third difference—the manner in which each of these objects may be imitated. For the medium being the same, and the objects the same, the poet may imitate by narration . . . or he may present all his *characters as living and moving before us* [imitators doing their work in and through action: EP 90]. (13)

   See also Aristotle under EVOLUTIONISM (AP 17-19), IMITATION (AP 11-13).

c.20 B.C.   Horace. *See* under STYLE (HAP 459).

1561   Scaliger   SP

Of dramatic poetry there are many subdivisions. . . . The earliest form is the pastoral, the latest is comedy and its offspring, tragedy. The epic is a mixed form, and because it is catholic in the range of subject matter, is the chiefest of all forms. (20) . . . We may make [a] classification of comedies according to subject matter. Some plays are wholly taken up with love affairs . . . some with calumny . . . and some with the civic conditions and customs of Rome. In other plays an absorbing *dénouement* is the end sought. . . . Still others hinge on deception. . . . By another classification we recognize plays as full of commotion and bustle, so-called noisy plays. . . . Other plays are more composed and free from this running to and fro—the so-called quiet plays. Other plays are jovial and convivial. . . . (48) . . . Although tragedy resembles . . . epic poetry, it differs in rarely introducing persons of the lower classes, such as messengers, merchants, sailors and the like. Comedies, on the other hand, never admit Kings, save in such a rare instance as the *Amphitryon* of Plautus. . . . The wanton characters of the satyric plays are drinking, joking, jolly, sarcastic fellows. The mime employs cloth-fullers, shoemakers, butchers, poulterers. . . . (57) . . . Now a tragedy, provided it is a genuine tragedy, is altogether serious. . . . There are, on the other hand, many comedies which end unhappily for some of the characters. . . . So too, there are not a few tragedies which end happily. . . . Hence it is by no means true, as has hitherto been taught, that an unhappy issue is essential to tragedy. It is enough that the play contain horrible events. (58-59)

   See also Scaliger under SUBJECT (SP 57, 69), TRAGEDY (SP 39).

1570   Castelvetro   CP

In questions of constituting the species of poetry, no account at all should be taken of [moral] goodness or badness, extreme or moderate: these things should be considered only in so far as the aim is to arouse pity and fear in the minds of the audience. (105) . . . The royal state and the private state are the considerations which divide poetry into species. (107) . . . The private action of a private citizen is the subject of comedy, as the actions of kings are the subject of tragedy. (135)

   See also Castelvetro under SUBJECT (CP 134-35), TRAGEDY (CP 95-96).

c.1583   Sidney   SDP

[All the contemporary poets'] plays be neither right tragedies nor right comedies, mingling kings and clowns, not because the matter so carrieth it, but thrust in the clown by head and shoulders to play a part in majestical matters, with neither decency nor discretion; so as neither the admiration and commiseration, nor the right sportfulness, is by their mongrel tragi-comedy obtained. (50)

1605   Jonson. *See* under POETIC JUSTICE (JBW).

1609   de Vega. *See* under IMITATION (VAWP 25), STYLE (VAWP 27).

1640   Jonson   JBW

But here's an Heresy of late let fall;
That Mirth by no means fits a *Pastoral*;
Such say so, who can make none, he presumes:
Else, there's no *Scene*, properly assumes
The Sock. For whence can sport in kind arise,
But from the Rural Routs and Families?
Safe on this ground then, we not fear today,
To tempt your laughter by our rustic *Play*. . . .
You shall have Love and Hate, and Jealousy,
As well as Mirth, and Rage, and Melancholy:
Or whatever else may either move,
Or stir affections, and your liking prove.
But that no style for *Pastoral* should go
Current, but what is stamp'd with *Ah*, and *O*;
Who judgeth so, may singularly err;
As if all *Poesy* had one Character:
In which what were not written, were not right, . . .

Prologue, *The Sad Shepherd*

1657   d'Aubignac. *See* under TRAGEDY (AAS 4: 146-47).

1660   Corneille. *See* under COMEDY (CFD 141), SUBJECT (CFD 142-43).

1668   Dryden. *See* under IMITATION (DW 1, 2: 126-27).

1671   Dryden. *See* under POETIC JUSTICE (DW 1, 2: 198-201).

1672   Dryden. *See* under GENRE DEFINITION (DW 1, 2: 213).

1731   Voltaire. *See* under SUBJECT (VE 284).

1751   Johnson   JW

Definitions are hazardous. Things modified by human understandings, subject to varieties of complication, and changeable as experience advances knowledge, or accident influences caprice, are scarcely to be included in any standing form of expression, because they are always suffering some alteration of their state. Definition is, indeed, not the province of man; every thing is set above or below our faculties. . . . Definitions have been no less difficult or uncertain in criticisms than in law. Imagination, a licentious and vagrant faculty, unsusceptible of limitations, and impatient of restraint, has always endeavoured to baffle the logician, to perplex the confines of distinction, and burst the inclosures of regularity. There is therefore scarcely any species of writing, of which we can tell what is its essence, and what are its constituents; every new genius produces some innovation, which, when invented and approved, subverts the rules which the practice of foregoing authors had established. (3: 93)

See also Johnson under VARIETY (JW 3: 241).

1758 Diderot. *See* under ACTION (DDP 291-92), TRAGEDY (DDP 296, 297).

1765 Johnson JS

Out of [the] chaos of mingled purposes and casualties the ancient poets, according to the laws which custom had prescribed, selected some of the crimes of men, and some their absurdities; some the momentous vicissitudes of life, and some the lighter occurrences; some the terrours of distress, and some the gayeties of prosperity. Thus rose the two modes of imitation, known by the names of *tragedy* and *comedy*, compositions intended to promote different ends by contrary means, and considered as so little allied, that I do not recollect among the *Greeks* or *Romans* a single writer who attempted both.

Shakespeare has united the powers of exciting laughter and sorrow not only in one mind, but in one composition. . . . That this is a practice contrary to the rules of criticism will be readily allowed; but there is always an appeal open from criticism to nature. The end of writing is to instruct; the end of poetry is to instruct by pleasing. That the mingled Drama may convey all the instruction of tragedy or comedy cannot be denied, because it . . . approaches nearer than either to the appearance of life. . . . (16) The players, who in their edition [of Shakespeare's plays] divided our author's works into comedies, histories, and tragedies, seem not to have distinguished the three kinds by any very exact or definite ideas. An action which ended happily to the principal persons, however serious or distressful through its intermediate incidents, in their opinion, constituted a comedy. This idea of comedy continued long among us; and plays were written, which, by changing the catastrophe, were tragedies to-day and comedies to-morrow. Tragedy was not in those times a poem of more general dignity or elevation than comedy; it required only a clamitous conclusion, with which the common criticism of that age was satisfied, whatever lighter pleasure it afforded in its progress. History was a series of actions, with no other than chronological succession, independent of each other, and without any tendency to introduce or regulate the conclusion. . . . A history may be continued through many plays; as it had no plan, it had no limits. (17-18)

See also Johnson under VARIETY (JS 15).

1767-1769 Lessing LSPW

I do not attempt to restrict comedy to . . . a species of the ludicrous; or tragedy to . . . extraordinary manifestations in the domain of morals that astonish our reason and rouse tumult in our breast. Genius laughs away all the boundary lines of criticism. Only so much is indisputable, that drama chooses its themes this side or beyond the frontiers of law, and only touches its objects in so far as they either lose themselves in the absurd, or extend to the horrible. (248) . . . What do we mean by the mixture of genres? In our primers it is right we should separate them from one another as carefully as possible, but if a Genius, for higher purposes amalgamates several of them in one and the same work, let us forget our primer and only examine whether he has attained these higher purposes. What do I care whether a play of Euripides is neither wholly a narrative nor wholly a drama, call it a hybrid, enough that this hybrid pleases me more, edifies me more, than the most rule-correct creations of your correct Racines or whatever else they may be called. Because the mule is neither a horse nor an ass, is it therefore the less one of the most useful Beasts of burden? (380) . . . It is not enough that [the poet's] work has an effect upon us, it must have that effect upon us which belongs to its species, and it must have that above all others. The lack of that can be in no wise replaced by other effects, especially if the species is of that importance, value and difficulty that all trouble and exertions would be in vain if it produced nothing but such effects as could be attained by an easier species requiring less preparation. (425)

See also Lessing under DRAMA (LSPW 418), TRAGEDY (LSPW 415).

1808   Schlegel   SCL

The *tragic* and *comic* bear the same relation to one another as *earnest* and *sport*. . . . Both, indeed, bear the stamp of our common nature; but earnestness belongs more to its moral, and mirth to its animal part. The creatures destitute of reason are incapable either of earnest or of sport. . . . Earnestness . . . is the direction of our mental powers to some aim. But as soon as we begin to call ourselves to account for our actions, reason compels us to fix this aim higher and higher, till we come at last to the highest end of our existence: and here that longing for the infinite which is inherent in our being, is baffled by the limits of our finite existence. . . . There is no bond of love without a separation, no enjoyment without the grief of losing it. . . . When we think upon all this, every heart which is not dead to feeling must be overpowered by an inexpressible melancholy, for which there is no other counterpoise than the consciousness of a vocation transcending the limits of this earthly life. This is the tragic tone of mind. . . . As earnestness in the highest degree is the essence of tragic representation; so is sport of the comic. The disposition to mirth is forgetfulness of all gloomy considerations in the pleasant feeling of present happiness. We are then inclined to view everything in a sportive light, and to allow nothing to disturb or ruffle our minds. The imperfections . . . of men are no longer an object of dislike and compassion, but serve, by their strange inconsistencies, to entertain the understanding and to amuse the fancy. The comic poet must therefore carefully abstain from whatever is calculated to excite moral indignation at the conduct, or sympathy with the situations of his personages, because this would inevitably bring us back again into earnestness. He must paint . . . the incidents which befall them as merely ludicrous distresses, which will be attended with no fatal consequences. (44-46) . . . In the history of poetry and the fine arts among the Greeks, their development was subject to an invariable law. Everything heterogeneous was first excluded, and then all homogeneous elements were combined, and each being perfected in itself, at last elevated into an independent and harmonious unity. Hence with them each species is confined within its natural boundaries, and the different styles distinctly marked. (46-47)

See also Schlegel under CHARACTER (SCL 148-49), COMEDY (SCL 149-51, 309-10), RULES (SCL 217), STYLE (SCL 370-71).

c.1810   Coleridge   CLSW

The *Tempest* is a specimen of the purely romantic drama, in which the interest is not historical, or dependent upon fidelity of portraiture, or the natural connection of events,—but is a birth of the imagination, and rests only on the coaptation and union of the elements granted to, or assumed by, the poet. It is a species of drama which owes no allegiance to time or space, and in which, therefore, errors of chronology and geography—no mortal sins in any species —are venial faults, and count for nothing. It addresses itself entirely to the imaginative faculty [of the spectator]; and although the illusion may be assisted by the effect on the senses of the complicated scenery and decorations of modern times, yet this sort of assistance is dangerous. For the principal and only genuine excitement ought to come from within,—from the moved and sympathetic imagination; whereas, where so much is addressed to the mere external senses of seeing and hearing, the spiritual vision is apt to languish, and the attraction from without will withdraw the mind from the proper and only legitimate interest which is intended to spring from within. (74)

1813-1814   Coleridge. See under GENRE DEFINITION (CSC 2: 229).

1816   Goethe. See under DRAMA (GLE 185).

1818   Coleridge. See under GENRE DEFINITION (CLSW 87).

c.1820   Hegel   HFA

In tragedy [the one-sided aspect of spiritual powers, which discover their self-stability in the dramatic character], . . . are opposed . . . in hostility [; whereas] in comedy, they are displayed within these characters themselves, without further mediation, in a condition of resolution. (4: 256) . . . Comedy . . . in the many-sided features of its worked-out intrigue, does not require such deliberate self-concentration as tragedy does. Romantic tragedy, however, is also in this respect more varied and less consistent in its unity than is classic tragedy. (4: 260) . . . We deduced from the fact of the drama's presenting an action distinct and independent in its actually visible development the conclusion that a fully complete sensuous reproduction is also essential, such as is for the first time possible under artistic conditions in the theatrical performance. In order that the action, however, may adapt itself to an external realization of this kind, it is necessary that both in poetic conception and detailed execution it should be absolutely definite and complete. This is only effected . . . by resolving dramatic poetry into *particular types*, receiving their typical character, which is in part one of opposition and also one of mediatory relation to such opposition, from the distinction, in which not only the end but also the characters, as also the conflict and entire result of the action, are manifested. The most important aspects emphasized by such distinction and subject to an historical development are those peculiar to tragedy and comedy respectively, as also the comparative value of either mode of composition. This inquiry in dramatic poetry is for the first time so essentially important that it forms the basis of classification for the different types. (4: 293) Dramatic poetry, which accepts as its centre of significance the collision of aims and characters, as also the necessary resolution of such a conflict, cannot do otherwise than deduce the principle of its separate types from the relation in which *individual persons* are placed relatively to their purpose and its content. The definition of this relation is, in short, the decisive factor in the determination of the particular mode of dramatic schism and the issue therefrom, and consequently presents the essential type of the entire process in its animated and artistic display. (4: 294)

See also Hegel under TRAGEDY (HFA 4: 300-301).

1824 Goethe   GCE

Tues. March 30. We spoke of the French drama, as contrasted with the German. "It will be very difficult," said Goethe, "for the German public to come to a kind of right judgment, as they do in Italy and France. We have a special obstacle in the circumstance, that on our stage a medley of all sorts of things is represented. On the same boards where we saw Hamlet yesterday, we see Staberle to-day. . . . Hence the public becomes confused in its judgment, mingling together various species, which it never learns rightly to appreciate and to understand. . . . Schiller had the happy thought of building a house for tragedy alone, and of giving a piece every week for the male sex exclusively. . . ." We talked about the plays of Iffland and Kotzebue, which, in their way, Goethe highly commended. "From this very fault," said he, "that people do not perfectly distinguish between *kinds* in art, the pieces of these men are often unjustly censured. We may wait a long time before a couple of such popular talents come again."

1864 Taine   TLA

In every simple or complex state, the social medium, that is to say, the general state of mind and manners, determines the species of works of art in suffering only those which are in harmony with it, and in suppressing other species, through a series of obstacles interposed, and a series of attacks renewed, at every step of their development. (104)

See also Taine under AESTHETIC (TLA 273-74).

1876   Sarcey   STT

The distinction between the comic and the tragic rests, not on a prejudice but on the very definition of drama; that this distinction may remain absolute without disadvantage; that there are disadvantages on the contrary if it is not observed; that nevertheless it may be disregarded—not without peril however —on this condition, that the disturbing element shall not interfere with the first impression which should remain single, and that it shall even heighten that impression by a slight effect of contrast. (48-49)

See also Sarcey under STYLE (STT 49-50), UNITY (STT 41-42).

1894   Brunetière   BLD

The types [of drama are not] always pure. In the history of literature or of art, as in nature, a type is almost never anything but an ideal, and consequently a limit. . . . There may be an alliance or mixture of farce and comedy, of drama and tragedy. . . . It is nevertheless useful to have carefully defined the species; and if the law should only teach authors not to treat a subject of comedy by the devices of farce, that would be something. . . . The dramatic species are distinguished by the nature of the obstacles encountered by [the will of the protagonist]. (79-80)

See also Brunetière under CONFLICT (BLD 77-80).

1908   Pirandello   POH

Now, if it were a matter of judging a work of the collective imagination, as in the case of a genuine epic poem which emerged vividly and powerfully from the primitive traditional legends of a certain people, we could somehow accept a broad and general definition. But when dealing with individual creations, particularly if they are works of humor, we can no longer be satisfied with that type of generalization. Using abstractly the type of English humor, Taine puts Swift, Fielding, Sterne, Dickens, Thackeray, Sydney Smith and Carlyle all together, and even includes Heine, Aristophanes, Rabelais and Montesquieu as well. Now, that is quite a collection! From humor understood in the broad sense and from the typical manner that, as a common characteristic, a particular people has of expressing its humor, we make a big jump to those singular and unique humoristic expressions which can be understood in a broad sense only at the cost of completely renouncing criticism—I mean the type of criticism that examines and brings out those individual traits that distinctly separate one expression, one art, one mode of being, and one style from any other. . . . The relations that each of these humoristic writers may have either with the national English humor or among themselves are entirely secondary and superficial; and they are totally irrelevant with respect to esthetic valuation. (22-23) . . . Controlled as it was by reason, Rhetoric perceived categories everywhere and saw literature as a kind of filing cabinet: for each compartment, a label. So many categories, so many corresponding genres; and each genre had its predetermined and inalterable form. It is true that Rhetoric often adjusted, but to yield, never. Whenever a rebel poet gave the filing cabinet a well-aimed kick and created a new form of his own, the rhetoricians would growl at him for quite a while. Eventually, however, if the new form succeeded in obtaining recognition, they would then take it, disassemble it like a little machine, give it a logical formation and catalogue it, perhaps by adding a new box to the file. This is what happened, for instance, with the historical drama of that barbarian, Shakespeare. Did Rhetoric give up? No; after growling for quite some time, it admitted historical drama to its ranks and prescribed the rules for it. But it is also true that whenever the dogs of Rhetoric got hold of a poor poet whose mind had become feeble, they would tear him to pieces and force him to mistreat his own work in which he had neglected to follow strictly the model imposed upon him. (30)

Compare with Pirandello under THOUGHT (POH 30-31).

GENRE DEFINITION

*Attempts have been made to differentiate plays on the model of natural species.
For more direct examination of the principles, see GENRE; for more extended
applications, see COMEDY and TRAGEDY.*

1561   Scaliger. *See* under GENRE (SP 20, 48, 57).

1668   Dryden. *See* under STYLE (DW 1, 2: 85-86).

1672   Dryden   **DW**

An heroick play ought to be an imitation, in little, of an heroick poem; and
consequently, that love and valour ought to be the subject of it. (1, 2: 213)

1711   Addison   **AW**

The tragi-comedy, which is the product of the English theatre, is one of the
most monstrous inventions that ever entered into a poet's thoughts. An author
might as well think of weaving the adventures of Aeneas and Hudibras into one
poem as of writing such a motley piece of mirth and sorrow. But the absurdity
of these performances is so very visible, that I shall not insist upon it. (1: 72)
The two great branches of ridicule in writing are comedy and burlesque. The
first ridicules persons by drawing them in their proper characters, the other by
drawing them quite unlike themselves. Burlesque is therefore of two kinds; the
first represents mean persons in the accoutrements of heroes; the other describes great persons acting and speaking like the basest among the people.
Don Quixote is an instance of the first, and Lucian's gods of the second. (1:
361)

1758   Diderot   **DDP**

Here is the whole field of drama: the gay comedy whose purpose it is to ridicule
and chastise vice; Serious comedy, whose office it is to depict virtue and the
duties of man; the sort of tragedy which is concerned with our domestic
troubles; and, finally, the sort of tragedy which is concerned with public
catastrophes and the misfortunes of the great. (287)

1765   Johnson   **JS**

That the mingled drama [tragicomedy] may convey all the instruction of
tragedy and comedy cannot be denied, because it includes both in its altera-

tions of exhibition and approaches nearer than either to the appearance of life, by shewing how great machinations and slender designs may promote or obviate one another, and the high and low cooperate in the general system of unavoidable concatenation. (16)

1767-1769   Lessing   LSPW

Tragi-comedy is the representation of an important action that takes place among noble persons and has a happy end. (389)
   See also Lessing under IMITATION (LSPW 399).

1778   Diderot   DPA

Satire deals with *a* tartufe; comedy with *the* Tartufe. Satire attacks the vicious; comedy attacks a vice. (49-50)

1808   Schlegel   SCL

New Comedy . . . is a mixture of earnestness and mirth. The poet no longer turns poetry and the world into ridicule, he no longer abandons himself to an enthusiasm of fun, but seeks the sportive element in the objects themselves; he depicts in human characters and situations whatever occasions mirth, in a word, what is pleasant and laughable. But the ridiculous must no longer come forward as the pure creation of his own fancy, but must be verisimilar, that is, seem to be real. . . . The subject of Tragedy . . . is the struggle between the outward finite existence, and the inward infinite aspirations. The subdued earnestness of the New Comedy, on the other hand, remains always within the sphere of experience. The place of Destiny is supplied by Chance, for the latter is the empirical conception of the former, as being that which lies beyond our power or control. . . . To unconditional necessity, moral liberty could alone be opposed; as for Chance, every one must use his wits, and turn it to his own profit as he best can. On this account, the whole moral of the New Comedy, just like that of the Fable, is nothing more than a theory of prudence. . . . [New Comedy] endeavors after strict coherence, and has, in common with Tragedy, a formal complication and dénouement of plot. Like Tragedy, too, it connects together its incidents, as cause and effect, only that it adopts the law of existence as it manifests itself in experience, without any such reference as Tragedy assumes to an idea. As the latter endeavours to satisfy our feelings at the close, in like manner the New Comedy endeavours to provide, at least, an important point of rest for the understanding. This, I may remark in passing, is by no means an easy task for the comic writer: he must contrive . . . to get rid of the contradictions which with their complication and intricacy have diverted us during the course of the action; if he really smooths them all off by making his fools become rational, or by reforming or punishing his villains, then there is an end at once of everything like a pleasant and comical impression. . . . [New Comedy mixes ingredients that are comic and tragic.] There is yet a third [ingredient] which in itself is neither comic nor tragic, in short, not even

poetic. I allude to portrait-like truthfulness. The ideal and caricature
. . . lay claim to no other truth than that which lies in their significance: their
individual beings even are not intended to appear real. Tragedy moves in an
ideal, and Old Comedy in a fanciful or fantastical world. . . . New Comedy
. . . [had] to afford some equivalent . . . and this was furnished by the probability of the subjects represented. . . . In so far as Comedy depicts the constitution
of social and domestic life in general, it is a portrait; from this prosaic side it
must be variously modified, according to time and place, while the comic
motives, in respect of their poetical principle, are always the same. [Does the
comic form itself require "individual reality"?] In the first place it is a
simulated whole, composed of congruous parts, agreeably to the scale of art.
Moreover, the subject represented is handled according to the laws of theatrical exhibition . . . [it is selective and more concentrated than real life]; over the
whole, viz., the situations and the characters, a certain clearness and distinctness of appearance is thrown, which the vague and indeterminate outlines of
reality seldom possess. Thus the form constitutes the poetic element of
Comedy, while the prosaic principle lies in the matter, in the required assimilation to something individual and external. (176-79)

   See also Schlegel under CHARACTER (SCL 183-84).

c.1810   Coleridge. *See* under GENRE (CLSW 74).

1813-1814   Coleridge   **CSC**

Fully to comprehend the nature of the Historic Drama, the difference should be
understood between the epic and tragic muse. The latter recognizes and is
grounded upon the free will of man; the former is under the control of destiny,
or, among Christians, an overruling Providence. In epic, the prominent character is ever under this influence, and when accidents are introduced, they are
the result of causes over which our will has no power. An epic play begins and
ends arbitrarily; its only law is, that it possess beginning, middle and end.
Homer ends with the death of Hector; the final fate of Troy is left untouched.
Virgil ends with the marriage of Aeneas; the historical events are left imperfect. In the tragic, the free will of man is the first cause, and accidents are never
introduced; if they are, it is considered a great fault. To cause the death of a
hero by accident, such as slipping off a plank into the sea, would be beneath the
tragic muse, as it would arise from no mental action. (2: 229)

1818   Coleridge   **CLSW**

The myriad-minded man, our, and all men's, Shakespeare, has in [*Comedy of
Errors*] presented us with a legitimate farce in exactest consonance with the
philosophical principles and character of farce, as distinguished from comedy
and from entertainments. A proper farce is mainly distinguished from comedy
by the license allowed, and even required, in the fable, in order to produce
strange and laughable situations. The story need not be probable, it is enough

that it is possible. A comedy would scarcely allow even the two Antipholuses; because, although there have been instances of almost indistinguishable likeness in two persons, yet these are mere individual accidents. . . . But farce dares add the two Dromios, and is justified in doing so by the law of its end and constitution. In a word, farces commence in a postulate, which must be granted. (87)

1818   Hazlitt. *See* under STYLE (HW 5: 347).

c.1820   Hegel   **HFA**

Midway between tragedy and comedy we have . . . a *third* fundamental type of dramatic poetry. . . . With . . . frequency in modern dramatic poetry we have the interplay of tragic and comic situation; and this is naturally so, because in modern compositions the principle of an intimate personal life has its place too in tragedy, the principle which is asserted by comedy in all its freedom, and from the first has been predominant, forcing as it does into the background the substantive character of the content in which the ethical forces . . . are paramount. The profounder mediation, however, of tragic and comic composition in a new whole does not consist in the juxtaposition or alternation of these contradictory points of view, but in a mutual accommodation, which blunts the force of such opposition. The element of subjectivity, instead of being exercised with all the perversity of the comic drama, is steeped in the seriousness of genuine social conditions and substantial characters, while the tragic steadfastness of volition and the depth of collisions is so far weakened and reduced that it becomes compatible with a reconciliation of interests and a harmonious union of ends and individuals. It is under such a mode of conception that in particular the modern play and drama arise. . . . The "Iphegenia" of Goethe is a genuine model of a play of this kind, and it is more so in his "Tasso." . . . As a rule . . . the boundary lines of [the] intermediate type fluctuate more than is the case with tragedy or comedy. It is also exposed to a further danger of breaking away from the true dramatic type, or ceasing to be genuine poetry. In other words, owing to the fact that the opposing factors, which have to secure a peaceful conclusion from out of their own division, are from the start not antithetical to one another with the emphasis asserted by tragedy; the poet is for this reason compelled to devote the full strength of his presentation to the psychological analysis of character, and to make the course of the situations a mere instrument of such characterization. Or . . . he admits a too extensive field for the display of the material aspect of historical or ethical conditions; and . . . he tends to restrict his effort to keep the attention alive to the interest of the series of events evolved alone. . . . They do not seek to affect us as genuine poetical productions as to reach our emotions generally as men and women; or they aim on the one hand simply at recreation, and on the other at the moral education of public taste. . . . (4: 305-308)

1894   Brunetière. *See* under CONFLICT (BLD 77-80).

1895   Shaw   **SDC**

[A good melodrama] only needs elaboration to become a masterpiece.
. . . It should be a simple and sincere drama of action and feeling, kept well
within the vast tract of passion and motive which is common to the philosopher
and the laborer, relieved by plenty of fun, and depending for variety of human
character . . . on broad contrasts between types of youth and age, sympathy and
selfishness, the masculine and the feminine, the serious and the frivolous, the
sublime and the ridiculous, and so on. The whole character of the piece must be
allegorical, idealistic, full of generalizations and moral lessons; and it must
represent conduct as producing swiftly and certainly on the individual the
results which in actual life it only produces on the race in the course of many
centuries. (48-49)

c. 1900   Shaw. *See* under TRAGEDY (SS 253).

1909   Shaw   **STPB**

The manufacture of well made plays [of Scribe and his school] is not an art: it is
an industry. . . . Nothing spoils a well-made play more infallibly than the least
alloy of high art or the least qualm of conscience on the part of the writer. 'Art
for art's sake' is the formula of the well made play, meaning in practice
'Success for money's sake.' Now great art is never produced for its own sake.
It is too difficult to be worth the effort. (xx) . . . The formula for the well made
play is . . . the manufacture of a misunderstandng. Having manufactured it, you
place its culmination at the end of the last act but one, which is the point at
which the manufacture of the play begins. Then you make your first act out of
the necessary introduction of the characters to the audience, after elaborate
explanations, mostly conducted by servants, solicitors, and other low life
personages (the principals must all be dukes and colonels and millionaires), of
how the misunderstanding is going to come about. Your last act consists, of
course, of clearing up the misunderstanding. . . . (xxii-xxiii)

GEST

The following statements by Bertolt Brecht concern his evolving concept of the significant "gesture."

1930   Brecht   **BBT**

The intention [in *Mahogonny*] was that a certain unreality, irrationality and lack of seriousness should be introduced at the right moment, and so strike with a double meaning. . . . This limited aim did not stop us from introducing an element of instruction, and from basing everything on the gest. The eye which looks for the gest in everything is the moral sense. In other words, a moral tableau. A subjective one, though. . . . (36)

c.1932   Brecht   **BBT**

DEFINITION: 'Gest' is not supposed to mean gesticulation: it is not a matter of explanation or emphatic movements of the hands, but of overall attitudes. A language is gestic when it is grounded in a gest and conveys particular attitudes adopted by the speaker towards other men. The sentence 'pluck the eye that offends thee out' is less effective from the gestic point of view than 'if thine eye offend thee, pluck it out.' The latter starts by presenting the eye, and the first clause has the definite gest of making an assumption; the main clause then comes as a surprise, a piece of advice, and a relief. WHAT IS A SOCIAL GEST? Not all gests are social gests. The attitude of chasing a fly away is not yet a social gest, though the attitude of chasing a dog may be one, for instance if it comes to represent a badly dressed man's continual battle against watch-dogs. One's efforts to keep one's balance on a slippery surface result in a social gest as soon as falling down would mean 'losing face'; in other words, losing one's market value. The gest of working is definitely a social gest, because all human activity directed toward the mastery of nature is a social undertaking, an undertaking between men. On the other hand a gest of pain, as long as it is kept so abstract and generalized that it does not rise above a purely animal category, is not yet a social one. But this is precisely the common tendency of art: to remove the social element in any gest. The artist is not happy till he achieves "the look of a hunted animal." The man then becomes just Man; his gest is stripped of any social individuality; it is an empty one, not representing any undertaking or operation among men by this particular man. The "look of a hunted animal" can become a social gest if it is shown that particular manoeuvres by men can degrade the individual man to the level of a beast; the social gest is the gest relevant to society, the gest that allows conclusions to be drawn about the social circumstances. (104-105)

1935   Brecht   BBT

The epic theatre . . . works out scenes where people adopt attitudes of such a sort that the social laws under which they are acting spring into sight. . . . The spectator is given the chance to criticize human behavior from a social point of view, and the scene is played as a piece of history. The idea is that the spectator should be put in a position where he can make comparisons about everything that influences the way in which human beings behave. This means, from the aesthetic point of view, that the actors' social gest becomes particularly important. The arts have to begin paying attention to the gest. (Naturally this means socially significant gest, not illustrative or expressive gest.) The gestic principle takes over, as it were, from the principle of imitation. (86)

   See also Brecht under DISTANCE (BBT 86).

1939   Brecht   BBG

It must be kept in mind that my chief work was for the theater; I was constantly thinking of the spoken word. And I had worked out for myself a definite technique for speaking, whether of prose or verse. I called it *gestural* (*gestisch*). This meant that the language had to accord entirely with the gesture of the person who was speaking. I will give an example. The sentence in the Bible: ''Pluck out thine eye if it offend thee'' has at bottom a gesture, one of command, but it is not expressed in a purely gestural way, since ''if it offend thee'' really has another gesture which is not expressed, namely, giving a reason. Expressed in a purely gestural way the sentence is as follows . . . ''If thine eye offend thee, pluck it out!'' One can see at a glance that this formulation is, with regard to gesture, much richer and purer. The first clause contains an hypothesis, and what is peculiar and special about it can be fully expressed in one's intonation. Then comes a short perplexed pause, and only *then* the startling exhortation. (34-35)

1940   Brecht   BBAn

All emotion must become visible and be developed into a gesture. The actor must find an appropriate expression for the emotions of his character; if possible, actions which will reveal those inner processes. . . . Outstanding elegance, strength and grace of gesture will result in [alienation]. The Chinese art of acting is mastery in the treatment of gesture. By openly watching his own movements, the Chinese actor attains [alienation]. (18)

1948   Brecht   BBBG

The province of the characters' attitude toward each other we call the *province of gesture*. The attitude of the body, vocal, and facial expression are determined by a *social gesture*: that is, the characters insult each other, compliment each other, teach each other, etc.... Though the theatrical image requires intensification, the actor must take care not to lose any of this gestural material. He should intensify the whole complex... [As an example of *gest*, note how Galileo bathes and drinks his milk in the opening scenes:] Isn't his pleasure in the drink and in the bath the same as his pleasure in new ideas? Do not forget: he thinks for the sake of sensual pleasure! (33)... In displaying such gestural material the actor masters his character by mastering the *plot*. Only from this, the distinct total event, is he able almost at one bound to reach the final characterization which combines all the individual details. If he has done everything to astonish himself at the contradictions in the various attitudes, knowing that in this way he will astonish his audience, the plot in its entirety allows him to fuse the contradictions. (35)... Each separate event has a basic gesture. *Richard Gloucester sues for the hand of his victim's widow. By means of a chalk circle the true mother is discovered.* (35-36)... When art mirrors life it does so with special mirrors.... Stylization should not eliminate what is natural but exaggerate it. At any rate a theatre that takes everything from gesture cannot do without choreography. The mere elegance of a movement and the charm of an ensemble are alienations, and pantomime is an aid to plot. (39)... Underlying the actual performance should be the gesture of *handing over* [to the audience] *a finished product.* (40)

   See also Brecht under PLOT (BBBG 17, 35, 36).

HERO

This category contains statements concerning the nature and significance of the protagonist of a drama.
     See also *FLAW and WILL*.

4th cent. B.C.   Aristotle   AP

The change of fortune presented must not be the spectacle of a virtuous man brought from prosperity to adversity: for this moves neither pity nor fear; it *merely* [morally: EP 364] shocks us. Nor, again, that of a bad man passing from adversity to prosperity: for nothing can be more alien to the spirit of Tragedy. . . . Nor, again, should the downfall of the utter villain be exhibited. . . . There remains, then, the character between these two extremes,—that of a man who is not eminently good and just, yet whose misfortune is brought about not by vice or depravity, but by some error or frailty. He must be one who is highly renowned and prosperous,—a personage like Oedipus, Thyestes, or other illustrious men of such families. (45-47)
     See also Aristotle under ACTION (AP 33-35), FLAW (AP 45), IDENTIFICATION (AR 159-60), UNITY (AP 33-35).

1561   Scaliger. *See* under TRAGEDY (SP 40).

1570   Castelvetro   CP

It appears that, as far as the subject of poetry, nobility or vileness constitute the difference: which nobility or vileness is not to be discerned by [moral] goodness or badness, but by bearing and address: a good deportment is a sign of nobility, an awkward one, of vileness. And by deportment I mean those things which witness not to the moral character but to the courtliness or the boorishness of the hero. (106) . . . [The saint falling into adversity] excites more pity and fear than does a character of moderate goodness: for spectators, leading a less saintly life, feel greater fear when they see a saint suffer, saying to themselves, "If this happens in the green tree, how much more so in the dry?" And who can cause more pity than a saint fallen into misfortune; if being unworthy of evil arouses pity, who is less worthy of evil than a saint? . . . The common people believe God incapable of injustice, and so they expend their wrath on the immediate causes of the saint's misery, absolving God from all responsibility . . . [but were He not absolved] the effect is not fatal to tragedy. . . . [A villain's adversity is not pitiful] but a villain achieving success is no less tragic than a saint falling into misery. (110-11)

See also Castelvetro under ACTION (CP 113), TRAGEDY (CP 96-97).

1657   d'Aubignac. See under TRAGEDY (AAS 4: 140).

1668   Dryden   **DW**

One character in all plays . . . will have advantage of all the others; and the design of the whole drama will chiefly depend on it. But this hinders not that there may be more shining characters in the play: many persons of a second magnitude, nay, some so very near, so almost equal to the first, that greatness may be opposed to greatness, and all the persons be made considerable, not only by their quality but their action. (1, 2: 89)

1668   Racine. See under FLAW (RP 154-55).

1671   Dryden. See under POETIC JUSTICE (DW 1, 2: 198-201).

1672   Dryden   **DW**

You see how little these great authors [, Homer and Tasso,] did esteem the point of honour, so much magnified by the French, and so ridiculously aped by us. They made their heroes men of honour; but so, as not to divest them quite of human passions and frailties: they content themselves to shew you, what men of great spirits would certainly do, when they were provoked, not what they were obliged to do by the strict rules of moral virtue. (1,2: 221)

1679   Dryden   **DW**

Shall we . . . banish all characters of villany? I confess I am not of that opinion; but it is necessary that the hero of the play be not a villain: that is, the characters which should move our pity ought to have virtuous inclinations, and degrees of moral goodness in them. As for a perfect character of virtue, it never was in nature; and therefore there can be no imitation of it. But there are alloys of frailty to be allowed for the chief persons; yet so that the good which is in them shall outweigh the bad, and consequently leave room for punishment on the one side, and pity on the other. (1,2: 270-71) . . . The chief character or hero in a tragedy . . . ought in prudence to be such a man, who has so much more in him of virtue than of vice, that he may be left amiable to the audience, which otherwise cannot have any concernment for his sufferings; and it is on this one character that the pity and terrour must be principally, if not wholly, founded: a rule which is extremely necessary. . . . For terrour and compassion work but weakly, when they are divided into many persons. (1, 2: 277)

1695   Dryden   **DW**

In a tragedy, or an epick poem, the hero of the piece must be advanced foremost to the view of the reader or spectator: he must outshine the rest of all the characters; he must appear the prince of them, like the sun in the Copernican system, encompassed with the less noble planets: because the hero is the centre of the main action; all the lines from the circumference tend to him alone: he is the chief object of pity in the drama. (3: 333)

See also Dryden under SUBJECT (DW 3: 312-13).

1711   Addison. See under SPECTACLE (AW 1: 74).

1712   Addison. See under ACTION (AW 1: 427).

1725   Voltaire. See under SUBJECT (VE 278-79).

1751   Johnson   **JW**

As the design of tragedy is to instruct by moving the passions, it must always have a hero, a personage apparently and incontestably superior to the rest, upon whom the attention may be fixed, and the anxiety suspended. For though, of two persons opposing each other with equal abilities and equal virtue, the auditor will inevitably, in time, choose his favourite, yet as that choice must be without any cogency of conviction, the hopes or fears which it raises will be faint and languid. Of two heroes acting in confederacy against a common enemy, the virtues or dangers will give little emotion, because each claims our concern with the same right, and the heart lies at rest between equal motives. (3: 242)

1755-1780   Diderot. See under TRAGEDY (DDE 291).

1766   Lessing. See under TRAGEDY (LSPW 31).

1808   Schlegel. See under ACTION (SCL 239-42).

1813-1814   Coleridge. See under GENRE DEFINITION (CSC 2: 229).

1819   Hazlitt. See under AFFECT (HW 8: 6).

c.1820   Hegel   **HFA**

The heroes of tragedy [are neither *guilty* nor *innocent*]. They act in accordance with a specific character, a specific pathos, for the simple reason that they are this character, this pathos. In such a case there is no lack of [moral decision] and no choice. The strength of great characters consists precisely in this that they do not choose, but are entirely and absolutely just that which they will and achieve. . . . A wavering attitude . . . is alien to these plastic creations. The bond between the psychological state of mind and the content of the will is for them indissoluble. . . . At the same time, however, such a pathos, with its potential resources of collision, brings in its train deeds that are both injurious and wrongful. They have no desire to avoid the blame that results therefrom. On the contrary, it is their fame to have done what they have done. One can in fact urge nothing more intolerable against a hero of this type than by saying that he has acted innocently. It is a point of honour with such great characters that they are guilty. They have no desire to excite pity or our sensibilities. For it is not the substantive, but rather the wholly personal deepening of the individual character, which stirs our individual pain. These securely strong characters, however, coalesce entirely with their essential pathos, and this indivisible accord inspires wonder, but does not excite heart emotions. (4: 320-21)

See also Hegel under CATHARSIS (HFA 4: 298-300), TRAGEDY (HFA 4: 295-99), UNIVERSALITY (HFA 4: 252-53).

1864   Taine   TLA

The aim of a work of art was to make known some leading and important character more effectually and clearly than objects themselves do. For that purpose the artist forms for himself an idea of that character, and according to his idea he transforms the actual object. This object thus transformed is found to *conform to the idea*, or, in other words, to the *ideal*. Things thus pass from the real to the ideal when the artist reproduces them by modifying them according to his idea, and he modifies them according to his idea when, conceiving and eliminating from them some notable character, he systematically changes the natural relationships of their parts in order to render this character more apparent and powerful. (180) . . . To give full prominence to a leading character is the object of a work of art. It is owing to this that the closer a work of art approaches this point the more perfect it becomes; in other words the more exactly and completely these conditions are complied with the more elevated it becomes on the scale. Two of these conditions are necessary; it is necessary that the character should be the most notable possible and the most dominant possible. (197) . . . A work of art is a system of parts, at one time drawn from every detail as it happens in architecture and in music, at another reproduced according to some real object as it happens in literature, sculpture and painting: . . . the purpose of art is to manifest by this *ensemble* some notable character. . . . The merit of the work is greater proportionately as this character becomes more notable and more predominant. We have distinguished in the notable character two points of view, according as it is more important, that is to say more stable and more elementary; and according as it is more beneficent, that is say, more capable of contributing to the preservation and the development of the individual and of the group in which he is comprehended. . . . The important or beneficent character is never but one force, measured at one time by its effects on others and, at another, by its effects on itself. . . . It takes a more powerful relief when the artist, employing all the elements of his work, makes all their effects converge. . . . Works of art are so much more beautiful as character is imprinted and expressed in them with a more universally predominant ascendency. The masterpiece is that in which the greatest force receives the greatest development. (351-53)

See also Taine under ACTION (TLA 318-19), AESTHETICS (TLA 76, 82-84, 273-74), CHARACTER (TLA 274-76).

1871   Nietzsche   NBT

The most sorrowful figure of the Greek stage, the hapless *Oedipus*, was understood by Sophocles as the noble man, who in spite of his wisdom was destined to error and misery, but nevertheless through his extraordinary sufferings ultimately exerted a magical, wholesome influence on all around him, which continues effective even after his death. The noble man does not sin; this is what the thoughtful poet wishes to tell us: all laws, all natural order, yea, the moral world itself, may be destroyed through his action, but through this very action a higher magic circle of influences is brought into play, which establish a new world on the ruins of the old that has been overthrown. This is what the poet, in so far as he is at the same time a religious thinker, wishes to tell us: as poet, he shows us first of all a wonderfully complicated legal mystery, which the judge slowly unravels, link by link, to his own destruction. The truly Hellenic delight at this dialectical loosening is so great, that a touch of surpassing cheerfulness is thereby communicated to the entire play, which everywhere blunts the edge of the horrible presuppositions of the procedure. (73-74) . . . All the celebrated figures of the Greek stage [before Euripides]— Prometheus, Oedipus, etc.—are but masks of [the] original [tragic] hero, Dionysus. The presence of a god behind all these masks is the one essential cause of the typical "ideality," so oft exciting wonder, of these celebrated figures. . . . The one truly real Dionysus appears in a multiplicity of forms, in the mask of a fighting hero and entangled, as it were, in the net of an individual will. . . . This hero is the suffering Dionysus of the mysteries, a god experiencing in himself the sufferings of individuation, of whom wonderful myths tell that as a boy he was dismembered by the Titans. . . . (81-82)

See also Nietzsche under AFFECT (NBT 70-71), EXPOSITION (NBT 98-100), MORALITY (NBT 78-79), THOUGHT (NBT 110-11), TRAGEDY (NBT 127, 159-60).

1886   Chekhov. *See* under LANGUAGE (CLF 70-71).

1894   Brunetière. *See* under WILL (BLD 73, 75).

1935   Brecht. *See* under CATHARSIS (BBT 87), IDENTIFICATION (BBT 87).

c.1952   Brecht   BBT

It is the theatre's job to present the hero in such a way that he stimulates conscious rather than blind imitation. (247)

HUMOR

Theories of the laughable or comical are considered under this category. For the comic as an art-form, see COMEDY.

4th cent. B.C.   Aristotle   ANE

Those who jest with good taste are called witty or versatile—that is to say, full of good turns; for such sallies seem to spring from the character. . . . [Such a temperate person] is further characterized by the quality of tact, the possessor of which will say, and allow to be said to him, only the sorts of things that are suitable to a virtuous man and a gentleman: since there is a certain propriety in which such a man will say and hear in jest, and the jesting of a gentleman differs from that of a person of servile nature, as does that of an educated from that of an uneducated man. The difference may be seen by comparing the old and the modern comedies; the earlier dramatists found their fun in obscenity, the moderns prefer innuendo, which marks a great advance in decorum. (247)

    See also Aristotle, under COMEDY (AP 21).

1570   Castelvetro. *See* under COMEDY (CP 134).

c. 1583   Sidney   SDP

Our comedians think there is no delight without laughter, which is very wrong; for though laughter may come with delight, yet cometh it not of delight, as though delight should be the cause of laughter; but well may one thing breed both together. Nay, rather in themselves they have, as it were, a kind of contrariety. For delight we scarcely do, but in things that have a conveniency to ourselves, or to the general nature; laughter almost ever cometh of things most disproportioned to ourselves and nature. Delight hath a joy in it either permanent or present; laughter hath only a scornful tickling. For example, we are ravished with delight to see a fair woman, and yet are far from being moved to laughter. We laugh at deformed creatures, wherein certainly we cannot delight. We delight in good chances, we laugh at mischances. We delight to hear the happiness of our friends and country, at which he were worthy to be laughed at that would laugh. We shall, contrarily, laugh sometimes to find a matter quite mistaken and go down the hill against the bias, in the mouth of some such men, as for the respect of them one shall be heartily sorry he cannot choose but laugh, and so is rather pained than delighted with laughter. Yet deny I not but that they may go well together. . . . But . . . all the end of the comical part be not upon such scornful matters as stir laughter only, but mixed with it that delightful teaching which is the end of poesy. And the great fault, even in that point of laughter, and forbidden plainly by Aristotle, is that they stir laughter in sinful things, which are rather execrable than ridiculous; or in miserable, which are rather to be pitied than scorned. For what is it to make folks gape at a wretched beggar or a beggarly clown, or, against law of hospitality, to jest at strangers because they speak not English so well as we do? What do we learn? (50-51)

1641 Jonson. *See* under COMEDY (JD 99-101).

1663 Molière. *See* under IMITATION (MP 4: 340).

1668 Dryden. *See* under COMEDY (DW 1, 2: 88-89).

1671 Dryden. *See* under COMEDY (DW 1, 2: 191-92), POETIC JUSTICE (DW 1, 2: 198-201).

1672 Dryden   **DW**

The language, wit, and conversation of our age, are improved and refined above the last; and . . . our plays have received some part of those advantages. (230) . . . Our improprieties are less frequent, and less gross than [the ancients]. One testimony of this is undeniable; that we are the first who have observed them; and, certainly, to observe errours is a great step to the correcting of them. (232) . . . I should now speak of the refinement of Wit. . . . The wit of the last age was yet more incorrect than their language. Shakespeare, who many times has written better than any poet in any language, is yet so far from writing wit always, or expressing that wit according to the dignity of the subject, that he writes in many places below the dullest writers of ours or of any precedent age. (243) . . . The wit of this age is much more courtly. (247) . . . I have always acknowledged the wit of our predecessors, with all the veneration which becomes me; but I am sure, their wit was not that of gentlemen; there was ever somewhat that was ill-bred and clownish in it, and which confessed the conversation of the authors. And this leads me to the last and greatest advantage of our writing, which proceeds from conversation. In the [former] age . . . there was less gallantry than in ours; neither did they keep the best company of theirs. (1, 2: 249)

1710 Addison. *See* under CLOSURE (AW 3: 263).

1711 Addison   **AW**

Among all kinds of writing, there is none in which authors are more apt to miscarry than in works of humour, as there is none in which they are more ambitious to excel. It is not an imagination that teems with monsters, a head that is filled with extravagant conceptions . . . ; and yet, if we look into the productions of several writers, who set up for men of humour, what wild irregular fancies, what unnatural distortions of thought, do we meet with? If they speak nonsense, they believe they are talking humour, and when they have drawn together a scheme of absurd inconsistent ideas, they are not able to read it over to themselves without laughing. These poor gentlemen endeavor to gain themselves the reputation of wits and humourists, by such monstrous conceits as almost qualify them for Bedlam; not considering that humour should always lie under the check of reason, and that it requires the direction of the nicest judgment, by so much the more as it indulges itself in the most boundless freedoms. There is a kind of nature that is to be observed in this sort of composition, as well as in all other; and a certain regularity of thought which must discover the writer to be a man of sense, at the same time that he appears altogether given up to caprice. (1: 64-65) . . . It is indeed much easier to describe what is not humour, than what is; and very difficult to define it otherwise than as Cowley has done wit, by negatives. Were I to give my own notions of it, I would deliver them after Plato's manner, in a kind of allegory, and by supposing Humour to be a person, deduce to him all his qualifications, according to the following genealogy. Truth was the founder of the family, and the father of Good Sense. Good Sense was the father of Wit, who married a lady of collateral line called Mirth, by whom he had issue Humour. Humour therefore being the youngest of this illustrious family, and descended from parents of such different dispositions, is very various and unequal in his temper; sometimes you see him putting on grave looks and a solemn habit, sometimes airy in his behaviour and fantastic in his dress; insomuch that at different times he appears as serious as a judge, and as jocular as a Merry-Andrew. But as he has a great deal of the mother in his constitution, whatever mood he is in, he never fails to make his company laugh. . . . Also Humour differs from the True, as a monkey does from a man. First of all, He is exceedingly given to little apish tricks and buffooneries. Secondly, He so much delights in mimickry, that it is all one to him whether he exposes by it vice and folly, luxury and avarice; or on the contrary, virtue and wisdom, pain and poverty. Thirdly, He is wonderfully unlucky, insomuch that he will bite the hand that feeds him, and endeavour to ridicule both friends and foes indifferently. For having but small talents, he must be merry where he can, not where he should. Fourthly, Being entirely void of reason, he pursues no point, either of morality or instruction, but is ludicrous only for the sake of being so. Fifthly, Being incapable of any thing but mock representations, his ridicule is always personal, and aimed at the vicious man, or the writer; not at the vice, or the writing. (1: 65)

See also Addison under GENRE DEFINITION (AW 1: 361).

1715 Addison. See under INSTRUCTION (AW 3: 244).

1738   Voltaire   **VW**

With regard to the stage . . . violent peals of universal laughter seldom rise but from some mistake: Mercury taken for Sofia; Menechmes for his brother. . . . There are a great many other species of the comic, and pleasantries, that cause a different sort of entertainment; but I never saw what we call laughing from the bottom of one's soul . . . except in cases nearly resembling those which [involve some mistake]. (10, 1: 271) . . . A bad man will never make us laugh, because laughter always arises from a gayety of disposition, absolutely incompatible with contempt and indignation; it is true, indeed, we laugh at Tartuffe, but not at his hypocrisy; it is at the mistake of the good old gentleman, who takes him for a saint: the hypocrisy once discovered we laugh no longer, but feel very different impressions. (10, 1: 272)

c.1749   Voltaire. *See* under COMEDY (VW 10, 1: 280).

1755-1780   Diderot   **DDE**

The starting point of comedy is the malice natural to all men. When the shortcomings of our fellow men are not pathetic enough to arouse passion, revolting enough to inspire fear, we regard these shortcomings with a self-satisfaction mixed with contempt. These images make us smile if they are depicted with delicacy. If the strokes of this malicious joy, as striking as they are unexpected, are sharpened by surprise, these images make us laugh. (287)
      See also Diderot under COMEDY (DDE 287).

1767-1769   Lessing. *See* under COMEDY (LSPW 307).

1808   Schlegel. *See* under CHARACTER (SCL 183-84),COMEDY (SCL 149-51), DISTANCE (SCL (256), GENRE (SCL 44-46), IRONY (SCL 369-70).

1815   Hazlitt   **HW**

The proper object of ridicule is *egotism*; and a man cannot be a very great egotist who every day sees himself represented on the stage. We are deficient in Comedy, because we are without characters in real life—as we have no historical pictures, because we have no faces proper for them. (1: 12) . . The alterations which have taken place in conversation and dress . . . have been by no means favourable to Comedy. The present prevailing style of conversation is not *personal*, but critical and analytical. It consists almost entirely in the discussion of general topics, in dissertations on philosophy or taste: and Congreve would be able to derive no better hints from the conversations of our toilettes or drawing-rooms, for the exquisite raillery or poignant repartee of his dialogues, than from a deliberation of the Royal Society. (1: 12)

1819   Hazlitt   HW

MAN is the only animal that laughs and weeps; for he is the only animal that is
struck with the difference between what things are, and what they ought to be.
We weep at what thwarts or exceeds our desires in serious matters: we laugh at
what only disappoints our expectations in trifles. We shed tears from sympathy
with real and necessary distress; as we burst into laughter from want of
sympathy with that which is unreasonable and unnecessary, the absurdity of
which provokes our spleen or mirth, rather than any serious reflections on it.
To explain the nature of laughter and tears, is to account for the condition of
human life; for it is in a manner compounded of these two! It is a tragedy or a
comedy—sad or merry, as it happens. The crimes and misfortunes that are
inseparable from it, shock and wound the mind when they once seize upon it,
and when the pressure can no longer be borne, seek relief in tears: the follies
and absurdities that men commit, or the odd accidents that befal them, afford
us amusement from the very rejection of these false claims upon our sympathy,
and end in laughter. If every thing that went wrong, if every vanity or weakness
in another gave us a sensible pang, it would be hard indeed: but as long as the
disagreeableness of the consequences of a sudden disaster is kept out of sight
by the immediate oddity of the circumstances, and the absurdity or unaccount-
ableness of a foolish action is the most striking thing in it, the ludicrous
prevails over the pathetic, and we receive pleasure instead of pain from the
farce of life which is played before us, and which discomposes our gravity as
often as it fails to move our anger or our pity! (8: 5) . . . The serious is the
habitual stress which the mind lays upon the expectation of a given order of
events, following one another with a certain regularity and weight of interest
attached to them. When this stress is increased beyond its usual pitch by
intensity, so as to overstrain the feelings of the violent opposition of good to
bad, or of objects to our desires, it becomes the pathetic or tragical. The
ludicrous, or comic, is the unexpected loosening or relaxing this stress below
its usual pitch of intensity, by such an abrupt transposition of the order of our
ideas, as taking the mind unawares, throws it off its guard, startles it into a
lively sense of pleasure, and leaves no time nor inclination for painful reflections. The essence of the laughable then is the incongruous, the disconnecting
one idea from another, or the jostling of one feeling against another. The first
and most obvious cause of laughter is to be found in the simple succession of
events, as in the sudden shifting of a disguise, or some unlooked-for accident,
without any absurdity of character or situation. The accidental contradiction
between our expectations and the event can hardly be said, however, to amount
to the ludicrous: it is merely laughable. The ludicrous is where there is the same
contradiction between the object and our expectations, heightened by some
deformity or inconvenience, that is, by its being contrary to what is customary
or desirable: as the ridiculous, which is the highest degree of the laughable, is
that which is contrary not only to custom but to sense and reason, or is a

voluntary departure from what we have a right to expect from those who are conscious of absurdity and propriety in words, looks, and actions. (8: 7-8) . . . There is nothing more powerfully humorous than what is called *keeping* in comic character, as we see it very finely exemplified in Sancho Panza and Don Quixote. The proverbial phlegm and the romantic gravity of these two celebrated persons may be regarded as the height of this kind of excellence. The deep feeling of character strengthens the sense of the ludicrous. Keeping in comic character is consistency in absurdity; a determined and laudable attachment to the incongruous and singular. The regularity completes the contradiction; for the number of instances of deviation from the right line, branching out in all directions, shews the inveteracy of the original bias to any extravagance or folly, the natural improbability, as it were, increasing every time with the multiplication of chances for a return to common sense, and in the end mounting up to an incredible and unaccountably ridiculous height, when we find our expectations invariably baffled. (8: 11) . . . Humour is the describing the ludicrous as it is in itself; wit is the exposing it, by comparing or contrasting it with something else. Humour is, as it were, the growth of nature and accident; wit is the product of art and fancy. Humour, as it is shewn in books, is an imitation of the natural or acquired absurdities of mankind, or of the ludicrous in accident, situation, and character: wit is the illustrating and heightening the sense of that absurdity by some sudden and unexpected likeness or opposition of one thing to another, which sets off the quality we laugh at or despise in a still more contemptible or striking point of view. Wit, as distinguished from poetry, is the imagination or fancy inverted, and so applied to given objects, as to make the little look less, the mean more light and worthless; or to divert our admiration or wean our affections from that which is lofty and impressive, instead of producing more intense admiration and exalted passion, as poetry does. (8: 15)

    See also Hazlitt under IRONY (HW 8: 10-11).

c.1820   Hegel. *See* under COMEDY (HFA 4: 301-304).

1878   Nietzsche   **NHH**

THE SOURCE OF THE COMIC ELEMENT.—If we consider that for many thousands of years man was an animal that was susceptible in the highest degree to fear, and that everything sudden and unexpected had to find him ready for battle, perhaps even ready for death; that even later, in social relations, all security was based on the expected, on custom in thought and action, we need not be surprised that at everything sudden and unexpected in word and deed, if it occurs without danger or injury, man becomes exuberant and passes over into the very opposite of fear—the terrified, trembling, crouching being shoots upward, stretches itself: man laughs. This transition from momentary fear into short-lived exhilaration is called the *Comic*. (173)

1908   Pirandello   POH

The inner and peculiarly essential process of humor is one that inevitably *dismantles*, splits and disrupts, whereas art taught in the schools by Rhetoric was primarily external composition, a logically ordered concordance. (31) . . . Humor requires above all an intimacy of style which in Italian literature has always been hindered by preoccupation over form and by all the rhetorical questions concerning language. Humor needs a highly spirited, free, spontaneous, and direct movement of language—a movement that can be achieved only when form creates itself anew each time. Now Rhetoric taught the writer not to *create* form but to *imitate* it, to compose it externally. It taught the writer to seek language from the outside as an object and naturally this type of language could only be found in books, in those books that rhetoric itself had imposed as models and as texts. What movement could one give to this external language, fixed and mummified, to this form not created anew each time but imitated, studied, and composed? Movement is only in living language and in form that creates itself. And the humor that cannot do without this movement, I repeat, we shall find it (both in its broad sense and in its proper sense) in the humoristic expressions in dialect, in macaronic poetry and in the writers who rebelled against Rhetoric. (35) . . . Having a profound belief, an ideal goal, having an aspiration and struggling to attain it, far from being conditions necessary to humor, are rather obstacles to it; and yet the person who has a belief, an ideal goal or an aspiration, and who struggles in his own way to achieve it, he, too, can be a humorist. In short, any such ideal, in itself, does not dispose anyone to humor but rather works as a handicap against it. But still the writer may well have an ideal, and when he does, humor, which stems from other causes, will certainly be affected by it just as it will be affected by all the other traits of the temperament of a certain humorist. In other words: humor does not require an ethical basis; it may or may not have one: this depends on the personality, on the temperament of the writer; but naturally, the presence or the lack of it will result in humor having different qualities and producing different effects, that is, in its being more or less bitter, more or less harsh, in its inclining more or less towards tragedy or comedy, or towards satire or burlesque, etc. People who believe that it is all a play of contrasts between the poet's ideal and reality, and who maintain that if that ideal is bitterly thwarted and scorned by reality, the result will be invective, irony, or satire; that if the poet is only slightly irritated by reality or if the contrast between the appearances of reality and himself causes him to laugh more or less heartily, then the result will be comedy, farce, jest, caricature, or the grotesque; and that finally humor will result if the poet's ideal does not become offended and does not react with indignation, but rather compromises good-naturedly, with a somewhat painful indulgence—these people show that they have an excessively one-sided and somewhat superficial view of humor. It is true that a great deal depends on the poet's temperament and that his ideal, confronted by reality, may react with indignation, or laughter, or compromise; but an ideal that compromises does not really show that it is sure of itself and profoundly rooted. And is this limitation of the ideal all that humor consists of? Not at all. The limitation of the ideal, if anything, would be not the cause but rather the result of the particular psychological process which is called humor. Let us therefore forget, once and for all, about ideals, faith, aspirations, and so forth. (93) . . . During the conception of all works of humor, reflection is not hidden, it does not remain invisible: it is not, that is, almost a form of feeling or almost a mirror in which feeling contemplates itself; rather, it places itself squarely before the feeling, in a judging attitude, and, detaching itself from it, analyzes it and disassembles its imagery; from this analysis and decomposition, however, there arises or emerges a new feeling which could be called and in fact I call the *feeling of the opposite*. I see an old lady whose hair is dyed and completely smeared with some kind of horrible ointment; she is all made-up in a clumsy and awkward fashion and is all dolled-up like a young girl. I begin to laugh. I *perceive* that she is *the opposite* of what a respectable old lady should be. Now I could stop here at this initial and superficial comic reaction: the comic consists precisely of this *perception of the opposite*. But if, at this point, reflection interferes in me to suggest that perhaps this old lady finds no pleasure in dressing up like an exotic parrot, and that perhaps she is distressed by it and does it only because she pitifully deceives herself into believing that, by making herself up like that and by concealing her wrinkles and gray hair, she may be able to hold the love of her much younger husband—if reflection comes to suggest all this, then I can no longer laugh at her as I did at first, exactly because the inner working of reflection has made me go beyond, or rather enter deeper into, the initial stage of awareness: from the beginning *perception of the opposite*, reflection has made me shift to a *feeling of the opposite*. And herein lies the precise difference between the comic and humor. (113) . . . Art, like all ideal or illusory constructions, also tends to fix life; it fixes it in one moment or in various given moments—the statue in a gesture, the landscape in a temporary immutable perspective. . . . Art generally abstracts and concentrates; that is, it catches and represents the essential and characteristic ideality of both men and things. Now it seems to the humorist that all this oversimplifies nature and tends to make life too reasonable or at least too coherent. It seems to him that art does not take into account, as it should, the causes, the *real* causes that often move this more human soul to the most mindless and totally unpredictable actions. For the humorist, the causes in real life are never as logical and as well ordered as they are in our common works of art, in which, basically, everything is arranged, organized and ordered according to the writer's proposed objective. Order? Coherence? But if we have within ourselves four or five different souls—the instinctive, the moral, the emotional, the social—constantly fighting among themselves? The attitude of our consciousness is contingent upon whichever of these souls is dominant; and we hold as valid and sincere that fictitious interpretation of ourselves, of our inner being—a being that we know nothing about because it never reveals itself in its entirety but now in one way and now in another way, according to the turn of the circumstances of life. Yes, an epic or dramatic poet may represent a hero of his in whom opposite and contrasting elements are shown in conflict, but we will *compose* a character from these elements and will want to represent him as consistent in every action. Well, the humorist does just the opposite: he will *decompose* the character into his elements and while the epic or dramatic poet takes pains to picture him as coherent in every action, the humorist enjoys representing him in his incongruities. The humorist does not recognize heroes, or rather he lets others represent them. For his part, he knows what a legend is and how it is created, what history is and how it is made: they are all compositions, more or less ideal; and the greater the pretense of reality, the more idealized they are. The humorist amuses himself by disassembling these compositions, although one cannot say that it is a pleasant amusement. (142-43) . . . The humorist knows that the ordinary happenings, the commonplace details—in short, the material substance of life, so varied and complex—harshly contradict [the] ideal simplifications; he knows that they incite actions and inspire thoughts and feelings that are contrary to all that harmonious logic of acts and characters created by the ordinary writers. And what about the unpredictable element in life? What about the abyss which exists in our souls? Don't we often feel within ourselves the flashes of strange thoughts, like flashes of madness, inconsequential thoughts we dare not confide even to ourselves, as if really issuing from a soul different from the one we normally recognize as ours? Hence comes, in the art of humor, all that searching of the most intimate and minute details—which may appear trivial or vulgar if compared with the idealized syntheses of art in general—and that search of contrasts and contradictions which is at the basis of the art of the humorist as opposed to the consistency sought by others; hence all that is disorganized, unraveled and whimsical, all the digressions which can be seen in the works of humor, as opposed to the ordered construction, the *composition* of the works of art in general. (144-45) . . . Humor consists in the feeling of the opposite produced by the special activity of reflection, which does not remain hidden and does not become, as usual in art, a form of feeling, but its opposite, though it follows closely behind the feeling as the shadow follows the body. The ordinary artist pays attention only to the body, the humorist pays attention to both, and sometimes more to the shadow than to the body: he notices all the tricks of the shadow, the way it sometimes grows longer and sometimes short and squat, almost as if to mimic the body, which meanwhile is indifferent to it and does not pay any attention to it. (145)

　　See also Pirandello under CHARACTER (POH 49, 59-60), IRONY (POH 5, 6-7, 7, 8, 39).

1931-1936   Artaud. *See* under TRAGEDY (AT 142-43).

IDEALISM

Attributes of philosophical idealism are suggested in statements about: ideas as real entities; objects as representing ideas; perfect or ideal standards; objects as self-contained and self-consistent; truth as something beyond and independent of surface reality; the search for essences.

1561   Scaliger   **SP**

We have presented the *ideas* of things in examples drawn from Vergil [in our *Poetics*], just as they might be taken from nature itself. Indeed, I think that the workmanship of his poetry finds an analogy in art, for sculptors and painters take from real life those conceptions which they use in imitating lines, light, shade, and background, and they embody in their own productions the peculiar excellencies of many objects, so that they do not seem to have been taught by nature, but to have vied with it, or even better to have given it its laws. Who, in fact, would say that nature ever produced a woman so beautiful that a connoisseur could not find some flaw in her beauty? For though the archetype of nature is altogether perfect in outline and proportions, the actual product suffers many hindrances through circumstances of parentage, climate, time, and place. So we have not been able to get from nature a single pattern such as the *ideas* of Vergil furnish us. (52)

1570   Castelvetro. *See* under IMITATION (CP 37-38, 40, 43-44).

c. 1583   Sidney. *See* under IMITATION (SDP 7-8. 9-10)

1657   d'Aubignac   **AAS**

The Stage . . . does not present things as they have been, but as they ought to be; for the Poet must in the Subject he takes reform every thing that is not accommodated to the Rules of his Art. (2: 65)

1668   Dryden. *See* under IMITATION (DW 1, 2: 126-27).

1695   Dryden. *See* under IMITATION (DW 3: 322-25).

1712   Addison   **AW**

Because the imagination can fancy to itself things more great, strange, or beautiful than the eye ever saw, and is still sensible of some defect in what it has seen; on this account it is the part of the poet to humour the imagination in our own notions, by mending and perfecting nature where he describes a reality, and by adding greater beauties than are put together in nature, where he describes a fiction. (2: 149)

1758   Diderot   **DDP**

In complicated plays, interest is the result rather of the plot than of the speeches; in simple plays, on the other hand, it is rather the speeches than the plot which arouse interest. But in whom is the interest to be aroused? In the characters, or in the minds of the audience? The spectators are merely ignorant witnesses of what passes. . . . If it were only understood that, although a drama is made to be produced, it was still necessary that both author and actor forget the spectator, and that all the interest should be centered in the characters, there would be less reading of Poetics. If you do this or that, you will produce this or that effect on the spectator. They should say: If you do this or that, this is what will happen to your characters. (298) . . . What will become of the actor, if you concentrate upon the audience? Do you imagine he will feel any more than what you have given him? If you think of the audience, he will think of them, too. You seek their applause; so will he. And then what will become of your illusion? . . . The actor performs badly what the poet wrote for the audience. . . . Whether you write or act, think no more of the audience than if it had never existed. Imagine a huge wall across the front of the stage, separating you from the audience, and behave exactly as if the curtain had never risen. (299)

1759   Johnson   **JW**

An ideal form is no less real than material bulk: yet an ideal form has no extension. It is no less certain, when you think on a pyramid, that your mind possesses the idea of a pyramid, than that the pyramid itself is standing. (1: 308)

1765   Johnson. *See* under UNIVERSALITY (JS 11-12).

1789   Goethe. *See* under IMITATION (GLE 59-61).

1798   Goethe. *See* under ILLUSION (GLE 52-57).

1808   Schlegel. *See* under CHARACTER (SCL 66, 148-49), FORM (SCL 340), GENRE (SCL 44-46, 46-47), POETRY OF THE THEATRE (SCL 36-37), SPECTACLE (SCL 59), TRAGEDY (SCL 67, 113), UNITY (SCL 242-45).

1813   Hazlitt. *See* under IMAGINATION (HW 1: 134).

1815   Coleridge. *See* under AESTHETIC (CBL 2: 232, 233-34, 238-39, 253, 256-57), CHARACTER (CBL 2: 33-34), IMAGINATION (CBL 1: 202,

2: 12), IMAGINATION (CBL 2: 259), ORDER (CBL 2: 262); compare with REALISM (CBL 1: 179).

1816   Hazlitt. *See* under AESTHETIC (HW 1: 68), IMITATION (HW 1: 72-74, 75), SUBJECT (HW 1: 75-76).

1817   Hazlitt. *See* under IMITATION (HW 1: 153).

c.1820   Hegel   HFA

We are justified in maintaining categorically that the beauty of art stands *higher* than Nature. For the beauty of art is a beauty begotten, a new birth of mind; and to the extent that Spirit and its creations stand higher than Nature and its phenomena; to that extent the beauty of art is more exalted than the beauty of Nature. . . . In predicating of mind and its artistic beauty a higher place in contrast to Nature, we do not denote a distinction which is merely relative. Mind, and mind alone, is pervious to truth, comprehending all in itself, so that all which is beautiful can only be veritably beautiful as partaking in this higher sphere and as begotten of the same (1: 2-3) [We must consider] the so-called realistic mode of expression, as opposed to a conventional speech of the theatre and its rhetoric. Diderot, Lessing, Goethe and Schiller also in their youth addressed themselves in modern times above all to this attitude of direct and natural expression. Lessing did so with the powers of a trained and sensitive observation. Schiller and Goethe did so with their predilection for the direct animation of unembellished robustness and force. That men should converse with one another as in the Greek, or with more insistence—and in this latter respect the criticism has a reasonable basis—as in French comedy and tragedy, was scouted as contrary to Nature. This type of naturalism, however, may very readily, with its superfluity of merely realistic traits, fall into the other extreme of dryness and prose, in so far, that is, as the characters are not developed in the essential qualities of their emotional life and action, but only as they happen to express themselves in the literal accuracy of their individual life, without indicating therein any more significant self-consciousness or any further sense of their essential position. The more natural the characterization is allowed to remain in this sense the more prosaic it becomes. In actual life men converse and strive with one another before everything else on the mere basis of their *distinct singularity*. If our object is to depict them simply as such it is impossible that they should also be represented in their truly substantive significance. . . . Between [the] two extremes of a purely formal generality and [the] natural expression of unpolished peculiarities we have the true universal, which is throughout neither formal nor destitute of individuality, but finds its concrete realization in a twofold way from the defined content of character and the objective presence of opinions and aims. Genuine poetry will therefore consist in the assertion of what belongs to immediate and actual life as characteristic and individual in the purifying medium of universality, both aspects being permitted to mediate each other. In this case we are conscious, even in respect to diction, that without being wholly banished from the basis of reality and its actual traits of truth, we are nevertheless carried into another sphere that is to say the ideal realm of art. (4: 265-67)

See also Hegel under ACTION (HFA 4: 252), AESTHETIC (HFA 1: 8-9, 10), AFFECT (HFA 4: 273, 276-77), CATHARSIS (HFA 4: 298-300), DRAMA (HFA 4: 254-55, 261-62), LANGUAGE (HFA 4: 264-65), TRAGEDY (HFA 4: 295-99, 300-301, 312-5).

c.1820   Hazlitt   HW

The *ideal* is not confined to creation, but takes place in imitation, where a thing is subjected to one view, as all the parts of a face to the same expression. (11: 463)

1823   Goethe. Compare with THOUGHT (GCE Nov. 14).

1824   Hazlitt   HW

The *ideal* is not the preference of that which is fine in nature to that which is less so. There is nothing fine in art but what is taken almost immediately, and, as it were, in the mass, from what is finer in nature. Where there have been the finest models in nature, there have been the finest works of art. (9: 379) . . . Sir Joshua [Reynolds] has constructed his theory of the *ideal* in art, upon the same mistaken principle of the negation or abstraction of *particular nature*. The *ideal* is not a negative but a positive thing. The leaving out the details or the peculiarities of an individual face does not make it one jot more ideal. To paint history, is to paint nature as answering to a general, predominant, or preconceived idea in the mind, of strength, beauty, passion, thought . . . ; but the way to do this is not to leave out the details, but to incorporate the general idea with the details;—that is, to show . . . the same character preserved consistently through every part of the body. Grandeur does not consist in omitting the parts, but in connecting all the parts into a whole, and in giving their combined and varied action: abstract truth or ideal perfection does not consist in rejecting the peculiarities of form, but in rejecting all those which are not consistent with the character intended to be given; and in following up the same *general idea* . . . through every ramification of the frame. But these modificatons of form or expression can only be learnt from nature, and therefore the perfection of art must always be sought in nature. The ideal properly applies as much to the *idea* of ugliness, weakness, folly, meanness, vice, as of beauty, strength, wisdom, magnanimity, or virtue. (9: 405)

Compare with Hazlitt under REALISM (HW 9: 378-79).

1830   Hazlitt   HW

The *ideal* is the abstraction of any thing from all the circumstances that weaken its effect, or lessen our admiration of it. Or it is filling up the outline of truth or beauty existing in the mind, so as to leave nothing wanting or to desire farther. The principle of the *ideal* is the satisfaction we have in the contemplation of any quality or object, which makes us seek to heighten, to prolong, or extend that satisfaction to the utmost; and beyond this we cannot go, for we cannot get beyond the highest conceivable degree of any quality or excellence diffused over the whole of an object. . . . The *ideal* is the impassive and immortal: it is that which exists in and for itself; or is begot by the intense *idea* and innate love of it. . . . The height of nature surpasses the utmost stretch of the imagination; the human form is alone the image of the divinity. . . . A thing is not more perfect by becoming something else, but by *being more itself*. If the face of the *Venus* had been soft and feminine, but the figure had not corresponded, then this would have been a defect of the *ideal*, which subdues the discordances of Nature in the mould of passion, and so far from destroying character, imparts the same character to all, according to a certain established idea or preconception in the mind. . . . To propose to *embody an abstraction* is a contradiction in terms. The attempt to carry such a scheme into execution would not merely supersede all the varieties and accidents of nature, but would effectually put a stop to the productions of art, or to reduce them to one vague and undefined abstraction. . . . That amalgamation, then, of a number of different impressions into one, which in some sense is felt to constitute the *ideal*, is not to be sought in the dry and desert spaces or the endless void of metaphysical abstraction, or by taking a number of things and *muddling* them all together, but by singling out some one thing or leading quality of an object, and making it the pervading and regulating principle of all the rest, so as to produce the greatest strength and harmony of effect. (9: 429-30) . . . The *ideal* is the enhancing and expanding of an idea from the satisfaction we take in it; or it is taking away whatever divides, and adding whatever increases our sympathy with pleasure and power ''till our content is absolute,'' or at the height. . . . The *ideal* is not in general the strong-hold of poetry. For description in words (to produce any vivid impression) requires a translation of the object into some other form, which is the language of metaphor and imagination; as narrative can only interest by a succession of events and a conflict of hopes and fears. Therefore, the sphere of the *ideal* is in a manner limited to Sculpture and Painting, where the object itself is given entire without any possible change of circumstances, and where, though the impression is momentary, it lasts forever. (9: 431-32) . . . The Greek tragedies may serve to explain how far the *ideal* and the *dramatic* are consistent; for the characters there are almost as ideal as their statues, and almost as impassive; and perhaps their extreme decorum and self-possession is only rendered palatable to us by the story which nearly always represents a conflict between Gods and men. The *ideal* part is, however, necessary at all times to the grandeur of tragedy, since it is the superiority of character to fortune and circumstances, or the larger scope of thought and feeling thrown into it, that redeems it from the charge of vulgar grossness or physical horrors. (9: 432)

1864   Taine. *See* under AESTHETICS (TLA 76, 76-77, 82-84, 273-74), EVOLUTIONISM (TLA 283-84), FORM (TLA 64, .73), HERO (TLA 180), IMITATION (TLA 51-53, 56-58), LANGUAGE (TLA 54-55).

1871   Nietzsche   **NBT**

The chorus is a living bulwark against the onsets of reality, because it—the satyric chorus—portrays existence more truthfully, more realistically, more perfectly than the cultured man who ordinarily considers himself as the only reality. The sphere of poetry does not lie outside the world, like some fantastic impossibility of a poet's imagination: it seeks to be the very opposite, the unvarnished expression of the truth, and must for this reason cast aside the false finery of that supposed reality of the cultured man. The contrast between this intrinsic truth of nature and the falsehood of culture, which poses as the only reality, is similar to that existing between the external kernal of things, the thing in itself, and the collective world of phenomena. (64)

  See also Nietzsche under DRAMA (NBT 60-61), LANGUAGE (NBT 55), TRAGEDY (NBT 127, 159-60), UNITY (NBT 27).

1873   Nietzsche. Compare with METAPHOR (NEG 178-88).

1887   Chekhov. Compare with REALISM (CL 57).

1888   Nietzsche. Compare with DISINTERESTEDNESS (NW 105-106), TRAGEDY (NEH 70-73).

1890   Shaw. Compare with REALISM (SMCE 31).

1898   Shaw   **SCP**

Idealism, which is only a flattering name for romance in politics and morals, is as obnoxious to me as romance in ethics or religion. . . . I can no longer be satisfied with fictitious morals and fictitious good conduct, shedding fictitious glory on robbery, starvation, disease, crime, drink, war, cruelty, cupidity. (734)

1908   Pirandello   **POH**

[Ariosto's] process of identification with his world consists in the fact that he, with his powerful imagination, *sees* as well carved out, or rather finished in all its forms, as precise, clearly-delineated, well-ordered, and alive, a world which others had assembled clumsily and had populated with beings so awkward, so ridiculous, so crudely inconsistent, and so on, that even their own authors could not take them seriously; a world also filled with wizards, fairies, and monsters which naturally increased its unreality and its unlikelihood. The poet lifts these beings out of their state as puppets and phantasms, and endows them with substance and consistency, vitality and character. Up to this point, he follows his own fantasy instinctively. Then the speculative faculty is introduced. . . . There is in that world an irreducible element . . . that the poet fails to objectify seriously without showing that he is conscious of its unreality. With that astonishing device . . . , he tries, however, to make it blend coherently with the whole. But his fantasy is not always helpful in this playful activity. And so he resorts to speculation: life loses its spontaneous movement and becomes a mechanical contrivance, an allegory. It is quite a strain. The poet strives to give a certain consistency to those fantastic constructions, which he senses have an irreducible unreality, by means of, let's say, a moral framework. It is a vain and misguided effort because the mere fact of giving an allegorical sense to a representation reveals clearly that the latter is already regarded as fable, devoid of both imaginative and real truth, and made up as a demonstration of a moral truth. One could confidently assert that the poet is not at all concerned with the demonstration of any moral truth and that those allegories were suggested to him by reflection, as a remedy. That was the world, and those were the elements that it made available. The element of magic and the marvelous in chivalric poetry could in no way be eliminated without altering the fundamental nature of that world. And thus the poet either tries to reduce it to a symbol, or he simply accepts it, but, of course, with a sense of irony. Even though a poet does not actually believe in the reality of his creation, he can still represent it as though he did believe in it . . . by not showing in the least that he is conscious of its unreality; he can also represent as real a thoroughly fantastic dream-world, which is regulated by its own laws, and which in the context of these laws is completely logical and consistent. When the poet creates with these conditions, the critic should no longer consider whether the artistic product is real or is a dream-world, but whether, as a dream-world, it is true: this is because the poet's intention was not to present an actual reality, but a dream having the appearance of reality, that is, of a reality which is dream-like, fantastic, and non-actual. (75-76) . . . In more than one place . . . [Ariosto] openly shows that he is conscious of the unreality of his creation. He also shows that when he gives a moral value and a logical (i.e., non-fantastic) coherence to the element of magic in that world. The poet does not want to create and represent a dream-world as true; he is not concerned only with the fantastic truth of his world, but also with its actual reality; he doesn't want his world to be inhabited by empty forms and puppets, but by men who are alive and real and who are affected and moved by our human passions. In short, the poet does not perceive the circumstances of that legendary past as having been converted into a fantastic reality through his artistic vision, but rather the reasons of the present carried to and embodied in that remote world. Naturally, when these reasons find, in that world, elements capable of accommodating them, the fantastic reality is saved; but when they do not find them, due to the unyielding resistance of those elements, then irony inevitably bursts out, and that reality is shattered. (76)

See also Pirandello under HUMOR (POH 93).

1913   Shaw. Compare with CLOSURE (SMCE 139-40, 142-43, 145), DRAMA (SMCE 144).

1918-1922   Stanislavski   SAS

Our modern theatre . . . should not on any account give us the bare reflection of life itself; it must rather reflect everything that exists in life in all its hidden heroic tension; in a simple form of what seems to be everyday life, but actually in precise and luminous images in which all the passions are ennobled and alive. The worst thing that can happen to a theatre is to produce a play in which tendentiousness is overemphasized, and in which ideas are thrust on the characters who are not even living people but puppets.(104) . . . A successful propaganda play . . . is not the task of a serious theatre, for that only means the inclusion of the theatre in the utilitarian needs of the hour. Theatre looks for only that which remains in the play as the grain of eternally pure human feelings and thoughts, only that which does not depend on the mounting of the play and is understood by everybody in every age and in every language. (105-106)

1931-1936   Artaud   AT

If in fact we raise the question of the origins and *raison d'être* (or primordial necessity) of the theater, we find, metaphysically, the materialization or rather the exteriorization of a kind of essential drama which would contain, in a manner at once manifold and unique, the essential principles of all drama, already *disposed* and *divided*, not so much as to lose their character as principles, but enough to comprise, in a substantial and active fashion (i.e., resonantly), an infinite perspective of conflicts. . . . And this essential drama, we come to realize, exists, and in the image of something subtler than Creation itself, something which must be represented as the result of one Will alone— and *without conflict*. We must believe that the essential drama, the one at the root of all the Great Mysteries, is associated with the second phase of Creation, that of difficulty and of the Double, that of matter and the materialization of the idea. (50-51)

See also Artaud under ACTION (AT 82).

1933   Stanislavski   SL

The spectator . . . is an accidental witness. Speak up so that he can hear you, place yourself in the right parts of the stage so that he can see you, but for the rest, forget entirely about the audience and put your mind solely on the characters in the play. It is not for the actor to be interested in the spectator but the other way around; the spectator should be engrossed in the actor. The best way to be in contact with the audience is to be in close relationship to the characters in the play. (134)

IDENTIFICATION

The passages presented under this heading imply, explicitly state, or attempt to explain a theory of the spectator's intellectual or emotional identification with a fictional character. For the most part these are reciprocal imitation theories, which is most extremely stated when it is suggested that the spectator can only imitate the character mentally when the character imitates the spectator physically. See also AFFECT and compare with ALIENATION.

4th cent. B.C.   Aristotle   **AP**

The poet should work out his play to the best of his power, with appropriate gestures; for those who feel emotion are most convincing *through natural sympathy with the characters they represent* [because they speak to the same natural tendencies in us: EP 486]; and one who *is agitated storms, one who is angry rages, with the most life-like reality* [rages or expresses dejection: EP 486]. Hence poetry *implies either a happy gift of nature or a strain of madness* [is an enterprise for the gifted <rather than> the manic individual: EP 486]. (61-63)

4th cent. B.C.   Aristotle   **AR**

We fear those who ought to be feared by our betters (since, if they can hurt our betters, rather will they be able to hurt us);—and, for the same reason, those whom our betters actually fear. (81-82) The appropriateness of the language helps to give probability to the *fact*; the hearer's mind draws the fallacious inference that the speaker is telling the truth, because, where such facts are present, men are thus affected; the hearer thinks, then, that the case stands as the speaker says, whether it does so stand or not, and invariably sympathises with the passionate speaker, even when he is an imposter. (159-60).

 See also Aristotle under AFFECT (APO 1340a: 1-25), FEAR (AP 45), IMITATION (APO 1340a: 11-25), PITY (AR 91).

c.20 B.C.   Horace. *See* under AFFECT (HAP 459).

1561   Scaliger. *See* under INSTRUCTION (SP 82-83).

1641   Jonson. *See* under AFFECT (JD 33).

1657   d'Aubignac   **AAS**

The Glory which one receives in publick for some handsom action; and the recital or representation of the Heroick Virtues of those who are not even in being, at the time we hear them, does nevertheless raise in us a presumptuous belief that we are able to perform the like; and this presumption becoming a nobler sort of Envy, called Emulation, produces in us an insatiable desire of Honour, and elevates our Courage to undertake any thing that may effect that Glorious Design. (1: 4)

See also d'Aubignac under PATHOS (AAS 3: 40-44), SUBJECT (AAS 2: 68-69).

1660   Corneille   CDENA

Kings are men just as the members of the audience, and fall into . . . misfortunes through the force of passions of which the audience is capable. . . . It helps us to choose the characters and the events which can excite both [pity and fear]. . . . Our audience is composed neither of very evil men nor of saints, but people of ordinary goodness, who are not so severely restrained by exact virtue that they are not susceptible to passions. . . . (3-4)

See also Corneille under CATHARSIS (CDT 816).

1669   Molière. Compare with AFFECT (MP 2: 37-38).

1679   Dryden. *See* under PITY (DW 1, 2: 270).

1695   Dryden   DW

All manner of imperfections must not be taken away from the characters; and the reason is, that there may be left some grounds of pity for their misfortunes. We can never be grieved for their miseries, who are thoroughly wicked, and have thereby justly called their calamities on themselves. Such men are the natural objects of our hatred, not of our commiseration. If on the other side their characters are wholly perfect, (such as for example, the character of a saint or martyr in a play,) his or her misfortunes would produce impious thoughts in the beholders; they would accuse the heavens of injustice, and think of leaving a religion where piety was so ill requited. (3: 308)

1712   Addison   AW

When we read of torments, wounds, deaths, and the like dismal accidents, our pleasure does not flow so properly from the grief which such melancholy descriptions give us, as from the secret comparison which we make between ourselves and the person who suffers. Such representations teach us to set a just value upon our own condition, and make us prize our good fortune, which exempts us from the like calamities. This is, however, such a kind of pleasure as we are not capable of receiving, when we see a person actually lying under the tortures that we meet with in a description; because, in this case, the object presses too close upon our sense, and bears so hard upon us, that it does not give us time or leisure to reflect on ourselves. Our thoughts are so intent upon the miseries of the sufferer, that we cannot turn them upon our own happiness.

Whereas, on the contrary, we consider the misfortunes we read in history or poetry, either as past or as fictitious; so that the reflection upon ourselves rises in us insensible, and overbears the sorrow we conceive for the sufferings of the afflicted. (2: 149)

1738 Voltaire. *See* under HUMOR (VW 10, 1: 272).

1758 Diderot. *See* under DRAMA (DDP 287-89).

1765 Johnson. *See* under ILLUSION (JS 28).

1766 Lessing **LSPW**

All stoicism is undramatical; and our sympathy is always proportioned to the suffering expressed by the object which interests us. It is true, if we see him bear his misery with a great soul, this grandeur of soul excites our admiration; but admiration is only a cold emotion, and its inactive astonishment excludes every warmer passion as well as every distinct idea. (11)

   See also Lessing under IMITATION (LSPW 23).

1767-1769 Lessing. *See* under FEAR (LSPW 404, 407), PITY (LSPW 409).

1778 Diderot. Compare with DISINTERESTEDNESS (DPA 7-8), DISTANCE (DPA 49).

1797 Goethe. *See* under MAGNITUDE (GED 338-39).

1808 Schlegel. *See* under AFFECT (SCL 39), DRAMA (SCL 44), IMITATION (SCL 32); compare with DISTANCE (SCL 184-86).

1817 Hazlitt. *See* under ILLUSION (HW 1: 232), IMITATION (HW 1: 153).

1818 Hazlitt **HW**

One mode in which the dramatic exhibition of passion excites our sympathy without raising our disgust is, that in proportion as it sharpens the edge of calamity and disappointment, it strengthens the desire of good. It enhances our consciousness of the blessing, by making us sensible of the magnitude of the loss. The storm of passion lays bare and shews us the rich depths of the human soul: the whole of our existence, the sum total of our passions and pursuits, of that which we desire and that which we dread, is brought before us by contrast; the action and re-action are equal; the keenness of immediate suffering only gives us a more intense aspiration after, and a more intimate participation with the antagonist world of good; makes us drink deeper of the cup of human life; tugs at the heartstrings; loosens the pressure about them; and calls the springs

of thought and feeling into play with tenfold force. (5: 6) . . . The objects of
dramatic poetry affect us by sympathy, by their nearness to ourselves, as they
take us by surprise or force us upon action, "while rage with rage doth
sympathise"; the objects of epic poetry affect us through the medium of the
imagination, by magnitude and distance, by their permanence and universality. The one fills us with terror and pity, the other with admiration and delight.
(5: 52)

    See also Hazlitt under AESTHETIC (HW 5: 1-2).

c.1820   Hegel. *See* under CATHARSIS (HFA 4: 298-300).

1864   Taine   **TLA**

Men, indeed, can only comprehend sentiments analogous to those they have
themselves experienced. Other sentiments, no matter how powerfully expressed, do not affect them; they look with their eyes, but the heart is dormant
and directly their eyes are averted. Imagine a man losing his fortune, country,
children, health and liberty, one manacled in a dungeon for twenty years, like
Pellico or Andryane, whose spirit by degrees is changed and broken, and who
becomes melancholy and a mystic, and whose discouragement is incurable;
such a man entertains a horror of cheerful music, and has not disposition to
read Rabelais; if you place him before the merry brutes of Rubens, he will turn
aside and place himself before the canvases of Rembrandt; he will enjoy only
the music of Chopin and the poetry of Lamartine or Heine. The same thing
happens to the public and to individuals; their taste depends on their situation.
(101)

    See also Taine under ACTION (TLA 318-19).

1871   Nietzsche   **NBT**

We may call the [Greek] chorus in its primitive stage in prototragedy, a
self-mirroring of the Dionysian man: a phenomenon which may be best exemplified by the process of the actor, who, if he be truly gifted, sees hovering
before his eyes with almost tangible perceptibility the character he is to
represent. The satyric chorus is first of all a vision of the Dionysian throng, just
as the world of the play is, in turn, a vision of the satyric chorus: the power of
this vision is great enough to render the eye dull and insensible to the impression of "reality," to the presence of the cultured men occupying the tiers of
seats on every side. (65-66) . . . The function of the tragic chorus is the
dramatic proto-phenomenon: to see one's self transformed before one's self,
and then to act as if one had really entered into another body, into another
character. This function stands at the beginning of the development of drama.
. . . We actually have a surrender of the individual by his entering into another
nature. Moreover this phenomenon appears in the form of an epidemic: a whole
throng feels itself metamorphosed in this wise. (67)

See also Nietzsche under AFFECT (NBT 64-65, 70-71) DRAMA (NBT 68-69, EXPOSITION (NBT 98-100).

1878   Nietzsche. *See* under IMITATION (NHH 193-94), PLEASURE (NHH 97).

1881   Nietzsche. *See* under MORALITY (NDD 237-38).

1888   Strindberg   **SSPP**

The fact that the heroine arouses our pity depends only on our weakness in not being able to resist the sense of fear that the same fate could befall ourselves. And yet it is possible that a very sensitive spectator might fail to find satisfaction in this kind of pity, while the man believing in the future might demand some positive suggestion for the abolition of evil. (11-12)

1913   Shaw. *See* under DRAMA (SMCE 144), THOUGHT (SMCE 137-39).

1926   Brecht. Compare with EPIC THEATRE (BBT 14-15).

c.1930   Stanislavski   **SCR**

The irresistibility, contagiousness, and power of direct communion by means of invisible radiations of the human will and feelings are great. It is used to hypnotize people. . . . Actors can fill whole auditoriums with the invisible radiations of their emotions. (106)

1931-1936   Artaud   **AT**

In order to reforge the chain, the chain of a rhythm in which the spectator used to see his own reality in the spectacle, the spectator must be allowed to identify himself with the spectacle, breath by breath and beat by beat. It is not sufficient for this spectator to be enchained by the magic of the play; it will not enchain him if we do not know *where to take hold of him*. There is enough chance magic, enough poetry which has no science to back it up. In the theatre, poetry and science must henceforth be identical. (140)

1935   Brecht   **BBT**

In aristotelean drama the plot leads the hero into situations where he reveals his innermost being. All the incidents shown have the object of driving the hero into spiritual conflicts. It is a possibly blasphemous but quite useful comparison if one turns one's mind to the burlesque shows on Broadway, where the public, with yells of "Take it off!," forces the girls to expose their bodies more and more. The individual whose innermost being is thus driven into the open then of course comes to stand for Man with a capital *M*. Everyone (including every spectator) is then carried away by the momentum of the events portrayed, so that in a performance of *Oedipus* one has for all practical purposes an auditorium full of little Oedipuses, an auditorium full of Emperor Jones for a performance of *The Emperor Jones*. (87)

   See also Brecht under CATHARSIS (BBT 87).

c. 1936   Brecht. *See* under EPIC THEATRE (BBA 20-21).

1938   Stanislavski. *See* under AFFECT (SAP 70).

1940   Brecht. *See* under AESTHETIC (BBT 145).

1948   Brecht   **BBBG**

Our delight in the theater must have become weaker than that of the ancients. . . . We grasp the ancient works through a comparatively new process: namely, *empathy* (*Einfühling*), which we can not get from them in any large amount. Thus the greatest part of our delight is fed from sources other than those [of] . . . our ancestors. We feel compensated with verbal beauties, with the elegant handling of the plot, with passages which call forth independent ideas, in brief, with the non-essentials of ancient works. (17) . . . Let the characters on our stage be socially motivated, and motivated differently according to their epoch. Then we make it difficult for our spectator to get inside the characters. He cannot simply feel: "That's how I would act," but can say at most: "*if* I had lived under such conditions." And if we perform plays of our own time as historical plays, then the conditions under which he acts may likewise appear strange to him. This is the beginning of criticism. (25) . . . To produce aliena-tion effects the actor had to forget everything he had learned about enabling an audience to feel its way . . . into his creations. Since his intention is not to put his audience into a trance he should not put himself into a trance. . . . Even when portraying someone who is possessed he ought not to seem possessed himself. Otherwise how could the spectators find out *what* possesses the possessed? (28) . . . Empathy with the character may be used in rehearsal [but] . . . is to be avoided in production. . . . (30)

   See also Brecht under ILLUSION (BBBG 28-29), UNIVERSALITY (BBBG 30).

1956   Brecht   **BBT**

However dogmatic it may seem to insist that self-identification with the character should be avoided in the performance, our generation can listen to this warning with advantage. However determinedly they obey it they can hardly carry it out to the letter, so the most likely result is that truly rending contradiction between experience and portrayal, empathy and demonstration, justification and criticism, which is what is aimed at. The contradiction between acting (demonstration) and experience (empathy) often leads the uninstructed to suppose that only one or the other can be manifest in the work of the actor (as if the Short Organum concentrated entirely on acting and the old tradition entirely on experience). In reality it is a matter of two mutually hostile processes which fuse in the actor's work; his performance is not just composed of a bit of the one and a bit of the other. His particular effectiveness comes from the tussle and tension of the two opposites, and also from their depth. The style in which the S[hort] O[rganum] is written is partly to blame for this. It is misleading often thanks to a possibly over-impatient and over-exclusive concern with the "principle side of the contradiction." (277-78)

ILLUSION

The discussions extracted here are concerned with the conditions of acceptance ("belief," "half-belief," "conscious fiction," and so on) of a work of art. Historically, the weight of theoretical interest has shifted from concepts of IMITATION (the relation of a work to an object) to those of ILLUSION (the relation of a work to a perceiver). There is a sense, therefore, in which IMITATION and ILLUSION should be considered together, as a concern with either the objective or the subjective (or intersubjective) dimensions of the work.

4th cent. B.C.   Aristotle   AA

Now it is clear that perception and intelligence are not the same thing. For all animals share in the one, but only a few in the other. . . . Perception of the objects of the special senses is always true and is found in all animals, while thinking may be false as well as true and is found in none which have not reason also. Imagination, in fact, is something different both from perception and from thought, and it is never found by itself apart from perception, any more than is belief apart from imagination. Clearly thinking is not the same thing as believing. For the former is in our own power, whenever we please: for we can represent an object before our eyes, as do those who range themselves under mnemonic headings and picture them to themselves. . . . Moreover, when we are of the opinion that something is terrible or alarming, we at once feel the corresponding emotion, and so, too, with what is reassuring. But when we are under the influence of the imagination we are no more affected than if we saw in a picture the objects which inspire terror or confidence. There are also different levels of belief; knowledge, opinion, intelligence and their opposites. (123)

c.1583   Sidney. *See* under IMAGINATION (SDP 35-37).

1657   d'Aubignac   AAS

[The actors] are to be look'd upon as representing, and . . . *Cinna* or *Horatius*, whom they represent, are to be consider'd as real and true persons, acting and speaking as *Cinna*, and *Horatius*, and not as those who represent them, and [the actors] must be look'd upon as transform'd into those men, whose names and concerns they take upon them, so that part of the *Hostel de Bourgogne* which is rais'd and adorn'd for a Stage, is the place representing, and the Image of another place which is represented at that time . . . ; and it must in the Play be look'd upon as the true place where all things pass, so the time which is employed in the Representation, being a part of our natural currant year, is but a representing time, but the day represented, and in which one supposes the action of the Stage to come to pass, ought to be taken for a real true time in regard to the Action. (1: 44-45) . . . The Stage is but a Representation of things; and yet we are not to imagine, that there is any thing of what we really see, but we must think the things themselves are there of which the Images are before us. (2: 99)

> *See also* d'Aubignac under PATHOS (AAS 3: 40-41), SPECTACLE (AAS 3: 93).

1668   Dryden   DW

The indecency of tumults [on the stage] is all which can be objected against fighting: for why may not our imagination as well suffer itself to be deluded with the probability of it, as with any other thing in the play? For my part, I can with as great ease persuade myself that the blows are given in good earnest, as I can, that they who strike them are kings or princes, or those persons which they represent. (1, 2: 90-91) . . . Imagination in a man or reasonable creature, is supposed to participate of reason; and when that governs, as it does in the belief of fiction, reason is not destroyed, but misled, or blinded: *that* can prescribe to the reason, during the time of the representation, somewhat like a weak belief of what it sees and hears; and reason suffers itself to be so hoodwinked, that it may better enjoy the pleasures of the fiction. But it is never so wholly made captive, as to be drawn headlong into a persuasion of those things which are most remote from probability. It is in that case a free-born subject, not a slave; it will contribute willingly its assent, as far as it sees convenient, but will not be forced. . . . Fancy and Reason go hand in hand; the first cannot leave the last behind; and though Fancy, when it sees the wide gulph, would venture over as the nimbler, yet it is withheld by Reason, which will refuse to take the leap, when the distance over it appears too large. (1, 2: 178-79)

> *See also* Dryden under DRAMATIZATION (DW 1, 2: 90-93), THREE UNITIES (DW 1, 2: 176-77, 183-84).

1672   Dryden   DW

Warlike instruments, and, even . . . presentations of fighting on the stage, are no more than necessary to produce the effects of the Heroick Play; that is, to raise the imagination of the audience, and to persuade them, for the time, that what they behold on the theatre is really performed. The poet is, then, to endeavour an absolute dominion over the minds of the spectators; for though our fancy will contribute to its own deceit, yet a writer ought to help its operation. (1, 2: 218)

1711   Addison. *See* under CONVENTION (AW 1: 75).

1751   Johnson. *See* under THREE UNITIES (JW 3: 241).

1755-1780   Diderot   **DDE**

In the arts of imitation the truth is nothing, verisimilitude everything, and not only does one not ask them to be real, one does not even want the pretence to be the exact resemblance. In tragedy it has been very justly observed that the illusion is not complete: (1) it cannot be; (2) it ought not be. It cannot be because it is impossible to disregard totally the actual place of the theatrical performance and its attendant inconsistencies. No matter how our imagination may be engaged, our eyes inform us that we are in Paris while the scene is in Rome; and the proof that we never lose sight of the actor in the character whom he portrays is that at the moment when we are the most moved, we exclaim: "Oh! How well it's acted!" Thus, we know that it is only acting. . . . But even if by perfect likeness it would be possible to create a total illusion, art would avoid it, just as sculpture does by not coloring the marble for fear of making it frightening. There are similar theatrical representations of which moderate illusion is pleasing, but of which total illusion would be revolting or painfully distressing. . . . But even if in comedy the illusion were complete, the spectator, imagining what he was seeing was nature, would forget the art and would be deprived by the illusion itself of one of the pleasures of theatrical representation. This is common to all the genres. The pleasure of being moved to pity and fear by the misfortunes of one's fellow men, and the pleasure of laughing at the expense of the failings and ridiculous traits of others are not the only ones which the stage offers us: the pleasure of seeing to what degree of power and truth genius and art can go, the pleasure of admiring in the scene presented the superiority of the depiction over the thing depicted—these would be lost if the illusion were complete. . . . It is the same with all kinds of imitation: at the same time we wish to enjoy both nature and art; we thus wish to be aware that art goes hand in hand with nature. (289)

1758   Diderot   **DDP**

Illusion is the end of both [the novel and the play], but upon what does the illusion depend? On circumstances. It is these which make illusion more or less difficult. Will you allow me to speak the language of geometry? You know what the geometrician calls an equation. Illusion stands to one side. It is an invariable quantity, equal to a sum of terms—some positive, others negative—whose number and possibility of combination can be varied in endless ways, but the total value of which is always the same. The positive terms represent ordinary circumstances and situations; the negatives, the extraordinary. One sort is compensated for by the others. Illusion is not voluntary. The poet who says, I wish to create an illusion, is like the man who says, I have a certain experience of life to which I shall pay no attention. When I say that an illusion is an invariable quantity, I mean to a man who judges of various productions, and not to various men. There are probably no two human beings in the world possessing the same measure of certainty, and yet the poet is forced to create an illusion for every one! (297-98)

   See also Diderot under IDEALISM (DDP 298,299).

1765   Johnson   JS

It is false, that any representation is mistaken for reality; that any dramatick fable in its materiality was ever credible, or, for a single moment, was ever credited. (26) . . . Delusion, if delusion be admitted, has no certain limitation; if the spectator can be once persuaded, that his old acquaintance are *Alexander* and *Caesar*, that a room illuminated with candles is the plain of *Pharsolia*, or the bank of *Granicus*, he is in a state of elevation above the reach of reason, or of truth. . . . There is no reason why a mind thus wandering in extasy should count the clock, or why an hour should not be a century in that calenture of the brains that can make the stage a field. The truth is, that the spectators are always in their senses, and know, from the first act to the last, that the stage is only a stage, and that the players are only players. (26-27) . . . It will be asked, how the drama moves if it is not credited. It is credited with all the credit due to a drama. It is credited, whenever it moves, as a just picture of a real original; as representing to the auditor what he would himself feel, if he were to do or suffer what is there feigned to be suffered or to be done. The reflection that strikes the heart is not, that the evils before us are real evils, but that they are evils to which we ourselves may be exposed. If there be any fallacy, it is not that we fancy the players, but that we fancy ourselves unhappy for a moment; but we rather lament the possibility than suppose the presence of misery, as a mother weeps over her babe, when she remembers that death may take it from her. . . . The delight of tragedy proceeds from our consciousness of fiction; if we thought murders and treasons real, they would please no more. Imitations produce pain or pleasure, not because they are mistaken for realities, but because they bring realities to mind. (28) . . . A play read, affects the mind like a play acted. It is therefore evident, that the action is not supposed to be real; and it follows, that between the acts a longer or shorter time may be allowed to pass, and that no more account of space or duration is to be taken by the auditor of a drama, than by the reader of a narrative, before whom may pass in an hour the life of a hero, or the revolutions of an empire. (28-29)

   See also Johnson under THREE UNITIES (JW 25).

1767-1769   Lessing   LSPW

If screams and contortions are fire then it is contestable that the actor can carry these too far. But if fire consists in the rapidity and vivacity with which all those parts that make the actor bring their properties to bear, to give to his acting the semblance of truth, then we should not desire to see this semblance of truth carried to the extremist illusion, if we deemed it possible that the actor could apply too much fire in this sense. (246) . . . Historical accuracy is not his [the dramatist's] aim, but only the means by which he hopes to attain his aim; he wishes to delude us and touch our hearts through this delusion. If it be true therefore that we no longer believe in ghosts; and if this unbelief must of necessity prevent this delusion, if without this delusion we cannot possibly sympathize, then our modern dramatist injures himself when he nevertheless dresses up such incredible fables, and all the art he has lavished upon them is vain. (260) . . . The tragedian should avoid everything that can remind the audience of their illusion, for as soon as they are reminded thereof the illusion is gone. (355)

See also Lessing under EXPOSITION (LSPW 484-85).

1778   Diderot   **DPA**

[*The First Speaker*]. It is Nature who bestows personal gifts—appearance, voice, judgment, tact. It is the study of the great models, the knowledge of the human heart, the habit of society, earnest work, experience, close acquaintance with the boards, which perfect nature's gifts. The actor who is merely a mimic can count upon being always tolerable; his playing will call neither for praise nor for blame. *The Second.* Or else for nothing but blame. *The First.* Granted. The actor who goes by Nature alone is often detestable, sometimes excellent. How should Nature without art make a great actor when nothing happens on the stage exactly as it happens in Nature, and when dramatic poems are all composed after a fixed system of principles? And how can a part be played in the same way by two different actors when, even with the clearest, the most precise, the most forceful of writers, words are no more, and never can be more, than symbols indicating a thought, a feeling, or an idea; symbols which need action, gesture, intonation, expression, and a whole context of circumstance, to give them their full significance? (14-15) . . . At the very moment when [the actor] touches your heart he is listening to his own voice; his talent depends not, as you think, upon feeling, but upon rendering so exactly the outward signs of feeling, that you fall into the trap. He has rehearsed to himself every note of his passion. He has learnt before a mirror every particle of his despair. He knows exactly when he must produce his handkerchief and shed tears; and you will see him weep at the word, at the syllable, he has chosen, not a second sooner or later. The broken voice, the half-uttered words, the stifled or prolonged notes of agony, the trembling limbs, the faintings, the bursts of fury—all this is pure mimicry, lessons carefully learned, the grimacing of sorrow, the magnificent aping which the actor remembers long after his first study of it, of which he was perfectly conscious when he first put it before the public, and which leaves him, luckily for the poet, the spectator, and himself, a full freedom of mind. Like other gymnastics, it takes only his bodily strength. He puts off the sock or the buskin; his voice is gone; he is tired; he changes his dress, or he goes to bed; and he feels neither trouble, nor sorrow, nor depression, nor weariness of soul. All these emotions he has given to you.

The actor is tired, you are unhappy; he has had exertion without feeling, you feeling without exertion. Were it otherwise the player's lot would be the most wretched on earth: but he is not the person he represents; he plays it, and plays it so well that you think he is the person; the deception is all on your side; he knows well enough that he is not the person. (16-17) . . . Pompous language can only be used by unfamiliar personages, spoken from poetical lips, with a poetical tone. Reflect a little as to what, in the language of the theatre, is *being true*. Is it showing things as they are in Nature? Certainly not. Were it so the true would be the commonplace. What, then, is truth for stage purposes? It is the conforming of action, diction, face, voice, movement, and gesture, to an ideal type invented by the poet, and frequently enhanced by the player. That is the strange part of it. This type not only influences the tone, it alters the actor's very walk and bearing. (22) . . . The likeness of passion on the stage is not then its true likeness; it is but extravagant portraiture, caricature on a grand scale, subject to conventional rules. (74)

1798   Goethe   GLE

Agent.—Theatrical representations by no means seem really true . . . but rather . . . have only an appearance of truth. . . . The feeling you have at the exhibition of an opera cannot be rightly called deception?

Spectator.—I agree. Still it is a sort of deception; something nearly allied to it.

Agent.—Tell me, do you not almost forget yourself?

Spectator.—Not almost, but quite, when the whole or some part is excellent. . . .

Agent.—You have already told when it is most apt to happen, namely, when all is in harmony. . . . We have denied to the opera the possession of a certain sort of truth. We have maintained that it is by no means faithful to what it professes to represent. But can we deny to it a certain interior truth, which arises from its completeness as a work of art?

Spectator.—When the opera is good, it creates a little world of its own, in which all proceeds according to fixed laws, which must be judged by its own laws, felt according to its own spirit.

Agent.—Does it not follow from this, that truth of nature and truth of art are two distinct things, and that the artist neither should nor may endeavor to give his work the air of a work of nature?

Spectator.—But yet it has so often the air of a work of nature. . . .

Agent.—Only to a wholly uncultivated spectator. . . .

Spectator.—Why does a perfect work of art appear like a work of nature to me also?

Agent.—Because it harmonizes with your better nature. Because it is above natural, yet not unnatural. A perfect work of art is a work of the human soul, and in this sense, also, a work of nature. But . . . above nature. It is comprehensible only to a mind that is harmoniously formed and developed, and such a one discovers that what is perfect and complete in itself is also in harmony with himself. (52-57)

1804   Coleridge   CSC

Stage presentations . . . produce a sort of temporary half-faith, which the spectator encourages in himself and supports by a voluntary contribution on his own part, because he knows that it is at all times in his power to see the thing as it really is. . . . The suspension of the act of comparison, which permits this sort of negative belief, is . . . assisted by the will. . . . The true stage-illusion in this and in all other things consists—not in the mind's judging it to be a forest, but, in its remission of the judgment that it is not a forest. . . . For not only are we never absolutely deluded—or anything like it, but the attempt to cause the highest delusion possible . . . is a gross fault, incident only to low minds, which, feeling that they cannot affect the heart or head permanently, endeavour to call forth the momentary affections. There ought never to be more pain than is compatible with co-existing pleasure, and to be amply repaid by thought. (1:178-81)

   See also Coleridge under DRAMA (CSC 1: 178-181).

1808   Schlegel   SCL

[The]idea of illusion has occasioned great errors in the theory of art. By this term there has often been understood the unwittingly erroneous belief that the represented action is reality. In that case the terrors of Tragedy would be a true torture to us, they would be like an Alpine load on the fancy. No, the theatrical as well as every other poetical illusion, is a waking dream, to which we voluntarily surrender ourselves. To produce it, the poet and actors must powerfully agitate the mind, and the probabilities of calculation do not in the least contribute towards it. This demand of literal deception, pushed to the extreme, would make all poetic form impossible; for we know well that the mythological and historical persons did not speak our language, that the impassioned grief does not express itself in verse, etc. (246)

   See also Schlegel under IMAGINATION (SCL 250), THREE UNITIES (SCL 236-51).

c.1810   Coleridge   CLSW

I find two extremes of critical decision (concerning the immediate end or object of drama);—the French, which evidently presupposes that a perfect delusion is to be aimed at,—an opinion which needs no fresh confutation; and the exact opposite to it, brought forward by Dr. Johnson, who supposes the auditors throughout in the full reflective knowledge of the contrary. In evincing the impossibility of delusion, he makes no sufficient allowance for an intermediate state, which I have before distinguished by the term, illusion. . . . [Both in the dream-state and in the experience of illusion] we simply do not judge the imagery to be unreal; there is a negative reality, and no more. Whatever, therefore, tends to prevent the mind from placing itself, or being placed, gradually in that state in which the images have such negative reality for the auditor, destroys the illusion, and is dramatically improbable. . . . So far as they tend to increase the inward excitement, [the excellences of the drama are all] means towards accomplishing the chief end, that of producing and supporting this willing illusion . . . (73)

    See also Coleridge under GENRE (CLSW 74).

1811   Coleridge. *See* under THREE UNITIES (CCSL 99).

1813   Goethe. *See* under IMAGINATION (GLE 175).

1815   Coleridge   **CBL**

That *illusion*, contra-distinguished from *delusion*, that *negative* faith, which simply permits the images presented to work by their own force, without either denial or affirmation of their real existence by the judgment, is rendered impossible by their immediate neighborhood to words and facts of known and absolute truth. (2: 107)

    See also Coleridge under AFFECT (CLB 2: 5-6), PROBABILITY (CBL 2: 189), REALISM (CBL 1: 179).

1817   Hazlitt   **HW**

Hamlet is a name; his speeches and sayings but the idle coinage of the poet's brain. What then, are they not real? They are as real as our own thoughts. Their reality is in the reader's mind. It is *we* who are Hamlet. This play has a prophetic truth, which is above that of history. Whoever has become thoughtful and melancholy through his own mishaps or those of others; whoever has borne about with him the clouded brow of reflection . . . ; whoever has seen the golden lamp of day dimmed by envious mists rising in his own breast, and could find in the world before him only a dull blank with nothing left remarkable in it. (1: 232)

1818   Coleridge   **CLSW**

[*The Tempest*] addresses itself entirely to the imaginative faculty; and although the illusion may be assisted by the effect on the senses of the complicated scenery and decorations of modern times yet this sort of assistance is dangerous. For the principal and only genuine excitement ought to come from within—from the moved and sympathetic imagination; whereas, where so much is addressed to the mere external senses of seeing and hearing, the spiritual vision is apt to languish, and the attraction from without will withdraw the mind from the proper and only legitimate interest which is intended to spring from within. (74)

1820   Hazlitt. *See* under DRAMA (HW 8: 417).

1871   Nietzsche   NBT

The true spectator [is] . . . always . . . conscious of having before him a work of art, and not an empiric reality. . . . We believe in an aesthetic public, and consider the individual spectator the better qualified the more he [is] capable of viewing a work of art as art, that is, aesthetically. (57-58) . . . [The fictional world of Greek drama] is not an arbitrary world placed by fancy betwixt heaven and earth; rather it is a world possessing the same reality and trustworthiness that Olympus with its dwellers possessed for the believing Hellene. The satyr, as being the Dionysian chorist, lives in a religiously acknowledged reality under the sanction of myth and cult. . . . Tragedy begins with him, . . . the Dionysian wisdom of tragedy speaks through him. . . . (60)

   See also Nietzsche under AFFECT (NBT 57-58, 70-71), TRAGEDY (NBT 127, 159-60).

1873   Nietzsche. *See* under METAPHOR (NEG 178-88).

1876   Sarcey   STT

Reality, if presented on the stage truthfully, would appear false to the monster with the thousand heads which we call the public. . . . (31)

   See also Sarcey under AFFECT (STT 34-41), CONVENTION (STT 26-27, 30), UNITY (STT 53).

1878   Nietzsche. *See* under CHARACTER (NHH 163-64).

1888   Strindberg. *See* under AFFECT (SSPP 20-21).

1888   Nietzsche. *See* under AESTHETIC (NW 289-90).

1889   Strindberg. *See* under THREE UNITIES (SMD 16).

1896   Shaw   SDC

Melodramatic stage illusion is not an illusion of real life, but an illusion of the embodiment of our romantic imaginings. (159-60) The function of the theatre is to realize for the spectators certain pictures which their imagination craves. . . . Nature is only brought in as an accomplice in the illusion . . . but the moment the illusion is sacrificed to nature, the house is up in arms and the play is chivied from the stage. (188-89)

1897   Shaw. *See* under IMAGINATION (SS 192).

1900   Shaw   **STPP**

The theatre is a place which people can endure only when they forget themselves: that is, when their attention is entirely captured, their interest thoroughly aroused, their sympathies raised to the eagerest readiness, and their selfishness utterly annihilated. (xiv)

1906   Shaw   **SDDGM**

There is no harder scientific fact in the world than the fact that belief can be produced in practically unlimited quantity and intensity, without observation or reasoning, and even in defiance of both, by the simple desire to believe founded on a strong interest in believing. (xvii)

1908   Pirandello   **POH**

We need to come to a clear understanding on the question of the poet's not believing in the reality of his poetic world or in whatever world he portrays. But it might be said that no representation exists that can be believed as a reality, and this holds not only for the artist but for anyone else as well, no matter if created by art or if it be the representation we humans make of ourselves, of other people, and of life. The artistic image and the image that normally comes to us through our senses are, in essence, one and the same. Nevertheless, we refer to the image obtained through our senses as *true*, and to the one created by art as *fictitious*. But to understand the difference between the two kinds of representation we must talk in terms not of *reality* but rather of *will*, and only insofar as artistic fiction is *willed* (by willed I do not mean obtained through an act of the will for purposes alien to artistic creation, but rather willed and loved for its own sake, devoid of any other motive), whereas the image of the senses does not depend on whether we will it or not: it comes into being merely because we are endowed with senses. Therefore the former is free, while the latter is not. And while one is an image or form of sensations, the other—artistic fiction—is a creation of form. The artistic process actually begins only when a figuration develops a will of its own in our mind; that is to say, when it *wills itself* in and by itself, and generates, by the mere fact that it wills itself, a movement (a technique) capable of bringing it into realization outside ourselves. If the figuration lacks this self-contained will, which is the movement itself of the image, then it is no more than a common psychic phenomenon—an image which is not willed by itself, an automatic spiritual phenomenon—insofar as it does not depend on our volition but comes into being in us as a result of our sense perception. (63-64) . . . There, I said the word: the magic of his style. [Ariosto] has realized that on one condition only could esthetic coherence and imaginative truth be given to that world, in which precisely magic plays such an important role: the condition that the poet become a magician himself and his style takes its traits and virtues from magic. And there is the illusion which the poet creates in us and at times also in himself by identifying himself with his subtle playing to the extent of wholly surrendering himself to it. Oh, that play seems so beautiful to him that he would gladly believe it to be reality. Which it isn't, unfortunately; so much so that, from time to time, the fine veil tears open and thus exposes true reality, the reality of the present. When this happens, the thinly-spread irony gathers quickly and then suddenly bursts into view. But these bursts are never too unpleasantly harsh and never come as sudden shocks, because we have always anticipated them. And in addition to the illusions which the poet creates for us and for himself, there are those that the characters create for themselves and also those which the sorcerers and fairies create for them. It is all phantasmagoric play of illusions, which does not so much involve the poetic world itself (as I have already mentioned, this representation often takes on the consistent aspect of reality), as it involves the style and the manner of representation adopted by the poet who, with remarkable perspicacity, has realized that only in this way, i.e., by competing with magic itself through his style, could he preserve the unalterable elements of his material and fit them coherently into the context of his poem. (66-67)

See also Pirandello under IDEALISM (POH 75-76)

c.1908   Strindberg   SOL

Since the theatre is an institution for the creation of illusion, there is nothing easier than to make oneself unreceptive to the illusion. One is contrary, the illusion does not come, but with that the purpose of going to the theater is counteracted, and the critic might better have stayed at home when he did not want to receive the delightful illusion that here a bit of life was presented. (128) . . . I have never committed . . . an unnecessary crime against historical accuracy when it has concerned universally known matters. . . . [The compression of remote historical events, however, is permissable because] the drama is an art form by means of which I must give illusion and an art form in which everything is illusory, language, dress, time above all. . . . (263)

1912   Shaw   SALOP

The main objection to the use of illusive scenery (in most modern plays scenery is not illusive: everything visible is as real as in your drawing room at home) is that it is unconvincing; whilst the imaginary scenery with which the audience transfigures a platform or tribune like the Elizabethan stage or the Greek stage used by Sophocles, is quite convincing. In fact, the more scenery you have the less illusion you produce. The wise playwright, when he cannot get absolute reality of presentation, goes to the other extreme, and aims at atmosphere and suggestion of mood rather than at direct simulative illusion. (72)

1921   Shaw. *See* under CHARACTER (SPC 248-49).

1931-1936   Artaud   **AT**

The images of the plague, occurring in relation to a powerful state of physical disorganization, are like the last volleys of a spiritual force that is exhausting itself, the images of poetry in the theatre are a spiritual force that begins its trajectory in the senses and does without reality altogether. (25) . . . The mind believes what it sees and does what it believes: that is the secret of the fascination. . . . However, there are conditions to be rediscovered in order to engender in the mind a spectacle capable of fascinating it: and this is not a simple matter of art. (27) . . . The public will believe in the theater's dreams on condition that it take them for true dreams and not for a servile copy of reality; on condition that they allow the public to liberate within itself the magical liberties of dreams which it can only recognize when they are imprinted with terror and cruelty. (86) . . . The theater will never find itself again—i.e. constitute a means of true illusion—except by furnishing the spectator with the truthful precipitates of dreams, in which his taste for crime, his erotic obsessions, his savagery, his chimeras, his utopian sense of life and matter, even his cannibalism, pour out, on a level not counterfeit and illusory, but interior. (92)

  See also Artaud under AESTHETIC (AT 97), POETRY OF THE THEATRE (AT 120-21).

1936   Stanislavski   **SAP**

Although such a thing as complete forgetting of self and unwavering belief in what is happening on the stage is possible, it occurs rarely.(269)

1936   Brecht   **BBB**

The Chinese performer does not act as if, in addition to the three walls around him there were also a fourth wall. *He makes it clear that he knows he is being looked at.* Thus, one of the illusions of the European stage is set aside. The audience forfeits the illusion of being unseen spectators at an event which is really taking place. (130)

  See also Brecht under STYLE (BBB 132).

1948   Brecht   **BBBG**

How long shall our souls, taking leave of our heavy bodies under a veil of darkness, steal into other dreamlike souls on the [stage] to share raptures denied us ordinary folk? (24) . . . The actor is on the stage in a double capacity (as Laughton and as Galileo), and the portraying Laughton is not swallowed up in the portrayed Galileo. This manner of acting has been called "Epic." This means nothing more in the end than that the real, the profane event is no longer veiled. Laughton is really standing on the stage and is showing us how Galileo seems to him. . . . The audience . . . will naturally not forget Laughton, even if he attempts a complete transformation. . . . Just as the actor should not deceive his audience into thinking that not he but the fictitious character is on the stage, so he should not deceive them into thinking that what happens on the stage has not been rehearsed but is happening for the first and only time. (28-29)

See also Brecht under IMITATION (BBBG 16), UNIVERSALITY (BBBG 30); compare with AFFECT (BBBG 21-23).

IMAGINATION

Statements in this category are concerned with the nature and employment of the imagination, understood as an act of forming images in the mind.

4th cent. B.C.   Aristotle   AA

Imagination is the faculty in virtue of which we say that an image presents itself to us, and if we exclude the metaphorical use of the term, it is some one of the faculties or habits in virtue of which we judge, and judge truly or falsely. Such faculties or habits are sensation, opinion, knowledge or intellect. It is clearly not sensation, for the following reasons. Sensation is either a faculty like sight or an activity like seeing. But we may have an image even when neither the one nor the other is present: for example, the images in dreams. Again sensation is always present but not so imagination. Besides, the identity of the two in actuality would involve the possibility, that all the brutes have imagination. . . . Moreover, sensations are always true, but imaginings prove for the most part false. . . . Neither, again, can imagination be ranked with the faculties, like knowledge or intellect, which always judge truly: it may also be false. It remains, then, to consider whether it be opinion, as opinion may be true or false. But opinion is attended by conviction, for it is impossible to hold opinions without being convinced for them: but no brute is ever convinced, though many have imagination. . . . Imagination [is] a motion generated by actual perception. And, since sight is the principal sense, imagination has derived even its name (*phantasia*) from light (*phaos*), because without light one cannot see. Again, because imaginations remain in us and resemble the corresponding sensations, animals perform many actions under their influence. . . . (125-29) . . . Men often act contrary to knowledge in obedience to their imaginings, while in the other animals there is no process of thinking or reasoning, but solely imagination. (151)

See also Aristotle under ILLUSION (AA 123).

1561   Scaliger. Compare with IMITATION (SP 59).

1570   Castelvetro   CP

What inconvenience the authority of Aristotle and the example of Agathon conduce. For if it is permitted to create kings who never existed, and to give them fictitious actions, it will also be permitted to create new mountains, new rivers, new lakes, new seas, new peoples, new kingdoms, and to transport old rivers into new districts, and, in short, it will be permitted to create a new world and to transform the old one. . . . [It might be argued that] the plot taken from history with part of its names delights every spectator, though few of them know that the action and part of the names are really historical; hence, it is not necessary that the action and part of the names should be historically true. . . . [Experience refutes this; plays greatly applauded give great displeasure when it is discovered that they are entirely fictitious], just as if [the spectators] had had a jewel and thinking it good, had rejoiced, but finding it artificial, had been cast into sorrow; whence the conclusion, the actions of kings and their names ought to be historically true and not imagined. (114-15).

See also Castelvetro under SUBJECT (CP 51-52); compare with ACTION (CP 113).

c.1583   Sidney   SDP

Of all writers under the sun the poet is the least liar; and though he would, as a poet can scarcely be a liar. The astronomer, with his cousin the geometrician, can hardly escape when they take upon them or measure the height of the stars. . . . Now for the poet, he nothing affirmeth, and therefore never lieth. For, as I take it, to lie is to affirm that to be true which is false; so as the other artists, and especially the historian, affirming many things, can, in the cloudy knowledge of mankind, hardly escape from many lies. But the poet . . . never affirmeth. The poet never maketh any circles about your imagination, to conjure you to believe for true what he writeth. He citeth not authorities of other histories, but even for his entry calleth the sweet Muses to inspire into him a good invention; in troth, not laboring to tell you what is or is not, but what should or should not be. And therefore though he recount things not true, yet because he telleth them not for true he lieth not. . . . What child is there that, coming to a play, and seeing Thebes written in great letters upon an old door, doth believe that it is Thebes? If then a man can arrive at that child's-age, to know that the poet's persons and doing are but pictures what should be, and not stories what have been, they will never give the lie to things not affirmatively but allegorically and figuratively written. And therefore as in history looking for truth, they may go away full-fraught with falsehood, so in poesy looking but for fiction, they shall use the narrative but as an imaginative ground-plot of a profitable invention. But hereto is replied that the poets give names to men they write of, which argueth a conceit of an actual truth, and so, not being true, proveth a falsehood. . . . But that is easily answered: their naming of men is but to make their picture the more lively, and not build any history. Painting men, they cannot leave men nameless. We see we cannot play at chess but that we must give names to our chess-men; and yet, me thinks, he were a very partial champion of truth that would say we lied for giving a piece of wood the reverend title of a bishop. The poet nameth Cyrus and Aeneas no other way than to show what men of their fames, fortunes, and estates should do. (35-37)

    See also Sidney under IMITATION (SDP 7-8, 9-10), THOUGHT (SDP 8), THREE UNITIES (SDP 49).

1641 Jonson   JD

Opinion is a light, vaine, crude, and imperfect thing, settled in the Imagination; but never arriving at the understanding, there to obtain the tincture of *Reason*. (6)

1660 Corneille. *See* under THREE UNITIES (CDENA 32)

1663 Molière. *See* under IMITATION (MP 6: 340).

1668 Dryden   DW

Poesy must resemble natural truth, but it must be ethical. Indeed the poet dresses truth, and adorns nature, but does not alter them. . . . That is not the best poesy, which resembles notions of things that are not, to things that are: though the fancy may be great, and the words flowing, yet the soul is but half satisfied when there is not truth in the foundation. (1, 2: 170)

    See also Dryden under ILLUSION (DW 1, 2: 178-79), THREE UNITIES (DW 1, 2: 176-77, 183-84).

1672 Dryden. *See* under ILLUSION (DW 1, 2: 218).

1712 Addison   AW

It is this sense [of sight] which furnishes the imagination with its ideas; so that by "the pleasures of the imagination," or "fancy," . . . I here mean such as arise from visible objects, either when we have them actually in our view, or when we call up their ideas into our minds by paintings, statues, descriptions, or any the like occasion. We cannot indeed have a single image in the fancy that did not make its first appearance through the sight; but we have the power of retaining, altering, and compounding those images, which we have once received, into all the varieties of picture and vision that are most agreeable to the imagination; for by this faculty a man in a dungeon is capable of entertaining himself with scenes and landscapes more beautiful than any that can be found in the whole compass of nature. (2: 137) . . . I divide these pleasures [of the imagination] into two kinds: my design being first of all to discourse of those primary pleasures of the imagination, which entirely proceed from such objects as are before our eyes; and in the next place to speak of those secondary pleasures of the imagination which flow from the ideas of visible objects, when the objects are not actually before the eye, but are called up into our memories or formed into agreeable visions of things that are either absent or fictitious. The pleasures of the imagination, taken in the full extent, are not so gross as those of sense, nor so refined as those of the understanding. The last are indeed more preferable, because they are founded on some new knowledge or improvement in the mind of man; yet it must be confessed, that those of the imagination are as great and as transporting as the other. A beautiful prospect delights the soul as much as a demonstration; and a description in Homer has charmed more readers than a Chapter in Aristotle. Besides, the pleasures of the imagination have this advantage above those of the understanding, that they are more obvious, and more easy to be acquired. It is but opening the eye, and the scene enters. The colours paint themselves on the fancy, with very little attention of thought or application of the mind in the beholder. We are struck, we know not how, with the symmetry of any thing we see, and immediately assent to the beauty of an object, without inquiring into the particular causes and occasions of it. . . . [The pleasures of the imagination] do not require such a bent of thought as is necessary to our more serious employments, nor at the same time, suffer the mind to sink into that negligence and remissness, which are apt to accompany our more sensual delights, but, like a gentle exercise to the faculties, awaken them from sloth and idleness, without putting them upon any labour or difficulty. . . . The pleasures of the fancy are more conducive to health than those of the understanding, which are worked out by dint of thinking, and attended with too violent a labour of the brain. Delightful scenes, whether in nature, painting, or poetry, have a kindly influence on the body, as well as the mind; and not only serve to clear and brighten the imagination, but are able to disperse grief and melancholy, and to set the animal spirits in pleasing and agreeable motions. (2: 138) . . . Those pleasures of the imagination which arise from the actual view and survey of outward objects . . . all proceed from the sight of what is great, uncommon, or beautiful. There may, indeed, be something so terrible or offensive, that the horror or loathsomeness of an object may overbear the pleasure which results from its greatness, novelty, or beauty; but still there will be such a mixture of delight in the very disgust it gives us, as any of these three qualifications are most conspicuous and prevailing. By greatness, I do not only mean the bulk of any single object, but the largeness of a whole view, considered as one entire piece. Such are the prospects of an open champaign country, a vast uncultivated desert, of huge heaps of mountains, high rocks and precipices. . . . Our imagination loves to be filled with an object, or to grasp at any thing that is too big for its capacity. We are flung into a pleasing astonishment at such unbounded views, and feel a delightful stillness and amazement in the soul at the apprehensions of them. . . . A spacious horizon is an image of liberty, where the eye has room to range abroad . . . and to lose itself amidst the variety of objects that offer themselves to its observation. Such wide and undetermined prospects are as pleasing to the fancy as the speculations of eternity or infinitude are to the understanding. . . . Every thing that is new or uncommon, raises a pleasure in the imagination because it fills the soul with an agreeable surprise, gratifies its curiosity, and gives it an idea of which it was not before possessed. . . . It is this that recommends variety, where the mind is every instant called off to something new, and the attention not suffered to dwell too long, and waste itself on any particular object. (2: 138-39) . . . As the fancy delights in every thing that is great, strange, or beautiful, and is still more pleased the more it finds of these perfections in the same object, so it is capable of receiving a new satisfaction by the assistance of another sense. Thus, any continued sound, as the music of birds, or a fall of water, awakens every moment the mind of the beholder, and makes him more attentive to the several beauties of the place that lie before him. Thus, if there arises a fragrancy of smells or perfumes, they heighten the pleasures of the imagination, and make even the colours and verdure of the landscape appear more agreeable; for the ideas of both senses recommend each other, and are pleasanter together than when they enter the mind separately; as the different colours of a picture, when they are well disposed, set off one another and receive an additional beauty from the advantages of their situation. (2: 140) . . . When I say the ideas we receive from statues, descriptions, or such-like occasions [, the secondary pleasures of the imagination], are the same that were once actually in our view, it must not be understood that we had once seen the very place, action, or person, that are carved or described. It is sufficient that we have seen places, persons, or actions in general, which bear a resemblance, or at least some remote analogy, with what we find represented; since it is in the power of the imagination, when it is once stocked with particular ideas, to enlarge, compound, and vary them at her own pleasure. . . . This secondary pleasure of the imagination proceeds from that action of the mind which compares the ideas arising from the original objects with the ideas we receive from the statue, picture, description, or sound, that represents them. (2: 145-46) . . . We may observe, that any single circumstance of what we have formerly seen often raises up a whole scene of imagery, and awakens numberless ideas that before slept in the imagination; such a particular smell or colour is able to fill the mind, on a sudden, with the picture of the fields or gardens where we first met with it, and to bring up into view all the variety of images that once attended it. Our imagination takes the hint, and leads us unexpectedly into cities or theatres, plains or meadows. We may further observe, when the fancy thus reflects on the scenes that have passed in it formerly, those which were at first pleasant to behold appear more so upon reflection, and that the memory heightens the delightfulness of the original. (2: 146-47)

See also Addison under AESTHETIC (AW 2: 139-40, 142), DISTANCE (AW 2: 148).

1751   Johnson. *See* under THREE UNITIES (JW 3: 241).

1758   Diderot. *See* under TRAGEDY (DDP 296, 297).

1765   Johnson. *See* under THREE UNITIES (JS 27).

1767-1769   Lessing   **LSPW**

Minute effects must never be carried to the extremity of repulsiveness. It is well if our heated fantasy can see blood . . . , but the eye must not really see it. (256)

1797   Goethe. Compare with AFFECT (GED 339).

1808   Schlegel   **SCL**

The capability of our mind to fly in thought, with the rapidity of lightning, through the immensity of time and space, is well known and acknowledged in common life; and shall poetry, whose very purpose it is to add all manner of wings to our mind, and which has at command all the magic of genuine illusion, that is, of a lively and enrapturing fiction, be alone compelled to renounce this universal prerogative? (250)

    See also Schlegel under THREE UNITIES (SCL 236-51), UNITY (SCL 242-45).

c.1808   Coleridge   **CSC**

We find undoubted proof in [Shakespeare's] mind of imagination, or the power by which one image or feeling is made to modify many others and by a sort of *fusion to force many into one.* . . . Various are the workings of this greatest faculty of the human mind—both passionate and tranquil. In its tranquil and purely pleasurable operation, it acts chiefly by producing out of many things, as they would have appeared in the description of an ordinary mind, described slowly and in unimpassioned succession, a oneness, even as nature, the greatest of poets, acts upon us when we open our eyes upon an extended prospect. . . . Or it acts by impressing the stamp of humanity, of human feeling, over inanimate objects. . . . And lastly, which belongs only to a great poet, the power of so carrying on the eye of the reader as to make him almost lose the consciousness of the words—to make him *see* everything—and this without exciting any painful or laborious attention, without any *anatomy* of description . . . but with the sweetness and easy movement of nature. (1: 188-89)

c.1810   Coleridge. *See* under GENRE (CLSW 74).

1811-1812   Coleridge. *See* under METAPHOR (CCSL 45), THREE UNITIES (CCSL 99).

1813 Goethe   GLE

Shakespeare's works are not for the physical vision. . . . The eye . . .may well
be called the clearest of the senses; but the inner sense is still clearer, and to it
by means of words belongs the most sensitive and clear receptivity. . . . Through
this, the picture-world of imagination becomes animated, and a complete
effect results, of which we can give no reckoning. Precisely here lies the
ground for illusion that everything is taking place before our eyes.
But . . . the works of Shakespeare . . . contain much more of spiritual truth than
of spectacular action. He makes happen what can easily be conceived by the
imagination, indeed what can be better imagined than seen. (175)

1813 Hazlitt   HW

By the help of arts and science, everything finds an ideal level. Ideas assume
the place of realities, and realities sink into nothing. Actual events and objects
produce little or no effect on the mind, when it has been long accustomed to
draw its strongest interest from constant contemplation. It is necessary that it
should, as it were, recollect itself—that it should call out its internal resources,
and refine upon its own feelings—place the object at a distance, and embellish
it at pleasure. By degrees all things are made to serve as hints, and occasions
for the exercise of intellectual activity. (1: 134)

‣ 1814 Hazlitt. *See* under IMITATION (HW 1: 162).

1815 Coleridge   CBL

[During] the mind's self-experience in the act of thinking [, t]here are evidently two powers at work, which relatively to each other are active and
passive; and this is not possible without an intermediate faculty, which is at
once both active and passive. (In philosophical language, we must denominate
this intermediate faculty in all its degrees and determinations, the IMAGINA-
TION. But, in common language, and especially on the subject of poetry, we
appropriate the name to a superior degree of the faculty, joined to a superior
voluntary controul over it.) (1: 86) . . .The IMAGINATION then, I consider
either as primary, or secondary. The primary IMAGINATION I hold to be the
living Power and prime Agent of all human Perception, and as a repetition in
the finite mind of the eternal act of creation in the infinite I AM. The secondary
Imagination I consider as an echo of the former, co-existing with the conscious
will, yet still as identical with the primary in the *kind* of its agency, and
differing only in *degree*, and in the *mode* of its operation. It dissolves,
diffuses, dissipates, in order to recreate; or where this process is rendered
impossible, yet still at all events it struggles to idealize and to unify. It is essentially *vital*, even as all objects (*as* objects) are essentially fixed and dead. (1:
202) . . . Fancy, on the contrary, has no other counters to play with, but fixities

and definites. The Fancy is indeed no other than a mode of Memory emancipated from the order of time and space; while it is blended with, and modified by that empirical phenomenon of the will, which we express by the word CHOICE. But equally with the ordinary memory the Fancy must receive all its materials ready made from the law of association. (1: 202)...The poet, described in *ideal* perfection, brings the whole soul of man into activity, with the subordination of its faculties to each other, according to their relative worth and dignity. He diffuses a tone and spirit of unity, that blends, and (as it were) *fuses*, each into each, by that synthetic and magical power, to which we have exclusively appropriated the name of imagination. This power, first put in action by the will and understanding, and retained under their irremissive, though gentle and unnoticed, controul (*laxis effertur habenis*) reveals itself in the balance of reconciliation of opposite or discordant qualities: of sameness, with difference; of the general, with the concrete; the idea, with the image; the individual, with the representative; the sense of novelty and freshness, with old and familiar objects; a more than usual state of emotion, with more than usual order; judgement ever awake and steady self-possession, with enthusiasm and feeling profound or vehement; and while it blends and harmonizes the natural and the artifical, still subordinates art to nature; the manner to the matter; and our admiration of the poet to our sympathy with the poetry. (2: 12)

1816   Hazlitt   HW

The two principles of imitation and imagination . . . are not only distinct, but also opposite. For the imagination is that power which represents objects, not as they are, but as they are moulded according to our fancies and feelings. (10: 83)

1816   Goethe. *See* under DRAMATIZATION(GLE 185-86).

1818   Hazlitt   HW

[Poetry] is strictly the language of the imagination; and the imagination is that faculty which represents objects, not as they are in themselves, but as they are moulded by other thoughts and feelings, into an infinite variety of shapes and combinations of power. This language is not the less true to nature, because it is false in point of fact; but so much the more true and natural, if it conveys the impression which the object under the influence of passion makes on the mind. Let an object, for instance, be presented to the senses in a state of agitation or fear—and the imagination will distort or magnify the object, and convert it into the likeness of whatever is most proper to encourage the fear. "Our eyes are made the fools" of our other faculties. . . . Things are equal to the imagination, which have the power of affecting the mind with an equal degree of terror, admiration, delight or love. When Lear calls upon the heavens to avenge his cause, "for they are old like him," there is nothing extravagant or impious in this sublime identification of his age with theirs; for there is no other image which could do justice to the agonising sense of his wrongs and his despair! (5: 4) . . . Objects must strike differently upon the mind, independently of what they are in themselves, as long as we have a different interest in them, as we see them in a different point of view, nearer or at a greater distance (morally or physically speaking) from novelty, from old acquaintance, from our ignorance of them, from our fear of their consequences, from contrast, from unexpected likeness. We can no more take away faculty of imagination, than we can see all objects without light or shade. . . . The province of the imagination is principally visionary, the unknown and undefined: the understanding restores things to their natural boundaries, and strips them of their fanciful pretensions. . . . It is the undefined and uncommon that gives birth and scope to the imagination; we can only fancy what we do not know. As in looking into the mazes of a tangled wood we fill them with what shapes we please, with ravenous beasts, with caverns vast, and drear enchantments, so in our ignorance of the world about us, we make gods or devils of the first object we see, and set no bounds to the wilful suggestions of our hopes and fears. (5: 8-9)

See also Hazlitt under AESTHETIC (HW 5: 1-2, 3), FORWARD MOVEMENT (HW 5: 10).

c.1820 **Hegel.** See under SPECTACLE (HFA 4: 258, 283-84).

1830 Hazlitt. See under IDEALISM ((9: 429-30, 431-32); compare with DISINTERESTEDNESS (HW 9: 431).

1835 Coleridge   CMC

The difference between the Fancy and the Imagination [is this:] that if the check of the senses and the reason were withdrawn, the first would become delirium, and the last mania. The Fancy brings together images which have no connection natural or moral, but are yoked together by the poet by means of some accidental coincidence. . . . The Imagination modifies images, and gives unity to variety; it sees all things in one. (435-36)

c.1863-1867 Taine. Compare with AESTHETIC (THEL 1, 18).

1871 Nietzsche   NBT

Nothing could be more certain than that the poet is a poet only in that he beholds himself surrounded by forms which live and act before him, into the innermost being of which his glance penetrates. By reason of a strange defect in our capacities, we modern men are apt to represent to ourselves the aesthetic proto-phenomenon as too complex and abstract. For the true poet the metaphor is not a rhetorical figure, but a vicarious image which actually hovers before him in place of a concept. The character is not for him an aggregate composed of a studied collection of particular traits, but an irrepressibly live person before his eyes, and differing only from the corresponding vision of the painter by its ever continued life and action. (66)

1878   Nietzsche. *See* under CHARACTER (NHH 163-64).

1888   Strindberg. *See* under SPECTACLE (SSPP 23).

1896   Shaw. *See* under ILLUSION (SDC 188-89).

1897   Shaw   SS

In The Tempest and A Midsummer Night's Dream . . . the best scenery you can get will only destroy the illusion created by the poetry. . . . The reason is, not that a man can *always* imagine things more vividly than art can present them to him, but that it takes an altogether extraordinary degree of art to compete with the pictures which the imagination makes when it is stimulated by such potent forces as the maternal instinct, superstitious awe, or the poetry of Shakespear. (192)

1908   Pirandello. *See* under IDEALISM (POH 75-76).

1910   Shaw   SMDLS

[I] use . . . the word imagination to denote two very different powers of mind. One is the power to imagine things as they are not: this I call the romantic imagination. The other is the power to imagine things as they are without actually seeing them; and this I will call the realistic imagination. . . . The wise man knows that imagination is not only a means of pleasing himself and beguiling tedious hours with romances and fairy tales and fools' paradises . . . but also a means of foreseeing and being prepared for realities as yet unexperienced, and of testing the feasibility and desirability of serious Utopias. (cxxii)

IMITATION

*The statements under this heading present theories concerning the relation-
ship of a work of art to reality. See also IDEALISM and REALISM for
discussions that bear on the conception of reality which is to be imitated. By
Aristotle's time the notion of imitation in art had aready become quite complex. The continued complexity of this issue is indicated by the number of
theorists addressing it, by the relative length of the extracts, and, especially,
by the diversity of views. To some extent concepts of illusion began to replace
those of imitation as a focus of interest early in the nineteenth century. See
ILLUSION.*

4th cent. B.C.   Aristotle   AP

Epic poetry and Tragedy, Comedy also and Dithyrambic poetry, and the music
of the flute and of the lyre in most of their forms, are all in their general
conception modes of imitation. They differ . . . in three respects—the medium,
the objects, the manner . . . of imitation . . . [but] taken as a whole, the imitation
is produced by rhythm, *language, or "harmony"* [speech, and melody: EP
17], either singly or combined. (7) . . . In dancing, rhythm alone is used
without "harmony"; for even dancing imitates character, *emotion* [experi-
ences: EP 17], and action *by rhythmical movement* [through their rhythms
incorporated in dance-figures: EP17]. (9) . . . The objects of imitation are men
in action, and these men must be either of a *higher or a lower type* [high or low
character: EP 68] (for moral character mainly answers to these divisions,
goodness and badness being the distinguishing marks of moral differences), it
follows that we must represent men either better than in real life or worse, or as
they are. . . . Homer, for example, makes men better than they are; Cleophon as
they are; Hegemon the Thrasian, the inventor of parodies, and Nicochares, the
author of *Deiliad*, worse than they are. . . . Comedy aims at representing men
as worse, Tragedy as better than in actual life. . . . The manner in which each of
these objects may be imitated [by] . . . the poet [includes] narration . . . or he
may present all *his characters as living and moving before us* [the imitators
doing their work in and through action: EP 90]. (11-13) . . . The instinct of
imitation is implanted in man from childhood, one difference between him and
the other animals being that he is the most imitative of living creatures, and
through imitation learns his earliest lessons; and no less universal is the
pleasure felt in things imitated. We have evidence of this in the facts of
experience. Objects which in themselves we view with pain, we delight to

contemplate when reproduced with minute fidelity: such as the forms of the most ignoble animals and of dead bodies. The cause of this again is, that to learn gives the liveliest pleasure, not only to philosophers but to men in general; whose capacity, however, of learning is more limited. Thus the reason why men enjoy seeing a likeness is, that in contemplating it they find themselves learning or inferring [what class each object belongs to: EP 125], and saying, perhaps, "Ah, that is he." For if you happen not to have seen the original, the pleasure will be due not to the imitation as such, but to the execution, the colouring, or some other cause. (15)...The poet being an imitator, like a painter or any other artist, must of necessity imitate one of three objects,—things as they were or are, things as they are said or thought to be, or things as they ought to be.... Within the art of poetry there are two kinds of faults,—those which touch its essence, and those which are accidental. If a poet has chosen to imitate something, [but has imitated it incorrectly] through want of capacity, the error is inherent in the poetry. But if the failure is due to a wrong choice—if he has represented a horse as throwing out both his off legs at once, or introduced technical inaccuracies in medicine, for example, or in any other art—the error is not essential to the poetry.... If [the poet] describes the impossible, he is guilty of an error; but the error may be justified, if the end of the art be thereby attained . . . if, that is, the effect of this or any other part of the poem is thus rendered more striking.... If it be objected that the description is not true to fact, the poet may perhaps reply,—"But the objects are as they ought to be": just as Sophocles said that he drew men as they ought to be; Euripides, as they are.... If, however, the representation be of neither kind, the poet may answer,—"This is how men say the thing is." This applies to tales about the gods. (97-101)

4th cent. B.C.   Aristotle   APO

[Songs] inspire enthusiasm, and enthusiasm is an emotion of the ethical part of the soul.... When men hear imitations, even apart from the rhythms and tunes themselves, their feelings move in sympathy. Since, then, music is a pleasure, and virtue consists in rejoicing and loving and hating aright, there is clearly nothing which we are so much concerned to acquire and to cultivate as the power of forming right judgments and of taking delight in good dispositions and noble actions. Rhythm and melody supply imitations of anger and gentleness, and also of courage and temperance, and of all the qualities contrary to these, and of the other qualities of character, which hardly fall short of the actual affections, as we know from our own experience, for in listening to such strains our souls undergo a change. The habit of feeling pleasure or pain at mere representations is not far removed from the same feeling about realities. (1340a: 11-25)

See also Aristotle under AESTHETIC (APA 16-17), AFFECT (APO 1340a: 1-25), CHARACTER (AP 27-29, 53-54, 56, 57), GENRE (AP 7, 11,

13), OBJECTIVITY (AP 13), PLEASURE (AP 15), PLOT (AP 25-29, 39, 39-41, 45-49, 49), TRAGEDY (AP 21-23, 23-25), UNIVERSALITY (AP 35).

c.20 B.C.   Horace   HAP

I would advise one who has learned the imitative art to look to life and manners for a model, and draw from thence living words. At times a play marked by attractive passages and characters fitly sketched, though lacking in charm, though without force and art, gives the people more delight and holds them better than verses void of thought, and sonorous trifles. (477)

1561   Scaliger   SP

Language served . . . in the search of the philosophers after truth, utility dictated its cultivation in statesmanship, and pleasure drew it to the theatre. . . . The third class contains two species . . . which employ narration, and use much embellishment. They differ, however, in that one professes to record the fixed truth . . . while the other either adds a fictitious element to the truth, or imitates the truth by fiction. . . . The latter was called Poetry, or Making, because it narrated not only actual events, but also fictitious events as if they were actual, and represented them as they might be or ought to be. Wherefore the basis of all poetry is imitation. (2) . . . While [historians] . . . represent things just as they are, in some sense like a speaking picture, the poet depicts quite another sort of nature, and a variety of fortunes; in fact, by so doing, he transforms himself almost into a second diety. . . . Poetry fashions images of those things which are not, as well as images more beautiful than life of those things which are. . . . (7-8) . . . When authors take their plots from history, they must be careful not to depart too widely from the records. . . . [Euripides] has been censured for bringing wicked and impure women into his plays. . . . But we reply that these women were not creatures of his imagination, but were taken from life. Forsooth, if we are to hear of no wickedness, history must be done away with. So those comedies should be prized which make us condemn the vices which they bring to our ears, especially when the life of impure women ends in an unhappy death. (59)

  See also Scaliger under IDEALISM (SP 52), THREE UNITIES (SP 60).

1570   Castelvetro   CP

Poetry is a narration, according to verisimilitude, of human actions. . . . Poetry is imitation, and its general mode is imitation. (31) . . . That imitation natural to many which is born in him from childhood, by which he learns what he first learns . . . and by the employment of which he is consequently delighted, that imitation is no other than following the example of others, and doing exactly the same thing as others do, without knowing its wherefore. But the [higher] imitation necessary to poetry not only neither follows the example given by others, nor makes the same thing as has already been made, without knowing why it is made so, but it makes something quite original, entirely different from what has been done up to that day; it is thus not a mere copying of something gone before, but itself makes a copy for later people to follow. (34-35) . . . [If, as Aristotle says, the lower kind of imitation were] the perfection of poetry, the nature of the object of imitation would be of no account whatever. . . . Poetry makes a fable and imitates a human action, not as it was, or is, or is said to be, but as it ought to be. . . . Art is not a thing different from nature, nor can it pass beyond the limits of nature: but it sets out to do the same as does nature . . . [but more perfectly; this is not an imitation of nature but] a rivalry between the poet and nature's arrangement of the course of earthly things. (37-38) . . . The poet must have in his mind continually an idea of the most perfect and delightful subject, from which he must never remove his attention when he is making his poem. (40) . . . Truth naturally existed before verisimilitude, and the thing represented before the thing representing: and as verisimilitude depends entirely on truth, and the thing representing depends entirely on the thing represented, so one cannot have a full and direct knowledge of the dependent things, without a previous full knowledge of those on which they depend: hence necessarily before one has a complete and direct knowledge of verisimilitude and of the thing representing, one must have a complete and direct knowledge of truth and of the thing represented, if one wishes to judge fully whether verisimilitude and the thing representing have or have not those qualities they should have in relation to the truth and the thing represented. [Hence the art of poetry depends entirely on the art of history, with which, for the greater part, it has its doctrine in common.] (43-44) . . . [Verisimilar are] those things which are like what has happened once; or are like those which, though apparently not "verisimile," nevertheless have happened in full detail or extent; or at least, those things which are an agglomeration of parts, each part of which is like some particular thing which has actually happened in diverse accidents and to diverse people, though the full series of events and things has never been present together in actuality. [It follows, therefore, that] a contradiction of history is a greater sin than a contradiction of verisimilitude. (48) . . . Poetry is similitude or imitation of history: and as history is divided into two parts, namely, matter and words, so poetry is divided into two parts similarly, namely, matter and words. But within these two parts poetry and history differ: the matter of history is the recorded facts, its words, those of ordinary human speech; the matter of poetry is solely the invention of the poet's genius, and its words are not those of ordinary speech, but are composed in a metrical arrangement by the poet's genius. . . . Now the matter of poetry ought to be similar to the matter of history and to imitate it; but it ought not be the same, since if it were the same, it would not be similar to it nor imitate it; and if it were not similar to it and did not imitate it, the poet, as far as concerns the matter of his poetry, would have employed no labour and would have displayed no fineness of genius in inventing it. (50-51) . . . There have been many famous lettered men in times past, and there are many at present, who believe that the poet ought to be most intimately learned in every science and in every art, and that without this encyclopaedic learning he cannot be a true poet. But Aristotle is against them: he believed that poetry could be praiseworthy and indeed perfect without the poet's having an exquisite or even a moderate knowledge of the sciences and the arts. (78) . . . In poetry there are possibly two modes of representing action, viz., either by words and things, or by words alone; one of these modes is more similar to the thing represented, the other less. (83)

See also Castelvetro under ACTION (CP 113), CHARACTER (CP 102).

c.1583 Sidney   SDP

There is no art delivered unto mankind that hath not the works of nature for his principal object, without which they could not consist, and on which they so depend as they become actors and players, as it were, of what nature will have set forth. . . . Only the poet, disdaining to be tied to any such subjection [to nature], lifted up with the vigor of his own invention, doth grow, in effect, into another nature, in making things either better than nature bringeth forth, or, quite anew, forms such as never were in nature, as the heroes, demi-gods, cyclops, chimeras, furies, and such like; so as he goeth hand in hand with nature, not enclosed within the narrow warrant of her gifts, but freely ranging within the zodiac of his own wit. Nature never set forth the earth in so rich tapestry as divers poets have done; neither with pleasant rivers, fruitful trees, sweet-smelling flowers, or whatsoever else may make the too-much-loved earth more lovely; her world is brazen, the poets only deliver a golden. (7-8) . . . Poesy . . . is an art of imitation, for so Aristotle termeth it in his [*mimesis*], that is to say, a representing, counterfeiting, or figuring forth; to speak metaphorically, a speaking picture, with this end,—to teach and delight. Of this have been three general kinds. The chief, both in antiquity and excellency, were they that did imitate the inconceivable excellencies of God. Such were David in his Psalms; Solomon in his Song of Songs, in his Ecclesiastes and Proverbs. . . . The second kind is of them that deal with matters philosophical: either moral, . . . natural, . . . or historical. . . . But because this second sort is wrapped within the fold of the proposed subject, and takes not the free course of his own invention, whether they properly be poets or no let grammarians dispute, and go to the third, indeed right poets, of whom chiefly this question ariseth. Betwixt whom and these second is such a kind of difference as betwixt the meaner sort of painters, who counterfeit only such faces as are set before them, and the more excellent, who having no law but wit, bestow that in colors upon you which is fittest for the eye to see. . . . For these third be they which most properly do imitate to teach and delight; and to imitate borrow nothing of what is, hath been, or shall be; but range, only reined with learned discretion, into the divine consideration of what may be and should be (9-10)... That imitation whereof poetry is, hath the most conveniency to nature of all other; insomuch that, as Aristotle saith, those things which in themselves are horrible, as cruel battles, unnatural monsters, are made in poetical imitation delightful. (24)

See also Sidney under THOUGHT (SDP 8).

1609   de Vega   VAWP

Yet the Comedy has its end established like every kind of poem or poetic art, and that has always been to imitate the actions of men and to paint the customs of their age. All poetic imitation whatsoever is composed of three things, which are discourse, agreeable verse, harmony, that is to say music, which so far was common also to tragedy: comedy being different from tragedy in that it treats of lowly and plebian actions, and tragedy of royal and great ones. (25)... Let [the poet] be on his guard against impossible things, for it is of the chiefest importance that only the likeness of truth should be represented. The lackey should not discourse of lofty affairs, nor express the conceits which we have seen in certain foreign plays; and in no wise let the character contradict himself in what he has said. (34)

See also de Vega under COMEDY (VAWP 25).

1609   Jonson   JBW

The ends of all, who for the *Scene* do write,
Are, or should be, to profit, and delight.
And still't hath been the praise of all best times,
So persons were not touch'd to tax the crimes.
Then, in this play, which we present tonight,
And make the object of your ear, and sight,
On forfeit of your selves, think nothing true:
Lest so you make the maker to judge you.
For he knows, *Poet* never credit gain'd
By writing truths, but things (like truths) well-feign'd.

Second Prologue, *Epicoene*

1641   Johnson   JD

In being able to counsell others, a Man must be furnish'd with an universall store in himselfe, to the knowledge of all *Nature*: That is the matter, and seed-plot; These are the seats of all Argument, and Invention. But especially you must be cunning in the nature of Man. (7)... The true Artificer will not run away from nature, as hee were afraid of her; or depart from life, and the likenesse of Truth; but speake to the capacity of his hearers. And though his language differ from the vulgar somewhat; it shall not fly from all humanity, with the *Tamerlanes*, and *Tamer-Chams* of the late Age, which had nothing in them but the *scenicall* strutting, and furious vociferation, to warrant them then to the ignorant gapers. Hee knowes it is his onely Art, so to carry it, as none but Artificers perceive it. (33)

See also Jonson under AESTHETIC (JD 59-60).

1657 d'Aubignac   AAS

I know very well that the Poet is the Master, and that he disposes the order of his Poem as he thinks fit . . . ; but still 'tis certain, that all [the elements of the play] must be so adjusted, as to seem to have naturally both the rise, progress, and end which he gives them; so that though he be the Author, yet he must write the whole with such Art, that it may not so much as appear that it was by him Invented. So in *Eschylus's* Tragedie of *Agamemnon*, all things appear as if really *Agamemnon* had been murder'd; and in *Sophocles*, as if *Ajax* were really furious; and so of all the other Pieces of the Ancients. And likewise when we judge of any Play on our Stage, we suppose the thing either true, or that ought to be so, and might be so; and upon that supposition we approve of all the Words or Actions that are done or said by those who speak or act; and of all those Events which might probably follow the first appearances; because that in this case we believe that things might really happen as they seem, nay that they have happened, and ought to happen so. (1: 35-36)

See also d'Aubignac under ACTION (AAS 1: 43-44, 2: 81), PROBABILITY (AAS 1: 38, 2: 75, 76), SPECTACLE (AAS 3: 95-98), THREE UNITIES (AAS 2: 97-99, 105, 111-13).

1660 Corneille. See under CHARACTER (CFD 144-46), THREE UNITIES (CTU 817).

1663 Molière   MP

All [the] ridiculous pictures which the stage presents should be regarded without prejudice by every one. They are public mirrors, in which we never ought to show we see ourselves; to be so scandalized at such reproofs is openly confessing our defects. (6: 335) . . . [It] is easier to be grand over [great] sentiments, brave adverse fortune, challenge destiny, and hurl defiance at the gods than to exhibit in a proper spirit the absurdities of men and show their failings pleasantly upon the stage. When you depict a hero you can make him what you choose. Such portraits follow fancy, and no one seeks resemblance; you trust the pinions of imagination, which often soars from truth to attain the marvellous. But when you picture men you must paint from nature. Those portraits must be likenesses; and if you do not make them recognized as the men and women of our day you have done nought. In a word, it is enough in serious works to say sound things in choicely written language; but in comedy we must be comic; and 'tis indeed a curious enterprise to make the honest public laugh. (6: 340)

1665   Dryden   **DW**

I believe it may be concluded impossible that any should speak as good verses
in rhyme, as the best poets have writ; and therefore, that which seems nearest
to what it intends, is ever to be preferred. Nor is great thoughts more adorned
by verse, than verse unbeautified by mean ones; so that verse seems not only
unfit in the best use of it, but much more in the worse, when a servant is called,
or a door bid to be shut, in rhyme. Verses . . . do in their height of fancy declare
the labour that brought them forth . . . ; and Nature, that made the poet capable,
seems to retire. (1, 2: 21-22)

1668   Dryden   **DW**

I acknowledge that the French contrive their plots more regularly, and observe
the laws of comedy, and decorum of the stage, . . . with more exactness than the
English. . . . Yet, after all, I am of opinion that neither our faults nor their
virtues are considerable enough to place them above us. For the lively imitation of nature being in the definition of a play, those which best fulfil that law,
ought to be esteemed superior to the others. 'Tis true, those beauties of the
French poesy are such as will raise perfection higher where it is, but are not
sufficient to give it where it is not: they are indeed the beauties of a statue, but
not of a man, because not animated with the soul of poesy, which is imitation of
humour and passions. (1, 2: 82-83) . . . [It is important to distinguish] betwixt
what is nearest to the nature of comedy, which is the imitation of common
persons and ordinary speaking, and what is nearest the nature of a serious play:
this last is indeed the representation of nature, but 'tis nature wrought up to an
higher pitch. The plot, the characters, the wit, the passions, the descriptions,
are all exalted above the level of common converse, as high as the imagination
of the poet can carry them, with proportion to verisimility. Tragedy, we know,
is wont to image to us the minds and fortunes of noble persons, and to portray
these exactly; heroick rhyme is nearest nature, as being the noblest kind of
modern verse. (1, 2: 126-27) . . . I never heard of any other foundation of
Dramatick Poesy than the imitation of nature; neither was there ever pretended
any other by the ancients, or moderns, or me, who endeavour to follow them in
that rule. (1, 2: 172)

    See also Dryden under IMAGINATION (DW 1, 2: 170), STYLE (DW 1,
2: 161), THREE UNITIES (DW 1, 2: 176-77).

1672   Dryden. *See* under STYLE (DW 1, 2: 209-10).

1679   Dryden. *See* under ACTION (DW 1, 2: 268-69), CHARACTER (DW
1, 2: 275-77), HERO (DW 1, 2: 270-71).

1695   Dryden   **DW**

Fiction is of the essence of poetry, as well as of painting: there is a resemblance
in one, of human bodies, things, and actions, which are not real; and in the

other, of a true story by a fiction. (3: 312)...To imitate nature well in whatsoever subject, is the perfection of both [painting and poetry]; and that picture, and that poem, which comes nearest to the resemblance of nature, is the best. But it follows not, that what pleases most in either kind is therefore good, but what ought to please. Our depraved appetites, and ignorance of the arts, mislead our judgments, and cause us often to take that for true imitation of nature, which has no resemblance of nature in it. . . . Aristotle tells us, that imitation pleases, because it affords matter for a reasoner to inquire into the truth or falsehood of imitation, by comparing its likeness or unlikeness with the original; but by this rule, every speculation in nature, whose truth falls under the inquiry of a philosopher, must produce the same delight; which is not true. I should rather assign another reason. Truth is the object of our understanding, as good is of our will; and the understanding can no more be delighted with a lie, than the will can choose an apparent evil. As truth is the end of all our speculations, so the discovery of it is the pleasure of them; and since a true knowledge of nature gives us pleasure, a lively imitation of it, either in poetry or painting, must of necessity produce a much greater: for both these arts . . . are not only true imitations of nature, but of the best nature, of that which is wrought up to a nobler pitch. They present us with images more perfect than the life in any individual; and we have the pleasure to see all the scattered beauties of nature united by a happy chemistry, without its deformities or faults. They are imitations of the passions, which always move, and therefore consequently please; for without motion there can be no delight, which cannot be considered but as an active passion. When we view these elevated ideas of nature, the result of that view is admiration, which is always the cause of pleasure. (3: 322-25)

1710-1711   Addison   AW

An opera may be allowed to be extravagantly lavish in its decorations, as its only design is to gratify the senses, and keep up an indolent attention in the audience. Common sense, however, requires, that there should be nothing in the scenes and machines, which may appear childish and absurd. . . . A little skill in criticism would inform us, that shadows and realities ought not to be mixed together in the same piece; and that scenes which are designed as the representations of nature, should be filled with resemblances, and not with the things themselves. If one would represent a wide champaign country filled with herds and flocks, it would be ridiculous to draw the country only upon the scenes, and to crowd several parts of the stage with sheep and oxen. This is joining together inconsistencies, and making the decoration partly real, and partly imaginary. I would recommend what I have said here to the directors, as well as to the admirers of our modern opera. (1: 23-24)

1711   Addison. *See* under GENRE DEFINITION (AW 1: 361); compare with CONVENTION (AW 1: 75), DRAMATIZATION (AW 1, 2: 75).

1712   Addison   **AW**

Though there are several of those wild scenes [in nature], that are more delightful than any artifical shows, yet we find the works of nature even more pleasant, the more they resemble those of art: for in this case our pleasure rises from a double principle; from the agreeableness of the objects to the eye, and from their similitude to other objects. We are pleased as well with comparing their beauties, as with surveying them, and can represent them to our minds, either as copies or originals. Hence it is that we take delight in a prospect that is well laid out, and diversified with fields and meadows, woods and rivers; in those accidental landscapes of trees, clouds, and cities, that are sometimes found in the veins of marble; in the curious fret-work of rocks and grottos; and, in a word, in any thing that hath such a variety or regularity as may seem the effect of design in what we call the works of chance. If the products of nature rise in value according as they more or less resemble those of art, we may be sure that artificial works receive a greater advantage from their resemblance of such as are natural; because here the similitude is not only pleasant, but the pattern more perfect. (2: 142)

   See also Addison under AFFECT (AW 2: 120), IMAGINATION (AW 2: 145-46).

1731   Voltaire. *See* under DRAMA (VE 283).

1738   Voltaire. *See* under COMEDY (VW 10, 1: 270).

1751   Johnson. *See* under VARIETY (JW 3: 241).

1758   Diderot. *See* under ACTION (DDP 291-92), TRAGEDY (DDP 296, 297).

1759   Johnson. *See* under UNIVERSALITY (JW 1: 222).

1765   Johnson. *See* under GENRE DEFINITION (JS 16), ILLUSION (JS 28, 28-29), OBJECTIVITY (JS 14), THREE UNITIES (JS 25, 27, 57), UNIVERSALITY (JS 11-12), VARIETY (JS 15).

1766   Lessing   **LSPW**

The drama designed for the living art of the actor should . . . be completed to confine itself more strictly within the limits of material art. In it we do not merely believe that we see and hear a shrieking Philoketes, we actually do see and hear him. The nearer the actor approaches to nature, the more will our eyes and ears be offended; for it is indisputable that they are so in nature itself when we meet with such loud and violent expressions of pain. Besides, bodily pain generally is not capable of exciting that sympathy which other ills awaken. Our imagination can discern too little in it for the mere sight of it to arouse in us anything of an equivalent emotion. (23) . . . Imitation is an effort to produce a resemblance, but can a person be said to aim at this whose changes overstep the line of necessity? Further, when a man thus exceeds, it is clear that it is not his design to produce resemblance; that, therefore, he has not imitated. (48-49)

1767-1769   Lessing   LSPW

It is true and yet not true that the comic tragedy of Gothic invention faithfully copied nature. It only imitates it faithfully in one half and entirely neglects the other, it imitates the nature of phenomena without in the least regarding the nature of our feelings and emotions. (399)

See also Lessing under IMAGINATION (LSPW 256).

1778   Diderot   DPA

One is one's self by nature; one becomes some one else by imitation; the heart one is supposed to have is not the heart one has. What, then, is the true talent? That of knowing well the outward symptoms of the soul we borrow, of addressing our selves to the sensations of those who hear and see us, of deceiving [the audience] by the imitation of these symptoms, by an imitation which aggrandises everything in their imagination, and which becomes the measure of their judgment; for it is impossible otherwise to appreciate that which passes inside us. And after all, what does it matter to us whether [the actors] feel or do not feel, so long as we know nothing about it? He, then, who best knows and best renders, after the best conceived ideal type, these outward signs, is the greatest actor. (74)

See also Diderot under AFFECT (DPA 17-18), CONVENTION (DPA 102), ILLUSION (DPA 4-5, 16-17, 22, 74).

c.1780   Johnson   JL

Whatever pleasure there may be in seeing crimes punished and virtue rewarded, yet, since wickedness often prospers in real life, the poet is certainly at liberty to give it prosperity on the stage. For if poetry has an imitation of reality, how are its laws broken by exhibiting the world in its true form? The stage may sometimes gratify our wishes; but, if it be truly the *mirror of life*, it ought to shew us sometimes what we are to expect. (2: 135)

c.1781   Johnson   JL

Nature is not the object of human judgment; for it is vain to judge where we cannot alter. If by nature is meant, what is commonly called *nature* by criticks, a just representation of things really existing and actions really performed, nature cannot be properly opposed to *art*; nature being, in this sense, only the best effect of *art*. (3: 255)

1789   Goethe   GLE

If an artist . . . turns to natural objects, uses all care and fidelity in the most perfect imitation of their forms and colors, never knowingly departs from nature . . . such an artist must possess high merit, for he cannot fail of attaining the greatest accuracy, and his work must be full of certainty, variety and strength. . . . A capable but limited talent can in this way treat but agreeable limited subjects. . . . This sort of imitation will thus be practiced by men of quiet, true, limited nature, in the representation of dead or still-life subjects. But man finds . . . such a mode . . . too timid and inadequate. He perceives a harmony among many objects, which can only be brought into the picture by sacrificing the individual. He gets tired of using Nature's letters each time to spell after her. He invents a way, devises a language for himself, so as to express in his own fashion the idea his soul has attained, and give to the object . . . a distinctive form, without having recourse to nature . . . or even without recalling exactly the individual form. . . . This species of imitation is applied with the best effect in cases where a great whole comprehends many subordinate objects . . . where the aim would be missed if we attended too closely to details, instead of keeping in view the idea of the whole. . . . When at last art, by means of imitation of Nature, of efforts to create a common language . . . has acquired a clearer and clearer knowledge of the peculiarities of objects . . . then will *Style* reach the highest point it is capable of. . . . Simple Imitation springs from quiet existence and an agreeable subject; Manner seizes with facile capacity upon an appearance; [but] Style rests upon the deepest foundations of knowledge, upon the essence of things, so far as we are able to recognize it in visible and comprehensible forms. (59-61)

1797   Goethe   GED

The worlds which are to be represented to view are common to both [the epic and drama]. . . .

1. The physical; and firstly, that most nearly approaching the one to which the persons represented belong, and by which they are surrounded. Here the dramatist as a rule confines himself strictly to one single point; the epic poet has more freedom of motion and his range of locality is much greater. Secondly, there is the remoter world, in which I include the whole of nature. This one the epic poet, who . . . has recourse to the imagination, seeks to bring nearer to us by means of similes or comparisons, of which the dramatist avails himself with less frequency.

2. The moral world is equally common to both. . . .

3. The world of phantasies, presentments, apparitions, accidents, and fatalities. This lies open to both, it being of course understood that it must approximate to the world of sensuous perception. (338)

1804   Coleridge. *See* under ILLUSION (CSC 1: 178-81).

1808 Schlegel   **SCL**

The invention of dramatic art, and of the theatre, seems a . . . natural one. Man has a great disposition to mimicry; when he enters vividly into the situation, sentiments, and passions of others, he involuntarily puts on a resemblance to them in his gestures. . . . It is one of the chief amusements [of children] to represent those grown people when they have had an opportunity of observing. . . . But one step more was requisite for the invention of drama, . . . to separate and extract the mimetic elements from the separate parts of social life, and to present them to itself again collectively in one mass. . . . (32) . . . [Lessing's] lingering faith in Aristotle, with the influence which Diderot's writings had had on him, produced a strange compound in his theory of the dramatic art. He did not understand the rights of poetical imitation, and demanded not only in dialogue, but everywhere else also, a naked copy of nature, just as if this were in general allowable, or even possible in the fine arts. (511)

 See also Schlegel under CHARACTER (SCL 148-9), DRAMA (SCL 30-2), GENRE DEFINITION (SCL 176-9), LANGUAGE (SCL 229-30, 366), PROBABILITY (SCL 182-3), SPECTACLE (SCL 59), THREE UNITIES (SCL 236-51).

1808 Coleridge. *See* under DRAMA (CSC 1: 177).

1811-1812 Coleridge. *See* under DISTANCE (CSC 2: 46), UNIVERSAL-ITY (CCSL 37).

1814 Hazlitt   **HW**

Nature is the soul of art. There is a strength in the imagination that reposes entirely on nature, which nothing else can supply. There is in the old poets and painters a vigour and grasp of mind, a full possession of their subject, a confidence and firm faith, a sublime simplicity, an elevation of thought, proportioned to their depth of feeling, an increasing force and impetus, which moves, penetrates, and kindles all that comes in contact with it, which seems, not theirs, but given to them. It is this reliance on the power of nature which has produced those masterpieces by the Prince of Painters, in which expression is all in all, where one spirit, that of truth, pervades every part, brings down heaven to earth, mingles cardinals and popes with angels and apostles, and yet blends and harmonises the whole by the true touches and intense feeling of what is beautiful and grand in nature. It was the same trust in nature that enabled Chaucer to describe the patient sorrow of Griselda; or the delight of that young beauty in the Flower and the Leaf. (1: 162)

1815 Coleridge   **CBL**

It is sufficient that philosophically we understand that in all imitation two elements must coexist, and not only coexist, but must be perceived as co-existing. These two constituent elements are likeness and unlikeness, or sameness and difference, and in all genuine creations of art there must be a union of these disparates. The artist may take his point of view where he pleases, provided that the desired effect be perceptibly produced,—that there be likeness in the difference, difference in the likeness, and a reconcilement of both in one. If there be likeness to nature without any check of difference, the result is disgusting, and the more complete the delusion, the more loathsome the effect. . . . In respect to a work of genuine imitation, you begin with an acknowledged total difference, and then every touch of nature gives you the pleasure of an approximation to truth. The fundamental principle of all this is undoubtedly the horror of falsehood and the love of truth inherent in the human breast. (2: 256) . . . The artist must first eloign [distance] himself from nature in order to return to her with full effect. Why this? Because if he were to begin by mere painful copying, he would produce masks only, not forms breathing life. He must out of his own mind create forms according to the severe laws of the intellect, in order to generate in himself that co-ordination of freedom and law, that involution of obedience in the prescript, and of the prescript in the impulse to obey, which assimilates him to nature, and enables him to understand her. (2: 258) . . . The artist must imitate that which is within the thing, that which is active through form and figure, and discourses to us by symbols—the *Natur-geist*, or spirit of nature, as we unconsciously imitate those whom we love; for so only can he hope to produce any work truly natural in the object and truly human in the effect. The idea which puts the form together cannot itself be the form. It is above form, and is its essence, the universal in the individual, or the individuality itself,—the glance and the exponent of the indwelling power. (2: 259)

See also Coleridge under AFFECT (CBL 2: 5-6).

1815   Hazlitt   HW

All art is built upon nature; and the tree of Knowledge lifts its branches to the clouds, only as it has struck its roots deep into the earth. He is the greatest artist, not who leaves the materials of nature behind him, but who carries them with him into the world of invention;—and the larger and more entire the masses in which he is able to apply them to his purpose, the stronger and more durable will his productions be. (2: 223)

See also Hazlitt under HUMOR (HW 1: 12), TRAGEDY (HW 1: 13).

1816   Hazlitt   HW

Objects in themselves disagreeable or indifferent, often please in the imitation. A brick-floor, a pewter-plate, an ugly cur barking . . . have been made very interesting as pictures by the fidelity, skill, and spirit, with which they have been copied. One source of the pleasure thus received is undoubtedly the surprise or feeling of admiration, occasioned by the unexpected coincidence between the imitation and the object. The deception, however, not only pleases at first sight, or from mere novelty; but it continues to please upon further acquaintance, and in proportion to the insight we acquire into the distinctions of nature and of art. By far the most numerous class of connoisseurs are the admirers of pictures of *still life*, which have nothing but the elaborateness of the execution to recommend them. One chief reason, it should seem then, why imitation pleases, is, because, by exciting curiosity, and inviting a comparison between the object and the representation, it opens a new field of inquiry, and leads the attention to a variety of details and distinctions not perceived before. This latter source of the pleasure derived from imitation has never been properly insisted on. . . . The painter of still life, as it is called, takes the same pleasure in the object as the spectator does in the imitation; because by habit he is led to perceive all those distinctions in nature, to which other persons never pay any attention till they are pointed out to them in the picture. The vulgar only see nature as it is reflected to them from art; the painter sees the picture in nature, before he transfers it to the canvass. He refines, he analyses, he remarks fifty things, which escape common eyes; and this affords a distinct source of reflection and amusement to him, independently of the beauty or grandeur of the objects themselves, or of their connection with other impressions besides those of sight. The charm of the Fine Arts, then, does not consist in any thing peculiar to imitation, even where only imitation is concerned, since *there*, where art exists in the highest perfection, namely, in the mind of the artist, the object excites the same or greater pleasure, before the imitation exists. Imitation renders an object, displeasing in itself, a source of pleasure, not by the repetition of the same idea, but by suggesting new ideas, by detecting new properties, and endless shades of difference, just as a close and continued contemplation of the object itself would do. Art shows us nature, divested of the medium of our prejudices. It divides and decompounds objects into a thousand curious parts, which may be full of variety, beauty, and delicacy in themselves, though the object to which they belong may be disagreeable in its general appearance, or by association with other ideas. (1: 72-74) . . . Imitation interests, then, by exciting a more intense perception of truth, and calling out the powers of observation and comparison: wherever this effect takes place the interest follows of course, with or without the imitation, whether the object is real or artificial. . . . It is not to be denied that the study of the *ideal* in art, if separated from the study of nature, may have the effect . . . of producing dissatisfaction and contempt for everything but itself, as all affectation must; but to the genuine artist, truth, nature, beauty, are almost different names for the same thing. (1: 75)

See also Hazlitt under IMAGINATION (HW 10: 83), SUBJECT (HW 1: 75-76), UNITY (HW 1: 76)

1817 Hazlitt **HW**

Players are the ''the abstracts and brief chronicles of the time''; the motley representatives of human nature. They are the only honest hypocrites. Their life is a voluntary dream; a studied madness. The height of their ambition is to be *beside themselves*, that they are nothing. Made up of mimic laughter and tears, passing from the extremes of joy or woe at the prompter's call, they wear the livery of other men's fortunes; their very thoughts are not their own. They are, as it were, train-bearers in the pageant of life, and hold a glass up to humanity, frailer than itself. We see ourselves at second-hand in them: they shew us all that we are, all that we wish to be, and all that we dread to be. The stage is an epitome, a bettered likeness of the world, with the dull part left out: and, indeed, with this omission, it is nearly big enough to hold all the rest. What brings the resemblance nearer is, that, as *they* imitate us, we, in our turn, imitate them. How many fine gentlemen do we owe to the stage? How many romantic lovers are mere Romeos in masquerade? How many soft bosoms have heaved with Juliet's sighs? (1: 153)

1818   Coleridge   CSC

But a moment's reflection suffices to make every man conscious of what every man must have before felt, that the drama is an *imitation* of reality, not a *copy*—and that imitation is contradistinguished from copy by this: that a certain quantum of difference is essential to the former, and an indispensable condition and cause of the pleasure we derive from it; while in a copy it is a defect, contravening its name and purpose. . . . Not only that we ought, but that we actually do, all of us judge of the drama under this impression, we need no other proof than the impassive slumber of our sense of probability when we hear an actor announce himself as a Greek, Roman, Venetian, or Persian in good mother English. (1: 115)

1818   Hazlitt. *See* under AESTHETIC (HW 5: 3), DRAMA (HW 5: 8), IMAGINATION (HW 5: 4), STYLE (HW 5: 347, 350-51), compare with LANGUAGE (HW 5: 12-13).

1820   Hazlitt. *See* under DRAMA (HW 8: 417), IDEALISM (HW 11: 463), PROBABILITY (HW 11: 463-64).

1823   Goethe. *See* under THOUGHT (GCE Nov. 14).

1824   Hazlitt   HW

The great works of art . . . owe their pre-eminence and perfection to one and the same principle,—*the immediate imitation of nature*. This principle predominated equally in the classical forms of [ancient Greece], and in the grotesque figures of Hogarth; the perfection of art in each arose from the truth and identity of the imitation with the reality; the difference was in the subjects; there was none in the mode of imitation. (9: 377) . . . There is nothing in nature, however mean or trivial, that has not its beauty and some interest belonging to it, if truly represented. (9: 389) . . . Sir Joshua [Reynolds] was perhaps the most original imitator that ever appeared in the world; and the reason of this, in a great measure, was, that he was compelled to combine what he saw in art, with what he saw in nature, which was constantly before him. (9: 398)

See also Hazlitt under IDEALISM (HW 9: 379).

1830   Hazlitt   HW

As the mind advances in the knowledge of nature, the horizon of art enlarges. . . . In addition to an infinity of details, even in the most common object, there is the variety of form and colour, of light and shade, of character and expression, of the voluptuous, the thoughtful . . . ; which are all to be found (separate or combined) in nature, which sufficiently account for the diversity of art. . . . All that we meet with in the master-pieces of taste and genius is to be found in the previous capacity of nature; and man, instead of adding to the store, or *creating* any thing either as to matter or manner, can only draw out a feeble and imperfect transcript, bit by bit, and one appearance after another, according to the peculiar aptitude and affinity that subsists between his mind and some one part. The mind resembles a prism, which untwists the various rays of truth, and displays them by different modes in several parcels. (9: 425)

1864   Taine   TLA

It is not alone the history of this or that great man which proves to us the necessity of imitating the living model, and of keeping the eye fixed on nature, but rather the history of every great school of art. Every school . . . degenerates and falls, simply through its neglect of exact imitation, and its abandonment of the living model. You see it in painting, in the fabricators of muscles and exaggerated attitudes who succeeded Michael Angelo [sic]; in the sciolists of theatrical decorations and in the brawny rotundities which have followed the great Venetians. . . . The same thing occurs in literature, with the versifiers and rhetoricians of the Latin decadence; with the sensual and declamatory playwrights closing the bright periods of the English drama. (45-46) . . . Is this [rule of imitation] true in every particular, and must we conclude that absolutely exact imitation is the end of art? If this were so . . . absolutely exact imitation would produce the finest works. But, in fact, it is not so. . . . If it were true . . . what would be . . . the best drama? A stenographic report of a criminal trial, every word of which is faithfully recorded. It is clear . . . that if we sometimes encounter in it flashes of nature and occasional outbursts of sentiment, these are but veins of pure metal in a mass of worthless dross; it may furnish a writer with materials for his art, but it does not constitute a work of art. . . . A broad sketch by Van Dyck is a hundredfold more powerful [than an illusionistic painting by Denner]. . . . Neither in painting nor in any other art are prizes awarded to deceptions. A second and stronger proof, that exact imitation is not the end of art, is to be found in this fact, that certain arts are purposely inexact. There is sculpture, for instance. A statue is generally of one color, either of bronze or of marble; and again, the eyes are without eyeballs. It is just this uniformity of tint, and this modification of moral expression, which completes its beauty. (51-53). . . . It is essential, then, to closely imitate something in an object; but not everything. . . . What [the artist has] to do is to reproduce [the model's] *relationships*, and first the proportions, that is to say, the relationships of magnitude. If the head is of a certain length, the body must be so many times longer than the head, the arm of a length equally dependent on that. . . . [The artist] is required to reproduce forms, or the relationships of position: this or that curve, oval, angle, or sinuosity in the model must be repeated in the copy by a line of the same nature. In short, [the artist's] object is to reproduce the aggregate of relationships, by which the parts are linked together, and nothing else; it is not the simple corporeal appearance that [the artist has] to give, but the *logic* of the whole body. Suppose, in like manner, [the artist is] contemplating some actual character, some scene in real life, high or low, and [is] asked to furnish a description of it. . . . What is expected of [the artist] is, not to record every word and motion, all the actions of the personage, or the fifteen or twenty figures that are figured before [him], but, as before, to note proportions, connections, and relationships; [the artist is] expected, in the first place, to keep exactly the proportion of the actions of the personage, in other words, to give prominence to ambitious acts, if he is ambitious, to avaricious acts, if he is avaricious, and to violent acts if he is violent; after this, to observe the reciprocal connection of these same acts; that is to say, to provoke one reply by another, to originate a resolution, a sentiment, an idea by an idea, a sentiment, a preceding resolution, and moreover by the actual condition of the personage; in addition to that, still by the general character bestowed on him. In short, in the literary effort, as in the pictorial effort, it is important to transcribe, not the visible outlines of persons and events, but the aggregate of their relationships and inter-dependencies, that is to say, their logic. (56-58)

See also Taine under AESTHETIC (TLA 76, 76-77, 273-74), LANGUAGE (TLA 54-55); compare with HERO (TLA 180), STYLE (TLA 322-23).

1871   Nietzsche   NBT

The *spectator* was brought upon the stage by Euripides. He who has perceived the material of which the Promethean tragic writers prior to Euripides formed their heroes, and how remote from their purpose it was to bring the true mask of reality upon the stage, will also know what to make of the wholly divergent tendency of Euripides. Through him the commonplace individual forced his way from the spectator's benches to the stage itself; the mirror in which formerly only great and bold traits found expression now showed the painful exactness that conscientiously reproduces even the abortive lines of nature. (87)

1876   Sarcey   STT

It is customary in seeking a definition of dramatic art to say that drama is the representation of life. Now, assuredly drama is the representation of life. But when one has said that, he has said no great thing. . . . All the arts of imitation are representations of life. All have for their purpose the placing of nature before our eyes. . . . But we see . . . that each of these arts has a different means of expression, that the conditions to which it is obliged to submit in order to represent life improve on each of them the employment of particular processes. (20-21)

1878   Nietzsche   NHH

Older than speech is the imitation of gestures, which is carried on unconsciously and which, in the general repression of the language of gesture and trained control of the muscles, is still so great that we cannot look at a face moved by emotion without feeling an agitation of our own face (it may be remarked that feigned yawning excites real yawning in any one who sees it). The imitated gesture leads the one who imitates back to the sensation it expressed in the face or body of the one imitated. Thus men learned to understand one another, thus the child still learns to understand the mother. . . . As soon as men understood each other by gestures, there could be established a *symbolism* of gestures. (193-94)

1880   Nietzsche   NHH 2

By imitation, the bad gains, the good loses credit—especially in art. (171)

1887   Chekhov. *See* under REALISM (CL 57).

1888   Nietzsche   NW

The compulsion to imitate: extreme irritability, by means of which a certain example becomes contagious—a condition is guessed and represented merely by means of a few signs. . . . A complete picture is visualized by one's inner consciousness, and its effect soon shows itself in the movement of the limbs,—in a certain suspension of the *will*. . . . This differentiates the artist from the layman (from the spectator of art): the latter reaches the height of his excitement in the mere act of apprehending: the former in giving—and in such a way that the antagonism between these two gifts is not only natural but even desirable. Each of these states has an opposite standpoint—to demand of the artist that he should have the point of view of the spectator (or the critic) is equivalent to asking him to impoverish his creative power. . . . (255-56)

1888   Chekhov. *See* under CHARACTER (CL 118-19).

1889   Strindberg   SMD

[Henri Becque's *Les Corbeaux*] is photography which includes everything, even the grain of dust on the lens of the camera. This is realism, a working method elevated to art, or the little art which does not see the forest for the trees. This is the misunderstood naturalism which holds that art merely consists of drawing a piece of nature in a natural way; it is not the great naturalism which seeks out the points where the great battles are fought, which loves to see what you do not see every day, which delights in the struggle between natural forces, ... which finds the beautiful or ugly unimportant if only it is great. (17)

1889   Chekhov. Compare with DRAMA (CLF 141).

1902   Shaw. *See* under THOUGHT (SAA 43).

1905   Stanislavski   SL

What does it really mean to be truthful on the stage? ... Truthfulness in those terms would be sheer triviality. There is the same difference between artistic and inartistic truth as exists between a painting and a photograph: the latter reproduces everything, the former only what is essential; to put the essential on canvas requires the talent of a painter. (20)

1908   Pirandello. *See* under CHARACTER (POH 49), RULES (POH 29-30).

1912   Shaw. *See* under REALISM (SALOP 73-74); compare with ILLU-SION (SALOP 72).

1918-1922   Stanislavski   SAS

You must make sure that the play is not a deplorable imitation of some classical masterpiece, but that it reflects life faithfully; for then you too will be able to reflect it through yourself on the stage as a slice of life. It does not matter if the name of the author is unknown so long as the people depicted in his play are not copies of some conventional stage figures but living people. ... [But] they should not represent some hackneyed ideals which one is, it seems, supposed to worship just because they have been 'acted' in this or that way for generations! (105)

Compare with Stanislavski under IDEALISM (SAS 104).

1921   Eliot. *See* under AESTHETICS (ESW 61).

1924   Eliot   EEE

It is essential that a work of art be self-consistent, that an artist should consciously or unconsciously draw a circle beyond which he does not trespass: on the one hand actual life is always the material, and on the other hand an abstraction from actual life is a necessary condition to the creation of the work of art. (11)

1930   Shaw   SCP

Between the two extremes of actual portraiture and pure fancy work suggested by a glance or an anecdote, I have copied nature with many degrees of fidelity combining studies from life in the same book or play with those types and composites and traditional figures of the novel and the stage which are called pure fictions. (678)

1931-1936   Artaud   AT

If we have all finally come to think of theatre as an inferior art, a means of popular distraction, and to use it as an outlet for our worst instincts, it is because we have learned too well what the theatre has been, namely, falsehood and illusion. It is because we have been accustomed for four hundred years, that is since the Renaissance, to a purely descriptive and narrative theater— storytelling psychology; it is because every possible ingenuity has been ex- erted in bringing to life on the stage plausible but detached beings, with the spectacle on one side, the public on the other—and because the public is no longer shown anything but the mirror of itself. (76)

Compare with Artaud under ACTION (AT 82), ILLUSION (AT 86).

1935   Brecht. *See* under GEST (BBT 86).

1936   Stanislavski   SAP

The great poets and artists draw from nature. . . . But they do not photograph her. Their product passes through their own personalities and what she gives them is supplemented by living material taken from their store of emotion memories. (163)

1936   Brecht. *See* under ALIENATION (BBB 131-36), ILLUSION (BBB 130), STYLE (BBB 132).

1938   Brecht. *See* under ACTION (BBEB 430).

1948   Brecht   BBBG

The pleasure afforded by images [of characters in the Greek, French and Elizabethan theatres] . . . hardly ever depended on the degree of resemblance between the picture and the object depicted. The pleasure was disturbed very little or not at all by inaccuracy or even extreme improbability, so long as the inaccuracy had a certain consistency and the improbability remained of the same kind. The illusion of a story that developed convincingly, an illusion created by all manner of poetical and theatrical devices, was enough. (16)

See also Brecht under STYLE (BBBG 23, 39-40); compare with AFFECT (BBBG 21-23).

1956   Brecht. *See* under THOUGHT (BBT 277, 279).

INSTRUCTION

Aristotle speaks of man's pleasure in learning, but it was Horace's formulation of the purpose of poetry, to teach and to please, which guided the thinking of many later theorists. (For discussions of the nature and function of drama, see DRAMA.) Presented here are concepts of drama's proposed instructive function, content, or means. See also MORALITY.

4th cent. B.C. Aristotle. *See* under IMITATION (AP 15), METAPHOR (AR 167-68), PLEASURE (AP 15).

c.20 B.C. Horace. *See* under DRAMA (HAP 479).

1561 Scaliger   SP

What . . . does the poet teach? Does he teach actions, which arise from mental states or dispositions . . . ? Or does he teach us how to become such men that the faculty of doing good is potent, and the principle of avoiding evil conduct is implanted? Aristotle ruled that since poetry is comparable to that civic institution which leads to happiness, happiness being nothing other than perfect action, the poet does not lead us to imitate character, but action. Surely he is right; we agree perfectly. . . . The poet teaches mental dispositions through action, so that we embrace the good and imitate it in our conduct, and reject evil and abstain from that. Action, therefore, is a mode of teaching; [moral] disposition that which is taught. Wherefore action is, as it were, the pattern or medium in a plot, disposition its end. (82-83)

    See also Scaliger under AESTHETIC (SP 53), DRAMA (SP 2, 3), IMITATION (SP 59), THREE UNITIES (SP 60).

1570 Castelvetro. *See* under PLEASURE (CP 128-29); compare with CATHARSIS (CP 123), DRAMA (CP 66, 67).

c.1583 Sidney   SDP

Whatever the philospher saith should be done, [the poet] giveth a perfect picture of it in some one by whom he presupposeth it was done, so as he coupleth the general notion with the particular example. A perfect picture, I say; for he yieldeth to the powers of the mind an image of that whereof the philosopher bestoweth but a wordish description, which doth neither strike, pierce, nor possess the sight of the soul so much as that other doth.

. . . No doubt the philosopher, with his learned definitions, . . . replenisheth the memory with many infallible grounds of wisdom, which notwithstanding lie dark before the imaginative and judging power, if they be not illuminated or figured forth by the speaking picture of poesy. (15-16) The question is, whether the feigned image of poesy, or the regular instruction of philosophy, hath the more force in teaching. . . . I say the philosopher teacheth, but he teacheth obscurely, so as the learned only can understand him; that is to say, he teacheth them that are already taught. But the poet is the food for the tenderest stomachs; the poet is indeed the right popular philosopher. Whereof Aesop's tales give good proof; whose pretty allegories, stealing under the formal tales of beasts, make many, more beastly than beasts, begin to hear the sound of virtue from those dumb speakers. (17-18) . . . A feigned example hath as much force to teach as a true example—for as for to move, it is clear, since the feigned may be tuned to the highest key of passion. (20) . . . The poet, with . . . delight, doth draw the mind more effectually than any other art doth. And so a conclusion not unfitly ensueth: that as virtue is the most excellent resting place for all worldly learning to make his end of, so poetry, being the most familiar to teach it, and most princely to move towards it, in the most excellent work is the most excellent workman. (26)

   See also Sidney under AFFECT (SDP 22, 25, 29), COMEDY (SDP 28), DRAMA (SDP 2-3), HUMOR (SDP 50-51), LANGUAGE (SDP 11), TRAG-EDY (SDP 28-29).

1601   Jonson. *See* under SYMBOL (JBW).

1605   Jonson. *See* under POETIC JUSTICE (JBW).

1610   Jonson   **JBW**

                    . . . This pen
Did never aim to grieve, but better men;
   . . . when the wholesome remedies are sweet,
And, in their working, gain, and profit meet,
He hopes to find no spirit so much diseas'd,
But will, with such fair correctives, be pleas'd.
For here, he doth not fear, who can apply.
If there by any, that will sit so nigh
Unto the stream, to look what it doth run,
They shall find things, they'ld think, or wish, were done;
They are so natural follies, but so shown,
As even the doers may see, and yet not own.

                              Prologue, *The Alchemist*

1641   Jonson. *See* under DISINTERESTEDNESS (JD 41-42), DRAMA (JD 90-91).

1657   d'Aubignac   AAS

The minds of those who are of the meanest Rank and Condition in a State, are generally so little acquainted with any notions of Morality, that the most general Maxims of it are hardly known to them; 'tis in vain therefore to make fine Discourses, full of convincing Reasons, and strengthened with Examples to them, they can neither understand the first, nor have any deference for the latter. All the elevated Truths of Philosophy are lights too strong for their weak Eyes.... All these [truths]...are Paradoxes to them, which makes them suspect Philosophy itself, and turn it into Ridicule; they must therefore be instructed by a more sensible way, which may fall more under their senses; and such are the Representations of the Stage, which may therefore properly be called the Peoples School. (1: 5)...I understand...by Didactick Discourses those Maxims and general Propositions which contain known Truths, and are only apply'd in the Play, according as the Subject will allow, tending more to instruct the Audience in the Rules of Morality, than to explain any part of the Intrigue.... As to these Didacktick Discourses, I distinguish them into two sorts, some I call Physical, and the others Moral ones. I call those Physical or Natural, which make a deduction or description of the Nature, Qualities, or Effects of any thing without distinction, whether it be in the rank of natural or supernatural things; or of the number of Artificial Compounds. Under the notion of Moral Discourses, I comprehend all those Instructions which contain any Maxim of Religion, or Politicks.... All these Didactick Discourses are of their own nature unfit for the Stage, because they are cold, and without motion, being general things which only tend to Instruct the mind, but not to move the heart, so that the action of the Stage, which ought to warm our affections, becomes by them dull and indifferent. (3: 32-33)...I confess that the Stage is a place of Instruction, but we must well understand how this is meant. The Poet ought to bring his whole Action before the Spectator, which ought to be so represented with all its circumstances, that the Audience be fully Instructed; for as Drammatick Poetry does but imitate human actions, it does it only to instruct us by them, and that it does directly, and properly: But for Moral Maxims, which may incite us either to the love of Virtue, or stir us up to hate Vice; it does it indirectly. (3: 35)

See also d'Aubignac under AFFECT (AAS 1: 6), DRAMA (AAS 1: 4, 7), POETIC JUSTIC (AAS 1: 5-6).

1660   Corneille   CFD

There are four kinds of plays in which there is some sort of moral intent. The first sort...is that which contains maxims and moral instructions, scattered throughout. These should be sparingly used and only on the rarest occasions inserted into general discourses, and then in small doses.... Every one of my [dramatic] poems would present a sorry approach if I eliminated that which I mixed into it; but again one must not accentuate them too much without applying the general to the particular . . . because it slackens the action. However well this exhibition of morality succeeds, we must always suspect it of being one of the vain ornaments which Horace orders us to curtail. The second use of dramatic poetry is in the simple description of the vices and virtues, which never misses its effect if well conceived, and if the marks of it are so clear that one cannot confuse the two nor take vice for virtue. The one, though unhappy, is loved, and the other is hated, though triumphant. The ancients were often satisfied with this description without troubling to have good actions rewarded and bad ones punished. . . . It is in [poetic justice] that the third use of theatre consists, just as the fourth consists in the purgation of the passions by means of pity and fear. (140-41)

    See also Corneille under DRAMA (CFD 140).

1668   Dryden. *See* under DRAMA (DW 1, 2: 43, 160).

1669   Molière. *See* under COMEDY (MP 2: 31-32).

1671   Dryden. *See* under POETIC JUSTICE (DW 1, 2; 198-201).

1679   Dryden   **DW**

The first rule which Bossu prescribes to the writer of an heroick poem, and which holds too by the same reason to all dramatick poetry, is, to make the moral of the work; that is, to lay down to yourself what that precept of morality shall be which you would insinuate into the people. . . . It is the moral that directs the whole action of the play to one centre; and that action or fable is the example built upon the moral, which confirms the truth of it to our experience. (1, 2: 274)

1682   Dryden. *See* under STYLE (DW 2: 329).

1695   Dryden   **DW**

The moral . . . is the first business of the poet, as being the groundwork of his instruction. This being formed, he contrives such a design, or fable, as may be most suitable to the moral; after this he begins to think of the persons whom he is to employ in carrying on his design; and gives them the manners which are most proper to their several characters. (3: 310-11)

    See also Dryden under DRAMA (DW 3: 311), IMITATION (DW 3: 322-25).

1697   Dryden. *See* under TRAGEDY (DW 3: 430-31).

1711   Dryden. *See* under DRAMA (DW 1, 2: 307).

1712   Addison   AW

Whatever vices are represented upon the stage, they ought to be so marked and branded by the poet, as not to appear either laudable or amiable in the person who is tainted by them. . . . There is another rule likewise, which was observed by authors of antiquity; and which these modern genuises have no regard to, and that was, never to choose an improper subject for ridicule. Now a subject is improper for ridicule, if it is apt to stir up horror and commiseration rather than laughter. For this reason, we do not find any comedy, in so polite an author as Terence, raised upon the violations of the marriage bed. The falsehood of the wife or husband has given occasion to noble tragedies; but a Scipio and Lelius would have looked upon incest or murder to have been as proper subjects for comedy. On the contrary, cuckoldom is the basis of most of our modern plays. . . . The truth of it is, the accomplished gentleman upon the English stage, is the person that is familiar with other men's wives, and indifferent to his own. . . . I do not know whether it proceeds from barrenness of invention, depravation of manners, or ignorance of mankind, but I have often wondered that our ordinary poets cannot frame to themselves the idea of a fine man who is not a whore-master, or a fine woman that is not a jilt. (2: 184-85)

1713   Addison. *See* under SYMBOL (AW 3: 149).

1715   Addison   AW

There are very good effects which visibly arose from the . . . performances [of Socrates, a propagator of morality], and others of the like nature; as, in the first place, they diverted raillery from improper objects, and gave a new turn to ridicule, which, for many years, had been exerted on persons and things of a sacred and serious nature. They endeavoured to make mirth instructive, and, if they failed in this great end, they must be allowed at least to have it innocent. If wit and humour begin again to relapse into their former licentiousness, they can never hope for approbation from those who know that raillery is useless when it has no moral under it, and pernicious when it attacks any thing that is either unblameable or praise-worthy. To this we may add . . . it is not difficult to be merry on the side of vice, as serious objects are the most capable of ridicule; as the party, which naturally favours such a mirth, is the most numerous. (3: 244).

    See also Addison under COMEDY (AW 3: 244).

c.1745-1752   Voltaire. *See* under TRAGEDY (VW 19: 141).

1750   Johnson   JW

The task of an author is, either to teach what is not known, or to recommend known truths by his manner of adorning them; either to let new light in upon the mind, and open new scenes to the prospect, or to vary the dress and situation of common objects, so as to give them fresh grace and more powerful attractions, to spread such flowers over the regions through which the intellect has already made its progress, as may tempt it to return, and take a second view of things hastily passed over, or negligently rewarded. (2: 11)

1755-1780 Diderot   DDE

Comedy is much more suited than tragedy to present instructive scenes. Tragic events are outside the ordinary course of nature, whereas every day instances occur where the successful outcome depends on good sense, on prudence, on moderation, on knowledge of the world, on decent behavior, or on some particular virtue, and where the opposite of these qualities produces disorder and confusion. Who would want to be the man so bereft of reason—one could say so brutish—as not to want to have before his eyes—in a thousand occasions on which depend his peace of mind, his honor, often the entire happiness of his life—exact and clearly defined models which would indicate to him in a striking fashion what is appropriate for him to do and what he should avoid? It would be in vain for him to want to consult treatises on morality; these works, no matter how excellent they may be, are presented in too general a manner. . . . For all the scenes of human life, only the comic theatre can provide true models of good and evil, of a reasonable way of behaving and a foolish one; besides, the instances are determined there by circumstances so precise that the spectator does not simply learn what he should do, he also learns how he should do it. Comedy does not limit itself to speculative wisdom, it adds practical wisdom, which is the only useful kind in life. (288)

See also Diderot under COMEDY (DDE 287), TRAGEDY (DDE 291).

1758 Diderot. See under AFFECT (DDP 289-90), DRAMA (DDP 287-89).

1765 Johnson. See under GENRE DEFINITION (JS 16), THREE UNITIES (JS 30).

1767-1769 Lessing. See under PROBABILITY (LSPW 236), WILL (LSPW 326); compare with COMEDY (LSPW 307), THOUGHT (LSPW 329).

1815 Hazlitt   HW

In proportion as comic genius succeeds in taking off the mask from ignorance and conceit, as it teaches us to "See ourselves as others see us,"—in proportion as we are brought out on the stage together, and our prejudices clash one against the other, our sharp angular points wear off; we are no longer rigid in absurdity, passionate in folly, and we prevent the ridicule directed at our habitual foibles, by laughing at them ourselves. (1: 11)

See also Hazlitt under COMEDY (HW 1: 10).

1815   Coleridge   **CBL**

The poet, speaking in his own person, may at once delight and improve us by sentiments, which teach us the independence of goodness, of wisdom, and even of genius, on the favors of fortune. (2: 105)

1817   Hazlitt. *See* under DISINTERESTEDNESS (HW 1: 200), DRAMA (HW 1: 154).

1818   Hazlitt. Compare with STYLE (HW 5: 347).

1827   Goethe   **GLE**

All poetry should be instructive, but unobviously so. It should draw the attention of a reader to the idea which is of value to be imported; but he himself must draw the lesson out of it, as he does out of life. (130).

1875   Nietzsche. Compare with CONFLICT (NTS 128-30).

1881   Nietzsche. Compare with MORALITY (NDD 237-38).

1888   Strindberg   **SSPP**

Like almost all other art, that of the stage has long seemed to me a sort of *Biblia Pauperum*, or a Bible in pictures for those who cannot read what is written or printed. And in the same way the playwright has seemed to me a lay preacher spreading the thoughts of his time in a form so popular that the middle classes, from which theatrical audiences are mainly drawn, can know what is being talked about without troubling their brains too much. For this reason the theatre has always served as a grammar school to young people, women, and those who have acquired a little knowledge, all of whom retain the capacity for deceiving themselves and being deceived—which means again that they are susceptible to illusions produced by the suggestions of the author. (10)

1888   Chekhov. Compare with THOUGHT (CL May 30).

1890   Chekhov. *See* under OBJECTIVITY (CL 141).

1896   Shaw   **SDC**

[I] attack every idea which has been full grown for ten years, especially if it claims to be the foundation of all human society. . . . I believe that when we begin to produce a genuine national drama, this apparently anarchic force . . . will underlie it. . . . (142)

1902   Shaw. *See* under THOUGHT (SAA 43).

1912   Shaw. *See* under REALISM (SALOP 73-74).

1918-1922   Stanislavski. Compare with IDEALISM (SAS 104, 105-106).

c.1936   Brecht. *See* under EPIC THEATRE (BBA 18-19, 20-21).

1948   Brecht   **BBBG**

What is the productive attitude toward nature and toward society which we
childen of a scientific age can accept with pleasure in the theatre? . . . The
attitude is a *critical* one. With respect to a river it consists in the regulation of
its flow; with respect to a fruit tree it consists in the grafting of fruit; with
respect to locomotion it consists in the construction of ships and planes; with
respect to society it consists in revolution. Our images of men's life together
will be made for river builders, fruit growers, shipbuilders, and social revolu-
tionaries. We invite them into our theatre, and we ask them not to forget their
joyful interest while they are there. For we hand the world over to their brains
and hearts; they will change it as they think best. (20) . . . Even if [theatres]
should not bother with many important matters, if these cannot contribute to
the pleasurableness, theaters are still free to find pleasure in instruction and
investigation. Out of practical images of society which are in a position to
influence society, the theater makes a thoroughly enjoyable game. It presents
to the builders of society the experience of society. . . . Let these people be
entertained by the wisdom which comes from the solution of problems; by the
anger into which pity for the oppressed would do well to change; by respect for
those who respect humanity, that is, for the friends of man; in short, by
everything which delights those who are productive. (21)

    See also Brecht under AESTHETIC (BBBG 13-14), PLEASURE (BBBG
15), STYLE (BBBG 39-40).

1952   Brecht. *See* under AFFECT (BBT 229).

c.1956   Brecht. *See* under EPIC THEATRE (BBT 276, 281), PLEASURE
(BBT 276), THOUGHT (BBT 277, 279).

IRONY

The citations below represent concepts of irony, primarily those identified as Sophoclean ("tragic" or "dramatic irony"), as verbal irony and as romantic irony; the quotations from Aristotle, d'Aubignac, and Schlegel define these variants in the order given. See also *REVERSAL*.

4th cent. B.C.   Aristotle. *See* under REVERSAL (AR 90-91).

1657   d'Aubignac   AAS

Irony is a Drammatick Figure, and of its own nature very Theatral; for by saying in jest or scorn the contrary of that which it really means, it carries a kind of disguise, and makes an agreeable Effect. (3: 55)

1808   Schlegel   SCL

What I mean by irony . . . is a sort of confession interwoven into the representation itself, and more or less distinctly expressed, of its overcharged one-sidedness in matters of fancy and feeling, and by means of which the equipoise is again restored. (227) . . . Nobody ever painted so truthfully as [Shakespeare] has done the facility of self-deception, the half-conscious hypocrisy towards ourselves, with which even noble minds attempt to disguise the almost inevitable influence of selfish motives in human nature. This secret irony of the characterization commands admiration as the profound abyss of acuteness and sagacity. . . . Here we therefore may perceive in the poet himself, notwithstanding his power to excite the most fervent emotions, a certain cool indifference of a superior mind, which has run through the whole sphere of human existence and survived feeling. The irony in Shakespeare has not merely a reference to the separate characters, but frequently to the whole of the action. Most poets who portray human events in a narrative or dramatic form take themselves a part, and exact from their readers a blind approbation or condemnation of whatever side they choose to support or oppose. The more zealous this rhetoric is, the more certainly it fails of its effect. In every case we are conscious that the subject itself is not brought immediately before us, but that we view it through the medium of a different way of thinking. When, however, by a dexterous manoeuvre, the poet allows us an occasional glance at the less brilliant reverse of the medal, then he makes, as it were, a sort of secret understanding with the select circle of the more intelligent of his readers or spectators; he shows them that he had previously seen and admitted the validity of their tacit objections; that he himself is not tied down to the represented subject, but soars freely above it; and that if he chose, he could unrelentingly annihilate the beautiful and irresistibly attractive scenes which his magic pen has produced. . . . Frequently an intentional parody of the serious part [of a play] is not to be mistaken in them. . . . The comic intervals everywhere serve to prevent the pastime from being converted into a business, to preserve the mind in the possession of its serenity, and to keep off that gloomy and inert seriousness which so easily steals upon the sentimental, but not tragical drama. (369-70)

1819 Hazlitt   HW

Wit is often the more forcible and pointed for being dry and serious, for it then seems as if the speaker himself had no intention in it, and we were the first to find it out. Irony, as a species of wit, owes its force to the same principle. In such cases it is the contrast between the appearance and the reality, the suspense of belief, and the seeming incongruity, that gives point to the ridicule, and makes it enter the deeper when the first impression is overcome. (8: 10-11)

1908 Pirandello   POH

Irony has both a rhetorical and a philosophical connotation. As a rhetorical figure, irony involves a deception which is absolutely contrary to the nature of genuine humor. It is true that this rhetorical figure implies a contradiction, but only an apparent one, between what is said and what is meant. The contradiction of humor is never, on the other hand, an apparent one, but rather an essential one . . . and one quite different in nature. (5) . . . The self, the only true reality, Hegel explained, can laugh at the vain appearance of the universe; since it can create this appearance, it can also abolish it. The self can choose not to take its own creation seriously, hence irony—a force which, according to Tieck, enables the poet to dominate his subject matter and because of which, says Friedrich Schlegel, the subject matter turns into a perpetual parody, a transcendental farce. (6-7) . . . Romantic irony is, or at least in a certain sense, can be related to, true humor and it certainly is more closely akin to true humor than rhetorical irony. Eventually romantic irony could even be made to derive from rhetorical irony, though not without some strain: in the latter one should not take seriously what is said while in the former one can choose not to take seriously what is done. As compared to romantic irony, rhetorical irony would be like the famous frog of the fable which—having been carried into the contrived world of German metaphysical idealism and filling itself up more with air than water—would successfully attain the enviable dimensions of an ox. The deception—that apparent contradiction of which rhetoric speaks—has here become, by dint of the continual swelling, the vain appearance of the universe. Now if humor consisted exclusively of the pin prick which deflates the blown-up frog, then irony and humor would be approximately the same thing. But humor . . . is more than just that puncture. (7) . . . Even when irony is employed towards a good end, one cannot remove from it the notion of a certain *mockery* and *mordancy*, two qualities that may also be found in writers who are unquestionably humorists but whose humor will certainly not consist of such biting mockery. (8) . . . Irony rarely reaches the comic dramatization that it does with true humorists; it always remains undramatically comic, and is therefore mere wit, jest, and more or less grotesque caricature. (39) . . . The irony [of Ariosto's poetry] resides in the vision the poet has not only of that fantastic world but of life itself and of man. Everything is fable and everything is true since it is inevitable that we accept as true the empty appearance emanating from our illusions and passions; to have illusions can be beautiful, but the deception of too much fantasizing always results in tears. This deception will appear to be comic or tragic depending on the degree of our involvement with the vicissitudes of those who suffer the deception, on the interest or sympathy which that passion or illusion arouses in us, and on the effects that the deception produces. Similarly we can see that the poet's ironic sense comes to the surface also in another aspect of the poem, and this time it does not stand out as obviously as before, but it shows itself through the artistic representation of the work in which it has transfused itself in a way that that representation feels and wants itself to be just the way it is. In short, the ironic sense, objectified, emerges from the artistic representation even in places where the poet does not openly show that he is aware of the unreality of that representation. (79-80)

   See also Pirandello under IDEALISM (POH 75-76).

1948   Brecht. *See* under GEST (BBBG 35-36).

LANGUAGE

The following are considerations of the nature, values, and purposes of dramatic language. See *METAPHOR, NOVELTY, STYLE, SYMBOL, and VARIETY.*

4th cent. B.C. Aristotle   **AP**

Fourth among the elements [of drama] enumerated comes Diction; by which I mean . . . the expression of the meaning in words; and its essence is the same both in verse and prose. (29)

   See also Aristotle under IDENTIFICATION (AR 159-60), STYLE (AR 148, AP 81-83, 87, 101, 105), THOUGHT (AP 25, 29), TRAGEDY (AP 23-25); compare with SUBJECT (AP 37).

c.20 B.C. Horace. *See* under NOVELTY (HAP 455), STYLE (HAP 459, 479).

1561 Scaliger. *See* under STYLE (SP 71), THOUGHT (SP 59-60), TRAGEDY (SP 39).

1570 Castelvetro. *See* under TRAGEDY (CP 95).

c.1583 Sidney   **SDP**

The greatest part of poets have apparelled their poetical inventions in that numberous [sic] kind of writing which is called verse. Indeed but apparelled, verse being but an ornament and no cause to poetry, since there have been many most excellent poets that never versified, and now swarm many versifiers that need never answer to the name of poets. . . . It is not riming and versing that maketh a poet . . . but it is that feigning notable images of virtues, vices, or what else, with that delightful teaching, which must be the right describing note to know a poet by. (11)

   See also Sidney under THREE UNITIES (SDP 47-48).

1609 de Vega. *See* under CLOSURE (VAWP 34), STYLE (VAWP 32-33).

1641 Jonson   **JD**

Of the two (if either were to bee wisht) I would rather have a plaine downe-right wisdome, then a foolish and affected eloquence. For what is so furious, and

Bet' lem like, as a vaine sound of chosen and excellent words, without any subject of *sentence* [i.e., thought], or *science* mix'd? (17) . . . Now [-a-days] nothing is good that is naturall: Right and naturall language seeme to have least of the wit in it; that which is writh'd and tortur'd, is counted the more exquisite. Cloath of Bodkin, or Tissue, must be imbrodered; as if no face were faire, that were not pouldred, or painted? . . . Nothing is fashionable, till it bee deform'd; and this is to write like a *Gentlemen*. All must bee as *affected*, and preposterous as our Gallants cloathes. . . . (25-26) . . . Many Writers preplexe their Readers, and Hearers with meere *Non-sense*. Their writings need sunshine. Pure and neat Language I love, yet plaine and customary. A barbarous Phrase hath often made mee out of love with a good sense; and doubtfull writing hath wrackt mee beyond my patience. (72)

    See also Jonson under IMITATION (JD 33), STYLE (JD 33, 74, 78).

1657   d'Aubignac. *See* under ACTION (AAS 3: 11-12), INSTRUCTION (AAS 3: 32-33, 35).

1665   Dryden. *See* under IMITATION (DW 1, 2: 21-22).

1668   Dryden. *See* under IMITATION (DW 1, 2: 126-27), STYLE (DW 1, 2: 85-86, 118-21, 161).

1672   Dryden. *See* under STYLE (DW 1, 2: 209-10).

1682   Dryden. *See* under STYLE (DW 2: 329).

1711   Addison. *See* under THOUGHT (AW 1: 70).

1725   Voltaire   **VE**

It is a very gross mistake to imagine that the versification is the least essential and least difficult part of a theatrical piece. . . . When the passions are to be described, nearly the same ideas occur to everybody; but it is in the expression of them that the man of genius is easily discerned from the wit, and the poet from the scribbler. (277-78)

    See also Voltaire under AFFECT (VE 277).

1731   Voltaire   **VE**

The English dramatists have more action in their plays than we have; they speak more directly. The French aim rather at elegance, harmony, style. It is certainly more difficult to write well than to fill the play with murders, wheels, gibbets, sorcerers, and ghosts. The tragedy of *Cato*, which does such great honor to M. Addison . . . owes its great reputation to no other element than its beautiful lines, its vigorous and true thoughts, expressed in harmonious verse.

. . . Often the unusual way of saying ordinary things, and the art of embellishing by literary style what all men think and feel—these are what make great poets. . . . M. Racine stands above others not because he has said the same things as he has, but because he has said them better than they. Corneille is not truly great except when he expresses himself as well as he thinks. (283)

See also Voltaire under SPECTACLE (VE 282).

1758 Diderot DDP

You can formulate any number of plots on the same subject and with the same characters; but, given the characters, there is only one way in which they may speak. These will say such and such things according to the situations in which you place them, but since they are always the same people, in any situation, they must be consistent. (292)

See also Diderot under ACTION (DDP 291-92), PLOT (DDP 292, 296).

1767-1769 Lessing LSPW

We cannot throughout take the old tragedies for our pattern. There all the personages speak and converse in a free public place, in presence of an inquisitive multitude. They must therefore nearly always speak with reserve and due regard to their dignity; they cannot give vent to their thoughts and feelings in the first words that come, they must weigh and choose them. But we moderns, who have abolished the chorus, who generally leave our personages between four walls, what reason have we to let them employ such choice stilted rhetorical speech notwithstanding? Nobody hears it except those whom they permit to hear it, nobody speaks to them but people who are involved in the action, who are therefore themselves affected and have neither desire nor leisure to control expressions. . . . It is . . . useless to invoke the high rank of the personages; aristocratic persons have learned how to express themselves better than the common man, but they do not affect incessantly to express themselves better than he. Least of all in moments of passion. . . . There can never be feeling with a stilted, chosen, pompous, language. If it is not born of feeling, it cannot evoke it. But feeling agrees with the simplest, commonest, plainest words and expressions. (393-94)

1778 Johnson JL

Language is the dress of thought; and as the noblest mien or most graceful action would be degraded and obscured by a garb appropriated to the gross employments of rusticks or mechanics, so the most heroick sentiments will lose their efficacy, and the most splendid ideas drop their magnificence, if they are conveyed by words used commonly upon low and trivial occasions, debased by vulgar mouths, and contaminated by inelegant applications.
. . . The diction, being the vehicle of the thoughts, first presents itself to the intellectual eye; and if the first appearance offends, a further knowledge is not

often sought. Whatever professes to benefit by pleasing must come at once. The pleasures of the mind imply something sudden and unexpected; that which elevates must always surprise. (1: 58-59)

1778   Diderot. *See* under ILLUSION (DPA 22).

1808   Schlegel   **SCL**

Even in our common discourses, we observe a certain continuity, we give a development both to arguments and objections, and in an instant passion will animate us to fulness of expression, to a flow of eloquence, and even to lyrical sublimity. The ideal dialogue of Tragedy may therefore find in actual conversation all the various tones and turns of poetry, with the exception of epic repose. (229-30) . . . There is in the human mind a desire that language should exhibit the object which it denotes, sensibly, by its very sound, which may be traced even as far back as in the first origin of poetry. As, in the shape in which language comes down to us, this is seldom the case, an imagination which has been powerfully excited is fond of laying hold of any congruity in sound which may accidentally offer itself, that by such means he may, for the nonce, restore the lost resemblance between the word and the thing. . . . Those who cry out against the play upon words [in Shakespeare] as an unnatural and affected invention, only betray their own ignorance of original nature. (366)
      See also Schlegel under POETRY OF THE THEATRE (SCL 36-37).

1813   Goethe. *See* under IMAGINATION (GLE 175).

1815   Coleridge. *See* under STYLE (CBL 2: 49-50, 50, 51, 115-16).

1817   Hazlitt   **HW**

The language of poetry is superior to the language of painting; because the strongest of our recollections relate to feelings, not to faces. (1: 271)

1818   Hazlitt   **HW**

Nothing . . . can be more absurd than the outcry which has been sometimes raised by frigid and pedantic critics, for reducing the language of poetry to the standard of common sense and reason . . . The impressions of common sense and strong imagination, that is, of passion and indifference, cannot be the same, and they must have a separate language to do justice to either. (5: 8) . . . There is nothing either musical or natural in the ordinary construction of language. It is a thing altogether arbitrary and conventional. Neither in the sounds themselves, which are the voluntary signs of certain ideas, nor in their grammatical arrangements in common speech, is there any principle of natural imitation, or correspondence to the individual ideas, or to the tone of feeling with which they are conveyed to others. The jerks, the breaks, the inequalities, and harshness of prose, are fatal to the flow of a poetical imagination, as a jolting road or a stumbling horse disturbs the reverie of an absent man. But poetry makes these odds all even. It is the music of language, answering to the music of the mind, untying as it were ''the secret soul of harmony.'' Wherever any object takes such a hold of the mind as to make us dwell upon it, and brood over it, melting the heart in tenderness, or kindling it to a sentiment of enthusiasm . . .—this is poetry. The musical in sound is the sustained and continuous; the musical in thought is the sustained and continuous also. . . . In ordinary speech we arrive at a certain harmony by the modulations of the voice: in poetry the same thing is done systematically by a regular collocation of syllables. It has been well observed, that everyone who declaims warmly, or grows intent upon a subject, rises into a sort of blank verse or measured prose. . . . An excuse might be made for rhyme. . . . It is but fair that the ear should linger on the sounds that delight it, or avail itself of the same brilliant coincidence and unexpected recurrence of syllables, that have been displayed in the invention and collocation of images. It is allowed that rhyme assists the memory. (5: 12-13)

See also Hazlitt under STYLE (HW 5: 347).

1818   Coleridge. See under SYMBOL (CMC 99).

c.1820   Hegel   **HFA**

The fact of the action is not the external aspect [of the drama] . . . but the exposition of the ideal spirit of the action, not merely in respect to the *dramatis personae* and their passion, pathos, resolve, interaction, and mediation, but also relatively to the universal essence of the action in its conflict and destiny. It is this ideally pregnant spirit, in so far as poetry gives embodiment to it in poetic form, which pre-eminently discovers an appropriate expression in the language of poetry, viewing this, as we should, as the most spiritual way of expressing emotions and ideas. . . . Genuine dramatic art consists in the expression of individuals in the conflict of their interests and the discord roused between their characters and their transitory passions. It is here that the twofold aspect of lyric and epic poetry will assert its power in true dramatic union: and we have then attached to this the aspect of positive external fact expressed likewise in the medium of language, as where we have, for instance, the departure and entrance of *dramatis personae* as a rule announced beforehand; not infrequently also their external habit or demeanour is indicated by other persons. (4: 264-65)

See also Hegel under IDEALISM (HFA 4: 265-67).

1830   Hazlitt. Compare with IDEALISM (HW 9: 431-32).

1864   Taine   **TLA**

The best half of dramatic poetry, every classic Greek and French drama, and the greater part of Spanish and English dramas, far from literally copying ordinary conversation, intentionally modify human speech. Each of these dramatic poets makes his characters speak in verse, casting their dialogue in rhythm, and often in rhyme. Is this modification prejudicial to the work? Far from it. One of the great works of the age, the "Iphigenia" of Goethe, which was at first written in prose and afterwards rewritten in verse, affords abundant evidence of this. It is beautiful in prose, but in verse what a difference! The modification of ordinary language, in the introduction of rhythm and metre, evidently gives to this work its incomparable accent, that calm sublimity, that broad, sustained tragic tone, which elevates the spirit above the low level of common life, and brings before the eye the heroes of ancient days. (54-55)

See also Taine under STYLE (TLA 321, 322-23).

1871   Nietzsche   **NBT**

Lyric poetry is dependent on the spirit of music just as music itself in its absolute sovereignty does not *require* the picture and the concept, but only *endures* them as accompaniments. The poems of the lyrist can express nothing which has not already been contained in the vast universality and absoluteness of the music which compelled him to use figurative speech. By no means is it possible for language adequately to render the cosmic symbolism of music, for the very reason that music stands in symbolic relation to the primordial contradiction and primordial pain in the heart of the the Primordial Unity, and therefore symbolises a sphere which is above all appearance and before all phenomena. (55)...Whatever rises to the surface in the dialogue of the Apollonian part of Greek tragedy, appears simple, transparent, beautiful. In this sense the dialogue is a copy of Hellene, whose nature reveals itself in the dance, because in the dance the greatest energy is merely potential, but betrays itself nevertheless in flexible and vivacious movements. The language of the Sophoclean heroes, for instance, surprises us by its Apollonian precision and clearness, so that we at once imagine we see into the innermost recesses of their being, and marvel not a little that the way to these recesses is so short. (72)

1875   Nietzsche. Compare with POETRY OF THE THEATRE (NTS 177, 177-78).

1886   Chekhov   **CLF**

May 10. Commonplaces such as "the setting sun bathing in the waves of the darkening sea, poured its purple gold, etc.,"... one ought to abandon. In descriptions of Nature one ought to seize upon the little particulars, grouping them in such a way that, in reading, when you shut your eyes, yet get the picture. For instance, you will get the full effect of a moonlight night if you write that on the mill-dam a little glowing star-point flashed from the neck of a broken bottle, and the round, black shadow of a dog, or a wolf, emerged and ran, etc. Nature becomes animated if you are not squeamish about employing comparisons of her phenomena with ordinary human activities, etc. In the sphere of psychology, details are also the thing. . . . Best of all is it to avoid depicting the hero's state of mind; you ought to try to make it clear from the hero's actions. It is not necessary to portray many characters. The centre of gravity should be in two persons: him and her. . . . (70-71)

1888   Nietzsche   NW

Compared with music, communication by means of words is a shameless mode of procedure; words reduce and stultify; words make impersonal; words make common that is uncommon. (254)

1908   Pirandello. *See* under HUMOR (POH 35), STYLE (POH 36).

1931-1936   Artaud   AT

How does it happen that the Occidental theater does not see theater under any other aspect than as a theater of dialogue? Dialogue—a thing written and spoken—does not belong specifically to the stage, it belongs to books, as is proved by the fact that in all handbooks of literary history a place is reserved for the theater as a subordinate branch of the history of the spoken langauge. I say that the stage is a concrete physical place which asks to be filled, and to be given its own concrete language to speak. (37)

   See also Artaud under THOUGHT (AT 46); compare with POETRY OF THE THEATRE (AT 12, 37, 78, 120-21, 123-24), SPECTACLE (AT 41, 68), THOUGHT (AT 39-40).

1932   Eliot. *See* under DRAMA (EJD 29).

1938   Stanislavski. *See* under ACTION (SBC 118), SUBTEXT (SBC 108-109), THOUGHT (SBC 169-71).

1939   Brecht. *See* under GEST (BBG 34-35).

1951   Eliot. *See* under AFFECT (EPD 24-25), STYLE (EPD 10-11, 13, 20-21, 26).

1953   Eliot. *See* under STYLE (ETVP 4, 8, 9-10).

MAGNITUDE

Aristotle's discussion of the "bulk" of tragedy was expanded by subsequent theorists into concepts of duration and conciseness (both included below) and also into strictures on the fictional content of tragedy (see THE THREE UNITIES).

4th cent. B.C.   Aristotle   AP

[Tragedy and Epic Poetry] differ in their *length* [bulk: EP 203]: for Tragedy endeavors, as far as possible, to *confine itself to a single revolution of the sun* [exist in a single daylight period: EP 203], or but slightly to exceed this limit; whereas, the Epic action has no limit as to time. (21-23) . . . There may be [such a thing as] a whole that is wanting in magnitude. A beautiful object . . . must not only have an orderly arrangement of parts, but must also be of a *certain magnitude* [a size that is not accidental: EP 282]; beauty depends on *magnitude and order* [size and arrangement: EP 283]. Hence a very small organism cannot be beautiful; for the view of it is confused, *the object being seen in an almost imperceptible moment of time.* Nor, again, can one of vast size be beautiful; for as the eye cannot take it all in at once, the unity and sense of the whole is lost for the spectator; as for instance if there was one a thousand miles long. As, therefore, in the case of animate bodies and organisms a certain magnitude is necessary, and a magnitude which may be easily embraced in one view; so in the plot, a certain length is necessary, and a length which can be easily embraced by the memory. . . . The *limit* [norm: EP 286] as fixed by the nature of the drama itself is this: the greater the length, the more beautiful will the piece be by reason of its size, provided that the whole be perspicuous. And to define the matter *roughly* we may say that the proper magnitude is comprised within such limits, that the sequence of events according to the law of probability or necessity, will admit of a change from bad fortune to good, or from good fortune to bad. (31-33) . . . Epic poetry has . . . a great—a special—capacity for enlarging its dimensions and we can see the reason. In Tragedy we cannot imitate several lines of action carried on at *one and the same time* [the time of their occurence: EP 602]; we must confine ourselves to the action on the stage and the part taken by the players. (91-93)

4th cent. B.C.   Aristotle   AA

In natural wholes there is always a limit or proportion which determines growth and size. (67)

See also Aristotle under DRAMA (AP 107-11), FORM (AP 31-33, 89), PLOT (AP 65-67), TRAGEDY (AP 21-23, 23-25).

c.20 B.C.   Horace   HAP

Of order, this . . . will be the excellence and charm that the author of the . . . poem shall say at the moment what at that moment should be said, reserving and omitting much for the present, loving this point and scorning that. (453, 455)

1561   Scaliger   SP

The content of a play should be as concise as possible, yet as varied and manifold as possible. (60)

1570   Castelvetro. *See* under ACTION (CP 89), WONDER (CP 88).

1609   de Vega   VAWP

Very seldom should the stage remain without someone speaking, because the crowd becomes restless in these intervals and the story spins itself out at great length; for, besides its being a great defect, the avoidance of it increases grace and artifice. (32)

1641   Jonson   JD

In the Constitution of a *Poeme*, the Action is aym'd at by the *Poet* . . . and that Action hath its largenesse, compasse, and proportion. (101) . . . If the Action be too great wee can never comprehend the whole together in our Imagination. . . . If it be too little, there ariseth no pleasure out of the object, it affords the view no stay: It is beheld and vanisheth at once. (102) . . . In every Action it behooves the *Poet* to know which is his utmost bound, how farre with fitnesse, and a necessary proportion, he may produce, and determine it. That is, till either good fortune change into the worse, or the worse into the better. For as a body without proportion cannot be goodly, no more can the Action, either in Comedy, or Tragedy without his fit bounds. And every bound for the nature of the Subject, is esteem'd the best that is largest, till it can increase no more: so it behooves the Action in *Tragedy* and *Comedy*, to be let grow, till the necessity aske a Conclusion: wherein two things are to be considered; First, that it exceed not the compasse of one Day: Next, that there be place left for digression, and Art. For the *Episodes*, and digressions in a Fable, are the same that household stuffe, and other furniture are in a house. And so farre for the measure, and extent of a *Fable Dramaticke*. (103)

1660   Corneille. *See* under THREE UNITIES (CTU 817).

1670   Racine   RP

It would be an easy task [to please my critics], had I wished to violate common sense a little. I should have but to abandon the natural for the extraordinary.

Instead of a simple plot, with very little material—as befits an action supposed to take place within the compass of a single day and which, proceeding by degrees toward the end, is sustained solely by the interest, sentiments and passions of the characters—I could just as well have crowded the very same story with a number of incidents which could not actually have happened within a whole month, with any number of stage-tricks, as astonishing as they would be false to nature, with a number of declamatory passages wherein the actors would utter the exact opposite of what they ought to utter. I might, for instance, have represented some hero as drunk, wishing to make his mistress hate him, out of sheer caprice. . . . How would I have dared appear . . . before those great men of antiquity whom I have taken for my models? (155)

1674   Racine   RP

I have for some time cherished the desire to try whether I could write a tragedy with the extremely simple plot so much admired by the ancients, for simplicity is one of the first precepts which they have left us. "Whatever you write," says Horace, "it must be simple and it must be one." . . . Nor must one assume that this rule was based entirely upon caprice; no, nothing but what is true to life can appeal to us in tragedy. But what sort of truth to life is there when within the space of one day a multitude of things happen that would in actual life occupy many weeks? There are some who believe that this simplicity is a confession of the author's poverty of invention. They are not aware that on the contrary an author's invention is most severely put to the test in making something out of nothing, and that the introduction of a host of incidents has always been the refuge of poets who felt their own want of genius, and power to interest their auditors through five acts of simple plot, sustained by the force of passion, beauty of ideas, and elegance of expression. . . (156)

1697   Dryden. *See* under TRAGEDY (DW 3: 430-31).

1712   Addison. *See* under AESTHETIC (AW 2: 142), IMAGINATION (AW 2: 138-39).

1797   Goethe   GED

[The illusiveness and expansiveness of the epic rhapsodist is exactly reversed by the stage-player (representing the drama)]. He comes before us as a distinct and determined individual. He wants us to interest ourselves exclusively in him and his immediate surroundings; he wants us to share his mental and bodily sufferings, to feel his perplexities, and to forget ourselves in following him. (338-39)
    See also Goethe under SUBJECT (GED 338).

1808   Schlegel   SCL

A tragedy cannot be indefinitely lengthened and continued, like the Homeric Epos for instance, to which whole rhapsodies have been appended; tragedy is too independent and complete within itself for this; nevertheless, several tragedies may be connected together in one great cycle by means of a common destiny running through the actions of all. Hence the restriction to the number three [in the trilogy] admits of a satisfactory explanation. It is the thesis, antithesis, and the synthesis. (81)...Aristotle [explains] that by "magnitude," as a requisition of beauty, he means, a certain measure which is neither so small as to preclude us from distinguishing its parts, nor so extensive as to prevent us from taking the whole in at one view. This is, therefore, merely an external definition of the beautiful, derived from experience, and founded on the quality of our organs of sense and our powers of comprehension. However, his application of it to the drama is remarkable.... "The composition will be the more beautiful the more extensive it is without prejudice to its comprehensibility." This assertion will be highly favourable for the compositions of Shakespeare and of other romantic poets, who have included in one picture a more extensive circle of life, characters, and events, than is to be found in the simple Greek tragedy.... (239)

   See also Schlegel under DRAMA (SCL 30-32), THREE UNITIES (SCL 236-51).

c.1820   Hegel. *See* under UNIVERSALITY (HFA 4: 252-53); compare with THREE UNITIES (HFA 4: 257-59).

1825   Goethe   **GCE**

Thurs., Feb. 24. "If I were still superintendent of the theatre," said Goethe, ... "I would bring out Byron's *Doge of Venice*. The piece is indeed too long, and would require shortening. Nothing, however, should be cut out, but the import of each scene should be taken, and expressed more concisely. The piece would thus be brought closer together, without being damaged by alterations, and it would gain a powerful effect, without any essential loss of beauty."

1827   Goethe. *See* under VARIETY (GCE Jan. 31).

1830   Goethe   **GCE**

Wed., March 17. "I am never quite pleased when I see [plays] too long to be represented as they are written.... [Schiller]...certainly committed this fault," [said] Goethe. "His first pieces particularly...seem as if they would never end. He had too much on his heart, and too much to say to be able to control it. Afterwards, when he became conscious of this fault, he took infinite trouble, and endeavored to overcome it by work and study; but he never perfectly succeeded. It really requires a poetical giant, and is more difficult than is imagined, to control a subject properly, to keep it from overpowering one, and to concentrates one's attention on that alone which is absolutely necessary."

1864   Taine   **TLA**

The characters which situations unfold to the mind are manifested to the senses only through language, and the convergence of . . . forces gives to the character all its prominence. The more the artist has discriminated and made converge in his work numerous elements . . . capable of effect, the more the character which he wishes to place in light becomes prominent. The whole of art lies in two words, *concentration* and *manifestation*. (323-24)

1888   Strindberg. *See* under AFFECT (SSPP 20-21).

1890   Chekhov. *See* under OBJECTIVITY (CL 141).

1928   Eliot. *See* under THREE UNITIES (ESE 45).

METAPHOR

Metaphor may be described as a fusion of images which produces altered perception, whether the images are cued by verbal or visual means. The terms metaphor *and* symbol *are employed in so many ways—sometimes interchangeably—that precise assignment of the extracts is impossible. Compare with* SYMBOL. See also *GEST, LANGUAGE, and POETRY OF THE THEATRE.*

4th cent. B.C.   Aristotle   AP

Metaphor is the application of an alien name by transference either from genus to species, or from species to genus, or from species to species, or by analogy, that is, proportion. Thus from genus to species, as: "There lies my ship"; for lying at anchor is a species of lying. From species to genus, as: "Verily ten thousand noble deeds hath Odysseus wrought"; for ten thousand is a species of large number, and here used for a large number generally. From species to species, as: "With blade of bronze drew away the life," . . . Analogy or proportion is when the second term is to the first as the fourth to the third. We may then use the fourth for the second, or the second for the fourth. Sometimes too we qualify the metaphor by adding the term to which the proper word is relative. Thus the cup is to Dionysus as the shield to Ares. The cup may, therefore, be called "the shield of Dionysus," and the shield "the cup of Ares." (77-79)

4th cent. B.C.   Aristotle   AR

All men take a natural pleasure in learning quickly; words denote something; and so those words are pleasantest which give us *new* knowledge. Strange words have no meaning for us; common terms we know already; it is *metaphor* which gives us most of this pleasure. Thus, when the poet calls old age "a dried stalk," he gives us a new perception by means of the common *genus*; for both the things have lost their bloom. Now poets' similes have the same effect; hence, when they are good, they have this sprightliness. A simile . . . is a metaphor with a preface; for this reason it is less pleasing because it is more lengthy; nor does it affirm that *this* is *that*; and so the mind does not even inquire into the matter. It follows that a smart style, and a smart enthymeme, are those which give us a new and rapid perception. (167-68)

   See also Aristotle under STYLE (AP 81-83, 87).

1641   Jonson   JD

Metaphors farfet[ched] hinder to be understood, and affected, lose their grace. Or when the person fetcheth his [metaphors] from a wrong place. As if a

Privie-Counsellor should at the Table take his *Metaphore* from a Dicing-house, or Ordinary, or a Vintners vault; or a Justice of Peace draw his similitudes from the *Mathematicks*; or a *Divine* from a Bawdy-house, or Tavernes. . . . *Metaphors* are thus many times deform'd. . . . (73) *Quintilian* warnes us, that in no kind of Translation, or *Metaphore*, or *Allegory*, wee make a turne from what wee began; As if wee fetch the originall of our *Metaphore* from the sea, and billowes; wee end not in flames and ashes; It is a most fowle inconsequence. Neither must wee draw out our *Allegory* too long, lest either wee make ourselves obscure, or fall into affectation, which is childish. (77)

1711   Addison. Compare with THOUGHT (AW 1: 70).

1712   Addison   **AW**

Allegories, when well chosen, are like so many tracks of light in a discourse, that make everything about them clear and beautiful. A noble metaphor, when it is placed to an advantage, casts a kind of glory round it, and darts a lustre through a whole sentence. These different kinds of allusion are but so many different manners of similitude; and that they may please the imagination, the likeness ought to be very exact or very agreeable, as we love to see a picture where the resemblance is just, or the posture and air graceful. (2: 152)

1767-1769   Lessing   **LSPW**

Wit . . . that does not depend on matters rooted in each other, but on the similar or dissimilar, if it ventures on a work that should be reserved to genius alone, detains itself with such events that have not further concern with one another except that they have occurred at the same time. To connect these, to interweave and confuse their threads so that we lose the one at every moment in following out the other and are thrown from one surprise into another, this is the part of wit and wit only. . . . Genius loves simplicity, and wit complication. (311)

1778   Johnson   **JL**

Wit, abstracted from its effects upon the hearer, may be more rigorously and philosophically considered as a kind of *discordia concors*; a combination of dissimilar images, a discovery of occult resemblances in things apparently unlike. (1: 20)

c.1808   Coleridge. *See* under IMAGINATION (CSC 1: 188-89).

1808   Schlegel. *See* under AESTHETIC (SCL 342-43).

1811-1812   Coleridge   **CCSL**

It is not always easy to distinguish between wit and fancy. When the whole pleasure received is derived from surprise at an unexpected turn of expression, than I call it wit; but when the pleasure is produced not only by surprise, but also by an image which remains with us and gratifies for its own sake, then I call it fancy. I know of no mode so satisfactory of distinguishing between wit and fancy. (45)

1815   Coleridge. *See* under IMAGINATION (CBL 2: 12), SYMBOL (CBL 1: 100).

1816   Hazlitt. *See* under AESTHETIC (HW 1: 71).

1818   Coleridge. *See* under SYMBOL (CMC 99).

1830   Hazlitt   **HW**

The *ideal* is not in general the strong-hold of poetry. For description in words (to produce any vivid impression) requires a translation of the object into some other form, which is the language of metaphor and imagination. . . . (9: 431)
    See also Hazlitt under IDEALISM (HW 9: 431-32).

1871   Nietzsche   **NBT**

For the true poet the metaphor is not a rhetorical figure, but a vicarious image which actually hovers before him in place of a concept. (66)
    See also Nietzsche under IMAGINATION (NBT 66), THOUGHT (NBT 110-11), TRAGEDY (NBT 127).

1873   Nietzsche   **NEG**

The ''Thing-in-itself'' . . . is . . . quite incomprehensible to the creator of language and not worth any great endeavor to obtain. He designates only the relations of things to men and for their expression he calls to his help the most daring metaphors. A nerve-stimulus, first transformed into a percept! First metaphor! The percept then copied into a sound! Second metaphor! And each time he leaps completely out of one sphere right into the midst of an entirely different one. . . . When we talk about trees, colours, snow and flowers, we believe we know something about the things themselves, and yet we only possess metaphors of the things, and these metaphors do not in the least correspond to the original essentials. . . . Every word becomes at once an idea not by having . . . to serve as a reminder for the original experience . . . but by having simultaneously to fit innumerable, more or less similar (which really means never equal, therefore altogether unequal) cases. Every idea originates through equating the unequal. . . . What therefore is truth? A mobile army of metaphors, metonymies, anthropomorphisms: in short a sum of human relations which become poetically and rhetorically intensified, metamorphosed, adorned, and after long usage seem to a nation fixed, canonic and binding; truths are illusions of which one has forgotten that they *are* illusions; worn out metaphors which have become powerless to effect the senses; coins which have their obverse effaced and now are no longer of account as coins but merely as metal.... Everything which makes man stand out in bold relief against the animal depends on [his] faculty of volatilising the concrete metaphors into a schema, and therefore resolving a perception into an idea. For within the range of those schemata something becomes possible that never could succeed under the first perceptual impressions: to build up a pryamidal order ... which now stands opposite the other perceptual world of first impressions and assumes the appearance of being the more fixed, general, known, human of the two and therefore the regulating and imperative one. Whereas every metaphor of perception is individual and without equal and therefore knows how to escape all attempts to classify it.... [But] the idea too, bony and hexahedral, and permutable as a die, remains however only as the *residuum of a metaphor*, and ... the illusion of the artistic metamorphosis of a nerve-stimulus into percepts is, if not the mother, then the grandmother of every idea.... [The] impulse towards the formation of metaphors [is a] fundamental impulse of man, which ... seeks for itself a new realm of action ... and finds it in *Mythos* and more generally in *Art*. (178-88).

1888   Chekhov. *See* under THOUGHT (CL Oct. 27).

1908   Pirandello. *See* under IDEALISM (POH 75-76).

1931-1936   Artaud   AT

The plague takes images that are dormant, a latent disorder, and suddenly extends them into the most extreme gestures; the theatre also takes gestures and pushes them as far as they will go: like the plague it reforges the chain between what is and what is not, between the virtuality of the possible and what already exists in materialized nature. It recovers the notion of symbols and archetypes which act like silent blows, rests, leaps of the heart, summons of the lymph, inflammatory images thrust into our abruptly wakened heads. The theatre restores us all our dormant conflicts and all their powers, and gives these powers names we hail as symbols: and behold! before our eyes is fought a battle of symbols: one charging against another in an impossible melée; for there can be theatre only from the moment when the impossible really begins and when the poetry which occurs on the stage sustains and superheats the realized symbols. (27-28) ... All true feeling is in reality untranslatable. To express it is to betray it. But to translate it is *to dissimulate it*. True expression hides what it makes manifest. It sets the mind in opposition to the real void of nature by creating in reaction a kind of fullness in thought. Or, in other terms, in relation to the manifestation-illusion of nature it creates a void in thought. All powerful feeling produces in us the idea of the void. And the lucid language which obstructs the appearance of this void also obstructs the appearance of poetry in thought. That is why an image, an allegory, a figure that masks what it would reveal have more significance for the spirit than the lucidities of speech and its analytics. (71)

See also Artaud under THOUGHT (AT 39-40).

c.1932   **Brecht.** *See* under GEST (BBT 104-105).

1934   **Eliot.** *See* under STYLE (EEE 189-90).

1948   **Brecht.** *See* under GEST (BBBG 33, 35).

MORALITY

The extracts presented here discuss the ethical content and influence of drama. See FLAW, INSTRUCTION.

4th cent. B.C.   Aristotle. *See* under CHARACTER (ANE 131, 133, AR 188-89), IMITATION (AP 11-13), PLOT (AP 45-49), REVERSAL (AP 67-69).

1561   Scaliger. *See* under INSTRUCTION (SP 82-83).

1570   Castelvetro   **CP**

[It is an error when the poet,] putting off that function of narration which is his own, . . . assumes the office of preacher and of censor of morals. (61)
     See also Castelvetro under HERO (CP 110-11).

c.1583   Sidney   **SDP**

To that which commonly is attributed [in] praise of history, in respect of the notable learning . . . gotten by marking the success [of virtue], as though therein a man should see virtue exalted and vice punished,—truly that commendation is peculiar to poetry and far off from history. For, indeed, poetry ever setteth virtue so out in her best colors, making Fortune her well-waiting handmaid, that one must needs be enamored of her. . . . And, of the contrary part, if evil men come to the stage, they ever go out—as the tragedy writer answered to one that misliked the show of such persons—so manacled as they little animate folks to follow them. But the historian, being captived to the truth of a foolish world, is many times a terror from well-doing, and an encouragement to unbridled wickedness. (21)

1605   Jonson   **JBW**

If men will impartially . . . look toward the offices, and function of a Poet, they will easily conclude to themselves, the impossibility of any man's being the good Poet, without first being a good man. . . . Now, especially in *dramatic*, or (as they term it) stage-*poetry*, nothing but ribaldry, profanation, blasphemy, all licence of offence to god, and man, is practis'd. . . . But [not] all are embark'd in this bold adventure to hell. . . . For my particular, I can (and from a clear conscience) affirm, that I have ever trembled to think toward the least profaneness; have loathed the use of such foul, and unwash'd bawdr'y, as is now made the food of the *scene*.

Dedication, *Volpone*

See also Jonson under POETIC JUSTICE (JBW).

1657   d'Aubignac. *See* under POETIC JUSTICE (AAS 1: 5-6).

1660   Corneille. *See* under POETIC JUSTICE (CFD 141).

1671   Dryden. *See* under POETIC JUSTICE (DW 1, 2: 198-201).

1677   Racine   **RP**

In no other of my plays have I given virtue so exalted a place as in this: the slightest evil is severely punished; the very thought of crime is made as horrible as the commission of it . . . vice is introduced in such wise as to make us detest it in all its horrible deformity. This should properly be the chief purpose of those who work for the public; this is what the ancients kept constantly in mind. . . . We should like our works to be as solid and full of useful instruction as were those of antiquity. . . . To instruct as well as please . . . auditors . . . [is] the true end of all tragedy. (157)

1679   Dryden. *See* under PITY (DW 1, 2: 270).

1709   Addison   **AW**

When . . . we see any thing divert an audience, either in tragedy or comedy, that strikes at the duties of civil life, or exposes what the best men of all ages have looked upon as sacred and inviolable, it is the certain sign of a profligate race of men, who are fallen from the virtues of their fathers, and will be contemptible in the eyes of their posterity. (3: 35) . . . [Socrates] was one day present at the first representation of a tragedy of Euripides. . . . In the midst of the tragedy . . . there chanced to be a line that seemed to encourage vice and immorality. This was no sooner spoken, but Socrates rose from his seat, and . . . showed himself displeased at what was said. . . . [The line] was in the part of Hyppolytus, who, when he was pressed by an oath, which he had taken to keep silence, returned for answer, "That he had taken the oath with his tongue, but not with his heart." Had a person of a vicious character made such a speech, it might have been allowed as a proper representation of the baseness of his thoughts: but such an expression out of the mouth of the virtuous Hyppolytus, was giving a sanction to falsehood, and establishing perjury by a maxim. (3: 36)

1711   Dryden   **DW**

Consider, if pity and terrour be enough for tragedy to move; and I believe, upon a true definition of tragedy, it will be found that its work extends farther, and that it is to reform manners, by a delightful representation of human life in great persons, by way of dialogue. If this be true, then not only pity and terrour are to be moved, as the only means to bring us to virtue, but generally love to virtue, and hatred to vice, by shewing the rewards of one, and punishments of the other; at least, by rendering virtue always amiable, though it be shewn unfortunate, and vice detestable, though it be shewn triumphant. If then, the encouragement of virtue, and discouragement of vice, be the proper ends of poetry in tragedy, pity and terrour, though good means, are not the only. For all the passions, in their turns, are to be set in a ferment; as joy, anger, love, fear, are to be used as the poet's commonplaces, and a general concernment for the principal actors is to be raised, by making them appear such in their characters, their words, and actions, as will interest the audience in their fortunes. (1, 2: 309-10)

1711   Addison. *See* under POETIC JUSTICE (AW 1: 71-72).

1712   Addison. *See* under DRAMA (AW 2: 184), INSTRUCTION (AW 2: 184-85).

1715   Addison. *See* under INSTRUCTION (AW 3: 244).

c.1745-1752   Voltaire. *See* under TRAGEDY (VW 19: 141).

1755-1780   Diderot. *See* under COMEDY (DDE 287).

1758   Diderot. *See* under DRAMA (DDP 287-89).

1765   Johnson   **JS**

[Shakespeare] sacrifices virtue to convenience, and is so much more careful to please than to instruct, that he seems to write without any moral purpose. From his writings indeed a system of social duty may be selected, for he that thinks reasonably must think morally; but his precepts and axioms drop casually from him; he makes no just distribution of good or evil, nor is always careful to shew in the virtuous a disapprobation of the wicked; he carries his persons indifferently through right and wrong, and at the close dismisses them without further care, and leaves their examples to operate by chance. . . . It is always a writer's duty to make the world better, and justice is a virtue independent of time or place. (21)

1767-1769   Lessing. *See* under CATHARSIS (LSPW 421), PROBABILITY (LSPW 236).

1808   Schlegel   **SCL**

The privilege of influencing an assembled crowd is exposed to most dangerous abuses. As one may disinterestedly animate them, for the noblest and best of purposes, so another may entangle them in the deceitful meshes of sophistry. ...Above all others must the comic poet...take heed, lest he afford an opportunity for the lower and baser parts of human nature to display themselves without restraint. When the sense of shame...is once weakened by the sight of others' participation in them, our inherent sympathy with what is vile will soon break out into the most unbridled licentiousness. (39)

   See also Schlegel under POETIC JUSTICE (SCL 254).

1817   Hazlitt. *See* under OBJECTIVITY (HW 1: 346-47).

c.1820   Hegel. *See* under CONFLICT (HFA 4: 318-20), TRAGEDY (HFA 4: 300-301, 312-15).

1827   Goethe. *See* under THOUGHT (GCE March 28).

1871   Nietzsche   **NBT**

[The myth of Prometheus shows that] the best and highest that men can acquire they obtain by a crime, and must now in their turn take upon themselves its consequences, namely the whole flood of sufferings and sorrows with which the offended celestials *must* visit the nobly aspiring race of man: a bitter reflection, which by the *dignity* it confers on crime, contrasts strangely with the Semitic myth of the fall of man, in which curiosity, beguilement, seducibility, wantonness,—in short, a whole series of preeminently feminine passions,—were regarded as the origin of evil. What distinguishes the Aryan representation is the sublime view of *active sin* as the properly Promethean virtue, which suggests at the same time the ethical basis of pessimistic tragedy as the *justification* of human evil—of human guilt as well as of the suffering incurred thereby. The misery in the essence of things—which the contemplative Aryan is not disposed to explain away—the antagonism in the heart of the world, manifests itself to him as a medley of different worlds, for instance, a Divine and a human world, each of which is in the right individually, but as a separate existence alongside of another has to suffer for its individuation. With the heroic effort made by the individual for universality, in his attempts to pass beyond the bounds of individuation and become the *one* universal being, he experiences in himself the primordial contradiction concealed in the essence of things, *i.e.*, he trespasses and suffers. (78-79)

1875   Shaw. *See* under DRAMA (SMCE 315-16).

1881   Nietzsche   NDD

The man who imagines that the effect of Shakespeare's plays is a moral one, and
that the sight of Macbeth irresistibly induces us to shun the evil of ambition, is
mistaken, and he is mistaken once more if he believes that Shakespeare himself
thought so. He who is truly obsessed by an ardent ambition takes delight in
beholding this picture of himself; and when the hero is driven to destruction by
his passion, this is the most pungent spice. . . . Did the poet feel this in any
way? How royally and with how little of the knave in him does his ambitious
hero run his course from the moment of his great crime! It is only from this
moment that he becomes "demonically" attractive, and that he encourages
similar natures to imitate him. . . . Do you think that Tristan and Isolde are
warnings against adultery, merely because adultery has resulted in the death of
both of them? (237-38)

1889   Chekhov   CLF

April 11. Flies purify the air, and plays,—the morals. (170)

1890   Chekhov. Compare with OBJECTIVITY (CL 141).

1896   Shaw. *See* under CHARACTER (SDC 135).

1902   Shaw   SAA

I am [not] one of those who claim that art is exempt from moral obligations,
and deny that the writing or the performance of a play is a moral act, to be
treated on exactly the same footing as theft or murder if it produces equally
mischievous consequences. I am convinced that fine art is the subtlest, the
most seductive, the most effective instrument of moral propaganda in the
world, excepting only the example of personal conduct; and I waive even this
exception in favor of the art of the stage, because it works by exhibiting
examples of personal conduct made intelligible and moving to crowds of
unobservant unreflecting people to whom real life means nothing. I have
pointed out again and again that the influence of the theatre in England is
growing so great that private conduct, religion, law, science, politics, and
morals are becoming more and more theatrical, whilst the theatre itself remains
impervious to common sense, religion, science, politics, and morals. (33)

1912   Shaw   SCP

It is ridiculous to say . . . that art has nothing to do with morality. What is true is
that the artist's business is not that of the policeman. . . . (69)

MOTIVATION

Motivation is the inquiry into the causes for the behavior of characters in a drama: the emotions and ideas expressed as the sources of action (see also under EMOTION and THOUGHT) or for which action is symptomatic (see also under SUBTEXT). See also WILL.

4th cent. B.C.   Aristotle   ANE

Now the cause of action (the efficient, not the final cause) is choice, and the cause of choice is desire and reasoning directed toward some end. Hence choice necessarily involves both intellect or thought and a certain disposition of character. . . . Thought by itself however moves nothing, but only thought directed to an end and dealing with action. . . . Hence choice may be called either thought related to desire or desire related to thought; and man, as an originator of action, is a union of desire and intellect. (329-31)

4th cent. B.C.   Aristotle   AR

All men do all things, either of themselves, or not of themselves. Of those things, which they do *not* of themselves, some are done by chance, some of necessity. And necessary acts are done either perforce or by nature; so that all things, which men do, *not* of themselves, are done either by chance or by nature or perforce. Actions which men do of themselves, and of which they are themselves the causes, are done either from habit or from appetite, rational or irrational. Now *wish* is an appetite of good; for no one wishes, unless he thinks the thing good: the irrational appetites are anger and lust. So that every act of men must have one of seven causes—chance, nature, force, habit, reason, passion, lust. (44)

   See also Aristotle under TRAGEDY (AP 23-25).

1657   d'Aubignac   AAS

[The Poet] examines first all that he designs to make known to the Audience, either by their Eyes or their Ears, and accordingly resolves either to let them see it, or to instruct them by some recital of the thing which they ought to know. But he does not make these Recitals or Spectacles only because the Spectators ought to know or see. How then? Why he must find in the Action, which is consider'd as true, some motive, colour, or apparent Reason, for which it may appear that these Shews or Recitals did probably happen, and ought to come to pass; and I may say that the greatest art of the Stage consists in finding out these Motives or Colours. An Actor must come upon the Stage, because the Spectator must know his Designs and Passions(1: 39) . . . 'Tis not enough that the Cause of some extraordinary Motion of the Mind be true, but it must also . . . be reasonable and probable, according to the receiv'd Opinions of Mankind; for . . .[otherwise the actor] would be look'd upon as a Mad man, instead of being pitied. (3: 42)

1679   Dryden   DW

The manners, in a poem, are understood to be those inclinations, whether natural or acquired, which move and carry us to actions, good, bad, or indifferent, in a play; or which incline the persons to such or such actions. . . . A poet ought not to make the manners perfectly good in his best persons; but neither are they to be more wicked in any of his characters, than necessity requires. To produce a villain without other reason than a natural inclination to villany, is in poetry, to produce an effect without a cause; and to make him more a villain than he has just reason to be, is to make an effect which is stronger than the cause. (1, 2: 274-75)

1755-1780   Diderot   DDE

Man falls into danger and into misfortune through a cause which is *outside him* or *within him*. *Outside him*, it is his destiny, his situation, his duties, his bonds, all the accidents of life, and the action which the gods, nature, and other men exercise on him. . . . *Within him*, it is his weakness, his imprudence, his passions, his vices, sometimes his virtues; of these causes the most fruitful, the most pathetic, and the most moral is passion combined with natural goodness. (290)

   See also Diderot under TRAGEDY (DDE 291).

1767-1769   Lessing   LSPW

[If] the poet chooses a martyr for his hero let him be careful to give to his actions the purest and most incontrovertible motives, let him place in an unalterable necessity of taking the step that exposes him to danger, let him not suffer him to seek death carelessly or insolently challenge it. Else his pious hero becomes an object of our distaste. (235) . . . I know full well that the sentiments in a drama must be in accordance with the assumed character of the person who utters them. They can therefore not bear the stamp of absolute truth, it is enough that they are poetically true, if we must admit that this character under these circumstances, with these passions could not have judged otherwise. But on the other hand this poetical truth must also approach to the absolute and the poet must never think so unphilosophically as to assume that a man could desire evil for evil's sake, that a man could act on vicious principles, knowing them to be vicious and boast of them to himself and to others. (239)

See also Lessing under PROBABILITY (LSPW 236), WILL (LSPW 326).

1808   Schlegel. See under ACTION (SCL 239-42), IRONY (SCL 369-70).

c.1810   Coleridge. See under UNITY (CLSW 117).

1813-1814   Coleridge. See under GENRE DEFINITION (CSC 2: 229).

1816   Hazlitt. See under TRAGEDY (HW 10: 96).

c.1820   Hegel. See under ACTION (HFA 4: 252, 259-61), DRAMA (HFA 4: 251, 278-80), TRAGEDY (HFA 4: 295-99, 300-301).

1878   Nietzsche   **NHH**

All ''evil'' actions are prompted by the instinct of preservation, or, more exactly, by the desire for pleasure and the avoidance of pain on the part of the individual; thus prompted, but not evil. ''To cause pain *per se*'' *does not exist*, except in the brains of philosophers, neither does ''to give pleasure, *per se*.'' . . . The individual can in the condition which lies before the State, act sternly and cruelly towards other creatures for the purpose of *terrifying*, to establish his existence firmly by such terrifying proofs of his power. Thus act the violent, the mighty, the original founders of States, who subdue the weaker to themselves. They have the right to do so, such as the State still takes for itself; or rather there is no right that can hinder this. . . . *Compulsion* precedes morality, indeed morality itself is compulsion for a time, to which one submits for the avoidance of pain. (97-99) . . . The aim of malice is *not* the suffering of others in itself, but our own enjoyment; for instance as the feeling of revenge, or a stronger nervous excitement. All teasing, even, shows the pleasure it gives us to exercise power on others. . . . Is it *immoral* to taste pleasure at the expense of another's pain? Is malicious joy [*Schadenfreude*] devilish . . . ? Pity aims just as little at the pleasure of others as malice at the pain of others *per se*. For it contains at least two (perhaps many more) elements of personal pleasure, and is so far self-gratification; in the first place as the pleasure of emotion, which is the kind of pity that exists in tragedy, and then, when it impels to action, as the pleasure of satisfaction in the exercise of power. (102-103)

1888   Strindberg   **SSPP**

[One thing in *Miss Julie* that] will offend simple brains is that my action cannot be traced back to a single motive, that the viewpoint is not always the same. An event in real life . . . springs generally from a whole series of more or less deep-lying motives, but of these the spectator chooses as a rule the one his reason can master most easily, or else the one reflecting most favourably on his power of reasoning. (13) . . . The psychological processes are what interest the people of our own day more than anything else. Our souls, so eager for knowledge, cannot rest satisfied with seeing what happens, but must also learn how it comes to happen! What we want to see are just the wires, the machinery. We want to investigate the box with the false bottom, touch the magic ring in order to find the suture, and look into the cards to discover how they are marked. (20)

1888   Nietzsche. *See* under WILL (NW 138-40).

1894   Brunetière. *See* under ACTION (BLD 75-76), WILL (BLD 73, 75, 81).

1908   Pirandello. Compare with HUMOR (POH 142-43).

c.1930   Stanislvaski   **SCR**

Life on the stage, as well as off it, consists of an uninterrupted series of objectives and their attainment. (51) . . . Both physical and psychological objectives must be bound together by a certain inner tie, by consecutiveness, gradualness, and logic of feeling. It sometimes happens that in the logic of human feelings one will find something illogical. . . . But on the stage it is necessary to be consecutive and logical. (55)

  See also Stanislavski under ACTION (SCR 48), SUBTEXT (SCR 51, 52, 77-79).

1936   Stanislavski. *See* under ACTION (SAP 43), FORWARD MOVEMENT (SAP 258), SUBTEXT (SAP 256).

1938   Stanislavski. *See* under THOUGHT (SBC 169-71).

1948   Brecht   **BBBG**

The powers of [the actor's] observations must . . . be able to take up readily fictitious additions to our basic [human] structure. This is done by turning social motivations into ideas or substituting for them other motivations. Through this procedure actual modes of behavior are made to appear somewhat unnatural. And thus actual *motivations* in turn are no longer "natural" but can be dealt with. . . . An alienating image is one which makes a circumstance recognizable and at the same time makes it seem strange. (26)

  See also Brecht under CHARACTER (BBBG 30), GEST (BBBG 33, 35, 35-36, 39), IDENTIFICATION (BBBG 17, 25, 28, 30).

NOVELTY

In general it seems that the concern with the fresh, the original, or the innovative has grown among theorists, and that the scope of that concern has grown from a focus on words (see, for instance, Aristotle on the pleasure of METAPHOR), through character, subject, and form, to embrace new art concepts (see, for instance, the claims of Brecht for EPIC THEATER). The statements presented here most explicitly discuss the nature and uses of originality.

c.20 B.C.   Horace   HAP

With a nice taste and care in weaving words together, you will express yourself most happily, if a skilful setting makes a familiar word new. . . . It has ever been, and ever will be, permitted to issue words stamped with the mint-mark of the day. (455) . . . It is hard to treat in your own way what is common: and you are doing better in spinning into acts a song of Troy than if, for the first time, you were giving the world a theme unknown and unsung. In ground open to all you will win private rights, if you do not linger along the easy and open pathway, if you do not seek to render word for word as a slavish translator, and if in your copying you do not leap into the narrow well, out of which either shame or the laws of your task will keep you from stirring a step. (461-63)

1561   Scaliger   SP

Novelty pleases us in things dramatic, even when a play is distorted to secure it. Thus in his playful way Plautus calls his *Jupiter in Disguise* a tragicomedy, for he attempted to combine the dignity of distinguished characters with the lowliness of comedy. (48)

1570   Castelvetro   CP

The essence of [poetry] is invention; no invention, no poet. (26) . . . [Actions to be the subject of tragedy must be known through history or legend, but] known only summarily and not particularly, so that without contradicting history or legend, the poet has a field for the exercise of his office, in that he can fashion the particularities concerning which history, being silent, cannot give him the lie. (116)

    See also Castelvetro under IMITATION (CP 34-35, 50-51), PLEASURE (CP 79).

1600   Jonson   JBW

If gracious silence, sweet attention,
Quick sight, and quicker apprehension,
(The lights of judgment's throne) shine anywhere;
Our doubtful author hopes this is their sphere.
And therefore opens he himself to those;
To other weaker beams, his labours close:
As loath to prostitute their virgin strain,
To ev'ry vulgar, and adult'rate brain.
In this alone, his *Muse* her sweetness hath,
She shuns the print of any beaten path;
And proves new ways to come to learned ears:
Pied ignorance she neither loves, nor fears.
Nor hunts she after popular applause,
Or foamy praise, that drops from common jaws:
The garland that she wears, their hands must twine,
Who can both censure, understand, define
What merit is: Then cast those piercing rays,
Round as a crown, instead of honour'd boys,
About his *poesy*; which (he knows) affords
Words, above action: matter, above words.

                                            Prologue, *Cynthia's Revels*

1641   Jonson   JD

Nothing doth more invite a greedy Reader, than an unlook'd for *subject*. And what more unlook'd for, then to see a person of an unblam'd life, made ridiculous, and odious, by the Artifice of lying? (15) . . . *Expectation* of the *Vulgar* is more drawne, and held with newnesse, then goodnesse; wee see it in *Fencers*, in *Players*, in *Poets*, in *Preachers*, in all, where *Fame* promiseth anything. (19)

        Compare with Jonson under LANGUAGE (JD 25-26).

1657   d'Aubignac. *See* under SUBJECT (AAS 2: 68-69).

1712   Addison. *See* under IMAGINATION (AW 2: 138-39, 140), SUR-
PRISE (AW 2: 312).

1713   Addison. *See* under SYMBOL (AW 3: 149).

1731   Voltaire. *See* under LANGUAGE (VE 283).

1750   Johnson. *See* under INSTRUCTION (JW 2: 11).

1808   Schlegel   **SCL**

[I reject] blind partiality for the ancients, which regards their excellence as a frigid faultlessness, and which exhibits them as models, in such a way as to put a stop to everything like improvement, and reduce us to abandon the exercise of art as altogether fruitless. I, for my part, am disposed to believe that poetry, as the fervid expression of our whole being, must assume new and peculiar forms in different ages. (50)

1815   Coleridge   **CBL**

I may remark that the pleasure arising from novelty must of course be allowed its due place and weight. This pleasure consists in the identity of two opposite elements, that is to say—sameness and variety. If in the midst of the variety there be not some fixed object for the attention, the unceasing succession of the variety will prevent the mind from observing the difference of the individual objects; and the only thing remaining will be the succession, which will then produce precisely the same effect as sameness. (2: 262)

1816   Hazlitt   **HW**

Knowledge is pleasure as well as power. A work of art has in this respect no advantage over a work of nature, except inasmuch as it furnishes an additional stimulus to curiosity. Again, natural objects please in proportion as they are uncommon, by fixing the attention more steadily on their beauties or differences. The same principle of the effect of novelty in exciting the attention, may account, perhaps, for the extraordinary discoveries and lies told by travellers, who, opening their eyes for the first time in foreign parts, are startled at every object they meet. (1: 75)

See also Hazlitt under AESTHETIC (HW 1: 68).

1818   Hazlitt   **HW**

In reasoning, truth and soberness may prevail, on which side soever they meet: but in works of imagination novelty has the advantage over prejudice; that which is striking and unheard-of, over that which is trite and known before, and that which gives unlimited scope to the indulgence of the feelings and the passions (whether erroneous or not) over that which imposes a restraint upon them. (5: 362)

1824   Goethe   **GCE**

Wed., Nov. 24. "The French," said Goethe, "do well to study and translate our writers; for, limited as they are both in form and motives, they can only look without for means. We Germans may be reproached for a certain formlessness; but in matter we are their superiors. The theatrical productions of

Kotzebue and Iffland are so rich in motives that they may pluck them a long time before all is used up. But, especially, our philosophical Ideality is welcome to them; for every Ideal is serviceable to revolutionary aims.''

1827   Goethe. Compare with SUBJECT (GCE Jan. 31).

1830   Hazlitt   **HW**

Originality is any conception of things, taken immediately from nature, and neither borrowed from, nor common to, others. To deserve this appellation, the copy must be both true and new. But herein lies the difficulty of reconciling a seeming contradiction in the terms of the explanation. For as any thing to be *natural* must be referable to a consistent principle, and as the face of things is open and familiar to all, how can any imitation be new and striking, without being liable to the charge of extravagance, distortion, and singularity? And, on the other hand, if it has no such peculiar and distinguishing characteristic to set it off, it cannot possibly rise above the level of the trite and the common-place. This objection would indeed hold good and be unanswerable, if nature were one thing, or if the eye or mind comprehended the whole of it at a single glance; in which case, if an object had been once seen and copied in the most cursory and mechanical way, there could be no farther addition to, or variation from, this idea, without obliquity and affectation; but nature presents an endless variety of aspects, of which the mind seldom takes in more than a part or than one view at a time; and it is in seizing on this unexplored variety, and giving some one of these new but easily recognised features, in its characteristic essence, and according to the peculiar bent and force of the artist's genius, that true originality consists. (9: 423-24)

1882   Nietzsche   **NJW**

What is originality? To *see* something that does not yet bear a name, that cannot yet be named, although it is before everybody's eyes. (207-208)
        See also Nietzsche under AESTHETIC (NJW 334-35)

1931-1936   Artaud. *See* under THOUGHT (AT 46), TRAGEDY (AT 142-43).

OBJECTIVE CORRELATIVE

Conceiving a disjunction between Shakespeare's intent and his expression in Hamlet, *and therefore a failure to achieve the intended effect, Eliot attempted to formulate the opposite of this "dissociation of sensibility." The formulation of the OBJECTIVE CORRELATIVE has been much debated. Like GEST, PATHOS, and SUBTEXT—from their very different perspectives—this was an attempt to more precisely relate the thing done (in the work) to the perception of it.*

1818   Coleridge. *See* under THOUGHT (CLSW 329-30).

c.1820   Hegel. *See* under PATHOS (HFA 4: 268-69).

1919   Eliot   **EEE**

The only way of expressing emotion in the form of art is by finding an "objective correlative"; in other words, a set of objects, a situation, a chain of events which shall be the formula of that *particular* emotion; such that when the external facts, which must terminate in sensory experience, are given, the emotion is immediately evoked. (61)

OBJECTIVITY

This term is used to refer to several concepts that are often alluded to in the theoretical literature: the absence of authorial intrusion in drama; the quality of drama that permits or requires the spectator to draw inferences; the semblance in drama of "the external facts."
    See also *ALIENATION and EPIC THEATER*.

4th cent. B.C.   Aristotle   **AP**

The poet may imitate by narration—in which case he can either take another personality as Homer does, or speak in his own person, unchanged—or [, as in drama,] he may present all *his characters as living and moving before us* [the imitators doing their work in and through action: EP 90].(13)

1765   Johnson   **JS**

[Shakespeare's] drama is the mirrour of life; . . . human sentiments in human language, by scenes from which a hermit may estimate the transactions of the world, and a confessor predict the progress of the passions. (14)
    See also Johnson under MORALITY (JS 21).

1767-1769   Lessing. *See* under DRAMA (LSPW 233).

1808   Schlegel. *See* under DRAMA (SCL 30-32).

c.1810   Coleridge. *See* under DRAMA (CLSW 116).

1817   Hazlitt   **HW**

Shakespear was in one sense the least moral of all writers; for morality (commonly so called) is made up of antipathies; and his talent consisted in sympathy with human nature, in all its shapes, degrees, depressions, and elevations. The object of the pedantic moralist is to find out the bad in everything: his was to shew that "there is some soul of goodness in things evil.' . . . In one sense, Shakespear was no moralist at all: in another, he was the greatest of all moralists. He was a moralist in the same sense in which nature is one. He taught what he had learnt from her. He shewed the greatest knowledge of humanity with the greatest fellow-feeling for it. (1: 346-47)

1820   Hazlitt. *See* under DRAMA (HW 8: 417).

c.1820   Hegel. *See* under AFFECT (HFA 4: 275), CHARACTER (HFA 4: 252), DRAMA (HFA 4: 248, 251, 278-80), LANGUAGE (HFA 4: 264-65), PATHOS (HFA 4: 268-69).

1827   Goethe. *See* under INSTRUCTION (GLE 130).

1871   Nietzsche. *See* under DRAMA (NBT 68-69).

1886   Chekhov. *See* under LANGUAGE (CLF 70-71).

1887   Chekhov. *See* under REALISM (CL 57).

1888   Chekhov. *See* under THOUGHT (CL May 30).

1890   Chekhov   **CL**

April 1. You abuse me for objectivity, calling it indifference to good and evil, lack of ideals and ideas, and so on. You would have me, when I describe horse-stealers, say: "Stealing horses is an evil." But that has been known for ages without my saying so. Let the jury judge them. . . . Of course it would be pleasant to combine art with a sermon, but for me personally it is extremely difficult and almost impossible, owing to conditions of technique. You see, to depict horse-stealers in seven-hundred lines I must all the time speak and think in their tone and feel in their spirit, otherwise, if I introduce subjectivity, the image becomes blurred and the story will not be as compact as all short stories ought to be. When I write I reckon entirely upon the reader to add for himself the subjective elements that are lacking in the story. (141)

1919   Eliot. *See* under CONVENTION (ESE 28).

1926   Brecht. *See* under EPIC THEATRE (BBT 14-15).

1931-1936   Artaud. *See* under DRAMA (AT 70),POETRY OF THE THEATRE (AT 39, 93), STYLE (AT 53).

1938   Brecht. *see* under ACTION (BBEB 430).

1948   Brecht. *See* under ALIENATION (BBBG 26-27), INSTRUCTION (BBBG 20,21).

1953   Eliot. *See* under STYLE (ETVP 9-10).

ORDER

The ancient idea of "order drawn from chaos" argues a fundamental operation of the aesthetic experience—that a sensed design emerges from an apparent disorder of elements. See also FORM and UNITY for qualities of the art object meant to satisfy the need for dynamic or emergent order.

4th cent. B.C.   Aristotle   AP

Even coincidences are most striking when they have an air of design. We may instance the statue of Mitys of Argos, which fell upon his murderer while he was a spectator at a festival, and killed him. Such events seem not due to mere chance. (39)

4th cent. B.C.   Aristotle   AM

Those who say mathematical number is first and go on to generate one kind of substance after another and give different principles for each, make the substance of the universe a mere series of episodes (for one substance has no influence on another by its existence or non-existence), and they give us many governing principles; but the world refuses to be governed badly. (1076 a: 1) . . . The observed facts show that nature is not a series of episodes, like a bad tragedy. (1090 b: 20)
  See also Aristotle under FORM (APA 8), PLOT (AP 39).

1789 Goethe. *See* under IMITATION (GLE 59-61).

1798 Goethe. *See* under ILLUSION (GLE 52-7).

1808 Schlegel. *See* under AESTHETIC (SCL 342-43), AFFECT (SCL 67-69), CLOSURE (SCL 254), DRAMA (SCL 273).

1810 Coleridge. *See* under TASTE (CLSW 369-70).

1815 Coleridge   CBL

Remember that there is a difference between form as proceeding, and shape as superinduced;—the latter is either the death or the imprisonment of the thing; —the former is its self-witnessing and self-effected sphere of agency. Art would or should be the abridgment of nature. Now the fulness of nature is without character, as water is purest when without taste, smell, or color; but this is the highest, the apex only,—it is not the whole. The object of art is to give the whole *ad hominem*; hence each step of nature hath its ideal, and hence the possibility of a climax up to the perfect form of a harmonized chaos. (2: 262)

c.1820   Hegel. *See* under AFFECT (HFA 4: 275), CONFLICT (HFA 4: 311-12), DRAMA (HFA 4: 321-23), TRAGEDY (HFA 4: 295-99,300-301, 312-15).

1827   Goethe. *See* under CATHARSIS (GLE 105).

1871   Nietzsche. *See* under DRAMA (NBT 60-61), MORALITY (NBT 78-79).

1873   Nietzsche. *See* under METAPHOR (NEG 178-88).

1875   Nietzsche. Compare with CONFLICT (NTS 128-30).

1888   Nietzsche. Compare with TASTE (NWP 448-50).

1909   Shaw. *See* under DRAMA (STPB xxiv).

1948   Brecht. *See* under AFFECT (BBBG 21-23).

PATHOS

For Aristotle, pathos is a particular kind of scene; but, as the extracts quoted here show, pathos for others could be an impending threat, a lament, or even a quality of character. The meaning shared in common appears to include an element in the dramatic work which is presumed to induce pity.

4th cent. B.C. Aristotle   AP

A third part [of plot] is the *Scene of Suffering* [Pathos: EP 356]. The Scene of Suffering is a destructive or painful action, such as death on the stage, bodily agony, wounds and the like [in the visible realm: EP 356]. (43)

    See also Aristotle under PITY (AP 49-53), PLOT (AP 65-67).

1570 Castelvetro   CP

An action destructive or sorrowful, either which actually happens, or which is impending. (98)

1657 d'Aubignac   AAS

[I] intend to shew with what Art a Pathetick, or Moving Discourse ought to be regulated so as to make it agreeable to the Spectators, by the impression it is to make on them. First then, The Cause which is to produce a Motion in the Actors themselves, and then in the Audience, ought to be something true, or believ'd to be so, not only by the Actor who speaks . . . but also by the Spectators, who probably would not be concern'd if they knew that the Subject he had to complain or rejoyce were fictitious; and if it so fall out, that by the rest of the story, the Spectator must know a thing contrary to the belief of the Actor: As for Example, that a Princess is alive, though a Lover believe her dead: I say, if in that case one would have the Passion take with the Audience, there must not be a long Complaint mingled with Sentiments of kindness and grief; but the Actor must be presently transported into Rage, that the spectators may be touched by his violent despair, and feel a great deal of compassion. . . . Secondly, 'Tis not enough that the Cause of some extraordinary Motion of the Mind be true, but it must also . . . be reasonable and probable, according to the receiv'd Opinions of Mankind; for if any Actor should fly into a passion of Anger, without reason, he would be look'd upon as a Mad man, instead of being pitied. . . . Thirdly, To make a Complaint that shall touch and concern the Audience, the Cause of it must be just, for else no body will enter into the Sentiments of the grieved Person. . . . Besides all these Considerations, if the

Pathetick Discourse be not necessary, that is to say, expected and desired by the Spectators, it will be very nauseous to them, let the Poets Art be what it will. . . . All passions that are not founded upon Opinions and Customs conformable to those of the Spectators, are sure to be cold, and of no effect, because they being already possessed with an Opinion contrary to the Action of the Player, cannot approve of any thing he says or does in another sense. (3: 40-44)

1712 Addison. *See* under IDENTIFICATION (AW 2: 149).

1808 Schlegel. *See* under CLOSURE (SCL 136).

c.1820 Hegel   **HFA**

We may . . . distinguish in the dialogue [of a play] between the expression of a pathos that is *subjective* and one that is *objective*. The first rather appertains to a given passion of more accidental a nature. . . . Poets, who endeavor to arouse the full movement of personal emotion by means of poignant scenes, are exceptionally partial to this type of pathos. Nevertheless, despite all their endeavor to depict personal suffering and unrestrained passion, or the unreconciled inward dissension of soul-life, it remains the fact that the human soul, in its depth, is less affected thereby than it is through a pathos, wherein at the same time a genuine objective content is evolved. For this reason the earlier plays of Goethe . . . make on the whole a weaker impression. . . . The poet may describe passion with all the overwhelming power possible. It is ineffective; the heart is merely rent in pieces [''stunned as by a blow''—translator], and turns aside from it. What we fail to find here is that which art can least dispense with, the positive aspect of reconciliation. The ancient tragedians, therefore, mainly sought for their effect by means of the objective type of pathos; nor is there wanting here genuine human individuality, so far as this was compatible with their art. The plays, also, of Schiller possess this pathos of a great spiritual force, a pathos which is penetrative throughout, and is manifested and expressed everywhere as fundamental to the action. . . . For that which produces a profound dramatic effect of universal and enduring appeal can be only the substantive in action—by which I mean, viewing it as a definite content, the ethical substance therein, or, in its more formal aspect, the grandeur of ideal reach and character, in which respect, again, Shakespeare is supreme. (4: 268-69)

    See also Hegel under HERO (HFA 4: 320-21), TRAGEDY (HFA 4: 295-99).

PITY

Pity, fear, and laughter have, since antiquity, been the most commonly dis-cussed and formulated of the special affective theories. The statements presented under this heading assert theoretical principles for evoking a com-passionate response from the spectator. Because pity is often conceived in relation to fear, compare with FEAR. See also PATHOS.

4th cent. B.C.   Aristotle   AP

Pity is aroused by unmerited misfortune. (45) . . . Let us determine what are the circumstances which strike us as terrible or pitiful. Actions capable of this effect must happen between persons who are either friends or enemies or indifferent to one another. If an enemy kills an enemy, there is nothing to excite pity either in the act or in the intention,—except so far as the suffering itself is pitiful. But when the *tragic incident* [painful deed: EP 413] occurs between those who are near or dear to one another—if, for example, a brother kills, or intends to kill, a brother, a son his father, a mother her son, a son his mother, or any other deed of the kind is done—these are the situations to be looked for by the poet. . . . The action may be done consciously and with knowledge of the persons in the manner of the older poets. It is thus, too, that Euripides makes Medea slay her children. Or, again, the deed of horror may be done in ignorance, and the tie of kinship or friendship be discovered after-wards. The Oedipus of Sophocles is an example. . . . Again, there is a third case, [to be about to act with knowledge of the persons and then not to act. The fourth case is] when someone is about to do an irreparable deed through ignorance, and makes the discovery before it is done. These are the only possible ways. For the deed must either be done or not done,—and that wittingly or unwittingly. But of all these ways, to be about to act knowing the persons, and then not to act, is the worst. It is shocking without being tragic, for no disaster follows. . . . The next and better way is that the deed should be perpetrated. Still better, that it should be perpetrated in ignorance, and the discovery made afterwards. There is then nothing to shock us, while the discovery produces a startling effect. The last case is best, as when in the Cresphoretes Mesope is about to slay her son, but, recognising who he is, spares his life. So in the Iphigenia, the sister recognizes the brother just in time. . . . (49-53)

4th cent. B.C.   Aristotle   AR

Pity may be defined as a pain for apparent evil, destructive or painful, befalling a person who does not deserve it, when we might expect such evil to befall ourselves or some of our friends, and when, moreover, it seems near. (89) The persons whom we pity are, first, our friends, if they are not very near friends; in the case of near friends, we feel as if we *ourselves* were threatened. . . . Now the dreadful is different from the piteous, and tends to drive out pity, and often serves to rouse its opposite. Again, men pity when the danger is near themselves. And they pity those like them in age, in character, in moral state, in rank, in birth; for all these examples make it more probable that the case may become their own; since here, again, we must take it as a general maxim that all things, which we fear for ourselves, we pity when they happen to others. (91)

See also Aristotle under ACTION (AP 37-39, 45), CATHARSIS (APO 1341 b: 36-1342 a: 29), POETIC JUSTICE (AP 48-49), REVERSAL (AR 90-91), TRAGEDY (AP 23-25).

1570   Castelvetro. *See* under HERO (CP 110-11), TRAGEDY (CP 98).

1660   Corneille. *See* under CATHARSIS (CDENA 3, CDT 816).

1679   Dryden   **DW**

It is absolutely necessary to make a man virtuous, if we desire he should be pitied. We lament not, but detest, a wicked man; we are glad when we behold his crimes are punished, and that poetical justice is done upon him. (1, 2: 270)

1695   Dryden. *See* under IDENTIFICATION (DW 3: 308).

1711   Dryden   **DW**

The pity which the poet is to labour for, is for the criminal, not for those or him whom he has murdered, or who have been the occasion of the tragedy. The terrour is likewise in the punishment of the same criminal, who, if he be represented too great an offender, will not be pitied; if altogether innocent, his punishment will be unjust. (1, 2: 307)

1712   Addison. *See* under DISTANCE (AW 2: 149), IDENTIFICATION (AW 2: 149).

1767-1769   Lessing   **LSPW**

Aristotle explains that which is fearful and that which merits pity by means of one another. All that, he says, is fearful to us, which if it had happened to another, or were to happen to him, would excite our pity; and we find all that worthy of our compassion, which we should fear if it were threatening us. It would not therefore be enough that the unfortunate person who excites our compassion does not deserve his misfortunes; he may have drawn them down upon himself by his own weakness, his tortured innocence or rather his too severely punished guilt would lose their effect upon us, would be incapable of awakening our pity if we saw no possibility that his sufferings might ever befall us. But this possibility arises, and becomes the more probable, if the poet does not make him out to be worse than mankind in general, if he lets him think and act as we should have thought and acted in his position, or at least as we might have thought and acted; in short, if he portrays him as one of ourselves. From similarity arises the fear that our destiny might as easily become like his as we feel ourselves to be like him, and this fear it is which would force compassion to full maturity. (409) . . . If we can feel compassion for others without fear for ourselves it remains incontestable that our compassion, strengthened by this fear, becomes far more vivid and intense than it would be without it. (412)

See also Lessing under AFFECT (LSPW 419), DRAMA (LSPW 426), SURPRISE (LSPW 377-78, 380-82), TRAGEDY (LSPW 415).

1808   Schlegel. Compare with DISTANCE (SCL 184-86).

c.1820   Hegel. *See* under CATHARSIS (HFA 298-300).

1878   Nietzsche. *See* under MOTIVATION (NHH 102-103).

1888   Nietzsche. *See* under CATHARSIS (NW 285-86).

PLEASURE

The pleasure of dramatic art, its source and its nature, is one of the earliest, most fundamental, and most durable of the issues that have concerned theorists of drama. Compare with INSTRUCTION, and see also NOVELTY, VARIETY and WONDER.

4th cent. B.C.   Aristotle   AP

To learn gives the liveliest pleasure, not only to philosophers but to men in general. . . . Thus the reason why men enjoy seeing a likeness is, that in contemplating it they find themselves learning or inferring [what class each object belongs to: EP 125] and saying, perhaps, "Ah, that is he." For if you happen not to have seen the original, the pleasure will be due not to the imitation as such, but to the execution, the colouring, or some other cause. (15)

4th cent. B.C.   Aristotle   APO

It sometimes happens that men make amusement the end, for the end probably contains some element of pleasure, though not any ordinary or lower pleasure; but they mistake the lower for the higher, and in seeking for the one find the other, since every pleasure has a likeness to the end of action. (1339 b: 32-35)

4th cent. B.C.   Aristotle   ANE

It might be held that all men seek to obtain pleasure, because all men desire life. Life is a form of activity, and each man exercises his activity upon those objects and with those faculties which he likes the most: for example, the musician exercises his sense of hearing upon musical tunes, the student his intellect upon problems of philosophy, and so on. And the pleasure of these activities perfects the activities, and therefore perfects life, which all men seek. Men have good reason therefore to pursue pleasure, since it perfects for each his life, which is a desirable thing. . . . [Pleasure and life] appear to be inseparably united; for there is no pleasure without activity, and also no perfect activity without its pleasure. (597-99)

    See also Aristotle under ACTION (AP 47-49), AESTHETIC (APA 16-17), CATHARSIS (APO 1341 b: 36-1342 a: 29), DRAMA (AP 107-11), IMITATION (AP 15; APO 1340 a: 11-25), METAPHOR (AR 167-68), PLOT (AP 45-49, 49), POETIC JUSTICE (AP 48-49),SUBJECT (AP 37), WONDER (AP 95).

c.20 B.C.   Horace. *See* under DRAMA (HAP 479), IMITATION (HAP 477), REALISM (HAP 479).

1561   Scaliger. *See* under AESTHETIC (SP 53); compare with DRAMA (SP 2).

1570   Castelvetro   CP

Poetry delights by the novelty of incident, [the pleasure being a delight in the marvelous]. (79) . . . [One of the sources of pleasure in the *Orestes* is that] we become aware of something which we believed could not happen, this being the proper pleasure arising from the marvelous. (126) . . . According to Aristotle there are four kinds of pleasure [in tragedy]. The first is the pleasure arising from the sad fate of a person, good or moderately good, who falls from happiness to misery: this pleasure . . . is caused obliquely [resulting from the recognition of our own inherent sense of injustice]. The second is the pleasure arising from the happy fate of a person, good or moderately good, and from the sad fate of the wicked; this pleasure we [call] direct. . . . The third is the pleasure of the happy fate common to persons of all kinds, friends and enemies: this pleasure can be called direct popular pleasure. The fourth is the pleasure caused by a fearful and monstrous spectacle; this can be called artificial, spectacular pleasure. Now Aristotle accepts in tragedy the first and second . . . and commends them, the first . . . more than the second: but he will not have them in comedy. [Thus from tragedy of the best kind we learn not to trust this world, but in a more delightful way than in a sermon:] we are delighted much more than we should be if Sir Priest taught us the same things directly in his discourses. (128-29)

    See also Castelvetro under DRAMA (CP 60-61, 66,67), FUNCTIONAL-ISM (CP 68), PROBABILILTY (CP 79), UNITY (CP 90-91).

c.1583   Sidney   SDP

Now therein of all sciences . . . is our poet the monarch. For he doth not only show the way, but giving so sweet a prospect into the way as will entice any man to enter into it. . . . He beginneth not with obscure definitions, which must blur the margent with interpretations, and load the memory with doubtfulness. But he cometh to you with words set in delightful proportion, either accompanied with, or prepared for, the well-enchanting skill of music; and with a tale, forsooth, he cometh unto you, with a tale which holdeth children from play, and old men from the chimney-corner, and, pretending no more, doth intend the winning of the mind from wickedness to virtue. (23)

    See also Sidney under HUMOR (SDP 50-51), IMITATION (SDP 9-10, 24).

1609   de Vega. *See* under VARIETY (VAWP 30).

1616   Jonson. *See* under REALISM (JBW).

1641   Jonson. *See* under DRAMA (JD 90-91), MAGNITUDE (JD 102).

1657   d'Aubignac. *See* under SPECTACLE (AAS 3: 93, 95-98), SUBJECT (AAS 2: 68-69).

1660   Corneille. *See* under DRAMA (CFD 140), POETIC JUSTICE (CFD 141), RULES (CDENA 32), THREE UNITIES (CDTU 237).

1663   Molière. *See* under RULES (MP 6: 344, 345).

1668   Dryden. *See* under DRAMA (DW 1, 2: 43, 160), VARIETY (DW 1, 2: 89).

1671   Dryden. *See* under COMEDY (DW 1, 2: 191-92), POETIC JUSTICE (DW 1, 2: 198-201).

1695   Dryden. *See* under DRAMA (DW 3: 311), IMITATION (DW 3: 322-25), RULES (DW 3: 318-19, 322).

1711   Dryden. *See* under DRAMA (DW 1, 2: 307).

1711   Addison. *See* under SPECTACLE (AW 1: 77-78).

1712   Addison. *See* under IMAGINATION (AW 2: 138-39, 140, 145-46), IMITATION (AW 2: 142), SURPRISE (AW 2: 312), WONDER (AW 2: 4).

1755-1780   Diderot. *See* under SUBJECT (DDE 287).

1765   Johnson   **JS**

Upon the whole, all pleasure consists in variety. (17)
      See also Johnson under WONDER (JS 32-33).

1767-1769   Lessing. *See* under THOUGHT (LSPW 329).

1804   Coleridge. *See* under ILLUSION (CSC 1: 178-81).

c.1810   Coleridge. *See* under TASTE (CLSW 369-70).

1811-1812   Coleridge   **CCSL**

[Poetry] is the art of communicating whatever we wish to communicate, so as both to express and produce excitement, but for the purpose of immediate pleasure; and each part is fitted to afford as much pleasure, as is compatible with the largest sum in the whole. (17)

See also Coleridge under DISTANCE (CCSL 25), METAPHOR (CCSL 45), UNITY (CLSW 20).

1815   Coleridge   **CBL**

Agreeable.—We use this word in 2 senses; in the first for whatever agrees with our nature, for that which is congruous with the primary constitution of our senses. Thus green is naturally agreeable to the eye. In this sense the word expresses, at least involves, a pre-established harmony between the organs and their appointed objects. In the second sense, we convey by the word *agreeable*, that the thing has by force of habit (thence called a second nature) been made to agree with us; or that it has become agreeable to us by its recalling to our minds some one or more things that were dear and pleasing to us; or lastly, on account of some after pleasure or advantage, of which it has been the constant cause or occasion. (231)

See also Coleridge under PROBABILITY (CBL 2: 189), STYLE (CBL 2: 49-50, 50, 51), UNITY (CBL 2: 10-11).

1816   Hazlitt. See under AESTHETIC (HW 1: 68), DRAMA (HW 1: 152, 154), IMITATION (HW 1: 72-74, 75).

c.1817   Coleridge. See under DRAMA (CBL 2: 220-21).

1818   Hazlitt   **HW**

The pleasure . . . derived from tragic poetry, is not any thing peculiar to it as poetry, as a fictitious and fanciful thing. It is not an anomaly of the imagination. It has its sources and ground-work in the common love of strong excitement. As Mr. Burke observes, people flock to see a tragedy; but if there were a public execution in the next street, the theatre would very soon be empty. It is not then the difference between fiction and reality that solves the difficulty. Children are satisfied with the stories of ghosts and witches in plain prose. . . . We are as fond of indulging our violent passions as of reading a description of those of others. We are as prone to make a torment of our fears, as to luxuriate in our hopes of good. If it be asked, Why we do so? the best answer will be, Because we cannot help it. The sense of power is as strong a principle in the mind as the love of pleasure. Objects of terror and pity exercise the same despotic control over it as those of love or beauty. It is as natural to hate as to love, to despise as to admire, to express our hatred or contempt, as our love or admiration. (5: 7)

See also Hazlitt under AESTHETIC (HW 5: 1-2).

1819   Hazlitt. See under HUMOR (HW 8: 5, 7-8).

c.1820 Hazlitt. *See* under AESTHETIC (HW 2: 463), TASTE (HW 11: 459-60).

1871 Nietzsche. *See* under TRAGEDY (NBT 127).

1878 Nietzsche   **NHH**

The feeling of pleasure on the basis of human relations generally makes men better; joy in common, pleasure enjoyed together is increased, it gives the individual security, makes him good-tempered, and dispels mistrust and envy, for we feel ourselves at ease and see others at ease. *Similar manifestations of pleasure* awaken the idea of the same sensations, the feeling of being like something; a like effect is produced by common sufferings, the same bad weather, dangers, enemies. Upon this foundation is based the oldest alliance, the object of which is the mutual obviating and averting of a threatening danger for the benefit of each individual. And thus the social instinct grows out of pleasure. (97)

1888 Nietzsche. *See* under TASTE (NWP 448-50).

1909 Shaw. *See* under DRAMA (STPB xxiv).

1930 Brecht. Compare with AESTHETIC (BBT 40-41).

1931-1936 Artaud. *See* under DRAMA (AT 116).

1938 Stanislavski. *See* under DRAMA (SKDC 10).

1948 Brecht   **BBBG**

It has always been the task of the theater, as of every other art, to entertain people. This task confers on it its special value. It requires no excuse for its existence other than that it provides amusement—it must be amusing under all circumstances. It could by no means be raised to a more exalted position, be made a market for morality, for example. It must rather take care that it is not degraded, as it would be if it did not make morality pleasurable, that is, pleasurable to the senses; from this, of course, morality can only be the gainer. The theater should not even be expected to teach, at any rate nothing more useful than how to be pleasurably moved, either physically or spiritually. It must be allowed to remain something superfluous. Of course, this means that we live for the superfluous. Pleasures stand need of defense less than anything else. . . . Thus, what the ancients required of tragedy, according to Aristotle, was nothing loftier nor humbler than that it entertain people. If it is said that the theater came from the realm of ritual, what is meant is that it became theater when it left that realm. From the mysteries it took nothing of the ritual *function* but only the pleasure associated with it, pure and simple. And the well-known Catharsis of Aristotle, the purification through terror and pity (or *of* terror and pity), is a cleansing which is effected not only in a pleasurable fashion but actually to the end of pleasure. To demand more of the theater or to interpret its function more broadly is to put too low a value on the end proper to it. . . . Art wishes to be free to operate as both high and low if it may thus be pleasing to people. . . . On the other hand, the theater affords weak (simple) and strong (complex) pleasures. The latter, which we find in great drama, reach a climax rather like that of sexual intercourse, though they have more ramifications, are richer in fine adjustments, more contradictory, and richer in consequences. (15)

   See also Brecht under AESTHETIC (BBBG 13-14), DRAMA (BBBG 13, 14, 19-20, 24), IMITATION (BBBG 16), INSTRUCTION (BBBG 20, 21).

c.1956   Brecht   BBT

It is not a matter of art presenting what needs to be learned in an enjoyable form. . . . Only once productivity has been set free can learning be transformed into enjoyment and vice versa. (276)

1956   Brecht. *See* under THOUGHT (BBT 277).

PLOT

*The plot is the arrangement of the story elements into a dramatic sequence;
hence plot is to be distinguished from* story, *which without a plot is a chronicle
of events in their actual or natural sequence (see SUBJECT). Whereas story
elements are incidents, characters, environments, and so forth, the plot is the
deployment of these in an order intended to enhance dramatic effectiveness.*
See also *ACTION, CLOSURE, COMPLICATION, FORM, FORWARD MOVE-
MENT, PATHOS, RECOGNITION, and REVERSAL.*

4th cent. B.C.   Aristotle   AP

Plot is the imitation of the action:—for by plot I mean the arrangement of the
incidents. (25) . . . Most important of all is the structure of the incidents. For
Tragedy is an imitation, not of men, but of an action and of life, and life
consists in action and its end is a mode of action, not a quality. *Now character
determines men's qualities* [The dramatic persons have certain qualities by
virtue of their "characters": EP 251], but it is by their actions that they are
happy or the reverse. Dramatic action, therefore, is not with a view to the
representation of character: character comes in as a subsidiary to the actions.
Hence the incidents and the plot are the end of a tragedy; and the end is the chief
thing of all. Again, without action there cannot be a tragedy; there may be
without [expressions of: EP 251] character. . . . Again, if you string together a
set of speeches expressive of character, and well-finished in a point of diction
and thought, you will not produce the essential tragic effect nearly so well as
with a play which, however deficient in these respects, yet has a plot and
artistically constructed incidents. Besides which, the most powerful elements
of emotional interest in Tragedy—Peripeteia or Reversal of the Situation, and
Recognition scenes—are parts of the plot. A further proof is, that novices in
the art attain to finish of diction and precision of portraiture before they can
construct a plot. It is the same with almost all the early poets. The Plot, then, is
the first principle, and, as it were, the soul of a tragedy: Character holds the
second place. A similar fact is seen in painting. The most beautiful colours,
laid on confusedly, will not give as much pleasure as the chalk outline of a
portrait. Thus Tragedy is the imitation of an action, and of the agents with a
view to the action. (25-29) . . . Of *all the* [simple: EP 323] plots and actions the
episodic are the worst. I call a plot "episodic" in which the episodes or acts
succeed one another without probable or necessary *sequence* [order: EP 323].
Bad poets compose such *pieces* [actions: EP 323] by their own fault, good

poets, to please the players; for as they write show pieces for competition, they stretch the plot beyond its capacity, and are often forced to break the natural continuity. (37-39) . . . Tragedy is an imitation not only of a complete action, but of events *inspiring* [replete with: EP 323] fear or pity. Such an effect is best produced when the events come on us by surprise [(yet) because of each other: EP 323]; and the effect is heightened when at the same time they follow as cause and effect. The *Tragic wonder* [quality of surprise: EP 323] will then be greater than if they happened of themselves or by accident; for even coincidences are most striking when they have an air of design. We may instance the statue of Mitys of Argos, which fell upon his murderer while he was a spectator at a festival, and killed him. Such events seem not due to mere chance. Plots, therefore, constructed on these principles are necessarily the best. (39) . . . Plots are either Simple or Complex, for the actions in real life, of which the plots are an imitation, obviously show a similar distinction. An action which is one and continuous . . . I call Simple when the change of fortune takes place without Reversal of the Situation and without Recognition. A complex action is one in which the change is accompanied by such a Reversal, or by a Recognition, or by both. These last should arise from the internal structure of the plot, so that what follows should be the necessary or probable result of the preceding action. It makes all the difference whether any given event is a case of ["therefore" or of "and then"]. (39-41) . . . A perfect tragedy should . . . be arranged not on the simple but the complex plan. It should, moreover, *imitate actions which excite pity and fear* [be an imitation of fearful and pitiable happenings: EP 364], this being the distinctive mark of tragic imitation. It follows plainly, in the first place, that the change of fortune presented must not be the spectacle of a virtuous man brought from prosperity to adversity: for this moves neither pity nor fear; it merely shocks us. Nor again, that of a bad man passing from adversity to prosperity: for nothing can be more alien to the spirit of Tragedy; it possesses no single tragic quality; it neither satisfies *the moral sense* [ordinary sympathy: EP 364] nor calls forth pity or fear. Nor, again, should the downfall of the utter villain be exhibited. A plot of this kind would, doubtless, *satisfy the moral sense* [arouse sympathy: EP 365], but it would inspire neither pity nor fear. . . . There remains, then, the character between these two extremes. . . . A well-constructed plot should, therefore, be single in its issue, rather than double as some maintain. The change of fortune should not be from bad to good, but, reversely, from good to bad. It should come about as the result not of vice, but of some great error or frailty in a character either such as we have described, or better rather than worse. . . . A tragedy, then, to be perfect according to the rules of art should be of this construction. Hence they are in error who censure Euripides just because he follows this principle in his plays, many of which end unhappily. It is, as we have said, the right ending. The best proof is that on the stage and in dramatic competition, such plays, if well worked out, are the most tragic in effect; and Euripides, faulty though he may be in the general management of his subject, yet is felt to be the most tragic of the poets. In the second rank comes the kind of tragedy which some place first. Like the Odyssey, it has a double thread of plot, and also an opposite catastrophe for the good and for the bad. It is accounted the best because of the weakness of the spectators; for the poet is guided in what he writes by the wishes of his audience. The pleasure, however, thence derived is not the true tragic pleasure. It is proper rather to Comedy, where those who, in the piece, are the deadliest enemies—like Orestes and Aegisthus—quit the stage as friends at the close, and no one slays or is slain. (45-49) . . . Fear and Pity may be aroused *by spectacular means* [from the costuming: EP 407]; but they may also result from the inner structure of the piece, which is the better way, and indicates a superior poet. For the plot ought to be so constructed that, even without the aid of the eye, he who hears the tale told will thrill with horror and melt to pity at what takes place. This is the impression we should receive from hearing the story of Oedipus. But to produce this effect by the *mere spectacle* [costume: EP 407] is a less artistic method, and dependent on *extraneous aids* [the services of a choragus: EP 407]. Those who employ spectacular means to create a sense not of the terrible but only of the monstrous, are strangers to the purpose of Tragedy; for we must not demand of Tragedy any and every kind of pleasure, but only that which is proper to it. And since the pleasure which the poet should afford is that which comes from pity and fear through imitation, it is evident that this quality must be impressed upon the incidents. (49) . . . This event should follow that by necessary or probable sequence. It is therefore evident that the unravelling of the plot, no less than the complication, must arise out of the plot itself, it must not be brought about by the *Deus ex Machina*—as in the Medea, or in the Return of the Greeks in the Iliad. The *Deus ex Machina* should be employed only for events external to the drama,—for antecedent or subsequent events, which lie beyond the range of human knowledge, and which require to be reported or foretold; for to the gods we ascribe the power of seeing all things. Within the action there must be nothing irrational. If the irrational cannot be excluded, it should be outside the scope of the tragedy. Such is the irrational element in the Oedipus of Sophocles. (55-57) . . . Every tragedy falls into two parts,—Complication and Unravelling or Dénouement. *Incidents extraneous to the action are frequently combined with a portion of the action proper, to form the Complication* [the events outside, and in many cases some of those inside, are the tying: EP 517]; the rest is the Unravelling. By the Complication I mean all that extends from the beginning of the action to the *part which marks the turning point* [scene which is the last before the shift: EP 517] to good or bad fortune. The Unravelling is that which extends from the change to the end. . . . These are four kinds of Tragedy, the Complex, depending entirely on Reversal of the Situation and Recognition; the *Pathetic* [fatal: EP 523] (where the motive is passion), the *Ethical* [moral: EP 523] (where the motives are ethical). . . . The fourth kind is the *Simple* [episodic: EP 517]. . . . In speaking of a tragedy as the same or different, the best test to take is the plot. Identity exists where the Complication and Unravelling are the same. Many poets tie the knot well but unravel it ill. *Both* arts, however, should always be mastered. Again, the poet should remember what has been often said, and not make an Epic *structure* [mass: EP 540] into a Tragedy—by an Epic structure I mean one with a multiplicity of *plots* [stories: EP 540]—as if, for instance, you were to make a tragedy out of the entire story of the Iliad. In the Epic poem, owing to its length, each part assumes its proper magnitude. In the drama the result is far from answering to the poet's expectation. The proof is that the poets who have dramatised the whole story of the Fall of Troy, instead of selecting portions, like Euripides; or who have taken the whole tale of Niobe, and not a part of her story, like Aeschylus, either fail utterly or meet with poor success on the stage. (65-67)

See also Aristotle under ACTION (AP 25-29, 33-35, 37-39, 45), CHARACTER (AP 27-29, 56, 69), FORM (AP 31-33), PITY (AP 49-53), RECOGNITION (AP 41-43, 57-61), REVERSAL (AP 41-43, 67-69), SUBJECT (AP 37, 53, 63-65), TRAGEDY (AP 23-25).

1561   Scaliger   SP

Aristotle laughs at those who think that the *Iliad* or the *Odyssey* is a complete organism with one plot, for he says that one may draw several plots from either one, because there are many parts and many episodes. (36)

See also Scaliger under ACTION (SP 62), THREE UNITIES (SP 60).

1570   Castelvetro   CP

The plot is the constitution of the things, i.e., the invention of the things or the subject: which invention or subject comprises the invention of the visible things and the invention of the invisible things. (101)

See also Castelvetro under ACTION (CP 89), CHARACTER (CP 102-103), FUNCTIONALISM (CP 68), WONDER (CP 88).

1609   de Vega. See under SURPRISE (VAWP 34).

1641   Jonson. See under ACTION (JD 105).

1657   d'Aubignac   AAS

The Dramatick Poet ought to shew all things in a state of decency, probability, and pleasingness. 'Tis true, that if Story is capable of all the Ornaments of Dramatick Poetry, the Poet ought to preserve all the true Events; but if not, he is well grounded to make any part of it yield to the Rules of his Art, and to the Design he has to please. (2: 66)

See also d'Aubignac under IMITATION (AAS 1: 35-36), SUBJECT (AAS 2: 64, 68-69).

1660   Corneille   **CSP**

The spectator loves to be absorbed in the action on the stage before him and not to be obliged, in order to understand what he sees, to think about what he has previously seen, and to cast back his memory on the first acts while the last are before his eyes. This is the inconvenience of complicated plays. . . . It is not found in plays with simple plots; but as the former doubtless need more wit to conceive them and more art to follow them through, the latter . . . require more force in the verse, the arguments and feelings to sustain them. (197-98)

   See also Corneille under SURPRISE (CSP 109).

1668   Dryden. *See* under VARIETY (DW 1, 2: 95-96).

1679   Dryden   **DW**

[A] necessary rule is, to put nothing into the discourse, which may hinder your moving of the passions. Too many accidents . . . incumber the poet as much as the arms of Saul did David; for the variety of passions which they produce are ever crossing and justling each other out of the way. He who treats of joy and grief together, is in a fair way of causing neither of those effects. (1, 2: 288)

1711   Addison   **AW**

The same objections which can be made to tragi-comedy, may in some measure be applied to all tragedies that have a double plot in them; . . . for though the grief of the audience, in such performances, be not changed into another passion, as in tragi-comedies; it is diverted upon another object, which weakens their concern for the principal action, and breaks the tide of sorrow, by throwing it into different channels. This inconvenience, however, may, in a great measure be cured, if not wholly removed, by the skillfull choice of an underplot, which may bear such a near relation to the principal design as to contribute towards the completion of it, and be concluded by the same catastrophe. (1: 72)

1711   Dryden. *See* under DRAMA (DW 1, 2: 302-303).

1712   Addison. *See* under ACTION (AW 1: 427), SURPRISE (AW 2: 312).

1713   Addison. *See* under SYMBOL (AW 3: 149).

1725   Voltaire. Compare with AFFECT (VE 277).

1758   Diderot   **DDP**

The plot is what holds a complicated play together; the speeches and the dialogue are what make people listen to and read a simple play. (292)
   . . . If you have few incidents, you will have few characters. Never introduce a superfluous character; and have the connecting links between your scenes

invisible. Above all, never introduce a thread that leads nowhere; if you interest me in a situation which is not developed you will scatter my attention. . . . The more complicated [the plot] is, the less true to life. . . . A plot is an interesting story, constructed according to the rules of dramatic form, which is in part the invention of the tragic poet and altogether that of the comic poet. (296)

> See also Diderot under COMPLICATION (DDP 291); compare with CHARACTER (DDP 290).

1767-1769   Lessing. *See* under SURPRISE (LSPW 377-78).

1797   Goethe   GED

Of motives I distinguish five different varieties [in the epic and drama]: 1. *Progressive*, which further the action, and are for the most part employed in drama. 2. *Retrogressive*, which draw the action away from its goal; these are almost exclusively confined to epic poetry. 3. *Retardative*, which delay the course or lengthen the way; these are used in both kinds of poetry [to] advantage. 4. *Retrospective*, by means of which events that have happened previously to the epoch of the poem are introduced into it. 5. *Anticipatory*, which anticipate that which will happen after the epoch of the poem. . . . (338)

1808   Schlegel   SCL

We [cannot] allow the common division into *Plays of Character and Plays of Intrigue* to pass. . . . A good comedy ought always to be both, otherwise it will be deficient either in body or animation. . . The development of the comic characters requires situations to place them in strong contrast, and these again can result from nothing but that crossing of purposes and events, which . . . constitute intrigue in the dramatic sense. Every one knows the meaning of intriguing in common life; namely, the leading of others by cunning and dissimulation, to further, without their knowledge and against their will, our own hidden designs. In the drama both these significations coincide, for the cunning of the one becomes a cross-purpose for the other. (181-82)

> See also Schlegel under ACTION (SCL 239-42), GENRE DEFINTION (SCL 176-79).

1815   Coleridge. *See* under UNITY (CBL 2: 11).

1818   Coleridge. *See* under SYMBOL (CMC 30).

c.1820   Hegel   HFA

Three . . . acts . . . will adapt itself most readily to intelligible theory. Of these the *first* discloses the appearance of the collision, which is thereupon emphasized in the *second* with all the animation of conflicting interests as the positive difference of such discord and its progression, until, *finally,* driven as it were upon the very apex of its contradiction, it is necessarily resolved. . . . In modern poetry the Spaniards mainly follow such a division into three acts. The English, French and Germans, on the contrary, for the most part divide the entire play into *five* acts. . . . (4: 264)

See also Hegel under ACTION (HFA 4: 253-54, 259-61), CONFLICT (HFA 4: 311-12), DRAMA (HFA 4: 261-62), FORM (HFA 4: 262-63).

1826 Goethe. *See* under SYMBOL (GCE July 26).

c.1900 Strindberg   **SEP**

An effective play should contain or make use of: Hints and intimations. A secret made known to the audience either at the beginning or toward the end. If the spectator, but not the actors, knows the secret, the spectator enjoys their game of blindman's bluff. If the spectator is not in on the secret, his curiosity is aroused and his attention held. An outburst of emotion, rage, indignation; A reversal, well-prepared; A discovery; A punishment (nemesis), a humiliation; A careful resolution, either with or without a reconciliation; A *quiproguo* [a misunderstanding: trans. note]; A parallelism; A reversal (*revirement*), an upset, a well-prepared surprise. (574-75)

1909 Shaw. *See* under GENRE DEFINITION (STPB xxii-xxiii).

c.1930 Stanislavski. *See* under CONFLICT (SCR 80).

1935 Brecht. *See* under IDENTIFICATION (BBT 87).

1937 Shaw   **SGCR**

Plot has always been the curse of serious drama, and indeed of serious literature of any kind. It is so out-of-place there that Shakespear never could invent one. Unfortunately, instead of taking Nature's hint and discarding plots, he borrowed them all over the place and got into trouble through having to unravel them in the last act. (135-36)

1948 Brecht   **BBBG**

Our theaters are no longer able or willing to tell stories clearly, not even the not-so-ancient stories of the great Shakespeare. That is they are not able or willing to make the "knotting-together" of the events credible. According to Aristotle the plot is the soul of the drama. We think so too. (17) . . . Everything depends on the plot. It is the heart of the theatrical presentation. From what happens *between* people comes whatever may be discussed, criticized, changed. . . . The great undertaking of theater is plot, the total complex of all the gestural occurrences, comprising the communications and impulses which should now go to the making of the audience's pleasure. (35) . . . Since the audience is not invited to throw itself into the plot as into a river to flounder vaguely about hither and yon, the individual events must be so knotted together that the knots are striking. The events should not follow each other without being noticed. . . . The parts of the plot must thus be carefully related to each other, each part having its own structure, a play within a play. This end is best accomplished by means of titles . . . [which] should contain the social ''points.'' (36)

See also Brecht under GEST (BBBG 35).

c.1956   Brecht   **BBT**

Analysis of the Play [:] Find out what socially valuable insights and impulses the play offers. Boil the story down to half a sheet of paper. Then divide it into separate episodes, establishing the nodal points, i.e., the important events that carry the story a stage further. Then examine the relationship of the episodes, their construction. Think of ways and means to make the story easily narrated and to bring out its social significance. (240-41)

POETIC JUSTICE

The closure of drama is identified as demonstrating poetic justice when a moral lesson is illustrated. This concept was a doctrine of neoclassical dramatic theory, primarily, but it continues to be a tenet of popular drama.

4th cent. B.C.   Aristotle   **AP**

[The plot should] *imitate actions which excite pity and fear* [be an imitation of fearful and pitiable happenings: EP 364], this being the distinctive mark of tragic imitation. It follows plainly . . . that the change in fortune presented must not be the spectacle of a virtuous man brought from prosperity to adversity: for this moves neither pity nor fear; it *merely* [morally: EP 364] shocks us. Nor again, that of a bad man passing from adversity to prosperity: for nothing can be more alien to Tragedy; it possesses no single tragic quality; it neither satisfies *the moral sense* [ordinary sympathy: EP 364] nor calls forth pity or fear. Nor, again, should the downfall of the utter villain be exhibited. A plot of this kind would, doubtless, *satisfy the moral sense* [arouse sympathy: EP 365], but it would inspire neither pity nor fear. . . . [A less perfect kind of tragedy] has a double thread of plot, and also an opposite catastrophe for the good and for the bad. It is accounted the best because of the weakness of the spectators; for the poet is guided . . . by the wishes of his audience. The pleasure, however, thence derived is not the true tragic pleasure. (48-49)

 Compare with Aristotle under PLOT (AP 45-49).

1561   Scaliger. *See* under ACTION (SP 62), IMITATION (SP 59).

c.1583   Sidney. *See* under MORALITY (SDP 21).

1603   Jonson   **JBW**

[The death of Sejanus] do we advance as a mark of Terror to all *Traitors*, & *Treasons*; to show how just the *Heavens* are in pouring and thundering down a weighty vengeance on their unnatural intents, even to the worst *Princes*. . . .
                                         The Argument, *Sejanus*

1605   Jonson   **JBW**

[The current abuses of the stage] hath not only 'rapp'd me to present indignation, but made me studius, heretofore . . . which may most appear in this my latest work . . . wherein I have labour'd [to show other playwrights], for their instruction, and amendment, to reduce, not only the ancient forms, but manners of the *scene*, the easiness, the propriety, the innocence, and last the doctrine, which is the principle end of *poesy*, to inform men, in the best reason of living. And though my *catastrophe* may, in the strict rigour of *comic* law, meet with censure, as turning back to my promise; I desire the learned, and charitable critic to have so much faith in me, to think it was done of industry. . . . My special aim being to put the snaffle in their mouths, that cry out, we never punish vice in our *enterludes*, &c. I took the more liberty; though not without some lines of example, drawn even in the ancients themselves, the goings out of whose *comedies* are not always joyful, but oft-times, the bawds, the servants, the rivals, yes, and the masters are muleted: and fitly, it being the office of a *comic Poet*, to imitate justice, and instinct to life, as well as purity of language, to stir up gentle affections.

Dedication, Volpone

1657   d'Aubignac   AAS

One of the Chiefest, and indeed the most indispensible Rule of Drammatick Poems, is, that in them Virtues always ought to be rewarded, or at least commended, in spight of all the Injuries of Fortune; and that likewise Vices be always punished, or at least detested with Horrour, though they triumph upon the Stage for that time. The Stage being thus regulated, what can Philosophy teach that won't become much more sensibly touching by Representation; 'tis there that the meanest Capacities may visibly see, that favours of Fortune are not real Enjoyments, when they see the ruin of the Royal Family of *Priamus*; all that they hear from the Mouth of *Hecuba* seems very probable, having before their Eyes the Sad Example of her Calamities; 'tis there that they are convinced that Heaven punishes the horrid Crimes of the Guilty with the remorse of them. (1: 5-6)

1660   Corneille   CFD

The ancients were often satisfied with . . . description [of virtue and vice] without troubling to have good actions rewarded and bad ones punished. . . . It is this interest which one has in the virtuous which forces one to come to this other manner of ending the dramatic poem, by the punishment of wicked actions and the reward of good ones which is not an art precept but a custom which we have adopted, which one can abandon only at one's own risk. It has existed since the time of Aristotle, and it may be that it did not please this philosopher to excess, since he says,—''It has had a vogue only by the imbecility of the judgment of the spectators, and those who practice it are gratifying the tastes of the populace.'' . . . Truly it is certain that we could not see an honest man in our theatre without wishing him prosperity and regretting his misfortune. That is why when he (the honest man) remains overcome by them, we leave with sorrow and carry away a kind of indignation against the author and the actor, but when the plot fills our expectations and virtue is rewarded, we leave with complete joy, and carry with us entire satisfaction, both of the work and those who represent it. The success of virtue against misfortunes and perils excites us to embrace it. . . . (141)

See also Corneille under INSTRUCTION (CFD 140-41).

1671 Dryden DW

It is charged upon me, that I made debauched persons (such as they say my Astrologer and Gamester are) my protagonists, or the Chief persons of the drama, and that I make them happy in the conclusion of my play; against the law of comedy, which is to reward virtue, and punish vice. I answer first, that I know no such law to have been constantly observed in comedy, either by the ancient or modern poets. . . . But now it will be objected, that I patronize vice by the authority of former poets, and extenuate my own faults by recrimination. I answer, that as I defend myself by their example, so that example I defend by reason, and by the end of all dramatick poesy. In the first place, therefore, give me leave to shew you their mistake, who have accused me. They have not distinguished as they ought, betwixt the rules of tragedy and comedy. In tragedy, where the actions and persons are great, and the crimes horrid, the laws of justice are more strictly to be observed; and examples of punishment to be made, to deter mankind from the pursuit of vice. Faults of this kind have been rare amongst the ancient poets. . . . Thus tragedy fulfils one great part of its institution; which is by example to instruct. But in comedy it is not so; for the chief end of it is divertisement and delight. . . . [Instruction] can be but its secondary end; for the business of the poet is to make you laugh: when he writes humour, he makes folly ridiculous; when wit, he moves you, if not always to laughter, yet to a pleasure that is more noble. . . . This being then established,—that the first end of comedy is delight, and instruction only the second, it may reasonbly be inferred, that comedy is not so much obliged to the punishment of the faults which it represents, as tragedy. For the persons in comedy are of a lower quality, the action is little, and the faults and vices are but sallies of youth, and the frailties of human nature, and not premeditated crimes: such to which all men are obnoxious, not such as are attempted only by few, and those abandoned to all sense of virtue; such as move pity and commiseration, not detestation and horrour; such, in short, as may be forgiven, not such as must of necessity be punished. (1, 2: 198-201)

1677 Racine. See under MORALITY (RP 157).

1679 Dryden. See under PITY (DW 1, 2: 270).

1711 Addison AW

The English writers of tragedy are possessed with a notion, that when they represent a virtuous or innocent person in distress, they ought not leave him till they have delivered him out of his troubles, or made him triumph over his enemies. This error they have been led into by a ridiculous doctrine in modern criticism, that they are obliged to an equal distribution of rewards and punishments, and an impartial execution of poetic justice. Who were the first that established this rule I know not; but I am sure it has no foundation in nature, in reason, or in the practice of the ancients. We find that good and evil happen alike to all men on this side of the grave; and as the principal design of tragedy is to raise commiseration and terror in the minds of the audience, we shall defeat this great end, if we always make virtue and innocence happy and successful. Whatever crosses and disappointments a good man suffers in the body of tragedy, they will make but a small impression on our minds, when we know that in the last act he is to arrive at the end of his wishes and desires. When we see him engaged in the depths of his afflictions, we are apt to comfort ourselves, because we are sure he will find his way out of them; and that his grief, how great soever it may be at present, will soon terminate in gladness. For this reason the ancient writers of tragedy treated men in their plays, as they are dealt with in the world, by making virtue sometimes happy and sometimes miserable, as they found it in the fable which they made choice of, or as it might affect their audience in the most agreeable manner. . . . I do not therefore dispute against [using poetic justice for] writing tragedies, but against the criticism that would establish this as the only method; and by that means would very much cramp the English tragedy, and perhaps give a wrong bent to the genius of our writers. (1: 71-72)

1711   Dryden. *See* under MORALITY (DW 1, 2: 309-10).

1731   Voltaire. *See* under SUBJECT (VE 284).

c.1780   Johnson. Compare with IMITATION (JL 2: 135).

1808   Schlegel   SCL

I cannot help considering [poetical justice] as a made-up example of a doctrine false in itself, and one, moreover, which by no means tends to the excitation of truly moral feelings. . . (254)
   See also Schlegel under AFFECT (SCL 67-69), CLOSURE (SCL 254).

1895   Shaw. *See* under GENRE DEFINITION (SDC 48-49).

POETRY OF THE THEATER

Of growing significance is a conception of drama, or of theatrical art, as a metalinguistic art form. The statements collected here suggest that the expressive qualities and metaphorical capacities of theatrical elements are equal or superior to language. See also *EPIC THEATER, GEST, and OBJECTIVE CORRELATIVE.*

1808   Schlegel   SCL

Visible representation is essential to the very form of drama; a dramatic work may always be regarded from a double point of view,—how far it is *poetical*, and how far it is theatrical. The two are by no means inseparable. Let not, however, the expression *poetical* be misunderstood: I am not now speaking of the versification and the ornaments of language; these, when not animated by some higher excellence, are the least effective on the stage; but I speak of the poetry of the spirit and design of a piece; and this may exist in as high a degree when the drama is written in prose as in verse. What . . . makes a drama poetical . . . makes other works so. It must . . . be a connected whole, complete and satisfactory within itself. But this is merely the negative definition of a work of art, by which it is distinguished from the phenomena of nature, which run into each other, and do not possess in themselves a complete and independent existence. To be poetical it is necessary that a composition should be a mirror of ideas, that is, thoughts and feelings which in their character are necessary and eternally true, and soar above this earthly life. . . . Without [these ideas] a drama becomes altogether prosaic and empirical . . . patched together . . . out of the observations . . . from literal reality. (36-37)

c.1820   Hegel   HFA

The Theatrical Art which is more Independent of Poetical Composition . . . liberates itself from the exclusive precedency of articulate poetry, and accepts as an independent end what was previously, to a more or less extent, a mere accompaniment or instrument, and elaborates the same on its own account. To carry out this emancipation, music and dance are quite as much essential features of the dramatic development as the art of the actor. . . . What we may define here as the position of the art of acting reversed consists in this, that the entire creation of the poet now tends to be purely an appendage or frame to and for the natural endowment, technical ability, and art of the actor. . . . The soul function of poetical composition is, in this view, to give the artist an opportunity to display and unfold in all its brilliance his emotional powers and art, to let us see the final outcome of his particular individuality. Among the Italians, the *commedia dell' arte* belongs to this type. . . . Among ourselves, the dramatic pieces of Iffland and Kotzebue, and many others besides, . . . unimportant or even bad compositions, nevertheless offer such an opportunity for the creative powers of the actor, who is compelled to initiate and shape something from such generally sketchy and artificial productions, which on account of a vital and independent performance of this kind receive a unique interest exclusively united to one and no other artist. It is here, more especially, that we find our much belauded realistic effects are displayed, a style carried to such lengths that a mere rumble and whisper of articulate speech, quite impossible to follow, will pass as an admirable performance. In protest to such a style, Goethe translated Voltaire . . . in order to compel [his] actors to drop this vulgar naturalism, and accustom themselves to a more noble exposition. And this is invariably the case with the French, who, even in all the animation of the farce, always keep the audience in view, and throughout address themselves to it. As a matter of fact, mere realism and imitation of our everyday expression is as little exhaustive of the real problem as the mere intelligibility and clever use made of charcterization. If an actor seeks to produce a really artistic effect in such cases, he will have to extend his powers to a genial virtuosity. . . . (4: 289-91)

1871   Nietzsche. *See* under LANGUAGE (NBT 55), TRAGEDY (NBT 127, 159-60).

1875   Nietzsche   NTS

In Wagner . . . the world of sounds seeks to manifest itself as a phenomenon for the sight; it seeks, as it were, to incarnate itself. His art always leads him into two distinct directions, from the world of the play of sound to the mysterious and yet related world of visible things and *vice versa*. He is continually forced—and the observer with him—to re-translate the visible into spiritual and primeval life, and likewise to perceive the most hidden interstices of the soul as something concrete and to lend it a visible body. This constitutes the nature of the *dithyrambic dramatist*, if the meaning given the term includes also the actor, the poet, and the musician. . . . Owing to his despair at having to appeal to people who were either only semi-musical or not musical at all, [he] violently opened a road for himself to the other arts in order to acquire the capacity for diversely communicating himself to others, by which he compelled the masses to understand him. . . . The real, emancipated artist cannot help himself, he must think in the spirit of all the arts at once, as the mediator and intercessor between apparently separated spheres, the one who reinstalls the unity and wholeness of the artistic faculty, which cannot be divined or reasoned out, but can only be revealed by deeds themselves. But he in whose presence this deed is done will be overcome by its gruesome and seductive charm. . . . Carried away from himself, he seems to be suspended in a mysterious fiery element; he ceases to understand himself, the standard of everything has fallen from his hands; everything stereotyped and fixed begins to totter; every object seems to acquire a strange colour and to tell its tale by means of new symbols. . . . (149-50) . . . Wagner, who was the first to detect the essential feeling in spoken drama, presents every dramatic action threefold: in a word, in a gesture, and in a sound. For, as a matter of fact, music succeeds in conveying the deepest emotions of the dramatic performers direct to the spectators, and while these see the evidence of the actor's states of soul in their bearing and movements, a third though more feeble confirmation of these states, translated into conscious will, quickly follows in the form of the spoken word. All these effects fulfill their purpose simultaneously, without disturbing one another in the least, and urge the spectator to a completely new understanding and sympathy, just as if his senses had suddenly grown more spiritual and his spirit more sensual, and as if everything which seeks an outlet in him and which makes him thirst for knowledge, were free and joyful in exultant perception. (177) . . . Because every essential factor in a Wagnerian drama is conveyed to the spectator with the utmost clearness, illumined and permeated throughout by music . . . their author can dispense with the expedients usually employed by the writer of the spoken play in order to lend light and warmth to the action. The whole of the dramatist's stock in trade could be more simple, and the architect's sense of rhythm could once more dare to manifest itself in the general proportions of the edifice; for there was no more need of the deliberate confusion and involved variety of styles, whereby the ordinary playwright strove in the interests of this work to produce that feeling of wonder and thrilling suspense which he ultimately enhanced to one of delighted amazement. The impression of ideal distance and height was no more to be induced by means of tricks and artifices. Language withdrew itself from the length and breadth of rhetoric into the strong confines of the speech of the feelings, and although the actor spoke much less . . . his innermost sentiments, which . . . had hitherto [been] ignored for fear of beng undramatic, [were] now able to drive the spectators to passionate sympathy, while the accompanying language of gestures could be restricted to the most delicate modulations. (177-78)

1898 Shaw. *See* under SPECTACLE (SMCE 220).

1928 Eliot   ESE

I say . . . that drama springs from religious liturgy, and that it cannot afford to depart far from religious liturgy. . . . When drama has ranged as far as it has in our own day, is not the only solution to return to religious liturgy? And the only dramatic satisfaction that I find now is in a High Mass well peformed. Have you not there everything necessary? And indeed, if you consider the ritual of the Church during the cycle of the year, you have the complete drama represented. The Mass is a small drama, having all the unities; but in the Church year you have represented the full drama of creation. (35)

1931-1936   Artaud   AT

Every real effigy has a shadow which is its double; and art must falter and fail from the moment the sculptor believes he has liberated the kind of shadow whose very existence will destroy his repose. Like all magic cultures expressed by appropriate hieroglyphs, the true theatre has its shadows too, and, of all languages and all arts, the theatre is the only one left whose shadows have shattered their limitations. The theatre, which is in *no thing*, but makes use of everything—gesture, sounds, words, screams, light, darkness—rediscovers itself at precisely the point where the mind requires a language to express its manifestations. And the fixation of the theatre in one language—written words, music, lights, noises—betokens its imminent ruin, the choice of any one language betraying a taste for the special effects of that language; and the dessication of the language accompanies its limitation. (12) . . . I say that this concrete language, intended for the senses and independent of speech, has first to satisfy the senses, that there is a poetry of the senses as there is a poetry of language, and that this concrete physical language to which I refer is truly theatrical only to the degree that the thoughts it expresses are beyond the reach of the spoken language. (37) . . . This very difficult and complex poetry [of concrete theatrical language] assumes many aspects: especially the aspects of all the means of expression utilizable on the stage, such as music, dance, plastic art, pantomime, mimicry, gesticulation, intonation, architecture, lighting, and scenery. Each of these means has its own intrinsic poetry, and a kind of ironic poetry as well, resulting from the way it combines with the other means of expression; and the consequences of these combinations, of their reactions and their reciprocal destructions, are easy to perceive. . . . [Poetry] can be fully effective only if it is concrete, i.e., only if it produces something objectively from the fact of its *active* presence on the stage;—only if a sound, as in the Balinese theatre, has its equivalent in a gesture and, instead of serving as a decoration, an accompaniment of a thought, instead causes its movement, directs it, destroys it, or changes it completely, etc. (39) . . . Beneath the poetry of the texts, there is the actual poetry, without form and without text. And just as the efficacity of masks in the magic practices of certain tribes is exhausted— and these masks are no longer good for anything except museums—so the poetic efficacity of a text is exhausted; yet the poetry and the efficacity of the theater are exhausted least quickly of all, since they permit the *action* of what is gesticulated and pronounced, and which is never made the same way twice. (78) . . . *Every spectacle will contain a physical and objective element, perceptible to all. Cries, groans, apparitions, surprises, theatricalities of all kinds,*

magic beauty of costumes taken from certain ritual models; resplendent light-
ing, incantational beauty of voices, the charms of harmony, rare notes of
music, colors of objects, physical rhythm of movements whose crescendo and
decrescendo will accord exactly with the pulsation of movements familiar to
everyone, concrete appearances of new and surprising objects, masks, effigies
yards high, sudden changes of light, the physical action of light which arouses
sensations of heat and cold, etc. (93)...The typical language of the theater
will be constituted around the *mise en scène* considered not simply as the
degree of refraction of a text upon the stage, but as the point of departure for all
theatrical creation. And it is in the use and handling of this language that the old
duality between author and director will be dissolved, replaced by a sort of
unique Creator upon whom will devolve the double responsibility of the
spectacle and the plot. (93-94)...For besides creating a performance with
palpable material means, the pure *mise en scène* contains, in gestures, facial
expressions and mobile attitudes, through a concrete use of music, everything
that speech contains and has speech at its disposal as well. Rhythmic repeti-
tions of syllables and particular modulations of the voice, swathing the precise
sense of words, arouse swarms of images in the brain, producing a more or less
hallucinatory state and impelling the sensibility and mind alike to a kind of
organic alteration which helps to strip from the written poetry the gratuitousness that commonly characterizes it. And it is around this gratuitousness that
the whole problem of theater is centered. (120-21)... Besides this need for the
theater to steep itself in the springs of an eternally passionate and sensuous
poetry available to even the most backward and inattentive portions of the
public, a poetry realized by a return to the primitive Myths, we shall require of
the *mise en scène* and not of the text the task of materializing these old conflicts
and above all of giving them *immediacy*; i.e., these themes will be borne
directly into the theater and materialized in movements, expressions, and
gestures before trickling away in words. Thus we shall renounce the theatrical
superstition of the text and the dictatorship of the writer. (123-24)

   See also Artaud under AESTHETIC (AT 96, 97), DRAMA (AT 31, 70,
116), ILLUSION (AT 25, 27, 86, 92), LANGUAGE (AT 37), METAPHOR
(AT 27-28, 71), SPECTACLE (AT 41, 68, 69), STYLE (AT 53), THOUGHT
(AT 39-40, 41, 46).

1938   Stanislavski. *See* under THOUGHT (SBC 258).

PROBABILITY

The statements presented here propose theoretical principles for establishing credibility in drama (compare with ILLUSION). In Aristotle's philosophical system probability is an inductive inference and necessity is a deductive inference.

4th cent. B.C.   Aristotle   AP

It is not the function of the poet to relate what has happened, but what may happen—what is possible according to the law of probability or necessity. The poet and historian differ not by writing in verse or in prose.... The true difference is that one relates what has happened, the other what may happen. Poetry, therefore, is more philosophical and a higher thing than history: for poetry tends to express the universal, history the particular. By the universal I mean how a person of a certain type will on occasion speak or act, according to the law of probability or necessity; and it is this universality at which poetry aims *in the names it attaches to personages* [tacking on names afterwards: EP 302]. The particular is—for example—what Alcibiades did or suffered. In Comedy this is already apparent: for here the poet first constructs the plot on the lines of probability, and then inserts characteristic names;—unlike the lampooners who write about particular individuals. But tragedians still keep to real names, the reason being that what is possible is credible: what has not happened we do not at once feel sure to be possible; but what has happened is manifestly possible: otherwise it would not have happened. Still there are even some tragedies in which there are only one or two well-known names, the rest being fictitious. In others, none are well known,—as in Agathon's Antheus, where incidents and names alike are fictitious, and yet they give none the less pleasure. (35-37)... The poet should prefer *probable impossibilities* [impossibilities that are (made) plausible: EP 623] to *improbable possibilities* [possibilities that are (left) implausible: EP 623]. The tragic plot must not be composed of irrational *parts* [incidents: EP 623]. Everything irrational should, if possible, be excluded; or, at all events, it should lie outside the action of the play (as, in the Oedipus, the hero's ignorance as to the manner of Lauis' death).... The plea that otherwise the plot would have been ruined, is ridiculous; such a plot should not in the first instance have been constructed. But once the irrational has been introduced and an air of likelihood imparted to it, we must accept it in spite of the absurdity. (95-97)... In general, the impossible must be justified by reference to artistic requirements, or to the higher reality, or to received opinion. With respect to the requirements of art, a probable impossibility is to be preferred to a thing improbable and yet possible. Again, it may be impossible that there should be men such as Zeuxis painted. "Yes," we say, "but the impossible is the higher thing; for the ideal type must surpass the reality." To justify the irrational, we appeal to what is commonly said to be. . . . The element of the irrational, and, similarly, depravity of character, are justly censured when there is no inner necessity for introducing them. Such is the irrational element in the introduction of Aegeus by Euripides and the badness of Menelaus in the Orestes. (105-107)

See also Aristotle under IMITATION (AP 97-101), REVERSAL (AP 41-43, 67-69), SUBJECT (AP 37), UNIVERSALITY (AP 35).

1570   Castelvetro   CP

History, recording things happened, has not need to regard verisimilitude or necessity, but only truth of fact; poetry, describing things possible to happen, regards only verisimilitude or necessity, to establish the possibility, since it cannot regard truth of fact. (41) . . . Incredible things cannot arouse the pleasure the marvelous excites. (79)

See also Castelvetro under ACTION (CP 113), COMEDY (CP 136).

1609   de Vega. See under IMITATION (VAWP 34).

1657   d'Aubignac   AAS

When [the Poet] considers in his Play the true Story of it, or that which is suppos'd to be so, he must particularly have a care to observe the Rules of probability in every thing, and to make all the Intrigues, Actions, Words, as if they had in reality come to pass; he must give fit thoughts and designs, according to the persons that are employed, he must write the Times with Places, and the Beginning with the Consequences; and in a word, he follows the nature of things so, as not to contradict neither the State, nor the Order, nor the Effects, nor the Property of them; and indeed has no other Guide but Probability and Decency, and rejects all that has not that Character upon it. (1: 38) . . . [Probability and Decency] is the bottom and ground work of all Dramatick Poems; many talk of it, but few understand it; but this is the general touchstone, by which all that comes to pass in a Play is to be tryed and examin'd, and it is the very Essence of the Poem, without which nothing rational can be done or said upon the Stage. (2: 74) . . . That which is simply possible is left a Subject for Plays, for many things may come to pass by the recounter of Natural Causes (or the adventures of humane Life) which yet would be ridiculous, and almost incredible, to be represented. 'Tis possible that a man may dye suddenly, and that happens often; but That Poet would be strangely laugh'd at, who to rid the Stage of a troublesome Rival, should make him dye of an Apoplexy, as of a common Disease; and it would need exceeding ingenious and artful preparations. There is nothing therefore but *Probability*, that can truly found a Dramatick Poem, as well as adorn and finish it; not that True and Possible things are banish'd off the Stage, but they are received upon it, only so far as they are Probable; and therefore all the Circumstances, that want this Character, are to be alter'd so as to attain it, if they hop'd to appear in publick. (2: 75) . . . The least Actions, brought upon a Stage, ought to be probable, or else they are entirely faulty, and should not appear there. There is no Action of Humane Life so perfectly single, as not to be accompanied by many little Circumstances, which do make it up; as are the Time, the Place, the Person, the Dignity, the Designs, the Means, and the Reasons of the Action; and since the Stage ought to be a perfect Image of Action, it ought to represent it entire, and that Probability and Decency be observ'd in all its parts. (2: 76)

See also d'Aubignac under ACTION (AAS 1: 43-44), IMITATION (AAS 1: 35-36), THREE UNITIES (AAS 97-99).

1660   Corneille   CFD

A subject of tragedy must not be merely probable. Aristotle himself cites as an example *The Flower* of Agathon wherein the names of people and things were purely fictitious, as in comedy. The great subjects which appeal to our emotions and in which our inclinations are set in conflict with the laws of duty and humanity, ought always to extend beyond the limits of the probable. Such plays would indeed find no audience capable of believing, unless they were aided by the authority of history, which is empirically persuasive, or by common knowledge, which supplies an audience of those whose attitudes are already formed. It is not "probable" that Medea should kill her children; that Clytemnestra should murder her husband; or Orestes stab his mother, but historical legend states these facts, and the representation of these great crimes excites no incredulity in the minds of the audience. It is neither true nor "probable" that Andromeda, at the mercy of a sea-monster, was rescued . . . by a flying knight . . . but this is a story which has been handed down, and which has been accepted by the ancients; and, since it has been transmitted even to us, no one would think of taking offense when he sees the story represented on the stage. . . . I do not mean to imply that the poet may invent at haphazard: that which truth or common belief takes for granted would be rejected were there no other basis for a play than mere verisimilitude or public opinion. . . . [Fortune] is the mistress of happenings, and the choice she allows us to make among these happenings . . . contains a mystic warning not to take advantage of her, nor to utilize for dramatic purposes any happenings which are not to her liking. (139)

See also Corneille under RULES (CDENA 32).

1668   Dryden. See under DRAMATIZATION (DW 1, 2: 90-93), THREE UNITIES (DW 1, 2: 93-94).

1679   Dryden   **DW**

[The] *probable* [is] that which succeeds or happens oftener than it misses. (1, 2: 269)

   See also Dryden under ACTION (DW 1, 2: 268-69).

1712   Addison   **AW**

Aristotle observes, that the fable of an epic poem should abound in circumstances that are both credible and astonishing; or, as the French critics choose to phrase it, the fable should be filled with the probable and the marvelous. This rule is as fine and just as any in Aristotle's whole Art of Poetry. If the fable is only probable, it differs nothing from a true history; if it is only marvellous, it is no better than a romance. The great secret, therefore, of heroic poetry is to relate such circumstances as may produce in the reader at the same time both belief and astonishment. This is brought to pass in a well-chosen fable, by the account of such things as have really happened, or at least of such things as have happened according to the received opinions of mankind. . . . Besides the hidden meaning of an epic allegory, the plain literal sense ought to appear probable. The story should be such as an ordinary reader may acquiesce in, whatever natural, moral, or political truth may be discovered in it by men of greater penetration. (2: 4)

   See also Addison under SURPRISE (AW 2: 312), WONDER (AW 2: 4).

1751   Johnson. *See* under THREE UNITIES (JW 3: 241).

1758   Diderot. *See* under WONDER (DDP 297).

1765   Johnson. *See* under THREE UNITIES (JS 25).

1767-1769   Lessing   **LSPW**

On the stage . . . everything that has to do with the character of the personages must arise from natural causes. We can only tolerate miracles in the physical world; in the moral everything must retain its natural course, because the theatre is to be the school of the moral world. The motives for every resolve, for every change of opinion or even thoughts, must be carefully balanced against each other so as to be in accordance with the hypothetical character, and must never produce more than they could produce in accordance with strict probability. (236) . . . Now Aristotle has long ago decided how far the tragic poet need regard historical accuracy: not farther than it resembles a well-constructed fable wherewith he can combine his intentions. He does not make use of any event because it really happened, but because it happened in such a manner as he will scarcely be able to invent more fitly for his present purpose. If he finds this fitness in a true case, then the true case is welcome; but to search through history books does not reward his labor. And how many know what has happened? If we only admit the possibility that something can happen from the fact that it has happened, what prevents us from deeming an entirely fictitious fable a really authentic occurrence, of which we have never heard before? What is the first thing that makes a history probable? Is it not its internal probability? And is it not a matter of indifference whether this probability be confirmed by no witnesses or traditions, or by such as have never come within our knowledge? (279) . . . Genius is only busied with events that are rooted in one another, that form a chain of cause and effect. To reduce the latter to the former, to weigh the latter against the former, everywhere to exclude chance, to cause everything that occurs to occur so that it could not have happened otherwise, this is the part of genius when it works in the domains of history and converts the useless treasures of memory into nourishment for the soul. (311)

　　See also Lessing under THREE UNITIES (LSPW 364-66).

1798　Goethe. *See* under ILLUSION (GLE 52-57).

1808　Schlegel　　　　　　　　　　　　　　　　　　　　　　**SCL**

[I admit that the *Play of Intrigue* (see PLOT SCL 1808)] deviates from the natural course of things, [but not] that it is [therefore] improbable. The poet . . . exhibits before us what is unexpected, extraordinary, and singular, even to incredibility; and often he even sets out with great improbability, as, for example, the resemblance between two persons, or a disguise which is not seen through; afterwards, however, all the incidents must have the appearance of truth, and all the circumstances by means of which the affair takes so marvellous a turn, must be satisfactorily explained. As in respect to the events which take place, the poet gives us but a light play of wit, we are the more strict with him respecting the *how* by which they are brought about. (182-83)

　　See also Schlegel under RULES (SCL 259), THREE UNITIES (SCL 236-51); compare with COMEDY (SCL 309-10).

1810　Coleridge　　　　　　　　　　　　　　　　　　　　　　**CLSW**

A sense of improbability . . . will depend on the degree of excitement in which the mind is supposed to be. Many things would be intolerable in the first scene of a play, that would not at all interrupt our enjoyment in the height of the interest. . . . Again on the other hand, many obvious improbabilities will be endured, as belonging to the groundwork of the story rather than to the drama itself, in the first scenes, which would disturb or disentrance us from all illusion in the acme of our excitement. . . . (73)

　　See also Coleridge under ILLUSION (CSLW 73).

1815　Coleridge　　　　　　　　　　　　　　　　　　　　　　**CBL**

A specific *dramatic* probability may be raised by a true poet, if the whole of his work be in harmony: a *dramatic* probability, sufficient for dramatic pleasure, even when the component characters and incidents border on impossibility. The poet does not require us to be awake and believe; he solicits us only to yield ourselves to a dream; and this too with our eyes open, and with our judgment *perdue* behind the curtain, ready to awaken us at the first motion of our will: and meantime, only, not to *dis*believe (2: 189)

c.1820   Hazlitt   HW

Invention is only feigning according to nature, or with a certain proportion between causes and effects. . . . I think invention is chiefly confined to poetry and words or ideas, and has little place in painting or concrete imagery, where the want of truth, or of the actual object, soon spoils the effect and force of the representation. (11: 463-64)

c.1820   Hegel. *See* under THREE UNITIES (HFA 4: 257-59).

1888   Nietzsche   NW

To combat determinism and teleology.—From the fact that something happens regularly, and that its occurrence may be reckoned upon, it does not follow that it happens *necessarily*. If a quantity of force determines and conducts itself in a certain way in every case, it does not prove that is has "no free will." "Mechanical necessity" is not an established fact: it is *we* who first read it into the nature of all phenomena. . . . The concept of "Cause and Effect" is a dangerous one, so long as people believe in something that *causes*, and a something that is caused. (58-59)

Compare with Nietzsche under WILL (NW 138-40).

1891   Shaw   SS

Pure accidents are not dramatic: they are only anecdotic. . . . They have no specifically dramatic interest. There is no drama in being knocked down or run over. . . . As a matter of fact no accident, however sanguinary, can produce a moment of real drama, though a difference of opinion between husband and wife as to living in town or country might be the beginning of an appalling tragedy or a capital comedy. (240)

1896   Shaw. *See* under ILLUSION (SDC 159-60).

1948   Brecht. *See* under IMITATION (BBBG 16), PLOT (BBBG 17, 35, 36).

RATIONALISM

The extracts collected here suggest the primacy of rationality (logic, factuality, argumentation, and so on) as the basis for art or drama.

4th cent. B.C.   Aristotle. *See* under AESTHETIC (APA 16-17), ILLUSION (AA 123), IMITATION (AP 15), LANGUAGE (AP 29), PLEASURE (AP 15), PLOT (AP 55-57), PROBABILITY (AP 95-97, 105-107), STYLE (AP 107).

1561   Scaliger. *See* under THREE UNITIES (SP 60).

1570   Castelvetro. *See* under AFFECT (CP 86), THREE UNITIES (CP 85).

c.1583   Sidney. *See* under THREE UNITIES (SDP 47-48, 49).

1600   Jonson. *See* under NOVELTY (JBW).

1604   Jonson. *See* under CHARACTER (JBW).

1611   Jonson   **JBW**

The commendation of good things may fall within a many, their approbation but in a few; for the most commend out of affection , self-tickling, an easiness, or imitation: but men judge only out of knowledge. This is the trying faculty.

To the Reader in Ordinaire, *Cataline*.

1641   Jonson. *See* under AESTHETIC (JD 59-60), COMEDY (JD 99-101), IMAGINATION (JD 6).

1657   d'Aubignac. *See* under ACTION (AAS 2: 81), PROBABILITY (AAS 2: 74, 76), RULES (AAS 1: 22-26), THREE UNITIES (AAS 2: 97-99, 99-100, 105, 111-13, 116-17).

1668   Dryden. *See* under THOUGHT (DW 1, 2: 170).

1711   Addison. *See* under HUMOR (AW 1: 64-65), THOUGHT (AW 1: 70).

1712   Addison. *See* under THOUGHT (AW 2: 41, 291).

1730 Voltaire. *See* under AESTHETIC (VE 279), THREE UNITIES (VE 280-81).

1751 Johnson. *See* under AESTHETIC (JW 2: 431), RULES (JW 3: 240), VARIETY (JW 3: 241), WONDER (JW 3: 147-48).

1758 Diderot. *See* under THOUGHT (DDP 291).

1765 Johnson. *See* under MORALITY (JS 21).

1767-1769 Lessing. Compare with THOUGHT (LSPW 329).

1778 Johnson. *See* under LANGUAGE (JL 1: 58-59).

1804 Coleridge. Compare with ILLUSION (CSC 1: 178-81).

1808 Schlegel. *See* under COMPLICATION (SCL 253-54), UNITY (SCL 242-45); compare with AESTHETIC (SCL 233, 237-38), CLOSURE (SCL 254).

1811-1812 Coleridge. *See* under THREE UNITIES (CCSL 99).

1815 Coleridge. Compare with STYLE (CBL 2: 115-16).

1818 Hazlitt. Compare with DRAMA (HW 5: 8), LANGUAGE (HW 5: 8).

c.1820 Hegel. *See* under AESTHETIC (HFA 1: 8-9), CATHARSIS (HFA 5: 298-300).

c.1863-1867 Taine. *See* under AESTHETIC (THEL 15, 18).

1871 Nietzsche. Compare with THOUGHT (NBT 110-11), WONDER (NBT 25-26).

1886 Nietzsche. Compare with WILL (NZ 134-36).

1888 Chekhov. Compare with THOUGHT (CL May 30).

1888 Nietzsche. Compare with TRAGEDY (NEH 70-73).

1890 Chekhov. Compare with AESTHETIC (CL 137).

1898 Shaw. Compare with THOUGHT (SPPU xx).

1908   Pirandello. Compare under RULES (POH 29-30).

1921   Eliot. Compare with THOUGHT (ESW 61).

1922   Stanislavski. Compare with STYLE (SL 154-55).

1926   Brecht. *See* under EPIC THEATRE (BBT 14-15).

1931-1936   Artaud. Compare with THOUGHT (AT 39-40).

1936   Brecht. *See* under ALIENATION (BBB 131-36).

1940   Brecht. *See* under AESTHETIC (BBT 145).

c.1940   Brecht. *See* under ALIENATION (BBAn 15-20).

1948   Brecht. *See* under ALIENATION (BBBG 26-27).

REALISM

Modern philosophical realism is the investment of primary value in the existence of a material world that is independent of perception and not reducible to abstractions or ideal forms. The statements presented here assert or imply such a premise. For realism as an art style, see STYLE.

4th cent. B.C. Aristotle. *See* under ACTION (AP 37-39).

c.20 B.C. Horace   **HAP**

Fictions meant to please should be close to the real, so that your play must not ask for belief in anything it chooses, nor from the Ogress's belly, after dinner, draw forth a living child. (479)
  See also Horace under IMITATION (HAP 477).

1561 Scaliger. *See* under THREE UNITIES (SP 60), TRAGEDY (SP 39).

1570 Castelvetro. *See* under ACTION (CP 113), AFFECT (CP 86), THREE UNITIES (CP 84, 85).

1616 Jonson   **JBW**

To make a child, now swaddled, to proceed
Man, and then shoot up, in one beard, and weed,
Past three score years: or, with three rusty swords,
And help of some few foot-and-half-foot words,
Fight over *York*, and *Lancaster's* long jars:
And in the tiring-house bring wounds, to scars.
[The author] prays, you will be pleas'd to see
One such, today, as other plays should be.
Where neither *Chorus* wafts you o'er the seas;
Nor creaking throne comes down, the boys to please;
  . . . But deeds and language such as men do use:
And persons, such as *Comedy* would choose,
When she would show an Image of the times,
And sport with human follies, not with crimes.
  . . . Which when you heartily [laugh], there's hope left, then,
You, that have so grac'd monsters, may like men.
                                     Prologue, *Every Man in his Humour*

1640   Jonson. *See* under GENRE (JBW).

1641   Jonson. *See* under IMITATION (JD 33).

1657   d'Aubignac. *See* under ACTION (AAS 1: 43-44).

1665   Dryden. Compare with STYLE (DW 1, 2: 19-20).

1668   Dryden. *See* under AFFECT (DW 1, 2: 88), THOUGHT (DW 1, 2: 170); compare with STYLE (DW 1, 2: 118-21, 161).

1672   Dryden. Compare with STYLE (DW 1, 2: 209-10).

1674   Racine. *See* under MAGNITUDE (RP 156).

1711   Addison. *See* under POETIC JUSTICE (AW 1: 71-72), SPECTACLE (AW 1: 74-75).

1730   Voltaire. *See* under AESTHETIC (VE 279).

1751   Johnson. *See* under RULES (JW 3: 240-41), VARIETY (JW 3: 241).

1758   Diderot. *See* under PLOT (DDP 296).

1765   Johnson. *See* under GENRE DEFINITION (JS 16), THREE UNITIES (JS 57), VARIETY (JS 15).

1778   Diderot. Compare with ILLUSION (DPA 4-5, 16-17, 22, 74).

c.1780   Johnson. *See* under IMITATION (JL 2: 135).

c.1781   Johnson. *See* under IMITATION (JL 3: 255).

1798   Goethe. *See* under ILLUSION (GLE 52-57).

1808   Schlegel. *See* under LANGUAGE (SCL 229-30), STYLE (SCL 370-71); compare with GENRE DEFINITION (SCL 176-79), ILLUSION (SCL 246), IMITATION (SCL 511), POETRY OF THE THEATRE (SCL 36-37), SPECTACLE (SCL 59), THREE UNITIES (SCL 236-51, 305).

1811-1812   Coleridge. Compare with DISTANCE (CCSL 25).

1815   Coleridge   **CBL**

It is to the true and original realism, that I would direct the attention. This believes and requires neither more nor less, than the object which it beholds or presents to itself, is the real and very object. In this sense, however much we may strive against it, we are all collectively born idealists, and therefore and only therefore are we at the same time realists. . . . The realism common to all mankind is far elder and lies infinitely deeper than [the idealistic] explanation of the origin of our perceptions, an explanation skimmed from the mere surface of mechanical philosophy. It is the table itself, which the man of common sense believes himself to see, not the phantom of a table, from which he may argumentatively deduce the reality of a table, which he does not see. If to destroy the reality of all, that we actually behold, be idealism, what can be more egregiously so, than the system of modern metaphysics, which banishes us to a land of shadows, surrounds us with apparitions, and distinguishes truth from illusion only by the majority of those who dream the same dream? (1: 179)

Compare with Coleridge under ILLUSION (CBL 2: 107), IMITATION (CBL 2: 256).

1816   Goethe. Compare with SPECTACLE (GLE 187-88).

1818   Hazlitt. Compare with DRAMA (HW 5: 8), IMAGINATION (HW 5: 4), LANGUAGE (HW 5: 12-13).

c.1820   Hegel. *See* under DRAMATIZATION (HFA 4: 280-82); compare with IDEALISM (HFA 4: 265-67), POETRY OF THE THEATRE (HFA 4: 289-91), THREE UNITIES (HFA 4: 257-59).

1823   Goethe. *See* under THOUGHT (GCE Nov. 14).

1824   Hazlitt   **HW**

The advocates for the *ideal system of art* would persuade their disciples, that the difference between Hogarth and the [ancient Greeks] does not consist in the different forms of nature which they imitated, but in this, that the one is like, and the other unlike nature. This is an error, the most detrimental, perhaps, of all others, both to the theory and practice of art. . . . What has given rise to the common notion of the *ideal*, as something quite distinct from *actual* nature, is probably the perfection of the Greek statues. Not seeing among ourselves any thing to correspond in beauty and grandeur, either with the features or form of the limbs in these exquisite remains of antiquity, it was an obvious, but a superficial conclusion, that they must have been created from the idea existing in the artist's mind, and could not have been copied from anything existing in nature. The contrary, however, is the fact. The general form, both of the face and figure, which we observe in the old statues, is not an ideal abstraction, is not a fanciful invention of the sculptor, but is . . . completely local and national. . . . It will not be denied that there is a difference of physiognomy as well as of complexion in different races of men. The Greek form appears to have been naturally beautiful, and they had, besides, every advantage of climate, of dress, of exercise, and modes of life to improve it. (9: 378-79)

   See also Hazlitt under IDEALISM (HW 9: 379), IMITATION (HW 9: 377, 389, 398).

1830   Hazlitt. *See* under IDEALISM (9: 429-30, 431-32), IMITATION (HW 9: 425).

1864   Taine. *See* under IMITATION (TLA 45-46, 51-53); compare with AESTHETIC (TLA 273-74), EVOLUTIONISM (TLA 283-84), LANGUAGE (TLA 54-55).

1871   Nietzsche. Compare with DISTANCE (NBT 58-60), IMITATION (NBT 87).

1873   Nietzsche. Compare with METAPHOR (NEG 178-88).

1876   Sarcey. Compare with AFFECT (STT 34-41), CONVENTION (STT 26-27, 28-29), STYLE (STT 49-50).

1887   Chekhov   **CL**

Jan. 14. That the world swarms with "dregs and scum" is perfectly true. Human nature is imperfect, and it would therefore be strange to see none but righteous ones on earth. But to think that the duty of literature is to unearth the pearl from the refuse heap means to reject literature itself. "Artistic" literature is only "art" in so far as it paints life as it really is. Its vocation is to be absolutely true and honest. . . . I agree that "pearls" are a good thing, but then a writer is not a confectioner, not a provider of cosmetics, not an entertainer; he is a man bound, under contract, by his sense of duty and his conscience; having put his hand to the plough he mustn't turn back, and, however distasteful, he must conquer his squeamishness and soil his imagination with the dirt of life. He is like an ordinary reporter. . . . To a chemist nothing on earth is unclean. A writer must be as objective as a chemist; he must lay aside his personal subjective standpoint and must understand that muck heaps play a very respectable part in a landscape, and that evil passions are as inherent in life as the good ones. (57)

1888   Chekhov. *See* under THOUGHT (CL May 30).

1889 Strindberg. Compare with IMITATION (SMD 17).

1890 Shaw   **SMCE**

The realist at last loses patience with ideals altogether, and sees in them only something to blind us, something to numb us, something to murder self in us. . . . The idealist says, "Realism means egotism; and egotism means depravity." The realist declares that when a man abnegates the will to live and be free in a world of the living and free, seeking only to conform to ideals for the sake of being, not himself, but a good man, then he is morally dead and rotten, and must be left unheeded to abide his resurrection, if that by good luck arrive before his bodily death. (31)

1897 Shaw. *See* under AESTHETIC (SDC 259-60).

1902 Shaw. Compare with THOUGHT (SAA 43).

1905 Stanislavski. Compare with IMITATION (SL 20).

1909 Shaw. *See* under CLOSURE (STPB xv-xvi).

1912 Shaw   **SALOP**

Theatrical art begins as the holding up to Nature of a distorting mirror. In this phase it pleases people who are childish enough to believe that they can see what they look like and what they are when they look at a true mirror. Naturally they think that a true mirror can teach them nothing. Only by giving back some monstrous image can the mirror amuse them or terrify them. It is not until they grow up to the point at which they learn that they know very little about themselves . . . that they become consumed with curiosity as to what they really are like, and begin to demand that the stage shall be a mirror of such accuracy and intensity of illumination that they shall be able to get glimpses of their real selves in it, and also learn a little how they appear to other people. (73-74)

1913 Shaw. *See* under DRAMA (SMCE 144).

1918-1922 Stanislavski. *See* under IMITATION (SAS 105).

c.1930 Stanislavski. *See* under CONFLICT (SCR 80).

1931-1936 Artaud. Compare with DRAMA (AT 70).

1936 Stanislavski. *See* under ACTION (SAP 43).

1948 Brecht. Compare with STYLE (BBBG 39-40).

RECOGNITION

Recognition is one kind of episode described by Aristotle in the complex plot. Later theorists have extrapolated principles of character self-knowledge or of spectator insight from the concept. See SURPRISE headnote.

4th cent. B.C.   Aristotle   AP

Recognition, as the name indicates, is a change from ignorance to knowledge, *producing love or hate* [pointing either to a state of close natural ties (blood relationship) or to one of enmity: EP 343] between the persons destined by the poet for good or bad fortune. The best form of recognition is coincident with a Reversal of the Situation, as in the Oedipus. There are indeed other forms. Even inanimate things of the most trivial kind may in a sense be objects of recognition. Again, we may recognise or discover whether a person has done a thing or not. But the recognition which is most intimately connected with the plot and action is, as we have said, the recognition of persons. This recognition, combined with Reversal, will produce either pity or fear; and actions producing these effects are those which by our definition, Tragedy represents. Moreover, it is upon such situations that the issues of good or bad fortune will depend. Recognition, then, being between persons, it may happen that one person only is recognised by the other—when the latter is already known—or it may be necessary that the recognition should be on both sides. Thus Iphigenia is revealed to Orestes by the sending of the letter; but another act of recognition is required to make Orestes known to Iphigenia. Two parts, then, of the Plot—Reversal of the Situation and Recognition—*turn upon surprises* [omitted in EP 356]. (41-43) . . . What Recognition is has already been explained. We will now enumerate its kinds. First, the least artistic form, which, from poverty of wit, is most commonly employed—recognition by signs. Of these some are congenital,—such as "the spear which the earth-born race bear on their bodies." . . . Others are acquired after birth; and of these some are bodily marks, as scars; some external tokens, as a necklace or the little ark in the Tyro by which the discovery is effected. Even these admit of more skilful treatment. Thus in the recognition of Odysseus by his scar, the discovery is made in one way by the nurse, in another by the swineherds. The use of tokens for the express purpose of proof—and, indeed, any formal proof with or without tokens—is a less artistic mode of recognition. A better kind is that which comes about by a turn of incident, as in the Bath Scene in the Odyssey. Next come the recognitions invented at will by the poet, and on that account wanting in art. For example, Orestes in the Iphigenia reveals the fact that he is Orestes. She, indeed, makes herself known by the letter; but he, by speaking himself, and saying what the poet, not what the plot requires. This, therefore, is nearly allied to the fault above mentioned:—for Orestes might as well have brought tokens with him. . . . The third kind depends on memory when the sight of some object awakens a feeling: as . . . where the hero breaks into tears on seeing the picture; or again . . . where [the hero] hearing the minstrel play the lyre, recalls the past and weeps; and hence the recognition. The fourth kind is by process of reasoning. Thus in the Choëphori:—''Some one resembling me has come: no one resembles me but Orestes: therefore Orestes has come.'' . . . Again, there is a composite kind of recognition involving false inference on the part of one of the characters, as in the Odysseus Disguised as a Messenger. A said [that no one else was able to bend the bow; . . . hence B (the disguised Odysseus) imagined that A would] recognise the bow which, in fact, he had not seen; and to bring about a recognition by this means—the expectation that A would recognise the bow—is false inference. But, of all recognitions, the best is that which arises from the incidents themselves, where the startling discovery is made by natural means. Such is that in the Oedipus of Sophocles, and in the Iphigenia; for it was natural that Iphigenia would wish to dispatch a letter. These recognitions alone dispense with the artificial aid of tokens or amulets. Next come the recognitions by process of reasoning. (57-61)

    See also Aristotle under PITY (AP 49-53), PLOT (AP 25-29, 39-41).

c.1900   Strindberg. *See* under PLOT (SEP 574-75).

REVERSAL

The Reversal of the Situation is one kind of episode described by Aristotle in the complex plot, but he suggests that the best examples are simultaneously Recognitions, and therefore these would occur in the same episode. Subsequent theorists have attempted to derive some basic principles of dramatic or tragic form from the concept of the Reversal. See also IRONY and SURPRISE.

4th cent. B.C.   Aristotle   AP

Reversal of Situation is a change by which the action veers round to its opposite, subject always to our rule of probability or necessity. Thus in the Oedipus, the messenger comes to cheer Oedipus and free him from his alarms about his mother, but by revealing who he is, he produces the opposite effect. Again in the Lynceus, Lynceus is being led away to his death, and Danaus goes with him, meaning to slay him; but the outcome of the preceding incidents is that Danaus is killed and Lynceus saved. . . . Two parts . . . of the Plot—Reversal of the Situation and Recognition—*turn upon surprise* [omitted in EP 356]. (41-43) . . . Even Agathon has been known to fail from this one defect [of "multiplicity of plots"]. In his Reversals of the Situation, however, he shows a marvelous skill in the effort to hit the popular taste—to produce a tragic effect that satisfies the moral sense. This effect is produced when the clever rogue, like Sisyphus, is outwitted, or the brave villain defeated. Such an event is probable in Agathon's sense of the word: "it is *probable* [plausible: EP 541]," he says, "that many things should happen contrary to probability." (67-69)

4th cent. B.C.   Aristotle   AR

It is piteous that an evil should befall from a quarter whence good fortune was due: or that this should happen often. It is piteous that some good should come, when all is over with a man; as when, after the death of Diopeithes, the presents from the Great King came down for him. It is piteous that no good should ever have happened to a man, or that, when it did happen, he should have been unable to enjoy it. (90-91)

    See also Aristotle under MAGNITUDE (AP 91-93), PLOT (AP 25-29, 39, 65-67).

1561   Scaliger. *See* under ACTION (SP 62).

1570   Castelvetro. *See* under WONDER (CP 88).

1609   de Vega. *See* under SURPRISE (VAWP 34).

1641   Jonson. *See* under MAGNITUDE (JD 103).

1657   d'Aubignac. *See* under CLOSURE (AAS 2: 131), SUBJECT (AAS 2: 68-69).

1660   Corneille. *See* under SURPRISE (CSP 109).

1712   Addison. *See* under ACTION (AW 1: 427), SURPRISE (AW 2: 312).

1758   Diderot. *See* under TRAGEDY (DDP 296, 297).

1827   Goethe   **GCE**

Wed., March 21. "We see in both [*Philoctetes* and *Oedipus in Colonos*] the extremely effective situation of a happy change, since one hero, in his disconsolate situation, has his beloved daughter restored to him, and the other, his no less beloved bow. The happy conclusions of these two pieces are also similar; for both heroes are delivered from their sorrows: Oedipus is blissfully snatched away, and as for Philoctetes, we are forewarned by the oracle of his cure, before Troy, by Aesculapius."

1876   Scarcey. *See* under STYLE (STT 49-50).

c.1900   Strindberg. *See* under PLOT (SEP 574-75).

RULES

The evolving attitude toward rules of art provides a compact pre-history of aesthetics. Initially it was assumed that there were rules if there was art, because an art was by definition an activity regulated by rules. But the accumulation of insights, stated as rules, began to appear contradictory; the question became which were the true rules. In the eighteenth century the rationalist premises for the rules became discredited and since the latter part of that century more fundamental principles have been sought. Aesthetics emerged as the philosophical discipline of that search.

4th cent. B.C.   Aristotle   AP

A tragedy . . . to be perfect according to the rules of art should be of [the] construction [described in *The Poetics: see* Plot (AP 45-49)].

c.20 B.C.   Horace   HAP

Let no play be either shorter or longer than five acts, if when once seen it hopes to be called for and brought back to the stage. And let no god intervene, unless a knot come worthy of such a deliverer, nor let a fourth actor essay to speak. Let the Chorus sustain the part and strenous duty of an actor, and sing nothing between acts which does not advance and fitly blend into the plot. (467)

1561   Scaliger   SP

The poetical art is a science, that is, it is a habit of production in accordance with those laws which underlie that symmetrical fashioning known as poetry. (18)

c.1583   Sidney. *See* under THREE UNITIES (SDP 49).

1603   Jonson   JBW

If it be objected, that what I publish is no true *Poem*; in the strict Laws of *Time*. I confess it: as also in the want of a proper *Chorus*, whose Habit, and Moods are such, and so difficult, as not any whom I have seen since the *Ancients* (no, not they who have most presently affected Laws) have yet come in the way off. Nor is it needful, or almost possible, in these our Times, and to such Auditors, as commonly Things are presented, to observe the old state, and splendour of *Dramatic Poems*, with preservation of any popular delight. . . . If in truth of Argument, dignity of Persons, gravity and height of Elocution, fullness and frequency of Sentence, I have discharg'd the other offices of a Tragic writer, let not the absence of these Forms be imputed to . . . want of a convenient knowledge. . . . Lest in some nice nostril, the *Quotations* might savour affected, I do let you know, that I abhor nothing more; and have only done it to show my integrity in the *Story*. . . .

To The Reader, *Sejanus*

1605 Jonson. *See* under THREE UNITIES (JBW).

1609 De Vega VAWP

Let each act have but four sheets, for twelve are well suited to the time and the patience of him who is listening. In satirical parts, be not clear or open, since it is known that for this very reason comedies were forbidden by law in Greece and Italy; wound without hate, for if, perchance, slander be done, expect not applause, nor aspire to fame. (36)

1641 Jonson JD

The Wretcheder [writers] are the obstinate contemners of all helpes, and Arts: such as presuming on theire owne *Naturals* (which perhaps are excellent) dare deride all dilligence, and seeme to mock at the termes, when they understand not the things; thinking that way to get off wittily, with their Ignorance. (32) . . . I take this labor in teaching others, that they should not be alwayes to bee taught; and I would bring my Precepts into practice. For rules are ever of lesse force, and valew, then experiments. Yet with this purpose, rather to shew the right way to those that come after, then to detect any that have slipt before by errour, and I hope it will be more profitable. . . . Among diverse opinions of an Art, and most of them contrary in themselves, it is hard to make election. . . . No precepts will profit a Foole; no more then beauty will the blind, or musicke the deafe. (68)

Compare with Jonson under AESTHETIC (JD 29).

1657 d'Aubignac AAS

Here are five objections which have been ordinarily made to me, against the Rules of the Ancients. First, That we are not to make Laws to our selves from Custom and Example, but from Reason; which ought to prevail over any Authority. Secondly, That the Ancients themselves have often violated their own Rules. Thirdly, That divers Poems of the Ancients had been translated, and acted upon our Stage with very ill success. Fourthly, That diverse of our modern Plays, though quite contrary to these Rules, have been acted with great applause. And last of all, That if these rigorous Maxims should be follwed, we should very often lose the greatest beauty of all true stories. Their Incidents having most commonly happened at different times, and in different places. As to the first Objection; I answer, That the Rules of the Stage are not founded upon Authority, but upon Reason; they are not so much settled by Example, as by the natural judgment of Mankind; and if we call them the Rules and the Art of the Ancients, 'tis only because They have practis'd them with great regularity, and must to their Glory; having first made many observations upon the Nature of Moral Actions, and upon the probability of Humane Accidents in this life, and thereby drawing the Pictures after the truth of the Original, and observing all due circumstances, they reduc'd to an Art this kind of Poem, whose Progress was very slow, though it were much in use among them, and much admir'd all the world over. . . . As for the second objection, it seems not considerable; for Reason, being alike all the world over, does equally require every bodies submission to it; and if our modern Authors, cannot without offence be dispens'd from the Rules of the Stage, no more could the Ancients; and where they have failed, I do not pretend to excuse them. My Observations upon *Plautus*, shew very well that I do propose the Ancients for Models, only in such things as they shall appear to have followed Reason in. . . . In all that depends upon common sence and reason, such as are the Rules of the Stage, there to take a license, is a crime; because it offends not Custom, but Natural light, which ought never to suffer an Eclipse. . . . The third Objection has no force, but in the Ignorance of those that allege it. For if some Poems of the Ancients, and even those which were most in Esteem with them, have not succeeded upon our Stage, the Subject, and not the want of Art, has been the cause of it; And sometimes likewise the Changes made by the Translators, which destroyed all the Graces of the Original. . . . To destroy the 4th Objection, we need only to remember, that those Plays of ours, which took with the people, and with the Court, were not lik'd in all their parts; but only in those things which were reasonable, and in which they were conformable to the Rules: When there were any passionate Scenes, they were prais'd; and when there was any great Appearance or noble Spectacle, it was esteem'd; and if some notable Event was well manag'd, there was great satisfaction shewn; but if in the rest of the Play, or even in these beauties of it, any irregularities were discover'd, or any fault against Probability and Decency, either in the persons, time, or place, or as to the state of the things represented, they were condemned as Faults. . . . Therefore that success so much bragg'd on, is so far from contradicting the Rules of the Stage, that quite contrary it establishes their Authority. For these Rules being nothing but an Art to cause the finest Incidents to please with decency and probability, it sufficiently appears how necessary they are, since by common consent, all that comes up to them is approved of, and all that varies from them is in some measure condemn'd. . . . The 5th Objection is absolutely ridiculous. For the Rules of the Stage do not at all reject the most notable Incidents of any Story, but they furnish us with Inventions, how so to adjust the Circumstances of the Action, Time, and Place, as not to go against all probable appearance, and yet not represent them always as they are in Story, but such as they ought to be, to have nothing but what's agreeable in them. 'Tis That then that we are to seek. (1: 22-26).

See also d'Aubignac under ACTION (AAS 2: 81), POETIC JUSTICE (AAS 1: 5-6), PROBABILITY (AAS 1: 38), THREE UNITIES (AAS 2: 97-99, 111-13), UNITY (AAS 2: 89).

1660   Corneille   CFD

It is evident that there are precepts because there is an art, but it is not evident just what the precepts are. We agree on the name but not on the thing; on the words but not on their meaning. The poet must observe unity of action, time and place. No one denies this, but it is a matter of no small difficulty to determine what unity of action is and to realize the extent and limit of the alotted unity of time and place. The poet must treat his subject according to "the probable" and "the necessary." This is what Aristotle says, and all his commentators repeat the words, which appear to them so clear and intelligible that not one of them has deigned . . . to tell us what [they] are. . . . We should, if possible, accommodate ourselves to [the precepts] and make them applicable to our practice. We have in our plays left out the chorus, and this has forced us to substitute more episodes than the Greeks used. This is an instance of going beyond the precepts. We should never go against them, even though in practice we do go beyond. We should know what these precepts are, but unfortunately, Aristotle and Horace after him, wrote in so obscure a fashion that they need interpreters . . . [who] were better versed in scholarship and metaphysics than in knowledge of the theatre. . . . (139-40) . . . I dare not attribute the success [of my early plays] to ignorance of the rules—which was very general at that time—inasmuch as the rules, well or poorly observed, must make their good or bad effect on those who, even without knowing them, abandon themselves to the current of natural feeling. (143-44)

See also Corneille under POETIC JUSTICE (CFD 141), UNITY (CFD 147).

1660   Corneille   CDENA

The goal of the poet is to please according to the rules of his art. To please, he sometimes has need to heighten the splendor of good actions, and to lessen the horror of disastrous ones. These are the necessities of embellishment when he can violate *particular* probability by some alteration in history, but can only rarely dispense with the *general*, and for things which are of the greatest beauty and so brilliant that they dazzle. . . . To please according to the rules of his art, he has need to confine his action to the unities of time and place; and as that is an absolute . . . necessity, he is permitted more [freedom] for these two . . . than for embellishments. (32)

See also Corneille under THREE UNITIES (CDTU 237).

1663   Molière   MP

[The "rules of art" are not mysteries but] only simple observations, made by common-sense, on things that may affect the pleasure people take in poems.

. . . And the same good sense which made these observations in the olden time makes them as easily in our day, without the help of Horace or of Aristotle. I would like to ask if the great rule of rules is not—*to please*; and if a play which attains that end upon the stage is not upon the high-road of good art. (6: 344) . . . If plays that follow rules don't please, and those that please don't follow rules, the reason must be, of necessity, the rules are bad. 'Tis best to laugh at all such quibbling criticism. . . . Let us enjoy in simple faith the things that please our inmost souls, and seek no arguments to spoil our pleasure. (6: 345).

Compare with Molière under AFFECT (MP 6: 324).

1668   Dryden. *See* under THREE UNITIES (DW 1, 2: 93-94).

1671   Dryden. *See* under POETIC JUSTICE (DW 1, 2: 198-201).

1674   Racine. *See* under AFFECT (RP 156), MAGNITUDE (RP 156).

1695   Dryden   **DW**

[Poetry and painting] must have rules, which may direct them to their common end. . . . The way to please being to imitate nature, both the poets and the painters in ancient times, and in the best ages, have studied her; and from the practice of both these arts the rules have been drawn, by which we are instructed how to please, and to compass that end which they obtained, by following their example; for nature is still the same in all ages, and can never be contrary to herself. Thus, from the practice of Aeschylus, Sophocles, and Euripides, Aristotle drew his rules for tragedy. . . . Thus, amongst the moderns, the Italian and French criticks, by studying the precepts of Aristotle and Horace, and having the example of the Grecian poets before their eyes, have given us the rules of modern tragedy. (3: 318-19) . . . To inform our judgments, and to reform our tastes, rules were invented that by them we might discern—when nature was imitated, and how nearly. . . . The imitation of nature is . . . justly constituted as the general, and indeed the only, rule of pleasing, both in poetry and painting. (3: 322) . . . Without rules there can be no art, any more than there can be a house without a door to conduct you into it. (3: 326)

1697   Dryden. *See* under THREE UNITIES (DW 3: 430-31).

1711   Addison. *See* under POETIC JUSTICE (AW 1: 71-72).

1714   Addison   **AW**

There is more beauty in the works of a great genius, who is ignorant of the rules of art, than in those of a little genius who knows and observes them. (2: 385)

1730 Voltaire. *See* under THREE UNITIES (VE 280-81).

1731 Voltaire VE

All [the] laws—not to fill the action with bloodshed, not to allow more than three characters to speak at the same time, and so on—are laws which . . . may have exceptions among us, as they did among the Greeks. There is a difference between the rules of decorum, which are always rather arbitrary, and those fundamental rules of the theater, which are the three unities: it would result only in feebleness and sterility to extend the action of a play beyond the proper time and place. Ask any one who has crowded too many events into his play, what the reason for this fault is: if he be honest, he will tell you that he lacked the inventive genius to fill his play with a single action. (282)

1751 Johnson JW

Among the laws of which the desire of extending authority, or ardour of promoting knowledge, has prompted the prescription, all which writers have received, had not the same original right to our regard. Some are to be considered as fundamental and indispensable, others only as useful and convenient; some as dictated by reason and necessity, others as enacted by despotick antiquity; some as invincible supported by their conformity to the order of nature and operations of the intellect; others as formed by accident, or instituted by example, and therefore always liable to dispute and alteration. (3: 240) . . . By what accident the number of acts was limited to five, I know not that any author has informed us; but certainly it is not determined by any necessity arising either from the nature of action, or propriety of exhibition. An act is only the representation of such a part of the business of the play as proceeds in an unbroken tenour, or without any intermediate pause. Nothing is more evident than that of every real, and by consequence of every dramatic action, the intervals may be more or fewer than five; and indeed, the rule is upon the English stage broken in effect, without any other mischief than that which arises from an absurd endeavour to observe it in appearance. Whenever the scene is shifted the act ceases, since some time is necessarily supposed to elapse while the personages of the drama change their place. (3: 240-41) . . . There are other rules more fixed and obligatory. It is necessary that of every play the chief action should be single; for since a play represents some transaction, through its regular maturation to its final event, two actions equally important must evidently constitute two plays. (3: 242)

See also Johnson under THREE UNITIES (JW 3: 241).

1758 Diderot DDP

The drama is a tissue of particular laws, from which the critics have deduced general precepts. It has been noticed that certain incidents produce great effects; and immediately it becomes a rule that all poets shall resort to the same means in order to produce like results. Now, if one had examined a little more closely, he would have seen that still greater effects might have been produced by entirely opposite means. Thus has the art of the drama become surcharged with rules; and the dramatists, in servilely subjecting themselves to them, have often gone to much pain and done less well than they might have done. (298)

1765   Johnson. *See* under THREE UNITIES (JS 24, 25, 27, 29, 30, 57).

1767-1769   Lessing   LSPW

The strictest observation of the rules cannot outweigh the smallest fault in a character. (370).

    See also Lessing under AFFECT (LSPW 273), GENRE (LSPW 248, 380), TASTE (LSPW 279), THREE UNITIES (LSPW 364-66), TRAGEDY (LSPW 415).

1808   Schlegel   SCL

The Chinese . . . have their standing national theatre, standing perhaps in every sense of the word; and I do not doubt, that in the establishment of arbitrary rules, and the delicate observance of insignificant conventionalities, they leave the most correct Europeans very far behind them. (34) . . . The affinity . . . [of Alfieri and Metastasio with French Tragedy] I trace [to] the total absence of the romantic spirit; in a certain fancifuless insipidity of composition; in the manner of handling mythological and historical materials, which is neither properly mythological nor historical; lastly, in the aim to produce a tragic purity, which degenerates into monotony. The unities of both place and time have been uniformly observed by Alfieri . . . [and] in his plots he aimed at the antique simplicity, while Metastasio, in his rich intrigues, followed Spanish models. . . . Yet the harmonious ideality of the ancients was as foreign to the one, as the other was destitute of the charm of the romantic poets, which arises from the indissoluble mixture of elements apparently incongruous. ["Purification"] often means emptying a thing of all its substance and vigour. . . . It originates in a chilling idea of regularity, once for all established for every kind alike, instead of ascertaining the spirit and peculiar laws of each distinct species. (217) . . . In so far as we have to raise a doubt of the unconditional authority of the rules followed by the old French tragic authors, of the pretended affinity between the spirit of their works and the spirit of the Greek tragedians, and of the indespensableness of many supposed proprieties, we find an ally in Voltaire. But in many other points he has, without examination, nay even unconsciously, adopted the maxims of his predecessors, and followed their practice. (235) . . . There is [an] aspect of French Tragedy from which it cannot appeal to the authority of the ancients: that is, the tying of poetry to a number of conventional proprieties. On this subject the French are

far less clear than on that of the rules; for nations are not usually more capable of knowing and appreciating themselves than individuals are. It is, however, intimately connected with the spirit of French poetry in general. . . . (236)
. . . Great importance is attached [by the French critics] to the principle that the stage should never in the course of an act remain empty. This is called binding the scenes [*liaison de scène*]. But frequently the rule is observed in appearance only, since the personages of the preceding scene go out at one door the very moment that those of the next enter at another. . . . A thousand times have we reason to repeat the observation of the [French] Academy, in their criticism on the *Cid*, respecting the crowding together so many events in the period of twenty-four hours: "From the fear of sinning against the rules of art, the poet has rather chosen to sin against the rules of nature." But this imaginary contradiction between art and nature could only be suggested by a low and narrow range of artistic ideas. (259)

    See also Schlegel under POETIC JUSTICE (SCL 254), THREE UNITIES (SCL 236-51); compare with ACTION (SCL 239-42).

c.1810   Coleridge   CLSW

There is a sort of improbability with which we are shocked in dramatic representation, not less than in a narrative of real life. Consequently, there must be rules respecting it; and as rules are nothing but means to an end previously ascertained—(inattention to which simple truth has been the occasion of all the pedantry of the French school),—we must first determine what the immediate end or objective of the drama is. (72-73)

1811-1812   Coleridge. *See* under THREE UNITIES (CCSL 99).

1815   Coleridge. *See* under TASTE (CBL 2: 63-64).

1819   Hazlitt. Compare with TASTE (HW 11: 456-57).

c.1819   Coleridge. *See* under UNITY (CLSW 110).

c.1820   Hazlitt   HW

Rules and models destroy genius and art; and the excess of the artificial in the end cures itself, for it in time becomes so uniform and vapid as to be altogether contemptible. (11: 464)

    Compare with Hazlitt under TASTE (HW 11: 459-60).

c.1820   Hegel. *See* under ACTION (HFA 4: 259-61), THREE UNITIES (HFA 4: 257-59).

1825   Goethe. *See* under THREE UNITIES (GCE Feb. 24).

1876   Sarcey   STT

Rules do not render any great service in criticizing any more than they do in creating. The best that can be said for them is that they may serve as directions or guide-posts. (19)

1888   Chekhov   CL

Nov. Those who have assimilated the wisdom of the scientific method . . . experience many alluring temptations. . . . The present day hot-heads want by science to conceive the inconceivable, to discover the physical laws of creative art, to detect the laws and formulae which are instinctively felt by the artist and are followed by him in creating. (103-104)

1894   Brunetière   BLD

I depart from the old school of criticism, that believed in the mysterious power of "Rules" in their inspiring virtues; and consequently we see the old-school critics struggling and striving, exercising all their ingenuity to invent additional Rules. . . . The truth is that there are no Rules in that sense; there never will be. There are only conventions, which are necessarily variable, since their only object is to fulfill the essential aim of the dramatic work, and the means of accomplishing this vary with the piece, the time, and the man. (69)

See also Brunetière under CONFLICT (BLD 77-80), THREE UNITIES (BLD 70).

1903   Shaw. *See* under AESTHETIC (SMS xxxvi).

1908   Pirandello   POH

According to Rhetoric, art was an activity that had to obey certain principles, which were universal and absolute as if the work of art were a statement to be formulated like a logical argument. Rhetoric said: "This is the way it is done; this is the way it must be done." Rhetoric collected numerous models of unchanging beauty as in a museum and required that they be imitated. Rhetoric and imitation are essentially the same thing. And unquestionably, the damages it caused to literature are, as everyone knows, incalculable. Founded on the prejudice of the so called "tradition," Rhetoric taught writers to imitate that which is inimitable: style, character, form. It did not understand that each form must be neither ancient nor modern but unique and inalienable, for it can belong to only one work of art, and that therefore no tradition can or should exist in art. (29-30)

See also Pirandello under GENRE (POH 30); compare with THOUGHT (POH 30-31).

1932   Eliot. *See* under THREE UNITIES (EUP 45-46).

SPECTACLE

Spectacle is Aristotle's term for the physical presentation of drama. Concepts and attitudes toward Spectacle have evolved among theorists, in general, from a position in which it is perceived as but one element—and one which, though useful, is not necessary—to a position which identifies enactment as the essential and unique quality of the art. See also DRAMATIZATION, EPIC THEATRE, GEST, POETRY OF THE THEATRE and SUBTEXT.

4th cent. B.C.   Aristotle   AP

The *Spectacle* [costuming: EP 274] has . . . an emotional attraction of its own, but, of all the parts, it is the least artistic, and connected least with the art of poetry. For the power of Tragedy we may be sure, is felt even *apart from representation* [without a competition: EP 274] and actors. Besides, the production of *spectacular effects* [the masks and costumes: EP 274] depends more on the art of the *stage machinest* [costumer: EP 274] than of the poet. (29-31) . . . In constructing the plot and working it out with the proper diction, the poet should place the scene, as far as possible, before his eyes. In this way, seeing everything with the utmost vividness, as if he were a spectator of the action, he will discover what is in keeping with it, and be most unlikely to overlook inconsistencies. (61)

    See also Aristotle under DRAMA (AP 107-11), PLOT (AP 49), TRAGEDY (AP 23-25), WONDER (AP 95).

c.20 B.C.   Horace. *See* under DRAMATIZATION (HAP 465-67).

1570   Castelvetro   CP

The opinion of Aristotle that as much delight can be had from a mere reading of tragedy as from a performance of it on the stage, is false. . . . Tragedy cannot effect its proper function with a reading without staging and acting. (83)

    See also Castelvetro under PLEASURE (CP 128-29).

1616   Jonson   JCD

A poet should detest a Ballet maker. (20)

1641   Jonson. *See* under COMEDY (JD 99-101).

1657   d'Aubignac   **AAS**

I call Representation, the Collection of all those things which may serve to represent a Drammatick Poem, consider'd in themselves and in their own Nature, as the Players, the Scenes, the Musick, the Spectators, and a great many other things. . . . That *Floridor* or *Beauchasteau* act the part of *Cinna*, that they are good or ill Actors, well or ill dress'd, that they are separated from the people by a Stage, which is adorn'd with painted cloth, representing Palaces and Gardens, that the Intervals of the Acts are mark'd by ill Fidlers, or excellent Musick; that an Actor goes behind the Stage, when he says he goes into the Kings Closet, and speaks to his Wife, instead of speaking to a Queen, that there are Spectatours, and those either from the Court, or the City; that they are silent or make a noise, . . . all these things are, and do depend on the Representation. (1: 43-44) . . . 'Tis certain that the Ornaments of the Stage with the Scenes, Machines, and Decorations, make the most sensible delight of that ingenious Magick which seems to make *Hero's* live again in the world after so many Ages; it sets before us a new Heaven, and a new Earth, and many other wonderful appearances of things which we imagine present, though we know at the same time that they are not so, and that we are agreeably deceiv'd: These Ornaments make the Poems themselves more illustrious; the people takes them for Enchantments, and the men of understanding are pleas'd to see the dexterity of the Artists. (3: 93) . . . Though the Court does not dislike these Ornaments, and that the People crowd to see them, yet I would not advise our Poet to busy himself in these *machine* Plays; our Players are neither Rich, nor Generous enough to make the Expence of them, and their Decorators want ability in the performance; I must add that our Authors themselv's have been so negligent in acquiring the knowledge of the Ancients ways in this matter, and in their means of Execution, that we need not wonder if we see so many ill Invented Embellishments of this Kind. (3: 94-95) . . . I consider all publick Spectacles and Decorations of the Scene three ways. Some are of *things*; when the Spectacles are permanent and immovable; as a Heaven open, a stormy sea, a Pallace, or the like Ornaments. Others are of *Actions*; when the Spectacle depends principally upon some extraordinary Fact; as that one should throw himself headlong from a Tower, or from a Rock in the Sea. The Third sort is of those that are mingled with *Things* and *Actions*, as a sea-fight, where at the same time is the Sea and Ships, and Men acting upon it. These may be all further distinguished into natural, artifical, and marvellous. The Natural ones are those which represent the most agreeable things in Nature, as a Desert, a Mountain on fire, Etc. The Artificial are those which shew us the most magnificent works of Art, as a Temple, a Pallace. The Marvellous are those which suppose some Divine Power or Magick Production, as the descent of some Body from Heaven, or the rising of some Fury from Hell. And of all these, the least considerable are the last, because there goes little contrivance to the inventing of them, there being hardly any wit so mean, who by this may not bring in, or carry off a great Intrigue. . . . All these Machines of Gods and Devils are to be us'd with great discretion, and great care to be taken that in the Execution they play easily; for else the people are apt to laugh. . . . I should not likewise advise our Poet to use frequently those, where Actions are to make the greatest Effect, because that all the success depends upon the Exactness of the *Comedians*, who are often so negligent in their performance. . . . That which remains then is the permanent Decorations, of what nature soever they are; and to these I would confine the Poet, but still with many Precautions: For, First, They are to be necessary, insomuch as the Play cannot be acted without these Ornaments. . . . Secondly, These ornaments must be agreeable to the Sight; for 'tis for that, that the People flock to them. . . . They must likewise be modest. . . . They must, besides, be easie to put in execution. . . . It will likewise be reasonable to consider, whether the Place represented by the Scene, will bear in truth that which is to be shewed in Image; for else it would be a gross Fault against Probability. . . . There must not likewise be any Decorations made which are not agreeable to the Unity of Place. . . . But particularly, the Poet must so order it, as that out of this Shew and Decoration some notable Event may result in the Body of the Play; that is, something that many contribute either to the perplexing of the Plot, or the easier unweaving of it. (3: 95-98)

See also d'Aubignac under INSTRUCTION (AAS 1: 5).

1668   Dryden. *See* under DRAMATIZATION (DW 1, 2: 90-93).

1710-1711   Addison. *See* under IMITATION (AW 1: 23-24).

1711   Addison   AW

Aristotle has observed, that ordinary writers in tragedy endeavor to raise terror and pity in their audience, not by proper sentiments and expressions, but by the dresses and decorations of the stage. There is something of this kind very ridiculous in the English theatre. When the author has a mind to terrify us, it thunders; when he would make us melancholy, the stage is darkened. But among all our tragic artifices, I am the most offended at those which are made use of to inspire us with magnificent ideas of the persons that speak. The ordinary method of making a hero, is to clap a huge plume of feathers upon his head, which rises so very high, that there is often a greater length from his chin to the top of his head, than to the sole of his foot. One would believe, that we thought a great man and a tall man the same thing. This very much embarrasses the actor, who is forced to hold his neck extremely stiff and steady all the while he speaks; and not withstanding any anxieties which he pretends for his mistress, his country, or his friends, one may see by his action, that his greatest care and concern is to keep the plume of feathers from falling off his head. For my own part, when I see a man uttering his complaints under such a mountain of feathers, I am apt to look upon him rather as an unfortunate lunatic than a distressed hero. (1: 74) . . . We are told, that an ancient tragic poet, to move the pity of his audience for his exiled kings and distressed heroes, used to make the actors represent them in dresses and clothes that were thread-bare and decayed. This artifice for moving pity, seems as ill-contrived as that we have been speaking of, to inspire us with a great idea of the persons introduced upon the stage. In short, I would have our conceptions raised by the dignity of thought and sublimity of expression, rather than by a train of robes or a plume of feathers. (1: 74-75) . . . Among all our methods of moving pity or terror, there is none so absurd and barbarous, and what more exposes us to the contempt and ridicule of our neighbours, than that dreadful butchering of one another, which is very frequent upon the English stage. To delight in seeing men stabbed, poisoned, racked, or impaled, is certainly the sign of a cruel temper: and as this is often practised before the British audience, several French critics, who think these are grateful spectacles to us, take occasion from them to represent us as a people that delight in blood. It is indeed very odd to see our stage strewed with carcasses in the last scenes of a tragedy; and to observe in the wardrobe of the playhouse several daggers, poniards, wheels, bowls for poison, and many other instruments of death. Murders and executions are always transacted behind the scenes in the French theatre; which in general is very agreeable to the manners of a polite civilized people: but as there are no exceptions to this rule on the French stage, it leads them into absurdities almost as ridiculous as that which falls under our present censure. . . . [Horace] never designed to banish all kinds of death from the stage: but only such as had too much horror in them, and which would have a better effect upon the audience when transacted behind the scenes. I would therefore recommend to my countrymen the practice of the ancient poets, who were sparing of their public executions, and rather chose to perform them behind the scenes, if it could be done with as great an effect upon the audience. At the same time I must observe, that though the devoted persons of the tragedy were seldom slain before the audience, . . . their bodies were often produced after their death, which has always in it something melancholy or terrifying; so that the killing on the stage does not seem to have been avoided only as an indecency, but also as an improbability. (1: 77-78)

See also Addison under CONVENTION (AW 1: 75), compare with DRAMATIZATION (AW 1, 2: 75).

1731 Voltaire   VE

The more the dramatist wishes to appeal to the eye with striking scenes . . . the greater becomes the necessity to saying sublime things; otherwise he will be but a decorator, and not a tragic poet. Nearly thirty years ago the tragedy of *Montézume* was produced at Paris; the scene disclosed was something of a novelty; a palace of magnificent and barbaric splendor. Montezuma himself wore an extraordinary costume; slaves armed with arrows stood at the back of the stage. . . . The scene charmed the audience: but this was the only beautiful thing in the tragedy. (282)

1765   Johnson. Compare with ILLUSION (JS 28-29).

1778   Diderot. *See* under ILLUSION (DPA 4-5, 16-17, 22, 74), IMITATION (DPA 74).

1804   Coleridge. *See* under ILLUSION (CSC 1: 178-81).

1808   Schlegel   SCL

The theatre, where many arts are combined to produce a magical effect; where the most lofty and profound poetry has for its interpreter the most finished action, which is at once eloquence and an animated picture; while architecture contributes her splendid decorations, and painting her perspective illusions, and the aid of music is called in to attune the mind, or to heighten by its strains the emotions which already agitate it; the theatre, in short, where the whole of the social and artistic enlightenment, which a nation possesses . . . are brought into play within the representation of a few short hours, has an extraordinary charm for every age, sex, and rank, and has ever been the favorite amusement of every cultivated people. (41) . . . The tragical imitation of the ancients was altogether ideal and rhythmical; and in forming a judgment of it, we must always keep this in view. It was ideal, in so far as it aimed at the highest grace and dignity; and rhythmical, insomuch as the gestures and inflections of voice were more solemnly measured than in real life. As the statuary of the Greeks, setting out, with almost scientific strictness, with the most general conception, sought to embody it again in various general characters which were gradually invested with the charms of life, so that the individual was the last thing to which they descended; in like manner in the mimetic art, they began with the idea (the delineation of persons with heroical grandeur, more than human dignity, and ideal beauty), then passed to character, and made passion the last of all; which, in the collision with the requisitions of either of the others, was forced to give way. Fidelity of representation was less their object than beauty; with us it is exactly the reverse. On this principle, the use of masks . . . was . . . absolutely essential; . . . the Greeks would certainly . . . have looked upon it as a makeshift to be obliged to allow a player with vulgar, ignoble, or strongly marked features to represent an Apollo or a Hercules; nay, rather they would have deemed it downright profanation. (59) . . . [On French tragedy:] In a princely palace no strong emotion, no breach of social etiquette is allowable; and as in a tragedy affairs cannot always proceed with pure courtesy, every bolder deed, therefore, every act of violence, every thing startling and calculated strongly to impress the senses, is transacted behind the scenes, and related merely by confidants or other messengers. And yet as Horace, centuries ago remarked, whatever is communicated to the ear excites the mind far more feebly than what is exhibited to the trusty eye, and the spectator informs himself of. What he recommends to be withdrawn from observation is only the incredible and the revoltingly cruel. The dramatic effect of the visible may, it is true, be liable to great abuse; and it is possible for a theatre to degenerate into a noisy arena of mere bodily events, to which words and gesture may be but superfluous appendages. But surely the opposite extreme of allowing the eye no conviction of its own, and always referring to something absent, is deserving of equal reprobation. In many French tragedies the spectator might well entertain a feeling that the great actions were actually taking place, but that he had chosen a bad place to be witness of them. (256-57)

See also Schlegel under THREE UNITIES (SCL 236-51).

c.1810   Coleridge. *See* under GENRE (CLSW 74).

1813   Goethe. Compare with IMAGINATION (GLE 175).

1816   Goethe   **GLE**

The primitiveness of the [Elizabethan] stage has been brought to our attention by scholars. There is no trace in it of that striving after realism, which we have developed with the improvement of machinery . . . from which we should find it hard to turn back to that childlike beginning of the stage,—a scaffolding, where one saw little, where everything was *signified*. . . . Who would be content today to put up with such a stage? But amid such surroundings, Shakespeare's plays were highly interesting stories, only told by several persons, who, in order to make somewhat more of an impression, had put on masks, and, when it was necessary, moved back and forth, entered and left the stage; but left to the spectator nevertheless the task of imagining at his pleasure Paradise and palaces on the empty stage. (187-88)

See also Goethe under DRAMA (GLE 185), SYMBOL (GLE 186); compare with DRAMATIZATION (GLE 185-86).

1818   Coleridge. Compare with ILLUSION (CLSW (73).

c.1820   Hegel   **HFA**

The drama is not, as the Epos, composed exclusively for the imaginative sense, but for the direct vision of our senses. In the sphere of the pure imagination we can readily pass from one scene to another. In a theatrical representation, however, we must not put too great a strain on the imaginative faculty beyond the point which contradicts the ordinary vision of life. Shakespeare, for example, in whose tragedies and comedies there is a very frequent change of scene, had posts put up with notices attached to them indicating the particular scene on view. A device of this kind is a poor sort of affair and can only impair the dramatic effect. . . . The most convenient course in this, as in other matters, is a happy mean; in other words, while not wholly excluding the claim of purely natural fact and perception, we may still permit ourselves considerable license in our attitude to both. (4: 258) . . . In the mere *perusal* and *reading aloud* of dramatic compositions we find a difficulty in deciding whether they are of a type which would produce the due effect from the stage. . . . If the character and object of the *dramatis personae* are on their own account great and substantive the manner of composition no doubt presents less difficulty. But as regards the motive force of interests, the various phases in the progress of the action, the suspended interest and development of situations, the just degree in which characters assert their effect on each other, the appropriate force and truth of their demeanour and speech—in all such respects the mere perusal unassisted by a theatrical performance can only in the rarest cases arrive at a reliable decision. Reading a work aloud is only under great qualification a further assistance. Speech in drama requires the presence of separate individuals. . . . When we listen to an action we desire to see the acting persons, their demeanour and surroundings; the eye craves for a completed vision, and finds instead before it merely a reciter, who sits or stands peacefully in a private house with company. Reading aloud or recitation is consequently always an unsatisfying compromise between the unambitious pretentions of private perusal, in which the aspect of realization is absent entirely and all is left to the imagination, and the complete theatrical presentation. (4: 283-84) . . . In tragedy, where the poetry is always the most essential thing, [an emphasis on] a lavish display of the sensuous side of things is no doubt not in its right place, although Schiller, in his "Maid of Orleans," shows a tendency here to run astray. . . . [However, even in opera,] we may entirely exhaust all the arts of scenic display, costume, instrumentation and the rest, but the fact remains that, if we are not really serious in earnest with that part of the content which concerns real dramatic action, the impression upon us can be at the strongest merely that of a perusal of the fairy-tale of "The Thousand and One Nights." (4: 291-92)

See also Hegel under AFFECT (HFA 4: 273), DRAMA (HFA 4: 248, 249-50, 251, 278-80), DRAMATIZATION (HFA 4: 280-82).

1825   Goethe   GCE

Wed., April 20. A poet who writes for the stage must have a knowledge of the stage, that he may weigh the means at his command, and know generally what is to be done, and what is to be left undone.

See also Goethe under THREE UNITIES (GCE Feb. 24).

1871   Nietzsche. See under AFFECT (NBT 70-71).

1888   Strindberg   **SSPP**

As far as the scenery is concerned, I have borrowed from impressionistic painting its asymmetry, its quality of abruptness, and have thereby in my opinion strengthened the illusion. Because the whole room and all its contents are not shown, there is a chance to guess at things—that is, our imagination is stirred into complementing our vision. (23)

1897   Shaw. *See* under IMAGINATION (SS 192).

1898   Shaw   **SMCE**

An allegory is never quite consistent except when it is written by someone without dramatic faculty, in which case it is unreadable. There is only one way of dramatizing an idea; and that is by putting on the stage a human being possessed by that idea, yet none the less a human being with all the human impulses which make him akin and therefore interesting to us. (188) . . . Wagner sought always for some point of contact between his ideas and the physical senses, so that people might not only think or imagine them in the eighteenth century fashion, but see them on stage, hear them from the orchestra, and feel them through the infection of passionate emotion. (220)

1912   Shaw. *See* under ILLUSION (SALOP 72).

1918-1922   Stanislavski. Compare with IDEALISM (SAS 105-106).

c.1930   Stanislavski. *See* under ACTION (SCR 48), IDENTIFICATION (SCR 106).

1931-1936   Artaud   **AT**

A theatre which subordinates the *mis en scène* and production, i.e., everything in itself that is specifically theatrical, to the text, is a theatre of idiots, madmen, inverts, grammarians, grocers, antipoets and positivists, i.e., Occidentals. (41) . . . This idea of the supremacy of speech in the theatre is so deeply rooted in us, and the theater seems to such a degree merely the material reflection of the text, that everything in the theater that exceeds this text, that is not kept within its limits and strictly conditioned by it, seems to us purely a matter of *mise en scène*, and quite inferior in comparison with the text. (68) . . . The idea of a play made directly in terms of the stage, encountering obstacles of both production and performance, compels the discovery of an active [theatrical] language, active and anarchic, a language in which the customary limits of feelings and words are transcended. (41) . . . One finds . . . that this language [of the theatre] is necessarily identified with the *mise en scène* considered: 1. as the visual and plastic materialization of speech, 2. as the language of everything that can be said and signified upon a stage independently of speech, everything that finds its expression in space, or that can be affected or disintegrated by it. (69)

See also Artaud under ACTION (AT 82), AESTHETIC (AT 96, 97), CONVENTION (AT 55), DRAMA (AT 70), IDENTIFICATION (AT 140), ILLUSION (AT 25, 27, 86, 92), LANGUAGE (AT 37), STYLE (AT 53), THOUGHT (AT 39-40, 41, 46).

1931   Brecht. *See* under CHARACTER (BBT 56).

1932   Eliot. *See* under DRAMA (EJD 29).

1936   Brecht. *See* under ALIENATION (BBB 131-36), ILLUSION (BBB 130), STYLE (BBB 132).

c.1940   Brecht. *See* under ALIENATION (BBAn 15-20).

STYLE

The extracts cited present concepts of style, understood here to be the choice of and the manner of employing the various elements and materials of the art. Early theorists generally understood style exclusively in terms of LANGUAGE and SUBJECT, while later theorists perceive style to include all that Aristotle called SPECTACLE. There is, in addition, an evolution of attitudes that might be characterized generally as one from unequivocally prescriptive genre formulations of style to one of recognition of various stylistic implications of period, culture, genre (or, for some, archetypal pattern), author and — increasingly—the particular purposes of the individual work of art. Of considerable importance to the development of these trends is the effort to dissolve the ancient distinctions of form and content. For issues related to "decorum" or rules for stylistic appropriateness, see DECORUM and GENRE DEFINITION.

4th cent. B.C.   Aristotle   AP

As, in the serious style, Homer is preeminent among poets, for he alone combined dramatic form, with excellence of imitation, so he too first laid down the main lines of Comedy, by dramatising the ludicrous instead of writing personal satire. His Margites bears the same relation to Comedy that the Iliad and Odyssey do to Tragedy. But when Tragedy and Comedy came to light, the two classes of poets still followed their natural bent: the lampooners became writers of Comedy, and the Epic poets were succeeded by Tragedians, since the drama was a larger and higher form of art. (17) . . . The perfection of style is to be clear without being mean. The clearest style is that which uses only current or proper words; at the same time it is mean:—witness the poetry of Cleophon and of Sthenelus. That diction, on the other hand, is lofty and raised above the commonplace which employs unusual words. By unusual, I mean strange (or rare) words, metaphorical, lengthened,—anything, in short, that differs from the normal idiom. Yet a style wholly composed of such words is either a riddle or a jargon; a riddle, if it consists of metaphors; a jargon, if it consists of strange (or rare) words. For the essence of a riddle is to express true facts under impossible combinations. Now this cannot be done by any arrangement of ordinary words, but by the use of metaphor it can. . . . A certain infusion, therefore, of these elements is necessary to style; for the strange (or rare) word, the metaphorical, the ornamental, and the other kinds above mentioned, will raise it above the commonplace and mean, while the use of proper words will make it perspicuous. (81-83)... It is a great matter to observe propriety in these several modes of expression, as also in compound words, strange (or rare) words, and so forth. But the greatest thing by far is to have a command of metaphor. This alone cannot be imparted by another; it is the work of genius, for to make good metaphors implies an eye for resemblances. (87)... In examining whether what has been said or done by some one is poetically right or not, we must not look merely to the particular act or saying, and ask whether it is poetically good or bad. We must also consider by whom it is said or done, to whom, when, by what means, or for what end; whether, for instance, it be to secure a greater good, or avert a greater evil. (101)... When a word seems to involve some inconsistency of meaning, we should consider how many senses it may bear in the particular passages.... The true mode of interpretation is the precise opposite of what Glaucon mentions. Critics, he says, jump at certain groundless conclusions; they give adverse judgment and then proceed to reason on it; and assuming that the poet has said whatever they happen to think, find fault if a thing is inconsistent with their own fancy. (105)... Things that sound contradictory should be examined by the same rules as in dialectical refutation—whether the same thing is meant, in the same relation, and in the same sense. We should therefore solve the question by reference to what the poet says himself, or to what is tacitly assumed by a person of intelligence. (107)

4th cent. B.C.   Aristotle   AR

We must disguise our art, then, and seem to speak naturally, not artificially; the natural is persuasive, the artificial is the reverse; for men are prejudiced against it, as against an insidious design, just as they are suspicious of doctored wines.... A successful illusion is wrought, when the composer picks his words from the language of daily life; this is what Euripides does, and first hinted the way to do. (148)

  See also Aristotle under METAPHOR (167-68).

c.20 B.C.   Horace   HAP

A theme for Comedy refuses to be set forth in verses of Tragedy; likewise the feast of Thyestes scorns to be told in strains of daily life that well nigh befit the comic sock. Let each style keep the beginning place allotted it. Yet at times even Comedy raises her voice, and an angry Chremes storms in swelling tones; so, too, in Tragedy Telephus and Peleus often grieve in the language of prose, when, in poverty and exile, either hero throws aside his bombast and Brobdingnagian words, should he want his lament to touch the spectator's heart. (459)... Whenever you instruct, be brief, so what is quickly said the mind may readily grasp and faithfully hold: every word in excess flows away from the full mind. (479)

1561   Scaliger   SP

The grand style is that which portrays eminent characters and notable events.
The sentiments are correspondingly choice, and they are couched in choice and
euphonious diction. . . . Choice sentiments are those which abhor vulgarity;
choice diction, that which is not trite; and pleasing language, that which
marries sense and sound. (71)

　　See also Scaliger under TRAGEDY (SP 39, 40).

c.1583   Sidney   SDP

I have found in divers small-learned courtiers a more sound style than in some
professors of learning; of which I can guess no other cause, but that the courtier
following that which by practice he findeth fittest to nature, therein, though he
know it not, doth according to art, though not by art; where the other, using art
to show art and not to hide art—as in these cases he should do—flieth from
nature, and indeed abuseth art. (54)

　　See also Sidney under GENRE (SDP 50), LANGUAGE (SDP 11).

1601   Jonson. *See* under SYMBOL (JBW).

1609   de Vega   VAWP

Menander . . . held the choruses in despite, as offensive. Terence was more
circumspect as to the principles; since he never elevated the style of comedy to
the greatness of tragedy, which many have condemned as vicious in Plautus;
for in this respect Terence was more wary. Tragedy has as its argument history,
and comedy fiction; for this reason it was called flat-footed, of humble
argument, since the actor performed without buskin or stage. (27) . . . Begin
. . . with simple language, do not spend sententious thoughts and witty sayings
on family trifles, which is all that the familiar talk of two or three people is
representing. But when the character who is introduced persuades, counsels or
disuades, then there should be gravity and wit; for then doubtless is truth
observed, since a man speaks in a different style from what is common when he
gives counsel, or persuades, or argues against anything. Aristides, the rhetori-
cian, gave us warrant for this; for he wishes the language of comedy to be pure,
clear, and flexible, and he adds also that it should be taken from the usage of
the people, this being different from that of polite society; for in the latter case
the diction will be elegant, sonorous, and adorned. Do not drag in quotations,
nor let your language offend because of exquisite words; for, if one is to imitate
those who speak, it should not be by the language of Panchaia, of the Metaurus,
of hippogriffs, demi-gods and centaurs. (32-33)

　　See also de Vega under ACTION (VAWP 30-31), VARIETY (VAWP
31).

1640   Jonson. *See* under GENRE (JBW).

1641 Jonson   **JD**

[The true Artificer] . . . in his Elocution to behold, what word is proper: which hath ornament: which height: what is beautifully translated: where figures are fit: which gentle, which strong to shew the composition *Manly*. And how hee hath avoyded, faint, obscure, obscene, sordid, humble, improper, or effeminate *Phrase*: which is not only prais'd of the most, but commended, (which is worse) especially for that it is naught. (33) . . . The chiefe vertue of a style is perspicuitie, and nothing so vitious in it, as to need an Interpreter. (74) . . . *Language* most shewes a man: speake that I may see thee. It springs out of the most retired, and inmost parts of us, and is the Image of the Parent of it, the mind. No glasse renders a mans forme, or likenesse, so true as his speech. (78)

    See also Jonson under IMITATION (JD 33), LANGUAGE (JD 17), 25-26, 72), METAPHOR (JD 73, 77), SURPRISE (JD 35).

1657 d'Aubignac. *See* under COMEDY (AAS 4: 141).

1665 Dryden   **DW**

Our best poets have differed from other nations . . . in usually mingling and interweaving mirth and sadness through the whole course of their plays, Ben Jonson only excepted, who keeps himself entirely to one argument. And I confess I am now convinced in my own judgment, that it is most proper to keep the audience in one entire disposition both of concern and attention; for when scenes of so different natures immediately succeed one another, it is probable the audience may not so suddenly recollect themselves, as to start into an enjoyment of the mirth, or into a concern for the sadness. Yet I dispute not but the variety of this world may afford pursuing accidents of such different natures: but yet, though possible in themselves to be, they may not be so proper to be presented; an entire connexion being the natural beauty of all plays, and language the ornament to dress them in; which, in serious subjects, ought to be great and easy, like a high-born person, that expresses greatness without pride or affectation. The easier dictates of nature ought to flow in Comedy, yet separated from obsceneness, there being nothing more impudent than the immodesty of words: wit should be chaste; and those that have it can only write well. (1, 2: 19-20) . . . [A] way of the ancients, which the French follow, and our stage has now lately practised, is, to write in rhyme; and this is the dispute betwixt many ingenious persons, whether verse in rhyme, or verse without the sound, which may be called *blank* verse, . . . is to be preferred. But take the question largely, . . . they are both proper, that is, one for a play, the other for a poem or copy of verses; a blank verse being as much too low for one, as rhyme is unnatural for the other. A poem being a premeditated form of thoughts upon designed occasions, ought not to be unfurnished of any harmony in words or sound; the other is presented as the present effect of accidents not thought of: so that it is impossible it should be equally proper to both these, unless it were possible that all persons were born so much more than poets, that verses were not to be composed by them, but already made in them. (1,2: 20)

1668   Dryden   DW

As for [the French playwright's] new way of mingling mirth with serious plot, I do not . . . condemn the thing, though I cannot approve their manner of doing it. [Lisideius] tells us, we cannot so speedily recollect ourselves after a scene of great passion and concernment, as to pass to another of mirth and humour, and to enjoy it with any relish: but why should he imagine the soul of man more heavy than his senses? Does not the eye pass from an unpleasant object to a pleasant in a much shorter time than is required to this? and does not the unpleasantness of the first commend the beauty of the latter? The old rule of logick might have convinced him, that contraries, when placed near, set off each other. A continued gravity keeps the spirit too much bent; we must refresh it sometimes, as we bait in a journey, that we may go on with greater ease. A scene of mirth, mixed with tragedy, has the same effect upon us which our musick has betwixt the acts; which we find a relief to us from the best plots and language of the stage, if the discourses have been long. I must therefore have stronger arguments, ere I am convinced that compassion and mirth in the same subject destroy each other; and in the mean time can not but conclude, to the honour of our nation, that we have invented, increased, and perfected a more pleasant way of writing for the stage, than was ever known to the ancients or moderns of any nation, which is tragi-comedy. (1, 2: 85-86) . . . in serious plays where the subject and characters are great, and the plot unmixed with mirth, . . . rhyme is there as natural and more effectual than blank verse. . . . What other conditions are required to make rhyme natural in itself, besides an election of apt words, and a right disposition of them? For the due choice of your words expresses your sense naturally, and the due placing them adapts the rhyme to it. . . . If then verse may be made natural in itself, how becomes it unnatural in a play? You say the stage is the representation of nature, and no man in ordinary conversation speaks in rhyme. But you foresaw when you said this, that it might be answered—neither does any man speak in blank verse, or in measure without rhyme. Therefore you concluded, that which is nearest nature is still to be preferred. But you took no notice that rhyme might be made as natural as blank verse, by the well placing of the words. . . . All the difference between them, when they are both correct, is, the sound in one, which the other wants; and if so, the sweetness of it, and all the advantage resulting from it . . . will yet stand good. As for that place of Aristotle, where he says, plays should be writ in that kind of verse which is nearest prose, it makes little for you; blank verse being properly but measured prose. (1, 2: 118-21)
. . . One great reason why prose is not to be used in serious plays, is, because it is too near the nature of converse. There may be too great a likeness; as the

most skilful painters affirm, that there may be too near a resemblance in a picture: to take every lineament and feature, is not to make an excellent piece; but to take so much only as will make a beautiful resemblance of the whole; and, with an ingenious flattery of nature, to heighten the beauties of some parts, and hide the deformities of the rest. (1, 2: 161)

1672   Dryden   DW

Whether Heroick Verse ought to be admitted into serious plays, is not now to be disputed: it is already in possession of the stage; and . . . very few tragedies, in this age, shall be received without it. All the arguments which are formed against it, can amount to no more than this,—that it is not so near conversation as prose; and therefore not so natural. But it is very clear to all who understand poetry, that serious plays ought not to imitate conversation too nearly. If nothing were to be raised above that level, the foundation of poetry would be destroyed. And if you once admit of a latitude, that thoughts may be exalted, and that images and actions may be raised above the life, and described in measure without rhyme, that leads you insensibly from your own principles to mine: you are already so far onward of your way, that you have foresaken the imitation of ordinary converse; you are gone beyond it; and, to continue where you are, is to lodge in the open field, betwixt two inns. You have lost that which you call natural, and have not acquired the last perfection of art. (1, 2: 209-10)

1679   Dryden. *See* under PLOT (DW 1, 2: 288), TRAGEDY (DW 1, 2: 266-67).

1682   Dryden   DW

The expressions of a poem, designed purely for instruction, ought to be plain and natural, and yet majestick; for here the poet is presumed to be a kind of law-giver, and those three qualities which I have named are proper to the legislative style. The florid, elevated, and figurative way is for the passions, for love and hatred, fear and anger, are begotten in the soul by shewing their objects out of their true proportion, either greater than the life, or less; but instruction is to be given by shewing them what they naturally are. A man is to be cheated into passion, but to be reasoned into truth. (2: 329)

1710-1711   Addison. *See* under IMITATION (AW 1: 23-24).

1711   Addison   AW

Our English blank verse . . . often enters into our common discourse, though we do not attend to it, and is such a due medium between rhyme and prose, that it seems wonderfully adapted to tragedy. I am therefore very much offended when I see a play in rhyme; which is as absurd in English, as a tragedy of hexameters would have been in Greek or Latin. . . . I would not however debar the poet from concluding his tragedy, or, if he pleases, every act of it, with two or three couplets, which may have the same effect as an air in the Italian opera after a long recitativo, and give the actor a graceful exit. (1: 70)

See also Addison under THOUGHT (AW 1: 70).

1712   Addison. See under TASTE (AW 2: 135-36).

1758   Diderot   **DDP**

[The style in serious drama is] more nervous, graver, more elevated, violent, more susceptible of what we term *feeling*, without which no style appeals to the heart. (288)

See also Diderot under ACTION (DDP 291-92).

1767-1769   Lessing. See under LANGUAGE (LSPW 393-94), METAPHOR (LSPW 311).

1778   Johnson. See under LANGUAGE (JL 1: 58-59).

1789   Goethe. See under IMITATION (GLE 59-61).

1808   Schlegel   **SCL**

[Samuel] Johnson founds the justification of the species of drama in which seriousness and mirth are mixed, on this, that in real life the vulgar is found close to the sublime, that the merry and the sad usually accompany and succeed one another. But it does not follow that because both are found together, therefore they must not be separable in the compositions of art. The observation is in other respects just, and this circumstance invests the poet with the power to adopt this procedure, because every thing in the drama must be regulated by the conditions of theatrical probability; . . . the mixture of such dissimilar; and apparently contradictory, ingredients, in the same works, can only be justifiable on principles reconcilable with the views of art. (370-71)

See also Schlegel under AESTHETIC (SCL 342-43), CHARACTER (SCL 148-49), GENRE DEFINITION (SCL 176-79), ILLUSION (SCL 246), LANGUAGE (SCL 229-30).

1815   Coleridge   **CBL**

I would trace the [*origin* of metre] to the balance in the mind effected by that spontaneous effort which strives to hold in check the workings of passion. It might be easily explained likewise in what manner this salutary antagonism is assisted by the very state, which it counteracts; and how this balance of antagonists became organized into *metre* . . . by a supervening act of the will and judgment, consciously and for the foreseen purpose of pleasure. (2:

49-50) . . . [There are] two legitimate conditions, which the critic is entitled to expect in every metrical work. First, that, as the *elements* of metre owe their existence to a state of increased excitement, so the metre itself should be accompanied by the natural language of excitement. Secondly, that as these elements are formed into metre *artificially*, by a *voluntary* act, with the design and for the purpose of blending *delight* with emotion, so the traces of present *volition* should throughout the metrical language be proportionately discernible. Now these two conditions must be reconciled and co-present. (2: 50) . . . I [also] argue from the EFFECTS of metre. As far as metre acts in and for itself, it tends to increase the vivacity and susceptibility both of the general feelings and of the attention. This effect it produces by the continued excitement of surprize, and by the quick reciprocations of curiosity still gratified and still re-excited, which are too slight indeed to be at any one moment objects of distinct consciousness, yet become considerable in their aggregate influence. (2: 51) . . . In poetry, in which every line, every phrase, may pass the ordeal of deliberation and deliberate choice, it is possible, and barely possible, to attain that ultimatum which I have ventured to propose as the infallible test of a blameless style; its *untranslatableness* in words of the same language without injury to the meaning. Be it observed, however, that I include in the *meaning* of a word not only its correspondent object, but likewise all the associations which it recalls. For language is framed to convey not the object alone, but likewise the character, mood and intentions of the person who is representing it. (2: 115-16)

See also Coleridge under TASTE (CBL 2: 63-64), UNITY (CBL 2: 258).

1818   Hazlitt   HW

There are four sorts or schools of tragedy with which I am acquainted. The first is the antique or classical. This consisted . . . in the introduction of persons on the stage, speaking, feeling, and acting *according to nature*, that is, according to the impression of given circumstances on the passions and mind of man in those circumstances, but limited by the physical conditions of time and place, as to its external form, and to a certain dignity of attitude and expression, selection in the figures, and unity in their grouping, as in a statue or bas-relief. The second is the Gothic or romantic, or as it might be called, the historical or poetical tragedy, and differs from the former, only in having a larger scope in the design and boldness in the execution; that is, it is the dramatic representation of nature and passion emancipated from the precise imitation of an actual event in place and time, from the same fastidiousness in the choice of materials, and with the license of the epic and fanciful form added to it in the range of the subject and the decorations of language. This is particularly the style or school of Shakespear and of the best writers of the age of Elizabeth, and the one immediately following. Of this class, or genus, the *tragedie bourgeoise* is a variety, and the antithesis of the classical form. The third sort is the French or common-place rhetorical style, which is founded on the antique as to its form and subject matter; but instead of individual nature, real passion, or imagination growing out of real passion and the circumstances of the speaker, it deals only in vague, imposing, and laboured declamations, or descriptions of nature, dissertations on the passions, and pompous flourishes which never entered any head but the author's, have no existence in nature which they pretend to identify, and are not dramatic at all, but purely didactic. The fourth and last is the German or paradoxical style, which differs from the others in representing men as acting not from the impulse of feeling, or as debating commonplace questions of morality, but as the organs and mouthpieces (that is, acting, speaking, and thinking, under the sole influence) of certain extravagant speculative opinions, abstracted from all existing customs, prejudices and institutions. (5: 347) . . . The great difference . . . which we find between the classical and the romantic style, between ancient and modern poetry, is, that the one more frequently describes things as they are interesting in themselves,—the other for the sake of the associations of ideas connected with them; that the one dwells more on the immediate impressions of objects on the senses—the other on the ideas which they suggest to the imagination. The one is the poetry of form, the other of effect. The one gives only what is necessarily implied in the subject, the other all that can possibly arise out of it. The one seeks to identify the imitation with the external object,—clings to it,—is inseparable from it,—is either that or nothing; the other seeks to identify the original impression with whatever else, within the range of thought or feeling, can strengthen, relieve, adorn or elevate it. Hence the severity and simplicity of the Greek tragedy, which excluded every thing foreign or unnecessary to the subject. Hence the Unities: for, in order to identify the imitation as much as possible with the reality, and leave nothing to mere imagination, it was necessary to give the same coherence and consistency to the different parts of a story, as to the different limbs of a statue. Hence the beauty and grandeur of their materials; for, deriving their power over the mind from the truth of the imitation, it was necessary that the subject which they made choice of, and from which they could not depart, should be in itself grand and beautiful. Hence the perfection of their execution; which consisted in giving the utmost harmony, delicacy, and refinement to the details of a given subject. Now, the characteristic excellence of the moderns is the reverse of all this. . . . The Muse of classical poetry should be represented as a beautiful naked figure: the Muse of modern poetry should be represented clothed, and with wings. The first has the advantage in point of form; the last in colour and motion. (5: 350-51)

See also Hazlitt under LANGUAGE (HW 5: 12-13).

1821-1822   Hazlitt   HW

We may observe an effeminacy of style, in some degree corresponding to effeminacy of character. Writers of this stamp are great interliners of what they indite, alterers of indifferent phrases, and the plague of printers' devils. By an effeminate style I would be understood to mean one that is florid, all fine; that cloys by its sweetness, and tires by its sameness. Such are what Dryden calls "calm, peaceable writers." They only aim to please, and never offend by truth or disturb by singularity. Every thought must be beautiful *per se*, every expression equally fine. They do not delight in vulgarisms, but in commonplaces, and dress out unmeaning forms in all the colours of the rainbow. They do not go out of their way to think—.... they cannot express a trite thought in common words—that would be a sacrifice of their own vanity. They are not sparing of tinsel, for it costs nothing. (6: 254)

1824   Goethe. *See* under GENRE (GCE March 30).

1824   Hazlitt. *See* under UNITY (HW 9: 404-405).

1827   Goethe. *See* under VARIETY (GCE Jan. 31).

1864   Taine   **TLA**

A phrase uttered is a combination of forces which at once awaken in the reader the logical instinct, the musical aptitude, the acquisitions of memory, and the fires of the imagination, and thrills the whole man through the nerves, the senses, and the habits. It is necessary therefore that the style should be in keeping with the rest of the work; there is therein a final convergence, and on this domain the art of the great writers is without limit; their tact is of extraordinary delicacy and their invention is of inexhaustible fertility. (321)
... Art is superior to nature; for the imaginary personage speaks better and more conformably to his character than the real personage. Without here entering into the subtleties of art, ... we easily perceive that verse is a sort of song and prose a sort of conversation that the stately alexandrine line raises the voice up to a sustained and noble accent, and that the short lyrical strophe is still more musical and still more exalted; ... in short, that every form of style determines a state of the soul, either expansion or tension, transport or indifference, order or disorder, and that therefore the effects of situations and of characters are diminished or heightened according as the effects of style follow in the contrary sense or in the same sense. Suppose that Racine should adopt the style of Shakespeare, and Shakespeare that of Racine, their work would be absurd or rather they would not be able to write. (322-23)
    See also Taine under LANGUAGE (TLA 54-55).

1871   Nietzsche   **NBT**

[Greek drama] is the Apollonian dream-state, in which the world of day is veiled, and a new world, clearer, more intelligible, more striking than the former, and nevertheless more shadowy, is ever born anew in a perpetual change before our eyes. We accordingly recognise in tragedy a thorough-going stylistic contrast: the language, colour, flexibility and dynamics of the dialogue fall apart in the Dionysian lyrics of the Chorus on the one hand, and in the Apollonian dream-world of the scene on the other, into entirely separate spheres of expression. (71)

See also Nietzsche under LANGUAGE (NBT 72).

1876   Sarcey . **STT**

We must come down to the middle of the eighteenth century to find in our literature a single comedy in which a situation turns toward the pathetic and is treated in a manner to bring tears to the eyes of the spectators. There is no doubt that the founders of our drama, and above all the immortal Moliere, had made the very simple observation that in life it often happens that the most joyful events face about suddenly and change joy into despair. . . . If the masters of the drama, who could not have failed to make so simple an observation, have nevertheless written as if it had been unknown to them, it is apparent that their sole purpose was not to exhibit life as it really is on the stage, that they had in view another object,—that of showing life in a certain aspect to twelve hundred persons assembled in a theater, and of producing on the multiple soul of this audience a certain impression. (49-50)

See also Scarcey under AFFECT (STT 34-38), GENRE (STT 48-49), UNITY (STT 41-42, 45, 53).

1880   Nietzsche **NHH 2**

To communicate a state, an inner tension of pathos by means of signs, including the tempo of these signs,—that is the meaning of every style. . . . Any style is *good* which genuinely communicates an inner condition, which does not blunder over the signs, over the tempo of the signs, or over *moods*— all the laws of phrasing are the outcome of representing moods artistically. . . . All this takes for granted, of course, that there exist ears that can hear, and such men as are capable and worthy of like pathos, that those are not wanting unto whom one may communicate one's self. (62-63)

1882   Nietzsche **NJW**

To ''give style'' to one's character—that is a grand and a rare art! He who surveys all that his nature presents in its strength and in its weakness, and then fashions it into an ingenious plan, until everything appears artistic and rational, and even the weaknesses enchant the eye—exercises that admirable art. (223)

See also Nietzsche under AESTHETIC (NJW 334-35).

1886   Chekhov. *See* under LANGUAGE (CLF 70-71).

1888   Chekhov **CLF**

May 30. You are . . . inclined to austere creation, which was developed in you by extensive reading of classic models, and by your love for these models.

Imagine your [play] written in verse, and you will see that its defects will take on a different aspect. If it were written in verse, nobody would notice that all its characters speak one and the same language, nobody would reproach your characters for uttering nothing but philosophy, and for "feuilletonizing" in the classic form,—all this would blend with the classic tone as smoke blends with the air,—and one would not observe . . . the absence of the commonplace language and the everyday, petty actions that the modern drama must provide in plenty. . . . Give your characters Latin names, attire them in togas, and you will get the same thing,—the defects of your play are irremediable because they are organic. (172)

c.1900   Shaw. *See* under TRAGEDY (SS 253).

1903   Shaw   **SMS**

"For art's sake" alone I would not face the toil of writing a single sentence. . . . But a true original style is never achieved for its own sake. . . . Effectiveness of assertion is the Alpha and Omega of style. He who has nothing to assert has no style and can have none: he who has something to assert will go far in power of style as its momentousness and his conviction will carry him. Disprove his assertion after it is made, yet its style remains. (xxxv)

1908   Pirandello   **POH**

It is the poet who must draw from language the individual form, that is, style. Language is knowledge, objectification; style is subjectivizing this objectification. In this sense, style is *creation* of form, i.e., is the hollow word being invested and animated, in us, by a particular feeling and moved by a particular will of ours. Therefore, it is not a matter of creating *ex nihilo*, for fantasy does not create in the strict sense of the word, that is, it does not produce forms that are genuinely new. In fact, even the most capricious arabesques and the strangest grotesques—centaurs, sphinxes, winged monsters—will always reveal images that relate to real perceptions, even though they are more or less altered through various combinations. Now, the art of language has a form that in a certain sense corresponds to the grotesque in the figurative arts—and this is in fact macaronic style, an arbitrary creation, a monstrous contamination of various elements of the cognitive world. (36)

   See also Pirandello under HUMOR (POH 35), ILLUSION (POH 66-67).

1919   Eliot   **ESE**

Cyrano satisfies . . . the requirements of poetic drama. It must take genuine and substantial human emotions, such emotions as observation can confirm, typical emotions, and give them artistic form; the degree of abstraction is a question for the method of each author. (29)

1922   Stanislavski   SL

Genuine grotesque is a vivid and bold exernalization based on such tremendous, all-embracing inner content that reaches the limits of exaggeration. An actor must not only feel and experience human passions in all their universal, component elements—he must over and above this condense them and produce a manifestation of them so vivid, so irresistable in its expressiveness, so audacious, so bold that it borders on the burlesque. The grotesque may not be unintelligible, there can be no question mark placed after it. . . . It would be too bad if any spectator, after seeing your grotesque, should ask: ''Tell me please, what is the meaning of those two crooked eyebrows and the black triangle on the cheek of Pushkin's Miser Knight or Salieri?'' . . . There lies the grave of the grotesque. It dies and in its place is born a simple riddle, as silly and naïve as the ones they publish in the illustrated magazines. (154-55)

1926   Eliot   EEE

The Poetic drama must have an emotional unity, let the emotion be whatever you like. It must have a dominant tone; and if this be strong enough, the most heterogeneous emotions may be made to reinforce it. (167)

1931-1936   Artaud   AT

The drama [of the Balinese theatre] does not develop as a conflict of feelings but as a conflict of spiritual states, themselves ossified and transformed into gestures—diagrams. In a word, the Balinese have realized, with the utmost rigor, the idea of pure theater, where everything, conception and realization alike, has value, has existence only in proportion to its degree of objectification *on the stage*. (53)

1932   Eliot. *See* under UNITY (EJD 60).

1934   Eliot   EEE

It is possible that what distinguishes poetic drama from prosaic drama is a kind of doubleness in the action, as if it took place on two planes at once. In this it is different from allegory, in which the abstraction is something conceived, not something differently felt, and from symbolism (as in the plays of Maeterlinck) in which the tangible world is deliberately diminished—both symbolism and allegory being operations of the conscious planning mind. In poetic drama a certain apparent irrelevance may be the symptom of this doubleness; or the drama has an underpattern, less manifest than the theatrical one. (189-90)

1936   Brecht   BBB

The Chinese performer . . . eschews complete transformation. He confines himself . . . to merely *quoting* the character. But with how much art he does this! He requires only a minimum of illusion. What he shows is worth seeing even to those who are not out of their senses. What western actor, with the exception of a comedian or so, could do what the Chinese actor Mei-Lan-Fang does—show the elements of his craft clad in evening dress in a room with no special lights before an audience of professionals? . . . He'd be like a conjurer at a fairground showing his magical tricks, which no one would want to see a second time. He would merely show how one *dissembles*. The hypnosis would pass and there would remain a couple of pounds of badly beaten-up mimicry. . . . (132)

See also Brecht under ALIENATION (BBB 131-36), ILLUSION (BBB 130).

1942   Eliot   **EOPP**

The history of blank verse illustrates two interesting and related points: the dependence upon speech and the striking difference, in what is prosodically the same form, between dramatic blank verse and blank verse employed for epical, philosophical, meditative and idyllic purposes. The dependence of verse upon speech is much more direct in dramatic poetry than in any other. In most kinds of poetry, the necessity for its reminding us of contemporary speech is reduced by the latitude allowed for personal idiosyncrasy: a poem by Gerard Hopkins, for instance, may sound pretty remote from the way in which you and I express ourselves . . . but Hopkins does give the impression that his poetry has the necessary fidelity to his way of thinking and talking to himself. But in dramatic verse the poet is speaking in one character after another, through a medium of a company of actors trained by a producer . . . : his idiom must be comprehensive of all the voices, but present at a deeper level than is necessary when the poet speaks only for himself. (33)

1943   Eliot   **EOPP**

Dramatic poetry . . . has a social function of a kind now peculiar to itself. For whereas most poetry to-day is written to be read in solitude, or to be read aloud in a small company, dramatic verse alone had as its function the making of an immediate, collective impression upon a large number of people gathered together to look at an imaginary episode acted upon a stage. Dramatic poetry is different from any other, but as its special laws are those of the drama its function is merged into that of the drama in general. (17)

1948   Brecht   **BBBG**

For about half a century [theater audiences] have been enabled to see somewhat more faithful images of men's life together, such as characters who rebelled against certain social evils or even against the whole structure of society. Their interest was so strong that they temporarily accepted extraordinary limitations in language, plot, and intellectual range; for the breeze of the scientific spirit reduced the customary "charm" of the theater almost to nothing. The sacrifice was hardly rewarding. The improvement [in the accuracy] of the images damaged one pleasure without putting another in its place. . . . Human relations became visible but . . . not clearly *seen*. Feelings generated in the old, magical way necessarily remained the old kind of feelings (23) . . . When art mirrors life it does so with special mirrors. Art does not become unrealistic if it alters proportions. It is unrealistic only if the proportions are altered in such a way that the spectator who uses art for practical insights and impulses finds he is at a loss in real life. Stylization should not eliminate what is natural but exaggerate it. At any rate a theater that takes everything from gesture cannot do without choreography. The mere elegance of a movement and the charm of an ensemble are alienations, and pantomime is an aid to plot. . . . Let us call in all the sister arts but not in order to produce a composite art work . . . in which they all surrender and lose themselves. They should, together with the art of acting, promote the common task each in its own way. Their intercourse with each other consists in reciprocal alienation. (39-40)

    See also Brecht under GEST (BBBG 39), ILLUSION (BBBG 28-29).

1951   Eliot   EPD

If poetry is merely a decoration . . . then it is superfluous. It must justify itself dramatically, and not merely be fine poetry shaped into a dramatic form. . . . No play should be written in verse for which prose is *dramatically* adequate.
. . . The audience, its attention held by the dramatic action, its emotions stirred by the situation between the characters, should be too intent upon the play to be wholly conscious of the medium. (10-11) . . . The chief effect of style and rhythm in dramatic speech . . . should be unconscious. . . . A mixture of prose and verse in the same play is generally to be avoided: each transition makes the auditor aware, with a jolt, of the medium. It is, we may say, justifiable when the author wishes to produce this jolt: when, that is, he wishes to transport the audience violently from one plane of reality to another. (13) . . . [Verse] intensifies the drama. . . . I do not think that this effect is felt only by those members of an audience who "like poetry" but also by those who go for the play alone. . . . These people . . . are the audiences whom the writer of [a play in verse] ought to keep in mind. (20-21) . . . No poet has begun to master dramatic verse until he can write lines which . . . are *transparent*. You are consciously attending, not to the poetry, but to the meaning of the poetry. (26)

1953   Eliot   ETVP

[The "three voices" of the poet:] The first is the voice of the poet talking to himelf—or to nobody. The second is the voice of the poet addressing an audience. . . . The third is the voice of the poet when he attempts to create a dramatic character speaking in verse . . . within the limits of one imaginary character addressing another imaginary character. The distinction between the first and the second voice . . . points to the problem of poetic communication;

the distinction between the poet addressing other people in either his own voice or an assumed voice, and the poet inventing speech in which imaginary characters address each other, points to the problem of the difference between dramatic, quasi-dramatic, and non-dramatic verse. (4) . . . The third, or dramatic voice, did not make itself audible to me until I first attacked the problem of presenting two (or more) characters, in some sort of conflict, misunderstanding, or attempt to understand each other, characters with each of whom I had to try to identify myself while writing the words for him or her to speak. (8) The poetry (I mean, the langauge of those dramatic moments when it reaches intensity) must be as widely distributed as characterisation permits; and each of your characters, when he has words to speak which are poetry and not merely verse, must be given lines appropriate to himself. The personage on the stage must not give the impression of being merely a mouthpiece for the author. Hence the author is limited by the kind of poetry, and the degree of intensity in its kind, which can be plausibly attributed to each character in his play. . . . The poet writing for the theatre may, as I have found, make two mistakes: that of assigning to a personage lines of poetry not suitable to be spoken by that personage, and that of assigning lines which, however suitable to the personage, yet fail to forward the action of the play. (9-10)

SUBJECT

The statements cited under this heading deal with the materials of dramatic art, whether drawn from the real world or from legends, myths, and stories. This is sometimes confounded with "plot," which here refers only to the ordering of story elements. Theories of imitation have tended to give particular significance to subject matter, at times even investing the artistic value of the work (beauty or originality, for instance) in the objects imitated. See also *IMITATION and REALISM. Genre theories, especially those proposed by pre-romantic theorists, also gives special weight to subject matter.* See also *GENRE and GENRE DEFINITION.* Compare with *STYLE.*

4th cent. B.C.   Aristotle   AP

The objects of imitation are men in action, and these men must be either of a *higher or a lower type* [high or low character: EP 68]. . . . (11) . . . We must not . . . at all costs keep to the received legends, which are the usual subjects of Tragedy. Indeed, it would be absurd to attempt it; for even subjects that are known are known only to a few, and yet give pleasure to all [for essentially the (same) reason: EP 315]. It clearly follows that the poet or "maker" should be the maker of plots rather than verses; since he is a poet because he imitates, and what he imitates are actions. And even if he chances to take an historical subject, he is none the less a poet; for there is no reason why some events that have actually happened should not conform to the law of the probable and possible, and in virtue of that quality in them he is their poet or maker. (37) . . . A few families only . . . furnish the subjects of tragedy. It was not art, but happy chance, that *lead the poets in search of subjects to impress the tragic quality upon their plots* [the poets stumbled upon the production of this kind of effect in their tragedies: EP 452]. They are compelled, therefore, to have recourse to those houses whose history contains moving incidents like these. [See PITY 4th cent. B.C. (AP 49-53)] (53) . . . As for the story, whether the poet takes it ready made or constructs it for himself, he should first sketch its general outline, and then fill in the episodes and amplify in detail. [To illustrate "the general plan" Aristotle recites the story of *Iphigenia at Tauros*.] . . . After this, the names being once given, it remains to *fill in the* [expand with: EP 503] episodes. We must see that they are relevant to the action. . . . In the drama, the episodes are short, but it is these that give *extension* [bulk: EP 503] to Epic poetry. Thus the story of the *Odyssey* can be stated briefly. A certain man is absent from home for many years; he is jealously watched by Poseidan, and left desolate. Meanwhile his home is in a wretched plight—suitors are wasting his substance and plotting against his son. At length, tempest-tost, he himself arrives; he makes certain persons acquainted with him; he attacks the suitors with his own hands, and is himself preserved while he destroys them. This is the essence of the plot; the rest is episode. (63-65)

See also Aristotle under ACTION (AP 33-35, 37-39), AFFECT (APO 1340a:1-25), IMITATION (AP 11-13).

c.20 B.C.   Horace. See under NOVELTY (HAP 461-63).

1561   Scaliger   **SP**

Tragedy and comedy are alike in mode of representation, but differ in subject matter and treatment. The matters of tragedy are great and terrible, as commands of kings, slaughters, despair, suicides, exiles, bereavements, parricides, incests, conflagrations, battles, the putting out of eyes, weeping, wailing, bewailing, funerals, eulogies, and dirges. In comedy we have jests, reveling, weddings with drunken carousals, tricks played by slaves, drunkenness, old men deceived and cheated of their money. (57) . . . Comedy also differs from tragedy in the fact that while the latter takes both its subject matter and its chief names from history, such as Agamemnon, Hercules, and Hecuba, in comedy all is fictitious, and names are assigned for the most part to suit the connection. (69)

See also Scaliger under GENRE (SP 20, 48), TRAGEDY (SP 39, 40).

1570   Castelvetro   **CP**

If it shall happen that a poet embodies in his poetry things happened, not, however, knowing at the time that they have happened, and consequently himself having imagined them, he will be a poet just as much as if the things had not happened, for he himself has employed that labour in invention by which the title of poet is earned. (51-52) . . . There are inexcusable errors in the art of poetry; and the first of them consists in choosing an unpoetic subject. (54) . . . [Such do those err] who treat the sciences, the arts and history in verse. (61) . . . Tragedy ought to have for subject an action which happened in a very limited extent of place and in a very limited extent of time, that is, in that place and in that time, in which and for which the actors representing the action remain occupied in acting; and in no other place and in no other time. (85) . . . [The greatest source of comedy] is deception, either through folly, drunkenness, a dream, delirium; or through ignorance of the arts, the sciences, and one's own powers; or through the novelty of the good being turned in a wrong direction or of the engineer hoist on his own petard; or through deceits fashioned by man or by fortune. (134-35)

See also Castelvetro under ACTION (CP 113), DRAMA (CP 41, 60-61), GENRE (CP 107, 135), IMITATION (CP 40, 43-44, 50-51), NOVELTY (CP 116).

c. 1583   Sidney   **SDP**

The best of the historian is subject to the poet; for whatsoever action or faction, whatsoever counsel, policy, or war-stratagem the historian is bound to recite, that may the poet, if he list, with his imitation make his own, beautifying it both for further teaching and more delighting, as it pleaseth him; having all, from Dante's Heaven to his Hell, under the authority of his pen. (20)

See also Sidney under AFFECT (SDP 24), THREE UNITIES (SDP 49).

1609   de Vega. See under ACTION (VAWP 30-31), AFFECT (VAWP 35-36), IMITATION (VAWP 25).

1641   Jonson. See under NOVELTY (JD 15).

1657   d'Aubignac   **AAS**

The way . . . of chusing a Subject, is to consider whether it be founded upon one of these three things; either upon Noble Passions, as *Marianne* and the *Cid*; or upon an intricate and pleasing Plot, as *Cleomedon* . . . ; or upon some extraordinary Spectacle and Show, as *Cyminda*, or the *Two Victims*; and if the Story will bear more Circumstances of this nature, or that the Poets imagination can fitly supply the Play with them, it will be still the better; provided, he observe a just moderation, for though a Poem ought not to be without a Plot, nor without Passions, or noble Spectacles, yet to load a subject with any of them, is a thing to be avoided. Violent Passions, too often repeated, do as it were numm the Soul, and its Sympathy; the multitude of Incidents and Intrigues distract the Mind, and confound the Memory; and much Show takes up more time than can be allowed it, and is hard to bring on well. (2: 64) . . . [I] propose three sorts of Subjects. The first consists of Incidents, Intrigues, and new events, when almost from Act to Act there is some sudden change upon the Stage, which alters all the Face of Affairs; when almost all the Actors have different designs; and the means they take to make them succeed come to cross one another, and produce new and unforeseen Accidents, all which gives a marvellous satisfaction to the Spectators, it being a continual diversion, accompanied with an agreeable Expectation of what the Event will be. The second sort of Subjects are of those rais'd out of Passions; when out of a small Fund the Poet does ingeniously draw great Sentiments and noble Passions, to entertain the Auditory; and when out of Incidents that seem natural to his subject, he takes occasion to transport his Actors into extraordinary and violent Sentiments, by which the Spectators are ravish'd, and their Soul continually mov'd with some new Impression. The last sort of Subjects are the mixt or compound of Incidents and Passions, when by unexpected Events, but Noble ones, the Actors break out into different Passions; and that infinitely delights the Auditory, to see at the same time surprising Accidents, and noble and moving

Sentiments, to which they cannot but yield with pleasure. Now 'tis certain, that in all these three sorts of Subjects the Poet may succeed, provided the disposition of his Play be ingenious; but yet I have observ'd some difference, according to which they take more or less. Subjects full of Plot and Intrigue are extremely agreeable at first, but being once known, they do not the second time please us so well, because they want the graces of Novelty, all our delight consisting in being surpriz'd, which we cannot be twice. The Subjects full of Passions last longer, and affect us more, because the Soul which receives the impression of them, does not keep them so long, nor so strongly, as our Memory does the Events of things; nay, often it happens, that they please us more at second seeing, because that the first time we are employed about the Event and disposition of the Play, and by consequent do less enter into the Sentiments of the Actors; but having once no need of applying our thoughts to the Story, we busie them about the things that are said, and so receive more Impressions of grief or fear. But it is out of doubt, that the mix'd or compound are the most excellent sort, for in them the Incidents grow more pleasing by the Passions which do as it were uphold them, and the Passions seem to be renew'd, and spring afresh, by the variety of the unthought of Incidents; so that they are both lasting, and require a great time to make them lose their Graces. (2: 68-69)

   See also d'Aubignac under ACTION (AAS 1: 43-44), AFFECT (AAS 2: 69-70), RULES (AAS 1: 22-26), TRAGEDY (AAS 4: 140, 146-47).

1660   Corneille   CFD

The requirements of the subject are different for tragedy and comedy... The latter... Aristotle defines simply [as] an imitation of low and knavish persons. I cannot refrain from saying that this definition does not satisfy me.... It is not entirely just for our time, in which even kings may come into comedy when their actions are not above it.... I do not think that even though the characters are illustrious the action [of a simple love intrigue] is sufficiently important to aspire to the dignity of tragedy. The dignity of tragedy needs some great State interest or passion nobler and more virile than love, such as ambition or vengeance, which leads us to expect greater misfortune than the loss of a mistress. It is fit to mix love in it because it always has much attraction and can serve as a basis of those other interests and other passions of which I speak. But it must content itself with second rank in the poem.... We see no tragedy [of the ancients] in which there is only a love-interest to unravel.... Comedy... differs from tragedy in that the latter requires an illustrious, extraordinary, serious subject while the former stops at a common playful subject. The latter demands great dangers for its hero; the former contents itself with the worry and displeasures of [its protagonists]. (142-43)

   See also Corneille under PROBABILITY (CFD 139), THREE UNITIES (CDTU 235-36, 237 and CDENA 32).

1664   Racine   RP

Love, which, ordinarily, assumed so important a role in tragedy, I have
practically neglected [in *La Thébaide*]; I doubt whether I should give it a more
important place were I to rewrite the play. It would be necessary to have one of
the brothers in love, or else both; but what chance had I to give them any other
interest but that famous hatred, which consumed them both? If I could not have
either of the brothers in love, there remained for me only to place the love-
interest in characters of secondary importance; and this is what I have done.
. . . I am of the opinion that lovers' tenderness and jealousies can have no
legitimate place amid all the incest, parricide, and other horrors. . . . (154)

1672   Dryden. *See* under GENRE DEFINITION (DW 1, 2: 213).

1679   Dryden. *See* under ACTION (DW 1, 2: 268-69).

1695   Dryden   DW

As all stories are not proper subjects for an epick poem or a tragedy, so neither
are they for a noble picture. The subjects both of the one and of the other, ought
to have nothing of immoral, low, or filthy in them . . . [but] must in general be
great and noble, . . . [the] great action of some illustrious hero. (3: 312-13)

1712   Addison. *See* under INSTRUCTION (AW 2: 184-85), PROBABIL-
ITY (AW 2: 4).

1725   Voltaire   VE

[Some contend] that domestic strife can never be a proper subject for a tragedy.
I beg leave to offer a few reflections on this prejudiced opinion. All tragic
pieces are founded either on the interests of a nation, or on the particular
interest of princes. Of the former kind are *Iphigenia in Aulis* . . . ; the *Horace*
. . . ; *Oedipus*. . . . Of the latter kind are *Britannicus, Phèdre, Mithridate*, and
so forth. In these last three pieces the whole interest is confined to the family of
the hero who is represented. The whole depends on passions which are equally
felt by all mankind, and the intrigue is as proper for comedy as for tragedy.
Change only the names, and Mithridates is but an old man in love with a young
girl, who is also passionately beloved by his two sons; and he makes use of a
low stratagem to find out which of the two is his happy rival. Phaedra is a
mother-in-law who, emboldened by her confidant, discovers her passion to her
son-in-law, who happens to be engaged elsewhere. . . . These are all subjects
which Molière might have handled as well as Racine. And, in fact, the intrigue
of *L'Avare* is exactly the same with that of *Mithridate*. Harpagon and the King
of Pontus are two amorous old men; both have their sons for rivals; both
contrive in the same manner to find out the correspondence that subsists
between their son and mistress; and both plays conclude with the marriage of

the young fellows. Molière and Racine have equally succeeded in handling this subject: the one amuses and diverts, the other moves us with terror and compassion. Molière exposes the ridiculous fondness of an old miser; Racine describes the foibles of a great king, and makes them even venerable. (278-79)

1730 Voltaire. *See* under THREE UNITIES (VE 280-81).

1731 Voltaire   VE

That love may be deserving of a place in tragedy it must have a necessary connection with the whole piece and not be arbitrarily introduced to fill up gaps, as it does in [English] tragedies as well as in our own, all of which are too long. It should in reality be a tragic passion, considered as a weakness, and opposed and contrasted by remorse. It should either lead to misfortune and crime, to convince us of its perils; or else virtue should triumph over it, to show that it is not invincible. Treated in any other way, love is of the same nature with that which is the subject of pastorals or comedies. (284)

See also Voltaire under LANGUAGE (VE 283).

1738 Voltaire. *See* under HUMOR (VW 10, 1: 271).

1751 Johnson. *See* under VARIETY (3: 241).

1755-1780 Diderot   DDE

Why should we forbid the painter of manners every subject that isn't laughable? Why would we regard man's likeable and reasonable side with less pleasure than his shortcomings and his ridiculous traits? It is undoubtedly very useful to expose the follies of man in their true light, but would it be less useful to offer examples of honest dealings, of noble sentiments, of decent behavior, of all the virtues of social life, so that these examples could touch us, move us, and make a lasting impression on us? And there is no need to fear that what is beautiful and virtuous is less suited to giving pleasure than what is ridiculous; on the contrary, we see that Plautus and Molière are nowhere more successful than when they are serious. Thus, without taking away anything of value from satiric and mirthful comedy, let us not close out theatres to comedy which entertains us by more noble pictures, and which instead of making us laugh at the failings of mankind delights us by the sight of its perfections. (287)

See also Diderot under TRAGEDY (DDE 291).

1758 Diderot   DDP

There are three kinds of subjects. History, which is a matter of facts; tragedy, where the poet adds to history whatever elements of interest he can; and comedy, where the poet invents everything. (296)

See also Diderot under DRAMA (DDP 287-89), GENRE DEFINITION (DDP 287).

1765   Johnson. *See* under GENRE (JS 16), VARIETY (JS 15).

1767-1769   Lessing. *See* under GENRE (LSPW 248), PROBABILITY (LSPW 279).

1797   Goethe   **GED**

The subjects of epic poetry and of tragedy should be altogether human, full of significance and pathos. . . . The epic poem represents above all things circumscribed activity, tragedy, circumscribed suffering. The epic . . . gives us man working outside of and beyond himself: battles, wanderings, enterprises of all kinds which demand a certain sensuous breadth. Tragedy gives us man thrown in upon himself, and the actions of genuine tragedy therefore stand in need of but little space. (338)

1808 Schlegel. *See* under GENRE DEFINITION (SCL 176-69), RULES (SCL 217), THREE UNITIES (SCL 236-51, 305), TRAGEDY (SCL 67).

c.1810   Coleridge. *See* under UNITY (CSLW 117).

1815   Hazlitt. *See* under HUMOR (HW 1: 12), TRAGEDY (HW 1: 13).

1816   Hazlitt   **HW**

The superiority of high art over the common or mechanical consists in combining truth of imitation with beauty and grandeur of subject. The historical painter is superior to the flower-painter, because he combines or ought to combine human interests and passions with the same power of imitating external nature; or, indeed, with greater, for the greatest difficulty of imitation is the power of imitating expression. The difficulty of copying increases with our knowledge of the object; and that again with the interest we take in it. The same argument might be applied to shew that the poet and painter of imagination are superior to the mere philosopher or man of science, because they exercise the powers of reason and intellect combined with nature and passion. They treat of the highest categories of the human soul, pleasure and pain. (1: 75-76)

    See also Hazlitt under TRAGEDY (HW 10: 96).

1817   Hazlitt   **HW**

Poetry is an interesting study, for this reason, that it relates to whatever is most interesting in human life. Whoever therefore has a contempt for poetry, has a contempt for himself and humanity. (1: 271)

1818   Hazlitt. *See* under STYLE (HW 5: 347, 350-51).

c.1820   Hegel. *See* under ACTION (HFA 4: 253-54), CONFLICT (HFA 4: 318-20), DRAMA (HFA 4: 261-62), TRAGEDY (HFA 4: 295-99, 300-301, 312-15).

1824   Goethe. *See* under NOVELTY (GCE Nov. 24).

1825   Goethe. *See* under THREE UNITIES (GCE Feb. 24), TRAGEDY (GCE May 12).

1827   Goethe   **GCE**

Wed., Jan 31. ''Our present poets should do like the ancients. They should not be always asking whether a subject has been used before, and look to south and north for unheard-of adventures, which are often barbarous enough, and merely make an impression as incidents. But to make something of a simple subject by a masterly treatment requires intellect and great talent, and these we do not find.''

   See also Goethe under THOUGHT (GCE March 28), TRAGEDY (GCE March 28).

1830   Goethe. *See* under MAGNITUDE (GCE March 17).

1894   Brunetière. *See* under ACTION (BLD 75-76), THREE UNITIES (BLD 70).

c.1908   Strindberg. *See* under ILLUSION (SOL 263).

1909   Shaw. *See* under CLOSURE (STPB xv-xvi), GENRE DEFINITION (STPB xx, xxii-xxiii).

1912   Shaw   **SALOP**

[*Overruled*] takes the form of a farcical comedy, because it is a contribution to the very extensive dramatic literature which takes as its special department the gallantries of married people. The stage has been preoccupied by such affairs for centuries, not only in the jesting vein of Restoration Comedy and Palais Royal farce, but in the more tragically turned adulteries of the Parisian school which dominated the stage until Ibsen put them out of countenance and relegated them to their proper place as articles of commerce. Their continued vogue in that department maintains the tradition that adultery is the dramatic subject *par excellence*, and indeed that a play that is not about adultery is not a play at all. (67-68)

1913   Shaw. *See* under DRAMA (SMCE 144).

1931-1936   Artaud. *See* under THOUGHT (AT 41).

1948   Brecht   BBBG

A theater [such as the Epic Theatre] which makes productivity its chief source of entertainment must also make productivity its theme. . . . The theater must engage itself with reality so that it can and may present effective images of reality. (21)

    See also Brecht under INSTRUCTION (BBBG 20, 21).

c.1956   Brecht. *See* under PLOT (BBT 240-41).

SUBTEXT

"Subtext" is a concept evolved by Stanislavski by which the actor could express an implicit psychological content through the overt behavior of dramatic characters.

1808 **Schlegel.** *See* under AFFECT (SCL 39).

1864 **Taine.** *See* under ACTION (TLA 318-19).

1875 **Nietzsche.** *See* under POETRY OF THE THEATRE (NTS 177, 177-78).

c.1930 **Stanislavski** SCR

[Character] objectives may be reasoned, conscious . . . or they may be emotional, unconscious. . . . A conscious objective can be carried out [by the actor] on the stage with almost no feeling or will; but . . . [he] can do no more than recite dry thoughts. (51) . . . The best creative objective is the unconscious one which immediately, emotionally, takes possession of an actor's feelings, and carries him intuitively along to the basic goal of the play. (52) In this innermost center, this core of the role, all the remaining objectives of the score converge . . . into one *superobjective*. That is the inner essence, the all-embracing goal, the objective of all objectives, the concentration of the entire score of the role, of all the major and minor units. The superobjective contains the meaning, the inner sense, of all the subordinate objectives of the play. . . . [Creativity in] an actor . . . consists of constant striving toward the superobjective and the expression of that striving in action. This striving . . . is the *through action of the role or play*. . . . (77-79)

    See also Stanislavski under ACTION (SCR 48), MOTIVATION (SCR 51, 55).

1936 **Stanislavski** SAP

In a play the whole stream of individual, minor objectives, all the imaginative thoughts, feelings, and actions of an actor, should converge to carry out the *superobjective* of the plot. The common bond must be so strong that even the most insignificant detail, if it is not related to the *superobjective*, will stand out as superfluous or wrong. All this impetus toward the superobjective must be continuous throughout the whole play. When its origin is *theatrical* or *perfunc-*

tory it will give only an approximately correct direction to the play. If it is human and directed toward the accomplishment of the basic purpose of the play it will be like a main artery, providing nourishment and life to both it and the actors. Naturally, too, the greater the literary work, the greater the pull of its superobjective. (256)

1938   Stanislavski   SBC

[The subtext] is the manifest, the inwardly felt expression of a human being in a part, which flows uninterruptedly beneath the words of the text, giving them life and a basis for existing. The subtext is a web of innumerable, varied inner patterns inside a play and a part, woven from "magic ifs," given circumstances, all sorts of figments of the imagination, inner movements, objects of attention, smaller and greater truths and a belief in them, adaptations, adjustments and other similar elements. It is the subtext that makes us say the words we do in a play. All these intentionally intertwined elements are like the individual threads in a cable, they run all through the play and lead to the ultimate superobjective. It is only when our feelings reach down into the subtextual stream that the "through line of action" of a play or a part comes into being. . . . The spoken word, the text of a play is not valuable in and of itself, but is made so by the inner content of the subtext and what is contained in it. . . . Without [the subtext] the words have no excuse for being presented on the stage. When they are spoken the words come from the author, the subtext from the actor. If this were not so the public would not make the effort of coming to the theatre, they would sit at home and read the printed play. (108-109)

   See also Stanislavski under AFFECT (SAP 70), THOUGHT (SBC 169-71, 258).

SURPRISE

The statements cited here concern the experience of the unexpected. In general, it appears that "dramatic surprise" refers to an arrangement of the elements such that an event is simultaneously unanticipated and prepared. Aristotle describes the principle underlying the REVERSAL in these terms, and therefore his particular description of the Reversal episode in the complex plot may be seen as a special form of dramatic surprise intended to produce IRONY. Similarly, RECOGNITION may be extrapolated in principle to involve the comprehension that the unexpected (the Reversal of the Situation) has been prepared; that is, if dramatic surprise lies first in the unexpected occurrence, its second and more profound effect lies in the unexpected inevitability of the occurrence. For discussions of the creation of expectation, see FORWARD MOVEMENT. See also WONDER.

4th cent. B.C. Aristotle   AP

Two parts . . . of the Plot—Reversal of the Situation and Recognition—turn upon surprises. (43)

> *See also* Aristotle under PLOT (AP 39), RECOGNITION (AP 41-43, 57-61), REVERSAL (AP 41-43, AR 90-91).

1609 de Vega   VAWP

In the first act set forth the case. In the second weave together the events, in such wise that until the middle of the third act one may hardly guess the outcome. Always trick expectancy; and hence it may come to pass that something quite far from what is promised may be left to the understanding. (34)

1641 Jonson   JD

[The true Artificer's] subtilty did not shew it sefle; his judgment thought that a vice. For the ambush hurts more that is hid. (35)

1657 d'Aubignac. *See* under CLOSURE (AAS 2: 131), SUBJECT (AAS 2: 68-69).

1660 Corneille   CSP

The oracle referred to in the first act [of *Horatius*] is fulfilled at the end of the fifth. It seems clear from the outset and makes one imagine the contrary; and I should prefer them thus on our stage than those which are entirely obscure, because the surprise of their true import is all the finer. (109)

1668   Dryden. *See* under VARIETY (DW 1, 2: 89).

1710   Addison. *See* under CLOSURE (AW 3: 263).

1712   Addison   AW

Surprise is so much the life of stories, that every one aims at it who endeavors to please by telling them. Smooth delivery, an elegant choice of words, and a sweet arrangement, are all beautifying graces, but not the particulars in this point of conversation which either long command the attention, or strike with the violence of a sudden passion, or occasion the burst of laughter which accompanies humour. I have sometimes fancied that the mind is in this case like a traveler who sees a fine seat in haste; he acknowledges the delightfulness of a walk set with regularity, but would be uneasy if he were obliged to pace it over, when the first view had let him into all its beauties from one end to the other. However, a knowledge of the success which stories will have when they are attended with a turn of surprise, as it has happily made the characters of some, so has it been the ruin of the characters of others. There is a set of men who outrage truth, instead of affecting us with a manner in telling it; who overleap the line of probability that they may be seen to move out of the common road; and endeavor only to make their hearers stare by imposing upon them with a kind of nonsense against the philosophy of nature, or such a heap of wonders told upon their own knowledge, and it is not likely one man should have ever met with. (2: 312)

    See also Addison under ACTION (AW 1: 427), AESTHETIC (AW 2: 139-40), IMAGINATION (AW 2: 138-39), WONDER (AW 2: 4).

1713   Addison. *See* under SYMBOL (AW 3: 149).

1751   Johnson. *See* under WONDER (JW 3: 147-48).

1755-1780   Diderot. *See* under COMEDY (DDE 287), HUMOR (DDE 287).

1767-1769   Lessing   LSPW

I know for certain, that for one instance where it is useful to conceal from the spectator an important event until it has taken place there are ten and more where interest demands the very contrary. By means of secrecy a poet effects a short surprise, but in what enduring disquietude could he have maintained us if he had made no secret about it! Whoever is struck down in a moment, I can only pity for a moment. But how if I expect the blow, how if I see the storm brewing and threatening for some time about my head or his? For my part none of the personages need know each other if only the spectator knows them all. Nay I would even maintain that the subject which requires such secrecy is a thankless subject, that the plot in which we have to take recourse to it is not as good as that in which we could have done without it. It will never give occasion for anything great. We shall be obliged to occupy ourselves with preparations that are either too dark or too clear, the whole poem becomes a collection of little artistic tricks by means of which we effect nothing more than a short surprise. If on the contrary everything that concerns the personages is known, I see in this knowledge the source of the most violent emotions. (377-78) . . . It is clear that all the plays whose prologues annoy [the critics of Euripides] so much would be completely and entirely comprehensible without these prologues . . . [and] would bring about excellent surprises, and those surprises would be sufficiently prepared without your being able to say they suddenly broke out like lightening from a white cloud. . . . Euripides knew as well as we that his 'Ion' for instance could stand without the prologue, that without this it was a play which sustained the interest and uncertainty of the spectator to the close, but he did not care for this uncertainty and expectation. For if the spectator only learned in the fifth act that Ion was the son of Creusa, then it is not for them her son, but a stranger, an enemy, whom she seeks to make away with in the third act; then it is not for them the mother of Ion on whom Ion seeks to avenge himself in the fourth act, but only a murderess. Whence then should fear and pity arise? . . . Say of this method what you will, enough if it has helped him to attain his goal, his tragedy is throughout what a tragedy should be, and if you are still dissatisfied that the form should give place to the essential then supply your learned criticism with nothing but plays where the essential is sacrificed to the form, and you are rewarded. . . . [Euripides] let the spectators foresee all the misfortunes that were to befall his personages, in order to gain their sympathy while these were yet far removed from deeming that they required sympathy. (380-82)

Compare with Lessing under CLOSURE (LSPW 377).

1778 Johnson. *See* under LANGUAGE (JL 1: 58-59).

1808 Schlegel. *See* under FORWARD MOVEMENT (SCL 119), PROBABILITY (SCL 182-83).

1811-1812 Coleridge. *See* under METAPHOR (CCSL 45).

1815 Coleridge. *See* under STYLE (CBL 2: 51).

1816 Hazlitt. *See* under NOVELTY (HW 1: 75).

1819 Hazlitt. *See* under AFFECT (HW 8: 6), HUMOR (HW 8: 7-8, 15).

c.1820   Hazlitt. Compare with AESTHETIC (HW 2: 463).

c.1821-1822   Hazlitt   **HW**

To *elevate and surprise* is the great rule for producing a dramatic or a critical effect. The more you startle the reader, the more he will be able to startle others with a succession of smart intellectual shocks. (6: 216)

c.1900   Strindberg. *See* under PLOT (SEP 574-75).

c.1932   Brecht. *See* under GEST (BBT 104-105).

1936   Brecht. *See* under WONDER (BBB 131).

1938   Brecht. *See* under ALIENATION (BBEB 432).

1939   Brecht. *See* under GEST (BBG 34-35).

c.1940   Brecht. *See* under ALIENATION (BBAn 15-20).

1948   Brecht. *See* under ALIENATION (BBBG 26-27), GEST (BBBG 35), PLOT (BBBG 36).

SYMBOL

There is considerable disagreement about the nature of "literary symbolism." As a mechanism of human perception, the symbolic process is the interpretation by convention of a token as standing for something else. Romantic theorists wished to discriminate allegory for disapproval from an approved method for conveying significance beyond the ostensive, which they called "symbolism." However, allegory is not an alternative to symbolism but a species of it, a system of symbols created by juxtaposing two frames of reference in which the elements of the ostensive frame of reference are tokens for the other. It seems that the Romantic concept of symbolism in art is actually a metaphorical process in which significance results from a fusion of images, of which one image is often "suppressed" or implied. In any case, the extracts cited here should be compared with those under METAPHOR. See also CONVENTION for discussions of one form of theatrical symbolism (in the strict sense).

4th cent. B.C. Aristotle. *See* under FEAR (AR 82).

c.1583 Sidney. *See* under THOUGHT (SDP 8).

1601 Jonson   **JBW**

Of base detractors, and illiterate apes, . . .
'Gainst these, have we put on this forc'd defence:
Whereof the *allegory* and hid sense
Is, that a well erected confidence
Can fright their pride, and laugh their folly hence.
Prologue, The Poetaster

1641 Jonson. *See* under METAPHOR (JD 77).

1712 Addison. *See* under METAPHOR (AW 2: 152), PROBABILITY (AW 2: 4).

1713 Addison   **AW**

An allegory may be both delightful and instructive; in the first place, the fable of it ought to be perfect, and, if possible, to be filled with surprising turns and incidents. In the next, there ought to be useful morals and reflections couched under it, which still receive a greater value from their being new and uncommon; as also from their appearing difficult to have been thrown into emblematical types and shadows. (3: 149).

1808   Schlegel   SCL

[In Greek drama] the ancient mythology is in general *symbolical*, although not *allegorical*; for the two are *certainly* distinct. Allegory is the personification of an idea, a poetic story invented solely with such a view; but that is symbolical which, created by the imagination for other purposes, or possessing an independent reality of its own, is at the same time easily susceptible of an emblematic explanation; and even of itself suggests it. (88)

See also Schlegel under CHARACTER (SCL 148-49).

1815   Coleridge   CBL

An IDEA, in the *highest* sense of that word, cannot be conveyed but by a *symbol*; and, except in geometry, all symbols of necessity involve an apparent contradiction. (1: 100)

See also Coleridge under CHARACTER (CBL 2: 187).

1816   Goethe   GLE

Strictly speaking, nothing is theatrical except what is immediately symbolical to the eye: an important action, that is, which signifies a still more important one. (186)

1818   Coleridge   CMC

[Allegory is] the employment of one set of agents and images with actions and accompaniments correspondent, so as to convey, while in disguise, either moral qualities or conceptions of the mind that are not in themselves objects of the senses, or other images, agents, actions, fortunes, and circumstances, so that the difference is everywhere presented to the eye or imagination while the likeness is suggested to the mind; and this connectedly so that the parts combine to form a consistent whole. Whatever composition answering to this definition is not a fable, is entitled an allegory. (30) . . . The symbolical cannot, perhaps, be better defined in distinction from the Allegorical, than that it is always itself a part of that, of the whole of which it is the representative.— "Here comes a sail," (that is, a ship) is a symbolical expression. "Behold our lion!" when we speak of some gallant soldier, is allegorical. Of most importance to our present subject is this point, that the latter (the allegory) cannot be other than spoken consciously;—whereas in the former (the symbol) it is very possible that the general truth represented may be working unconsciously in the writer's mind during the construction of the symbol;—and it proves itself by being produced out of his own mind. . . . The advantage of symbolical writing over allegory is, that it presumes no disjunction of faculties, but simple predominance. (99)

1818   Hazlitt. *See* under AESTHETIC (HW 5: 3), LANGUAGE (HW 5: 12-13).

c.1820   Hegel. *See* under AFFECT (HFA 4: 273-74).

1826   Goethe   **GCE**

Wed. July 26. I asked [Goethe] how a piece must be constructed so as to be fit for the theater. ''It must be symbolical,'' replied Goethe; ''that is to say, each incident must be significant in itself, and lead to another still more important. The *Tartuffe* of Moliere is, in this respect, a great example. Only think what an introduction is the first scene! From the very beginning everything is highly significant, and leads us to expect something still more important that is to come.''

1871   Nietzsche. *See* under LANGUAGE (NBT 55), TRAGEDY (NBT 127, 159-60).

1875   Nietzsche. *See* under POETRY OF THE THEATRE (NTS 149-50).

1880   Nietzsche. *See* under STYLE (NHH 2: 62-63).

1898   Shaw. *See* under SPECTACLE (SMCE 188).

1908   Pirandello. *See* under IDEALISM (POH 75-76).

1925   Pirandello   **PPSC**

I hate symbolic art in which the presentation loses all spontaneous movement in order to become a machine, an allegory—a vain and misconceived effort because the very fact of giving an allegorical sense to a presentation clearly shows that we have to do with a fable which by itself has no truth either fantastic or direct; it was made for the demonstration of some moral truth. The spiritual need [of philosophical writers] . . . cannot be satisfied . . . by such allegorical symbolism. This latter starts from a concept, and from a concept which creates or tries to create for itself an image. The former, [the spiritual need,] on the other hand seeks in the image—which must remain alive and free throughout—a meaning to give it value. (365)

1931-1936   Artaud. *See* under METAPHOR (AT 27-28, 71), STYLE (AT 53), THOUGHT (AT 39-40).

c.1932   Brecht. *See* under GEST (BBT 104-105).

1934   Eliot. *See* under STYLE (EEE 189-90).

TASTE

"Taste" is the appreciation of excellence in art or sensitivity to aesthetic forms and qualities. Like "sensibility," this metaphor became fashionable in the eighteenth century to indicate a faculty beyond the reach of rationality. Historically it is important as an admission of the irrational to the very basis of art. Because it undermines respect for rules and gives special importance to the individual, the doctrine of taste was an important pre-Romantic development.

1712 Addison   AW

Most languages make use of [the metaphor of taste], to express that faculty of the mind which distinguishes all the most concealed thoughts and nicest perfections in writing. . . . A man of fine taste in writing will discern . . . not only the general beauties and imperfections of an author, but discover the several ways of thinking and expressing himself, which diversify him from all other authors. . . . After having thus far explained what is generally meant by a fine taste in writing . . . , I think I may define it to be "that faculty of the soul which discerns the beauties of an author with pleasure, and the imperfections with dislike." . . . It is very difficult to lay down rules for the acquirement of such a taste. . . . The faculty must in some degree be born with us; and it very often happens, that those who have other qualities in perfection are wholly void of this. . . . But, notwithstanding this faculty must in some measure be born with us, there are several methods for cultivating and improving it. . . . The most natural method for this purpose is to be conversant among the writings of the most polite authors. A man who has any relish for fine writing, either discovers new beauties, or receives stronger impressions, from the masterly strokes of a great author every time he peruses him; besides that he naturally wears himself into the same manner of speaking and thinking. . . . It is likewise necessary for a man who would form to himself a finished taste of good writing, to be well versed in the works of the best critics, both ancient and modern. (2: 135-36)

1767-1769 Lessing   LSPW

Not every one who can feel the beauties of one drama, the correct play of one actor, can on that account estimate the value of all others. He has no taste who has only a one-sided taste; but he is often the more partisan. True taste is general; it spreads over beauties of every kind, and does not expect more enjoyment or delight from each than its nature can afford. (230)...It is permitted to everybody to have their own taste, and it is laudable to be able to give the reasons why we hold such taste. But to give to the reasons by which we justify it a character of generality, and thus make it out to be the only true taste if these be correct, means exceeding the limits permitted to the investigating amateur and instituting oneself an independent lawgiver.... A true critic deduces no rules from his individual taste, but has formed his taste from rules necessitated by the nature of the subject. (279)

1778   Diderot   DPA

Work, [French] poets, for a nation given to vapours, and sensitive; content yourselves with the tender, harmonious, and touching elegies of Racine; this nation would flee the butcheries of Shakespeare; its feeble spirit cannot stand violent shocks; beware of offering too violent a picture.... (56)

1808   Coleridge   CSC

Taste ... may be defined [as] a distinct perception of any arrangement conceived as external to us, co-existent with some degree of dislike or complacency conceived as resulting from that arrangement, and this immediately, without any prospect of consequences, tho' this is indeed implied in the word co-existent. (1: 160-61)

c. 1810   Coleridge   CLSW

By taste, ... as applied to the fine arts, we must be supposed to mean an intellectual perception of any object blended with a distinct reference to our own sensibility of pain or pleasure, or, *vice versa*, a sense of enjoyment or dislike co-instantaneously combined with, appearing to proceed from, some intellectual perception of the object;—intellectual perception, I say; for otherwise it would be a definition of taste in its primary [i.e., of the taste buds] rather than in its metaphorical sense. Briefly, taste is a metaphor taken from one of our mixed senses, and applied to objects of the more purely organic senses, and of our moral sense, when we would imply the coexistence of immediate personal dislike or complacency. In this definition of taste, therefore, is involved the definition of fine arts, namely, as being such the chief and discriminitive purpose of which it is to gratify the taste,—that is, not merely to connect, but to combine and unite, a sense of immediate pleasure in ourselves, with the perception of external arrangement. (369-70)

1815   Coleridge   CBL

If it be asked, by what principles the poet is to regulate his own style, if he does not adhere closely to the sort and order of words which he hears in the market, wake, high-road, or plough-field? I reply; by principles, the ignorance or neglect of which would convict him of being no *poet*, but a silly or presumptuous usurper of the name! By the principles of grammar, logic, psychology! In one word by such a knowledge of the facts, material and spiritual, that most appertain to his art, as, if it have been governed and applied by *good sense*, and rendered instinctive by habit, becomes the representative and reward of our past conscious reasonings, insights, and conclusions, and acquires the name of TASTE. (2: 63-64) . . . TASTE is the intermediate faculty which connects the active with the passive powers of our nature, the intellect with the senses; and its appointed function is to elevate the *images* of the latter, while it realizes the *ideas* of the former. We must therefore have learned what is peculiar to each, before we can understand that ''Third something,'' which is formed by a harmony of both. (2: 227)

1818   Hazlitt   HW

TASTE is nothing but sensibility to the different degrees and kinds of excellence in the works of art or nature. . . . Taste is the power of perceiving the excellence . . . produced [by a genius] in its several sorts and degrees, with all their force, refinement, distinctions, and connections. In other words, taste (as it relates to the productions of art) is strictly the power of being properly affected by works of genius. It is the proportioning admiration to power, pleasure to beauty: it is entire sympathy with the finest impulses of the imagination, not antipathy, not indifference to them. The eye of taste may be said to reflect the impressions of real genius, as the even mirror reflects the objects of nature in all their clearness and lustre, instead of distorting or diminishing them. (11: 450) . . . The ultimate and only conclusive proof of taste is . . . not indifference, but enthusiasm; and before a critic can give himself airs of superiority for what he despises, [h]e must first lay himself open to reprisals, by telling us what he admires. (11: 454)

1819   Hazlitt   HW

Fine taste consists in sympathy, not in antipathy; and the rejection of what is bad is only to be accounted a virtue when it implies a preference of and attachment to what is better. (11: 454) . . . To perceive the height of any excellence, it is necessary to have the most exquisite sense of that kind of excellence through all its gradations: to perceive the want of any excellence, it is merely necessary to have a negative or abstract notion of the thing, or perhaps only of the name. Or, in other words, even the most crude and mechanical idea of a given quality is a measure of positive deficiency, whereas none but the most refined idea of the same quality can be a standard of superlative merit. . . . It may be asked . . . whether mere extravagance and enthusiasm are proofs of taste? And I answer, no, where they are without reason and knowledge. Mere sensibility is not true taste, but sensibility to real excellence is. To admire and be wrapt up in what is trifling or absurd, is a proof of nothing but ignorance or affectation: on the contrary, he who admires most what is most worthy of admiration . . . shows himself neither extravagant nor "unwise." . . . The highest taste is shown in habitual sensibility to the greatest beauties; the most general taste is shown in a perception of the greatest variety of excellence. . . . Those who are pleased with the fewest things, know the least; as those who are pleased with every thing, know nothing. (11: 456-57)

c.1820   Hazlitt   HW

TASTE relates to that which, either in the objects of nature, or the imitation of them or the Fine Arts in general is calculated to give pleasure. . . . There is no dogmatic or bigoted standard of taste, like a formula of faith. . . . There is no standard of taste whatever. . . . Certain things are not more apt to please than others. . . . There are not others that give most pleasure to those who have studied the object. . . . If we were . . . to insist on an universal standard of taste, it must be that, not which *does*, but which *would* please universally, supposing all men to have paid an equal attention to any subject and to have an equal relish for it, which can only be guessed at by the imperfect and yet more than casual agreement among those who have done so from choice and feeling. Taste is nothing but an enlarged capacity for receiving pleasure from works of imagination. (11: 459-60)

1864   Taine. *See* under IDENTIFICATION (TLA 101).

1888   Nietzsche   NWP

It is a question of *strength* (of an individual or a people) *whether* and *when* the judgment "beautiful" is applied. . . . *A preference for questionable and terrifying things* is a symptom of *strength*; while a taste for the *pretty and dainty* belongs to the weak and the delicate. *Pleasure* in tragedy characterizes *strong* ages and natures: their *non plus ultra* is perhaps the *divina commedia*. It is the *heroic* spirits who say Yes to themselves in tragic cruelty: they are hard enough to experience suffering as a pleasure. Supposing, on the other hand, that the weak desire to enjoy an art that is not meant for them; what would they do to make tragedy palatable for themselves? They would interpret *their own value feelings* into it; e.g., the "triumph of the moral world-order" or the doctrine of the "worthlessness of existence" or the invitation to "resignation." . . . It is a sign of one's *feeling of power and well-being* how far one can acknowledge the terrifying and questionable character of things; and *whether* one needs some sort of "solution" at the end. (448-50)

1903   Shaw. *See* under AESTHETIC (SMS xxxvi).

THOUGHT

The parameters of this category have been interpreted broadly in order to permit inclusion of radically different conceptions of the kind of significance that drama has or may have and the means by which that significance is generated. The term is from Aristotle, for whom dianoia *(thought) is largely identifiable with the logic of a character's language, a logic made explicit by proofs and argumentation. At the opposite pole is Artaud, for whom the significance of drama lies in the experience it creates for the spectator out of its totality, a significance neither identifiable in a passage or part nor paraphrasable as a theme or idea.*

4th cent. B.C.   Aristotle   **AP**

Thought is required wherever a statement is proved, or, it may be, a general truth enunciated. (25) . . . Thought . . . is the faculty of saying what is *possible* [involved: EP 263] and pertinent in given circumstances. In the case of oratory, this is the function of the political art and of the art of rhetoric: and so indeed the older poets make their characters speak *the language of civic life* [in a "political" fashion: EP 263]; the poets of our time, the language of the rhetoricians. . . . Speeches . . . in which the speaker does not choose or avoid anything whatever, are not expressive of character. Thought, on the other hand, is found where something is proved to be or not to be, or a general maxim is enunciated. (29) . . . Concerning Thought, we may assume what is said in the Rhetoric, to which inquiry the subject more strictly belongs. Under Thought is included every effect which has to be [deliberately: EP 561] produced by speech, the subdivisions being,—proof and refutation; the excitation of the feelings, such as pity, fear, anger, and the like; the suggestion of importance or its opposite. Now, it is evident that *the dramatic incidents must be treated from the same points of view as the dramatic speeches* [in tragic actions also one must use 'thought' under the same categories: EP 561], when the object is to evoke the sense of pity, fear, importance, or probability. The only difference is, that the incidents should speak for themselves without verbal exposition; while the effects aimed at in speech should be produced by the speaker, and as a result of the speech. For what were the *business* [need: EP 561] of a speaker, if the thought were *revealed quite apart from what he says* ["brought home" even without his speech?: EP 562]? (69-71)

4th cent. B.C.   Aristotle   AA

Thought . . . is different from sense-perception and seems to include imagination on the one hand and conception on the other. (125) . . . If thinking is analogous to perceiving, it will consist in a being acted upon by the object of thought or in something else of this kind. This part of the soul, then, must be impassive, but receptive of the form and potentially like this form, though not identical with it: and, as the faculty of sense is to sensible objects, so must intellect be related to intelligible objects. . . . We cannot reasonably conceive [the mind] to be mixed with the body: for in that case it would acquire some particular quality, cold or heat, or would even have some organ, as the perceptive faculty has. But as a matter of fact it has none. (131)

4th cent. B.C.   Aristotle   AR

Proofs are either artificial or inartificial. By "inartificial" I mean such things as have not been supplied by our own agency, but were already in existence,— such as witnesses, depositions under torture, contracts, and the like: by "artificial" I mean such things as may be furnished by our method and by our own agency; so that, of these, the "inartificial" have only to be used; the "artificial" have to be invented. Of proofs provided by the speech there are three kinds; one kind depending on the character of the speaker; another, on disposing the hearer in a certain way; a third, a demonstration or apparent demonstration in the speech itself. Ethical proof is wrought when the speech is so spoken as to make the speaker credible; for we trust good men more and sooner, as a rule, about everything; while, about things which do not admit of precision, but only of guesswork, we trust them absolutely. Now this trust, too, ought to be produced by means of the speech,—not by a previous conviction that the speaker is this or that sort of man . . . The hearers themselves become the instruments of proof when emotion is stirred in them by the speech; for we give our judgments in different ways under the influence of pain and of joy, of liking and of hatred. . . . Proof is wrought through the speech itself when we have demonstrated a truth or an apparent truth by the means of persuasion available in a given case. These being the instruments of our proofs, it is clear that they may be mastered by a man who can reason; who can analyse the several types of Character and the Virtues, and thirdly, the Emotions—the nature and quality of each emotion, the sources and modes of its production. (6-7) . . . The speech has two parts:—it is necessary to *state* the matter which is our subject and to *prove* it. We cannot, then, have a statement without a demonstration, or a demonstration without a previous statement; for the demonstrator must demonstrate something, and the expositor set a thing forth, in order to prove it. (179)

   See also Aristotle under TRAGEDY (AP 23-25).

1561   Scaliger   SP

When a sentiment has two modes of expression, the tragedy throughout is to rest upon each, for together they constitute, as it were, a sustaining column or pillar for the entire structure. A sentiment may be put simply and definitely, as when we say, "Death makes the good happy," or it may be expressed figuratively at greater length, as when the above sentiment is thus expressed: "Be not willing to think of good men as perishing, whose souls, *per se* immortal take their flight from out these miseries to those seats whence they had departed." (59-60)

c.1583   Sidney   SDP

Any understanding knoweth the skill of each artificer standeth in that idea, or fore-conceit of the work, and not in the work itself. And that the poet hath that idea is manifest, by delivering them forth in such excellency as he hath imagined them. Which delivering forth, also, is not wholly imaginative, as we are wont to say by them that build castles in the air; but so far substantially it worketh, not only to make a Cyrus, which had been but a particular excellency as nature might have done, but to bestow a Cyrus upon the world to make many Cyruses, if they will learn aright why and how that maker made him. (8)

See also Sidney under INSTRUCTION (SDP 15-16, 17-18).

1600   Jonson. See under NOVELTY (JBW).

1601   Jonson. See under SYMBOL (JBW).

1641   Jonson. See under LANGUAGE (JD 17, 72). SURPRISE (JD 35).

1660   Corneille. See under INSTRUCTION (CFD 140-41).

1668   Dryden   DW

I am of opinion that they cannot be good poets, who are not accustomed to argue well. False reasonings and colours of speech are the certain marks of one who does not understand the stage; for moral truth is the mistress of the poet, as much as of the philosopher. Poesy must resemble natural truth, but it must be ethical. Indeed the poet dresses truth, and adorns nature, but does not alter them. (1, 2: 170)

1695   Dryden. See under INSTRUCTION (DW 3: 310-11).

1709   Addison. See under MORALITY (AW 3: 36).

1711   Addison   AW

Our English poets have succeeded much better in the styles, than in the sentiments of their tragedies. Their language is very often noble and sonorous, but the sense either very trifling, or very common. On the contrary, in the ancient tragedies, and indeed in those of Corneille and Racine, though the expressions are very great, it is the thought that bears them up and swells them. . . . I prefer a noble sentiment that is depressed with homely language, infinitely before a vulgar one that is blown up with all the sound and energy of expression. . . . I believe it might rectify the conduct both of [the language and the sentiment] if the writer laid down the whole contexture of his dialogue in plain English, before he turned it into blank verse; and if the reader . . . would consider the naked thought of every speech in it, when divested of all its tragic ornaments. . . . When our thoughts are great and just, they are often obscured by the sounding phrases, hard metaphors, and forced expressions in which they are clothed. Shakespeare is often very faulty in this particular. (1: 70)

1711   Dryden. *See* under DRAMA (DW 1, 2: 302-303).

1712   Addison   AW

Longinus has observed that there may be a loftiness in sentiments where there is no passion, and brings instances out of ancient authors to support this his opinion. The pathetic, as that great critic observes, may animate and inflame the sublime, but is not essential to it. Accordingly, as he further remarks, we very often find that those who excel most in stirring up the passions very often want the talent of writing in the great and sublime manner, and so on the contrary [sic]. (2: 41) . . . No thought is beautiful which is not just; and no thought can be just which is not founded in truth, or at least in that which passes for such. (2: 291)
     See also Addison under PROBABILITY (AW 2: 4).

1713   Addison. *See* under SYMBOL (AW 3: 149).

1758   Diderot   DDP

One good scene contains more ideas than is possible in a whole play of incident; and it is to ideas we return, that we listen to and never grow tired of; these affect us in every age. (291)
     See also Diderot under DRAMA (DDP 287-89).

1767-1769   Lessing   LSPW

Drama . . . makes no claim upon a single definite axiom flowing out of its story. It aims at the passions which the course and events of its fable arouse and treat, or it aims at the pleasure accorded by a true and vivid delineation of characters and habits. Both [drama and the fable] require a certain integrity of action, a certain harmonious end which we do not miss in the moral tale because our attention is solely directed to the general axiom of whose especial application the story affords such an obvious instance. (329)

1778   Johnson. *See* under LANGUAGE (JL 1: 58-59).

1808   Schlegel   SCL

We must consider [the Greek chorus] as a personified reflection on the action which is going on; the incorporation into the representation itself of the sentiments of the poet, as the spokesman of the whole human race. . . . In a word, the Chorus is the ideal spectator. It mitigates the impression of a heartrending or moving story, while it conveys to the actual spectator a lyrical and musical expression of his own emotions, and elevates him to the region of contemplation. Aristotle affords no satisfactory solution. . . . Its office is better painted by Horace, who ascribes to it a general expression of moral sympathy, exhortation, instruction, and warning. (69-70)

   See also Schlegel under CLOSURE (SCL 254), POETRY OF THE THEATRE (SCL 36-37), SYMBOL (SCL 88), TRAGEDY (SCL 67).

1813   Goethe   GLE

It would be hard to find a poet each of whose works was more thoroughly pervaded by a definite and effective idea than [Shakespeare's]. Thus *Coriolanus* is permeated by the idea of anger at the refusal of the lower classes to recognize the superiority of their betters. . . . *Antony and Cleopatra* expresses with a thousand tongues the idea that pleasure and action are ever incompatible. (178)

1817   Hazlitt. *See* under OBJECTIVITY (HW 1: 346-47).

1818   Coleridge   CLSW

As soon as the human mind is intelligibly addressed by an outward image exclusively of articulated speech, so soon does art commence. But please observe that I have laid particular stress on the words "human mind," meaning to exclude thereby all results common to man and all other sentient creatures, and consequently confining myself to the effect produced by the congruity of the animal impression with the reflective powers of the mind; so that not the thing presented, but that which is represented by the thing shall be the source of pleasure. In this sense nature itself is to a religious observer the art of God; and for the same cause art itself may be defined as of a middle quality between a thought and a thing, or, as I said before, the union and reconciliation of that which is nature with that which is exclusively human. It is the figured language of thought, and is distinguished from nature by the unity of all the parts in one thought or idea. Hence nature itself would give us the impression of a work of art if we could see the thought which is present at once in the whole and in every part; and a work of art will be just in proportion as it adequately conveys the thought, and rich in proportion to the variety of parts which it holds in unity. (329-30)

See also Coleridge under SYMBOL (CMC 30).

1818   Hazlitt. *See* under STYLE (HW 5: 347).

c.1820   Hegel. *See* under AFFECT (HFA 4: 275-77).

1823   Goethe   **GCE**

Fri., Nov. 14. . . . "I have," said I, "a peculiar feeling towards Schiller. Some scenes of his great dramas I read with genuine love and admiration; but presently I meet with something which violates the truth of nature, and I can go no further. . . . I cannot but think that Schiller's turn for philosophy injured his poetry, because this led him to consider the idea far higher than all nature; indeed, thus to annihilate nature. What he could conceive must happen, whether it were in conformity with nature or not." "It was sad," said Goethe, "to see how so highly gifted a man tormented himself with philosophical disquisitions which could in no way profit him."

1826   Goethe. *See* under SYMBOL (GCE July 26).

1827   Goethe   **GCE**

Wed. March 28. "Hinrichs, in considering Greek tragedy, sets out from the *idea;* and . . . he looks upon Sophocles as one who, in the invention and arrangement of his pieces, likewise set out from an idea, and regulated the sex and rank of his characters accordingly. But Sophocles . . . by no means started from an *idea*; on the contrary, he seized upon some ancient ready-made popular tradition in which a good idea existed, and then only thought of adapting it in the best and most effective manner for the theater." . . . "I do not object," said Goethe, "to a dramatic poet having a moral influence in view; but when the point is to bring his subject clearly and effectively before his audience, his moral purpose proves of little use, and he needs much more a faculty for delineation and familiarity with the stage to know what to do and what to leave undone. If there be a moral in the subject, it will appear, and the poet has nothing to consider but the effect and artistic treatment of the subject."

See also Goethe under INSTRUCTION (GLE 130).

1864   Taine. *See* under HERO (TLA 180).

1871   Nietzsche   NBT

Socrates, the dialectical hero in Platonic drama, reminds us of the kindred nature of the Euripidean hero, who has to defend his actions by arguments and counter-arguments, and thereby so often runs the risk of forfeiting our tragic pity; for who could mistake the *optimistic* element in the essence of dialectics, which celebrates a jubilee in every conclusion, and can breathe only in cool clearness and consciousness: the optimistic element, which, having once forced its way into tragedy, must gradually overgrow its Dionysian regions, and necessarily impel it to self-destruction—even to the death-leap into the bourgeois drama. . . . Optimistic dialectics drives *music* out of tragedy with the scourge of syllogisms: that is, it destroys the essence of tragedy, which can be explained only as a manifestation and illustration of Dionysian states, as the visible symbolisation of music, as the dream-world of Dionysian ecstasy. (110-11)

   See also Nietzsche under MORALITY (NBT 78-79).

1873   Nietzsche. *See* under METAPHOR (NEG 178-88).

1888   Nietzsche   NW

Thought is the strongest and most persistently exercised function in all stages of life—and also in every act of perception or apparent experience! Obviously, it soon becomes the *mightiest* and *most exacting* of all functions, and in time tyrranises over other powers. Ultimately it becomes a "passion in itself." (105)

1888   Chekhov   CL

May 30. It seems to me it is not the writers of fiction to solve such questions as that of God, of pessimism, etc. The writer's business is simply to describe who has been speaking about God or about pessimism, how, and in what circumstances. The artist must be not the judge of his characters and of their conversations, but merely an impartial witness. I have heard a desultory conversation of two Russians about pessimism—a conversation which settles nothing—and I must report that conversation as I heard it; it is for the jury, that is, my readers, to decide on the value of it. My business is merely to be talented—to know how to distinguish important statements from unimportant, how to throw light on the characters, and to speak their language. . . . It is time that writers, especially those who are artists, recognized that there is no making out anything in this world, as once Socrates recognized it, and Voltaire, too. The mob thinks it knows and understands everything. . . . If a writer whom the mob believes in has the courage to say that he does not understand anything of what he sees, that alone will be something gained in the realm of thought and a great step in advance. (88-89) Oct. 27. That in [the artist's] sphere there are no questions, but only answers, can only be maintained by those who have never written and have had no experience of thinking in images. An artist observes, selects, guesses, combines—and this in itself presupposes a problem: unless he had set himself a problem from the very first there would be nothing to conjecture and nothing to select. . . . If one denies that creative work involves problems and purposes, one must admit that an artist creates without premeditation or intention, in a state of aberration. . . . You are right in demanding that an artist should take an intelligent attitude to his work, but you confuse two things: *solving a problem* and *stating a problem correctly*. It is only the second that is obligatory for the artist. . . . It is the business of the judge to put the right questions, but the answers must be given by the jury according to their own lights. (100)

1889   Chekhov. *See* under CHARACTER (CL 119).

1896   Shaw. *See* under INSTRUCTION (SDC 142).

1898   Shaw   **SPPU**

It is quite possible for a piece to enjoy the most sensational success on the basis of a complete misunderstanding of its philosophy: indeed, it is not too much to say that it is only by a capacity for succeeding in spite of its philosophy that a dramatic work of serious poetic import can become popular. (xx)

   See also Shaw under CONFLICT (SMCE 217), SPECTACLE (SMCE 188, 220).

1902   Shaw   **SAA**

Only in the problem play is there any real drama, because drama is no mere setting up of the camera to nature: it is the presentation in parable of the conflict between Man's will and his environment: in a word, of problem. (43)

1903   Shaw. *See* under STYLE (SMS xxxv).

1908   Pirandello   **POH**

For Rhetoric, thought originated first, then came form; that is, it was not like Minerva dressed in armor as she issued forth from Jupiter's head. Thought was born all naked, the poor thing, and Rhetoric dressed it. The garment was the form. Rhetoric, in short, was like a wardrobe of eloquence to which naked thoughts went to get dressed. The clothes in that wardrobe were all ready to wear, all cut on old models, more or less adorned, made with humble, common, or magnificent cloth, divided into so many compartments, nicely hung and placed in the care of a wardrobe lady whose name was Convenience. She would prescribe the most appropriate clothes for the naked thoughts that went to her. . . . Thoughts were like mannequins dressed with the apparel of form. That is, form was not properly form but *formation*: it was not *born*, it was *made*. By following predetermined rules, it was composed externally, like an object. Therefore it was artifice, not art; a copy, not creation. (30-31)

1913   Shaw   SMCE

An interesting play cannot in the nature of things mean anything but a play in which problems of conduct and character of personal importance to the audience are raised and suggestively discussed. . . . The play in which there is no argument and no case no longer counts as serious drama. (137-39)

    See also Shaw under ACTION (SMCE 138-39), CLOSURE (SMCE 138-39, 139-40, 142-43, 145), CONFLICT (SMCE 139).

1921   Eliot   ESW

Goethe's demon [Mephistopheles in *Faust*] inevitably sends us back to Goethe. A creation of art should not do that: he should *replace* the philosophy. Goethe has not, that is to say, sacrificed or consecrated his thought to make the drama; the drama is still a means. (59) . . . The moment an idea has been transferred from its pure state in order that it may become comprehensible to the inferior intelligence it has lost contact with art. It can remain pure only by being stated simply in the form of general truth, or by being transmuted, as the attitude of Flaubert toward the small bourgeois is transformed in *Education Sentimentale*. It has there become so identified with the reality that you can no longer say what the idea is. (61)

1925   Pirandello. *See* under SYMBOL (PPSC 365).

1926   Brecht. *See* under EPIC THEATRE (BBT 14-15).

1930   Brecht. *See* under GEST (BBT 36).

1931-1936   Artaud   AT

By "unperverted" pantomime I mean direct Pantomime where gestures— instead of representing words or sentences, as in our European Pantomime . . . —represent ideas, attitudes of mind, aspects of nature, all in an effective, concrete manner, i.e., by constantly evoking objects or natural details, like that Oriental language which represents night by a tree on which a bird that has already closed one eye is beginning to close the other. (39-40) . . . I am well aware that the language of gestures and postures, dance and music, is less capable of analyzing a character, revealing a man's thoughts, or elucidating states of consciousness clearly and precisely than is verbal language, but who ever said the theatre was created to analyze a character, to resolve the conflicts of love and duty, to wrestle with all the problems of a topical and psychological nature that monopolize our contemporary stage? (41) . . . To make metaphysics out of a spoken language is to make the language express what it does not ordinarily express: to make use of it in a new, exceptional, and unaccustomed fashion; to reveal its possibilities for producing physical shock; to divide and distribute it actively in space; to deal with intonations in an absolutely concrete manner, restoring their power to shatter as well as really to manifest something; to turn against language and its basely utilitarian, one could say alimentary, sources, against its trapped—beast origins; and finally, to consider language as the form of *Incantation*. Everything in this active poetic mode of envisaging expression on the stage leads us to abandon the modern humanistic and psychological meaning of the theater, in order to recover the religious and mystic preference of which our theatre has completely lost the sense. (46)

    See also Artaud under POETRY OF THE THEATRE (AT 37, 39, 123-24).

c.1932   Brecht. *See* under GEST (BBT 104-05).

1932   Eliot. *See* under THREE UNITIES (EUP 45-46).

1933   Eliot. *See* under AFFECT (EUP 153).

1938   Stanislavski   **SBC**

The simplest entrance or exit on the stage, any action taken to carry out a scene, to pronounce a phrase, words, soliloquy and so on, must have a perspective and an ultimate purpose (the superobjective). . . . In . . . the perspective used in conveying a thought, logic and coherence play an important part in the unfolding of the thought and the establishing of the relation of the various parts of the whole expression. This perspective is achieved with the aid of a long series of key words and their accents which [add] sense to the phrase. . . . It is only when we study a play as a whole and can appreciate its overall perspective that we are able to fit the various planes correctly together, make a beautiful arrangement of the component parts, mold them into harmonious and well rounded forms in terms of words. (169-71) . . . *Everything happens for the sake of these two elements, perspective and the through line of action. They contain the principal significance of creativeness, of art, of our approach to acting.* (176) . . . The problem for our art and consequently for our theatre is—to create an inner life for a play and its characters, to express in physical and dramatic terms the fundamental core, the idea which impelled the writer, the poet, to produce his composition. (258)

c.1936   Brecht. *See* under EPIC THEATRE (BBA 20-21).

c.1940   Brecht. *See* under ALIENATION (BBAn 15-20).

1948   Brecht. *See* under DRAMA (BBBG 24), IDENTIFICATION (BBBG 25).

1952   Brecht. *See* under AFFECT (BBT 229).

1956   Brecht   **BBT**

The theatre of the scientific age is in a position to make dialectics into a source of enjoyment. The unexpectedness of logically progressive or zigzag development, the instability of every circumstance, the joke of contradiction and so forth: all these are ways of enjoying the liveliness of men, things and processes, and they heighten both our capacity for life and our pleasure in it. Every art contributes to the greatest art of all, the art of living. (277) . . . A quotation from Lenin: ''It is impossible to recognize the various happenings in the world in their independence of movement, their spontaneity of development, their vitality of being, without recognizing them as a unity of opposites.'' [*On the Question of Dialectics*] . . . It is a matter of indifference whether the theatre's main object is to provide knowledge of the world. The fact remains that the theatre has to represent the world and that its representations must not mislead. If Lenin's view is right, then they cannot work out satisfactorily without knowledge of dialectics—and without making dialectics known. Objection: What about the kind of art which gets its effects from dark, distorted, fragmentary representations? What about the art of primitive peoples, madmen and children? If one knows a great deal and can retain what one knows, it may be possible perhaps to get something out of such representations; but we suspect that unduly subjective representations of the world have anti-social effects. (279)

THREE UNITIES

The idea of the unities of time and place may derive from a misunderstanding of Aristotle's discussion of the magnitude of drama. (In Athenian drama competitions each tragedian had from dawn until dusk to present his work.) Whatever the case, this category presents a near microcosm of the history—the trends, the arguments, the premises—of the theory of the drama. The third unity, Action, is omitted here; see ACTION and UNITY.

4th cent. B.C.   Aristotle   AP

[Tragedy and Epic poetry] differ in their *length* [bulk: EP 203]: for Tragedy endeavours, as far as possible, to *confine itself to a single revolution of the sun* [exist in a single daylight period: EP 203], or but slightly to exceed this limit; whereas, the Epic action has no limits of time. (21-23)

See also Aristotle under MAGNITUDE (AP 91-93), TRAGEDY (AP 21-23, 23-25).

1561   Scaliger   SP

The events . . . should be made to have such sequence and arrangement as to approach as near as possible to truth, for the play is not acted solely to strike the spectator with admiration or consternation— . . . but should also teach, move, and please. We are pleased either with jests, as in comedy, or with things serious, if rightly ordered. Disregard of truth is hateful to almost every man. Therefore, neither those battles or sieges at Thebes which are fought through in two hours please me, nor do I take it to be the part of a discreet poet to pass from Delphi to Athens, or from Athens to Thebes, in a moment of time. . . . As the whole time for a stage-representation is only six or eight hours, it is not true to life to have a storm arise, and the ship founder, in a part of the sea from which no land is visible. (60)

1570   Castelvetro   CP

The time of the representation and that of the action represented must be exactly coincident. . . . The scene of the action must be constant, being not merely restricted to one city or one house, but indeed to that one place alone which could be visible to one person. (84) . . . [The action must be limited to twelve hours] for people owing to bodily needs, could not possibly remain in the theatre longer than that. . . . (85)

See also Castelvetro under ACTION (CP 89), AFFECT (CP 86), SUBJECT (CP 85), WONDER (CP 88).

c.1583   Sidney   SDP

[*Gorboduc*] is full of stately speeches and well-sounding phrases, climbing to the height of Seneca's style, and as full of notable morality, which it doth most delightfully teach, and so obtain the very end of poesy; yet in truth it is very defectious in the circumstances, which grieveth me, because it might not remain as an exact model of all tragedies. For it is faulty both in place and time, the two necessary companions of all corporal actions. For where the stage should always represent but one place, and the uttermost time presupposed in it should be, both by Aristotle's precept and common reason, but one day; there is [in *Gorboduc*] both many days and many places inartificially imagined. (47-48) . . . [The poets ask,] how then shall we set forth a story which containeth both many places and many times? And do they not know that a tragedy is tied to the laws of poesy, and not of history; not bound to follow the story, but having liberty either to feign a quite new matter, or to frame the history to the most tragical conveniency? Again, many things may be told which cannot be showed,—if they know the difference betwixt reporting and representing. As for example I may speak, though I am here, of Peru, and in speech digress from that to the description of Calicut; but in action I cannot represent it without Pacolet's horse. . . . If [the poets] will represent a history . . . they must come to the principal point of that one action which they will represent. (49)

1605   Jonson   JBW

[The author] presents quick *comedy*, refined,
    As best Critics have designed,
The laws of time, place, persons he observeth,
    From no needful rule he swerveth.

Prologue, *Volpone*

1609   de Vega   VAWP

The subject once chosen, write in prose, and divide the matter into three acts of time, seeing to it, if possible, that in each one the space of the day be not broken. (31)
    See also de Vega under ACTION (VAWP 30-31)

1616   Jonson. *See* under REALISM (JBW).

1640   Jonson   JBW

Hear what his sorrows are; and, if they wound
Your gentle breasts, so that the *End* crown all,
Which in the Scope of one day's chance may fall. . . .

Prologue, *The Sad Shepherd*

1641   Jonson. *See* under MAGNITUDE (JD 103).

1657   d'Aubignac   AAS

After the Poet has order'd his Subject according to the Rules . . . he must
reflect, that the best part of it must be represented by Actors, which must be
upon Stage fix'd and determinated; for to make his Actors appear in different
places, would render his Play ridiculous, by the want of Probability, which is
to be the foundation of it. This Rule of Unity of Place begins now to be look'd
upon as certain. . . . For the truely Learned, they are thoroughly convinc'd of
the necessity of this Rule, because they see clearly that Probability can no ways
be preserv'd without it. . . . *Aristotle* has said nothing of it, and I believe he
omitted it, because that this Rule was in his time too well known; the Chorus's,
which ordinarily remain'd upon the Stage from one end of the Play to the other,
marking the unity of the *Scene* too visibly to need a Rule for it; and indeed,
would it not have been ridiculous, that in the Play call'd the *Seven before
Thebes*, the young Women who make the Chorus, should have found themselves sometimes before the Palace of the King, and sometimes in the Camp of
the Enemies, without ever stirring from the same place. (2: 97-99) . . . The
place cannot change in the rest of the Play, since it cannot change in the
Representation, for one and the same Image remaining in the same state,
cannot represent two different things; now it is highly improbable, that the
same space, and the same floor, which receive no change at all, should
represent two different places. (2: 99-100) . . . They are mistaken, that suppose
in one side of the Stage one part of the Town, as for example, the *Louvre*, and
on the other side another part, as the *Place Royal*; thinking by this fine
Invention to preserve the unity of Place. Indeed if two Parts or Quarters of a
Town, thus suppos'd, were not far from one another, and the space between
were really empty of Houses, such a thing were not improper; but if between
the two places, there are many Houses and solid bodies, I would then ask, how
it comes to pass that those Houses do not fill up the empty place of the Stage.
(2: 105) . . . A Dramatick Poem has two sorts of Time, each of which has a
different and proper lasting. The first is the true time of the Representation; for
though this sort of Poem be but an Image, and so ought to be consider'd as
having a representative Being; nevertheless one ought to consider, that there is
a reality in the very Representation, for really the Actors are seen and heard,
the Verses are really pronounc'd, and one suffers really either pleasure or pain
in assisting at these Representations, and there is a real time spent in amusing
the Audience, that is from the opening of the Stage to the end of the Play: This
time is call'd the lasting of the Representation. Of this time, the measure can be
no other, but so much time as will reasonably spend the patience of the
Audience, for this sort of Poem being made for pleasure, it ought not to weary
and fatigate the mind. . . . In all this, Experience is the faithfullest Guide, and
tells most commonly, that a Play cannot last above three hours without
wearying of us, nor less without coming short of pleasing us. . . . The other

Time of the Dramatick Poem, is that of the Action represented, so [f]ar as it is considered as a true Action, and containing all that space which is necessary to the performing of those things, which are to be expos'd to the knowledge of the Spectators, from the first to the last Act of the Play. . . . [Aristotle] set down the Rule, or rather renew[ed] it from the Model of the Ancients, saying, That Tragedy ought to be comprehended in the Revolution of one Sun. (2: 111-13) . . . It remains then to say, [Aristotle] means the Diurnal Revolution; but . . . the day is considered two ways, . . . the Natural day, and . . . the Artificial Day. It is necessary to observe that *Aristotle* means only the Artificial Day. (2: 115) . . . We can never better understand *Aristotle*, than by those three Excellent Tragick Poets, whom he always proposes for Examples, who have regularly observ'd, not to give above 12 hours to their Plays. . . . It were even to be wish'd, that the Action of the Poem did not take up more time, than that of the Representation, but that being hard, and almost impossible, in certain occasions the Poet has the Liberty to suppose a longer time by some hours, in which the Musick that marks the Intervals of the Acts, and the Relations of the Actors upon the Stage, while the others are busie off of it, with the natural desire of the Spectators to see the Event, do all contribute very much, and help to deceive the Audience, so as to make them think, there has passed time enough for the performance of the things represented. (2: 116-17)

See also d'Aubignac under ILLUSION (AAS 1: 44-45), SPECTACLE (AAS 3: 95-98).

1660   Corneille   CDENA

It is difficult to find . . . enough . . . events, both illustrious and worthy of tragedy, in which the . . . execution can happen in the same place and on the same day without doing a little violence to the common order of things. . . . There are fine subjects where it cannot be avoided. . . . I would give [the playwright] . . . advice which perhaps he would find salutory: that is, to prefix no specific time to his poem, and no set place in the location of his actors. The imagination of the audience has greater liberty to go along with the action if it is not fixed. . . . (32)

1660   Corneille   CTU

The dramatic poem is an imitation, or better yet, a portraiture of the actions of men; and it is beyond question that portraitures are more excellent in proportion as they better resemble the original. The [dramatic] representation lasts two hours, and would be a perfect resemblance if the action portrayed did not demand more to make it seem real. So let us not stop either with twelve or with twenty-four hours; but let us confine the action of the poem to the smallest space of time that we can, that the representation may better approach resemblance and perfection. . . . As to the unity of place, I can find no precept regarding it either in Aristotle or Horace. . . . I should wish, in order not to annoy the spectator, that what is represented before him in two hours be able actually to take place in two hours, and that what he is shown on the stage (which does not change) be able to happen in a private room or salon, whichever might be desired; but often that is so awkward, not to say impossible, that some enlargement of place must of necessity be found, also of time. (817)

1660 Corneille   CDTU

I find that there are some subjects so difficult to confine in so little time that not only do I accord them the entire twenty-four hours [of a natural day], but I will even avail myself of the liberty that [Aristotle] gives of exceeding them a little, and will, without scruple, extend them to thirty hours. (235-36) . . . I simply do not know how to reconcile ancient rules with modern pleasures any better. (237)

    See also Corneille under RULES (CFD 139-40, 143-34, CDENA 32).

1668 Dryden   DW

[The French] are too strictly bounded by . . . their servile observations of the unities of time and place, and integrity of scenes. They have brought on themselves that dearth of plot, and narrowness of imagination, which may be observed in all their plays. How many beautiful accidents might naturally happen in two or three days, which cannot arrive with any probability in the compass of twenty-four hours? There is time to be allowed also for maturity of design, which, amongst great and prudent persons, such as are often represented in tragedy, cannot, with any likelihood of truth, be brought to pass at so short a warning. Farther; by tying themselves strictly to the unity of place, and unbroken scenes, they are forced many times to omit some beauties which cannot be shewn where the act began; but might, if the scene were interrupted, and the stage cleared for the persons to enter in another place; and therefore the French poets are often forced upon absurdities: for if the act begins in a chamber, all the persons in the play must have some business or other to come thither, or else they are not to be shewn that act; and sometimes their characters are very unfitting to appear there. (1, 2: 93-94) . . . Though the stage cannot be two places, yet it may properly represent them, successively, or at several times. . . . [We must] distinguish place, as it relates to plays, into real and imaginary. The real place is that theatre, or piece of ground, on which the play is acted. The imaginary, that house, town, or country, where the action of the drama is supposed to be; or more plainly, where the scene of the play is laid. . . . It is neither impossible, nor improper, for one real place to represent two or more imaginary places, so it be done successively; which in other words is no more than this,—that the imagination of the audience, aided by the words of the poet, and painted scenes, may suppose the stage to be sometimes one place, sometimes another; now a garden, or wood, and immediately a camp: which, I appeal to every man's imagination, if it be not true. (1, 2: 176-

77) . . . What has been said of the unity of place, may easily be applied to that of time. I grant it to be impossible, that the greater part of time should be comprehended in the less, that twenty-four hours should be crowded into three: but there is no necessity of that supposition.—For as *place*, so *time* relating to a play, is either imaginary or real: the real is comprehended in those three hours, more or less, in the space of which the play is represented; the imaginary is that which is supposed to be taken up in the representation, as twenty-four hours more or less. Now no man ever could suppose that twenty-four real hours could be included in the space of three: but where is the absurdity of affirming that the feigned business of twenty-four imagined hours may not more naturally be represented in the compass of three real hours, than the like feigned business of twenty-four years in the same proportion of real time? For the proportions are always real, and much nearer, by his permission, of twenty-four to three, than of four thousand to it. (180) . . . The imaginary time of every play ought to be contrived into as narrow a compass as the nature of the plot, the quality of the persons, and variety of accidents will allow. In comedy I would not exceed twenty-four or thirty hours: for the plot, accidents, and persons of comedy are small, and may be naturally turned in a little compass: but in tragedy the design is weighty, and the persons great; therefore there will naturally be required a greater space of time in which to move them. (1, 2: 183-84)

1670   Racine. *See* under MAGNITUDE (RP 155).

1697   Dryden   **DW**

There is no such absolute necessity that the time of a stage-action should so strictly be confined to twenty-four hours, as never to exceed them; for which Aristotle contends, and the Grecian stage has practised. Some longer space, on some occasions, I think may be allowed, especially for the English theatre, which requires more variety of incidents than the French. Corneille himself, after long practice, was inclined to think, that the time allotted by the ancients was too short to raise and finish a great action; and better a mechanick rule were stretched or broken, than a great beauty omitted. (3: 430-31)

1730   Voltaire   **VE**

The French were among the first of the modern nations to revive [the] wise rules of the drama: the other nations long remained unwilling to submit to a yoke which seemed so irksome; but as the yoke was necessary, and as reason always triumphs in the end, they all submitted. And nowadays, in England, certain dramatists have informed the audience before the play begins that the duration of the action is identical with that of its representation on the stage. . . . All nations are beginning to consider as barbarous those ages when the rules were ignored by the greatest geniuses, such as Lope de Vega and

Shakespeare; these nations even acknowledge their obligation to us for having brought the rules out of that state of barbarism. . . . What is a play? The representation of an action. Why of one action only, and not of two or three? Because the human brain cannot focus its attention upon several objects at the same time; because the interest which is dispersed when there is more than one action, soon disappears; because we are shocked to observe two events in the same picture; because, finally, nature herself has given us this precept, which ought to be like her, immutable. For the same reason, unity of place is essential: a single action obviously cannot transpire in several places at once. If the characters which I see are at Athens in the first act, how can they be in Persia in the second? . . . I cannot imagine an intelligent and enlightened nation *not* inclined toward an observance of the rules, which are based upon good sense, and made in order to enhance our pleasure. . . . Unity of time naturally goes hand in hand with the other two unities. And here, I believe, is an obvious proof. I see tragedy: that is, the representation of an action. The subject is concerned with the working-out of that action alone. There is a conspiracy against Augustus in Rome; I wish to know what will happen to Augustus and the conspirators. If the poet makes the action last fifteen days, he must account for what passes during these fifteen days, because I am in the theater to learn what happens: nothing superfluous *must* happen. Now, if he causes to pass before my eyes the events of fifteen days, there will be at least fifteen different actions, no matter how small and unimportant they may be. It is not in this case merely the bringing to a head of this conspiracy toward which the poet must quickly lead his play: he must of necessity drag out his story until it no longer interests and is no longer living. All these things are very far from the decisive moment which I am waiting for. I do not come in order to learn the whole history of the hero, I come only to see a single happening in his life. Further, the spectator is in the theater only three hours: therefore the action must not last longer than three hours. The action in *Cinna, Andromaque, Bajazet,* in *Oedipe* . . . lasts no longer. If other plays perchance require more time, the liberty can be allowed only where the play makes up for the loss in compensating beauties. The greater the liberty, the more open it is to censure. We often extend the limit of unity of time to twenty-four hours, and that of unity of place to the walls of a whole palace. A greater severity than this would sometimes render some beautiful subjects impracticable, while greater liberty might open the way to greater abuses. For were it once established that the action of a play could extend over a period of two days, it would not be long before one poet would take two weeks, and another two years. . . . An observance of these laws not only prevents faults, but even leads the poet to true beauty, just as the rules observed in the best sort of architecture must of necessity result in a building that is sure to please the eye. It is seen, therefore, that with unity of time, action, and place, it is difficult to write a play which shall not be simple. This is the great merit of M. Racine's plays; this was demanded by Aristotle. (280-81)

1731   Voltaire. *See* under RULES (VE 282).

1751   Johnson   **JW**

With no . . . right to our obedience have the criticks confined the dramatic
action to a certain number of hours. Probability requires that the time of action
should approach somewhat nearly to that of exhibition, and those plays will
always be thought most happily conducted which crowd the greatest variety
into the least space. But since it will frequently happen that some delusion must
be admitted, I know not where the limits of the imagination can be fixed. It is
rarely observed that minds, not prepossessed by mechanical criticism, feel any
offence from the extension of the intervals between the acts; nor can I conceive
it absurd or impossible, that he who can multiply three hours into twelve or
twenty-four, might imagine with equal ease a greater number. (3: 241)

1755-1780   Diderot. *See* under ILLUSION (DDE 289).

1765   Johnson   **JS**

[The unities are] those laws which have been instituted and established by the
joint authority of poets and of criticks. (24) . . . The necessity of observing the
unities of time and place arises from the supposed necessity of making the
drama credible. The criticks hold it impossible, that an action of months and
years can be possibly believed to pass in three hours; or that the spectator can
suppose himself to sit in the theatre, while ambassadors go and return between
distant kings. . . . The mind [supposedly] revolts from evident falsehood, and
fiction loses its force when it departs from the resemblance of reality. (25)
. . . The drama exhibits successive imitations of successive actions; and why
may not the second imitation represent an action that happened years after the
first, if it be so connected with it, that nothing but time can be supposed to
intervene? Time is, of all modes of existence, most obsequious to the imagination; a lapse of years is as easily conceived as a passage of hours. In contemplation we easily contract the time of real actions, and therefore willingly permit it
to be contracted when we only see their imitation. (27) . . . As nothing is
essential to the fable, but unity of action, and as the unities of time and place
arise evidently from false assumptions, and, by circumscribing the extent of
the drama, lessen its variety, I cannot think it much to be lamented, that they
were not known by him [Shakespeare], or not observed. (29) . . . [Because] the
unities of time and place are not essential to a just drama, [and] though they
may sometimes conduce to pleasure, they are always to be sacrificed to the
nobler beauties of variety and instruction; and that a play, written with nice
observation of critical rules, is to be contemplated as an elaborate curiosity, as
the product of superfluous and ostentatious art, by which is shewn, rather what
is possible, than what is necessary. (30) . . . An act is so much of the drama as
passes without intervention of time or change of place. A pause makes a new

act. In every real, and therefore in every imitative action, the intervals may be more or fewer, the restriction of five acts being accidental and arbitrary. (57)

   See also Johnson under ILLUSION (JS 26-27, 28-29).

1767-1769   Lessing   LSPW

If we consider all the events occurring in [Voltaire's] "Merope," as occurring one day, what a number of absurdities we must conceive. . . . It is true, I see no physical hindrances why all the events could not have occurred in this space of time, but I see the more moral obstacles. It is certainly not impossible that a woman should be wooed and married within twelve hours. . . . But if it occurs do we not require the most cogent and urgent reasons for such forcible speed? . . . What good does it do the poet, that the particular actions that occur in every act would not require much more time for their real occurrence than is occupied by the representation of each act; and that this time, including what is absorbed between the acts, would not nearly require a complete revolution of the sun; has he therefore regarded the unity of time? He has fulfilled the words of the rule, but not their spirit. For what he lets happen in one day, can be done in one day it is true, but no sane mortal would do it in one day. Physical unity of time is not sufficient, the moral unity must also be considered, whose neglect is felt by every one, while the neglect of the other, though it generally involves an impossibility, is yet not so generally offensive because this impossibility can remain unknown to many. If, for instance, in a play a person must travel from one place to another and this journey alone would require more than a day, the fault is only observed by those who know the distance of the locality. Not everyone knows geographical distances, while everybody can feel in themselves for what actions they would allow themselves one day, for what several. The poet therefore who does not know to preserve physical unity of time except at the expense of moral unity, who does not hesitate to sacrifice the one to the other, consults his own interests badly and sacrifices the essential to the accidental. (364-66)

1808   Schlegel   SCL

The consideration of the dramatic regularity for which [the French] critics contend brings us back to the so-called Three Unities of Aristotle. We shall therefore examine the doctrine delivered by the Greek philosopher on this subject: how far the Greek tragedians knew or observed these rules; whether the French poets have in reality overcome the difficulty of observing them without the sacrifice of freedom and probability, or merely dexterously avoided it; and finally, whether the merit of this observance is actually so great and essential as it has been deemed, and does not rather entail the sacrifice of still more essential beauties. The far-famed Three Unities, which have given rise to a whole Iliad of critical wars, are the Unities of Action, Time, and Place. The validity of the first is universally allowed, but the difficulty is to agree about its true meaning. . . . The Unities of Time and Place are considered by some quite a subordinate matter, while others lay the greatest stress upon them, and affirm that out of the pale of them there is no safety for the dramatic poet. . . . The only one of [these of] which [Aristotle] speaks with any degree of fulness is the first, . . . [of the second,] Time, he merely throws out a vague hint; while of . . . Place he says not a syllable. I do not therefore find myself in a polemical relation to Aristotle. . . . I only claim a greater latitude with respect to place and time for many species of drama, nay, hold it essential to them. . . . With respect to the Unity of Time . . . Aristotle is not giving a precept . . . , but only making historical mention of a peculiarity which he observed in the Grecian examples before him. . . . Corneille . . . prefers [a] lenient interpretation, . . . to extend the duration of the action . . . to thirty hours. Others, however, . . . insist on the principle that the action should not occupy a longer period than that of its representation, that is to say, from two to three hours. . . . The latter plead a sounder case than the more lenient. . . . For the only ground of the rule is the observation of a probability which they suppose to be necessary for illusion, namely, that the actual time and that of the representation should be the same. If once a discrepancy be allowed, such as the difference between two hours and thirty, we may upon the same principle go much farther. . . . Our body is subjected to external astronomical time, because the organical operations are regulated by it; but our mind has its own ideal time, which is no other but the consciousness of the progressive development of our beings. In this measure of time the intervals of an indifferent inactivity pass for nothing, and two important moments, though they lie years apart, link themselves immediately to each other. . . . It is the same with dramatic exhibition: our imagination overleaps with ease the times which are presupposed and intimated, but which are omitted because nothing important takes place in them; it dwells solely on the decisive moments placed before it, by the compression of which the poet gives wings to the lazy course of days and hours. [Unity of Time] does not apply to the ancients: what they observe is nothing but the *seeming* continuity of time. . . . They unquestionably allow much more to take place during the choral songs than could really happen within the actual duration. . . . [The Greeks] had, however, a particular reason for observing the seeming continuity of time in the constant presence of the Chorus. When the Chorus leaves the stage, the continuous progress is interrupted [as] in the *Eumenides* of Aeschylus. . . . The moderns have, in the division of their plays into acts, . . . a convenient means for extending the period of representation without any ill effect. . . . The romantic poets take the liberty even of changing the scene during the course of an act. . . . The objection to the change of scene is founded on the same erroneous idea of illusion [previously] discussed. To transfer the action to another place would, it is urged, dispel the illusion. But now if we are in reality to consider the imaginary for the actual place, then must stage decoration and scenery be altogether different from what it now is. (It is calculated merely for a single point of view: seen from every other point, the broken lines betray the imperfection of the imitation.) Johnson, a critic who, in general, is an adovacte for the strict rules, very justly observes . . . [he cites ILLUSION 1765 (JS 26-27)]. Confined within the narrow limits of time, the poet is in many subjects obliged to mutilate the action, by beginning close to the last decisive stroke, or else he is under the neccessity of unsuitably hurrying on its progress: on either supposition he must reduce within petty dimensions the grand picture of a strong purpose, which is no momentary ebullition, but a firm resolve undauntedly maintained in the midst of all external vicissitudes, till the time is ripe for execution. (236-51) . . . The Unities of Place and Time are inconsistent with the essence of many tragical subjects, because a comprehensive action is frequently carried on in distant places at the same time, and because great determinations can only be slowly prepared. This is not the case in Comedy: here Intrigue [i.e., the scheming of a character] ought to prevail, the active spirit of which quickly hurries towards its object; and hence the unity of time may here be almost naturally observed. The domestic and social circles in which Comedy moves are usually assembled in one place, and, consequently, the poet is not under the necessity of sending our imagination abroad. (305)

See also Schlegel under RULES (SCL 217); compare with CONVENTION (SCL 256), IMAGINATION (SCL 250).

c.1810   Coleridge. *See* under GENRE (CLSW 74).

1811-1812   Coleridge   **CCSL**

The limit allowed by the rules of the Greek stage was twenty-four hours; but, inasmuch as, even in this case, time must have become a subject of imagination, it was just as reasonable to allow twenty-four months, or even years. The mind is acted upon by such strong stimulants, that the period is indifferent; and when once the boundary of possibility is passed, no restriction can be assigned. In reading Shakespeare, we should first consider in which of his plays he means to appeal to the reason, and in which to the imagination, faculties which have no relation to time and place, excepting as in the one case they imply a succession of cause and effect, and in the other form a harmonious picture, so that the impulse given by the reason is carried on by the imagination. (99)

c.1819   Coleridge. *See* under UNITY (CLSW 110).

c.1820   Hegel   **HFA**

The inalterability of one exclusive *locale* of the action . . . belongs to the type of those rigid rules, which the French in particular have deduced from classic tragedy and . . . Aristotle. As a matter of fact, Aristotle merely says that the duration of the tragic action should not exceed at the most the length of a day.

He does not mention the unity of place at all; moreover, the ancient tragedians have not followed such a principle in the strict sense adopted by the French. To a still lesser extent [than the ancients] can our more modern dramatic writing, in its effort to portray a more extensive field of collision . . . and . . . an action the ideal explication of which requires . . . an external environment of greater breadth, subject itself to the yoke of rigid identity of scene. Modern poetry, in so far . . . as its creations are in harmony with the romantic type, which as a rule displays more variety and caprice in its attitude to external condition, has . . . freed itself from any such demand. If, however, the action is in truth concentrated in a few great motives, so that it can avoid all complexity of external exposition, there will be no necessity for considerable alternation of scene. Indeed, the reverse will be a real advantage. The unity of *time* is a precisely similar case. In the pure realm of imaginative idea we may no doubt, with no difficulty, combine vast periods of time; in the direct vision of perception we cannot so readily pass over a few years. If the action is, therefore, of a simple character . . . we shall do best to concentrate the time of such a conflict, from its origin to its resolution, to a restricted period. If, on the contrary, it demands character richly diversified, . . . then the formal unity of a purely relative and entirely conventional duration of time will be essentially impossible. To attempt to remove such a representation from the domain of dramatic poetry . . . would simply amount to making the prose of ordinary facts the final court of appeal, as against the truth of poetic creation. Least of all need we waste time in discussing the purely empirical probability that as audience we could, in the course of a few hours, witness . . . directly through our senses merely the passage of a short space of time. For it is precisely in the case where the poet is most at pains to illustrate this conclusion that . . . he well-nigh invariably perpetuates the most glaring improbabilities. (4: 257-59)

1825   Goethe   GCE

Feb. 24. Goethe . . . laughed to think that Lord Byron, who, in practical life, could never adapt himself, and never even asked about a law, finally subjected himself to the stupidest of laws—that of the *three unities*. "He understood the purpose of this law," said he, "no better than the rest of the world. *Comprehensibility* is the purpose, and the three unities are only so far good as they conduce to this end. If the observance of them hinders the comprehension of a work, it is foolish to treat them as laws, and to try to observe them. Even the Greeks, from whom the rule was taken, did not always follow it. . . . It is obvious that good representation of their subject was with them more important than blind obedience to law, which, in itself, is of no great consequence. The pieces of Shakespeare deviate, as far as possible, from the unities of time and place; but they are comprehensible—nothing more so—and on this account, the Greeks would have found no fault in them. The French poets have endeavored to follow most rigidly the laws of the three unities, but they sin against comprehensibility, inasmuch as they solve a dramatic law, not dramatically, but by narration. I call to mind . . . *Goetz von Berlichingen*, which deviates as far as possible from the unity of time and place; but which, as everything is visibly developed to us, and brought before our eyes, is . . . truly dramatic and comprehensible. . . . The unities . . . were natural . . . only when a subject is so limited in its range that it can develop itself before our eyes with all its details in the given time; but with a large action, which occurs in several places, there is no reason to be confined to one place, especially as our present stage arrangements offer no obstacle to a change of scene.''

1889 Strindberg   SMD

[Èmile Zola, author of *Thérèse Raquin*,] had had the feeling . . . that through greater unity of place his audience would receive a more complete illusion, by which the action would impress its main feature more forcefully on the spectators. At every curtain rise, the spectator had to be haunted by the memories of the preceding act and thus through the impact of the recurring milieu be captivated by the action. But because of the difficulty in having a before and after the crime sequence, Zola commits the error of letting a year elapse between the first and second acts. Presumably he did not dare offend against the prevailing law about a year's widowhood, otherwise a day between the acts would have been enough, and the play would have made a more unified impression. (16)

1894 Brunetière   BLD

Shall we oblige the dramatic author to observe the Three Unities? I reply that he will not be hampered by them, if he can choose, like Racine, subjects which properly or necessarily adjust themselves of their own accord, so to speak, to the rule: "Bérénice," "Iphigénie," "Esther." . . . But if he chooses, like Shakspere [*sic*], subjects which are checked by it in their free development, or diverted merely, we will relieve him of the Rule: and "Othello," "Macbeth," "Hamlet," will still be drama. This is another example of a Rule which can be turned in various ways. (70)

1928 Eliot   ESE

The Unities have for me . . . a perpetual fascination. I believe they will be found highly desirable for the drama of the future. For one thing, we want more concentration. All plays are now much too long. . . . A continuous hour and a half of *intense* interest is what we need. . . . The Unities do make for intensity, as does verse rhythm. (45)

1932 Eliot   EUP

Unity of place and time is a stumbling-block so old that we think it long since worn away. . . . But . . . the unities differ radically from human legislation in that they are laws of nature. . . . The laws (*not* rules) of unity of place and time remain valid in that every play which observes them *in so far as its material allows* is in that respect and degree superior to plays which observe them less. I believe that in every play in which they are not observed we only put up with their violation because we feel that something is gained which we could not have if the law *were* observed. This is not to establish another law. There *is* no other law possible. It is merely to recognise that in poetry as in life our business is to make the best of a bad job. Furthermore, we must observe that the Unities are not three separate laws. They are three aspects of one law: we may violate the law of Unity of Place more flagrantly if we preserve the law of Unity of Time, or vice versa; we may violate both if we observe more closely the law of Unity of Sentiment. (45-46)

    See also Eliot under UNITY (EJD 60).

TRAGEDY

The statements included here are exercises in GENRE DEFINITION which present their authors' conceptions of the nature or characteristics of tragedy. Though for Aristotle the term tragedy *applied to any noncomic drama, it has since come to refer to a particular kind of drama or to an honorific quality of drama or to a particular effect of drama—indeed it has acquired nondramatic applications, as well. As new techniques and fashions of drama succeeded those of the Greek theater, and its conventions fell away, Aristotle's particular description of serious drama came to seem increasingly distinctive and exclusive. As a result the new dramas were taken as specimen of new genres, which first slowly and then rapidly proliferated. The generation of definitions of the new genres permitted the definition of tragedy to go virtually unchanged. A further result is the periodic announcement of "the death of tragedy," usually a much belated obituary for the conventions of the classical Greek theater. Tragedy is often defined in contrast with COMEDY. See also CATHARSIS, FLAW, HERO, PATHOS, RECOGNITION, and REVERSAL.*

4th. cent. B.C.   Aristotle   AP

Epic poetry agrees with Tragedy in so far as it is an [large sized: EP 203] imitation in verse of *characters of a higher type* [serious matters: EP 203]. They differ, in that Epic poetry admits but one kind of metre, and is narrative in form. They differ, again, in their *length* [bulk: EP 203]: for Tragedy endeavours, as far as possible, to *confine itself to a simple revolution of the sun* [exist in a single day-light period: EP 203], or but slightly to exceed this limit; whereas the Epic action has no limits of time. . . . Whoever . . . knows what is good or bad Tragedy, knows also about Epic poetry. All the elements of an Epic poem are found in Tragedy, but the elements of a Tragedy are not all found in the Epic poem. (21-23) . . . Tragedy, then, is an imitation of an action that is serious, complete and *of a certain magnitude* [has bulk: EP 221]; in language embellished with each kind of artistic ornament, the several kinds being found in separate parts of the play; *in the form of* [with persons performing the: EP 221] action, not of narrative; *through pity and fear effecting the proper purgation of these emotions* [carrying through to completion, through a course of events involving pity and fear, the purification of those painful or fatal acts which have that quality: EP 221]. By language embellished, I mean language into which rhythm, "*harmony*" [melody: EP 221], and song enter. By the several kinds in separate parts, I mean, that some parts are rendered through the medium of verse alone, others again with the aid of song. Now as tragic imitation implies persons acting, it necessarily follows, in the first place, that *Spectacular equipment* [the adornment of their physical appearance: EP 233] will be a part of tragedy. Next, Song and Diction, for these are the medium of imitation. By "Diction" I mean the mere metrical arrangement of the words: as for "Song," it is a term whose sense everyone understands. Again, Tragedy is the imitation of an action; and *an action implies personal agents*, who necessarily possess certain distinctive qualities both of character and of thought; for it is by these that we qualify actions themselves, and these—thought and character—are the two natural causes from which actions spring, and on actions again all success or failure depends. Hence, the Plot is the imitation of the action:—for by plot I here mean the arrangement of the incidents. By Character I mean that in virtue of which we ascribe certain [moral: EP 238] qualities to the agents. Thought is required wherever a statement is proved, or, it may be, a general truth enunciated. Every Tragedy, therefore, must have six parts, which parts determine its quality—namely, Plot, Character, Diction, Thought, Spectacle, Song. Two of the parts constitute the medium of imitation, one the manner, and three the objects of imitation. And these complete the list. (23-25)

    See also Aristotle under CHARACTER (AP 27-29, 69), IMITATION (AP 11-13), PLOT (AP 49), SUBJECT (AP 53), WONDER (AP 95).

1561   Scaliger   SP

Tragedy, like comedy, is patterned after real life, but differs from comedy in the rank of the characters, in the nature of the action, and in the outcome. These differences demand, in turn, differences in style. Comedy employs characters from rustic, or low city life. . . . The beginning of a comedy presents a confused state of affairs, and this confusion is happily cleared up at the end. The language is that of everyday life. Tragedy, on the other hand, employs kings and princes, whose affairs are those of the city, the fortress, and the camp. A tragedy opens more tranquilly than a comedy, but the outcome is horrifying. The language is grave, polished, removed from the colloquial. All things wear a troubled look; there is a pervading sense of doom, there are exiles and deaths. (39) . . . I do not wish to attack [Aristotle's definition of tragedy] other than by adding my own: A tragedy is the imitation of the adversity of a distinguished man; it employs the form of action, presents a disastrous *dénouement*, and is expressed in impressive metrical language. . . . The mention of "purgation" is too restrictive, for not every subject produces this effect. (40)

1570   Castelvetro   CP

Tragedy is an imitation of an action, magnificent, complete, which has magnitude, and comprises each of those species, which represent with speech made delightful separately in its parts, and not by narration, and, moreover, induces through pity and fear, the purgation of such passions. (95) . . . The excitment of pity and fear being the end of tragedy [any dramatic species which excites these emotions is tragedy]. (95-96) . . . Tragedy can have either a happy or a sorrowful ending, as can comedy; but the joy and sorrow of the tragic ending is different from [that] of the comic ending. The joyful dénouement of tragedy is formed by the cessation to the hero or to one dear to him, of impending death or sorrowful life or threatened loss of kingship: and the sorrowful dénouement is formed by the occurrence of these things. The happy dénouement of comedy is formed by the removal of insult from the hero or from one dear to him, or the cessation of a long-standing shame, or by the recovery of an esteemed person or possession which was lost, or by the fulfillment of his love: and the sorrowful dénouement of comedy is formed by the occurrence of the opposite of these things. (96-97) . . . Tragedy without the sad ending cannot excite and does not excite, as experience shows, either fear or pity.. (98)

  See also Castelvetro under ACTION (CP 113), HERO (CP 110-11), SUBJECT (SP 57, 69), WONDER (CP 80).

c.1583 Sidney   SDP

Tragedy . . . openeth the greatest wounds, and showeth forth the ulcers that are covered with tissue; [it] maketh kings fear to be tyrants, and tyrants manifest their tyrannical humors; . . . with stirring the effects of admiration and commiseration [tragedy] teacheth the uncertainty of this world, and upon how weak foundations gilden roofs are builded. . . . How much [tragedy] can move, Plutarch yieldeth a notable testimony of the abominable tyrant Alexander Pheraeus; from whose eyes a tragedy, well-made and represented, drew abundance of tears, who without all pity had murdered infinite numbers, and some of his own blood; so as he that was not ashamed to make matters for tragedies, yet could not resist the sweet violence of a tragedy. And if it wrought no further good in him, it was that he, in despite of himself, withdrew himself from hearkening to that which might mollify his hardened heart. (28-29)

1609 de Vega. *See* under IMITATION (VAWP 25), STYLE (VAWP 27).

1657 d'Aubignac   AAS

[Ancient] Tragedy represented the Life of Princes and great People full of disquiets, suspicions, troubles, rebellions, wars, murders, and all sorts of violent passions. . . . To distinguish Tragedys by their *Catastrophe*, they were of two sorts; the one were calamitous and bloody in their Events, ending generally by the death, or some great misfortune of the *Hero*; the others were more happy, and concluded by the felicity of the chief persons upon the Stage, and yet because the Poets out of compliasance to the *Athenians*, who loved spectacles of horrour, ended often their Tragedys by unfortunate *Catastrophes*;

many people have thought that the word *Tragical* never signifi'd any thing but some sad, bloody Event; and that a Drammatick Poem could not be call'd a *Tragedy*, if the *Catastrophe* did not contain the death of the chief persons in the Play; but they are mistaken, that word, in its true signification, meaning nothing else but a *Magnificent, serious, grave Poem, conformable to the Agitations and sudden turns of the fortune of great people*. And accordingly in the nineteen Tragedys of *Euripides*, many of them have a happy conclusion. (4: 140) . . . [Ancient] *Tragedy* and *Comedy* were two Poems so distinct, that not only the Adventures [and] Persons . . . of the one, had nothing common with the other; but even the *Tragedians* never acted Comedys, nor the *Comedians Tragedy*: They were as it were two different Trades or Professions. . . . The chief distinctive mark of these two Poems was the matter of their *Incidents*, and the condition of the persons in each Poem; for where Gods and Kings acted according to their gravity and dignity, that was call'd *Tragedy*; but when the *Intrigues* of the Stage were founded upon the tricks and behavior of young *Debauchees*, women and slaves, that was Comedy. (4: 146-47)

1660   Corneille. *See* under PROBABILITY (CFD 139), SUBJECT (CFD 142-43).

1664   Racine. *See* under SUBJECT (RP 154).

1668   Dryden. *See* under IMITATION (DW 1, 2: 126-27).

1671   Dryden. *See* under POETIC JUSTICE (DW 1, 2: 198-201).

1679   Dryden   **DW**

Tragedy[,] thus defined by Aristotle[,] . . . is an imitation of one entire, great, and probable action, not told, but represented; which, by moving in us fear and pity, is conducive to the purging of those two passions in our minds. More largely thus: Tragedy describes or paints an action, which action must have all the properties above named. First, it must be one or single, that is, it must not be a history of one man's life, . . . but one single action. . . . This condemns all Shakspeare's historical plays, which are rather chronicles represented, than tragedies; and all double action of plays. . . . The natural reason of this rule is plain; for two different independent actions distract the attention and concern-ment of the audience, and consequently destroy the intention of the poet. If his business be to move terrour and pity, and one of his actions be comical, the other tragical, the former will divert the people, and utterly make void his greater purpose. Therefore, as in perspective, so in tragedy, there must be a point of sight in which all the lines terminate; otherwise the eye wanders, and the work is false. (1, 2: 266-67)

    See also Dryden under ACTION (DW 1, 2: 268-69).

1695   Dryden. *See* under SUBJECT (DW 3: 312-13).

1697   Dryden   **DW**

Tragedy is the miniature of human life; an epick poem is the draught at length. . . . To raise, and afterwards to calm the passions, to purge the soul from pride, by the examples of human miseries which befall the greatest; in a few words, to expel arrogance, and introduce compassion, are the great effects of tragedy: great, I must confess, if they were altogether as true as they are pompous. . . . The effects of tragedy . . . are too violent to be lasting. (3: 430-31)

1711   Dryden. *See* under MORALITY (DW 1, 2: 309-10).

1711   Addison. *See* under POETIC JUSTICE (AW 1: 71-72).

1712   Addison. *See* under ACTION (AW 1: 427).

1725   Voltaire. *See* under SUBJECT (VE 278-79).

1731   Voltaire. *See* under SPECTACLE (VE 282).

c.1745-1752   Voltaire   **VW**

True tragedy is the school of virtue, and the only difference between a refined theatre and books of morality is, that the instruction of the former is all in action, that it is more interesting, and heightened by the charms of an art invented to make earth and heaven happy, and which was therefore truly called the language of the gods. (19: 141)

1755-1780   Diderot   **DDE**

A form of tragedy which keeps in check the agitations of the heart is thus a political lesson at the same time as a lesson in manners and morals. Hatred, anger, vengeance, ambition, black envy, and above all love spread their devastion in all stations of life, in all the ranks of society. These are the true domestic enemies, and it is most essential that we be made to fear them by the depiction of those misfortunes to which they can lead us, since they have brought to similar misfortunes men often less weak, more prudent, and more virtuous than we. . . . The aim of tragedy is to correct manners and morals by imitating them, by an action which serves as an example: then, whether or not the victim of passion is famous, whether or not his ruin is dazzling, the lesson is no less general in import. The same cause which spreads desolation in a state can spread it in a family. Love, hate, ambition, jealousy, and vengeance poison the sources of domestic happiness just as they poison those of the public good. (291)

    See also Diderot under CHARACTER (DDE 291).

1758   Diderot   DDP

Tragedy demands dignity in the method; comedy, delicacy. (296) . . . The known portion which the tragic poet borrows from history makes us accept the imaginative part as if it were history. The part he invents is given a verisimilitude from the historic part. But nothing is given to the comic poet; therefore he is less able to rely upon extraordinary combinations of events. Furthermore, fate and the will of the gods, which inspire terror in the hearts of men whose destiny is in the hands of superior beings before whom they are helpless, which follows them and strikes them the moment they believe themselves secure— this is more necessary to tragedy. If there is anything sad in life, it is the spectacle of a man rendered guilty and unhappy in spite of himself. In comedy, men must play the rôle which gods play in tragedy. Fate is the basis of tragedy; human malignity that of comedy. (297)

See also Diderot under ACTION (DDP 291-92), GENRE DEFINTION (DDP 287).

1766   Lessing   LSPW

To awaken the sensation . . . is the sole aim of the tragic stage. Its heroes must exhibit feeling, must express their pain, and let simple nature work within them. If they betray [manifest] training and restraint, they leave our hearts cold. (31)

1767-1769   Lessing   LSPW

A tragedy is a poem which excites compassion. According to its genus it is the imitation of an action, like the epopee and comedy, but according to its species, the imitation of an action worthy of compassion. From these two definitions all the rules can be perfectly deduced and even its dramatic form may be determined. (415)

See also Lessing under IMITATION (LSPW 399).

1778   Diderot   DPA

A tragedy is, to my thinking, nothing but a fine page of history divided into a certain number of marked periods. (58)

1797   Goethe. See under SUBJECT (GED 338).

1808   Schlegel   SCL

Inward liberty and external necessity are the two poles of the [Greek] tragic world. It is only by contrast with its opposite that each of these ideas is brought into full manifestation. As the feeling of an internal power of self-determination elevates the man above the unlimited dominion of impulse and the instincts of nature; in a word, absolves him from nature's guardianship, so the necessity, which alongside of her he must recognize, is no mere natural necessity, but one lying beyond the world of sense in the abyss of infinitude;

consequently it exhibits itself as the unfathomable power of Destiny.
. . . In Tragedy the gods either come forward as the servants of destiny, and
mediate executors of its decrees; or else approve themselves godlike only by
asserting their liberty of action, and entering upon the same struggles with fate
which man himself has to encounter. (67) . . . [The essence of tragedy lies] in
the prevailing idea of Destiny, in the Ideality of the composition, and in the
significance of the Chorus. (113)

   See also Schlegel under ACTION (SCL 239-42), AFFECT (SCL 67-69),
CHARACTER (SCL 66), DISTANCE (SCL 72), GENRE DEFINITION (SCL
176-79).

1815   Hazlitt   HW

Aristotle has long since said, that Tragedy purifies the mind by terror and pity;
that is, substitutes an artificial and intellectual interest for real passion. Tragedy, like Comedy, must therefore defeat itself; for its patterns must be drawn
from the living models within the breast, from feeling or from observation; and
the materials of Tragedy cannot be found among a people, who are the habitual
spectators of Tragedy, whose interests and passions are not their own, but
ideal, remote, sentimental, and abstracted. It is for this reason chiefly, we
conceive, that the highest efforts of the Tragic Muse are in general the earliest;
where the strong impulses of nature are not lost in the refinements and glosses
of art. . . . Shakespeare, with all his genius, could not have written as he did, if
he had lived in the present times. (1: 13)

1816   Hazlitt   HW

The object of modern tragedy is to represent the soul utterly subdued as it were,
or at least convulsed and overthrown by passion or misfortune. That of the
ancients was to show how the greatest crimes could be perpetrated with the
least remorse, and the greatest calamities borne with the least emotion. Firmness of purpose, and calmness of sentiment, are their leading characteristics.
. . . Contradictory motives are not accumulated; the utmost force of imagination and passion is not exhausted to overcome the repugnance of the will to
crime; the contrast and combination of outward accidents are not called in to
overwhelm the mind with the whole weight of unexpected calamity. The dire
conflict of the feelings, the desperate struggle with fortune, are seldom there.
All is prepared and submitted to with inflexible constancy, as if Nature were
only an instrument in the hands of Fate. (10: 96)

1818   Hazlitt. *See* under STYLE (HW 5: 347, 350-51).

c.1820   Hegel   HFA

With respect to *tragedy*, I will here confine myself to a consideration of only
the most general and essential characteristics. . . . The genuine content of

tragic action subject to the *aims* which arrest tragic characters is supplied by the world of those forces which carry in themselves their own justification, and are realized substantively in the volitional activity of mankind. Such are the love of husband and wife, of parents, children, and kinsfolk . . . the life of communities, the patriotism of citizens, the will of those in supreme power . . . the life of churches. . . . It is of a soundness and thoroughness consonant with these that the really tragical *characters* consist. They are throughout that which the essential notion of their character enables them and compels them to be. . . . It is at some . . . elevation, where the mere accidents of unmediated individuality vanish altogether, that we find the tragic heroes of dramatic art, . . . they stand forth as works of sculpture, and as such interpret . . . the essentially more abstract statues and figures of gods, as also the lofty tragic characters of the Greeks more completely than is possible for any other kind of elucidation or commentary. Broadly speaking, we may, therefore affirm that the true theme of primitive tragedy is the godlike. . . . In this form the spiritual substance of volition and accomplishment is ethical life. . . . These ethical forces . . . are *distinctively defined* in respect to their content and their individual personality. . . . If, then, these particular forces, in the way presupposed by dramatic poetry, are attached to the external expression of human activity, and are realized as the determinate aim of a human pathos which passes into action, their concordancy is cancelled, and they are asserted *in contrast* to each other in interchangeable succession. Individual action will then, under given conditions, realize an object or character, which, under such a presupposed state, inevitably stimulates the presence of a pathos [Trans. note: Hegel appears to understand by pathos here little more than a psychological state.] opposed to itself, because it occupies a position of unique isolation in virtue of its independently fixed definition, and, by doing so, brings in its train unavoidable conflicts. Primitive tragedy, then, consists in this, that within a collision of this kind both sides of the contradiction, if taken by themselves, are *justified*; yet, from a further point of view, they tend to carry into effect the true and positive content of their end and specific characterization merely as the negation and *volition* of the other equally legitimate power, and consequently in their ethical purport and relatively to this so far fall under *condemnation*. . . . Whatever may be the claim of the tragic final purpose and personality, whatever may be the necessity of the tragic collision, it is . . . no less a claim that is asserted . . . by the tragic resolution of this division. It is through *this* latter result that Eternal Justice is operative in such aims and individuals under a mode whereby it restores the ethical substance and unity in and along with the downfall of the individuality which disturbs its repose. For, despite the fact that individual characters propose that which is itself essentially valid, yet they are only able to carry it out under the tragic demand in a manner that implies contradiction and with a one-sidedness that is injurious. What, however, is substantive in truth, and the function of which is to secure realization, is not the battle of particular unities, however much such a conflict is essentially involved in the notion of a real world and human action; rather it is the reconciliation in which definite ends and individuals unite in harmonious action without mutual violation and contradiction. That which is abrogated in the tragic issue is merely the *onesided* particularity which was unable to accommodate itself to this harmony, and consequently in the tragic course of its action, through inability to disengage itself from itself and its designs, either is committed in its entirety to destruction or at least finds itself compelled to fall back upon a state of resignation in the execution of its aim in so far as it can carry this out. . . . (4: 295-99) Over and above mere fear and tragic sympathy we have . . . the feeling of *reconciliation*, which tragedy is vouched for in virtue of its vision of eternal justice, a justice which exercises a paramount force of absolute contingency on account of the relative claim of all merely contracted aims and passions; and it can do this for the reason that it is unable to tolerate the victorious issue and continuance in the truth of the objective world of such a conflict with and opposition to those ethical powers which are fundamentally and essentially concordant. . . . All that pertains to tragedy preeminently rests upon the contemplation of such a conflict and its resolution. . . . In tragedy . . . that which is eternally substantive is triumphantly vindicated under the mode of reconciliation. It simply removes from the contentions of personality the false one-sidedness, and exhibits instead that which is the object of its volition, namely, positive reality, no longer under an asserted mediation of opposed factors, but as the real support of consistency. And in contrast to this in *comedy* it is the purely *personal experience*, which retains the mastery in its character of infinite self-assuredness. And it is only these two fundamental aspects of human action which occupy a position of contrast in the classification of dramatic poetry into its several types. In tragedy individuals are thrown into confusion in virtue of the abstract nature of their sterling volition and character, or they are forced to accept that with resignation, to which they have been themselves essentially opposed. In comedy we have a vision of the victory of the intrinsically assured stability of the wholly personal soul-life, the laughter of which resolves everything through the medium and into the medium of such life. (4: 300-301) . . . The fundamental type [of tragedy] which determines its entire organization and structure is to be sought for in the emphasis attached to the substantive constitution of final ends and their content, as also of the individuals dramatized and their conflict and destiny. In the tragic drama . . . the general basis or background for tragic action is supplied . . . by that world-condition which I have [called] the *heroic*. For only in heroic times, when the universal ethical forces have neither acquired the independent stability of definite political legislation or moral commands and obligations, can they be presented in their primitive jocundity as gods, who are either opposed to each other in their personal activities, or themselves appear as the animated content of a free and human individuality. If, however, what is intrinsically ethical is to appear throughout [the drama] as the . . . universal ground . . . from which . . . personal action [appears] with equal force in its disunion, and is no less brought back again . . . into unity, we shall find that there are two distinct modes under which the ethical content of human action is asserted. *First*, we have the simple consciousness, which . . . in its veneration, its faith, and its happiness . . . is incapable of . . . any definite action; . . . although it does, while remaining itself incapable of action, esteem . . . that spiritual courage which asserts itself resolutely. The *second* mode under which this ethical content is asserted is that . . . which urges the active characters to their moral self-vindication into the opposition they occupy relatively to others, and brings them thereby into conflict. The individuals . . . are neither what . . . we describe as characters, nor are they mere abstractions. They are rather placed in the vital midway sphere between both . . . —elevated, absolutely determinate characters, whose definition, however, discovers its content and basis in a particular ethical power. . . . The tragic situation first appears in the *antagonism* of individuals who are thus empowered to act. . . . It results from the specific character of this alone that a particular quality so effects the substantive [ethical] content of a given individual, that the latter identifies himself with his entire interest and being in such a content, and penetrates it throughout with the glow of passion. . . . These two modes or aspects—of which the one is as important for the whole as the other—namely the unrevered consciousness of the godlike, and the combating human action, asserted, however, in godlike power and deed, which determines and executes the ethical purpose—supply the two fundamental elements, the mediation of which is displayed by Greek tragedy in its artistic compositions under the form of *chorus* and *heroic figures* respectively. (4: 312-15)

See also Hegel under GENRE (HFA 4: 256. 260, 293).

1825 Goethe   GCE

Thurs. May 12. "Moliere," said Goethe, "is so great, that one is astonished anew every time one reads him. He is a man by himself—his pieces border on tragedy; they are apprehensive. . . . His *Miser*, where the vice destroys all the natural piety between father and son, is especially great, and in a high sense tragic. But when, in a German [adaptation], the son is changed into a relation, the whole is weakened, and loses its significance. They feared to show the vice in its true nature, as he did; but what is tragic there, or indeed anywhere, except what is intolerable?"

1827 Goethe   GCE

Wed., March 28. "I am sorry that a man of undoubted innate power . . . like Hinrichs, should be so spoilt by the philosophy of Hegel as to lose all unbiased and natural observation and thought, and gradually to get into an artificial and heavy style, both of thought and expression . . . and we no longer know what we are reading. . . . What must the English and French think of the language of our philosophers, when we Germans do not understand them ourselves? . . . His idea of the relation between family and state,'' said Goethe, ''and the tragical conflicts that may arise from them, is certainly good and suggestive; still I cannot allow that it is the only right one, or even the best for tragic art. We are indeed all members both of a family and of a state, and a tragical fate does not often befall us which does not wound us in both capacities. Still we might be very good tragical characters, if we were merely members of a family or merely members of a state; for, after all, the only point is to get a conflict which admits of no solution, and this may arise from an antagonistical position in any relation whatever. . . . Thus Ajax falls a victim to the demon of wounded honor, and Hercules to the demon of jealousy. In neither of these cases is there the least conflict between family piety and political virtue; though this, according to Hinrichs, should be the [essence] of Greek tragedy.'' ''One sees clearly,'' says I, ''that in this theory he merely had *Antigone* in mind.''

1830 Hazlitt. *See* under IDEALISM (HW 9:432).

1871 Nietzsche   **NBT**

In the phenomenon of the lyrist . . . music strives to express itself with regard to its nature in Apollonian images. If we now reflect that music in its highest potency must seek to attain also to its highest symbolization, we must deem it possible that it also knows how to find the symbolic expression of its inherent Dionysian wisdom; and where shall we have to seek for this expression if not in tragedy and, in general, in the conception of the *tragic*? From the nature of art, as it is ordinarily conceived according to the single category of appearance and beauty, the tragic cannot honestly be deduced at all; it is only through the spirit of music that we understand the joy in the annihilation of the individual. For in the particular examples of such annihiliation only is the eternal phenomenon of Dionysian art made clear to us, which gives expression to the will in its omnipotence, as it were, behind the *principium individuationis*, the eternal life beyond all phenomena, and in spite of all annihilation. The metaphysical delight in the tragic is a translation of the instinctively unconscious Dionysian wisdom into the language of the scene: the hero, the highest manifestation of the will, is disavowed for our pleasure, because he is only phenomenon, and because the eternal life of the will is not affected by his annihilation. (127) . . . Tragedy absorbs the highest musical orgasm into itself, so that it absolutely brings music to perfection among the Greeks, as among ourselves; but it then places alongside thereof tragic myth and the tragic hero, who, like a mighty Titan, takes the entire Dionysian world on his shoulders and disburdens us thereof; while, on the other hand, it is able by means of this same tragic myth, in the person of the tragic hero, to deliver us from the intense longing for this existence, and reminds us with warning hand of another existence and a higher joy, for which the struggling hero prepares himself presentiently by his destruction, not by his victories. Tragedy sets a sublime symbol, namely the myth, between the universal authority of its music and the receptive Dionysian hearer, and produces in him the illusion that music is only the most effective means for the animation of the plastic world of myth. Relying upon this noble illusion, she can now move her limbs for the dithyrambic dance, and abandon herself unhesitatingly to an orgiastic feeling of freedom, in which she could not venture to indulge as music itself, without this illusion. The myth protects us from the music while, on the other hand, it alone gives the highest freedom thereto. By way of return for this service, music imparts to tragic myth such an impressive and convincing metaphysical significance as could never be attained by word and image, without this unique aid; and the tragic spectator . . . experiences thereby the sure presentiment of supreme joy to which the path through destruction and negation leads; so that he thinks he hears, as it were, the innermost abyss of things speaking audibly to him. (159-60)

See also Nietzsche under CATHARSIS (NBT 166).

1875   Nietzsche. See under CONFLICT (NTS 128-30).

1888   Nietzsche   **NTI**

The psychology of orgaism conceived as the feeling of a superabundance of vitality and strength, within the scope of which even pain acts as a *stimulus*, gave me the key to the concept *tragic* feeling, which has been misunderstood not only by Aristotle, but also even more by our pessimists. Tragedy is so far from proving anything in regard to the pessimism of the Greeks . . . that it ought rather to be considered as the categorical repudiation and *condemnation* thereof. The saying of Yea to life, including even the most strange and most terrible problems, the will of life rejoicing over its own inexhaustibleness in the *sacrifice* of its highest types—this is what I call Dionysian, this is what I divined as the bridge leading to the psychology of the tragic poet. Not in order to escape from terror and pity, not to purify one's self of a dangerous passion by discharging it with vehemence—this is how Aristotle understood it—but to be far beyond terror and pity and to be the eternal lust of Becoming itself—that lust which also involves the *lust of destruction*. (119-20)

1888   Nietzsche   **NEH**

I was the first to see the actual contrast [between the Socratic and the Dionysian phenomena]: the degenerate instinct which turns upon life with a subterranean lust of vengeance (Christianity . . .—in short, the whole of idealism in its typical forms), as opposed to a formula of the highest yea-saying to life—a yea-saying free from all reserve, applying even to suffering and guilt, and all that is questionable and strange in existence. . . . I had by means of these doctrines discovered the idea of "tragedy," the ultimate explanation of what the psychology of tragedy is, [as] I discussed finally in *The Twilight of the Idols*. In this sense I have the right to regard myself as the first *tragic philosopher*—that is to say, the most extreme antithesis and antipodes of a pessimistic philosopher. Before my time no such thing existed as this translation of the Dionysian phenomenon into philosophic emotion: tragic wisdom was lacking. . . . The yea-saying to the impermanence and annihilation of things, which is the decisive feature of a Dionysian philosophy; the yea-saying to contradiction and war, the postulation of Becoming, together with the radical rejection even to the concept Being. . . . (70-73)

See also Nietzsche under CATHARSIS (NW 285-86), TASTE (NWP 448-50).

c.1900   Shaw   SS

After Dickens, Comedy completed its development into the new species, which has been called tragicomedy when any attempt has been made to define it. Tragedy itself never developed. . . . (253)

1931-1936   Artaud   AT

In order to understand the powerful, total, definitive, absolute originality . . . of films like *Animal Crackers* and *Monkey Business*, you would have to add to humor the notion of something disquieting and tragic, a fatality (neither happy nor unhappy, difficult to formulate) which would hover over it like the cast of an appalling malady upon an exquisitely beautiful profile. (142-43)

UNITY

Unity considers the nature of the "singleness" of a play and how the sense of that quality is produced. In general, the trend is from an early emphasis on external characteristics of the work to more internal characteristics and from objective or logical criteria to those more subjective or perceptual. See also FORM, ORDER, THREE UNITIES.

4th cent. B.C.   Aristotle   AP

Imitation . . . is one instinct of our nature. Next there is the instinct for *"harmony"* [melody: EP 125], and rhythm, metres being manifestly sections of rhythm. (15) . . . Unity of plot does not, as some persons think, consist in *the unity of the hero* [having to do with one individual: EP 296]. For infinitely various are the incidents in one man's life which cannot be reduced to unity; and so, too, there are many actions of one man out of which we cannot make one action. Hence the error, as it appears, of all poets who have composed a Heracleid, a Theseid, or other poems of the kind. They imagine that as Heracles was one man, the story of Heracles must also be a unity. But Homer, as in all else he is surpassing merit, here too—whether from art or natural genius—seems to have happily discerned the truth. In composing the Odyssey he did not include all the adventures of Odysseus—such as his wound on Parnassus, or his feigned madness at the mustering of host—incidents between which there was no necessary or probable connexion: but he made the Odyssey, and likewise the Iliad, to centre round an action that in our sense of the word is one. As therefore, in the other imitative arts, the imitation is one when the object imitated is one, so the plot, being the imitation of an action, must imitate one action and that a whole, the structural union of the parts being such that, if any one of them is displaced or removed, the whole will be disjointed and disturbed. For a thing whose presence or absence *makes no visible difference* [does not lend any greater clarity: EP 300], is not an organic part of the whole. (33-35)

    See also Aristotle under ACTION (AP 25-29, 33-35), AESTHETIC (APA 16-17), DRAMA (AP 107-11), FORM (AM 1023b: 26-31, 1024a: 1-4, and AP 31-33, 89), MAGNITUDE (AP 91-93), ORDER (AM 1076a: 1, 1090b: 20), PLOT (AP 37-39, 39-41, 45-49).

1561   Scaliger. Compare with ACTION (SP 62).

1570 Castelvetro   CP

There is no doubt that there is more pleasure in listening to a plot containing
many and diverse actions than in listening to that which contains one.
. . . Singleness of plot is not in the least introduced on account of its necessity,
but on account of the poet's eagerness for glory and to demonstrate the
excellence and the singularity of his genius. (90-91)

    See also Castelvetro under ACTION (CP 89).

1609 de Vega. *See* under ACTION (VAWP 30-31).

1641 Jonson   JD

The Fable is call'd the *Imitation* of one intire, and perfect Action; whose parts
are so joyned, and Knitt together, as nothing in the structure can be chang'd; or
taken away, without imparing, or troubling the whole; of which there is a
proportionable magnitude in the members. (101)

    See also Jonson under ACTION (JD 105).

1657 d'Aubignac   AAS

[The Poet] must remember, that his Action ought to be not only one, but
continued, that is, That from the opening of the Stage, to the very closing of the
Catastrophe, from the first Actor, that appears upon the Scene, to the last that
goes off; the principal Persons of the Play must be always in Action; and in
Theatre must carry continually, and without any interruption the face of some
Designes, Expectations, Passions, Troubles, Disquiets, and other such like
Agitations, which may keep the Spectators in a belief, that the Action of the
Theatre is not ceased, but still going on. This is one of the Precepts of *Aristotle*,
as well as of Reason; and his Interpreters have always observed the Cessation
of Action for one of the greatest Faults of the Drama. (2: 89)

    See also d'Aubignac under ACTION (AAS 2: 81).

1660 Corneille   CFD

I say that [the first act] must contain the seed of all that is going to happen . . . so
that no actors come into the following act who are not known by the first, or at
least named. . . . This maxim is new and rather strict; I have not always kept it,
but I judge that it helps a great deal to create a veritable unity of action by the
binding of all those which come in the poem. (147)

    See also Corneille under ACTION (CDTU 235), COMPLICATION
(CTU 816).

1664 Racine   RP

This subject had already been treated by Rotrou, in his *Antigone*; but he killed
off the two brothers at the beginning of the third act. The remainder of the

drama was in a way the beginning of another tragedy, introducing entirely new interests. It combined within itself two distinct plots. . . . I saw that the double plot tended to spoil his play, which was, however, full of beautiful things. (154)

1668   Dryden   DW

[The French playwrights'] plots are single; they carry on one design, which is pushed forward by all the actors, every scene in the play contributing and moving towards it. Our plays, besides the main design, have under-plots or by-concernments, of less considerable persons and intrigues, which are carried on with the motion of the main plot. . . . If contrary motions may be found in nature to agree; if a planet can go east and west at the same time;—one way by virtue of his own motion, the other by the force of the first mover;—it will not be difficult to imagine how the under-plot, which is only different, not contrary to the great design, may naturally be conducted along with it. . . . The unity of action is sufficiently preserved, if all the imperfect actions of the play are conducing to the main design; but when . . . petty intrigues of a play are so ill ordered, that they have no coherence with the other . . . [they] want of due connexion; for coordination in a play is as dangerous and unnatural as in a state. . . . Our variety, if well ordered, will afford a greater pleasure to the audience. (1, 2: 86-87)

See also Dryden under VARIETY (DW 1, 2: 89).

1670   Racine   RP

Personally, I have always believed that since tragedy was the imitation of a complete action—wherein several persons participate—that action is not complete until the audience knows in what situation the characters are finally left. Sophocles always informs us of this. . . . (155)

1679   Dryden. See under INSTRUCTION (DW 1, 2: 274).

1712   Addison. See under ACTION (AW 1: 385), AESTHETIC (AW 2: 139-40).

1730   Voltaire. See under THREE UNITIES (VE 280-81).

1751   Johnson. See under RULES (JW 3: 242).

1765   Johnson. See under FORM (JS 24-25).

1767-1769   Lessing. See under THREE UNITIES (LSPW 364-66).

1789   Goethe. See under IMITATION (GLE 59-61).

1798   Goethe. *See* under ILLUSION (GLE 52-57).

1808   Schlegel   **SCL**

Action, according to [Aristotle], must have beginning, middle, and end, and consequently consist of a plurality of connected events. But where are the limits of this plurality? Is not the concatenation of causes and effects, backwards and forwards, without end? and may we then, with equal propriety, begin and break off wherever we please? . . . Completeness would therefore be altogether impossible. . . . The difference [Corneille] assumed between tragic and comic Unity is altogether unessential. [*see* COMPLICATION CTU 1660] For the manner of putting the play together is not influenced by the circumstance, that the incidents in Tragedy are more serious, as affecting person and life; the embarrassment of the characters in Comedy when they cannot accomplish their design and intrigues, may equally be called a danger. Corneille, like most others, refers all to the idea of connexion between cause and effect. No doubt when the principal persons, either by marriage or death, are set at rest, the drama comes to a close; but if nothing more is necessary to its Unity than the uninterrupted progress of an opposition, which serves to keep up the dramatic movement, . . . without violating this rule of Unity, we may go on to an almost endless accumulation of events, as in the *Thousand and One Nights.* . . . De la Motte . . . would substitute for Unity of action, the *Unity of interest.* If the term be not confined to the interest in the destinies of some single personage, but is taken to mean in general the direction which the mind takes at the sight of an event, this explanation . . . seems most satisfactory and very near the truth. . . . The idea of *One* and *Whole* is in no way whatever derived from experience, but arises out of the primary and spontaneous activity of the human mind. . . . The external sense perceives in objects only an indefinite plurality of distinguishable parts; the judgment, by which we comprehend these into an entire and perfect unity, is in all cases founded on a reference to a higher sphere of ideas. . . . The separate parts of a work of art . . . must not be taken in by the eye and ear alone, but also comprehended by the understanding. Collectively, however, they are all subservient to one common aim, namely, to produce a joint impression on the mind. . . . The Unity lies in a higher sphere, in the feeling or in the reference to ideas. This is all one; for the feeling, so far as it is not merely sensual and passive, is our sense, our organ for the Infinite, which forms itself into ideas for us. Far . . . from rejecting the law of perfect Unity in Tragedy as unnecessary, I require a deeper, more intrinsic, and more mysterious unity than that [with] which most critics are satisfied. . . . Logical coherence, the causal connexion, I hold to be equally essential to Tragedy and every serious drama, because all the mental powers act and react upon each other, and if the Understanding be compelled to take a leap, Imagination and Feeling . . . follow . . . with equal alacrity. . . . Why should not the poet be allowed to carry on several, and, for a while, independent streams of human passions and endeavours, down to the moment of their raging junction, if only he may overlook the whole of their course? (242-45)

See also Schlegel under ACTION (SCL 239-42), COMEDY (SCL 149-51), COMPLICATION (SCL 253-54), POETRY OF THE THEATRE (SCL 36-37).

c.1810   Coleridge   CLSW

In order that a drama may be properly historical, it is necessary that it should be the history of the people to whom it is addressed. In the composition, care must be taken that there appear no dramatic improbability, as the reality is taken for granted. It must, likewise, be poetical;—that only, I mean, must be taken which is the permanent in our nature, which is common, and therefore deeply interesting to all ages. The events themselves are immaterial, otherwise than as the clothing and manifestation of the spirit that is working within. In this mode, the unity resulting from succession is destroyed, but is supplied by a unity of a higher order, which connects the events by reference to the workers, gives a reason for them in the motives, and presents men in their causative character. It takes, therefore, that part of history which is the least known, and infuses a principle of life and organization into the naked facts, and makes them all the framework of an animated whole. (117)

1811-1812   Coleridge   CLSW

Poetry, or rather a poem, is a species of composition, opposed to science, as having intellectual pleasure for its object, and as attaining its end by the use of language natural to us in a state of excitement—but distinguished from other species of composition, not excluded by the former criterion, by permitting a pleasure from the whole consistent with a consciousness of pleasure from the component parts;—and the perfection of which is, to communicate from each part the greatest immediate pleasure compatible with the largest sum of pleasure on the whole. (20)

1815   Coleridge   CBL

A poem is that species of composition, which is opposed to works of science, by proposing for its immediate object pleasure, not truth; and from all other species (having this object in common with it) it is discriminated by proposing to itself such delight from the whole, as is compatible with a distinct gratification from each component part. (2: 10) . . . If the definition sought for be that of a legitimate poem, . . . it must be one, the parts of which mutually support and explain each other; all in their proportion harmonizing with, and supporting the purpose and known influences of metrical arrangement. The philosophic critics of all ages coincide with the ultimate judgment of all countries, in equally denying the praises of a just poem, on the one hand, to a series of striking lines or distiches, each of which, absorbing the whole attention of the reader to itself, disjoins it from its context, and makes it a separate whole, instead of an harmonizing part; and on the other hand, to an unsustained composition, from which the reader collects rapidly the general result, unattracted by the component parts. The reader should be carried forward, not merely or chiefly by the mechanical impulse of curiosity, or by a restless desire to arrive at the final solution; but by the pleasurable activity of mind excited by the attractions of the journey itself. (2: 10-11) . . . In short, whatever *specific* import we attach to the word, poetry, there will be found involved in it, as a necessary consequence, that a poem of any length neither can be, or ought to be, all poetry. Yet if an harmonious whole is to be produced, the remaining parts must be preserved *in keeping* with the poetry; and this can be no otherwise effected than by such a studied selection and artificial arrangement, as will partake of *one*, though not a *peculiar* property of poetry. And this again can be no other than the property of exciting a more continuous and equal attention than the language of prose aims at, whether colloquial or written. (2: 11)

    See also Coleridge under AESTHETIC (CBL 2: 232, 233-34, 238-39, 253, 256-57), FORWARD MOVEMENT (CBL 2: 10-11), IMAGINATION (CBL 1: 202; 2: 12), ORDER (CBL 2: 262).

1816   Hazlitt   HW

True genius . . . combines truth of imitation with effect, the parts with the whole, the means with the end. The mechanic artist sees only that which nobody else sees, and is conversant only with the technical language and difficulties of his art. A painter, if shewn a picture, will generally dwell upon the academic skill displayed in it. . . . The poet will be struck with the harmony of versification, or the elaborateness of the arrangement in a composition (1: 76)

    See also Hazlitt under AESTHETIC (HW 1: 68).

c.1817   Coleridge   CBL

In every work of art there is a reconcilement of the external with the internal; the conscious is so impressed on the unconscious as to appear in it. . . . He who combines the two is the man of genius. (2: 258)

1818   Coleridge. *See* under SYMBOL (CMC 30), THOUGHT (CLSW 329-30).

c.1819   Coleridge   CLSW

We have had occasion to speak at large on the subject of the three unities, time, place, and action, as applied to the drama in [the] abstract, and to the particular stage for which Shakespeare wrote. . . . We succeeded in demonstrating that the two former, instead of being rules, were mere inconveniences attached to the local peculiarities of the Athenian drama; that the last alone deserved the name of a principle, and that in this Shakespeare stood pre-eminent. Yet

instead of unity of action I should great[ly] prefer the more appropriate tho'
scholastic and uncouth words—homogeneity, proportionateness, and totality
of interest. (110)

1820   Hegel. *See* under ACTION (HFA 4: 259-61).

c.1820   Hazlitt. *See* under AESTHETIC (HW 2: 463).

1824   Hazlitt HW

The modern French and English schools . . . are both wrong. The English seem
generally to suppose, that if they only leave out the subordinate parts, they are
sure of the general result. The French, on the contrary, as erroneously imagine,
that, by attending successively to each separate part, they must infallibly arrive
at a correct whole; not considering that, besides the parts, there is their relation
to each other, and the general expression stamped upon them by the character
of the individual, which to be seen must be felt; for it is demonstrable, that all
character and expression, to be adequately represented, must be perceived by
the mind, and not by the eye only. The French painters give only lines and
precise differences; the English only general masses, and strong effects. Hence
the two nations reproach one another with the differences of their styles of
art,—the one as dry, hard, and minute,—the other as gross, gothic, and
unfinished; and they will probably remain for ever satisfied with each other's
defects, as they afford a very tolerable fund of consolation on either side.
(9:404-405)

   See also Hazlitt under IDEALISM (HW 9: 405), UNIVERSALITY (HW
9: 402).

1826   Goethe GCE

Wed., July 26. "[Calderon's] pieces are throughout fit for the boards; there is
not a touch in them which is not directed towards the required effect."

1835   Coleridge. *See* under IMAGINATION (CMC 435-36).

1864   Taine TLA

Art, like nature, casts its objects in every mould; only, in order that the object
be viable it is necessary, in art as in nature, that the parts should constitute a
whole, and that the least part of the least element should be subordinate to the
whole. (332-33)

   See also Taine under AESTHETIC (TLA 76, 76-77, 87), CLOSURE
(TLA 311, 324).

1871   Nietzsche NBT

At the [Dionysian] evangel of cosmic harmony, each one feels himself not only
united, reconciled, blended with his neighbour, but as one with him, as if the

veil of Mâyâ had been torn and were now merely fluttering in tatters before the mysterious Primordial Unity. . . . Man is no longer an artist, he has become a work of art: the artistic power of all nature here reveals itself in the tremors of drunkenness to the highest gratification of the Primordial Unity. (27)

1876   Sarcey   **STT**

To be strong and durable an impression must be single. All dramatists have felt this instinctively; and it is for this reason that the distinction between the comic and the tragic is as old as art itself. (41-42) . . . Try to recall your past theatrical experience; you will find that in all the melodramas, in all the tragedies, whether classic or romantic, into which the grotesque has crept, it has always been obliged to take an humble place, to play an episodic part; otherwise it would have destroyed the unity of impression which the author always strives to produce. (45) . . . This great law of the unity of impression—without which there is no possibility of illusion for an audience of twelve hundred persons— has been observed instinctively by all the playwrights who were truly endowed with the comic genius. (53)

1889   Strindberg. *See* under THREE UNITIES (SMD 16).

1898   Shaw. Compare with CONFLICT (SCP 729).

1908   Pirandello. *See* under IDEALISM (POH 75-76).

1926   Eliot. *See* under STYLE (EEE 167).

1932   Eliot   **EJD**

More *unity of poetic feeling* (which is the only unity that matters) can be obtained *as a rule*, with a minimum of difference between times and places. I say *as a rule*, for some actions obviously cannot be represented at all without making great leaps of time or space. (60)

1936   Stanislavski. *See* under ACTION (SAP 43), FORWARD MOVEMENT (SAP 258), SUBTEXT (SAP 256).

1938   Stanislavski   **SBC**

As long as there exist only separate sounds, ejaculations, notes, exclamations instead of music, or separate spasmodic jerks instead of coordinated move-ment—there can be no question of music, singing, design or painting, danc-ing, architecture, sculpture nor, finally, of dramatic art. (61)

   See also Stanislavski under ACTION (SBC 118), FOREWARD MOVE-MENT (SBC 211-12), SUBTEXT (SBC 108-109), THOUGHT (SBC 169-71).

UNIVERSALITY

The concept of "universality" raises one of the fundamental issues of art theory: what should be the balance (or fusion) of the abstract and the concrete and how may that balance be achieved. An extended historical example of the working out of this principle and its application may be seen in CHARACTER, with the concept of DECORUM representing the neoclassical emphasis on typicality and SUBTEXT representing a post-Romantic concern with individuation.

4th cent. B.C.   Aristotle   AP

Poetry tends to express the universal, history the particular. By the universal I mean how a person of a certain type will on occasion speak or act, according to the law of probability or necessity; and it is this universality at which poetry aims *in the names she attaches to personages* [tacking on names afterward: EP 302]. The particular is—for example—what Alcibiades did or suffered. (35)

4th cent. B.C.   Aristotle   AM

We must not only raise these questions about the first principles, but also ask whether they are universal or what we call individuals. If they are universal, they will not be substances; for everything that is common indicates not a "this" but a "such," but substance is a "this." And if we are to be allowed to lay down that a common predicate is a "this" and a single thing, Socrates will be several animals—himself and "man" and "animal," if each of these indicates a "this" and a single thing. (1003a: 5-12) . . . The universal is common, since that is called universal which is such as to belong to more than one thing. (1038b: 10-12)

    See also Aristotle under IMITATION (AP 15), PROBABILITY (AP 35-37).

c.1583   Sidney   SDP

[In poetry,] all virtues, vices, and passions so in their own natural states [are] laid to the view, that we seem not to hear of them, but clearly to see through them. (17) . . . Aristotle himself, in his Discourse of Poesy, . . . say[s] that poetry is . . . more philosophical and more studiously serious than history. His reason is, because poesy dealeth with . . . the universal consideration, and the history with . . . the particular. (18)

    See also Sidney under THOUGHT (SDP 8).

1648   Corneille. *See* under AUTHORITY (CSP 8-9).

1711   Addison. *See* under HUMOR (AW 1: 65).

1725   Voltaire. *See* under SUBJECT (VE 278-79).

1755-1780   Diderot. *See* under TRAGEDY (DDE 291).

1759   Johnson   **JW**

The business of a poet . . . is to examine, not the individual, but the species; to remark general properties and large appearances: he does not number the streaks of the tulip, or describe the different shades in the verdure of the forest. He is to exhibit, in his portraits of nature, such prominent and striking features, as recall the original to every mind; and must neglect the minuter discriminations, which one may have remarked, and another have neglected, for those characteristics which are alike obvious to vigilance and carelessness. (1: 222)

1765   Johnson   **JS**

The poet of nature . . . holds up to his readers a faithful mirrour of manners and of life. His characters are not modified by the customs of particular places . . . ; by the peculiarities of studies or professions. . . . His persons act and speak by the influence of those general passions and principles by which all minds are agitated, and the whole system of life is continued in motion. (11-12)

1767-1769   Lessing. *See* under CHARACTER (LSPW 456-67).

1778   Diderot   **DPA**

The Miser, *The* Tartufe, [*The* Misanthrope] were drawn from [all the misers, hypocrites and misanthropes] in the world; they contain their broadest and most marked features, but there is in them no exact portrait of a given individual; and that is why the real people don't recognize themselves in their types. (49)

1808   Schlegel. *See* under CHARACTER (SCL 148-49), SPECTACLE (SCL 59).

c.1810   Coleridge. *See* under UNITY (CLSW 117).

1811   Coleridge   **CSNL**

Shakespeare's characters are all *genera* intensely individualized; the results of meditation, of which observation supplied the drapery and the colors necessary to combine them with each other. He had virtually surveyed all the great component powers and impulses of human nature,—had seen that their different combinations and subordinations were in fact the individualisers of men, and showed how their harmony was produced by reciprocal dispropor- tions of excess or deficiency. (91)

1811-1812   Coleridge   **CCSL**

When I use the term meditation, I do not mean that our great dramatist [Shakespeare] was without observation of external circumstances: quite the reverse; but mere observation may be able to produce an accurate copy, and even to furnish to other men's minds more than the copyist professed; but what is produced can only consist of parts and fragments, according to the means and extent of observation. Meditation looks at every character with interest, only as it contains something generally true, and such as might be expressed in a philosophical problem. (37)

1813   Goethe. *See* under CHARACTER (GLE 177).

1815   Coleridge. *See* under CHARACTER (CBL 2: 33-34, 159,187), IMI- TATION (CBL 2: 259).

1817   Hazlitt. *See* under DISINTERESTEDNESS (HW 1: 200).

c.1820   Hegel   **HFA**

Inasmuch . . . as the interest, in a dramatic sense, restricts itself to the personal aim, whose hero the active personality is, and it is only necessary in the artistic work to borrow from the external world so much as is bound in an essential relation to this purpose, which originates in self-conscious life, for this reason the drama is *primarily* of a more abstract nature than the epic poem. . . . The action, in so far as it reposes in the self-determination of character, . . . does not presuppose the epic background of an entire world through all the varied aspects . . . of its positive realization, but is concentrated in the simpler definition of circumstances subject to which the individual man is absorbed in his immediate purpose and carries the same to accomplishment. . . . We have not here the type of personality which [manifests] the *entire complexity* of national qualities as such are displayed by the epic, but rather character viewed in *direct* relation to its action, character which possesses a definite end directed to spirit life in its universality. . . . Consequently . . . in relation to the active personality, dramatic poetry ought to be more simply concentrated than epic poetry. The same generalization is applicable to the number and variety of characters represented. (4: 252-53)

 See also Hegel under ACTION (HFA 4: 253-54,259-61), AFFECT (HFA 4: 273), IDEALISM (HFA 4: 265-67), LANGUAGE (HFA 4: 264-65), PATHOS (HFA 4: 268-69).

c. 1820   Hazlitt. *See* under TASTE (HW 11: 459-60).

1824   Hazlitt   **HW**

The highest perfection of . . . art depends, not on separating but on uniting general truth and effect with individual distinctness and accuracy. (9: 402)

1871   Nietzsche. *See* under MORALITY (NBT 78-79).

1918-1922   Stanislavski. *See* under IDEALISM (SAS 105-106).

1931-1936   Artaud. *See* under DRAMA (AT 116).

1936   Brecht. Compare with ALIENATION (BBB 131-36).

1948   Brecht   **BBBG**

[Not only the illusion of the "first time," in Epic Theatre, but] a further illusion had to be relinquished: that *everyone* behaves as a particular character does. "I do this" became "I did this," and now "He did this" must become "He did *this*, not something else." It is an oversimplification to make action exactly fit character and character exactly fit action. The contradictions evidenced by the actions and characters of real people cannot thus be exhibited. The laws of social mobility cannot be demonstrated by ideal cases, since "impurity" (contradictoriness) is inherent in mobility. It is only necessary—but this is essential—that something like the conditions of an experiment be set up, that is, that a control experiment is always conceivable. In general, society should be treated . . . as though it does what it does experimentally. (30)

Compare Brecht under CHARACTER (BBBG 25, 30) and ILLUSION (BBBG 28-29).

VARIETY

The statements here concern the nature of and justifications for the diversity of elements and qualities in a single play. Variety as an art standard was a Gothic taste more often excused by working playwrights in the Renaissance than by theorists. On the other hand, variety assumed such significance for Romantic theorists that it sometimes seems more important to them than unity. A beneficial effect of the Romantic interest in variety was that theorists were forced to find more subtle concepts of unity, less dependent on ostensive features than were those of neoclassic theory.

4th cent. B.C. Aristotle   AP

Sameness of incident soon produces satiety, and makes tragedies fail on the stage. (93)

Compare with Aristotle under PLOT (AP 49).

1561 Scaliger. *See* under ACTION (SP 62), AESTHETIC (SP 53), COMEDY (SP 17), MAGNITUDE (SP 60).

1570 Castelvetro. *See* under UNITY (CP 90-91).

1609 de Vega   VAWP

Tragedy mixed with comedy and Terence with Seneca, tho it be like another minotaur of Pasiphae, will render one part grave, the other ridiculous; for this variety causes much delight. Nature gives us good example, for through such variety it is beautiful. (30)

1641 Jonson. *See* under MAGNITUDE (JD 103).

1657 d'Aubignac. *See* under SUBJECT (AAS 2: 68-69).

1665 Dryden. Compare with STYLE (DW 1, 2: 19-20).

1668 Dryden   DW

'Tis evident that the more the [characters] are, the greater will be the variety of the plot. If then the parts are managed so regularly, that the beauty of the whole be kept entire, and that the variety become not a perplexed and confused mass of accidents, you will find it infinitely pleasing to be led, in a labyrinth of design, where you see some of your way before you, yet discern not the end till you arrive at it. (1, 2: 89) . . . If [the French] content themselves, as Corneille did, with some flat design, which, like an ill riddle, is found out ere it be half proposed, such plots we can make every way regular, as easily as they; but whenever they endeavor to rise to any quick turns and counterturns of plot . . . you see they write as irregularly as we, though they cover it more speciously. Hence the reason is perspicuous, why no French plays, when translated, have, or ever can succeed on the English stage. For, if you consider the plots, our own are fuller of variety; if the writing, ours are more quick and fuller of spirit. . . . Our plots are weaved in English looms; we endeavor therein to follow the variety and greatness of characters which are derived to us from Shakespeare and Fletcher; the copiousness and well-knitting of the intrigues we have from Jonson. (1, 2: 95-96)

    See also Dryden under STYLE (DW 1, 2: 85-86).

1670   **Racine.**Compare with MAGNITUDE (RP 155).

1674   **Dryden.** *See* under PLOT (DW 1, 2: 288).

1697   **Dryden.** *See* under THREE UNITIES (DW 3: 430-31).

1712   **Addison.** *See* under AESTHETIC (AW 2: 139-40, 142), IMAGINA-TION (AW 2: 138-39, 146-47).

1751   **Johnson**   **JW**

For what is there in the mingled drama [tragicomedy] which impartial reason can condemn? The connection of important with trivial incidents, since it is not only common but perpetual in the world, may surely be allowed upon the stage, which pretends only to be the mirror of life. (3: 241)

1765   **Johnson**   **JS**

Shakespeare's plays are not in the rigorous and critical sense either tragedies or comedies, but compositions of a distinct kind; exhibiting the real state of sublunary nature, which partakes of good and evil, joy and sorrow, mingled with endless variety of proportion and innumerable modes of combination; and expressing the course of the world, in which the loss of one is the gain of another. (15)

    See also Johnson under PLEASURE (JS 17), THREE UNITIES (JS 29, 30).

1808   **Schlegel.** *See* under AESTHETIC (SCL 342-43), DRAMA (SCL 273), RULES (SCL 217).

1815   **Coleridge.** *See* under AESTHETIC (CBL 2: 232, 256-57), NOVELTY (CBL 2: 262).

c.1820   Hegel. *See* under UNIVERSALITY (HFA 4: 252-53).

1824   Goethe. Compare with GENRE (GCE March 30).

1827   Goethe   **GCE**

Wed., Jan. 31 "Plays," [said I,] especially tragedies, in which an uniform tone uninterrupted by change prevails, have always something wearisome about them. . . . " "Perhaps," said Goethe, "the lively scenes introduced into Shakespeare's plays rest upon this 'law of required change,' but it does not seem applicable to the higher tragedy of the Greeks, where, on the contrary, a certain fundamental tone pervades the whole." "The Greek tragedy," said I, "is not of such a length as to be rendered wearisome by one pervading tone. Then there is an interchange of chorus and dialogue. . . . " "You may be right," said Goethe; "and it would be well worth the trouble to investigate how far the Greek tragedy is subject to the general 'law of required change.' "

1830   Hazlitt. *See* under NOVELTY (HW 9: 423-24).

1864   Taine. Compare with STYLE (TLA 321, 322-23).

1926   Eliot. Compare with STYLE (EEE 167).

1932   Eliot   **EJD**

A very little examination of Elizabethan drama, and especially of Shakespeare, will convince us that the comic is not really "relief" at all, but on the contrary, at its best an intensification of the sombreness. The Porter in *Macbeth*, the Gravedigger in *Hamlet*, the Fool in *Lear*, the drunkenness of Lepidus in *Antony and Cleopatra*—there is no "relief" in these; they merely make the horror or tragedy more real by transposing it for a moment from the sublime to the common. (61)

1932   Eliot   **EUP**

The desire for "comic relief" on the part of an audience is, I believe, a permanent craving of human nature; but that does not mean that it is a craving that ought to be gratified. It springs from a lack of the capacity for concentration. Farce and love-romances especially if seasoned with scabrousness, are the two forms of entertainment upon which the human mind can most easily, lovingly and for the longest time maintain its attention; but we like some farce as a relief from our sentiment, however salacious, and some sentiment as a relief from our farce, however broad. (41)

1951   Eliot. Compare with STYLE (EPD 13).

WILL

In Aristotle's theory, purposiveness is imbedded in the structure of the play itself, essentially independent of the will or purpose of the protagonist. This is a distinction which, if Aristotle makes it at all, is only implied in his comment that tragedy can exist without "character" (ethos), which is the particularized representation of "moral purpose." The emphasis on character by early Romantic theorists, intensified by the focus on character-in-conflict of nineteenth-and twentieth-century theorists generally, has made the striving will of the protagonist the primary vehicle for dramatic purposiveness (in theory if not always in practice). Little serious effort has been made to analyze purposiveness in dramatic art except in the dramatization of human will. See also MOTIVATION *for discussions of specific purposes in the dramatic character,* CLOSURE, *and FORWARD MOVEMENT for discussions of purposiveness in dramatic structure.*

1758 Diderot. *See* under CHARACTER (DDP 290).

1767-1769 Lessing   **LSPW**

We are justified in demanding purpose and harmony in all the characters a poet creates. . . . A character in which the instructive is lacking, lacks purpose. To act with a purpose is what raises man above the brutes, to invent with a purpose, to imitate with a purpose, is that which distinguishes genius from the petty artists who only invent to invent, imitate to imitate. . . . (326)

1808 Schlegel. *See* under ACTION (SCL 239-42).

c.1810 Coleridge. *See* under DRAMA (CLSW 116).

1813-1814 Coleridge. *See* under GENRE DEFINITION (CSC 2: 229).

c.1820 Hegel. *See* under ACTION (HFA 4: 252, 253-54), COMEDY (HFA 4: 327-30), CONFLICT (HFA 4: 318-20), DRAMA (HFA 4: 251, 278-80), GENRE DEFINITION (HFA 4: 305-308), HERO (HFA 4: 320-21), TRAGEDY (HFA 4: 295-99, 300-301, 312-15).

1864 Taine. *See* under ACTION (TLA 318-19).

1871 Nietzsche. *See* under TRAGEDY (NBT 127).

1878   Nietzsche. *See* under MOTIVATION (NHH 97-99, 102-103).

1886   Nietzsche   NZ

"Will to Truth" do ye call it, ye wisest ones, that which impelleth you and maketh you ardent? Will for the thinkableness of all being: thus do *I* call your will! All being would ye *make* thinkable: for ye doubt with good reason whether it be already thinkable. But it shall accommodate and bend itself to you! So willeth your will. . . . That is your entire will, ye wisest ones, as a Will to Power; and even when ye speak of good and evil, and of estimate of value. Ye would still create a world before which ye can bow the knee: such is your ultimate hope and ecstasy. . . . To be sure, ye call it will to procreation, or impulse towards a goal, towards the higher, remoter, more manifold: but all that is one and the same secret. . . . That I have to be struggle, and becoming, and purpose, and cross-purpose—ah, he who divineth my will, divineth well also on what *crooked* paths it had to tread! Whatever I create, and however much I love it,—soon must I be adverse to it, and to my love: so willeth my will. And even thou, discerning one, art only a path and footstep of my will: verily, my Will to Power walketh even on the feet of thy Will to Truth! (134-36)

1888   Nietzsche   NW

For ages we have always ascribed the value of an action, of a character, of an existence, to the *intention*, to the *purpose* for which it was done, acted or lived: this primeval idiosyncrasy of taste ultimately takes a dangerous turn—provided the lack of intention and purpose in all phenomena comes ever more to the front in consciousness. . . . In conformity with this valuation, people were forced to place the value of life in a "life after death," or in the progressive development of ideas, or of mankind, or of the people, or of man to superman; but in this way the *progressus in infinitum* of purpose had been reached. . . . In regard to this point, "purpose" needs a somewhat more severe criticism: it ought to be recognised that an action *is never caused by a purpose*. . . . Science does *not* inquire what impels us to will: on the contrary, it *denies* that *willing* takes place at all, and supposes that something quite different has happened—in short, that the belief in "will" and "end" is an illusion. It does not inquire into the *motives* of an action, as if these had been present in consciousness previous to the action: but it first divides the action up into a group of phenomena, and then seeks the previous history of this mechanical movement—but *not* in the terms of feeling, perception, and thought. . . . The problem of science is precisely to explain the world, *without* taking perceptions as the cause: for that would mean regarding *perceptions* themselves as the *cause* of perceptions. . . . Thus: either there is *no* such thing as will,—the hypothesis of science,—or the will is *free*. The latter assumption represents the prevailing feeling, of which we cannot rid ourselves, even if the hypothesis of science were *proved*. The popular belief in cause and effect is founded on the principle that free will *is the cause of every effect:* thereby alone do we arrive at the feeling of causation. And thereto belongs also the feeling that every cause is *not* an effect, but always only a cause—if will is the cause. "Our acts of will are *not necessary*"—this lies in the very *concept of "will."* (138-40)

See also Nietzsche under CONFLICT (NW 130), TRAGEDY (NTI 119-20).

1894   Brunetière   BLD

In drama or farce, what we ask of the theater, is the spectacle of a *will* striving towards a goal, and conscious of the means which it employs. (73) . . . That is what may be called *will*, to set up a goal, and to direct everything toward it, to strive to bring everything into line with it. (75) . . . One drama is superior to another drama according as the quantity of will exerted is greater or less, as the share of chance is less, and that of necessity greater. (81)

See also Brunetière under ACTION (BLD 75-76), CONFLICT (BLD 77-80), GENRE (BLD 79-80).

1906   Shaw. *See* under ILLUSION (SDDGM xvii).

1908   Pirandello   POH

We all have, to some extent, a will that generates those movements which enable us to create our own lives. This creation, which everyone makes of his own life, needs, in greater or lesser degree, the cooperation of the functions and activities of the spirit, that is, of the intellect and imagination, as well as of the will; and he who has more of these faculties and puts them to use, will succeed in creating for himself a higher, broader and more vigorous life. (64)

1938   Stanislavski. *See* under ACTION (SBC 118).

WONDER

From Plato and Longinus to Kenneth Burke and Suzanne Langer writers have ascribed to truly successful works of art a quality or several qualities variously described as ecstasy, sublimity, wonderful, the marvelous, awesome, a strangeness, the noumenous, epiphinal, and so on. The statements cited here indicate, describe, or attempt to explain the causes for these experiences.

4th cent. B.C. Aristotle   AP

The element of the *wonderful* [astonishing: EP 622] is required in Tragedy. The irrational, on which *the wonderful* [astonishment: EP 622] depends for its chief effects, has wider scope in Epic poetry, because there the person acting is not seen. . . . Now the *wonderful* [astonishing: EP 622] is pleasing: as may be inferred by the fact that everyone tells a story with some addition of his own, knowing that his hearers like it. (95)

    See also Aristotle under MOTIVATION (ANE 329-31), PLOT (AP 39).

1570 Castelvetro   CP

[In tragedy] the state of marvel induced is the culmination of pity and fear. . . . The end of poetry is delight, and the marvelous specially excites delight. (80) . . . It is more marvellous when a great mutation of a hero's fortune is made, in a very limited time and a very limited place, than when it is made in a longer time and in varied and larger places. . . . The more the time of action . . . is restricted, the more praiseworthy it will be: the more place is restricted, the more commendable it will be. (88)

    See also Castelvetro under PLEASURE (CP 79, 126).

1657 d'Aubignac. *See* under SPECTACLE (AAS 3: 95-98).

1670 Racine. Compare with MAGNITUDE (RP 155).

1712 Addison   AW

[A] method of reconciling miracles with credibility, is by a happy invention of the poet: as in particular, when he introduces agents of a superior nature, who are capable of effecting what is wonderful, and what is not to be met with in the ordinary course of things. Ulysses's ship being turned into a rock, and Aeneas's fleet into a shoal of water-nymphs, though they are very surprising accidents, are nevertheless probable when we are told, that they were the gods who thus transformed them. It is this kind of machinery which fills the poems both of Homer and Virgil with such circumstances as are wonderful but not impossible, and so frequently produce in the reader the most pleasing passion that can rise in the mind of man, which is admiration. (2: 4)

See also Addison under IMAGINATION (AW 2: 138-39), PROBABILITY (AW 2: 4).

1751   Johnson   JW

That wonder is the effect of ignorance, has been often observed. The awful stillness of attention, with which the mind is overspread at the first view of an unexpected effect, ceases when we have leisure to disentangle complications and investigate causes. Wonder is a pause of reason, a sudden cessation of the mental progress, which lasts only while the understanding is fixed upon some single idea, and is at an end when it recovers force enough to divide the object into its parts, or mark the intermediate gradations from the first agent to the last consequence. (3: 147-48)

1758   Diderot   DDP

There sometimes occurs in the natural order of things an extraordinary chain of incidents. It is this same order that distinguishes the marvelous from the miraculous. Dramatic art rejects miracles. If nature never brought about situations of an extraordinary sort, then everything imagined by the poet outside the simple and cold uniformity about him would be unbelievable. . . . [The poet] either uses the extraordinary combinations which he finds in nature, and which, owing to our want of knowledge often seems like a fatal association of circumstances, [or] the poet insists that throughout his work there be a visible and credible relation, and in this respect his work is less true, but more natural and true to life, than that of the historian. (297)

1765   Johnson   JS

Such is the power of the marvellous even over those who despise it, that every man finds his mind more strongly seized by the tragedies of *Shakespeare* than of any other writer; others please us by particular speeches, but he always makes us anxious for the event, and has perhaps excelled all but *Homer* in securing the first purpose of a writer, by exciting restless and unquenchable curiosity and compelling him that reads his work to read it through. (32-33)

1767-1769   Lessing. *See* under GENRE (LSPW 248).

1808   Schlegel. *See* under DISTANCE (SCL 72), DRAMA (SCL 273), PROBABILITY (SCL 182-83).

c.1820   Hegel. *See* under HERO (HFA 4: 320-21).

1871   Nietzsche   **NBT**

Schopenhauer has described to us the stupendous *awe* which seizes upon man when of a sudden he is at a loss to account for the cognitive forms of a phenomenon, in that the principle of reason, in some one of its manifestations, seems to admit of an exception. Add to this awe the blissful ecstasy which rises from the innermost depths of man, ay, of nature, at this same collapse of the *principium individuationis*, and we shall gain an insight into the being of the *Dionysian* [principle of art]. (25-26)

   See also Nietzsche under HERO (NBT 81-82).

1875   Nietzsche. *See* under POETRY OF THE THEATRE (NTS 177-78).

1922   Brecht. *See* under ALIENATION (BBT 9).

1936   Brecht   **BBB**

[The Chinese actor] wishes to appear alien to the spectator. Alien to the point of arousing surprise. This he manages by seeing himself and his performance as alien. In this way the things he does on stage become astonishing. By this craft everyday things are removed from the realm of the self-evident. (131)

c.1936   Brecht. *See* under ALIENATION (BBA 19-20).

1948   Brecht. *See* under ALIENATION (BBBG 26-27).

GUIDE TO AUTHORS'
BIOGRAPHIES, BIBLIOGRAPHIES, AND
INDEXES TO QUOTATIONS

JOSEPH ADDISON (1672-1719). English essayist, critic, poet and play-wright. With Richard Steele, Addison wrote most of the numbers of *The Tatler* (1709-1711) and *The Spectator* (1711-1712 and 1714). Of his plays the most notable was the tragedy *Cato* (1713). Among his literary allies were John Dryden (q.v.), William Congreve, and Jonathan Swift; but he was scathingly satirized by Alexander Pope as "Atticus" in *An Epistle to Dr. Arbuthnot*. Addison is generally credited with an important influence on the course of English literary history through his critical writings. In the practice of art and of criticism he sought to enforce standards of morality and classicism.

Bibliography

AW   *The Works of Joseph Addison*. 3 vols. New York: Harper and Brothers, 1868.

Index

ACTION 1712; *see also* under PLOT 1711.
AESTHETIC 1712; *see also* under IMAGINATION 1712, IMITATION 1712.
AFFECT 1712; *see also* under ACTION 1712, AESTHETIC 1712, DRAMA 1712, DRAMATIZA-
       TION 1711, FORM 1712, IMAGINATION 1712, PLOT 1711, POETIC JUSTICE
       1711, SPECTACLE 1711; compare with THOUGHT 1711, 1712.
AUTHORITY 1713.
CATHARSIS 1711; *see also* under IMAGINATION 1712.
CHARACTER *see* under GENRE DEFINITION 1711.
CLOSURE 1710; *see also* under STYLE 1711.
COMEDY 1715.
COMPLICATION *see* under PLOT 1711.
CONVENTION 1711; *see also* under SPECTACLE 1711, STYLE 1711.
DISTANCE 1712; *see also* under AFFECT 1712, INDENTIFICATION 1712.
DRAMA 1712; *see also* under CATHARSIS 1711.
DRAMATIZATION 1711.
FEAR *see* under DISTANCE 1712.
FORM 1712; *see also* under AESTHETIC 1712, compare with IMAGINATION 1712.
FORWARD MOVEMENT *see* under SURPRISE 1712.
GENRE DEFINITION 1711.
HERO *see* under ACTION 1712, SPECTACLE 1711.
HUMOR 1711; *see also* under CLOSURE 1710, GENRE DEFINITION 1711, INSTRUCTION
       1715.
IDEALISM 1712.
INDENTIFICATION 1712.
ILLUSION *see* under CONVENTION 1711.
IMAGINATION 1712; *see also* under AESTHETIC 1712, DISTANCE 1712.

ARISTOTLE (384-322 B.C.). Greek philosopher. Aristotle was born in Stagira on the northwestern Aegean where his father was court physician to Amyntas II, father of Philip of Macedon. At 17 Aristotle became a student at Plato's Academy in Athens. After Plato's death in 347 B.C. Aristotle went to Assus in Asia Minor for three years to teach and then to Lesbos for two years to study marine biology. In 342 B.C. he went to Pella at the invitation of Philip to instruct his son Alexander, which he did until his pupil's accession to the throne in 336 B.C. Aristotle then returned to Athens and established the Peripatetic School. Most of Aristotle's extant work was written as lectures for his school. It is not known whether the *Poetics* is in its original form, is a summary, or is an extrapolation from lecture notes. The latter assumption is usually credited. Aristotle's influence on European thought in science, logic, philosophy, and art is incalculable.

Bibliography

AA   *De Anima*. Translated by R. D. Hicks. Cambridge: At the University Press, 1910.

AM   *Metaphysics*. Translated by W. D. Ross. 2d ed. Oxford: Clarendon Press, 1928.

ANE   *The Nicomachean Ethics*. Translated by H. Rackham. New York: G. P. Putnam's Sons, 1934.

AP   *Aristotle's Theory of Poetry and Fine Art*. Translated by S. H. Butcher. 4th ed. London: Macmillan and Co., 1922.

APA   *The Parts of Animals*, trans. W. Ogle. London: Kegan Paul, 1882.

APO   *Politics*. Translated by Benjamin Jowett. Oxford: Clarendon Press, 1921.

AR   *The Rhetoric of Aristotle*. Translated by R. C. Jebb. Cambridge: At the University Press, 1909.

EP   *Poetics: The Argument*. Translated by Gerald F. Else. Cambridge, Mass.: Harvard University Press, 1957.

Index

ILLUSION.

IMAGINATION (twice); *see also* under ILLUSION.

IMITATION (twice); *see also* under AESTHETIC, AFFECT, CHARACTER, GENRE, OB-
    JECTIVITY, PLEASURE, PLOT, TRAGEDY, UNIVERSALITY.

INSTRUCTION *see* under IMITATION, METAPHOR, PLEASURE.

IRONY *see* under REVERSAL.

LANGUAGE; *see also* under IDENTIFICATION, STYLE, THOUGHT, TRAGEDY; compare
    with SUBJECT.

MAGNITUDE (twice); *see also* under DRAMA, FORM, PLOT, TRAGEDY.

METAPHOR (twice); *see also* under STYLE.

MORALITY *see* under CHARACTER, IMITATION, PLOT, REVERSAL.

MOTIVATION (twice); *see also* under TRAGEDY.

OBJECTIVITY.

ORDER (twice); *see also* under FORM, PLOT.

PATHOS; *see also* under PITY, PLOT.

PITY (twice); *see also* under ACTION, CATHARSIS, POETIC JUSTICE, REVERSAL,
    TRAGEDY.

PLEASURE (three entries); *see also* under ACTION, AESTHETIC, CATHARSIS, DRAMA,
    IMITATION (twice), METAPHOR, PLOT, POETIC JUSTICE, SUBJECT, WONDER.

PLOT; *see also* under ACTION, CHARACTER, FORM, PITY, RECOGNITION, REVERSAL,
    SUBJECT, TRAGEDY.

POETIC JUSTICE; compare with PLOT.

PROBABILITY; *see also* under IMITATION, REVERSAL, SUBJECT, UNIVERSALITY.

RATIONALISM *see* under AESTHETIC, ILLUSION, IMITATION, LANGUAGE, PLEA-
    SURE, PLOT, PROBABILITY, STYLE.

REALISM *see* under ACTION.

RECOGNITION; *see also* under PITY, PLOT.

REVERSAL (twice); *see also* under MAGNITUDE, PLOT.

RULES.

SPECTACLE; *see also* under DRAMA, PLOT, TRAGEDY, WONDER.

STYLE (twice); *see also* under METAPHOR.

SUBJECT; *see also* under ACTION, AFFECT, IMITATION.

SURPRISE; *see also* under PLOT, RECOGNITION, REVERSAL.

SYMBOL *see* under FEAR.

THOUGHT (three entries); *see also* under TRAGEDY.

THREE UNITIES; *see also* under MAGNITUDE, TRAGEDY.

TRAGEDY; *see also* under CHARACTER, IMITATION, PLOT, SUBJECT, WONDER.

UNITY; *see also* under ACTION, AESTHTEIC, DRAMA, FORM, MAGNITUDE, ORDER,
    PLOT.

UNIVERSALITY (twice); *see also* under IMITATION, PROBABILITY.

VARIETY; compare with PLOT.

WONDER; *see also* under MOTIVATION, PLOT.

ANTONIN ARTAUD (1896-1948). French poet, essayist, critic, playwright,
actor and director. He initially received attention as a poet (his first collection
was published in Paris in 1923) and as a critic. Artaud began to act in films in
1924, but he chose theatre as the medium for the total art form that he sought.
Though associated with the Surrealists briefly (1924-1926), he attempted to
formulate an aesthetic distinct from theirs. He was a director and founder of

theatres (Alfred Jarry Theatre and The Theatre of Cruelty) but proved un-successful in his theatrical activities. Artaud was a prolific writer, best known for his *The Theatre and Its Double* (written between 1931 and 1936, published in 1938). Throughout his life Artaud's bouts of mental disturbance led to periodic internment in hospitals, with a continuous stay between 1937 and 1946. On his release he resumed his writing and was revising a play commissioned by French radio at his death. Susan Sontag says of him that "he has had an impact so profound that the course of serious theatre in Western Europe and the Americas can be said to divide into two periods—before Artaud and after Artaud. No one who works in the theatre now is untouched by the impact. . . ." Only Brecht (q.v.) rivals Artaud's influences on the theatre in the second half of the twentieth century.

Bibliography

All citations for Artaud are dated 1931-1936.

AT   *The Theatre and Its Double*. Translated by Mary Caroline Richards. New York: Grove Press, 1958.

Index

ACTION.
AESTHETIC; *see also* under POETRY OF THE THEATRE.
AFFECT *see* under AESTHETIC, METAPHOR, POETRY OF THE THEATRE.
CATHARSIS.
CHARACTER *see* under DRAMA, THOUGHT.
CONFLICT; *see also* under THOUGHT, and compare with DRAMA, IDEALISM.
CONVENTION.
DRAMA; *see also* under CATHARSIS, IDEALISM, METAPHOR.
HUMOR *see* under TRAGEDY.
IDEALISM; *see also* under ACTION.
IDENTIFICATION.
ILLUSION; *see also* under AESTHETIC, POETRY OF THE THEATRE.
IMITATION; compare with ACTION, ILLUSION.
LANGUAGE; *see also* under THOUGHT (p. 46); compare with POETRY OF THE THEATRE, SPECTACLE, THOUGHT (pp. 39-40).
METAPHOR; *see also* under THOUGHT.
NOVELTY *see* under THOUGHT, TRAGEDY.
OBJECTIVITY *see* under DRAMA, POETRY OF THE THEATRE, STYLE.
PLEASURE *see* under DRAMA.
POETRY OF THE THEATRE; *see also* under AESTHETIC, DRAMA, ILLUSION, LAN-GUAGE, METAPHOR, SPECTACLE, STYLE, THOUGHT.
RATIONALISM compare with THOUGHT.
REALISM compare with DRAMA.
SPECTACLE; *see also* under ACTION, AESTHETIC, CONVENTION, DRAMA, IDENTIFI-CATION , ILLUSION, LANGUAGE, STYLE, THOUGHT.
STYLE.
SUBJECT *see* under THOUGHT.
SYMBOL *see* under METAPHOR, STYLE, THOUGHT.
THOUGHT; *see also* under POETRY OF THE THEATRE.

TRAGEDY.
UNIVERSALITY *see* under DRAMA.

FRANÇOIS HÉDELIN ABBE' D'AUBIGNAC (1604-1676).

French cleric and critic. He participated in the literary discussions in Paris in the mid-seventeenth century as a major instrument of Cardinal Richelieu's efforts to improve the quality of drama. He wrote plays (extant are *Cyminde, La Pucelle d' Orléans* and *Zénobie*) and a study of dramatic technique, commissioned by the Cardinal, *La Practique du Théâtre*. A great admirer of the work of Corneille (q.v.), d'Aubignac was influential in the formation of French classical doctrine; on the other hand, he had little grasp of contemporary comedy and was probably associated with the coteries satirized in *Les Précieuses ridicules* by Molière.

Bibliography

AAS   *The Whole Art of the Stage.* London: William Cademan, 1684.

Index

All citations for d'Aubignac are dated 1657.
ACTION; *see also* under PROBABILITY, THREE UNITIES.
AFFECT; *see also* under DRAMA, EXPOSITION, INSTRUCTION, PATHOS, POETIC JUS-
          TICE, SPECTACLE, SUBJECT, THREE UNITIES.
AUTHORITY; *see also* under ACTION, RULES.
CHARACTER *see* under TRAGEDY.
CLOSURE; *see also* under EXPOSITION, TRAGEDY.
COMEDY; *see also* under TRAGEDY.
DRAMA; *see also* under INSTRUCTION.
DRAMATIZATION; *see also* under ACTION, AFFECT, EXPOSITION, MOTIVATION.
EXPOSITION; *see also* under MOTIVATION.
FORWARD MOVEMENT *see* under SUBJECT, UNITY.
FUNCTIONALISM *see* under THREE UNITIES.
GENRE *see* under TRAGEDY.
HERO *see* under TRAGEDY.
IDEALISM.
IDENTIFICATION; *see also* under PATHOS, SUBJECT.
ILLUSION; *see also* under PATHOS, SPECTACLE.
IMITATION; *see also* under ACTION, PROBABILITY, SPECTACLE, THREE UNITIES.
INSTRUCTION; *see also* under AFFECT, DRAMA, POETIC JUSTICE.
IRONY.
LANGUAGE *see* under ACTION, INSTRUCTION.
MORALITY *see* under POETIC JUSTICE.
MOTIVATION.
NOVELTY *see* under SUBJECT.
PATHOS.
PLEASURE *see* under SPECTACLE, SUBJECT.
PLOT; *see also* under IMITATION, SUBJECT.
POETIC JUSTICE.
PROBABILITY; *see also* under ACTION, IMITATION, THREE UNITIES.
RATIONALISM; *see* under ACTION, PROBABILITY, RULES, THREE UNITIES.
REALISM *see* under ACTION.

REVERSAL *see* under CLOSURE, SUBJECT.
RULES; *see also* under ACTION, POETIC JUSTICE, PROBABILITY, THREE UNITIES,
    UNITY.
SPECTACLE; *see also* under INSTRUCTION.
STYLE *see* under COMEDY.
SUBJECT; *see also* under ACTION, AFFECT, RULES, TRAGEDY.
SURPRISE *see* under CLOSURE, SUBJECT.
THREE UNITIES; *see also* under ILLUSION, SPECTACLE.
TRAGEDY.
UNITY; *see also* under ACTION.
VARIETY; *see* under SUBJECT.
WONDER *see* under SPECTACLE.

BERTOLT BRECHT (1898-1956). German essayist, song writer, poet,
playwright, and director. As a theatrical producer and theorist he dominated
the European theatre of the 1950s. Brecht studied medicine in Munich, 1917-
1921, interrupted by army service in 1918. His first play, *Baal*, was produced
in 1923. In Berlin from 1924 to 1933 he worked briefly with Max Reinhardt
and Irwin Piscator but most of his activities involved his own group of
associates, most notably Kurt Weill with whom he wrote operas. In those years
he became a Marxist and developed his theory of "epic theatre." In 1933 he
went into exile, first to Scandinavia (1933-1941) and then to the United States
(1941-1947). Between 1937 and 1941 he wrote some of his most important
plays and theoretical essays. However, the best known essay, the *Klienes
Organum für das Theater*, was written after his return to Europe in 1947. He
went to Berlin in 1949 to help stage *Mütter Courage* in the Soviet sector which
led to the formation of his own company, the Berliner Ensemble, and to
permanent residence. Through Brecht's theoretical statements—which sometimes make universal principles of his personal preferences—his influence on
drama and theatrical practice became a force that continues to this date.
Unfortunately there often is insufficient awareness of the tentative, exploratory, and evolving nature of Brecht's thought.

Bibliography

BBA   "Theatre for Learning." Translated by Edith Anderson. *Tulane Drama Review 6, No. 1
        (September 1961): 18-25.*
BBAn   *"A Short Description of a New Technique of the Art of Acting which Produces an Effect
        of Estrangement." World Theatre* 4, no. 1 (1955): 15-29.
BBB   "On Chinese Acting." Translated by Eric Bentley. *Tulane Drama Review* 6, no. 1
        (September 1961): 130-136.
BBBG   "A Little Organum for the Theater." Translated by Beatrice Gottlieb. *Accent* 11, no. 1
        (Winter 1951): 13-40.
BBEB   "A Model for an Epic Theatre." Translated by Eric Bentley. *Sewanee Review* 57, no. 3
        (Summer 1949): 425-436.
BBG   "On Unrhymed Lyrics in Irregular Rhythms." Translated by Beatrice Gottlieb. *Tulane
        Drama Review* 2, no. 1 (November 1957): 33-38.
BBT   *Brecht on Theatre.* Translated and edited by John Willet. New York: Hill and Wang, 1964.

SURPRISE *see* under ALIENATION 1938, c.1940, 1948, GEST c.1932, 1939, 1948, PLOT
1948, WONDER 1936.
SYMBOL *see* under GEST c.1932.
THOUGHT 1956; *see also* under AFFECT 1952, ALIENATION c.1940, DRAMA 1948, EPIC
THEATRE 1926, c.1936, GEST 1930, c.1932,IDENTIFICATION 1948.
UNIVERSALITY 1948; compare with ALIENATION 1936, CHARACTER 1948, ILLUSION
1948.
WONDER 1936; *see also* under ALIENATION 1922, c.1936, 1948.

FERDINAND BRUNETIÈRE (1849-1906). French essayist, critic, and
literary historian. He was educated in Marseille and Paris. Appointed to a chair
at the École Normale in 1886, and later as editor of the *Revue des deux mondes*,
Brunetière became famous for a theory of the evolution of literary genres
(which he later abandoned) and for the impetus he gave to the development of
comparative literature as a scholarly discipline. In Brunetière's dramatic
theories the tradition of French classicism is still strong, but with new justifications and new content: a Darwinian and Hegelian focus on struggle, clash, and
a purposiveness that connects the individual to a higher purpose. Perhaps his
most important contribution to the theory of the drama lay in clarifying and
simplifying some of Hegel's (q.v.) central doctrines, making them more
accessible to others (for example, Stanislavski).

Bibliography

BLD   *The Law of the Drama*. Translated by Philip M. Hayden. New York: Dramatic Museum
of Columbia University, 1914.

Index

All citations for Brunetière are dated 1894.
ACTION.
AESTHETIC *see* under WILL.
CHARACTER *see* under ACTION.
CONFLICT; *see also* under GENRE.
CONVENTION *see* under RULES.
DRAMA *see* under ACTION.
FORWARD MOVEMENT *see* under WILL.
GENRE; *see also* under CONFLICT.
GENRE DEFINITION *see* under CONFLICT.
HERO *see* under WILL.
MOTIVATION *see* under ACTION, WILL.
RULES; *see also* under CONFLICT, THREE UNITIES.
SUBJECT *see* under ACTION, THREE UNITIES.
THREE UNITIES.
WILL; *see also* under ACTION, CONFLICT, GENRE.

LODOVICO CASTELVETRO (1505-1571). Italian scholar, critic, and
theorist. He attended the universities of Bologna, Ferrara, Padua, and Siena,
taking a degree in law at Siena. Forced into exile when a literary dispute

became the subject of inquiry into heresy, he was excommunicated in 1561. He lectured on literary matters in Switzerland and published his *Poetica* in Vienna in 1570. It was Castelvetro who carried the rationalist and realist premises of his time to their logical conclusions by his rigorous definition of the unities of time and place.

Bibliography

CP   Charlton, H. B. *Castelvetro's Theory of Poetry*. Manchester: University Press, 1913.

Index

ANTON PAVLOVICH CHEKHOV (1860-1904). Russian writer of short stories as well as of one-act and long plays. Chekhov began to support his family by writing humorous stories while a medical student. Not long after receiving his degree in Moscow in 1884 he decided to make a literary career. His early stories led to a friendship with Alexi Suvorin, publisher of an influential newspaper, with whom he maintained a literary correspondence until their break over Chekhov's support for Dreyfus. Chekhov wrote hundreds of short stories in his lifetime, but his international fame rests largely on a few full-length plays. *Ivanov*, written in 1887, was his first professional venture, after which he wrote a number of short plays. *Chaika (The Seagull)* failed when first produced in 1896 but was a great success when performed by the newly founded Moscow Art Theatre in 1898 under the direction of Konstantin Stanislavski (q.v.). Most of Chekhov's critical and theoretical statements are contained in his letters, including those to Suvorin and to his brother Michael. In his letters he often forswears any theoretical understanding of literary principles. It is his plays which have been the primary source of his influence on artistic practice and also a provocation to theorists.

Bibliography

CL   *Letters of Anton Chekhov To His Family and Friends*. Translated by Constance Garnett. New York: Macmillan, 1920.
CLF   *Letters on the Short Story, the Drama, and Other Literary Topics*. Translated by Louis S. Friedland. New York: Minton, Balch and Co., 1924.

Index

SAMUEL TAYLOR COLERIDGE (1772-1834). English poet, lecturer, journalist, critic, theorist and sometime playwright, philosopher, and minister.

Coleridge's interests ranged widely over contemporary thought, first in the vein of idealistic socialism, later in that of the neo-Platonic idealism of Plotinus. Among his early friends were Charles Lamb, Robert Southey, and William Wordsworth. With Wordsworth, his long friendship included a brief period of collaboration which resulted in the joint publication of the *Lyrical Ballads* in 1798, usually considered to be the beginning of the Romantic movement in England. While that volume of poetry was being published its authors left England for Germany, where Coleridge matriculated at Göttingen in February 1799, returning to England in July of that year. Journalism, travels to Malta and Italy, illness, penury, and politics largely displaced his literary efforts for the next nine years, but in January of 1808 he began an important series of lectures on poetry for the Royal Institution. He gave a second series of lectures from November 1811 to January 1812 on Shakespeare and Milton and later in 1812 a third series of lectures on drama. In 1813 his play *Remorse* had a considerable success. In 1815 he began to dictate the *Biographia Literaria*. In the last twenty years of his life Coleridge enjoyed a degree of financial security and a very considerable reputation and influence in England not unlike that of Goethe, his older contemporary, in Germany. Much admired by younger poets of the time such as Shelley, Keats, and Byron, he was nevertheless the subject of satire in Charles Lloyd's novel *Edmund Oliver* (1798) and of attacks by William Hazlitt (q.v.) in the *Edinburgh Review* and the *Examiner*. As a theorist of poetry and drama Coleridge has been perhaps more influential in this century than in his own.

Bibliography

CBL   *Biographia Literaria*. Edited by J. Shawcross. 2 vols. London: Oxford University Press, 1907.

CCSL   *Seven Lectures on Shakespeare and Milton*. Edited by J. P. Collier. New York: Burt Franklin, 1968.

CLSW   *Lectures Upon Shakespeare and Other Dramatists*. Edited by W. G. T. Shedd. Vol. 4. (*The Complete Works of Samuel Taylor Coleridge*.) New York: Harper and Brothers, 1884.

CMC   *Coleridge's Miscellaneous Criticism*. Edited by Thomas Middleton Raysor. Cambridge: Harvard University Press, 1936.

CSC   *Shakespearean Criticism*. Edited by Thomas Middleton Raysor. 2 vols. New York: E. P. Dutton, 1960.

CSNL   *Shakespeare, Ben Jonson, Beaumont and Fletcher: Notes and Lectures*. Liverpool: Edward Howell, 1874.

Index

CONFLICT *see* under DRAMA c.1810.

DISINTERESTEDNESS *see* under AESTHETIC 1815.

DISTANCE 1811-1812; *see also* under IMITATION 1815, 1818.

DRAMA 1804, c.1810, 1815; *see also* under ILLUSION 1804, c.1810, RULES c.1810.

EPIC THEATRE *see* under UNITY c.1810.

EVOLUTIONISM *see* under DRAMA c.1810, UNITY c.1810.

FORM 1815; *see also* under AESTHETIC 1815, ORDER 1815, PLEASURE 1811-1812, UNITY 1815.

FORWARD MOVEMENT 1815; *see also* under NOVELTY 1815, UNITY 1815.

GENRE c.1810; *see also* under GENRE DEFINITION 1813-1814, 1818.

GENRE DEFINITION 1813-1814, 1818; *see also* under GENRE c.1810.

HERO *see* under GENRE DEFINITION 1813-1814.

IDEALISM *see* under AESTHETIC 1815, CHARACTER 1815, IMAGINATION 1815, IMITATION 1815, ORDER 1815; compare with REALISM 1815.

ILLUSION c.1810, 1814, 1815, 1818; *see also* under AFFECT 1815, DRAMA 1804, GENRE c.1810, PROBABILITY 1815, REALISM 1815, THREE UNITIES 1811-12.

IMAGINATION c.1808, 1815, 1835; *see also* GENRE c.1810, METAPHOR 1811-1812, THREE UNITIES 1811-1812.

IMITATION 1815, 1818; *see also* under AFFECT 1815, DISTANCE 1811-1812, DRAMA 1808, ILLUSION 1804, UNIVERSALITY 1811-1812.

INSTRUCTION 1815.

LANGUAGE *see* under STYLE 1815, SYMBOL 1818.

METAPHOR 1811-1812; *see also* under IMAGINATION c.1808, 1815; SYMBOL 1815, 1818.

MOTIVATION *see* under GENRE DEFINITION 1813-1814, UNITY c.1810.

NOVELTY 1815.

OBJECTIVE CORRELATIVE *see* under THOUGHT 1818.

OBJECTIVITY *see* under DRAMA c.1810.

ORDER 1815; *see also* under TASTE c.1810.

PLEASURE 1811-1812, 1815; *see also* under DISTANCE 1811-1812, DRAMA c.1817, ILLUSION 1804, METAPHOR 1811-1812, PROBABILITY 1815, STYLE 1815, TASTE c.1810, UNITY 1811-1812, 1815.

PLOT *see* under SYMBOL 1818, UNITY 1815.

PROBABILITY c.1810, 1815; *see also* under ILLUSION c.1810.

RATIONALISM *see* under THREE UNITIES 1811-1812; compare with ILLUSION 1804, STYLE 1815.

REALISM 1815; compare with DISTANCE 1811-1812, ILLUSION 1815, IMITATION 1815.

RULES c.1810; *see also* under TASTE 1815, THREE UNITIES 1811-1812, UNITY c.1819.

SPECTACLE *see* under GENRE c.1810, ILLUSION 1804; compare with ILLUSION 1818.

STYLE 1815; *see also* under TASTE 1815, UNITY 1815.

SUBJECT *see* under UNITY c.1810.

SURPRISE *see* under METAPHOR 1811-1812, STYLE 1815.

SYMBOL 1815, 1818; *see also* under CHARACTER 1815.

TASTE 1808, c.1810, 1815.

THOUGHT 1818; *see also* under SYMBOL 1818.

THREE UNITIES 1811-1812; *see also* under GENRE c.1810, UNITY c.1819.

UNITY c.1810, 1811-1812, 1815, c.1817, c.1819; *see also* under AESTHETIC 1815, FORWARD MOVEMENT 1815, IMAGINATION 1815, 1835, SYMBOL 1818, THOUGHT 1818, ORDER 1815.

UNIVERSALITY 1811, 1811-1812; *see also* under CHARACTER 1815, IMITATION 1815, UNITY c.1810.

VARIETY *see* under AESTHETIC 1815, NOVELTY 1815.

WILL *see* under DRAMA c.1810, GENRE DEFINITION 1813-1814.

PIERRE CORNEILLE (1606-1684). French playwright, creator of French classical tragedy, in which form he was excelled only by his younger contemporary, Racine (q.v.). Corneille received a classical education from a Jesuit lycée in Rouen and practiced law there, as he began to write plays. His first successes were in comedy, but after coming to the attention and the patronage of Cardinal Richelieu he wrote primarily tragicomedy and tragedy. His most famous play, *The Cid* (1637), sparked a controversy and a report of the French Academy which clarified the French ideals of dramatic poetry. Corneille prefaced the second collection of his plays, published in 1660, with three essays on dramatic theory. In addition he wrote *Examens* of his plays. The playwright's publicly articulated theories reflect the vocabulary of ideas and concepts authorized in his time, and the goals which he set for himself. They also provide frames of reference for his reader. The modifications of the established doctrine he introduced, compelled by his experience in the theatre, may have significantly influenced the understanding and the development of those concepts and are of independent interest to modern scholarship. In any case, Corneille established a model of drama that dominated continental Europe for centuries.

Bibliography

CDENA   "Discourse on Tragedy and the Methods of Treating it, According to Probability and Necessity" in *Dramatic Essays of the Neoclassic Age*. Edited by Henry H. Adams and Baxter Hathaway. New York: Columbia University Press, 1950.

CDT   "A Discourse on Tragedy." Translated by J. H. Smith in *The Great Critics*. Edited by J. H. Smith and W. W. Parks. 3d ed. New York: W. W. Norton, 1951.

CDTU   "Third Discourse on the Three Unities of Action, of Time, and of Place." Translated by A. H. Armstrong in *Dramatic Theory and Criticism*. Edited by B. F. Dukore. New York: Holt, Rinehart and Winston, 1974.

CFD   "First Discourse on the Uses and Elements of Dramatic Poetry." Translated by B. S. MacClintock in *European Theories of the Drama*. Edited by Barrett H. Clark. Cincinnati: Stewart and Kidd, 1918.

CSD   "Second Discourse on Tragedy and the Means of Treating It According to the Probable or the Necessary." Translated by A. H. Armstrong in *Dramatic Theory and Criticism*. Edited by Bernard F. Dukore. New York: Holt, Rinehart and Winston, 1974.

CSP   *Seven Plays*. Translated by Samuel Solomon. New York: Random House, 1969.

CTU   "A Discourse on the Three Unities." Translated by J. H. Smith in *The Great Critics*. Edited by J. H. Smith and E. W. Parks. 3d ed. New York: W. W. Norton, 1951.

Index

CONVENTION *see also* under EXPOSITION.
DRAMA; *see also* under AFFECT.
EXPOSITION; *see also* under UNITY.
FEAR *see* under CATHARSIS.
FLAW *see* under CATHARSIS.
FORM *see* under ACTION.
FORWARD MOVEMENT *see* under ACTION, SURPRISE.
GENRE *see* under COMEDY, SUBJECT.
IDENTIFICATION; *see also* under CATHARSIS.
IMAGINATION *see* under THREE UNITIES.
IMITATION *see* under CHARACTER, THREE UNITIES.
INSTRUCTION; *see also* DRAMA.
MAGNITUDE *see* under THREE UNITIES.
MORALITY *see* under POETIC JUSTICE.
PITY *see* under CATHARSIS.
PLEASURE *see* under DRAMA, POETIC JUSTICE, RULES, THREE UNITIES.
PLOT; *see also* under SURPRISE.
POETIC JUSTICE; *see also* under INSTRUCTION.
PROBABILITY; *see also* under RULES.
REVERSAL *see* under SURPRISE.
RULES (twice); *see also* under POETIC JUSTICE, THREE UNITIES, UNITY.
SUBJECT; *see also* under PROBABILITY, THREE UNITIES.
SURPRISE.
THOUGHT *see* under INSTRUCTION.
THREE UNITIES (three entries); *see also* under RULES.
TRAGEDY *see* under PROBABILITY, SUBJECT.
UNITY; *see also* ACTION, COMPLICATION.
UNIVERSALITY *see* under AUTHORITY 1648.

DENIS DIDEROT (1713-1784). French encyclopedist, philosopher, essayist, novelist, and playwright. Educated for the priesthood, in 1729 Diderot moved to Paris instead of taking religious orders. There he studied at the Jansenist Collége d'Harcourt, was awarded an M.A. at the University of Paris in 1732, and studied law for a time. From 1734 to 1744 he worked as a publisher's hack. In 1745 he was approached by a publisher to translate Chamber's *Cyclopaedia*. Once in Diderot's hands this assignment changed into an ambitious project to systematize all knowledge and to mobilize radical forces. The first volume of Diderot's *Encyclopédie* was published in 1751, the last in 1772, the whole consisting of 17 volumes of text and 11 of plates. Diderot contributed many articles to the *Encyclopédie*, among the more important are those on the history of philosophy and on aesthetics ("The Beautiful"). He wrote several plays, none of which was successful, but his special interest in the theatre is shown in his essays *Dialogue on the Natural Son* (1757), *Of Dramatic Poetry* (1758), and *The Paradox of Acting* (1773-1778; published in 1830). Diderot's dramatic theories, especially those favoring bourgeois drama and stage realism, had an immediate effect on Lessing (q.v.) and, in the longer term, on early nineteenth-century melodrama and the plays of Augier and Dumas *fils*. His definition of the actor as a fabulous puppet for whom the poet holds the strings and his ideas about acting and stage illusion have also been influential.

Bibliography

DDE   (Editor). *Encyclopedia* (1775-1780). Translated by Daniel C. Gerould in *Dramatic Theory and Criticism*. Edited by Bernard F. Dukore. New York: Holt, Rinehart and Winston, 1974.

DDP   "On Dramatic Poetry." Translated by Barrett H. Clark in *European Theories of the Drama*. Edited by Barrett H. Clark. New York: D. Appleton and Co., 1918.

DPA   *The Paradox of Acting*. Translated by Walter Herries Pollock. London: Chatto and Windus, 1883.

LANGUAGE 1758; *see also* under ACTION 1758, ILLUSION 1778, PLOT 1758.
MORALITY *see* under COMEDY 1755-1780, DRAMA 1758.
MOTIVATION 1755-1780; *see also* under TRAGEDY 1755-1780.
PLEASURE *see* under SUBJECT 1755-1780.
PLOT 1758; *see also* under COMPLICATION 1758; compare with CHARACTER 1758.
PROBABILITY *see* under WONDER 1758.
RATIONALISM *see* under THOUGHT 1758.
REALISM compare with ILLUSION 1778, PLOT 1758.
REVERSAL *see* under TRAGEDY 1758.
RULES 1758.
SPECTACLE *see* under ILLUSION 1778, IMITATION 1778.
STYLE 1758; *see also* under ACTION 1758.
SUBJECT 1755-1780, 1758; *see also* under DRAMA 1758, GENRE DEFINITION 1758,
      TRAGEDY 1755-1780.
SURPRISE *see* under COMEDY 1755-1780, HUMOR 1755-1780.
TASTE 1778.
THOUGHT 1758; *see also* under DRAMA 1758.
THREE UNITIES *see* under ILLUSION 1755-1780.
TRAGEDY 1755-1780, 1758, 1778; *see also* under ACTION 1758, CHARACTER 1755-1780,
      GENRE DEFINITION 1758.
UNIVERSALITY 1778; *see also* under TRAGEDY 1755-1780.
WILL *see* under CHARACTER 1758.
WONDER 1758.

JOHN DRYDEN (1631-1700). English poet, playwright, critic, and theorist. Dryden was educated at Westminster and Trinity College, Cambridge. After the completion of his degree in 1654 he went to London where he first worked as secretary to Sir Gilbert Pickering, his cousin, and began publishing his poetry. After the Restoration in 1660 he turned to the revived theatre and achieved success first as a writer of comedy and then of rhymed "heroic" drama. Though his conception of drama was greatly influenced by the French (he often adapted French materials) he perceived his relation to English dramatic traditions and upheld their validity against the claims of classical and contemporary French practices. A good deal of his critical and theoretical thinking appears in the prefaces and dedications to his plays. In 1668 he wrote *Of Dramatic Poesie, An Essay* in which he addressed himself directly to current issues of dramatic theory and practice. The *Essay* is presented as a dialogue in which one speaker, Neander, generally represents Dryden's positions. All four speakers are used as vehicles for attitudes Dryden wishes to set against each other. In that same year Dryden was appointed Historiographer Royal and poet laureate, positions which he held until the king's abdication in 1688. His work was satirized in Villier's *The Rehearsal* (1671). Later Dryden proved he too was a brilliant satirist in *Mac Flecknoe* (1678), a verse attack on the playwright Thomas Shadwell. The origin of his dispute with Shadwell was a disagreement over the quality of the wit of Ben Johnson (q.v.). Dryden's thinking about drama was shaped almost equally by his respect for English dramatic tradition and neoclassical doctrines.

Bibliography

DW   *The Critical and Miscellaneous Prose Works of John Dryden.* Edited by Edmond Malone. 3 vols. London: H. Baldwin and Son, 1800.

Index

REALISM *see* under AFFECT 1668, THOUGHT 1668; compare with STYLE 1665, 1668, 1672.
RULES 1695; *see also* under POETIC JUSTICE 1671, THREE UNITIES 1668, 1697.
SPECTACLE *see* under DRAMATIZATION 1668.
STYLE 1665, 1668, 1672, 1682; *see also* under PLOT 1679, TRAGEDY 1679.
SUBJECT 1695; *see also* under ACTION 1679, GENRE DEFINITION 1672.
SURPRISE *see* under VARIETY 1668.
THOUGHT 1668; *see also* under DRAMA 1711, INSTRUCTION 1695.
THREE UNITIES 1668, 1697.
TRAGEDY 1679, 1697; *see also* under ACTION 1679, IMITATION 1668, MORALITY 1711,
    POETIC JUSTICE 1671, SUBJECT 1695.
UNITY 1668; *see also* under INSTRUCTION 1679, VARIETY 1668.
VARIETY 1668; *see also* under PLOT 1674, STYLE 1668, THREE UNITIES 1697; compare
    with STYLE 1665.

THOMAS STEARNS ELIOT (1888-1965). American poet, playwright, essayist, and critic. Educated at Harvard, Paris, and Oxford Universities, Eliot established himself in London in 1914 as an editor and poet. In 1922 he published *The Waste Land*, a long poem which brought him considerable fame and influence. In 1927 he became a British citizen. He began to experiment with dramatic verse in 1932 and wrote a number of plays thereafter; probably his two most successful dramatic works are the *Sweeney Agonistes* fragment and *Murder in the Cathedral* (1935). Eliot's first collections of critical essays, *The Sacred Wood* (1920) and *Homage to John Dryden* (1924), established his reputation as a critic. He was a traditionalist, both neoclassically and religiously orthodox, in a conscious effort to connect with deeper levels of human experience than those suggested by novelties in thought and fashions of style.

Bibliography

EEE   *Elizabethan Essays*. New York: Haskell House, 1964.
EJD   *John Dryden: The Poet, The Dramatist, The Critic*. New York: Haskell House, 1932.
EOPP   *On Poetry and Poets*. London: Faber and Faber, 1957.
EPD   *Poetry and Drama*. Cambridge, Mass.: Harvard University Press, 1951.
ESE   *Selected Essays*. New York: Harcourt, Brace and Company, 1950.
ESW   *The Sacred Wood*. New York: Alfred A. Knopf, 1921.
ETVP   *The Three Voices of Poetry*. 2nd ed. New York: Cambridge University Press, 1955.
EUP   *The Use of Poetry and the Use of Criticism*. London: Faber and Faber, 1964.

Index

AESTHETIC 1921; *see also* under IMITATION 1924, OBJECTIVE CORRELATIVE 1919,
    THOUGHT 1921.
AFFECT 1933, 1951; *see also* under CONVENTION 1919, OBJECTIVE CORRELATIVE
    1919, STYLE 1943, 1951, THREE UNITIES 1928, 1932, UNITY 1932, VARIETY
    1932.
CHARACTER 1919, 1930; *see also* under STYLE 1942, 1953.
CONVENTION 1919; *see also* under STYLE 1951.
DISTANCE *see* under STYLE 1951.
DRAMA 1921, 1932; *see also* under AESTHETIC 1921, STYLE 1943.

EMOTION *see* under CHARACTER 1919, OBJECTIVE CORRELATIVE 1919, STYLE 1919, 1926.
FORM 1921; *see also* under STYLE 1919.
FORWARD MOVEMENT *see* under STYLE 1953.
FUNCTIONALISM *see* under STYLE 1951.
IMITATION 1924; *see also* under AESTHETIC 1921.
LANGUAGE *see* under AFFECT 1951, DRAMA 1932, STYLE 1951, 1953.
MAGNITUDE *see* under THREE UNITIES 1928.
METAPHOR *see* under STYLE 1934.
OBJECTIVE CORRELATIVE 1919.
OBJECTIVITY *see* under CONVENTION 1919, STYLE 1953.
POETRY OF THE THEATRE 1928.
RATIONALISM compare with THOUGHT 1921.
RULES *see* under THREE UNITIES 1932.
SPECTACLE *see* under DRAMA 1932.
STYLE 1919, 1926, 1934, 1942, 1943, 1951, 1953; *see also* under UNITY 1932.
SYMBOL *see* under STYLE 1934.
THOUGHT 1921; *see also* under AFFECT 1933, THREE UNITIES 1932.
THREE UNITIES 1928, 1932; *see also* under UNITY 1932.
UNITY 1932; *see also* under STYLE 1926.
VARIETY 1932 (twice); compare with STYLE 1926, 1951.

JOHANN WOLFGANG VON GOETHE (1749-1832).

German journalist, statesman, historian, theatre manager, critic, scientist, philosopher, novelist, poet, and playwright. He has been called the last Renaissance man. Goethe studied law at the University of Leipzig where, like many young Germans, he resented the strong French cultural influence (but he was never a Francophobe, as many were). Though his earliest published work was poetry, his first love was the theatre; it was his play *Götz von Berlichingen* (1773) which launched his fame and was the first major work of the *Sturm und Drang* movement. In 1775 he went on a visit to Weimar and, except for his travels, remained there for the rest of his life. By 1786, however, Goethe became restive; he had begun but not completed several major and quite ambitious works, his fame and the comforts and distractions of his official duties at the Weimar court were impeding his growth, and a long platonic relationship with the wife of a court official had become finally unbearably frustrating and sterile. He fled Weimar, in effect, to make a long-postponed journey to Italy which he later celebrated as a death and rebirth in which he found renewal as a man and as an artist. He rediscovered classicism, which transformed his thought and his work and gave them new energy.

Goethe's thought is complex and subtle, and it is also, inevitably, self-contradictory over so long and productive a life; indeed, his career illustrates at many levels one of the major tenets of his thought, that its ultimate objective is the discovery of principles that reconcile apparently opposing extremes and tendencies.

Bibliography

GCE   *Conversations of Goethe with Eckermann and Soret*. Translated by John Oxenford. London: George Bell, 1883.

GED   ''Epic and Dramatic Poetry.'' Translated by W. R. Rönnfeldt in *European Theories of the Drama*. Edited by Barrett H. Clark. Cincinnati: Stewart and Kidd, 1918.

GLE   *Goethe's Literary Essays*. Edited by J. E. Spingarn. New York; Harcourt, Brace and Company, 1921.

Index

SYMBOL 1816, 1826.
THOUGHT 1813, 1823, 1827; *see also* under INSTRUCTION 1827, SYMBOL 1826.
THREE UNITIES 1825.
TRAGEDY 1825, 1827; *see also* under SUBJECT 1797.
UNITY 1826; *see also* under ILLUSION 1798, IMITATION 1789.
UNIVERSALITY *see* under CHARACTER 1813.
VARIETY 1827; compare with GENRE 1824.

WILLIAM HAZLITT (1778-1830). English journalist, lecturer, critic, philosophical essayist, and painter. As a child Hazlitt read voluminously. He was trained to be a painter and studied art at the Louvre in 1802-1803. In 1804 he painted the portrait of Charles Lamb which hangs in the National Portrait Gallery. However, he turned from painting to philosophy. In 1805 and the following two years he published several philosophical works. Financial difficulties drove him to journalism and to lecturing in London on philosophy in 1811, in both of which he was soon successful. His *Characters of Shakespeare's Plays* was published in 1817 and a collection of his dramatic criticism was published as *A View of the English Stage* in 1818. In the latter year he delivered a course of lectures *On the English Poets* and in the next year another *On the English Comic Writers*. His last course of lectures was *On the Dramatic Literature of the Age of Elizabeth*. In one decade Hazlitt had drawn himself out of poverty and obscurity to become one of the leading romantic critics of the time. He was close to most of the best-known writers of his period, having known Wordsworth and Coleridge (q.v.) since 1798. He was admired by Shelley and Keats, the latter of whom he championed against his critics. Just as Samuel Johnson's (q.v.) common sense guarded him from the excesses of neoclassicism, the same native English propensity protected Hazlitt to some degree from the excesses of romanticism, though he had not the rigor and clearheadedness of Johnson.

Bibliography

HW   *The Collected Works of William Hazlitt*. Edited by A. R. Waller and Arnold Glover, 12 vols. New York: McClure, Phillips, and Company, 1902-1904.

Index

AESTHETIC 1815, 1816, 1818, c.1820; *see also* under EVOLUTIONISM 1814, FORWARD MOVEMENT 1818, IDEALISM 1824, 1830, IMAGINATION 1813, IMITATION 1830, SUBJECT 1816, UNIVERSALITY 1824.
AFFECT 1817, 1819; *see also* under AESTHETIC 1818, c.1820, FORWARD MOVEMENT 1818, HUMOR 1819, IMAGINATION 1818, IMITATION 1814, 1816, 1817, LANGUAGE 1818, METAPHOR 1830, NOVELTY 1818, TRAGEDY 1815, UNITY 1816, UNIVERSALITY 1824.
CATHARSIS 1817; *see also* under TRAGEDY 1815.
CHARACTER 1821-1822; *see also* under COMEDY 1817, EMOTION 1817.
COMEDY 1815, 1817.
CONFLICT *see* under HUMOR 1819.
CONVENTION *see* under AESTHETIC 1816.

GEORG WILHELM FRIEDRICH HEGEL (1770-1831). German philosopher. Hegel was educated at the Stuttgart grammar school and then at the University of Tübingen, where he studied the classics and philosophy, receiving his Ph.D. in 1790. Though he continued the study of theology thereafter, he decided not to take religious orders. Hegel's thinking was first influenced by Kant and by his friend F. W. J. Schelling who helped him with his first academic employment at Jena in 1801. In 1805 he was appointed Extraordinary Professor there, and in 1806, on Goethe's (q.v.) intervention, began to receive a stipend. In 1807 he published his first important work, *The Phenomenology of Mind*. From 1808 to 1816 he was rector of a school in Nurenberg, where he published his *Science of Logic* (1812 and 1816). In 1816 he accepted the chair of philosophy at Heidelberg and then, in 1818, at Berlin. Hegel's lectures on *Aesthetics*, later published by his students, derive more from his philosophical system than from his experience as a spectator of the drama, but he was a frequent and appreciative visitor to the theatre and art galleries. He kept notes and newspaper clippings about the theatre to give concrete illustrations to his lectures. Hegel's philosophical point of view might be described as theological and historical (in contrast with a description of Aristotle's as biological, Kant's as physical, and Nietzsche's as aesthetic). It is grounded in faith and spiritual progress through history; spirit knows itself as spirit only by contrast with nature, and therefore each particularization, finite where spirit is infinite, is a step toward greater self-realization because tension is created for the necessarily unrealized (because infinite) spirit. Thus there is a "dialectical" process in nature, history, human reason, and art—not only in the development of art but in its structure and in the nature of its appeal. Hegel's system has been characterized as both idealism and realism at once, and disciples have developed these strains variously. Hegel's influence has been enormous; his concept of drama as clash and reconcilation (known best as the "conflict theory") has dominated modern theories of drama.

Bibliography

HFA   *The Philosophy of Fine Art*. Translated by F. P. B. Osmaston. London: G. Bell and Sons, 1920.

Index

HORACE (Quintus Horatius Flaccus) (65-8 B.C.). Roman poet and critic. His father, a freed slave, was able to educate him in Rome and Athens. Horace fought on the losing side of the battle of Philippi (42 B.C.) and returned destitute to Rome under an amnesty. He became perhaps the first professional man of letters and gained a permanent reputation as a skilled and humane but not a profound poet. His critical and theoretical comments on literature are scattered; the best known of his writing in this vein is an epistle usually called *Ars poetica*. This longest and one of the last of his works acquired an authority in the Renaissance that it hardly deserves. It contains practical and sensible advice but it is neither analytical nor coherent, relying on aphorism rather than connected argument.

Bibliography

HAP   *Satires, Epistles, and Ars Poetica.* Translated by H. Rushton Fairclough. New York: G. P. Putnam's Sons, 1929.

SAMUEL JOHNSON (1709-1784). English poet, critic, journalist, essayist, and lexicographer. Educated in Lichfield grammar school and his father's book shop, he attended Pembroke College, Oxford, for four terms before he was compelled to leave for want of money. Marriage in 1735 brought a dowry which enabled him to set up a school in Lichfield, but at the end of two years the school was forced to close. With one of his former students, David Garrick, Johnson went to London in 1737 to seek his fortune. Garrick found his way quickly as an actor, playwright, and producer but Johnson's came more slowly and as a result of great labor. He made some reputation as a satirical poet, writer of political tracts, and journalist with *Gentleman's Magazine*. In 1745 he published his *Miscellaneous Observations on the Tragedy of Macbeth*. In 1749 Garrick produced Johnson's tragedy *Irene* at Drury Lane. In 1750 he began to publish the twice-weekly *Rambler*, each issue containing a single essay. The series lasted two years. In 1755 his *Dictionary of the English Language* was completed after nearly nine years of work; this and the *Rambler* essays established Johnson as virtual literary dictator in England. He wrote many prefaces, introductions, articles, and tracts thereafter. In 1756 he began to accept subscriptions for his edition of Shakespeare, which was published in eight volumes in 1765. A pension of £300 a year from the king in 1762 greatly eased his financial straits. He was enabled to travel and to write at a more leisurely pace (as recently as 1759 he had written *Rasselas* in a week's time to raise money to pay for his mother's final illness and funeral expenses). In 1777 he agreed to write the *Lives of the English Poets*, the publication of which was completed in 1781, his last major work. As a literary and dramatic theorist Johnson's thought is marked by his classical learning, his strong moralism, his pragmatism, and his paradoxical attitude toward the theatre. On the one hand his criticism is always informed by his consciousness that art is created to be perceived, which for dramatic art logically requires performance. Yet, on the other hand, he almost totally lacks appreciation for the contributions of the stage to the realization of dramatic art—he treats the stage as merely a lively illustration of a literary art. Johnson is generally accounted the single most influential critic of English literature.

Bibliography

JL   *Lives of the English Poets*. Edited by George Birkbeck Hill. 3 vols. New York: Octagon Books, 1967.

JS   *Johnson on Shakespeare*. Edited by Walter Raleigh. New York: Oxford University Press, 1929.

JW   *The Works of Samuel Johnson. Edited by F. P. Walesby. 9 vols. Oxford: Talboys and Wheeler, 1825.*

Index

IDENTIFICATION *see* under ILLUSION 1765.
ILLUSION 1765; *see also* under THREE UNITIES 1751, 1765.
IMAGINATION *see* under THREE UNITIES 1751, 1765.
IMITATION c.1780, c.1781; *see also* under GENRE DEFINITION 1765, ILLUSION 1765,
    OBJECTIVITY 1765, THREE UNITIES 1765, UNIVERSALITY 1759, 1765, VARI-
    ETY 1751, 1765.
INSTRUCTION 1750; *see also* under GENRE DEFINITION 1765, THREE UNITIES 1765.
LANGUAGE 1778.
METAPHOR 1778.
MORALITY 1765.
NOVELTY *see* under INSTRUCTION 1750.
OBJECTIVITY 1765; *see also* under MORALITY 1765.
PLEASURE 1765; *see also* under WONDER 1765.
POETIC JUSTICE compare with IMITATION c.1780.
PROBABILITY *see* under THREE UNITIES 1751, 1765.
RATIONALISM *see* under AESTHETIC 1751, LANGUAGE 1778, MORALITY 1765, RULES
    1751, VARIETY 1751, WONDER 1751.
REALISM *see* under GENRE DEFINITION 1765, IMITATION c.1780, c.1781, RULES 1751,
    THREE UNITIES 1765, VARIETY 1751, 1765.
RULES 1751; *see also* under THREE UNITIES 1751, 1765.
SPECTACLE compare with ILLUSION 1765.
STYLE *see* under LANGUAGE 1778, VARIETY 1751.
SUBJECT *see* under GENRE 1765, VARIETY 1765.
SURPRISE *see* under LANGUAGE 1778, WONDER 1751.
THOUGHT *see* under LANGUAGE 1778.
THREE UNITIES 1751, 1765; *see also* under ILLUSION 1765.
UNITY *see* under FORM 1765, RULES 1751.
UNIVERSALITY 1759, 1765.
VARIETY 1751, 1765; *see also* under PLEASURE 1765, THREE UNITIES 1765.
WONDER 1751, 1765.

BEN JONSON (1573[?]-1637). English critic, poet, composer of masques
and plays. Jonson was educated at a private school in St. Martin's Church and
at Westminster School; he may also have worked as an apprentice bricklayer
for his stepfather. Sometime prior to 1592 he soldiered in the Low Countries,
and he married on his return to London. He became a strolling player and hack
writer for Philip Henslowe. He was cited among those playwrights "who are
best for tragedy" by Francis Meres in 1598. In the fall of that year Shakespeare's
company performed *Every Man in His Humour*, which was the true beginning
of the career Jonson was to have. A traditionalist and classicist, as early as
1599 he was gently satirized by Marston as a pedant in the *Histrio-mastix*. It
has been suggested that Jonson's argument with his contemporaries was not
over neoclassical theories, which all accepted in principle, but over the rigor
and consistency of the practice that he demanded. This may be; in any case,
there was no attempt to define a system of countervailing principles of
Elizabethan poetics until Schlegel's (q.v.) at the beginning of the nineteenth
century. Jonson expounded his principles in prefaces, dedicatory poems, and

in *Timber or Discoveries* (published 1640); his views are also reported by William Drummond in *Conversations with Drummond*. The Renaissance commonplaces that Jonson propounded are not in any way as interesting, flexible, or subtle as Jonson's practice, nor as coherently or profoundly understood by him as by Philip Sidney (q.v.). The true measure of Jonson's intelligence is to be found in his great comedies, with their realism, morality, complexity, clarity, and joy. Jonson's most fundamental intellectual sympathies were at least as much neo-Platonic as neo-Aristotelean.

Bibliography

JBW *The Works of Ben Jonson*. Edited by William Gifford. Boston: Phillips, Sampson & Co., 1855.
  Alchemist (Prologue).
  Cataline (To the Reader in Ordinarie).
  Cynthia's Revels (Prologue).
  Epicoene (Second Prologue).
  Every Man in His Humour (Preface).
  Poetaster (Prologue).
  ''Prefatory Poem'' for Thomas Wright's *The Passions of the Mind in General*.
  The Sad Shepherd (Prologue).
  Sejanus (To the Readers; The Argument).
  Volpone (Dedication; Prologue).
JD *Discoveries and Conversations with William Drummond of Hawthomden*. Edited by G. B. Harrison. London: John Lane, The Bodley Head, 1923.

Index

PLEASURE *see* under DRAMA 1641, MAGNITUDE 1641, REALISM 1616.
PLOT *see* under ACTION 1641.
POETIC JUSTICE 1603, 1605.
RATIONALISM 1611; *see also* AESTHETIC 1641, CHARACTER 1604, COMEDY 1641, IMAGINATION 1641, NOVELTY 1600.
REALISM 1616; *see also* under GENRE 1640, IMITATION 1641.
REVERSAL *see* under MAGNITUDE 1641.
RULES 1603, 1641; *see also* under THREE UNITIES 1605; compare with AESTHETIC 1641.
SPECTACLE 1616; *see also* under COMEDY 1641.
STYLE 1641; *see also* under GENRE 1640, IMITATION 1641, LANGUAGE 1641, META-PHOR 1641, SURPRISE 1641, SYMBOL 1601.
SUBJECT *see* under NOVELTY 1641.
SURPRISE 1641.
SYMBOL 1601; *see also* under METAPHOR 1641.
THOUGHT *see* under LANGUAGE 1641, NOVELTY 1600, SURPRISE 1641, SYMBOL 1601.
THREE UNITIES 1605, 1640; *see also* under MAGNITUDE 1641, REALISM 1616.
UNITY 1641; *see also* under ACTION 1641.
VARIETY *see* under MAGNITUDE 1641.

GOTTHOLD EPHRAIM LESSING (1729-1781). German playwright, critic, and theorist. Lessing entered the University of Leipzig in 1746 to study theology, but he soon became enamoured of the theatre and wrote a number of comedies which were produced by the Neuber company. He fled Leipzig in 1748 to avoid debtor's prison, spending the next four years in Berlin turning out translations, criticism, and diverse essays. Lessing took a medical degree at Wittenberg in 1752 and then returned to Berlin where he published a six-volume collection of his works, including the first German bourgeois tragedy, *Miss Sara Sampson* (1755). In his critical essays for journals in this period Lessing attacked the imitation of French dramatic models by Germans, urging the development of a national drama like that of Shakespeare. In 1766 he published his famous treatise *Laokoön*, an attempt to define the particular qualities of painting and sculpture as space arts and poetry as a time art. An argument with Voltaire (q.v.), then living at the court of Frederick the Great, prevented him from receiving an appointment as director of the royal library; therefore in 1766 he accepted an offer to act as adviser and critic for the new privately funded National Theatre in Hamburg. The theatre closed after only one year, but Lessing wrote over fifty performance notices which he published in 104 parts as the *Hamburg Dramaturgie* (1767-1769). Again he attacked French classical drama, disputing especially the ideas of Corneille (q.v.) and Voltaire but he applauded the "common realism" of Diderot (q.v.). Though greatly respected in his own time, and enormously influential on the course of German drama, Lessing died tired, lonely, and poor.

Bibliography

LSPW   *Selected Prose Works of G. E. Lessing*. Translated by E. C. Beasley and Helen Zimmern. Edited by Edward Bell. London: George Bell and Sons, 1879.

Index

MOLIÈRE [Jean Baptiste Paquelin] (1622-1673). French actor, theatrical producer, and playwright. Born in Paris into the upper middle class, he studied law in Orleans after four years at the Jesuit College de Clermont. He returned to Paris, perhaps without receiving his degree, and in 1643 he joined with ten other actors to form a company called L'Illustre Theatre, taking the name Molière for the stage. After three years in Paris with more creditors in attendance than spectators, the young company went into the provinces and toured for twelve years. Through the intervention of the Duc d'Anjou, Molière was able to take his troupe to Paris to present Corneille's *Nicomede*, followed by an interlude written by Molière, before the king. The king was so pleased that he permitted the company to remain in Paris and perform on alternate nights at the Petit-Bourbon. Thereafter Molière became established as a court favorite. Unquestionably it is his dramaturgical practice rather than his theories that has been most influential. Typically, his attitudes are pragmatic, aiming to please rather than to obey the rules. In the absence of a perfect set of rules or an adequate theory of drama, the goal to please at least enforces close observation of the relationship between the things done on the stage and their effects on the spectator. Molière had an excellent laboratory, and he observed and learned well.

Bibliography

MP   *The Plays of Molière*. Translated by Katherine Prescott Wormeley. 6 vols. New York: Athenaeum Society, 1894.

Index

FRIEDRICH NIETZSCHE (1844-1900). German philosopher and philologist. Nietzsche was educated at the Universities of Bonn and Leipzig in classical philology. In 1869 he was appointed to the University of Basel (one of the youngest to receive a professorship) and became a Swiss citizen. An early apostle of Wagner, he later broke with him over Wagner's chauvinism, anti-semitism, and religious hypocrisy. Released from the restraints of Wagner's more conventional attitudes, Nietzsche's thought became increasingly and profoundly iconoclastic, anti-religious, anti-idealistic, psychologically exploratory, existentialistic, and phenomenological.Little-known until Georg Brandes began to lecture on Nietzsche at the University of Copenhagen in 1888, within a decade he was world-famous. In 1879 Nietzsche resigned from the university to devote his time to his writing. He was astonishingly prolific until his mental breakdown in 1889. After that time the works published in his name were largely compiled by his sister from his notes—and there is evidence that she suppressed, modified, and reorganized his writing. Though Nietzsche was quite capable of changing his mind, even refuting his own earlier ideas, some apparent contradictions in those works that Nietzsche saw into print and those edited by his sister, or those compiled during the Nazi era in Germany, must be dealt with warily.

Among Nietzsche's heroes was Goethe (q.v.), whom he described as one who was capable of tolerance because of his strength—a man of great passion under complete control, a man for whom there was no longer anything forbidden because he was beyond good and evil; in other words, Goethe was for him a near approximation of the Superman, the state of power over self. Modern philosophy and aesthetics have been greatly influenced by Nietzsche's ideas, as may be seen in the thought of Gilbert Murray, Henri Bergson, Sigmund Freud and Jean-Paul Sartre as well as in the dramatic theories of Francis Ferguson, Antonin Artaud (q.v.), and G. B. Shaw (q.v.).

Bibliography

NBT   *The Birth of Tragedy.* Translated by William A. Haussmann in *The Complete Works of Friedrich Nietzsche.* Edited by Oscar Levy. Vol. 1. New York: Russell and Russell, 1964.

NDD   *The Dawn of Day.* Translated by J. M. Kennedy in *The Complete Works of Friedrich Nietzsche.* Edited by Oscar Levy. Vol. 9. London: T. N. Foulis, 1911.

NEG   *Early Greek Philosophy and Other Essays.* Translated by Maxmilian A. Mügge in *The Complete Works of Friedrich Nietzsche.* Edited by Oscar Levy. Vol. 2. New York: Russell and Russell, 1964.

NEH   *Ecce Homo.* Translated by Anthony M Ludovici in *The Complete Works of Friedrich Nietzsche.* Edited by Oscar Levy. Vol 17. New York: Russell and Russell, 1964.

NGM   *The Genealogy of Morals, Peoples and Countries.* Translated by H. B. Samuel in *The Complete Works of Friedrich Nietzsche.* Edited by Oscar Levy. Vol. 13. London: George Allen and Unwin, 1910.

NHH   *Human, All-Too-Human, Part I.* Translated by Helen Zimmern in *The Complete Works of Friedrich Nietzsche.* Edited by Oscar Levy. Vol. 6. New York: Russell and Russell, 1964.

NHH2   *Human, All-Too-Human, Part 2.* Translated by Paul V. Cohn in *The Complete Works of Friedrich Nietzsche.* Edited by Oscar Levy. Vol. 7. London: George Allen and Unwin, 1911.

NJW   *The Joyful Wisdom.* Translated by Thomas Cimmon in *The Complete Works of Friedrich Nietzsche.* Edited by Oscar Levy. Vol.10. London: T. N. Foulis, 1910.

NTI   *The Twilight of the Idols*. Translated by Anthony M. Ludovici in *The Complete Works of Friedrich Nietzsche*. Edited by Oscar Levy. Vol. 16. London: George Allen and Unwin, 1911.

NTS   *Thoughts Out of Season, Part 1*. Translated by Anthony Ludovici in *The Complete Works of Friedrich Nietzsche*. Edited by Oscar Levy. Vol. 4. London: George Allen and Unwin, 1909.

NTS2   *Thoughts Out of Season, Part 2*. Translated by Adrian Collins in *The Complete Works of Friedrich Nietzsche*. Edited by Oscar Levy. Vol. 5. New York: Russell and Russell, 1964.

NW   *The Will to Power*. Translated by Anthony M. Ludovici in *The Complete Works of Friedrich Nietzsche*. Edited by Oscar Levy. Vol. 15. New York: Russell and Russell, 1964.

NWP   *The Will to Power*. Translated by Walter Kaufmann and R. J. Hollingdale. New York: Random House, 1967.

NZ   *Thus Spoke Zarathustra*. Translated by Thomas Common in *The Complete Works of Friedrich Nietzsche*. Edited by Oscar Levy. Vol. 11. New York: Russell and Russell, 1964.

Index

ILLUSION 1871; *see also* under AESTHETIC 1888, AFFECT 1871, CHARACTER 1878, METAPHOR 1873, TRAGEDY 1871.

IMAGINATION 1871; *see also* under CHARACTER 1878.

IMITATION 1871, 1878, 1880, 1888.

INSTRUCTION compare with CONFLICT 1875, MORALITY 1881.

LANGUAGE 1871, 1888; compare with POETRY OF THE THEATRE 1875.

METAPHOR 1871, 1873; *see also* under IMAGINATION 1871, THOUGHT 1871, TRAGEDY 1871.

MORALITY 1871, 1881.

MOTIVATION 1878; *see also* under WILL 1888.

NOVELTY 1882; *see also* under AESTHETIC 1882.

OBJECTIVITY *see* under DRAMA 1871.

ORDER *see* under DRAMA 1871, METAPHOR 1873, MORALITY 1871; compare with CONFLICT 1875, TASTE 1888.

PITY *see* under CATHARSIS 1888, MOTIVATION 1878.

PLEASURE 1878; *see also* under TASTE 1888, TRAGEDY 1871.

POETRY OF THE THEATRE 1875; *see also* under LANGUAGE 1871, TRAGEDY 1871.

PROBABILITY 1888; compare with WILL 1888.

RATIONALISM compare with THOUGHT 1871, TRAGEDY 1888, WILL 1886, WONDER 1871.

REALISM compare with DISTANCE 1871, IMITATION 1871, METAPHOR 1873.

SPECTACLE *see* under AFFECT 1871.

STYLE 1871, 1880, 1882; *see also* under AESTHETIC 1882, LANGUAGE 1871.

SUBTEXT *see* under POETRY OF THE THEATRE 1875.

SYMBOL *see* under LANGUAGE 1871, POETRY OF THE THEATRE 1875, STYLE 1880, TRAGEDY 1871.

TASTE 1888.

THOUGHT 1871, 1888; *see also* under METAPHOR 1873, MORALITY 1871.

TRAGEDY 1871, 1888 (twice); *see also* under CATHARSIS 1871, 1888, CONFLICT 1875, TASTE 1888.

UNITY 1871.

UNIVERSALITY *see* under MORALITY 1871.

WILL 1886, 1888; *see also* under CONFLICT 1888, MOTIVATION 1878, TRAGEDY 1871, 1888.

WONDER 1871; *see also* under HERO 1871, POETRY OF THE THEATRE 1875.

LUIGI PIRANDELLO (1867-1936). Italian playwright and novelist. Pirandello studied in Palermo and the University of Rome and at Bonn (1888-1891) where he received a doctorate in philology. He published a volume of poetry in 1889 but his first significant works were stories and novels. Though he began to write for the theatre in 1898, it was not until the great success of *Right You Are (If You Think You Are)* (1917) that he made drama important in his career. It was in the theatre that he acquired an international reputation (he received the Nobel Prize for Literature in 1934). Pirandello's theoretical and critical writing is contained largely in prefaces, in lectures, and in his essay *On Humor* (1908). His plays, with their strong interest in philosophy, psychology, and dramatic form, have been his most influential writing.

Bibliography

POH   *On Humor*. Translated by Antonio Illiano and Daniel P. Testa. Chapel Hill, N.C.: University of North Carolina Press, 1960.

PPSC   "Preface to *Six Characters in Search of an Author*." Translated by Eric Bentley in *Naked Masks*. Edited by Eric Bentley. New York: E. P. Dutton, 1952.

Index

AESTHETIC *see* under GENRE 1908, HUMOR 1908, ILLUSION 1908.
AFFECT *see* under IRONY 1908.
CHARACTER 1908; *see also* under HUMOR 1908.
CONFLICT *see* under HUMOR 1908.
DISINTERESTEDNESS 1908; *see also* under ILLUSION 1908.
DISTANCE *see* under HUMOR 1908.
FORM 1925; *see also* under HUMOR 1908, RULES 1908, STYLE 1908, THOUGHT 1908.
GENRE 1908; *see also* under THOUGHT 1908.
HUMOR 1908; *see also* under CHARACTER 1908, IRONY 1908.
IDEALISM 1908; *see also* under HUMOR 1908.
ILLUSION 1908; *see also* under IDEALISM 1908.
IMAGINATION *see* under IDEALISM 1908.
IMITATION *see* under CHARACTER 1908, RULES 1908.
IRONY 1908; *see also* under IDEALISM 1908.
LANGUAGE *see* under HUMOR 1908, STYLE 1908.
METAPHOR *see* under IDEALISM 1908.
MOTIVATION compare with HUMOR 1908.
RATIONALISM *see* under RULES 1908.
RULES 1908; *see also* under GENRE 1908; compare with THOUGHT 1908.
STYLE 1908; *see also* under HUMOR 1908, ILLUSION 1908.
SYMBOL 1925; *see also* under IDEALISM 1908.
THOUGHT 1908; *see also* under SYMBOL 1925.
UNITY *see* under IDEALISM 1908,
WILL 1908.

JEAN RACINE (1630-1699).French poet, playwright, and historian. Racine was educated in the puritanical doctrines of Cornelius Jansen at Port Royal and, in Paris, at the Collège d'Harcourt. He first gained attention in Paris as a poet. In 1664 Molière (q.v.) produced his play *La Thébaïde* at the Palais-Royale. Racine was a younger contemporary and rival of Corneille (q.v.); together they established the supremacy of classical ideals. All of Racine's plays are classical in spirit and, except for the final biblical plays, in subject as well. Unlike Corneille, Racine wrote very little about his work or about the principles of dramatic art. Most of Racine's theoretical statements are contained in the prefaces to his plays, all of which have some degree of polemical and apologetic intent. His friend and literary counselor, Boileau, published his *L'art Poetique* in 1674, which may have an even closer relation to Racine's thought than does d'Aubignac's (q.v.) to Corneille. If it was Racine's ultimate objective to attain advancement at court through his playwriting, he succeeded, but that achievement aborted a brilliant playwriting career. His few poetic tragedies became a standard for French classicism thereafter.

Bibliography

RP   Prefaces:
        "Preface to *La Thébaïde*" (1664)
        "First Preface to *Andromaque*" (1668)
        "First Preface to *Britannicus*"(1670)
        "Preface to *Bérénice*" (1674)
        "Preface to *Phédre*" (1677)
        In *European Theories of the Drama*. Edited by Barrett H. Clark. Cincinnati: Stewart
        and Kidd, 1918.

Index

FRANCISQUE SARCEY (1827-1899). French critic and reviewer. Born in Dourdan, Sarcey studied at the École Normale, and subsequently taught at Chaumont and Grenoble. In 1858 he resigned his professorship in order to go to Paris to pursue a career in literature. He wrote prodigiously but unsuccessfully, and in 1860 he took employment with the newspaper *L'Opinion nationale* as drama critic. In 1867 he transferred to the prestigious *Le Temps*, where he remained until his death. For much of his forty-year career as a reviewer of plays in Paris, Sarcey was the despot of the French theatre. His views were sane, middle-class, and logical rather than adventurous. He was an ardent advocate of the "well-made play."

Bibliography

STT   *A Theory of the Theater*. Translated by H. H. Hughes. New York: Dramatic Museum of
        Columbia University, 1916.

Index

AUTHORITY *see* under STYLE.
CONVENTION.
DRAMA; *see also* under CONVENTION, IMITATION.
GENRE; *see also* under STYLE, UNITY.
ILLUSION; *see also* under AFFECT, CONVENTION, UNITY.
IMITATION.
REALISM compare with AFFECT, CONVENTION, STYLE.
REVERSAL *see* under STYLE.
RULES.
STYLE; *see also* under AFFECT, GENRE, UNITY.
UNITY.

JULIUS CAESAR SCALIGER (1485-1558). Italian physician, scientist, and classical scholar. Scaliger settled in France in 1525, becoming a French citizen. He wrote a number of treatises on zoology, botany, grammar, and poetics, much of which was published posthumously; his *Poetics* was published in 1561. Perhaps the most widely respected of the Renaissance commentators on Aristotle, Scaliger's views were seminal in the formation of neoclassic dramatic doctrine, especially in France.

Bibliography

SP   *Select Translations from Scaliger's Poetics*. Translated by Frederick Morgan Padelford. New York: Henry Holt, 1905.

Index

All citations for Scaliger are dated 1561.
ACTION; *see also* under CHARACTER, INSTRUCTION
AESTHETIC.
AFFECT *see* under ACTION, AESTHETIC, INSTRUCTION, THREE UNITIES.
AUTHORITY *see* under IDEALISM, TRAGEDY.
CATHARSIS *see* under TRAGEDY.
CHARACTER; *see also* under COMEDY, TRAGEDY.
CLOSURE *see* under ACTION, TRAGEDY.
COMEDY; *see also* under SUBJECT, TRAGEDY.
DRAMA; *see also* under INSTRUCTION, THREE UNITIES.
GENRE; *see also* under SUBJECT, TRAGEDY.
GENRE DEFINITION *see* under GENRE.
HERO *see* under TRAGEDY.
IDEALISM.
IDENTIFICATION *see* under INSTRUCTION.
IMAGINATION compare with IMITATION.
IMITATION ; *see also* under IDEALISM, THREE UNITIES.
INSTRUCTION; *see also* under AESTHETIC, DRAMA, IMITATION, THREE UNITIES.
LANGUAGE *see* under STYLE, THOUGHT, TRAGEDY.
MAGNITUDE.
MORALITY *see* under INSTRUCTION.
NOVELTY.
PLEASURE *see* under AESTHETIC; compare with DRAMA.
PLOT; *see also* under ACTION, THREE UNITIES.
POETIC JUSTICE *see* under ACTION, IMITATION.

RATIONALISM *see* under THREE UNITIES.
REALISM *see* under THREE UNITIES, TRAGEDY.
REVERSAL *see* under ACTION.
RULES.
STYLE; *see also* under TRAGEDY.
SUBJECT; *see also* under GENRE, TRAGEDY.
THOUGHT.
THREE UNITIES.
TRAGEDY.
UNITY compare with ACTION.
VARIETY *see* under ACTION, AESTHETIC, COMEDY, MAGNITUDE.

AUGUST WILHELM VON SCHLEGEL (1767-1845). German translator, critic, and lecturer. Schlegel studied classical philology and aesthetics at Göttingen (1787-1791). With his younger brother, Friedrich, he founded *The Atheneum* (1798-1800), a periodical which became the organ of the romantic movement. Appointed professor at Jena University in 1798, he began his translations of Shakespeare which became the German standard. He also translated many of the plays of Calderón. In 1801 Schlegel lectured on literature and art in Berlin, identifying Dante, Shakespeare, Calderón and Camôes as the authors of the romantic classics of modern Europe. He subsequently made his critique of neoclassicism more explicit in *A Comparison Between the Phèdre of Racine and that of Euripides* (1807).In 1803 his wife left him and he met and travelled with Mme. de Staël. During his travels, in the spring of 1808, he gave a series of *Lectures on Dramatic Art and Literature* in Vienna, a much translated and influential historical, critical, and theoretical account of the development of world drama which firmly established the romantic point of view in European thought. In later years Schlegel founded Sanskrit studies at Bonn. His own poetry and drama are uninspired, but his theories continue to be an inspiration for others.

Bibliography

SCL   *Course of Lectures on Dramatic Art and Literature*. Translated by John Black. London: Henry G.Bohn, 1846.

Index

All citations for Schlegel are dated 1808.
ACTION; *see also* under COMPLICATION, DRAMA, THREE UNITIES.
AESTHETIC; *see also* under FORM, POETRY OF THE THEATRE, STYLE, UNITY.
AFFECT; *see also* under CHARACTER, CLOSURE, DRAMA, EXPOSITION, FORWARD MOVEMENT, GENRE, MORALITY, POETIC JUSTICE, THOUGHT, UNITY; compare with MAGNITUDE.
AUTHORITY; *see also* under AFFECT, NOVELTY, RULES.
CATHARSIS *see* under AFFECT.
CHARACTER; *see also* under ACTION, COMEDY, PLOT.
CLOSURE; *see also* under UNITY.
COMEDY; *see also* under CHARACTER, DISTANCE, GENRE DEFINITION, PLOT, THREE UNITIES.

COMPLICATION; *see also* under ACTION.
CONFLICT *see* under ACTION, AFFECT, CHARACTER, COMPLICATION, UNITY.
CONVENTION; *see also* under RULES, SPECTACLE.
DISINTERESTEDNESS *see* under AFFECT.
DISTANCE; *see also* under GENRE, IRONY, THOUGHT; compare with DRAMA.
DRAMA.
DRAMATIZATION *see* under EXPOSITION.
EVOLUTIONISM *see* under GENRE, LANGUAGE.
EXPOSITION; *see also* under DRAMA.
FORM; *see also* under CHARACTER, COMEDY, GENRE, GENRE DEFINITION, POETRY
      OF THE THEATRE, UNITY.
FORWARD MOVEMENT; *see also* under ACTION, AFFECT, COMEDY, DRAMA, EXPOSI-
      TION, PLOT, UNITY.
FUNCTIONALISM *see* under CHARACTER; compare with AESTHETIC.
GENRE; *see also* under CHARACTER, COMEDY, RULES, STYLE.
GENRE DEFINITION; *see also* under CHARACTER.
HERO *see* under ACTION.
HUMOR *see* under CHARACTER, COMEDY, DISTANCE, GENRE, IRONY.
IDEALISM *see* under CHARACTER, FORM, GENRE, POETRY OF THE THEATRE, SPEC-
      TACLE, TRAGEDY, UNITY.
IDENTIFICATION *see* under AFFECT, DRAMA, IMITATION; compare with DISTANCE.
ILLUSION; *see also* under IMAGINATION, THREE UNITIES.
IMAGINATION; *see also* under THREE UNITIES, UNITY.
IMITATION; *see also* under CHARACTER, DRAMA, GENRE DEFINITION, LANGUAGE,
      PROBABILITY, SPECTACLE, THREE UNITIES.
IRONY.
LANGUAGE; *see also* under POETRY OF THE THEATRE.
MAGNITUDE; *see also* under DRAMA, THREE UNITIES.
METAPHOR *see* under AESTHETIC.
MORALITY; *see also* under POETIC JUSTICE.
MOTIVATION *see* under ACTION, IRONY.
NOVELTY.
OBJECTIVITY *see* under DRAMA.
ORDER *see* under AESTHETIC, AFFECT, CLOSURE, DRAMA.
PATHOS *see* under CLOSURE.
PITY compare with DISTANCE.
PLOT; *see also* under ACTION, GENRE DEFINITION.
POETIC JUSTICE; *see also* under AFFECT, CLOSURE.
POETRY OF THE THEATRE.
PROBABILITY; *see also* under RULES, THREE UNITIES; compare with COMEDY.
RATIONALISM; *see* under COMPLICATION, UNITY; compare with AESTHETIC, CLOSURE.
REALISM *see* under LANGUAGE, STYLE: compare with GENRE DEFINITION, ILLUSION,
      IMITATION, POETRY OF THE THEATRE, SPECTACLE, THREE UNITIES.
RULES; *see also* under POETIC JUSTICE, THREE UNITIES; compare with ACTION.
SPECTACLE; *see also* under THREE UNITIES.
STYLE; *see also* under AESTHETIC, CHARACTER, GENRE DEFINITION, ILLUSION,
      LANGUAGE.
SUBJECT *see* under GENRE DEFINITION, RULES, THREE UNITIES, TRAGEDY.
SUBTEXT *see* under AFFECT.
SURPRISE *see* under FORWARD MOVEMENT, PROBABILITY.
SYMBOL; *see also* under CHARACTER.
THOUGHT; *see also* under CLOSURE, POETRY OF THE THEATRE, SYMBOL, TRAGEDY.

THREE UNITIES; *see also* under RULES; compare with CONVENTION, IMAGINATION.
TRAGEDY; *see also* under ACTION, AFFECT, CHARACTER, DISTANCE, GENRE DEFINITION.
UNITY; *see also* under ACTION, COMEDY, COMPLICATION, POETRY OF THE THEATRE.
UNIVERSALITY *see* under CHARACTER, SPECTACLE.
VARIETY *see* under AESTHETIC, DRAMA, RULES.
WILL *see* under ACTION
WONDER *see* under DISTANCE, DRAMA, PROBABILITY.

GEORGE BERNARD SHAW (1856-1950). Irish journalist, essayist, critic, novelist, and playwright. Shaw was educated in Dublin at Wesley College. He went to London at twenty determined to have a literary career. There he lived with his mother, who had separated from his father, until his marriage in 1898. In the ten years after his arrival in London he wrote a series of novels, of which several were published serially, earning an income from them of less than ten shillings a year. In 1885 he met William Archer who found him employment as a book reviewer for the *Pall Mall Gazette*, as an art critic for the *World*, and as a music critic for the *Star* and *World*. In 1895 he became drama critic for the *Saturday Review*. Shaw's first play, *Widower's Houses* (performed 1892) seems to have been revised to reflect his admiration for Ibsen, whose *A Doll's House* reached London in 1889, followed by *Ghosts* in 1891. Shaw wrote *The Quintessence of Ibsenism* (1891; republished with additions in 1913) to clear the way for the new drama in England, including—as it turned out—his own. Shaw had not only a long life but an astonishingly vigorous career as a playwright. (*Saint Joan*, perhaps his greatest play, was written when he was sixty-seven.) He was more influential as a critic, in the immediate term, and as a playwright, in the longer term, than he was as a theorist; indeed, most of his speculative thinking concerned social rather than aesthetic matters. His primary influences on dramatic theory probably lay in his insistence that entertainment could have intellectual content and that ideas entertain.

Bibliography

SAA   ''The Author's Apology,'' *Plays by George Bernard Shaw*. New York: New American Library, 1960.
SALOP   *Androcles and the Lion, Overruled and Pygmalion*. New York: Brentanos, 1914.
SCP   *The Complete Prefaces of Bernard Shaw*. London: Paul Hamlyn, 1965.
SDC   *Shaw's Dramatic Criticism* (1895-1898). Edited by John F. Matthews. New York: Hill and Wang, 1959.
SDDGM   *The Doctor's Dilemma, Getting Married, The Shewing-up of Blanco Posnet*. New York: Brentanos, 1911.
SGCR   *Geneva, Cymbeline Refinished, and Good King Charles*. New York: Dodd, Mead and Co. 1947.
SMCE   *Major Critical Essays. The Quintessence of Ibsenism. The Perfect Wagnerite. The Sanity of Art*. London: Constable, 1932.
SMDLS   *Misalliance, The Dark Lady of the Sonnets and Fanny's First Play*. New York: Brentano, 1914.
SMS   *Man and Superman*. New York: Brentanos, 1920.

Index

UNITY compare with CONFLICT 1898.
WILL *see* under ILLUSION 1906.

SIR PHILIP SIDNEY (1554-1586).

SIR PHILIP SIDNEY (1554-1586). English soldier, statesman, novelist, poet, and theorist. Educated at Shrewsbury school and Christ Church, Oxford, Sidney completed his education with a two-year tour of the Continent that ended in his twentieth year. His Latin, French, and Italian were excellent. Born and educated for state duties, Sidney was given little of a serious nature to do, and so he wrote. His *An Apologie for Poetrie* was probably written in response to Stephen Gosson's *The Schoole of Abuse* (1579), but its precise date is not known. In it Sidney shows both his knowledge of the best current thinking and his own powerful intellect. He wrote without the example of Shakespeare and so, unlike later English theorists, was not required to test neoclassical principles against the practice of a Romantic genius. His taste was impeccable, and he praised the best English poetry then available. He was the first to introduce Renaissance theories of art into England, primarily those of Scaliger (q.v.).

Bibliography

SDP   *The Defense of Poesy.* Edited by Albert S. Cook. Boston: Ginn, 1890.

Index

All citations for Sidney are dated c.1583.
AFFECT; *see also* under COMEDY, GENRE, INSTRUCTION, TRAGEDY.
CHARACTER *see* under COMEDY.
COMEDY.
DRAMA; *see also* under THREE UNITIES.
EXPOSITION *see* under THREE UNITIES.
GENRE.
HUMOR.
IDEALISM *see* under IMITATION.
ILLUSION *see* under IMAGINATION.
IMAGINATION; *see also* under IMITATION, THOUGHT, THREE UNITIES.
IMITATION; *see also* THOUGHT.
INSTRUCTION; *see also* under AFFECT, COMEDY, DRAMA, HUMOR, LANGUAGE, TRAGEDY.
LANGUAGE; *see also* under THREE UNITIES.
MORALITY.
PLEASURE; *see also* under HUMOR, IMITATION.
POETIC JUSTICE *see* under MORALITY.
RATIONALISM *see* under THREE UNITIES.
RULES *see* under THREE UNITIES.
STYLE; *see also* under GENRE, LANGUAGE.
SUBJECT; *see also* under AFFECT, THREE UNITIES.
SYMBOL *see* under THOUGHT.
THOUGHT; *see also* under INSTRUCTION.
THREE UNITIES.
TRAGEDY.
UNIVERSALITY; *see also* under THOUGHT.

KONSTANTIN SERGEEVICH ALEKSEEV STANISLAVSKI (1863-1938). Russian actor, director, and theoretician. Stanislavski began acting at age fifteen with an amateur group. In 1888 he founded the Society of Art and Literature, which became one of the most popular amateur theatrical companies in Moscow. In 1897 he was invited by V. I. Nemirovich-Danchenko, playwright and director of a drama school, to join with him in founding the Moscow Art Theatre. Danchenko was responsible for literary and administrative matters, Stanislavski for production. Stanislavski's first great success was with *The Seagull* of Chekhov (q.v.) in 1898; thereafter he, the Moscow Art Theatre, and Chekhov became internationally celebrated. Stanislavski's enduring reputation rests on his published theories of acting and acting-pedagogy, in which he urges a total inner realism that is more psychological and spiritual than empirical.

Bibliography

SAP   *An Actor Prepares*. Translated by Elizabeth Reynolds Hapgood. New York: Theatre Arts Books, 1936.

SAS   *Stanislavsky on the Art of the Stage. Translated by David Magarshack*. New York: Hill and Wang, 1961.

SBC   *Building a Character*. Translated by Elizabeth Reynolds Hapgood. New York: Theatre Arts Books, 1949.

SCR   *Creating a Role*. Translated by Elizabeth Reynolds Hapgood. Edited by Hermine Popper. New York: Theatre Arts Books, 1961.

SKDC *Discipline or Corruption*. London: Fact and Fiction, 1966.

SL   *Stanislavski's Legacy*. Translated and edited by Elizabeth R. Hapgood. New York: Theatre Arts Books, 1968.

MOTIVATION c.1930; *see also* under ACTION c.1930, 1936, FORWARD MOVEMENT 1936, SUBTEXT c.1930, 1936, THOUGHT 1938.
PLEASURE *see* under DRAMA 1938.
PLOT *see* under CONFLICT c.1930.
POETRY OF THE THEATRE *see* under THOUGHT 1938.
REALISM 1936; *see also* under ACTION 1936, CONFLICT c.1930, IMITATION 1918-22; compare with IMITATION 1905.
SPECTACLE *see* under ACTION c.1930, IDENTIFICATION c.1930; compare with IDEALISM 1918-1922.
STYLE 1922.
SUBTEXT c.1930-1938; *see* text for additional citations under other headings.
THOUGHT 1938.
UNITY 1938; *see also* ACTION 1936, 1938, FORWARD MOVEMENT 1936, 1938, SUBTEXT 1936, 1938, THOUGHT 1938.
UNIVERSALITY *see* under IDEALISM 1918-1922.
WILL *see* under ACTION 1938.

(JOHAN) AUGUST STRINDBERG (1849-1912). Swedish playwright, novelist, essayist, and autobiographer. Strindberg studied intermittently at Uppsala University, leaving without a degree. He worked as a journalist for several years, meanwhile revising and resubmitting his first important play, *Mäster Olof* (1872). He achieved his first fame with the novel *The Red Room* in 1879. In his dramatic work Strindberg explored the Romantic historical play under the influence of Shakespeare and early Ibsen. Then he developed the realistic thesis-drama—his most often revived plays. Finally he wrote a series of antirealistic proto-expressionistic plays which took something from French symbolist drama, something from medieval drama, something else from Swedenborgian mysticism and Nietzschean (q.v.) philosophy, and a great deal from his own autobiographical self-examinations. Strindberg's dramatic theories are contained in some prefaces (most notably that to *Miss Julie*, 1888) and in his autobiographical accounts. As with many playwrights, Strindberg's primary influence on dramatic theory derives from his plays rather than from his theoretical pronouncements, both by what the plays seem to confirm and the new questions they provoke.

Bibliography

SEP *An Effective Play*. Translated by Evert Sprinchorn in *Dramatic Theory and Criticism*. Edited by Bernard Dukore. New York: Holt, Rinehart and Winston, 1974.

SMD *On Modern Drama and Modern Theatre*. Translated by Børge Gedsø Medsen in *Playwrights on Playwriting*. Edited by Toby Cole. New York: Hill and Wang, 1961.

SOL *Open Letters to the Intimate Theater*. Translated by Walter Johnson. Seattle: University of Washington Press, n.d.

SSPP *Plays by August Strindberg: Miss Julie, The Stronger*. Translated by Edwin Björkman. New York: Charles Scribner's Sons, 1912.

Index

AFFECT 1888; *see also* under plot c.1900, SPECTACLE 1888, THREE UNITIES 1889.
CHARACTER 1888, 1908.

CLOSURE *see* under PLOT c.1900.
CONVENTION *see* under FORM 1908.
DRAMA *see* under IDENTIFICATION 1888, ILLUSION c.1908.
EMOTION *see* under PLOT c.1900.
FORM 1908.
FORWARD MOVEMENT *see* under PLOT c.1900.
IDENTIFICATION 1888.
ILLUSION c.1908; *see also* under AFFECT 1888, THREE UNITIES 1889.
IMAGINATION *see* under SPECTACLE 1888.
INSTRUCTION 1888.
MAGNITUDE *see* under AFFECT 1888.
MOTIVATION 1888.
PLOT c.1900.
REALISM compare with IMITATION 1889.
RECOGNITION *see* under PLOT c.1900.
REVERSAL *see* under PLOT c.1900.
SPECTACLE 1888.
SUBJECT *see* under ILLUSION c.1908.
SURPRISE *see* under PLOT c.1900.
THREE UNITIES 1889.
UNITY *see* under THREE UNITIES 1889.

HIPPOLYTE ADOLPHE TAINE (1828-1893). French literary critic, art critic, aesthetician, and historian. Educated privately at home, in 1848 Taine entered the École Normale in Paris; failing to graduate in 1851 because of his adherence to Spinoza's philosophy, Taine taught for a year and then returned to Paris to prepare two doctoral dissertations. He received his doctorate in 1853. He contributed literary and historical articles to a number of journals. In 1861 he published a revised version of his dissertation on La Fontaine as *La Fontaine and his Fables*, following the publications of *French Philosophers of the XIX Century* (1857), and *Essays of Criticism and History* (1858). His four-volume *History of English Literature* was published in 1863-1864. Taine was appointed professor of aesthetics and art history at the École des Beaux-Arts in Paris in 1864. His published lectures include *The Philosophy of Art* (1865) and *Of the Ideal in Art* (1867). Taine was devoted to the application of the scientific method to all areas of human thought, including art. He helped provide a theoretical basis for the literary movement of Naturalism; the novel, he said, should be a "collection of experiments." He attempted to unify rationalism and positivism with the idealism of Hegel (q.v.). Taine's concern with the "three great conditioning facts" of art—race, environment, and historical situation—encouraged biographical and historical criticism.

Bibliography

THEL   *History of English Literature*. Translated by H. Van Laun. Vol 1. London: Chatto and Windus, 1899.

TLA   *Lectures on Art*. Translated by John Durrand. New York: Henry Holt, 1875.

Index

ACTION 1864.

AESTHETIC 1863-1867, 1864; *see also* under CHARACTER 1864, DRAMA 1863-1867, EVOLUTIONISM 1863-1867, HERO 1864, UNITY 1864.

AFFECT *see* under AESTHETIC 1864, CHARACTER 1864, DRAMA 1863-1867, STYLE 1864.

CHARACTER 1864; *see also* under ACTION 1864, AESTHETIC 1864, CLOSURE 1864, HERO 1864, IMITATION 1864, MAGNITUDE 1864.

CLOSURE 1864.

COMEDY 1864; *see also* under AESTHETIC 1864.

DECORUM *see* under IMITATION 1864, STYLE 1864.

DRAMA 1863-1867; *see also* under ACTION 1864, HERO 1864.

EMOTION *see* under ACTION 1864, IDENTIFICATION 1864.

EVOLUTIONISM 1863-1867, 1864; *see also* under AESTHETIC 1863-1867, 1864, GENRE 1864.

FORM 1864; *see also* under ASTHETIC 1864, HERO 1864, IMITATION 1864.

FUNCTIONALISM *see* under FORM 1864, HERO 1864, UNITY 1864.

GENRE 1864; *see also* under AESTHETIC 1864.

HERO 1864; *see also* under ACTION 1864, AESTHETIC 1864, CHARACTER 1864.

IDEALISM *see* under AESTHETIC 1864, EVOLUTIONISM 1864, FORM 1864, HERO 1864, IMITATION 1864, LANGUAGE 1864.

IDENTIFICATION 1864; *see also* under ACTION 1864.

IMAGINATION compare with AESTHETIC 1863-1867.

IMITATION 1864; *see also* under AESTHETIC 1864, LANGUAGE 1864; compare with HERO 1864, STYLE 1864.

LANGUAGE 1864; *see also* under STYLE 1864.

MAGNITUDE 1864.

RATIONALISM *see* under AESTHETIC 1863-1867.

REALISM *see* under IMITATION 1864; compare with AESTHETIC 1864, EVOLUTIONISM 1864, LANGUAGE 1864.

STYLE 1864; *see also* under LANGUAGE 1864.

SUBTEXT *see* under ACTION 1864.

TASTE *see* under IDENTIFICATION 1864.

THOUGHT *see* under HERO 1864.

UNITY 1864; *see also* under AESTHETIC 1864, CLOSURE 1864.

VARIETY compare with STYLE 1864.

WILL *see* under ACTION 1864.

LOPE DE VEGA [Lope Félix de Vega Carpio] (1562-1635). Spanish poet, novelist, and playwright. De Vega studied at the Theatine College and the University of Salamanca but left without a degree and without taking religious orders (which he did much later). He served in the army from 1583-1587. In 1588 de Vega was banished for eight years from Madrid and sailed with the Spanish Armada against England. On his return he lived in Valencia, a center of dramatic activity, and began writing plays. De Vega's literary output for the rest of his life (he claimed to have written an average of twenty sheets a day) was phenomenal; his first biographer gives a total of 1800 plays and over 400 *auto sacramentales*, as well as diverse other writing. He is considered to be the creator of the Spanish *comedia* and to have introduced classical principles into Spanish drama. Nevertheless, de Vega's verse apologia for his plays, which contains his most explicit theoretical statements, is most interesting for the tension shown between the abstract principles he thinks he *should* be applying to his work and the affective principles he does employ.

Bibliography

VAWP   *The New Art of Writing Plays*. Translated by William T. Brewster. New York: Dramatic Museum of Columbia University, 1914.

Index

(FRANÇOIS MARIE AROUET) VOLTAIRE (1694-1778). French scientist, philosopher, essayist, novelist, poet, and playwright. Voltaire was educated by Jesuits at the College of Louis-le-Grand in Paris. First as a wit (but an indiscreet epigram resulted in a term in the Bastille in 1717), and then as a playwright (*Oedipe*, 1718), Voltaire quickly won a reputation in Paris as Racine's successor. He became interested in English culture and literature. When exiled from France in 1726, he went to London where he became acquainted with the most eminent English men of letters, philosophers, and politicians. He returned to France in 1728 confirmed in his admiration for English freedom of speech and overwhelmed by the experience of Shakespearean theatre. His wan imitations of Shakespeare were not successful in Paris, however. Finally, it was with such spectacular and exotic plays as *Zaïre*

(1732) that he regained for a time the leadership of the French stage. In 1734 his book *Philosophical Letters* created a scandal that again drove him from Paris to escape arrest. Thereafter, except for brief visits, he remained an exile from Paris for the remainder of his life. In 1758, like Candide—the novel of that title was published in the same year—Voltaire retired ''to cultivate one's garden'' in Ferney, a Swiss estate on the French border; there the famous of Europe came to visit him. Voltaire became increasingly uncomfortable with the pre-Romantic developments which he had earlier encouraged. He attempted to halt the growing interest in Shakespeare and in 1776 attacked the translation of Shakespeare into French in his *Letter to the Academy*. In his last plays he returned to the strict classicism of his predecessors.

Bibliography

VE   ''Preface to *Herod and Mariamne*,'' Letter to Father Poree, and ''A Discourse on Tragedy'' in *European Theories of the Drama*. Edited by Barrett H. Clark. Cincinnati: Stewart and Kidd, 1918.

VW   *The Works of Voltaire*. Translated by William F. Fleming. 22 vols. Akron, Ohio: St. Hubert Guild, c. 1901.

Index

INDEX OF NAMES AND TITLES

INDEX OF
TERMS AND TOPICS

This is an analytical index of terms or synonyms and general topics of significance to theories of dramatic art as they appear in extracts quoted in the text.
When spelled-out numbers appear in parentheses following page numbers,
these indicate that the reference is to more than one quoted extract on that page;
similarly, when two consecutive, hyphenated page numbers are given (such as
66-67) the reference is to an extract that starts on the first page given and ends
on the second, though other extracts on either or both of those pages also may
be referred to in the index (for example: 66, 66-67, 67).

327, 331, 340, 341 (two), 357-58, 360,
361, 362, 368, 378, 384, 415, 424 (two),
426, 429, 430, 438, 440, 451, 453, 454,
458; as embodied standards for self-
criticism, 57, 284; as first teacher for
playwrights, 57; as guidance to be tested
by experience, 56; as justification for
one's position, 57, 58; as models for
imitation, 58; questioning of, 359;
rejection of, 58, 206, 365, 428, 430-31;
as unnecessary, 360; as unqualified guide
to fundamental precepts, 56. *See also*
Rule(s)

Balinese drama, 111, 336, 386
Beautiful, the, 18-19, 64, 143, 158, 171, 194,
208, 209, 250, 262, 273, 274, 284, 285,
288, 357, 369, 377, 378, 379, 395, 396,
427, 429, 447, 452, 462
—as aim of poetry, 15
—defining characteristics of, 13, 14, 16-17,
20; absolute, 17, 18; association of ideas,
14, 16, 17 (two), 18, 19; disinterestedness, 17, 117 (two), 122 (rejected);
harmony, 16-17, 19-20; higher interest,
137; ideal, 16, 369; independence from
three unities, 428, 430, 431-32;
magnitude and order, 163, 260, 282, 285;
multëity in unity, 16-17, 421;
novelty, symmetry, and harmony, 18;
order, 12, 165, 260, 421; relative, 14
(two); symmetry, 236; uniformity, 260;
variety, 462; virtue, 91
—discerned only by taste, 408, 408-9, 410,
411 (two)
—greater in art than nature, 207, 245, 251, 252
—greater in fanciful images than in nature,
235
—greater in nature than in art, 14
—literature instructs through, 136
—models of, 364
—not a sufficient criterion for poetry, 29
—pleasures of, 13, 119, 132, 205-6, 236-37,
252; anticipation, 46
—rejection of, 140
—sources of: Apollonian dialogue of Greek
tragedy, 280; custom, 17-18;
distinguished from the agreeable and the
good, 17; human beings not things, 24;
nature, 255, 257, 258, 349-50; the object,
18; painting, 65-66, 257; parody, 81;

poetical impression of any object, 19,
205-6; poetry, 116, 130, 206, 245; poet's
imitation of history, 392; profound
personal experience, 44-45; rhythm and
metre, 280; sculpture, 259-60, 349;
subjects of Greek tragedy, 382. *See also*
Aesthetic; Psychology, of aesthetic
experience
Beginnings of plays, 155 (two), 156 (two),
157, 158, 163, 164 (two), 165, 169, 171,
187, 342, 415, 433, 453; arbitrary in epic
plays, 185; as crisis, 166; definition of,
163, 166-67; should be disregarded, 172.
See also Crisis; Premise(s)
Behavior, 50, 53, 75, 81, 82, 93, 97, 122, 189
(two), 225, 253, 269, 300, 371, 395, 440,
461
Belief, 21, 29, 38, 39, 44, 56, 66-67, 120,
147, 202, 211, 214, 220, 221, 224, 226,
227, 229 (two), 231 (two), 234, 249, 252,
255, 273, 289, 310, 340, 341, 343, 347,
349, 351, 400, 466, 469; as illusion, 226;
negative, assisted by the will, 226; self-
deception as, 24. *See also* Illusion
Bourgeois theatre, the, 51, 418; tragedy of,
381. *See also* Genre definition
Burlesque, 80, 202, 217, 386; definition of,
183. *See also* Genre definition

Caricature, 72-73, 80-81, 81, 185, 202, 225,
274
Catastrophe, 85, 88, 89, 102, 103, 108, 135-
36, 155, 170, 177, 183, 323, 325, 329,
330, 439-40, 443, 451; tragic, 161. *See
also* Closure
Catharsis, 33, 37, 39, 59-64, 117, 127, 145,
217-18, 236, 266-67, 320, 437, 439, 440,
441. *See also* Closure
—contrived to refute Plato, 59
—definition of, 443, 448 (two); as
achievement of equilibrium on stage, 62;
as awakening of rational inhibition, 60
(two), 61; as consciousness expansion,
60, 64; as consciousness that things can
be changed, 64; as Dionysian
transcendence, 63; as homeopathic, 59,
63 (rejected); as life-enhancing, 63; as
mean between emotional extremes, 61; as
perception of thematic content, 61; as
pleasurable release of emotion, 61; as
wonder, 468;

—without restraint in comedy, 97

Irony, 102, 107, 202, 211, 230, 272-74, 336, 354 (two), 442; definition of, 272, 272-73, 273, 273-74; romantic, 272-73, 273. *See also* Distance; Humor

Irrationality, 20, 54, 200, 203, 468

Italian: critics, 360; drama, 180, 334, 357; literature, 202

Joke (jest), 85, 92 (two), 96, 102, 196, 202, 272, 274, 397, 422, 423. *See also* Humor

Judgment (or criticism) induced by art, 56, 98, 218, 224, 240, 244, 253, 265. *See also* Affect; Insight; Thought; *Compare with* Criticism (or judgment) of art

—applied to: characters' actions, 11, 48, 49, 53, 122, 150, 189, 195, 218-19, 327, 413; every sentence of the character, 51; society, 52 (two), 53-54, 122, 189, 218, 271; vices and the ridiculous in comedy, 95

—as basis for verisimilitude, 246

—employs faculties of imagination, sensation, opinion, knowledge, and intellect, 233

—in epic theatre, 150, 218

—must be made by audience, not artist, 419

—role of, in experience of stage-illusion, 226, 227 (two), 343

—spectator convicted of meanly false, 89

—technique for inducing; check of freedom in humor, 198, 203; from historical perspective, 218; through objective representation of chorus, 76; pleasure or pain, 28, 413; produced by comedy but not farce, 94

Language, 12, 15, 18-19, 25, 32, 65, 75, 76, 82, 92, 110, 111, 112 (two), 113, 119, 128, 131, 134-36, 139, 140, 143, 174, 188, 189, 197, 202, 207-8, 209, 212, 213, 224, 225, 226, 230, 239, 240, 243, 245, 246-47, 247, 248, 249 (two), 250 (two), 254, 261, 266, 275-81, 283, 286, 287, 287-88, 289 (two), 290, 301, 306, 325, 330, 333, 335, 336-37, 339, 356, 367-68, 369-70, 376, 378, 380-81, 381, 384, 385 (three), 387, 389, 400, 402, 406, 408, 409-10, 414 (two), 415, 416-17, 418, 420-21, 421, 424, 427, 438, 441, 447, 447-48, 454, 455 (two), 457, 458, 459, 469. *See also* Dialogue; Epigram; Literature; Monologue; Poetic drama; Repartée; Rhyme; Verse

—in comedy, 92

—conventions of, 277

—definition of, 438; drawn from daily life, 375 (two), 376, 378, 380, 438; as eloquence, 19, 34, 419; rationalistic, 275, 277-78; rationalistic definition rejected, 278-79; reason and imagination require different kinds, 278; reductive, impersonal, and commonplace compared with music, 281; semiotic analysis, 278-79; as window to inner sense of imagination, 239

—exalted by poetry, 383

—excellence of, the most essential thing in tragedy, 371

—fiction not verse distinguishes artists in, 275

—figurative, 30, 31

—inadequate to render cosmic symbolism of music, 280

—obscenity in, 92

—origin in metaphor, 289-90

—pleasing, 376

—purpose of, 125; display, 6; feeling best expressed in colloquial, 277; ideal spirit of action conveyed, 279; must be expressive of feeling, 277, 278; must be expressive of thought, 277-78; reveals the person, 377; as state of the soul, 383; thought best expressed in eloquent, 277-78

—rejection of, 281 (two), 290-91

—skepticism toward, as expression of truth of character, 76-77

—as source of interest in simple plays, 206, 325

—sources of: characters, 277; relation to action, 7, 11; in tragedy, idealization of ordinary conversation, 278

—stage spectacle requires its own concrete, 281

—sublimity of, most necessary accompaniment to spectacular effects, 368

—supremacy of, rejected, 372

—techniques of: distancing devices, 279-80; elliptical detail as stimulating perception, 280-81; justified by subtext, 400; realism, 347; style, 374-75, 375

271, 280, 284, 290, 297, 298, 303, 304,
306, 308, 308-9, 327, 332, 349, 351,
358, 360, 361, 363, 376, 378-79, 381-82,
383, 396, 402, 410, 411, 414, 416-17,
417, 419, 420, 436, 442, 443 (two), 452,
456, 457, 459 (two), 462, 463, 469, 470;
definition of, 253; as source of ideal
essences perceived by artists, 259; as
source of rules, 429. *See also* Reality
Nazi Period, 26, 54. *See also* Fascism
Neoclassical tragedy, 381-82
New Comedy, 73, 96; definition of, 184-85;
distinguished from Old Comedy, 185,
196. *See also* Comedy
Novel, the, 10, 77, 116, 143, 222, 263;
bourgeois, 149; as opposite in purpose
from drama, 10; "romance," 341. *See
also* Literature
Novelty, 4, 38, 51, 89, 151, 240, 256, 301-4,
368, 405-6; always relates to real
perceptions, 385; beauty gives finishing
to, 13; in comedy, 391; definition of, 304
(two); essential to higher imitation, 245-
46; gives birth to the imagination, 241;
historical relativity of, 303; importance
of, 46, 301 (two); limitations of, in plot,
393; makes great poet, 277; more
important than genre, 301; pleasure of,
defined, 303; rejected by rhetoricians,
182; rejected when overleaping
probability, 402; rejection of, 276, 302,
397; as source of pleasure, 18, 236-37,
316; subverts the rules, 177; as true
observation of nature's variety, 304; in
the use of language, 421; value of, 268-69

Objective (as goal), 9, 10, 67, 75, 76, 100,
171, 300, 326, 399, 399-400, 433, 444-
45, 460, 466, 467. *See also* Motivation;
Subtext; Superobjective
Objective correlative, 278, 289, 311, 334-35,
386, 420; definition of, 305; relation of
things seen to emotions felt, 50. *See also*
Aesthetic; Affect
Objectivity, 53, 55, 76, 87, 97, 111, 116, 131,
132, 134-36, 137, 139, 149, 211, 270,
271, 272, 279, 281, 294, 306-7, 311,
336-37, 350, 385, 386, 389, 412, 418; as
action from which inferences may be
drawn, 306; as multiple perspectives,
307; as nonjudging sympathy, 306; as the

presentation of action, 306; qualification
of, 40
Observation, 25, 50 (two), 72-73, 80, 97, 125,
207, 229, 255, 257, 300, 333, 358, 359-
60, 384, 385, 419, 443, 446, 459, 460
Obstacle, 8, 9, 103, 104, 106, 107-8, 108,
181, 372, 433. *See also* Conflict
Occidental drama, 281, 372, 387
Ode, 165. *See also* Literature
Old Comedy, 72, 92 (two), 96-97;
distinguished from New Comedy, 185,
196; parabasis in, 97. *See also* Comedy
Onomatopoeia, 278. *See also* Language
Opera, 25, 106, 225, 251, 371; Italian, 380
Orchestra, 42
Order, 20, 195, 240, 308-9, 361, 383, 409,
411
—in the art object: in art not nature, 203;
creation of, distinguishes man from
animal, 290; the creation (of artists) out of
chaos, 138, 210-11; as equilibration in
tragedy, 62; events should approach
truth, 423; French view of, 132; as
general equanimity in comedy, 101;
makes thoughts intelligible, 165; in the
parts of a fable, 164; in the parts of a
poem, 128, 454-55; in the parts of a
tragedy, 163, 321; perception of, a
criterion of taste, 409; plots
without, called "episodic," 321; as
recognized by poet, 455; role of, in the
tragical and comic, 200; as supreme
equilibrium in theatre, 63; as unifying
point of view, 308-9, 421; in variety, 452;
whole, in conflict with individuals, 106
—in the beautiful, 15, 163, 165, 282, 421
—lack of, only supportable in genius, 165
—more manifest in celestial bodies than on
earth, 164
—in nature, 12, 417, 469
—as product of art: air of design, 308, 322;
created by regulating principle, 209;
dramatist must master divine order of
world, 41; exalted world order should be
visible in romantic tragedy, 105; no
relevation of higher, in French tragedy,
86; revelation of a higher design, 37;
sought by spectator, 47; vision of, in
ancient art, 15
—as source of pleasure, 252, 322, 409, 454-55
—as underlying principle, 308

376, 382, 412, 419; as imitation, 364. *See also* Language

Rhyme, 167, 250, 275, 279, 280, 377, 378, 379; justification for, 279; rejection of, 379-80. *See also* Language; Style

Rhythm, 15, 28, 36, 46, 107, 167, 171, 174, 217, 243, 244, 280, 335, 337, 369, 388, 435, 437, 450. *See also* Spectacle; Verse

Ridicule. *See also* Humor
—enhanced by contrast, 273
—of follies not essential to the comic, 99, 101
—makes comedy wear itself out, 98
—not used in New Comedy, 184
—produces: in comedy, correction of vices, 95, 183, 269; humor, 198; laughter not delight, 196-97; pleasure, 99; in satire, correction of vices, 93
—role of: in comedy, 91, 199, 222, 249, 331; in comedy rejected, 95; in comedy versus burlesque, 183; in parody, 81
—subjects of: characters in romances, 77; egotism, 199; improper, 100, 128, 268 (two), 302, 395; philosophy, 266; serious objects, 268

Ritual, 25, 319-20, 335-36, 337, 421. *See also* Convention

Roman: comedy, definition of, 90; drama, 112, 128, 177, 380; history as subject for plays, 175; literature, 259; rhetoric, 259

Romantic, 210, 228; definition of, 15; distinguished from classical, 105; drama, 9, 107, 179, 253, 285, 432, 434; imagination, 242; irony, 273-74; spirit, 362; tragedy, 179, 381-82. *See also* Gothic

Rule(s), 5, 8, 9, 12, 25, 32 (two), 33 (two), 35, 36, 56, 57 (three), 65-66, 66, 69, 85, 89, 90, 126, 127, 131-32, 153, 163, 177 (two), 178, 182, 192 (two), 205, 224, 250, 251, 259, 266, 267, 268, 279, 284, 322, 324, 325, 326, 330, 332, 339, 341, 354, 356-64, 368, 375, 378, 404, 408, 409, 420, 424, 425, 427, 430, 431, 433 (three), 434, 435, 440, 451, 453, 455, 457. *See also* Aesthetic; Authority; Law; Principle; Rationality
—apology for not following, 356
—applied to: *liaison de scène*, 363; number of acts, 356, 357, 361, 362-63; plot, 356 (two); three unities, 356, 358, 359 (two), 361; tragedy and comedy, 331

—arbitrary, distinguished from fundamental, 361 (two)
—in conflict with popular delight, 356-57
—as contradicting themselves, 357
—as conventions, 364
—defense of, 357-58, 360, 363, 428-29
—derived from: affect, 33, 359-60, 360, 361-62; authority, 356-57, 357-58, 362; common sense, 358, 359-60; definitions of tragedy, 442; means to an end previously ascertained, 363; rhetoric, 364; the writer's instinct, 359
—as distinct from pleasure and more fundamental, 359
—fulfill the word but not the spirit of the, 431
—as guide-posts, 364
—ignorance of the, 357
—inform critical judgment and reform taste, 360
—observation of, outweighed by characterization, 362
—questioning of, 359
—rejection of, 359-60, 360, 361-62, 362-63, 363, 364, 428, 430, 433-34
—teaching of the, 357

Satire, 80, 90, 93, 98, 99, 102, 202, 357, 374, 395; definition of, 184; generalized characterization in, 184. *See also* Genre definition; Humor

Satyr play, 122, 137, 175, 210, 216, 228. *See also* Classical

Schema, 290. *See also* Archetype; Idea

Science, 21 (two), 22, 24 (two), 26, 53, 55, 79, 115, 126, 132-33, 140-41, 151, 152-53, 166, 217, 229, 239, 247, 251, 271, 276, 296, 316, 350, 356, 364, 369, 387, 391, 396, 422, 454 (two), 461, 466; as astronomy, 234

Sculpture, 12, 17, 21, 72, 88, 135, 153 (two), 194, 203, 205, 209, 222, 235-37, 250, 259, 308, 322, 336, 349-50, 369, 381-82, 444, 457. *See also* Fine art

Sensation, 20, 72, 150, 233, 235-37, 239, 253, 261, 266, 278, 286, 319, 336-37, 369, 370, 372, 378, 382, 383, 406, 409, 410-11, 413, 416, 434, 442, 453; distinguished from perception, 409

Sensuous experience, 13, 15, 16 (two), 18, 20, 22, 31, 36 (two), 40, 64, 68, 96, 123,

About the Authors

OSCAR LEE BROWNSTEIN is Chairman of the Playwriting Department at the Yale School of Drama. He has contributed to many scholarly publications, including *Shakespeare Quarterly*, and *Rhetoric: A Tradition in Transition*, edited by W. R. Fisher.

DARLENE M. DAUBERT, until recently an Instructor in the Rhetoric Program at the University of Iowa in Iowa City, is presently employed by the Institute for Social and Policy Studies at Yale University.